Conservation of Historic Brick Structures

This publication was developed under a grant from the National Park Service and the National Center for Preservation Technology and Training. Its contents are solely the responsibility of the authors and do not necessarily represent the official position or policies of the National Park Service or the National Center for Preservation Technology and Training.

Conservation of Historic Brick Structures

Case Studies and Reports of Research

Edited by

N.S. Baer, S. Fitz, and R.A. Livingston

Text and Production Editor

J.R. Lupp

DONHEAD

First published in the United Kingdom in 1998 by
Donhead Publishing Ltd
Lower Coombe
Donhead St Mary
Shaftesbury
Dorset SP7 9LY
Tel: +44 (0) 1747 828422
www. donhead.com

ISBN 978 1 873394 34 2

Reprinted in 2009 by Donhead Publishing Ltd

Cover picture: façade details of the Chorin Convent, located north of Berlin

Conservation of historic brick structures
1. Building, Brick   2. Historic buildings - Conservation and restoration
I. Baer, N. S. II. Fitz, S. III. Livingston, R. A.
693 .2' 1' 0288

ISBN I 873394 34 9

British Library Cataloguing in Publication Data
Printed in Great Britain by Cromwell Press Group

Contents

CASE STUDIES

Preface

The present work finds its origins in a NATO-CCMS Pilot Study entitled, "The Conservation of Historic Brick Buildings and Monuments."

In addition to its military component, NATO has several nonmilitary committees. The Science Committee, formed in 1959, operates an extensive program of international study institutes, research workshops and collaborative research in many areas. Because of its success in promoting cooperation among the NATO member countries, it was recommended that the concept be extended to other aspects of civilian life. The Committee on the Challenges of Modern Society (CCMS) was established in 1969 to study issues affecting the physical and social environment (Campbell 1979). The work of CCMS is decentralized with projects called Pilot Studies carried out by groups of NATO countries that provide their own resources. Pilot studies have been conducted on a wide range of topics ranging from air pollution modeling to emergency medical evacuation. In 1979, CCMS undertook its first Pilot Study in the cultural field on the conservation of stone monuments (NAS 1982). At the conclusion of that Pilot Study, several recommendations were made for further work, among them the conservation of historic brick structures (NATO 1985). In September, 1986, representitives of West Germany, The Netherlands, Norway, Portugal, Spain, and the United States met in Brussels to draft a broad outline for a future Pilot Study on the Conservation of Brick Buildings (NATO-CCMS 1986)

The suggestion of a Pilot Study on brick conservation was embraced by West Germany. A proposal was prepared and accepted by CCMS on May 11, 1987 (Appendix I). Five major topics were identified in the proposal:

1. Development of an Atlas of Damage to Historic Brick Structures,
2. Diagnosis of Damage,
3. Field and Accelerated Aging Tests,
4. Instrumental Methods Development and Standardization of Procedures with Emphasis on Non-Destructive Testing,
5. Treatment and Conservation Methods.

It was recognized that a brick building does not consist of bricks alone, but rather is a system composed of the bricks themselves, the mortar, and in many cases, a plaster rendering or stucco covering the surface of the brick.

West Germany assumed leadership of the Pilot Study, designating the Umweltbundesamt (Federal Environmental Agency) in Berlin as the coordinating agency. Participants came from Belgium, East Germany, The Netherlands, Norway, Italy, Turkey, Great Britain, and the United States.

One of the remarkable aspects of the Pilot Study was its witness to history as "the Wall" proved less durable than the Pilot Study. From the first Experts Meeting held in

1987 at the facilities of the Umweltbundesamt, in what was then West Berlin, to the 8th and final meeting in 1994 in Leuven, Belgium (see Appendix II for a complete listing of the dates and venues of the Experts Meetings), the political landscape of Europe was transformed.

The meeting in Leuven also marked a significant further development in the conservation of historic brick structures as it coincided with a major conference organized by DG-XII of the European Commission, marking an important source of support for research in this area.

It had been the custom of the Pilot Study Coordinator to prepare Postprints of the papers presented at the Experts Meetings. These postprint papers, revised and supplemented with new results, are the basis for the individual case studies and research reports that form the chapters of this book.

In 1997, Blaine Cliver, a participant at several of the Experts Meetings, observed that the papers in the postprints contained a wealth of useful information but were generally unavailable to an audience beyond the participants. He suggested that they be edited and consolidated in a single volume. This book is a direct consequence of his initiative.

— Norbert S. Baer, Stephan Fitz, Richard A. Livingston, editors
June, 1998

ACKNOWLEDGEMENTS

The Editors acknowledge with deep gratitude the heroic efforts of their Text and Production Editor, Ms. Julia Lupp, who brought the high professional standards and skills that she exercises as Head of the Editorial Staff of the Dahlem Konferenzen to this book. The Editors also wish to acknowledge the encouragement and support of Blaine Cliver without whose intervention the publication effort would not have been undertaken.

As noted more formally elsewhere, the Editors acknowledge the National Center for Preservation Technology of the National Park Service for financial support towards the preparation of the manuscript. They also wish to thank their Project Officer at the Center, Dr. Mary F. Striegel for her advice and encouragement.

The Editors also acknowledge the encouragement and advice of Terence M.W. Moran, who as Programme Director of NATO-CCMS was an enthusiastic and effective supporter of Pilot Studies on cultural property issues.

REFERENCES

Campbell, E. 1979. CCMS: The First Decade – A Report to Commemorate the Tenth Anniversary of the NATO Committee on the Challenges of Modern Society.

National Academy of Sciences (NAS). 1982. Conservation of Historic Stone Buildings and Monuments. Washington, D.C.: National Academy Press.

NATO. 1985. Final Report: Pilot Study on the Conservation/Restoration of Stone Monuments, Document AC/255-D111, Brussels.

NATO-CCMS. 1986. Proposal for a New Pilot Study: The Conservation of Brick Buildings: Note by the Programme Director, Document AC/274-D/216, Brussels.

1

Introduction

N.S. BAER[1], S. FITZ[2], and R.A. LIVINGSTON[3]

[1]Conservation Center, New York University, 14 East 78th Street,
New York, NY 10021, U.S.A.
[2]Umweltbundesamt, Bismarckplatz 1, 14193 Berlin, Germany
[3]Office of Highway Engineering, R&D HNR–2, Federal Highway Administration,
6300 Georgetown Pike, McLean VA 22101

Brick has been used as a building material since ancient times and is the construction material for many historic buildings in Europe and the United States. Among the causes of damage to brick are air pollution, acid rain, biodeterioration, salts, and freeze-thaw cycles. Although conservation of this form of the architectural heritage is a high priority, relatively little scientific research has been undertaken concerning the deterioration of this material, especially in comparison to the vast resources devoted to the study of stone deterioration.

As reviewed in the Preface, a NATO-CCMS Pilot Study, coordinated by the Umweltbundesamt (German Environmental Protection Agency), encouraged research efforts on the conservation of historic brick structures in five areas:

1. Development of an Atlas of Damage to historic brick structures,
2. Diagnosis of damage,
3. Field and accelerated aging tests,
4. Development of instrumental methods and standardization of procedures with emphasis on nondestructive testing,
5. Treatment and conservation methods.

The thirty-nine chapters that follow report on the results achieved by the participants in the Pilot Study. Although the Pilot Study has concluded, the programs begun under its aegis continue under other sponsorship, principally that of the European Community. While this volume represents a significant advance in our knowledge base for the conservation of historic brick structures, it also represents a research agenda as the individual research papers identify topics for future study. In the following discussion, organized by the five research areas listed above, a number of these research opportunities are described.

ATLAS OF BRICK DAMAGE

The Atlas, initially intended as a stand alone descriptive tool, has become an integral part of an expanded effort (Van Balen 1997) to develop a Masonry Damage Diagnostic System (MDDS). The Atlas provides descriptions and characterizations of the state of historic brick structures and of the materials themselves. It serves as the basis for:

- Identification of the causes of damage,
- Documentation of the extent of damage to a given building,
- Determination of appropriate treatment methods.

The development of the Atlas consisted of two steps. The first was the compilation of a standardized list of characteristic symptoms of brick and mortar deterioration, including photographs of each type of damage at various stages of the deterioration process, as well as verbal descriptions.

The second aspect involved the application of the Atlas to a survey of a number of historic brick buildings in Europe. Extensive documentation was made for each building. This included:

1. Characterization of the chemical composition and physical condition of the materials and structure, as well as any deterioration products, using an array of geological, physical, and chemical methods.
2. Characterization of the environmental influences on the building, such as air pollution, biodeterioration, microclimate, and soluble salts.
3. Description of the structural condition of the building, including design, foundations, settling, etc.
4. Historical documentation including former uses, major damages due to fire, flood, war, etc., and major repairs.
5. Mapping of the extent of damage.

Van Balen (Chapter 12) provides an introduction to the Atlas and a completed questionnaire for a historic brick structure in Belgium. The MDDS and Atlas show considerable promise as possible teaching aids, e.g., the user may follow the logical sequence leading to a diagnosis for an example of damage to a monument illustrated in the Atlas.

A projected further application of the system incorporating proposed treatment strategies is in development.

DIAGNOSIS OF DAMAGE

This part of the Pilot Study concerned improvements in the ability to diagnose the causes of damage through a better knowledge of the damage processes themselves. These papers and the associated case studies include research on the mechanisms through which environmental agents produce damage. The influence of the composition of materials and workmanship on the damage process was also investigated. This kind of research requires the use of a wide range of techniques beyond the resources of a single laboratory and so the work was shared internationally among a number of laboratories.

For mortars, the research was led by Middendorf and Knöfel of the University of Siegen, [West] Germany. This covered the chemical and mineralogical examination of samples of historic mortars for such factors as:

- Type of binder, e.g., gypsum, lime, Portland cement,
- Proportions of binders and aggregates,
- Nature of the aggregates,
- Admixtures including salts or organic compounds.

Physical properties of the mortar samples including:

- Elastic modulus,
- Swelling value,
- Strength of mortar,
- Porosity and water absorption.

Chapters 17 and 18 report on this work to characterize ancient lime and gypsum mortars from Germany and the Netherlands. In an appendix (17.I), the authors present in flow chart format a comprehensive approach to the chemical-mineralogical characterization of mortars. Further results on ancient mortar specimens from historic monuments in Turkey are reported by Güleç (Chapter 19). Included are calcination analyses, porosimetric data, and photomicrographs documenting petrographic examination.

In an extensive series of studies on renderings, Hoffmann and Niesel describe their work on the effects of air pollutants (Chapter 22), the effects of orientation, and the development of specific reaction zones in the field (Chapter 23). In an introductory chapter (21), they detail their experimental protocols and the background to their study. To place the several studies of air pollution effects in context, Fitz (Chapter 20) reviews trends in air pollution in Germany. As has been observed in many of the developed nations, sulfur dioxide emissions are in substantial decline while oxides of nitrogen are increasing, complicating the analysis of retrospective damage studies. Arnold (Chapter 39) examines historic renderings on churches in Brandenburg. Interactions between the mortar and the brick were studied by Franke and Grabau (Chapter 15), Elsen (Chapter 16), and Hoffmann and Niesel (Chapter 31).

The study of the bricks themselves involved cooperation among the Technical University of Hamburg-Harburg, the Turkish National Museum, the Architectural Conservation Laboratory of Venice, the National Institute of Standards and Technology (U.S.), and the University of Maryland. Samples of bricks from a number of sites in Hamburg and in Lübeck were obtained and analyzed by a variety of chemical and mineralogical methods, including X-ray diffraction (XRD), X-ray fluorescence, optical microscopy, and SEM. Additional samples from Istanbul, Venice, Amsterdam,

Antwerp, and Copenhagen were collected. In the United States, samples were obtained from Colonial Williamsburg, Annapolis, and St. Mary's City, Maryland.

Among the studies were the subsequent determinations of the firing temperature of brick (Franke and Schumann, Chapter 3). The authors also provided a brief history of brickmaking in northern Germany (Chapter 2). In a related study (Chapter 11), Livingston and co-workers attempted to develop a durability index based on the ratio of cristobalite/quartz XRD intensities. While in agreement with durability observations for bricks from Colonial Williamsburg, the technique proved inapplicable to historic German brick. The study suggested that there was a fundamental difference in the mineralogy of German brick when compared to that of this example of American brick.

As with the mortar analysis, the purpose of the Diagnosis of Damage part of the study was to characterize the brick damage as a function of materials properties including:

- Chemical composition of fluxes, e.g., K, Na, Ca,
- Nature and proportion of nonplastics, e.g., quartz grains,
- Presence of minerals formed during firing, e.g., plagioclase,
- Pore-size distribution.

Manufacturing practices, such as the addition of salt to the brick, were investigated for their influence on durability (Chapters 3 and 11). The presence of damaging salts, such as sulfates and nitrates from air pollutants, chlorides from deicing salts or sea water, and carbonates from grouting, was the subject of several studies (Chapters 6, 7, 15, and 24). Guillitte (Chapter 8) reviews the vegetation and bioreceptivity of brick structures, observing that moisture is the main factor in determining kinetics, biomass, and composition. Biodeterioration, including scaling, cracking of brick, peeling and crumbling of mortar, and disjointing, are ascribed to the main organisms which colonize brick structures.

FIELD AND ACCELERATED LABORATORY TESTS

Work to develop quantitative relations that describe the rate of damage as a function of time and the intensity of the agent of damage was done through a combination of exposures at field sites and accelerated aging tests in the laboratory (Chapters 4, 5, 6, 8, 13, 22, and 23). The laboratory tests provide a way to isolate the effect of one cause of damage, e.g., SO_2, while keeping all others constant. The field tests, on the other hand, provide confirmation of the damage functions in the real world (Livingston 1997). Of particular note is the attempt to achieve levels of environmental characterization comparable to those of the laboratory while retaining the benefits of field exposure by constructing full-scale models (Chapter 13). Binda and her group introduced moisture and salts under carefully controlled and monitored conditions. These data, combined with detailed monitoring of the decay process, produced significant results while developing important new test methods.

DEVELOPMENT OF INSTRUMENTAL METHODS
AND STANDARDIZATION OF PROCEDURES

A major objective of the Pilot Study was the application of advanced methods of materials science to historic brick problems. The feasibility of each of the methods for the analysis of brick and mortar needed to be evaluated, requiring testing on specimens of known characteristics. Once feasibility was established, the procedures were to be standardized so the results from one laboratory would be comparable to those of another. Results are reported on a range of NDT methods including acoustic tomography (Chapter 10), XRD (Chapter 11), neutron scattering (Chapter 14), and physical methods (Chapters 9 and 13). Of particular interest is the use of acoustic tomography to follow the course of an injection grouting repair to a test pier (Chapter 10). Nappi and Côte (1997), in their parallel review of NDT methods applied to stone masonry, give similar examples of the use of ultrasonic tomography in evaluating the effectiveness of injection grouting in consolidating deteriorated stone in such monuments as a bell tower in Chioggia, Italy, and the Pont Neuf, Paris.

A special need in this area is a standardized method for measuring brick durability. The reliability of tests involving sodium sulfate crystallization has been questioned. Cyclical freeze-thaw tests also have problems (Ritchie 1979). A most promising durability test method is the Clemens Hardness Tester used by the Royal Institute for Cultural Heritage in Brussels (De Witte et al. 1977). Another technique based on abrasion measurements was developed by the [West] German Federal Institute for Materials Research and Testing (UBA 1988).

In addition to measurement methods, other aspects also need to be standardized. These include procedures for taking samples, and for preparing them for testing in the field or in the laboratory. Standard protocols for measurement of environmental factors are also necessary.

Finally, of particular interest is the development of portable equipment that can be used in the field to make nondestructive tests. Among these are portable X-ray fluorescence, the neutron probe, infrared thermography, ground penetrating radar, and a number of sonic methods (Livingston and Frassetto 1987). Several of these methods were evaluated in the United States, using an historic brick building in Colonial Williamsburg (Chapter 37).

TREATMENT AND CONSERVATION METHODS

After the damage problem at a given building has been correctly diagnosed, decisions must be made about the best way to deal with it. Alternatives include application of treatments such as water repellents or consolidants. Other possible actions may include the installation of waterproof barriers to prevent rising groundwater in the walls. Methods of removing salt from contaminated brick walls are reviewed by Friese (Chapter 29) and a number of case studies deal with the effects of salts and approaches to desalination (Chapters 32, 34, 37, 40). Most dramatic is the preservation challenge presented by the brick grinding house and other structures of a potash mine with huge salt depositions in the brick fabric (Chapter 40). Here the quantitites of salt are thought to preclude desalination, leading to a decision to rely on internal climate control to arrest salt migration.

Specific conservation treatments are examined for adobe brick (Chapter 25), water-repellent treatment of an exposed brick facade (Chapter 26), the development of water-resistant mortars (Chapter 27), and injection grouting (Chapter 28).

It is often necessary in the conservation of an historic structure to replace missing brick or mortar. The analytical methods described above for diagnosis of damage can also be applied to determine the brick or mortar composition for replacement materials that is the most suitable match to the original material. Petrographic analysis and XRD are demonstrated to be of particular relevance in the characterization of historic mortars and plasters.

SOME OBSERVATIONS

Case Studies

As part of the Pilot Study, a number of case studies were conducted where individual monuments were examined in detail and in some cases treated. The extensive documentation and conservation program at St. Pancras Chambers is outlined by Davies (Chapter 33). The unusual case of a fire-damaged structure, Uppark (Chapter 38), the earthquake response of Hagia Sophia (Chapter 35), and the restoration of a significantly altered structure, The Octagon (Chapter 36), provide real world supplements to the laboratory studies. The important related material, terracotta, is the subject of an investigation and conservation treatment at Schwerin Castle (Chapter 30).

Historical Correlations

In the northern European countries participating, there seems to be general agreement that brickmaking technology was imported from Lombardy around A.D. 1100–1150. Subsequently, brick shape, appearance, and dimensions seem to have varied in ways that can be correlated with historical periods. Also there seem to be some correlations between the historical period and the durability of the brick. This tends to support the idea that significant changes in brick manufacturing over history (kiln design, fuel type, additives, etc.) have implications for durability. Similarly, the collaboration of conservators, scientists, and architectural historians (Chapter 39) has demonstrated that historic renderings and mortars are a fruitful subject for interdisciplinary study.

Salt Deterioration

One of the primary motivations for the Pilot Study was concern about the effects of air pollution and acid rain. It was initially thought that these agents of attack would be important for lime mortars, but not for the bricks themselves because of their silicate-based composition. Nevertheless, one discovery of this Pilot Study was that bricks are in fact sensitive to acidic deposition because of the migration of calcium-rich solution from the mortar into the brick's pore space. This leads to the formation of calcium carbonate in the pores, which can then be attacked by SO_2 or acid rain.

On the other hand, these pollutants may be less significant in the future. The trends observed in Germany, demonstrating a substantial reduction in SO_2 emissions, find parallels throughout the major industrial nations (UN ECE 1998). However, attack by soluble salts, particularly sodium chloride and the less soluble gypsum, have been identified as a major problem in several countries, even where there are no local sources of natural salt. This suggests that salt may have been deliberately added in the process of brickmaking, in the mortar or in the plaster or whitewash. Research is needed on the phase relationships of these salts, particularly for the thermodynamics of complex mineral assemblages formed from solutions containing several cations (e.g., K, Ca, Na) and anions including Cl, SO_4, NO_3. The response of these mineral assemblages to changes in temperature or relative humidity needs to be characterized to understand the mechanisms of damage in porous materials. In recent times, salt damage has been aggravated by the introduction of heating systems into previously unheated structures. Microclimate studies are an area for further investigation.

Hand-molded vs. Machine-Made Brick

It is evident that one cannot make a simple classification of monuments on the basis of whether they were built with hand-molded or with machine-made brick. Due to extensive alterations or repairs, even medieval buildings contain a certain amount of nineteenth or twentieth century machine-made brick. Some of the most prominent brick deterioration observed in these buildings occurs in the machine-made bricks. It may be that some of these were made in the transition period around the turn of century, when the stiff-mud extrusion process and tunnel kiln firing was coming into use. Lack of experience with these techniques resulted in brick that has a definite laminated structure or a thin, hard outer skin. This shows up in characteristic patterns of deterioration that involve spalling or wrinkling of the surface. In conjunction with an experts meeting in Berlin, an Hoffmann kiln adapted to the production of hand-molded brick for the restoration of historic buildings in Brandenburg was visited. An historic preservation challenge is presented by the need to keep such historic technologies in production.

Protective Coatings

Another common theme is the intermittent use of coatings, either thin layers of white-wash or thick layers of stucco. During certain periods, these coatings were in fashion, but during others, bare brick was preferred. A builder planning to apply stucco or lime-wash could use poorer quality brick. Conversely, if only inferior brick were being made, such coatings would have been unavoidable. The prevailing style in the use of coatings should be factored into the evaluation of the correlation between historical period of construction and durability. In terms of restoration, it is evident that the decision of whether or not to apply such a coating depends on the prevailing attitude at the time of construction rather than on modern taste.

CONCLUSIONS

The CCMS Pilot Study approach has been applied to the study of the conservation of historic brick. It has been possible to coordinate the research of a number of institutions in several European countries and the United States. The ability to share resources and expertise made it possible to achieve far more than any one laboratory could have accomplished alone. The Pilot Study case studies and research reports make an important contribution to the scientific study of brick conservation.

The value of such a Pilot Study lies in the ability to identify promising new directions of research. However, given the organizational structure and the limited time frame of the Pilot Study, the results do not represent a comprehensive and complete research program. Consequently, other research programs should continue the work started here to apply the methods to a wider range of bricks and historic structures.

REFERENCES

De Witte, E., P. Huget, and P. Van Den Broeck. 1977. A comparative study of three consolidation methods on limestone. *Studies in Conservation* **22**:190–196.
Livingston, R.A. 1997. Development of air pollution damage functions. In: Saving Our Architectural Heritage: The Conservation of Historic Stone Structures, ed. N.S. Baer and R. Snethlage, pp. 37–62. Dahlem Workshop Report. Chichester: Wiley.
Livingston, R.A., and R. Frassetto. 1987. Nondestructive diagnosis of building condition. In: Proc. 8th ICOMOS General Assembly, pp. 362–370.Washington, D.C.: US/ICOMOS.
Nappi, A., and P. Côte. 1997. Nondestructive test methods applicable to historic stone structures. In: Saving Our Architectural Heritage: The Conservation of Historic Stone Structures, ed. N.S. Baer and R. Snethlage, pp. 151–166. Dahlem Workshop Report. Chichester: Wiley.
Ritchie, T. 1979. Brick Durability Tests and the Method of Freezing. Vth Intl. Brick Masonry Conference, Rome, pp. 46–48.

UBA (Umweltbundesamt). 1988. NATO-CCMS Pilot Study "Conservation of Historic Brick Structures." Minutes of the 2nd Expert Meeting of the NATO-CCMS Pilot Study. Berlin: UBA.

UN ECE. 1998. Workshop on Quantification of Effects of Air Pollutants on Materials. Oral Presentations, May, 1998.

Van Balen, K.E.P. 1997. Monitoring of degradation: Selection of treatment strategies. In: Saving Our Architectural Heritage: The Conservation of Historic Stone Structures, ed. N.S. Baer and R. Snethlage, pp. 167–180. Dahlem Workshop Report. Chichester: Wiley.

2

A Brief History of Brickmaking in Northern Germany

L. FRANKE and I. SCHUMANN

Technische Universität Hamburg-Harburg, Arbeitsbereich Bauphysik und Werkstoffe im Bauwesen, Eißendorfer Straße 42, 21071 Hamburg, Germany

ABSTRACT

A brief overview is given of the development of brick production in northern Germany and its influence on brick quality. Until the late 19th century, bricks were produced manually by hand-molding, then it was increasingly replaced by extrusion methods. The conditions of firing are critical to the final brick quality. In former times and with early kiln types, the skill of the brick-maker had a great influence on the quality and aging properties of brick since it was virtually impossible to control and influence the firing once the fire was ignited.

HISTORY OF BRICKMAKING

The production of brick can roughly be divided into two categories:

- hand-molded
- industrially produced.

The manual period lasted from ca. 13,000 B.C. until the latter part of the 19th century. The earliest unburnt bricks were found in Egypt and have been dated back to 13,000 B.C. The earliest fired bricks were found in Mesopotamia and have been dated back to 4000 B.C. (Bender and Händle 1982). According to Richards (1990), brickmaking spread eastward and then westward via Egypt, Asia Minor, and Greece towards Rome, where such monuments as the Coliseum were built mostly out of Roman brick. The art of brickmaking was carried all over the known world by the Roman legionnaires.

The technique of using fired clay as building material and not only for pottery is said to have come to northern Germany via Italy after A.D. 1150 (Bender and Händle 1982).

Hand-molding, as illustrated in Figure 2.1, was the exclusive method of brick production until the 16th century when the first attempts at mechanization were made.

Figure 2.1 Hand-molding (illustration taken from: "Die Bauleute" Ständebuch von Chr. Weigel, Nürnberg 1698 in Noah (1986)).

Here, a wooden mold was placed on a table covered with sand. Then, a clot of excess clay was thrown into the mold so that it was completely filled. Afterwards the excess clay was sheared off with an oak plate, and the green bricks were dried slowly for about 3–6 weeks before burning.

In Ostfriesland during medieval times, the procedure of firing was divided into three parts (Noah 1986):

- for the first 2–3 days, the fire was kept low to allow remnant moisture to evaporate,
- for the next 2–3 days, the heat was kept medium,
- finally, the temperature was increased to 800°–1100°C.

After the bricks were thoroughly burnt, the fire was extinguished by closing the air holes. The kiln was then left to cool down naturally. Depending on the number of bricks, the kind of fuel, and the weather, the complete firing procedure took 2–4 weeks.

Kilns

The earliest type was the clamp kiln. Green clay bricks were stacked together with fuel in such a way that the pile formed chimneys within. The sides of the pile, which could be as high as 3.5 m, were smeared with a mixture of clay and straw, and the top was covered with layers of grass pads (see Figure 2.2). The fire was then ignited (Noah 1986). This type of kiln had several disadvantages:

- It could only be used once, because it had to be disassembled to remove the bricks.
- It was virtually impossible to influence the fire once it was ignited.
- The smoke and associated pollutants came into contact with the green bricks and could settle on their surface.

To avoid these disadvantages, beginning with the 16th century or perhaps even earlier, the clamp kiln was replaced by the so-called scove or "Scotch" kiln (Zoller 1982). This type of kiln utilized a variety of different constructions and firing systems. One type was used in the Netherlands until the 19th century and consisted of three masonry of U-shaped walls (Schulz 1805). One of the short fronts and the top were left open; the front could be erected according to the number of bricks that were to be burnt and the top was closed with clay and/or green bricks.

Figure 2.2 Clamp kiln for the production of brick (after Bender and Händle 1982).

Another type of medieval kiln was found in Narzym/Neidenburg. The kiln consisted of a chamber dug into the slope of a small hill. This was done to reduce the distance from the quarry, where the clay was dug, to the oven and to insulate the kiln better. The walls of the kiln were stabilized with natural stone masonry and after loading with the green bricks, the front was closed apart from some holes that were left for air and refilling with firing material. The quality of the burnt bricks found within the kiln in Narzym was very good (Dethlefsen 1915).

The early types of kilns required large quantities of wood, thus there was soon a shortage of firing material. Based on the formulas given by Buchin and Erdmann (1986), the amount of wood necessary to fire 10,000 bricks (each weighing 4 kg) at 1000°C can roughly be calculated to be 11,700 kg or 21 m³ of beechwood. The high price of wood necessitated a more economical firing method at a lower temperature, which had a disadvantageous effect on brick quality. This change in quality between romanesque and medieval bricks can easily be recognized in northern Germany (Holst, pers. comm.).

Wood, however, was not the only possible firing material. In coastal areas like the Netherlands, Ostfriesland, and Nordfriesland, peat was commonly used. Apart from that "coal, straw, bracken and billberry bushes" also sufficed as firing material (Bender and Händle 1982).

The technique of brickmaking hardly changed over the centuries. Bricks were still produced by hand-molding. One worker could produce 150–350 green bricks per hour, or more than 5,000 bricks a day (Noah 1986). Until 1769, the only mechanization involved replacement of manpower by waterpower or horsepower for the preparation of the clay.

In 1769, James Watt invented the steam machine, which made further progress possible. The first to make use of this invention were the English, but only for the preparation of the clay; the shaping was still done by hand. In 1799, a machine was constructed to imitate hand-molding. From then on, efforts were made to replace hand-molding by machines: the first extruder was developed in 1860 and shortly thereafter came the first soft mud-molding machine. The production of these machines were placed in series just before A.D. 1900 (Bender and Händle 1982).

Influence of Technique on Quality

Figure 2.3, which illustrates two bricks from different eras of production, clearly shows how the technique influenced the quality of the bricks produced. The brick in

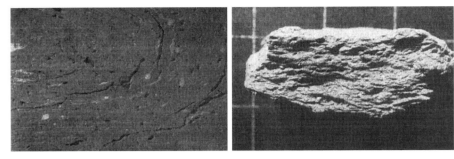

Figure 2.3   (a) Brick produced by hand-molding; (b) green brick produced by extrusion.

Figure 2.3a was produced by hand-molding. The structure within the brick is directly due to the method of manufacture. The pattern traced by the streaks and large pores derives from kneading the clay and throwing it into the mold. With romanesque bricks we can even see the hand-molding structure as "squeezing folds" or flutes on the surface of the bricks if they are not molded properly (Holst, pers. comm.).

Figure 2.3b shows the layers of clay minerals in a green clay brick. This brick was produced industrially by means of extrusion through a de-airing auger. The pressure and rotation of the auger causes the sheet minerals to adjust themselves accordingly. Thus we find a concentric layering of clay minerals. Sometimes this pattern is traced by the pores that develop after firing. The whole structure of the brick changes with industrial production, as seen in Figure 2.4. The material is mixed more thoroughly and is thus more homogeneous. Furthermore one does not see large pores as are evident in Figure 2.3.

The way the different kinds of brick weather supports the hypothesis that the pattern which is laid out by production is often followed by the flaking or detachment, or crumbling or breaking, respectively.

Most important for the quality of the bricks is the temperature at which they were fired. Production of a sound brick of excellent quality requires temperatures greater than 900°C. This was difficult to control with ancient kilns, especially with the clamp

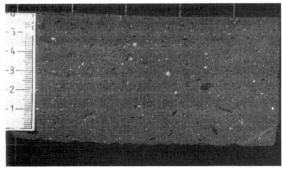

kiln, which is said to have been commonly used on the west coast of Schleswig-Holstein. The quality of bricks produced this way differed very much even in one charge: part of the charge was of good quality, but the larger part was overburnt, underfired, or scrap (Bender and Händle 1982).

Figure 2.4   Industrially produced burnt brick.

REFERENCES

Bender, W., and F. Händle, eds. 1982. Handbuch für die Ziegelindustrie: Verfahren und Betriebspraxis in der Grobkeramik. Wiesbaden, Berlin: Bauverlag.

Buchin, K., and W. Erdmann. 1986. Keramiktechnologie und Brennofen: Untersuchung und Rekonstruktionen zur Töpferei des 13. Jahrhunderts am Koberg zu Lübeck. *Lübecker Schriften zur Archäologie und Kulturgeschichte* 12:41–66.

Dethlefsen. 1915. Ein mittelalterlicher Ziegelofen. *Die Denkmalpflege* 17(1):12–14.

Noah, R. 1986. Der Backstein. Berichte zur Denkmalpflege in Niedersachesen. 6. Jg., Nr. 2, pp. 38–42.

Richards, W.R. 1990. Brick manufacturing from past to present. *Ceramic Bull.* 69(5):807–813.

Schulz, F.J.E. 1805. Einige Bemerkungen über die holländische Ziegelfabrikation. Königsberg: Goebbels & Unzer.

Zoller, D. 1982. Ziegelöfen des Zisterzienserklosters Heide, Ldkr. Oldenburg. *Archäol. Mitteilungen aus Nordwestdeutschland* 5:49–54.

3

Subsequent Determination of the Firing Temperature of Historic Bricks

L. FRANKE and I. SCHUMANN

Technische Universität Hamburg-Harburg, Arbeitsbereich Bauphysik und Werkstoffe im Bauwesen, Eißendorfer Straße 42, 21071 Hamburg, Germany

ABSTRACT

The firing temperature, or more specifically, the combination of temperature and time, is an important parameter in characterizing the durability of bricks. Attempts were made to develop a reliable, easy, and quick method for its subsequent determination. Several methods were checked for their applicability but only X-ray diffraction turned out to be reliable. With the help of reference samples of known firing temperature and chemical composition and with analyses of their strongest hematite peak, the approximate firing temperature of an unknown brick sample could be determined.

INTRODUCTION

Experiments showed that firing temperature is an important parameter in characterizing the durability of bricks, especially where resistance to acid rain and other aggressive substances is concerned (Schumann 1997). In assessing the durability of brick, with respect to frost and salt crystallization resistance and other detrioration mechanisms, efforts were made to develop a method for the subsequent determination of the firing temperature. This method had to fulfil certain requirements:

- be part of an industrial laboratory's analyses (no extra devices necessary) to enable a greater number of laboratories to use it,
- commonly applicable (no new standards necessary for a brick of unknown origin),
- easy to handle and rapid, to make its use as inexpensive as possible.

REFERENCE MATERIALS

Reference materials were produced to have a basis for comparison. Illitic clays from two different pits in northern Germany (Hamburg/Neuenfelde and Lübeck/Hansa) were hand-molded; to three portions of the Hamburg clay, salt mixtures were added. These samples were then fired at increasing temperatures (700°, 800°, 900°, 970°, 1040°, 1100°, and 1150°C) in two different laboratories (Technical University of Hamburg-Harburg and Keram-Labor, Hamburg) and their characteristics examined. To give an impression of how the material behaved under the same firing conditions, especially in the case of the historic brick, selected reference samples and historic bricks were refired at 1100°C for four hours.

The chemical composition, especially the iron oxide, calcium and magnesium oxide content as well as the fluxes, is of some importance. Therefore, the oxidized composition of the reference materials and selected samples of historic brick were analyzed by X-ray fluorescence.

Color

A very rough indication of the firing temperature is the color of the brick. The higher the temperature, the more intense the color. This red tonality is due to a change in the degree of oxidation of the iron. However, color is an inaccurate and uncertain means of determination, because important parameters remain unknown for the historic bricks, such as:

- atmosphere during firing (oxidizing/reducing),
- original content of calcium,
- exact firing temperature.

Due to variations in the oxidizing/reducing nature of the atmosphere, the predominant color can vary from red to black; depending on the amount of calcium, the brick can develop colors from red to yellow, as the calcium-silicates incorporate Fe_2O_3 in their lattices (Heimann 1979).

Change in Porosity

Firing causes changes in such porosity characteristics as:

- total intrusion volume (TIV),
- median pore radius (MPR) (according to volume or area),
- average pore radius (APR),
- bulk density (BD) and apparent density (AD).

For almost every case mentioned, a trend is recognizable with increasing temperature. However, results also revealed that porosity is dependent on such production conditions as molding or extrusion, grain size distribution of the components, water content, etc. Furthermore, differences in material composition, like additional fluxes, often influence porosity characteristics. Pore-size characteristics are therefore not a reliable means for the subsequent determination of the firing temperature.

High Temperature Dilatometer Measurements

The dimensions of a clay specimen change with increasing temperature: most significant is shrinkage at temperatures above approximately 900°C. For an already fired sample, shrinkage starts again at temperatures higher than the original firing temperature (Heimann 1978). This effect can be used to determine the firing temperature of unknown samples. Two different procedures were applied and compared (Heimann 1978) to determine the firing temperature:

- single heating of the sample,
- repeated heating of the sample (Roberts 1963; Tite 1969).

Results of these measurements for standards and historic brick revealed that the high temperature dilatometer (HTD) is not reliable in determining the firing temperature of an unknown brick sample. The amount of shrinkage upon heating is dependent on too many factors, such as the mineral composition of the clay, carbonate content, and maximum temperature used in the HTD.

Change in Mineral Composition

Another method tested for use in determining the firing temperature of old bricks is based on the development of the mineral phase composition of a clay specimen with increasing temperature, as shown in Figure 3.1, for one of the reference materials.

Most striking is the reduction of clay minerals and feldspars and the increase in hematite. However, neither clay minerals, quartz, nor feldspar could be used because their amounts in the original material as well as the fired product are difficult to determine. Only the amount of hematite (Fe_2O_3) can easily be measured by X-ray fluorescence.

According to Deer et al. (1985), the formation of hematite is limited to the range between 200°–700°C and 1388°C[1]. This feature was taken for the determination of the firing temperatures. Figure 3.2 shows the increase in absolute intensity of the strongest hematite peak, y, for the samples from Hamburg and Lübeck. Here, for temperatures higher than 800°C, a straight line can be fitted through the points for absolute intensity,

$$T \ [°C] = 0.84 \cdot y + 757 , \qquad (3.1)$$

with a standard deviation of ±25°C. This increase is independent of the amount of iron oxide in the sample.

---

[1] Hematite may start to develop at temperatures as low as 200°C depending on the history of the sample; however, the amounts formed are too small to be detected with standard X-ray diffraction (XRD) routines.

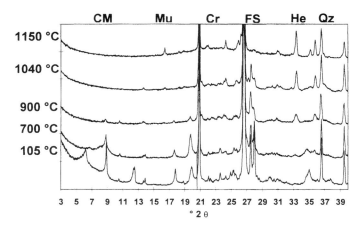

Figure 3.1   Change in mineral composition according to XRD measurements with firing temperature (CM = clay minerals, FS = feldspar, Cr = cristobalite, He = hematite, Mu = mullite, Qz = quartz).

However, the amount of hematite present in a sample is reflected in the combination of absolute intensity (AI) and half-width (HW). Therefore, an extended method was developed based on this feature (Figure 3.3). It revealed that with less iron oxide, hematite will (a) first be detected at a higher temperature and (b) reach the point of "saturation"[2] at a lower temperature than in a material with a higher content in iron

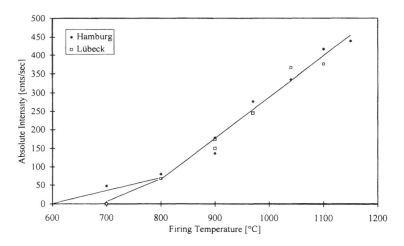

Figure 3.2   Change in the absolute intensity for the strongest hematite peak, $2\theta \approx 34$.

---

[2]   Temperature above which no increase in hematite content can be detected.

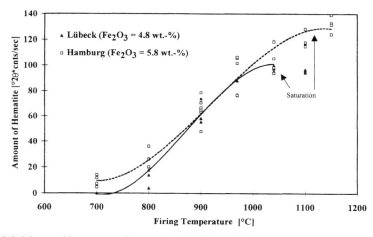

Figure 3.3 Measurable amount of hematite (AI·HW) vs. firing temperature for both materials.

oxide. The minimum content Fe_2O_3 has to be 3–4 wt.%. The graph is represented by the following equation:

$$T\,[°C] = a_3 \cdot y^3 - a_2 \cdot y^2 + a_1 \cdot y + a_0 \qquad (3.2)$$

with $y = AI \cdot HW$. This calculation should be applied only in cases where the simple method yields temperatures lower than 900°C.

It must be kept in mind, however, that these equations cannot be applied to results of measurements obtained with other X-ray diffractometers. Although the form of the graph stays the same, the conditions of measurement influence the values of AI and HW. The respective constants of both equations have to be determined for each diffractometer with the help of reference material and the historic brick must be analyzed under the same conditions.

After the methods were checked against our own standards, they were applied to determine the firing temperature (FT) of the historic bricks in their original condition and in refired state. Table 3.1 shows the results of the calculations schematically.

The diagnosis "inferior firing" could be confirmed with the help of the color or indicator minerals like clay minerals. In a related X-ray diffraction study of these same brick specimens, Livingston et al. (Chapter 11, this volume) attempted to apply a

Table 3.1 Calculated firing temperatures (FT) of Wixtore bricks.

	Original Condition	Refired
FT correct:	in most cases (900°–1100°C)	with sufficient iron oxide content
FT too low if:	inferior firing reducing kiln atmosphere	too little iron oxides and/or too much calcium

Table 3.2   Calculated vs. actual firing temperatures (FT) for fired clay samples.[1]

		Calculated FT (°C) for Sample	
		A	B
Method:	simple	830	860
	extended	890	920
Actual FT:		900	900

[1]L. v. d. Klugt, TNO, Delft, Netherlands.
Samples A and B differ in origin and composition of clay.

cristobalite index for durability. However, this index, developed for American bricks, does not appear suitable for the German ones. In the case of refired samples, correct FTs resulted if the material contained enough iron oxide and/or had only small amounts of calcium containing compounds.

Additionally, fired clay samples were obtained from a Dutch institute (TNO) and used to check the method. Table 3.2 shows that the calculated FTs are in good accordance with the actual FT. It can be concluded that X-ray diffraction analysis of the strongest hematite peak is a reliable and routinely applicable method for the subsequent determination of the FT of fired clay specimen.

LIMITATION OF THE METHODS

Two conditions are necessary for the XRD classification of FT. First, the sample must contain iron oxide, and the chemical composition must be known (especially the Fe, Mg, and Ca contents), since a high calcium and/or magnesium content may hinder the development of hematite. This is particularly the case when hematite is fine and homogeneously distributed throughout the clay body. If it is solely contained in yellow streaks, the red matrix can be used to determine the firing temperature.

Second, the sample must have been fired under an oxidizing atmosphere. The amount of hematite produced changes with the quantity of oxygen present in the atmosphere of the kiln. The higher the oxygen content, the higher the quantity of hematite produced at a given temperature.

CONCLUSIONS

The results presented show that for the characterization of FT of a brick sample, the chemical composition (especially the content of iron and calcium oxides) as well as the XRD intensity and half-width of the strongest hematite peak must be known. When calibrated against reference samples, the FT of the brick can then be subsequently determined. Within the limits mentioned, the analytical methods presented are a reliable and rapid method for determining the firing temperature.

ACKNOWLEDGEMENTS

The authors wish to thank the UBA for their financial support this research work. This paper results, in part, from a thesis by I. Schumann (1997).

REFERENCES

Deer, W.A., R.A. Howie, and J. Zussman. 1985. An introduction to the rock forming minerals. In: 15th Impression 1985, pp. 428–429. Essex: Longman Group Ltd.

Heimann, R.B. 1978. Mineralogische Vorgänge beim Brennen von Keramik und Archäothermie. *Acta praehistorica et archaelogica* **9(10)**:79–102

Robert, J.P. 1963. Determination of the firing temperature of ancient ceramics by measurement of thermal expansion. *Archaeometry* **6**:21–25.

Scholze, H. 1977. Glas: Natur, Struktur und Eigenschaften, 2. Auflage, p. 158. Berlin: Springer-Verlag.

Schumann, I. 1997. Zur nachträglichen Bestimmung der Brenntemperatur und zum Einfluß der Brenntemperatur auf die chemische Beständigkeit von Ziegel. Hamburg-Harburg, Techn. Univ., Dissertation. Aachen: Shaker Verlag.

Tite, M.S. 1978. Determination of the firing temperatures of ancient ceramics by measurement of thermal expansion. *Nature* **222**:81.

Weast, R.C., ed. 1970. Handbook of Chemistry and Physics. 51st Edition. Ohio: The Chemical Rubber Co.

4

Causes and Mechanisms of the Decay of Historic Brick Buildings in Northern Germany

L. FRANKE and I. SCHUMANN

Technische Universität Hamburg-Harburg, Arbeitsbereich Bauphysik und Werkstoffe im Bauwesen, Eißendorfer Straße 42, 21071 Hamburg, Germany

ABSTRACT

Based on the results of the analyses of buildings in northern Germany, it is possible to identify the main causes of deterioration, i.e., either salt or frost damage. In some cases, a combination of both can be demonstrated. The dominant salt causing damage to outdoor brick is gypsum. It is formed by the reaction of acid rain with calcium-containing constituents of brick and/or mortar. The gypsum precipitates as a kind of crust within the weathered front in decreasing amounts towards the center of the brick. The type of deterioration caused by the gypsum (flaking or sanding off) may be due to the velocity of drying. A new method to detect the frost susceptibility of brick is described.

THE BUILDINGS

The buildings surveyed are located in northern Germany and are situated in three different types of environment:

1. Hamburg, a large city not far from the coast,
2. Lübeck, a small town near the Baltic Sea,
3. Eiderstedt and Föhr, rural areas with a coastal climate.

The age of the monuments ranges from 80 to 700 years, covering a wide range of age and exposure. The damage affecting the buildings can be classified into two different types: indoor and outdoor, of which only the latter will be dealt with in detail in this chapter.

RESULTS

Description of the Materials: Brick and Mortar

Since brick is an artificial building material made of natural raw materials, firing can result in a variety of colors, phases, and mechanical and chemical behavior/performance. The final product is dependent on the composition of the raw material and the degree of firing. This has to be taken into account with historic bricks, since in the early days of brick production, the technical means of production and firing were not able to guarantee bricks of comparatively constant quality (see Chapter 2, this volume).

Even for ancient mortars it can be assumed that – with regard to private buildings where funds were limited – the materials used would not meet present requirements: instead of fresh water, brackish water, or salt water might have been used, and instead of river sand, sea sand. All this may have led to a reduction in quality and may have contributed to the decay of the masonry over time.

When judging the damage of the sampled buildings, these factors have to be taken into account. To enable mechanical classification of the characteristics of the historic materials, compressive strength, water absorption, bulk density, and porosity were measured for samples from 12 of the 15 buildings. For the remaining three buildings, the amount of sample material was too small to carry out the above-mentioned tests.

A correlation between the mechanical features and the degree of deterioration can not be seen; only a smaller variation in density is noticeable for industrially produced bricks (Bundesstraße, Hiobshospital, Kate) compared with the manually produced ones. Due to a lack of sample material, the above-mentioned tests could not be carried out for historic mortars. The application of modern hard and densely cemented mortars for restoration (repointing) of historic buildings with their comparatively soft bricks can cause damage, i.e., result in spalling of the surface of the brick in the depth of the repointing.

For two of the younger buildings in Hamburg, Hiobshospital and Bundesstraße 58, adhesive strength experiments were carried out at different depths of the same brick. For both buildings, adhesive strength shows a distinct gradient from the core to the surface of the stone, and in case of the Hiobshospital, the adhesive strength for the deteriorated material is lower than that of the nondeteriorated material (see Table 4.1). This leads to the conclusion that adhesive strength tests in varying depths of predrilled or sliced samples are a reliable means of mechanically detecting damage or planes of weakness.

CHARACTERIZATION OF BRICK DAMAGE

The types of outdoor damage found in the buildings can be classified in three categories: spalling, flaking, sanding off. In most cases, joints were also affected. This classification follows the definitions of damage types given in the "Damage Atlas" (Franke, Schumann et al. 1998).

Table 4.1 Adhesive strength profiles for damaged (G) and undamaged brick (U) from two different buildings.

Name	Adhesive strength β_{HZ} [N/mm²]		
	β_{HZ}	β_{min}	β_{max}
Hiob U vv	0.70	0.65	0.75
v	0.93	0.89	0.97
m	1.06	0.85	1.29
h	0.99	0.72	1.20
Hiob G vv	0.11	0	0.22
v	1.01	0.98	1.04
m	1.12	0.92	1.41
h	1.10	0.78	1.32
Bund U vv	0.75	0.65	0.85
v	1.49	1.44	1.53
m	1.61	1.11	2.02
h	1.27	0.91	1.84
Bund G vv	1.34	1.13	1.55
v	1.75	1.71	1.78
m	1.43	1.23	1.63
h	0.96	0.52	1.17

As far as salts are concerned, the zone of deterioration only affects the outer brick front, which for most of the analyzed bricks is thinner than 0.5 cm. Between 0.5 and 1 cm depth, remarkable amounts of salts could still be found; however, for the majority of the buildings, these were not sufficient to cause damage. Thus we generally have a gradient of salt distribution over the depth of the brick.

Compared with flaking, spalling can reach deeper than 1 cm and may affect the brick as a whole, e.g., as in the *Neue Mauer* in Lübeck. We tried to determine whether apparently nondeteriorated zones of bricks were predamaged on a microscale by frost or salt action. This might result in a reduced performance for the zones with microcracks compared with the original material. It proved to be difficult to find a suitable method to make these changes recognizable. Mercury porosimetry cannot be used, since the sample can only be used once with this method and, on the other hand, the expected changes due to formation of microcracks would fall in the range of variation. Experiments with frost-cycled and uncycled material gave no significant differences in porosity. The measurement of nitrogen adsorption on the inner surface of a sample (BET) also turned out not to be exact enough. The attempts to make these cracks visible under the light microscope or by SEM were also unsuccessful.

It may be assumed that faults like microcracks, and cracks in general, appear along zones of weakness formed in production, like textures. This is especially valid for modern, extruded bricks with their concentric texture of clay minerals parallel to the weathered surface. This texture can still be latently present after firing.

Soluble Content and Salts

An important part of the investigation was the analysis of the soluble contents of the bricks: those water-soluble as well as those soluble in perchloric acid and hydrochloric acid. Furthermore, the mineral phases and salts were identified.

For all of these examinations, bricks were cut into slices parallel to their weathered front (see Figure 4.1) and ground to pass through a 90 μm sieve and then passed on to the respective analyses. Table 4.2 shows the results in the form of the calculated salts. For reasons of clarity, only the contents of the weathered front (vv) and the back (h) are stated. As far as mortars are concerned, a calculation of the salt concentrations can only be given for selected buildings, as data concerning cation and anion contents were not available for all mortars. From Table 4.2, it can be seen that an enrichment of gypsum has taken place in cases of outdoor deterioration for the greater part of the bricks. The amount of other soluble salts is, however, low.

This enrichment of gypsum is limited to a thin subsurface layer, as the content decreases with increasing depth. Figure 4.2 shows this gradient for mortar and brick of the Hiobshospital, Hamburg.

In those cases where deteriorated and nondeteriorated areas were sampled on the same building, a difference can be seen in gypsum content. The deteriorated areas show concentrations of gypsum increased by factor 2 to 15. An exception here is the *Neue Mauer* in Lübeck. These bricks do not show the purely superficial deterioration characteristic of salt efflorescence, but a much more severe damage of the brick as well as a low salt content.

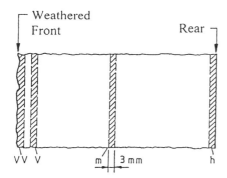

Figure 4.1 Scheme of saw cuts for chemical analyses.

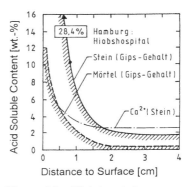

Figure 4.2 Hiobshospital: gypsum concentrations for mortar and brick. Stein = an individual brick.

These results show clearly that inspite of the different appearance of the damage and the manifold causes for deterioration assumed up to now, gypsum is the cause for deterioration in most of the outdoor cases. It is thus evident that this phenomenon, described for calcite-containing natural stones so far, occurs with bricks, as well.

Frost Susceptibility

For 10 of the 15 sampled buildings, frost resistance tests were carried out according to a newly developed dilatometer method (Franke and Bentrup 1990b). The bricks were cut into prisms 80 × 40 × 40 mm, stored in water for 3 days, according to DIN 52252 and immediately afterwards exposed to 50 frost-thaw cycles within the device. The recorded elongation due to ice formation (ε_E) during the exposure and the remaining elongation after the test (ε_R) led to a classification of the material as frost resistant or nonfrost resistant. A brick is termed frost resistant if no ice elongation is detectable or if no noticeable increase in ice elongation and no remaining elongation has taken place after 50 cycles. A material is classified as not frost resistant if a spontaneous rupture has occurred during the test or, if over the period of testing, a continuous increase in remaining elongation has taken place, which is often connected with a continuous increase in ice elongation. Table 4.3 shows the classification of the tested historic material (Franke and Bentrup 1990a).

DISCUSSION AND CONCLUSIONS

Relative Damage Factors

Based on the results presented so far, we are able to identify the main causes of deterioration for buildings that sustained outdoor damage. For St. Katharinen (Hamburg), St. Petri (Lübeck), Am Hafen 37 (Tönning), Packhaus (Tönning) and Kirche (Garding (II)), damage was caused by the formation of a gypsum crust in the surface layer of brick and mortar, as the gypsum content within the surface layer was high and no frost susceptibility was detectable.

For Bundesstraße 58 (Hamburg), Hiobshospital (Hamburg), Paradieshof (Hamburg), and Kirche (Tönning), it can be assumed that in addition to the mechanism of gypsum formation, a damaging effect of frost must also be taken into account, since the bricks of these buildings turned out to be potentially susceptible towards frost. Especially for the bricks of Bundesstraße 58, the aspect of frost should not be neglected as the gypsum contents were relatively low in the surface layer. The *Neue Mauer* in Lübeck obviously shows damage due to frost alone, even if the respective laboratory tests could not be carried out because of the fragile material. Still the salt contents were too low and the damage too severe and thorough to ascribe the deterioration to salt crystallization alone; there is also earth on the rear side off the wall serving as a supply for the damp necessary to cause frost damage.

Table 4.2 Results of chemical analyses for 14 buildings (other S = other sulfates; content of sulfates and nitrates without hydrate water; **boldface** = indoor samples). Tests were not possible on the *Neue Mauer* (see text).

No	Name		Salt content in surface layer [wt. %] — acid soluble Calcite	Gypsum	other S	water soluble Chlorides	Nitrates	Salt content in the rear [wt. %] — acid soluble Calcite	Gypsum	water soluble Gypsum	other S	Chlorides	Nitrate
Hamburg													
1	Bundesstr.	G	0.4	1.38	0	0.1_{Na}	0.07_K	0.3	0.9	0.04	0.05_{Mg}	0.07_{Na}	0.05_K
		U	0.8	0.24	0	<0.1	0	0.8	<0.36	0.05	0	0.02_{Na}	0
2	Hiobshospital	G	0.5	28.44	1.09_{Mg}	0.03	$<0.1_{K,Na}$	0.8	1.26	1.22	0	<0.1	n.m.
		U	0.5	2.16	0	<0.1	<0.1	0.6	1.08	0.99	0	<0.1	<0.1
3	Kate	G	0.5	0.39	0	<0.1	<0.1	n.m.	0.39	0.04	0	<0.1	<0.1
		U	1.3	1.26	0	<0.1	<0.1	0.9	<0.36	0.05	0	$<0.08_{Na}$	$<0.27_{Ca}$
4	Paradieshof		0.3	19.38	0.94_{Mg}	<0.1	0.10_K	1.5	30.6	2.5	0.13_{Mg}	$<0.19_{Na}$	0.21_{Na}
5	St. Katharinen		0.8	13.34	0	<0.1	<0.1	1.9	<0.36	0.05	0	<0.1	<0.1
Lübeck													
6	**Dankwart**	**0**	2.8	<0.36	0	2.47_{Na}	$2.87_{Ca,N}$						
		5	3.8	<0.36	0	0.79	0.7_K						
7	**Marlesgr.**	**10**	2.6	11.32	1.29_{Mg}	$<0.05_{Na}$	$<0.05_K$	0.4	0.08	<0.14	0	$<0.05_{Na}$	$<0.05_K$
		12	3.1	0.14	0	$<0.05_{Na}$	$<0.05_K$	2.2	0.04	0.11	0	$<0.05_{Na}$	$<0.05_K$
8	St. Petri	I	0.8	11.32	1.29_{Mg}	$<0.05_{Na}$	$<0.05_K$						
		II	0.3	0.14	0	$<0.05_{Na}$	$<0.05_K$						
		I_K	15.2	0.54	0	n.m.							
		II_K	3.14	<0.36	0	0.02_{Na}							

(continued)

Table 4.2 *continued*

No	Name	Salt content in surface layer [wt. %]					Salt content in the rear [wt. %]					
		acid soluble			water soluble		acid soluble		water soluble			
		Calcite	Gypsum	other S	Chlorides	Nitrates	Calcite	Gypsum	Gypsum	other S	Chlorides	Nitrate
9	**Burgtor**	0	1.8	0.15_{Mg}	<0.1	0.19_{Na}	0.2	1.77	1.69	$<0.1_{Mg}$	0	0.21_{Na}
11	Kirche I	0.5	14.68	0	$<0.31_{Na}$	0.1	3.3	<0.36	<0.03	0	$<0.05_{Na}$	0.05_K
	II	0.3	12.56	0	0.19_{Na}	0.08_K	2.7	0.36	0.04	0	$<0.05_{Na}$	0.05_K
12	Am Hafen I	0.7	0.48	0	<0.1	<0.1	0.8	0.48	0.03	n.m.	<0.1	<0.1
	II	0.8	4.61	0	$<0.03_{Na}$	$<0.05_K$	0.8	0.35	0.44	0	$<0.03_{Na}$	0.04_K
	III	0.5	11.13	0	<0.1	<0.1	0.7	0.69	0.04	0	<0.1	<0.1
13	Packhaus	0.8	17.62	0	0.03_{Na}	0.06_K	3.5	<0.36	0.39	0	n.m.	0.12_{Ca}
	Garding											
14	**Kirche** I	5.6	3.35	0	1.16Na	1.30_{Na}	7.0	0.28	0.28	0	1.35_{Na}	1.32_{Na}
	II	3.5	2.26	0	$<0.05_{Na}$	$<0.04_{Ca}$	4.7	0.04	0.12	0	$<0.05_{Na}$	$<0.04_{Ca}$
	IIIr	4.8	<0.36	0	0.36_{Na}	0.33_{Ca}						
	IIIs	3.4	7.23	0	0.63_{Na}	0.61_{Ca}						
	Föhr											
15	**Kirche**	0.3	1.91	0	0.35_{Na}	0.13	0.4	0.1	<0.04	0	0.23_{Na}	0.06

Table 4.3   Results of frost dilatation tests for the historic bricks (average).

Building	Water saturation after 3 days [%] S_{3d}	Elongation ε due to ice formation [mm] after 1 and 50 freeze-thaw cycles $\varepsilon_{E,1}$	$\varepsilon_{E,50}$	Remaining ε after 50 freeze-thaw cycles $\varepsilon_{R,50}$	Frost Resistant
St. Petri	63.6	<0.01	<0.01	0	yes
St. Katharinen	78.9	0.12	0.12	0	yes
Garding	80.5	0	0	0	yes
Hiobshospital	77.8	0.53	1.57	1.40	no
Paradieshospital	83.4	0.35	0.90	1.23	no
Bundesstraße	74.0	0.06	*	*	no
Kate	74.0	0.37	0.45	0	yes
Tö: Am Haf. (5)	78.7	0.11	0.19	0.04	yes[1]
Tö: Am Haf. (7)	75.1	0.20	0.22	0.10	yes[1]
Tö: Kirche	85.7	0.20	**	**	no
Tö: Packhaus	80.9	0.53	1.15	0	yes

[1]   Frost resistant, shows only minimal increase in remaining elongation after 50 freeze-thaw cycles (Franke et al. 1993).
*   Cracked after 9 freeze-thaw cycles.
**   Cracked after 1–4 freeze-thaw cycles.

For those cases where there were samples taken from a deteriorated and a nondeteriorated part of the same building, it is remarkable that the deteriorated bricks had a higher content of water/dampness than the undeteriorated bricks (Hiobhospital, Am Hafen) although hygroscopic salts were not found. Long-lasting and deep-penetrating dampness is thus a supporting, if not necessary, feature for the formation of gypsum crusts, as the aggressive solutions need time to work. This is especially obvious for the Hiobshospital, where both areas sampled are on the same wall. The bricks of the lower part of the wall (up to approximately 2 m) are badly deteriorated, whereas the bricks above show no visible damage thus far.

Mechanism of Acid Attack and Encrustation

The mechanism of the formation of a gypsum crust proceeds as follows: Potentially aggressive pollutants, such as SO_2, CO_2, and NO_x, in combination with humidity are the causes for this type of deterioration. They are transported to the brick, which usually contains minerals that are acid-sensitive, like calcite or feldspar. The acid solution dissolves these minerals and transports them towards the surface, where Ca^{2+} from calcite or feldspar precipitates together with SO_4^{2-} of the sulfuric acid as gypsum.

Damage to the brick occurs as soon as the outer layer of pores is filled with gypsum. The pressure due to further crystallization leads to sanding off or flaking of the outer layer.

Laboratory simulations of the procedure proved that the necessary calcium is taken from the brick and the sulfate is delivered by acid deposition. The comparatively high capillarity of the bricks enables a progression of the aggressive solutions towards the inner part of the brick and thus guarantees the calcium supply necessary to cause damage over time. This is especially true since the joints are affected, as well. An intake by rising damp, dust, etc. is not necessary. With several of the buildings, the calcite content shows a decrease from the core towards the crust of the brick. This supports the theory of transformation of calcite into gypsum or the dissolution as calcium nitrate, respectively. In some cases, this gradient reveals an opposite behavior, which is caused either by an enhanced solution of part of the calcite content of the joint mortar of the masonry or by a dissolution of calcite in the core and precipitation of the same beneath the surface. The subsequent transformation of this calcite into gypsum *in situ* is connected with an increase in volume, which can lead to destruction of the material, provided there is a sufficient degree of filling of the pores.

Effects of Salt Crystallization

As only a single salt mineral is responsible for all of the observed damage, it remains to be explained why the damage occurs sometimes as sanding off and other times as flaking. Experiments by Binda et al. (1988) revealed that the type of damage depends on the velocity of drying. The longer the time for crystallization within one cycle, the earlier the damage occurs. Delamination, cracks, and fissures predominate. If the cycle of drying included heating, pulverization results.

Applied to damage on buildings, we can conclude that for parts of buildings that stay wet over a long period or are exposed to frequent rainfall (NE/NW), flaking off should predominate. Facades that dry quickly (S/SE) should primarily show sanding off.

This theoretical data is supported by the appearance of the damage of our historic buildings. Damage described as *sanding off* is stated for the S/SE facades of Paradieshof, Kirche, and House *Am Hafen 37* in Tönning. Even for the SE facade of Hiobshospital, sanding off occurs together with a flaking off of the encrustation. However, the position of the facade alone should not be solely considered to be the cause of damage; shade from bushes and trees must also be taken into account too, as they can change the conditions of drying completely. It should be mentioned that the production of a brick can support a certain way of weathering: bricks produced by extrusion should be more susceptible to flaking and spalling due to the concentric layers of clay minerals whereas hand-molded bricks should be affected by sanding off.

As noted earlier, firing has an important effect on the performance and quality of the brick. Results concerning the subsequent determination of the firing temperature for this group of bricks are described further in Chapter 3 (this volume) and Schumann (1997).

The contribution of the nitrifying bacteria to the observed damage should be investigated, as well, especially with respect to how much the nitrificants support the formation of gypsum crusts by transforming the calcium of the minerals of the core of the brick into more soluble compounds.

ACKNOWLEDGEMENT

We wish to thank the Umweltbundesamt Berlin for their financial support of our research.

REFERENCES

Bender, W., and F. Händle, eds. 1982. Handbuch für die Ziegelindustrie. Wiesbaden, Berlin: Bauverlag.

Binda, L., G. Baronio, and A.E. Charola. 1988. Deterioration of porous materials due to salt crystallization under different thermohygrometric conditions. I. Brick. In: Proc. 6th Intl. Congress on Deterioration and Conservation of Stone, ed. J. Ciabach pp. 279–287. Torun, Poland: Nicholas Copernicus Univ.

Franke, L., and H. Bentrup. 1990a. Ein neues Frostprüfverfahren für Ziegel mittels Dilatometrie. Vortrag / TUHH-BauForum Hamburg, TUHH.

Franke, L., and H. Bentrup. 1990b. Kritische Betrachtung der aktuellen Frostprüfverfahren für Mauerziegel. *Ziegelindustrie Intl.* **9**: 493–500.

Franke, L., H. Bentrup, and I. Schumann. 1993. Ursachen der Steinschädigung an historischen Backsteinbauten in Norddeutschland, Teil 1 und 2. *Bautenschutz + Bausanierung* **16**: 13–16, 45–48.

Franke, L., and I. Schumann. 1994. Beeinträchtigung von Sichtmauerwerk durch Luftschadstoffe und sauren Regen. 12. ibausil (Weimar). Beitrag Nummer 1.32

Franke, L., I. Schumann, R.P.J. van Hees, L.J.A.R. van der Klugt, S. Naldini, L. Binda, and G. Baronio. 1998. Damage Atlas: Classification and Analysis of Damage Patterns Found in Brick Masonry. Stuttgart: Fraunhofer IRB Verlag.

Schumann, I. 1997. Zur nachträglichen Bestimmung der Brenntemperatur und zum Einfluß der Brenntemperatur auf die chemische Beständigkeit von Ziegel. Hamburg-Harburg, Tech. Univ., Dissertation. Aachen: Shaker Verlag.

5

Indoor Brick Damage

Investigation of the Roles of Pore Size and Salts

L. FRANKE and I. SCHUMANN

Technische Universität Hamburg-Harburg, Arbeitsbereich Bauphysik und Werkstoffe im
Bauwesen, Eißendorfer Straße 42, 21071 Hamburg, Germany

ABSTRACT

The degree of deterioration due to salt action is influenced by pore characteristics, the
performance of the brick and the amount and type of salt present. Results of theoretical
calculations are presented which allow an estimation of both the general susceptibility of brick
to salt action as well as the danger caused by the amount of salts. Explanations are offered as to
why different damage types (sanding, spalling, etc.) are observed.

INTRODUCTION

Deterioration of brick and stone, in general, appears to be mainly an outdoor problem.
Yet severe indoor damage was observed at several buildings in northern Germany. The
results of standard analyses are only a background topic of this report. They serve as a
basis for further consideration of the underlying mechanisms of indoor decay (and
consequently outdoor decay) and can be regarded as a continuation and completion of
earlier articles on outdoor damage (see Franke and Schoppe 1991; Chapter 4, this
volume).

OBSERVED DAMAGE PATTERNS

In contrast to outdoor damage, where the cause of decay can mainly be ascribed to the
formation of gypsum crusts and/or frost action, the cause of indoor damage can not so
easily be assigned.

Comparing indoor and outdoor damage, the patterns of decay appear different.
With weathered facades we mainly find encrustation, blistering and superficial sanding off, whereas indoor damage is – with our buildings – more protruding: the bricks
fall apart into sharp-edged pieces (Dankwartsgrube/Marlesgrube) or only sand

remains of the former brick (St. Laurentius, Föhr; Kirche in Garding). There was one building in our study where the indoor bricks seemed not to have deteriorated (Burgtor, Lübeck).

RESULTS

Since the results of the chemical and mechanical analyses of the main part of the buildings were presented earlier (Franke and Schoppe 1991), the following two sections offer a summary and generalization in order to make the topic more understandable.

Mechanical Properties

Bricks removed from indoor walls revealed no extraordinarily striking features compared to those taken out of weathered surfaces. The only remarkable features were a high density and a low coefficient of capillary uptake of water in the bricks of the two houses in Lübeck.

Chemical Analyses

The results of the chemical analyses revealed a difference in salt content between exposed and indoor facades as well as between the different types of indoor walls.

In unsheltered facades, gypsum was identified almost exclusively as the soluble salt. The walls of the two private buildings in Lübeck contain chlorides and nitrates whereas the walls above the domes of the churches show both a declining gypsum content from the surface of the bricks to the rear/center as well as an almost constant content of chlorides and nitrates with the same brick.

Nevertheless, the salt contents of the indoor bricks are low (max. < 5–6 wt.%) compared to the outdoor ones (max. < 30 wt.%). This observation leads to the assumption that crystallization pressure cannot be the only cause for decay.

Calculation of Crystallization Pressures

Material-independent Crystallization Pressures

According to several reports, crystallization of salt (or ice) for energetic reasons preferentially takes place in the larger pores (Everett 1961; Snethlage 1983; Weiss 1992; Kühne 1997). The values for the smallest pore radius in which crystallization can take place range between 1–5 μm. However, Kühne found salts in amorphous form in pores of less than 1 μm radius if the material contained no pores bigger than 1 μm. The same authors could show that differences appear in the crystallization and precipitation behavior of readily soluble $MgSO_4$ and slightly soluble gypsum ($CaSO_4 \cdot H_2O$).

Furthermore, it is well known that the surface of a building material with mainly large pores will dry sooner than that with smaller pores.

The previously mentioned result implies that for further investigation of the causes of decay, the pore-size distribution of the bricks has to be examined, as the pores are the locations were the salts crystallize. Snethlage (1983) and Rossi-Manaresi (1991) also

Table 5.1   Material-independent crystallization pressure according to Snethlage (1983).

Pore class (µm)	0.005	0.05	0.5	5
tcp (N/mm²)	32	3.2	0.32	0.032

base their calculations of crystallization pressure on this consideration. Based on the thesis of Everett (1961) on the growth of ice crystals within a pore system, Snethlage is of the opinion that a salt crystal growing in a small pore has a higher chemical potential than one growing in a large pore. As a consequence, crystal growth in larger pores is favored. Only if the larger pore is filled with salt and there is still solution within the small pore will the crystal grow into the latter. This is enabled by increasing the chemical potential of the bulk crystal via pressure rise, which creates a storage of energy within the system through the difference in inner pressure, Δ_p. The effect is a higher thermodynamic potential for the already present salt crystal. This leads to an expression for calculation of the crystallization pressure for a definite pore size:

$$\Delta_p = \frac{2\sigma}{r} \ . \tag{5.1}$$

Snethlage assumed 8 dyn/cm² ($8 \cdot 10^{-2}$ N/mm²) to be a good enough value for the surface tension, σ, of a salt solution close to saturation for most salts. For calculations, the pore radii, r, were classified and the mean value of each pore class taken (0.005, 0.05, 0.5, 5 µm). With these values, results for the theoretical crystallization pressure (*tcp*) within each of the previously mentioned pore classes are obtained (Table 5.1).

For the calculation of the *tpc* of our samples, the *tcp* of the smallest pore class had to be changed to 21.33 N/mm², as only pores down to 0.004 µm were recorded. For all of the samples, pore sizes larger than 100 or 200 µm were recorded as well; however, the *tcp* was not adapted, as the associated effects are negligible.

Material-dependent Crystallization Pressures

These results do not, however, explain the fact that different bricks show varying performance because the mentioned *tpc*'s are material-independent. As a consequence, Snethlage (1983) offers two different volume factors for correcting these values according to the specific pore-size distribution of each sample: V_1 and V_2. They represent different pore geometries. The volume factor V_1

$$V_1 = \frac{V_r}{V_R} \tag{5.2}$$

compares the amount of the respective smaller pore class, r, with the amount of the first pore-size maximum, R. The underlying model of pore geometry is that the smaller pore-size classes are connected with the first maximum and serve as supply of solution for the growing crystal. In contrast, the volume factor V_2

$$V_2 = \frac{V_r}{\Sigma V_R} \qquad (5.3)$$

is based on another pore geometry. Here the amount of each smaller pore class r is compared with the sum of the amount of all larger pore classes ΣV_R. This represents a pore system where the sum of larger pores is connected with the next smaller class. While Snethlage uses V_2 and the part of V_r and V_R of the open porosity for his calculations, Rossi-Manaresi (1991) applies V_1 and the percentage of each pore class of the total intrusion volume. For the following calculations, the model of Rossi-Manaresi was applied and Table 5.2 shows the results for this so-called material-dependent crystallization pressure (*mdcp*) obtained for six buildings, five of which revealed indoor deterioration and for comparison one with good outdoor performance.

Applying this method to all porosity samples, we get an average *mdcp* for each sampled building area, as shown in Table 5.3. This *mdcp* is now compared with the average compressive strength (column three), although the tensile strength of a material is the

Table 5.2 Scheme of *mdcp* calculation for some of the buildings according to the Rossi-Manaresi model (1991).

Building		Pore-size class (μm)					Total pressure (N/mm²)
		0.005	0.05	0.5	5	50	
theoretical pressure		21.33	3.2	0.32	0.032	0.0032	*mdcp*
Bundesstraße	A	0.18	0.95	36.65	55.72	6.50	
(outdoor)	B	0.003	0.017	0.66	8.57		
	C	0.064	0.054	0.211	0.274		0.7
Dankwartsgrube	A	1.41	8.99	84.82	2.71	2.21	
(indoor)	B	0.017	0.106	31.23	38.29		
	C	0.362	0.339	9.994	1.225		11.9
Marlesgrube	A	1.08	19.31	61.99	6.65	11.07	
(indoor)	B	0.017	0.312	9.45	5.60		
	C	0.363	0.0998	3.024	0.179		4.6
Garding I	A	10.16	35.25	41.44	6.39	6.23	
(indoor)	B	0.25	0.851	6.49	14.62		
	C	5.333	2.723	2.077	0.467		10.6
St. Laurentius	A	5.63	33.52	57.49	2.03	1.06	
(indoor)	B	0.098	0.58	28.32	54.24		
	C	2.09	1.856	9.062	1.736		14.7
St. Petri	A	0.47	3.66	47.08	43.58	5.14	
(core II)	B	0.01	0.078	1.08	9.16		
	C	0.213	0.2496	0.346	0.293		1.1

A = percentage of pore-size class of total intrusion volume.
B = correction factor $V_1 = V_r / V_R$.
C = calculated pressure $\cdot$ V_1.

value which characterizes the resistance of a building material against salt crystallization. The tensile strength is always lower than the compressive strength (*cs*).

Figure 5.1 clearly shows that with bricks falling apart without any direct influence
of the weather (open circles), the highest *mdcp*'s – even higher than the brick *cs* – were
calculated. Bricks of these buildings are likely to suffer from crystallization pressure
because of their pore-size distribution.

Thus, Figure 5.1 shows the potential for bricks or porous building material in general to be affected by salt crystallization as the horizontal axis represents, from left to
right, a rising resistance against crystallization pressure whereas the vertical axis
shows rising stress, from bottom to top. The bricks most likely to decay by salt crystallization fall above the isobar of Figure 5.1. However, many of the exposed brick, which
according to this illustration are not likely to show damage due to salt action, deteriorate as well.

One gains a different impression if the tensile strength is plotted against the *mdcp*.
Here all the brick should suffer from crystallization since for all of them the *mdcp* is
higher than the material's calculated minimum tensile strength.

Table 5.3 Average theoretical crystallization pressures (*cp*) and compressive strengths (*cs*);
STRESS: actual maximum pore filling (PF) × *mdcp*.*

Building	Av. theor. *cp* (N/mm²)	Av. *cs* (N/mm²)	STRESS
Bundesstraße	0.65	10.7	2.4
Hiobshospital	2.81	27.4	252.1
Kate	4.77	21.9	16.5
Paradieshospital	0.60	11.2	27.0
St. Katharinen	1.11	16.0	39.5
Marlesgrube 8	5.40	13.5	60.5
Dankwartsgrube	8.04	13.9	116.7
St. Petri II	0.64	19.3	0.4
St. Petri i	1.25	18.2	3.1
Am Hafen 37 I	1.82	11.8	1.8
Am Hafen 37 II	1.09	13.6	10.3
Am Hafen 37 III	2.12	18.5	50.4
Packhaus	0.96	18.3	30.5
Kirche (Tönning) I	1.59	26.1	74.3
II	1.21	13.1	30.7
Garding, Kirche I	13.13	14.7	195.5
dto. II dunkel	1.85	18.8	8.7
St. Laurentius	13.14	15.8	51.3

* As some samples contain salt mixtures and expandable salts, the results obtained here contain
  errors, which means that the calculated pore filling may be to low.

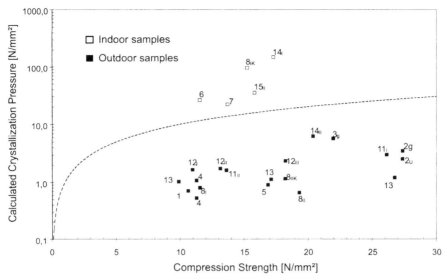

Figure 5.1 Material-dependent crystallization pressure vs. compressive strength (numbers indicate building according to Table 4.2; see Chapter 4, this volume). The dashed line indicates points where crystallization pressure = compressive strength).

It can be stated, that both versions do not offer sufficient explanation for the varying observed behavior of the building material towards salt crystallization.

Material- and Salt Content-dependent Crystallization Pressures (STRESS Index)

The results of the *mdcp* calculations for the historic buildings imply that the *mdcp* has to be regarded as the maximal crystallization pressure that can occur in the pore system. For the estimation of the actual likeliness of deterioration, the degree of pore filling is taken into consideration and a STRESS index is introduced.

For the calculation of the STRESS index, the salt content S_S (in g/100 g sample; = wt.%) is transformed into a brick-related salt content S_B (in g/100 g brick), which is then changed into a volume S_V (g/cm³) via its respective density:

$$S_S \, [wt.\%] = \frac{salt \; content \, [g]}{100 \, g \; sample \; material} \Rightarrow S_B = \frac{salt \; content \, [g]}{100 \, g \; brick \; material} \quad (5.4)$$

$$S_V \, [\%] = \frac{S_B}{density} \, [cm^3 \, / \, 100 \; g]. \quad (5.5)$$

Division of total intrusion volume (*TIV*) (Hg porosimetry [cm³/100 g]) by the calculated salt volume leads to the degree of pore filling (*PF*) of the total pore volume in %

$$PF \, [\%] = \frac{S_V \cdot 100}{TIV}. \quad (5.6)$$

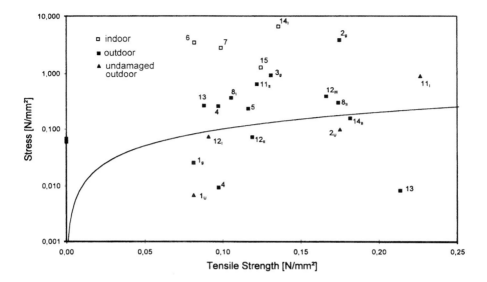

Figure 5.2 Material- and salt content-dependent crystallization pressure (STRESS index) vs. tensile strength; numbers indicate building according to Table 4.2, this volume.

Multiplication of *PF* with *mdcp* leads to the results stated in column STRESS of Table 5.3. The illustrated version is given in Figure 5.2, with the STRESS index vs. the calculated minimum tensile strength[1]. This figure clearly indicates that an unfavorable combination of STRESS and tensile strength is a better explanation for the deterioration.

LABORATORY SIMULATION OF SALT ACTION

As explained above, salts can be harmful to the brick because they exert pressure on the walls of the pores upon crystallization or hydration. To study these effects, devices were constructed to allow measurement of the dilation of the samples ($10 \times 4 \times 4$ cm) due to the hydration/crystallization pressure of salts. The samples were soaked in saturated salt solution, dried and exposed to changing relative humidity ($50 \rightarrow 100\%$) and the dilation recorded twice a day.

For $MgSO_4$, the dilation was approximately ten times higher than for Na_2SO_4, which is probably due to their different behavior towards humidity in the range in question:

---

[1] According to Schubert (1990), the tensile strength can be approximated from the compressive strength. It is 1% to 10% of its value.

Table 5.4   Salt distribution (MgSO₄) over the sample.

Prism	inside	middle [wt.-%]	surface	Exposition
F6 II	3.51	5.39	1.79	changing RH
F6 V	2.95	2.95	5.50	desiccator

- Sodium sulfate takes up water and hydrates and dehydrates.
- Magnesium sulfate only hydrates.

Both salts may dissolve and recrystallize in the course of the experiment.

Following this, new specimens were prepared and soaked twice (with drying in between) in the specific solution. While the sodium probes crumbled and disintegrated after a short second immersion in the solution, the magnesium samples developed only small fissures/cracks. During the dilation test that followed, the double-soaked samples showed a smaller degree of dilation than the single-soaked ones. An explanation can be offered for this observation considering the fact, that the double-soaked probes experienced a pre-dilation during the second soaking which was not recorded.

The results of the chemical analyses for the Mg Prisms II and V indicate that the salt distribution over the sample is not homogenous but concentrates below the surface of the probe (Table 5.4). Prism II was exposed to changing relative humidity (RH), whereas prism V was stored in a desiccator.

Most striking is the observation that fissures and detachment were found below the flakes that are pressed off, but no salts were visible. A closer look, by light microscope, on a surface perpendicularly cut through one of the disintegrated sodium prisms reveals there are not enough salts underneath the outward layer to press the latter off. Figure 5.3 illustrates this clearly.

This may lead to the conclusion that the mechanism causing detachment could be a one other than simply pressure. The hydrating or crystallizing salts in the outer crust expand and exert pressure on the walls of the surrounding pores. This results in a dilation of the outer layer whereas the core of the sample remains rigid and undisturbed. Tensions arise between crust and core which, in the end, cannot be compensated anymore by the material, and the crust finally looses it adhesion to the body. Visual signs are blisters and flaking.

INFLUENCE OF THE PORE-SIZE DISTRIBUTION

It can be concluded that the location and appearance of crystallization and its related damage depends on several conditions:
- pore-size distribution,
- rate of evaporation,
- composition of the salt(s),
- condition and strength of the building material surface.

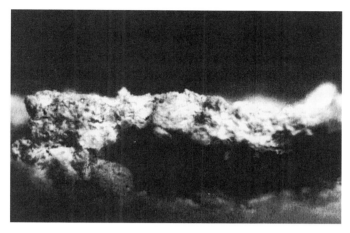

Figure 5.3   Cut Na sulfate-treated prism under the light microscope.

Variation of *mdcp* and *cs*

Since the STRESS index in itself is not sufficient explanation for the appearance of the different deterioration patterns found with bricks and the pore-size *distribution* may have an influence on the damage pattern, further investigations are needed.

Only if the variation of *mdcp* and *cs* is also taken into account, will a satisfying description of the mechanism of decay be possible. Table 5.5 gives the observed variations. It clearly reveals that for some of the samples, the ratio between maximum and minimum *mdcp* is very high (≥ 2), which represents a rather uneven distribution of crystallization pressure. The result here is a point-by-point sanding off (alveolization), this the more so if the ratio between minimum and maximum *cs* is low. With samples removed indoors in Lübeck (Marlesgrube, Dankwartsgrube) the relative as well as the absolute deviation of *mdcp* is high, with the samples from Föhr (St. Laurentius) and Garding (Kirche I) the relative deviation (= max./min. value) of *mdcp* is low, but the absolute deviation (= max. – min. value) is high. This offers an explanation for the failure of single bricks of these buildings, too.

These considerations, together with the conclusions of Rossi-Manaresi, lead to general hypotheses about the mechanisms of salt decay, taking into account the deviation of *cs* as well. Table 5.6 shows the four different possibilities of combining the degrees of deviations of *cs* and *mdcp* and their respective effects.

The first combination of features represents a homogeneous distribution of pressure within the surface with the effect that according to the prevailing drying conditions, areal sanding off or spalling of encrustation is observed (see Chapter 4, this volume). The sensitivity to salt decay for this category is mainly based on the absolute *cs* of the brick in question.

Table 5.5   Possible damage patterns due deviation in *mdcp* and *cs*.

Degree of Deviation			Effects
	mdcp	*cs*	
1	low	low	areal sanding, spalling
2	low	high	alveolization, blistering
3	high	low	alveolization, blistering
4	high	high	sound and deteriorated areas close together

For the second and third combination of the varying *mdcp* and *cs*, salt crystallization creates alveolization or blistering, respectively (depending on the drying conditions) because the material strength is exceeded within small, limited areas.

The fourth mode differs from the others as the combination of absolute values of
mdcp and *cs* can lead to areas of totally different performance within both the brick itself and wall. As a result we may find sound and deteriorated areas as well as sanding
off/flaking within larger areas and alveolization/blistering within limited areas.

Consolidation of Stone by Salt Crystals

Salt may have favorable effects on the material characteristics, such as bending
strength and compressive strength, since a kind of composite material is created. The
salts fill the pores and thereby increase their host's compressive strength, and they can
create connections via the pore system which results in a higher bending strength.

A similar effect was observed by Weiss (1992) during his salt expansion tests with
sandstone and sodium sulfate. In a first phase, the salt accumulated in the pore system
and led to an increase in its strength, then in a second phase the deterioration began.

As a result of this temporary increase in strength, larger blisters can be built up,
flaking and spalling takes a longer time to become visible/detectable, and the stone
appears sound for a longer period.

Rossi-Manaresi (1991) observed that for sandstone having a high porosity and for
marble having almost no small pores, the calculated *mdcp* are too low to create any
damage. She concluded that salt crystallization should result in a cementation of the
surface within these stones.

According to our measurements of the pore-size distribution in salt-containing
and salt-free bricks, the calculated *mdcp* was higher for surface samples containing
gypsum than for the original salt-free material. Washing of a salt-containing sample
(only with limited effect, as gypsum is only slightly soluble) leads to a decrease of the
mdcp as some bigger pores are at least partly salt-free now. The calculated *mdcp* thus
increases with increasing salt content.

Table 5.6 Absolute and relative deviation of *mdcp* and compressive strength for 13 historical buildings and their observed damage

Building	mdcp [N/mm²]		max. / min.	βSt [N/mm²]		max. / min.	Damage
	min.	max.		min.	max.		
Bundesstraße	0.60	0.70	1.16	8.6	12.7	1.48	S
Hiobshosp. U o.h	2.10	2.18	1.03	18.2	35.4	1.95	P
Kate	1.15	6.50	5.65	13.9	29.9	2.15	Bl, P
Paradieshof	0.58	0.63	1.09	10.7	11.7	1.09	S, P
St. Katharinen	0.61	1.42	2.33	11.4	20.5	1.80	Al, P
St. Petri II	0.59	0.64	1.08	19.3	32.1	1.66	B, Kr
Dankwartsgrube	4.56	11.92	2.61	12.6	15.3	1.21	Cr
Marlesgrube	2.60	6.70	2.58	11.0	16.8	1.53	Cr
Tönning: Kirche I	1.25	1.93	1.54	23.4	30.0	1.37	ok
II	0.66	1.76	2.67	11.9	14.1	1.18	Al
Tönning: Packhaus	0.78	1.14	1.46	9.9	26.8	2.71	R
Tönning: Hafen I	1.21	2.43	2.01	8.4	12.5	1.49	R
II	1.10	–	–	12.2	15.9	1.30	S
III	1.84	2.39	1.30	15.5	19.5	1.26	S
Garding II	1.74	4.93	2.83	18.3	23.1	1.26	P
I	10.60	15.66	1.49	14.7	21.2	1.44	S
St. Laurentius	11.55	14.74	1.28	13.5	18.2	1.35	S

B = flaking, P = spalling, S = sanding off, Bl = blistering, Al = alveolization, Kr = crusts, Cr = crumbling, R = rough surface, – = no data.

FURTHER INFLUENCES ON THE MECHANISM OF (SALT) DECAY

Besides the effects of mechanical properties and pore-size distribution, there are other factors that influence the development of deterioration patterns. The effect of drying condition was discussed in Chapter 4 (this volume).

Furthermore, the method of production has an effect on the damage type as the texture may include voids and pores of preferential elongation which can serve as a place for crystallization. The performance of a brick or its durability respectively, will demand a good firing of the brick. Inferior burning can leave salts or clay minerals in the brick and mistakes during the firing process can, for example, lead to cracks or black cores.

For indoor bricks, insufficient firing and/or mistakes during firing may have contributed to the observed damage.

CONCLUSIONS

The application of Snethlage's correction factors for the calculation of material-dependent crystallization pressure allows an assessment of the susceptibility of building materials towards salt crystallization.

With increasing salt content, the pore structure changes towards smaller pores due to a filling of the pores. This altered pore-size distribution may leave the salts with less room for further crystallization. A calculation of *mdcp* for this reduced pore system results in higher *mdcp* values with the salt-containing sample. Therefore, a STRESS index is introduced which takes this pore filling into consideration and enables an assessment of the actual likelihood of decay due to salt action.

Depending on the combination of *mdcp* and material strength (and drying conditions), bricks show different deterioration patterns, like sanding off or spalling. They can even appear to be consolidated by small amounts of salt.

ACKNOWLEDGEMENT

We wish to thank the Umweltbundesamt Berlin for their financial support of our reserach.

REFERENCES

Everett, D.H. 1961. The thermodynamics of frost damage to porous solids. *Trans. Faraday Soc.* **57**:1541–1551.

Franke, L., and I. Schoppe. 1991. Schädigung historischer Backsteinbauten durch Luftschadstoffe. In: Proc. Intl. Brick/Block Masonry Conf., Berlin, Germany, Oct. 13–16, 1991, vol. 3, pp. 1465–1472. Bonn: Dt. Gesellschaft Mauerwerksbau.

Kühne, H.-C. 1997. Zum Kristallisationsverhalten von Salzen in porösen baukeramischen Materialien. 13th Intl. Baustofftagung ibausil, Weimar. Tagungsbericht **1**:1.1021–1.1040.

Rossi-Manaresi, R., and A. Tucci. 1991. Pore structure and the disruptive or cementing effect of salt crystallisation in various types of stone. *Studies in Conservation* **36**:53–58.

Schubert, P. 1990. Eigenschaften von Mauerwerk, Mauersteinen und Mauermörtel. Mauerwerkskalender 1990, pp. 121–130. Berlin: Ernst & Sohn Verlag,

Snethlage, A. 1983: Steinkonservierung, 1979–83. Berichte für die Stiftung Volkswagenwerk, Arbeitshefte des Bayr. LA für Denkmalpflege.

Weiss, G. 1992. Die Eis- und Salzkristallisation im Porenraum von Sandsteinen und ihre Auswirkungen auf das Gerfüge unter besonderer Berücksichtigung gesteinsspezifischer Parameter. *Münchener Geowiss. Abh.* **9**(B):1–118.

6

Stages of Damage in the Structure of Brick Due to Salt Crystallization

E.N. CANER-SALTIK[1], I. SCHUMANN[2], and L. FRANKE[2]

[1]Material Conservation Laboratory, Department of Architecture, Middle East Technical University, Ankara 06531, Turkey
[2]Technische Universität Hamburg-Harburg, Arbeitsbereich Bauphysik und Werkstoffe im Bauwesen, Eißendorfer Straße 42, 21071 Hamburg, Germany

ABSTRACT

Salt damage is an important decay phenomenon and its assessment is important for the conservation of historic brick structures. This study presents work related to understanding the process and the extent of salt damage to brick and introduces data for sound historic bricks. Historic brick samples from a 14th century bath in Anatolia, representing sound material, were subjected to salt crystallization tests. Investigations were done on salt crystallization sites and pores by optical and scanning electron microscopy. Change in the durability of brick during salt crystallization cycles was examined with the help of pore-size distribution data from mercury porosimetry and such simple tests as water absorption and water vapor sorption. It is shown that salt crystallization changes the pore structure. An increase in the percentage of finer pores, in total porosity, spontaneous water absorption, and water vapor sorption have been observed.

INTRODUCTION

Salt crystallization is a complex process and is not yet well understood, although the involvement of hydration and crystallization pressures (Mortensen 1933; Correns 1949) has been known for some time, and attempts have been made to calculate them (Cooke and Smalley 1968; Winkler and Wilhelm 1970; Evans 1970; Cooke 1979). Salt crystallization is a major concern to the conservator for a variety of monuments and structures because it presents itself as efflorescence at the brick or stone surface and causes the development of cracks, flaking, powdering, etc. Studies concerning salt crystallization pressures as well as the occurrence and progress of salt damage in the structures are summarized; thereafter, experimental work is presented and discussed.

Salt Crystallization Pressures

Thermodynamically, salt will not crystallize spontaneously from an undersaturated solution since the free energy of crystallization of an undersaturated solution is positive. This means that energy must be supplied to the system to cause solid salt to deposit (Lewin 1989). Saturated salt solution in contact with a crystal phase is at equilibrium and involves no free energy change or crystallization; a supersaturated solution, however, deposits crystals as a spontaneous process, since free energy is released (Lewin 1989). Free energy released during crystallization from a supersaturated solution can be calculated by using the data on free energies of formation. The energy released is available for expansive work, which can be sufficient to cause mechanical failure (Lewin 1989). This is the origin of the crystallization pressure concept.

There is no direct experimental data on crystallization pressures. It has been calculated through theoretical assumptions by considering the degree of saturation and the temperature of salt solution as variables (Correns 1949; Winkler and Singer 1972), or by using the pore radii and interfacial tension of salt solution as variables (Rossi-Manaresi and Tucci 1991).

Mechanical salt weathering has been reviewed by Evans (1970), covering theories on growth pressure. Pressure may be generated by growing crystals (in particular linear growth pressure), by hydration (hydration pressure), or by thermal expansion. Although several standard tests of rock durability based on salt crystallization have been developed, there is still much to be learned about the nature of the salt weathering process. The Correns (1949) calculation for crystallization pressure gives:

$$P = \frac{RT}{V} \ln \frac{C}{C_s}, \tag{6.1}$$

where P is the pressure exerted by growing crystals (atmospheres), R is the gas constant (0.082 liter atmospheres/ K^0), V is the molar volume of solid salt (liter/mole), and C/C_s is the degree of supersaturation (C is the existing solute concentration and C_s is the saturation concentration).

The Correns calculations are based on the Riecke principle, which indicates that a crystal under hydrostatic pressure has a greater solubility than an unstressed crystal. Winkler and Singer (1972) have calculated the crystallization pressures for several salts at various degrees of supersaturation and temperatures.

Cooke (1979) found that crystal growth of salt and related processes are directly related to porosity, water absorption capacity, or saturation coefficient of the rock (Correns 1949; Wander Velden 1981).

Soluble salts in a porous building material can lead to salt decay only for particular pore structures (Rossi-Manaresi and Tucci 1989). Rossi-Manaresi and Tucci have calculated the salt crystallization pressures theoretically:

$$P = 2\sigma\left(\frac{1}{r} - \frac{1}{R}\right), \tag{6.2}$$

where σ is the interfacial tension of salt solution, r is the radius of small pore, and R is the radius of coarse pore. Fitzner and Snethlage (1982a, b) discuss this in analogy with the thermodynamics of frost mechanisms in porous building materials developed by Everett (1961). Calculations were in agreement with the observed weathering stages of the subject sandstone (Rossi-Manaresi and Tucci 1989).

High crystallization pressure appears to be associated with structures with a substantial percentage of small pores (less than one micron radius) along with large-sized pores (Rossi-Manaresi and Tucci 1989). However, different salt concentrations have not been considered in these calculations and an average interfacial tension of 80 dynes/cm has been used.

Cassaro et al. (1982) measured linear expansion of limestone prisms soaked in saturated salt solution. The induced pressure was then calculated from the equations:

$$\in = \Delta L / L \quad \text{and} \quad \pi = E \in , \tag{6.3}$$

where $\Delta L/L$ is the expansion, L is the length of specimen, E is the modulus of elasticity, $\in$ is the strain, and π is the induced pressure.

Their linear expansion data were not, however, representative of the samples, since the salt was concentrated at the surface layers during drying. To measure the expansion with reference to the length of the brick, the salt concentration should be uniform throughout the brick, which can be accomplished by freeze-drying the bricks after immersion in salt solution (Felix and Furlan 1981).

Occurrence and Progress of Salt Damage in the Structures

Salt accumulation in walls originates from ions that have been (a) leached out of soils, stones, mortars, and other materials used on buildings, (b) deposited from the polluted atmosphere, (c) generated by metabolisms of organisms, etc. All water present in the walls is more or less in the form of solutions. The evaporation of water occurs only through and from the exposed surfaces and, consequently, salt deposition occurs at the surface and in the zone below the surface.

Two different types of precipitation from a supersaturated salt solution have to be considered: when salts precipitate within an aqueous solution, and when salts precipitate on a material surface by hygroscopic reactions with humid air (Arnold and Zehnder 1989). Salt precipitation in a solution is possible when it is supersaturated, i.e., when the actual ion activity product is greater than the equilibrium constant. It is known that saturated salt solutions establish definite relative humidities in test chambers. There is a clear relationship between the variations in relative humidity of the nearby atmosphere and the crystallization and dissolution of salts on walls. When the ambient relative humidity becomes lower than the equilibrium relative humidity of the concerned salt solution, a salt can crystallize (Arnold and Zehnder 1989). When the ambient relative humidity rises, previously crystallized salts redissolve. For example, sodium nitrate, with an equilibrium relative humidity of 73.9% as pure salt, crystallizes on walls when the relative humidity drops below 60%, and it redissolves when it rises again above this value (Arnold and Zehnder 1989). It is understood that by varying the relative humidity of the air, one can produce crystallization cycles.

In an area of rising damp on a wall, the transported salts in solution precipitate in a spatial sequence according to the mineral assemblage of the salt phases in the system. Since evaporation starts as the solution moves upwards aboveground, slightly soluble salts will become supersaturated and precipitate first on a given level while more soluble ions move further upward (Arnold and Zehnder 1989). Observations and analyses show that in the lower zone of the rising damp area, less-soluble and less-hygroscopic sulfates and carbonates are mainly present. In the upper zone, chlorides and nitrates forming very hygroscopic solutions accumulate (Arnold and Zehnder 1989).

Portland cement or water glass used in restoration may cause serious problems of salt crystallization in monuments. They introduce alkali ions which react with existing alkaline earth sulfates, nitrates, and chlorides and are transformed into alkali sulfates, nitrates and chlorides, which in turn crystallize easily and frequently in a humid climate. Thus, alkaline building materials not only supply more salts into the walls but also transform less harmful salts into more harmful ones (Arnold and Zehnder 1989).

A relationship between the crystal morphology and local conditions of crystallization has been summarized by Arnold and others (Arnold 1982; Arnold and Kueng 1985; Zehnder and Arnold 1988). Crystal morphology is determined by internal (structural) factors, such as the crystal lattice, and by external factors, such as supersaturation, composition, impurities of the solution, and the shape and current of the solution nourishing the growing crystal. External factors such as temperature, air humidity, and shape of the solution seem to be most important. The relationship between the substrate humidity and the crystal habits has been demonstrated (Puhringer 1983; Zehnder and Arnold 1988).

Crystals with bulky (isomeric) shapes similar to their euhedral forms, which are commonly aggregated to crusts, grow from wet substrate in solution or in a thick solution film. Needle-shaped whisker crystals, forming bristly or fluffy efflorescences, grow from a nearly dry substrate, when the solution film on the substrate becomes very thin. In between, all transitions from euhedral shapes to prisms, needles, and hair-like crystals are formed according to the decreasing thickness of the solution film while the substrate is drying out (Zehnder and Arnold 1988).

The progress of salt damage and its influence on the durability of the brick needs to be described by some measurable parameters. The durability of stone has been studied far more than that of brick. The parameters and relationships used for stone are also helpful in examining the durability of brick.

Durability in regard to strength properties of stone material has been examined and relationships have been established between strength, water absorption and durability (Robertson 1982; Accardo et al. 1978; Winkler 1986). Wet-to-dry strength ratios are being used as a measure of durability for stone materials (Felix 1981; Winkler 1986) on a scale of zero to one. Durability is also estimated by the ratio of the dry strength (MPa) to porosity plus swelling strain (Rodrigues and Jeremias 1990), the ratio less than two falling in the range of poor durability. This study was based on limestone weathering by salt crystallization tests (Rodrigues and Jeremias 1990).

The relationship of strength and water absorption property is important (Winkler 1986). Water vapor sorption increases as the salt crystallization proceeds. An increase in moisture absorption is a good indication of an increase in the finest pores (< 0.5 microns) (Winkler 1986; De Castro 1978; Massa and Amaduri 1990).

Dependence of durability on the relative proportions of large and small pores connected to the surface was first indicated by Scott Russell (in a private communication to R.J. Schaffer (1932)). He measured the large pore-size distribution and also the total porosity by saturation with water and large pores by using an optical microscope. The difference between the total porosity and the volume of macro-pores was estimated to be the volume of small pores less than five microns diameter, which was thought to decrease the durability. Several techniques have since been used to measure the relative proportions of large and small pores, such as water suction methods (De Castro 1978). Suction and moisture absorption methods can also be used to make a pore distribution diagram. Although the procedure is lengthy, it is a simple method and can be repeated several times on the same sample of brick subjected to damage until a good view of the state of pore structure can be developed (De Castro 1978).

Changes in the durability of stone and brick in relation to the pore structure by mercury porosimetry have been investigated in several studies (Accardo et al. 1978; Robertson 1982; Punuru et al. 1990; Maage 1984; Robinson 1984; Winslow et al. 1988).

Punuru et al. (1990) defined a durability factor (DF) for limestone based on the percentages of fine, medium, and large pores:

$$DF = A1V1 + A2V2 + A3V3 , \qquad (6.4)$$

where $V1$, $V2$, and $V3$ are the percentage pore volumes in the pore ranges of 5, 0.5–5, and <0.5 microns, $A1$, $A2$, and $A3$ are constants with the values 1.2338, 2.6220, and –0.9841, respectively. The performance of limestone layers of the pyramids in Egypt and their pore-size distributions were the basis of the durability factor. Punuru et al. calculated the pore-size distribution by intrusion of mercury into the pores followed by extrusion and reintrusion. In the pore system of a material, interconnected large and small pores may exist. During the porosity measurements by mercury porosimetry, a good view of pore-size distribution may not be obtained since a small connecting pore will allow the entry of mercury into a large pore at the pressure adequate for the breakthrough of this small pore. This type of small and large pore assembly is called an "ink bottle" pore. If ink bottle pores are predominant in the structure, one-way intrusion data of pore-size distribution is not relevant, whereas extrusion and reintrusion data obtained after the first intrusion give an idea about the percentages of ink bottle pores, and the amount of large pores. The area of the hysteresis curve is also a relative indication of durability (Robertson 1982). The other studies (Accardo et al. 1978; Maage 1984; Robinson 1984; Winslow et al. 1988) are based on one-way intrusion of mercury, and their data may not represent the actual pore-size distribution due to the presence of ink bottle pores in the structure.

Maage (1984) proposed the following durability relationship for frost resistance based on pore sizes measured by one-way intrusion of mercury, which has been used as a durability factor in other studies (Winslow et al. 1988):

$$F = 3.2 / P_V + 2.3P_3 , \qquad (6.5)$$

where F is the relative frost resistance, P_V is the volume of the pores (cm^3) per unit mass, and P_3 is the volume of pores larger than 3 μm expressed as percentage of P_V.

Values larger than 70 indicate durable brick while values less than 55 indicate brick prone to damage by freeze-thaw cycles.

Finally, the studies based on the mineral content, petrographic properties, and chemical weathering characteristics that are quantified and expressed as weatherability index (Aires-Barros and Mouraz-Miranda 1989; Aires-Barros et al. 1994) have to be mentioned among the studies describing the state of damage and durability.

EXPERIMENTS AND RESULTS

Sound 14th century brick samples from a bath in Bursa, Turkey, were subjected to cycles of salt crystallization. The size of the authentic bricks is $41 \times 24 \times 4$ cm, and they are of high porosity (37.2%). Due to the small size of the samples, the strength properties were measured by point load tests and converted to uniaxial compressive strength by using geometrical correction factors (ISRM point load test 1985; Brook 1985) (Table 6.1).

Table 6.1 Porosity, uniaxial compressive strength[1], wet-to-dry strength ratio, and dry strength-to-porosity ratio of bath brick.

Bath brick	P^2	Dry UCS MPa	Wet UCS MPa	Wet/Dry UCS	Dry UCS/P
01	37.2	31.6	22.8	0.72	0.85

[1] ISRM point load test.
[2] P, porosity; UCS, uniaxial compressive strength.

A wet-to-dry strength ratio of 0.72 indicates good brick durability (Felix 1981; Winkler 1986) whereas a dry strength-to-porosity ratio of 0.85 indicates poor durability according to the durability equation established by Rodrigues and Jeremias (1990).

The brick samples were cut to 4 cm cubes and subjected to salt crystallization tests by soaking them in 10% sodium sulfate solution for four hours and by drying at 60°C for at least sixteen hours (Price 1978; Knöfel et al. 1987). The brick cubes subjected to this salt crystallization test lose weight as the cycles are repeated. A 10% weight loss is measured from about the 10th to 15th cycle of crystallization (Figure 6.1). Afterwards, the samples were washed free of salt by soaking them in distilled water. Water sorption, water vapor sorption, and pore structure were subsequently investigated on the bricks. It is observed that bricks subjected to salt crystallization show an increase in initial water sorption and an increase in total porosity (Figures 6.2 and 6.3). Thin-

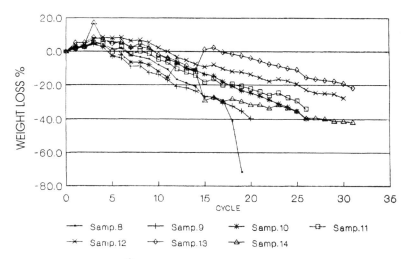

Figure 6.1   Weight loss of 14th century bricks subjected to salt crystallization.

section examination of the brick samples at different cycles of salt crystallization revealed a considerable increase in the size of the larger pores with crystallization.

It was also seen that water vapor sorption increases after repeated cycles of salt crystallization (Figure 6.4). Increase in moisture sorption is a good indication of an increase in the finest pores which are less than 0.5 μm (De Castro 1978; Massa and Amadori 1990). As a result, the finest pore volumes make the brick hygroscopic during changes of relative humidity.

Salt crystallization sites in the network of pores are of particular interest for a better understanding of the crystallization phenomenon. While larger pores are more likely

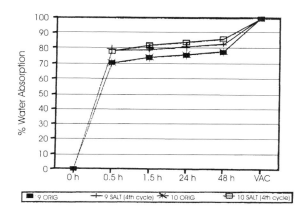

Figure 6.2   Rate of water absorption of washed bricks after salt crystallization tests; final points are under vacuum (VAC).

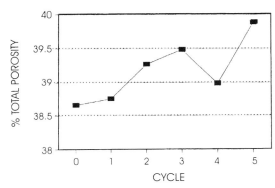

Figure 6.3 Porosity change of bricks after salt crystallization as determined by water absorption.

to be the sites of crystallization (Rossi-Manaresi and Tucci 1991), the finer capillaries connected to them also have the possibility of accommodating some crystal growth (Fitzner and Snethlage 1982a; 1982b). In our experimental work, cross-sections of bricks that were subjected to salt crystallization tests and investigated under scanning electron microscope support this view. In Figure 6.5 it can be seen that a large pore is filled with salt and the adjoining fine capillary pore also contains some salt. Sulfur distribution of the image in Figure 6.5 allows us to locate the sodium sulfate salt in the structure. In investigations of medieval bricks, Larsen and Nielsen (1990) found the preferred sites for salt crystals in pore sizes to be smaller than 15 µ; this was not the case in our salt crystallization experiments. Thus preferred crystallization sites need to be studied further.

Pore-size distribution measurements by mercury porosimetry show an increase in the percentage of finer pores after salt crystallization (Figures 6.6 and 6.7). Data have been obtained by intrusion and extrusion except for one sample, where the data were obtained by intrusion, extrusion, and further reintrusion of mercury. Since the ink bottle pores predominate in the brick samples studied, one-way intrusion data of pore-size distribution is not relevant, whereas extrusion and reintrusion data obtained after the first intrusion give an idea about the percentages of ink bottle pores (Robertson 1982).

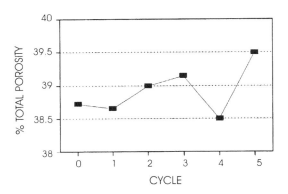

Relative durabilities have been calculated by using the Maage relative frost resistance equation. The results show a decrease in durability by salt crystallization (Table 6.2). However, they are still classified as good frost-resistant bricks since the F values are above 70. Actually, these bricks have lost considerable weight during salt crystallization, and further crystallization will speed up the loss (Figure 6.1).

Figure 6.4 Moisture absorption of washed bricks after repeated cycles of salt crystallization (kept at 80% RH for 28 hours).

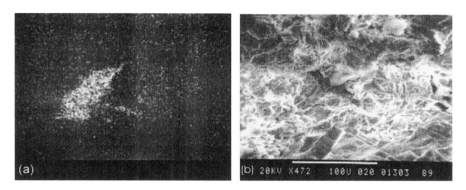

Figure 6.5   Cross-section of salt-tested brick viewed by scanning electron microscopy: (a) sulfur map, (b) SEM view of the identical area in (a).

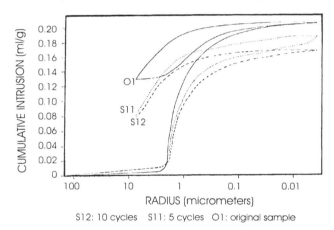

S12: 10 cycles   S11: 5 cycles   O1: original sample

Figure 6.6 Pore-size distribution of bricks before and after salt crystallization (O1 original sample; S11, five cycles; S12, ten cycles).

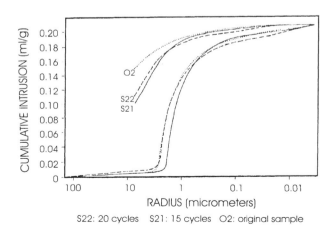

S22: 20 cycles   S21: 15 cycles   O2: original sample

Figure 6.7 Pore-size distribution of bricks before and after salt crystallization (O2 original sample; S21, fifteen cycles; S22, twenty cycles).

Table 6.2 Relative durability of bricks before and after salt crystallization as calculated by Maage's equation.

Sample	No. of cycles	$P_V{}^1$	P_3	Durability
01	0	0.1828	63.85	170
S11	5	0.1873	42.10	101
S12	10	0.1694	46.04	129
02	0	0.2082	72.04	188
S21	15	0.2083	48.00	130
S22	20	0.2038	52.99	143

[1] P_V, volume of pores (cm^3) per unit mass; P_3, volume of pores < 3 μm expressed as percentage of P_V.

CONCLUSIONS

Salt crystallization changes the pore structure. The percentage of finer pores increases considerably. Increase in total porosity, spontaneous water absorption, and water vapor sorption is also observed.

Durability calculations based on pore-size distribution do not satisfactorily describe the behavior of brick. The Maage equation is not sufficient to describe the situation of brick damaged by salt crystallization, partly because the equation is derived from one-way intrusion data of mercury to the pore structure. Changes in the pore structure need to be evaluated better. It also seems necessary to include strength parameters (for dry and wet states) in the durability expressions together with the pore-size parameters and a weatherability parameter, depending on the petrographic properties.

Preferred crystallization sites are not clearly understood. Further investigations in different pore systems and for different salt crystallization conditions should be made.

ACKNOWLEDGEMENT

A NATO-CCMS grant for collaborative research in the pilot study on the conservation of historic brick structures is gratefully acknowledged (ENC-S).

REFERENCES

Accardo, A., S. Massa, P. Rossi-Doria, and M. Tabasso. 1978. Measures of porosity and mechanical resistance in order to evaluate the state of deterioration of some stones. In: Deterioration and Protection of Stone Monuments Intl. Symp., 2.1. Paris: UNESCO-RILEM.
Aires-Barros, L., and A. Moura-Miranda. 1989. Weathering and weatheribility of rocks and its significance in geotechnics. In: Weathering: Its Products and Deposits, vol. 2, Products-Deposits-Geotechnics, ed. S.A. Zographou, pp. 605–645. Athens: Theophrastus Publications.

Aires-Barros, L., C. Gomes da Silva, C. Figueiredo, and P.R. Figueiredo. 1994. Weatherability of calcareous rocks: Quantitative preliminary approach. 7th Intl. IAEG Congr., pp. 3591–3594. Rotterdam: Balkeme.

Arnold, A. 1982. Rising damp and saline minerals. In: 4th Intl. Congr. Deterior. Preserv. Stone Objects, pp.11, Louisville: Univ. of Louisville Press.

Arnold, A., and A. Kueng. 1985. Crystallization and habits of salt efflorescences on walls: Part I: Methods of investigation and habits. In: 5th Intl. Congr. Deterior. Consv. Stone, ed. G. Felix, pp. 255. Lausanne: Presses Polytechniques Romandes.

Arnold, A., and K. Zehnder. 1989. Salt weathering on monuments. In: The Conservation of Monuments in the Mediterranean Basin, Proc. 1st Intl. Symp., Bari, ed. F. Zezza, pp. 31–58. Brescia: Grafo.

Brook, N. 1985. The equivalent core diameter method of size and shape correction in point load testing. *Intl. J. Rock Mech. Min. Sci. & Geomech. Abstr.* **22(2)**:61–70

Cassaro, M.A., K.L. Gauri, M. Sharifinassab, and A. Sharifian. 1982. On the strength and deformation properties Indiana limestone and concrete in the presence of salts. In: Proc. 4th Intl. Congr. on the Deterioration and Preservation of Stone Objects, ed. K.L. Gauri and J.A. Gwinn, pp. 57–76. Louisville: Univ. of Louisville Press.

Cooke, P.V., and I.J. Smalley. 1968. Salt weathering in deserts. *Nature* **220**:1226.

Cooke, R.V. 1979. Laboratory simulation of salt weathering processes in arid environments. *Earth Surface Processes* **4**:347

Correns, C.W. 1949. Growth and dissolution of crystals under linear pressure. *Trans. Faraday Soc.* **5**:267–271.

De Castro, E. 1978. Les methodes de succion dans l'etude de l'alteration des pierres. In: Deterioration and Protection of Stone Monuments Intl. Symp., 2.2. Paris: UNESCO-RILEM.

Evans, I.S. 1970. Salt crystallization and rock weathering. *Rev. de Geomorph. Dynam.* **19**:153.

Everett, D.H. 1961. The thermodynamics of frost damage to porous solids. *Trans. Faraday Soc.* **57**:1541.

Felix, C. 1981. Caractéres pétrographiques et comportement par rapport a l'eau de grés molassiques du Plateau Suisse. Comparaison avec d'autres gres. In: The Conservation of Stone, IIA, Intl. Symp. Centro Conservazione Sculture all'Aperto, ed. R. Rossi-Manaresi, pp. 219–232. Bologna: Centro Per la Conservazione Delle Sculture All'aperto.

Felix, C., and V. Furlan. 1981. Mesures automatiques sur des facies greseux de la dilatation lineaire isotherme par absorption d'eau dans differentes conditions. In: The Conservation of Stone, IIA, Intl. Symp. Centro Conservazione Sculture all'Aperto, ed. R. Rossi-Manaresi, pp. 127–134. Bologna: Centro Per la Conservazione Delle Sculture All'aperto.

Fitzner, B., and R. Snethlage. 1982a. Einfluss der Porenradienverteilung auf das Verwitterungsverhalten ausgewahlter Sandsteine. *Bautenschutz + Bausanierung* **3**:97–103.

Fitzner, B., and R. Snethlage. 1982b. Über Zusammenhänge zwischen Salzkristallisationsdruck und Porenradienverteilung. *GP News Lett.* **3**:13.

ISRM, Point Load Test. 1985. Suggested method for determining point load strength. *Intl. J. Rock Mech. Min. Sci. & Geomech. Abstr.* **22(2)**:53–60.

Knöfel, D.K., D. Hoffmann, and R. Snethlage. 1987. Physico-chemical weathering reactions as a formulary for time-lapsing ageing tests. *Mat. and Struct.* **20**:116, 127, 19R7.

Larsen, E.S., and C.B. Nielsen. 1990. Decay of bricks due to salt. *Mat. and Struct.* **23**:16–25.

Lewin, S.Z. 1989. The susceptibility of calcareous stones to salt decay. In: The Conservation of Monuments in the Mediterranean Basin, Proc. 1st Intl. Symp., Bari, ed. F. Zezza, pp. 59–64. Brescia: Grafo.

Maage, M. 1984. Frost resistance and pore-size distribution in bricks. *Materiaux et Construction* **17**:345.

Massa, S., and M. L. Amadori. 1990. The environment and moisture content of the bricks. In: Proc. 4th Expert Meetings, NATO-CCMS Pilot Study, Conservation of Historic Brick Structures, ed. S. Fitz, pp. 41–45. Berlin: Umweltbundesamt.

Mortensen, H., 1933. Die Salzpregnung und ihre Bedeutung für die regional klimatische Gliederung der Wüsten. Petermann's Geol., 130 pp.

Price, C.A. 1978. The use of the sodium sulphate crystallization test for determining the weathering resistance of untreated stone In: Deterioration and Protection of Stone Monuments Intl. Symp. 3.6 Paris: UNESCO-RILEM.

Puhringer, J. 1983. Salzwanderung und Verwitterung durch Salze. In: Werkstoff, Wissenschaften und Bausanierung, ed. F.H. Wittman, pp. 361–367. Ostfeldern: Lack and Chemie.

Punuru, A.R., A.N. Chowdhury, N.P. Kulshresnthe, and K.L. Gauri. 1990. Control of porosity on durability of limestones at the Great Sphinx, Egypt. *Environ. Geol. Water Sci.* **15**:225–232.

Robertson, W.D. 1982. Evaluation of the durability of limestone masonry in historic buildings. In: 4th Intl. Congr. on Deterioration and Preservation of Stone Objects, ed. K.L.Gauri and J.A. Gwinn, pp. 261–278. Louisville: Univ. Louisville Press.

Robinson, G.C. 1984. The relationship between pore structure and durability of brick. *Ceram. Bull. Am. Ceram. Soc.* **63**:295–300.

Rodrigues, J.D., and F.T. Jeremias. 1990. Assessment of rock durability through index properties, 6th Intl. IAEG Congress, vol. 4, pp. 3055–3060. Rotterdam: Balkeme.

Rossi-Manaresi, R., and A. Tucci. 1989. Pore structure and salt crystallization. In: The Conservation of Monuments in the Mediterranean Basin, Proc. 1st Intl. Symp., Bari, ed. F. Zezza, pp. 97–102. Brescia: Grafo.

Rossi-Manaresi, R., and A. Tucci. 1991. Pore structure and the disruptive or cementing effect of salt crystallization in various types of stone. *Studies in Conservation* **36**:53–58.

Schaffer, R.J. 1932. The weathering of natural building stones. Dept. of Scientific and Industrial Research, Building Research: Special Report Nr. 18. Building Reseach Station, Garston, Near Watford.

Vander Velden, J.H. 1981. Water absorption of ceramics. *Ziegelindustrie Intl.* **12**:704–715.

Winkler, E.M. 1986. A durability index for stone. *Bull. Assoc. Eng. Geol.* **23**:344–347.

Winkler, E.M., and E.J. Wilhelm. 1970. Salt burst by hydration pressure in architectural stone in urban atmosphere. *Bull. Geol. Soc. of Am.* **81(2)**:567–572.

Winslow, D.N., C.L. Kilgour, and R.W. Crooks. 1988. Predicting the durability of bricks. *JTVA* **16(6)**:527–531.

Zehnder, K., and A. Arnold. 1988. New experiments on salt crystallization. In: 6th Intl. Congress on Deterioration and Conservation of Stone, ed. J. Ciabach. Torun, Poland: Nicholas Copernicus Univ.

7

Influence of Salt Content on the Drying Behavior of Brick

L. FRANKE and J. GRABAU

Technische Universität Hamburg-Harburg, Arbeitsbereich Bauphysik und Werkstoffe im Bauwesen, Eißendorfer Straße 42, 21071 Hamburg, Germany

ABSTRACT

We know that the drying behavior of brickwork is affected by hygroscopic salts. Slightly soluble salts like gypsum affect brick similarly when they crystallize beneath the fired surface. Tests were carried out to study these phenomena.

Results show that a layer with a thickness of a few hundred micrometers of crystallized gypsum in the pores of a brick near the surface is enough to influence the drying behavior strongly. After capillary water transport from inside the bricks, evaporation and vapor diffusion are dramatically reduced.

INTRODUCTION

Damage to brick caused by salts has been examined and described in detail in the literature. Deterioration is a result of hydration and crystallization pressures and the effects of hygroscopic salts (WTA 1992; Winkler 1994). This paper discusses the influence of salts on the drying behavior of bricks. The starting point for this work was determination of the salt distribution in brickwork as a function of pore volume and pore-size distribution. As gypsum often appears to be the damaging salt in historic brickwork, our aim was to induce an enrichment of this compound by capillary uptake of saturated solutions of the salt, and then to let the water evaporate over the brick surface. We thought that this could be achieved within a few days, since capillary uptake of pure water and gypsum solutions do not differ. Unexpectedly, these initial tests were not successful. Thus, systematic investigation of this effect was undertaken.

EVAPORATION OF SALT SOLUTIONS

The experimental setup for these tests is shown in Figure 7.1. The sides of the brick samples were sealed with a water-tight sealant so that uptake could only proceed from the bottom. Evaporation was only possible through the top surface of the sample.

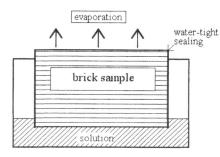

Figure 7.1 Experimental setup for evaporation tests.

The specimens were then put into one of three test solutions:

- pure water,
- magnesium sulfate solution (concentration 0.012 mol/l),
- saturated gypsum solution.

The amount of evaporated water was determined over different time intervals by gravimetry. The tests were conducted for three weeks.

Figure 7.2 shows the results for bricks without fired skins. The evaporation rate is plotted as a function of time.

During the first few days, all samples behaved similarly: after water saturation, as a result of capillary suction, the evaporation flow was nearly constant. Eventually, a significant decrease (down to about 10% of the initial value) in the evaporation rate could be detected with the gypsum-soaked samples, whereas the flow remained unchanged in the other solutions. Similar results were obtained from bricks with a fired surface. A

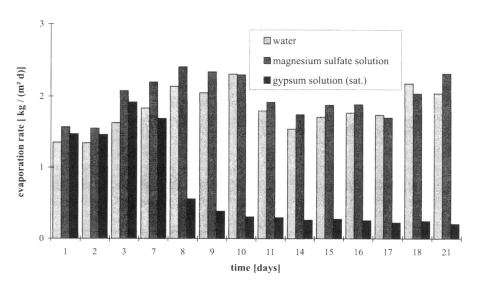

Figure 7.2   Evaporation rates of different solutions for brick without fired surfaces.

blocking effect could also be detected in bricks with the magnesium sulfate solution, but only after a longer test time.

Several experiments were conducted to establish the cause of this phenomenon. The sulfate contents of the bricks were determined. The values were in the range of about 0.5 to 1 wt.% in the first 2 mm of the samples. No sulfate enrichment could be detected at depths greater than 2 mm.

Pore blocking, examined by mercury intrusion porosimetry, could not be proven as the calculated effects of changes were in the same order of magnitude as the uncertainty of the measured quantity. It was possible to get relationships between salt content and changes in pore volume and pore-size distribution when analyzing other samples with higher salt contents after natural weathering.

Using a scanning electron microscope (SEM), more accurate information on salt distribution in the sample was obtained. Salt enrichment could be detected within the first 100–200 μm of the samples. This was confirmed by X-ray fluorescence (XRF) analysis using the SEM.

Figure 7.3 shows the relative XRF peak intensities relative to silicon plotted as a function of different depths.

As the signals (and therefore content) of aluminum, iron, and potassium are nearly constant over a depth of about 400 μm, a strong calcium enrichment can be detected within the first 150–200 μm of the sample.

Thus, there is a change in the pore structure that strongly reduces the capillary transport but which does not completely obstruct water evaporation.

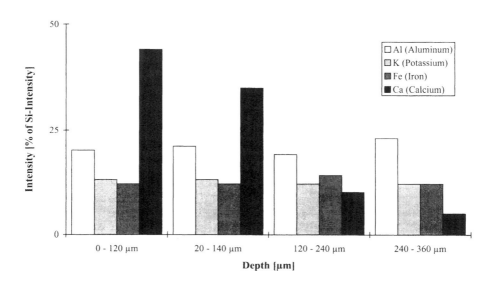

Figure 7.3   Salt distribution by XRF analysis results relative to Si.

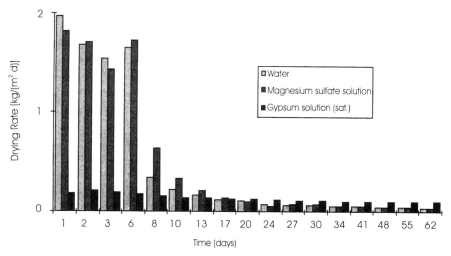

Figure 7.4   Drying rates as function of time after evaporation cycle.

DRYING BEHAVIOR AFTER EVAPORATION TESTS

Drying behavior of the samples, after removing the capillary supply of solution and sealing the bottom surface, is of interest. Results of these tests are shown in Figure 7.4.

The drying rates are plotted as a function of time. In the beginning, the samples soaked with water and magnesium sulfate solution quickly give off a large amount of water; thereafter, the drying rate decreases. The resultant values are of the same order of magnitude as for the gypsum-soaked material from the beginning of this drying cycle. Samples soaked with water and magnesium sulfate solution are dry after about 150 days, while gypsum-containing material needs more than 300 days to reach this point.

There are different mechanisms of water transport during the drying process of porous materials. A theoretical graph by Krischer (Klopfer 1989; Krischer and Kast 1978), plotted in Figure 7.5, shows the drying rates as a function of water/moisture content.

Three periods of drying can be distinguished: In the first period with high water content, evaporation proceeds at a constant rate. The flow is supplied by capillary transport of liquid water from the interior of the material. In this period there is a constant drying rate.

At salient point KN1, capillary transport is no longer strong enough to maintain constant evaporation. The water content adjacent to the surface of the samples decreases in the same manner as the drying rate. Thus, capillary transport and transport of water vapor due to pressure gradients, i.e., vapor diffusion, are significant.

After all liquid water has evaporated, only vapor diffusion may cause further transport. This occurs after salient point KN2. Plotting the results of the evaporation tests as a function of water content, Figure 7.6 is obtained.

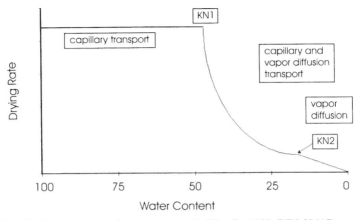

Figure 7.5   Drying processes of porous materials (Klopfer 1989; DIN 52617).

The typical curve was observed for bricks soaked with water and with magnesium sulfate solution. However, the drying rate of gypsum-containing material is very low and seems to be determined by the rate of water vapor diffusion. The rate is of the same order of magnitude as it was at the end of the experiments with capillary supply of gypsum solution. This means that the samples in these tests had not been fully saturated with water but must have had a decreased water content in the surface area. These gypsum-containing samples appeared visibly drier than the others. This phenomenon must be connected with a decrease of the relative humidity at the sample surface which is normally taken as 100%.

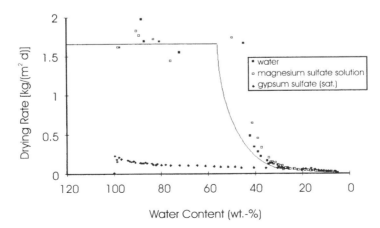

Figure 7.6   Drying rate as function of water content.

CAPILLARY SUCTION AND DRYING BEHAVIOR

If there is pore blocking, capillary suction should be affected as well. To test this, a capillary suction test was conducted according to DIN 52617 (May, 1987). The bricks used in these tests were those that had been tested during the evaporation and drying cycles. Penetration of water proceeded over portions of the surface where evaporation and drying had occurred.

The water adsorption coefficients (related to the coefficient after an one-hour test) are plotted as a function of time in Figure 7.7. Obviously, the coefficient of gypsum-containing material is reduced in the first ten to twenty minutes. This period is probably due to the process of gypsum dissolution. After this initial process, a rather constant coefficient value was measured, as was the case from beginning of the tests for those of bricks in water or magnesium sulfate solutions.

The samples were then stored in sulfuric acid (pH 3.5) for another three days to enable suction. The acid was used to simulate acid rain.

We were interested in determining the drying rates after water suction. Thus the drying behavior had to be reanalyzed. These results are shown in Figure 7.8. It is obvious that the drying process of the sample with gypsum enrichment is significantly lower than that of other samples.

Another periodic test was conducted to simulate alternate wetting-drying cycles: samples with the dimensions $5 \times 4 \times 3$ cm were prepared as in Figure 7.1. An uptake and evaporation test (with gypsum solution) was run over eight hours. The samples were then allowed to dry over 16 hours; drying could occur at both areas of capillary uptake and evaporation. This procedure was repeated fourteen times. Results for samples with (A) and without (B) a fired surface surface are plotted in Figure 7.9.

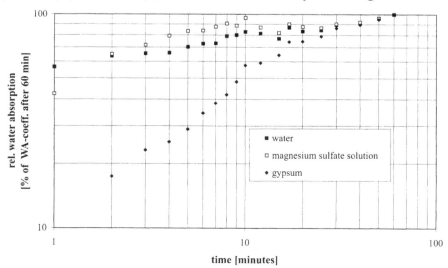

Figure 7.7   Capillary suction of samples with or without salt.

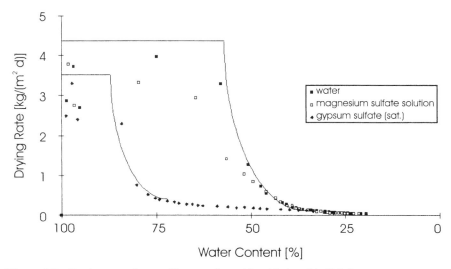

Figure 7.8   Drying rate after capillary suction with sulfuric acid pH 3.5.

An increasing gypsum content leads to a decreasing drying rate: initially 80% of the water which was taken up evaporates. At the end of the test, only 20% of the water can leave the sample within 16 hours of drying.

The significance to existing buildings is that water penetration into the bricks of a facade with low gypsum content during a long driving rain does not significantly differ from that with a facade without any salts. The drying process, however, is considerably slowed in the first case.

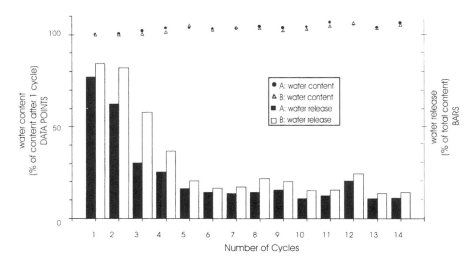

Figure 7.9   Water content and water release.

WATER VAPOR DIFFUSION

Water vapor diffusion is important to the drying process. The influence of salts on the rate of this process was also examined. Samples taken after 21 days of an evaporation cycle (with pore blocking after transport of gypsum solution) were used during these tests. The test was set up according to DIN 52615 (November, 1987) and is shown in Figure 7.10.

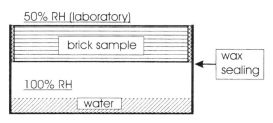

Values were determined at a vapor pressure gradient of 100% to 50% RH at 23°C. Results (thickness of samples 10 mm) are summarized in Table 7.1.

Gypsum enrichment at the exposed surface also leads to a decrease of water vapor transport. The values were approximately halved. This happens likewise with samples with and without fired surfaces. Similar results were obtained when analyzing the water vapor diffusion of historic bricks.

Figure 7.10   Test for water vapor diffusion.

What do these effects mean to the moisture behavior of a building? After rainwater uptake due to capillary saturation, the drying process is slowed. Niesel and Hoffmann (1990) have also shown this in their tests with brick stacks.

The effect is important to buildings subjected to rising damp or water uptake caused by water supply from the interior. These buildings can only dry out at rates on the order of magnitude of vapor diffusion. In addition, this process is also slowed down by the pore blocking effect caused by gypsum.

Table 7.1   Water vapor diffusion values for brick samples containing different salt solutions.

Solution in Brick	with fired surface	without fired surface
	water vapor diffusion [kg / (m² d)]	
Water	0.032	0.065
Magnesium sulfate solution	0.033	0.062
Gypsum solution	0.018	0.029
	diffusion resistance coefficient [μ]	
Water	75	37
Magnesium sulfate solution	60	35
Gypsum solution	130	80

The occurrence of the drying blocking effect depends on such brick properties as porosity and density. At the same time, it is also a question of how soluble a salt is, as was shown by comparing magnesium and calcium sulfate. Both salt solutions used in the tests had the same molarity. Gypsum is less soluble than magnesium sulfate and causes the blocking effect.

SUMMARY

- During evaporation of salt-containing solutions in bricks, the salts crystallize when their saturation concentration is exceeded.
- A layer of a few hundred micrometers enriched with low soluble salts is enough to influence the drying characteristics of a brick. Acording to Krischer (Krischer and Kast 1978), the first period of drying, which is rate-determined by vapor transport, cannot be detected or is already complete at higher water contents. The evaporation front is not shifted from the surface to the inner part of the sample. Evaporation and drying processes are then controlled by water vapor diffusion. This mechanism is less efficient than capillary transport of liquid water. The effect requires a sufficient amount of deposited salt.
- Salt incrustation not only influences the type of water transport but also decreases the rate of vapor diffusion transport.
- Salts more soluble than gypsum also lead to a drying time extension due to the possibility that greater amounts of water can evaporate without salt crystallization. Salts like magnesium sulfate also tend to crystallize on the surface and not in the brick pore system as gypsum does. Crystallization at the surface does not greatly influence water transport because the salts can be washed off during rainfall.
- The blocking of pores has a significant influence on the drying behavior of facades. An increase in salt content leads to a decrease in the drying rate, so that water remains in the bricks longer.
- The rate of capillary suction, however, decreased only in the first minutes of the tests. This could be higher if a sample has a higher salt content. This possibility is currently being examined at our institute. In these tests, natural stones will also be studied.
- A change in the drying behavior is very important to the health of the bricks. A slower drying rate may cause higher probabilities of frost damage. A higher moisture content may also increase the sorption of acid pollution gases, which can cause further material damage.
- In addition to the well-known damage caused by hydration and crystallization pressures or higher moisture contents as a result of hygroscopic salts, the blocking effect of salt ought to be taken into consideration.

REFERENCES

DIN 52615. November, 1987. Testing of Thermal Insulation: Determination of Water Vapour Permeability of Building and Insulating Materials. Berlin: Beuth Verlag GmbH.

DIN 52617. May, 1987. Determination of the Water Absorption Coefficient of Building Materials. Berlin: Beuth Verlag GmbH.

Hoffmann, D., and K. Niesel. 1990. Vorgänge des kapillaren Feuchtigkeitsaufstiegs und der Verdunstung in porösen Baustoffen. In: Schriftenreihe der Sektion Architektur der Technischen, Heft 30, pp. 110–115. Dresden: Universität Dresden.

Klopfer, H. 1989. III. Feuchte. In: Lehrbuch der Bauphysik, ed. Lutz, Jenisch, Klopfer, Freymuth, and Krampf, 1st edition, pp. 311–485. Stuttgart: B.G. Teubner.

Krischer, O., and W. Kast. 1978. Die wissenschaftlichen Grundlagen der Trocknungstechnik, 3rd edition. Berlin: Springer-Verlag.

Winkler, E.M. 1994. Stone in Architecture. Berlin: Springer-Verlag.

WTA. 1992. Schriftenreihe Heft 1: Die Rolle von Salzen bei der Verwitterung von mineralischen Baustoffen, ed. E.W. Nägele. WTA Baierbrunn Mai.

8

Bioreceptivity and Biodeterioration of Brick Structures

O. GUILLITTE

Laboratoire d'écologie, Faculté universitaire des Sciences Agronomiques,
Passage des Déportés, 2, 5030 Gembloux, Belgium

ABSTRACT

The vegetation and bioreceptivity of brick structures are reviewed. Moisture is the main factor determining the kinetics, the biomass, and the composition of this vegetation. The vegetation colonizing brick structures is therefore described according to the differences in moisture exposure. Other environmental factors (e.g., frost, pollution and light) and the intrinsic characteristics of the brick, the mortar and their interactions are also discussed. The biodeterioration (including scaling, cracking of the bricks, peeling and crumbling of the mortar, and disjointing) caused by the main organisms which colonize brick structures is described in relation to these structures, based on a review of the literature and personal observations in the field and in a laboratory exposure chamber.

INTRODUCTION

The biological colonization of brick structures depends both on the characteristics of these structures and on environmental factors. Bioreceptivity is a new concept introduced by Guillitte (1994) to define all chemical and physical parameters of materials that might influence potential colonization by organisms when these organisms grow in the most favorable ecological conditions.

The literature dealing with biological colonization and in particular with the biodeterioration of brick structures is very limited. In contrast, there are numerous references to stone-built houses and historical monuments, although they seldom contain much information on the quality of the building materials used. However, as the biological colonization of brick structures is based mainly on mortar, the vegetation type does not differ fundamentally from that developing on alkali materials, such as concrete, asbestos-cement, limestone, and stone mortar. It is therefore possible to extrapolate from the behaviors on other types of material. Over the past ten years, we have also elaborated upon and improved an experimental design in laboratory exposure chambers for accelerating plant colonization and biodeterioration in building materials (Guillitte 1993, Guillitte and Dreesen 1994, 1995). These experiments clarify the earlier information aquired from the literature and from field observations.

A large number of plant species, without including a varied microflora, potentially have the ability to colonize brick structures. Nevertheless, the species most commonly found on these structures are few in number. It is the deterioration caused by these organisms that is elaborated upon here.

BIORECEPTIVITY

Three basic requirements are necessary for organisms to become established and to survive on any substrate:

1. a surface on which they can get anchorage;
2. enough nutrients to sustain their development and growth;
3. adequate amounts of water to support their main physiological functions and, in many cases, their multiplication and dissemination (cyanobacteria, algae, mosses and lichens).

Several intrinsic characteristics of structures and types of materials, such as bricks and grouting mortar, meet these requirements and therefore influence biological colonization. For example, surface roughness is a major anchorage factor for diaspores from numerous plants and fungi (glazed bricks are rarely colonized). Porosity influences the rates of water absorption and retention, and hence the development of a profuse plant population (Jaton et al. 1985). The material pH also has a screening effect on organism population. Acidophilic species prefer brick whereas calcicolous species prefer mortar. Microcracks resulting from poor repointing or brick manufacturing (shrinkage cracks) may harbor a wide diversity of organisms.

Laboratory chamber experiments have shown that there are similar successive stages in the development of a biofilm on mortar and bricks. Cyanobacteria and green algae are the first colonizing organisms and produce a continuous biofilm on the material surface when there is sufficient moisture. This biofilm thickens, the species number increases, new taxa appear (other cyanobacteria and diatoms), green algae decrease, and a stratification of different species appears. The most heliophilous and xerophilous species (e.g., *Calothrix parietina*) grow within the upper layer of the biofilm and the most sciaphilous and hygrophilous species (e.g., *Microcystis grevillei* and diatoms) stay within the lower layer. When the biofilm is thick enough (about 100 μm), spores of mosses can germinate and develop protonemas which turn into leafy stems after a few weeks. At this stage, numerous hygrophilous species increase the biomass on the material and the humification starts. After this stage, the growth of higher plants is possible, particularly if there are preexisting microcracks where the humus has accumulated. In drier conditions, colonization by higher plants often follows lichen settlements.

These experiments demonstrate that the bioreceptivity of old historic brick is comparable with or even higher than the bioreceptivity of historic mortar or stony materials. This is not the case for modern bricks manufactured by industry; these bricks have a lower bioreceptivity because of their smoother surfaces and the absence of microcracks (Guillitte and Dreesen 1994, 1995).

Environmental factors (e.g., frost and pollution) and biological actions (see below) increase the anchorage and the nutrient-releasing abilities of the material. These actions often occur after a long colonization by woody plants, which are able to destroy brick structure. The kinetics of these stages of development depend mainly on environmental factors.

ECOLOGICAL FACTORS DETERMINING COLONIZATION

Biological colonization is influenced mainly by factors associated with the building environment which generally masks the effect of intrinsic bioreceptivity. This can be explained by the fact that moisture is the major limiting factor. Any material exposed to weather ends up being colonized if there is enough moisture. Moisture may originate from climatic agents (e.g., rain, fog and snow), from the soil (surface or capillary water) and, more rarely, from water pipes (e.g., fountains) and from plants themselves (water translocated by the mycelium of dry rot, *Serpula lacrimans*).

Air (or surface water) pollution is another major external factor that can inhibit the development of many species. Conversely, in some cases, pollution can result in nutrients becoming available to pollution-resistant organisms by dissolving substances (e.g., $CaCO_3$) contained in the materials.

Based on these factors and on materials exposed to atmospheric agents and moisture, the following four types of structures have been identified.

Facades

These structures are the best protected against physical and chemical degradation as only one side of the wall is exposed to external agents. The upper part of the structure is generally protected by the roof, and the lower part is relatively well insulated against soil moisture. Although facades are usually the driest building structures, their degree of wetness can vary widely according to wall exposure to prevailing rain and environmental conditions (e.g., shading, trees and valley floors).

Outer Walls, Connecting Walls, Low Walls, and Ruins

Both sides and the top of the wall are exposed to atmospheric agents. The lower part often receives large quantities of capillary water from the soil. These structures are characterized by a higher than average moisture content.

Partly Submerged Walls (e.g., wharfs and castle moats)

One part of the wall is always in contact with water while the other parts are strongly affected by water moving upwards by capillarity from the free water or the soil. The upper part of the wall is not always protected. This is the most humid condition.

Other Structures (e.g., bridges, viaducts and tunnels)

These structures are made up of the elements described above. In all cases, vertical and horizontal – or near horizontal – brick structures are to be considered separately. The initial stage of plant colonization in vertical structures often depends solely on the mortar. In horizontal structures, the first stages of plant establishment are also influenced by the exposed side of bricks.

VEGETATION ON BRICK WALLS

The importance and ecological preferences of various taxonomic groups of plants observed on brick walls in Western Europe are shown in Table 8.1. Each species can be classified according to its ecological preferences:

- Moisture: Aquatic, hygrophilous, mesophilous, xerophilous.
- Nutrients: Basophilous, neutrophilous, acidophilous, nitrophilous, halophilous.
- Light: Heliophilous, sciaphilous.
- Pollution: Toxitolerant, toxiphobic.

All plants with similar ecological requirements form plant associations. Each invaded brick structure is characterized by one or several plant associations.

One plant, *Tortula muralis*, can be found on all brick structures (except on submerged parts) regardless of their environment and exposure. This moss is able to survive over prolonged dry periods. Its leaves contain glandular cells and it can be easily identified by the presence of a long white hair at the tip. The fern *Asplenium ruta-muraria* has a much more restrictive ecological niche than *Tortula* as it develops only in cracks in mortar, although it can be found in almost all situations.

Facade Vegetation

In general, facades are only lightly colonized by plants. Colonization can occur in specific conditions, particularly in very moist locations:

- under window sills,
- at the juncture of protruding structures,
- in unrepaired accidental cracks,
- on wall parts exposed to accidental water flows (e.g., overspills or gutter breakage),

Table 8.1 Taxonomic groups of plants colonizing brick structures.

Taxonomic Groups	Number	Structure	Position	Location
Cyanobacteria	Min. 20	IV	V	B, M
Algae (Chlorophyta, Phaeophyta, Diatoms)	Min. 20	IV	V	B, M
Lichens				
— foliose species	Min. 30	II, (I)	<u>H</u>, V	B, M
— crustose species	Min. 30	I, II	V, H	B, M
Mosses and Liverworts	Min. 40	IV	H, V	<u>M</u>, B
Ferns	Min. 10	II, (I)	<u>V</u>, H	M
Phanerogams	Min. 100	IV	<u>H</u>, V	<u>M</u>, B
Fungi (only macromycetes)	Min. 10	I	H, V	<u>M</u>, B

Key: Number = Number of species found from personal observations and in the
literature (e.g., Segal 1969; De Ridder 1971–1974; Gallé 1973; Gérard
1978; Hruska Dell'Uomo 1979; Nimis et al. 1987, 1992)
  I = Front walls   V = Vertical
  II = Outer walls   H = Horizontal
  III = Submerged walls M = Mortar
  IV = All walls   B = Brick
Note: The underlined letter indicates the preferred situation.

- on heavily shaded wall parts that are always wet (e.g., facade exposed to rain and surrounded by trees),
- on the lower part of the facade in contact with the ground.

The vegetation is often hygrophilous (but can tolerate dry conditions for long periods of time), sciaphilous, nitrophilous and toxitolerant (facades are often located in fairly polluted urban areas).

The main taxonomic groups are Cyanobacteria (*Lyngbya* spp., *Gloeocapsa* sp., *Anabaena variabilis*,...), algae (*Desmococcus vulgaris*, *Chlorella* spp., *Klebsormidium flaccidum*, diatoms, ...), mosses (including *Rhynchostegium murale* and *Bryum* spp.) and lichens (including *Lepraria incana* and *Lecanora* spp.) (Figures 8.1–8.3).

Mosses are more likely to develop on the joints between flat bricks. Conversely, lichens tend to colonize the surface of bricks although they are also influenced by the type of pointing mortar. Brightman and Seaward (1977) have noted that *Caloploca heppiana* grows onto the brick from the joint. In England, Brightman (1965) stressed the importance of water absorption capacity, pH and roughness in lichen colonization. For instance, many foliose species, including several *Physcia* species and two crustose species, *Ochrolechia parella* and *Lecanora sulphurea*, develop on acidic bricks (pH 5.8) with a moisture content of 12%. Only *Lecanora conizaeoides* was observed on less acidic (pH 6) and drier (9% moisture content) bricks. On smooth bricks, *Lecidea lucida* was the only growing species where the bricks contained enough moisture.

(a)

(b)

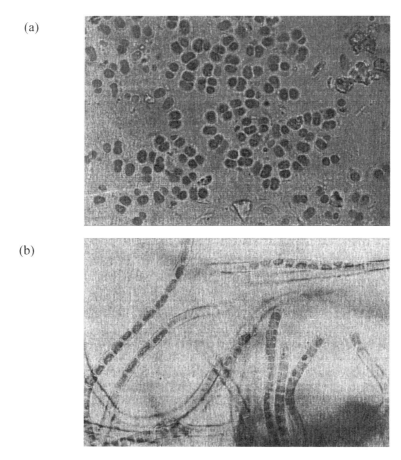

Figure 8.1 Microscopic views of organisms commonly colonizing bricks: (a) *Gloeocapsa* sp., a cyanobacterium having a thick mucilaginous sheet (scale: × 300); (b) *Klebsormidium flaccidum*, a hygrophilous filamentous green algae (scale: × 300).

It would appear that glazed bricks are not colonized (Brightman and Seaward 1977). However, Bouly de Lesdain (1951) mentions a few species that grow on similar materials (china and coated earthenware), such as *Physcia ascendens, Lecidea umbrina, Lecanora muralis* and *Bacidia inundata.*

Phanerogams and ferns develop generally under major water flows. However, some xerophilous and thermophilous plants grow in drier conditions (e.g., *Corydalis lutea, Cheiranthus cheirii* and *Parietina judaieca*). *Buddlea davidii,* an exotic and thermophilous shrub, expands constantly on brick masonry in urban areas. Climbing species

(a)

(b)

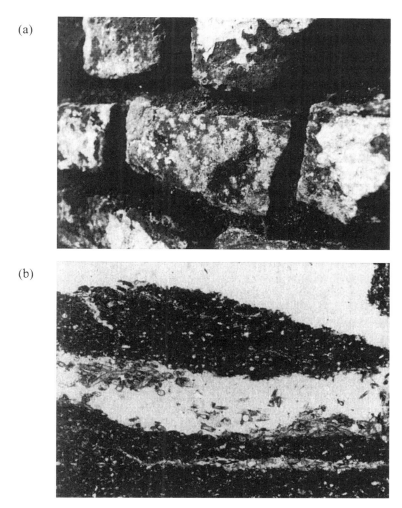

Figure 8.2 Natural biological colonization of an old historical brick wall. (a) Vegetation on a front wall of a water mill in Gembloux (Belgium). The moss with a dark green color has colonized mortar joints and microcracks of the bricks. Conversely, the lichen with a yellow-orange color, *Caloplaca* sp., has colonized the surface of the bricks (scale: × 1/5). (b) Microscopic view of a thin-section in a brick from this wall. The rhizoids of *Tortula* have penetrated in preexisting microcracks and induced a scaling of the surface of the brick (scale: × 30).

are sometimes planted by people at the bottom of walls as cover plants. The most common climbers are ivy (*Hedera helix*) and Virginia creeper (*Parthenocissus* spp.).

The inner part of facades is also colonized by dry rot (*Serpula lacrimans*). This fungus pest of wooden frames can grow through brickworks and invade joints. It is

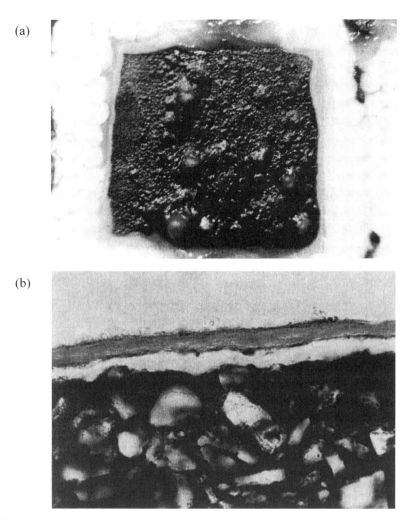

Figure 8.3 Artificial accelerated biological colonization of brick samples. (a) Thick biofilm (100 μm) with cyanobacteria, green algae, diatoms and protonema of mosses covering completely the surface of a historical brick after six month of experimentation (scale: × 1/1). (b) Microscopic view of a thin-section in a modern brick after six months of experimentation. The thin, dried biofilm (10 μm) has removed some material fragments from the brick surface (scale: × 400).

increasingly found in houses due to poor insulation techniques (Rammeloo et al. 1992). Other less aggressive xylophageous fungi develop their mycelium only on the surface of the masonry (e.g., *Coniophora* spp., Antrodia spp., and *Asterostroma ochroleucum*).

Vegetation on Outer Walls, Connecting Walls, Low Walls, and Ruins

This vegetation is highly diversified due to the varied ecological conditions in the numerous niches in these structures. Moreover, these structures are often less well maintained than facades, resulting in many cracks.

The upper part of walls is colonized by xerophilous and heliophilous plants (foliose lichens such as *Xanthoria parietina* and *Lecanora muralis*; mosses such as *Tortula, Orthotrichum diaphanum, Bryum muralis* and *Grimmia pulvinata*; and several phanerogams such as *Poa compressa, Hieracium murorum, H. pilosella, Taraxacum* sp., *Sedum acre* and *Corydalis lutea*).

The lower and shaded parts of walls are colonized by a more hygrophilous and sciaphilous flora (mosses such as *Rhynchostegium, Amblystegium serpens* and *Brachythecium rutabulum*; lichens such as *Lepraria* and *Cladonia chlorophea*; and several ferns such as *Athyrium* spp. and *Dryopteris* spp.).

Asplenium ruta-muraria and *Cymbalaria muralis,* a dicotyledonous plant with small blue flowers, invade vertical structures. Several woody species, particularly the elder (*Sambucus* sp.), are found in wider cracks.

Polluted areas are colonized mainly by crustose lichens (*Caloplaca* spp., *Candariella* spp., *Lecanora dispersa* and even *L. conizoides*, a species that is normally epiphytic, although highly toxitolerant).

Vegetation on Partly Submerged Walls

The submerged part of walls is covered with a very distinctive aquatic flora consisting mainly of mosses and algae.

The above-water part is covered by many hygrophilous species (mosses, lichens and phanerogams). The latter group is often represented by the following species: *Sagina procubems, Lycopus europaeus, Rumex* spp., *Alnus* and *Salix.*

Wharfs and dikes in the sea or in brackish waters are colonized by only a few halophilous plants. The most salt-resistant mosses and lichens are *Bryum argenteum* and various *Xanthoria* species, respectively.

BIODETERIORATION

The damage caused by plants is often the result of one or more other types of deterioration or occurs concurrently with this deterioration: high humidification, cracking due to frost, and chemical alterations (Segal 1969; Kieslinger 1932; Krumbein 1972; Krumbein and Schönborn-Krumbein 1986). This makes it difficult to evaluate the importance of each of these agents in the damage observed.

The types of deterioration caused by plants vary immensely: unsightly marks, disjointing, desquamation, cracking, arenization by dissolution of the cement or by physical pressure, crystallization and various types of efflorescence.

The description of the main types of damage is based on personal observations made in field chiefly in Belgium (a number of observations were also made in the Trieste area of Italy, the Munich area of Germany, the Pas de Calais area of France and the Grand Duchy of Luxembourg) and on a review of the literature, broadly extended to encompass other materials, particularly a homologous material, terracotta tiles, since literature focusing specifically on the biodeterioration of bricks is virtually nonexistent. Laboratory exposure chamber studies have completed the field observations (Guillitte 1993; Guillitte and Dreesen 1994, 1995; Saiz-Jimenez et al. 1995).

MICROBIOLOGICAL DETERIORATION

Before turning to the deterioration caused by plants proper, it is important to stress the important role that microorganisms (bacteria, actinomycetes and microfungi) can play in the degradation of stone materials (Eckhardt 1985; Krumbein and Schönborn-Krumbein 1986; Sand et al. 1991). There have been few reports of the damage caused by these organisms on bricks (Barcellona Vero and Montesila 1978; Palmer 1991).

These organisms have the ability to produce substances, often mineral acids (e.g., sulfuric acid is produced by bacteria of the *Thiobacillus* genus) or organic acids (such as oxalic, citric and gluconic acids), which affect the deterioration of minerals in the brick or, more often, those in the repointing mortar (particularly calcium compounds). Several mechanisms of deterioration are now classically recognized: reduction or oxidation of mineral cations, acidolysis by organic and inorganic acids produced by microorganisms and complexing.

The molds most commonly found on stone structures belong to the following genera: *Penicilium, Cladosporium, Aspergillus, Aureobasidium, Torula,* and *Alternaria*.

These molds can also cause unsightly marks. This is particularly true of *Alternaria*, which produces masses of blackish spots in very confined environments where the relative humidity is high. We very often found it on brick walls in cellars.

DETERIORATION CAUSED BY MACROMYCETES

When load-bearing pieces of wood (particularly lintels) are incorporated into the brick structure, they can become damaged by xylophagous fungi, causing the brick structure to weaken, crack and even collapse. The fungi most frequently responsible for this type of damage are *Serpula lacrimans, Coniophora puteana, Antrodia vaillantii* and *Donkioporia expensa,* but 20 or so other species may also be involved (Leclercq and Seutin 1989; Rammeloo et al. 1992).

Peculiar to dry rot, *Serpula lacrimans*, is a mycelium that is stimulated at alkaline pH values (Coggins 1980) and readily crosses masonry. When masonry is riddled with this mycelium it can become damaged as a result of joints becoming crumbly, first by cement dissolution produced by the acid secretions of the mycelium, then by the effect of frost which is facilitated by the humidification produced by the mycelium, and finally by the mechanical effect of pressure exerted by the mycelium during the formation of rhizomorphs (condensed mycelium made up of dense-walled hyphae).

Dry rot and other fungi also cause more or less continuous superficial marks on brick masonry (the most impressive are those of the *Coniophora* genus in the form of blackish arachniform mats).

DETERIORATION CAUSED BY CYANAOBACTERIA
(BLUE ALGAE)

The Cyanophytes are also capable of dissolving minerals, particularly limestone, which certain species recover by reprecipitation to form their sheath (*Lyngbya, Scytonema, Aphanothece*, etc.) (Trotet et al. 1973; Grant and Bravery 1985).

Many blue algae, particularly those in the order Nostacales (e.g., *Nostoc, Anabeana* and *Lyngbya*), produce mucilagenous holdfasts, which attach them firmly to the colonized surface (Albertano et al. 1991; Saiz-Jimenez et al. 1995).

On sudden desiccation, the retraction of the colonies can cause slight surface flaking (Guillitte 1993; Guillitte and Dreesen 1995).

Some species are capable of being endolithic and could cause desquamation (Krumbein and Jens 1981). This phenomenon has not been reported on bricks. Finally, in all cases, they leave often very obvious green (bluish or dark) marks.

DETERIORATION CAUSED BY ALGAE

Chlorophytes (e.g., *Chlorella, Protococcus, Klebshormidium, Stichococcus* and *Apatococcus*) and Chrysophytes (various diatoms) cause physico-chemical damage which is often more superficial and more limited than that caused by blue algae because their development is also very superficial and their attachment to the surface less tenacious (absence of mucilage).

These agents nevertheless leave marks in the form of greenish trails (most Chlorophytes), brownish-yellow trails (diatoms) or orange trails (*Trentepohlia aurea*) when they are fresh. They can develop very quickly in favorable conditions and turn a wall green in a few days. All of them turn a grayish to blackish color on severe desiccation, resembling dust trails (Grossin and Dupuy 1978; Grant and Bravery 1985). During decomposition, a saprophytic mold (*Epicoccum purpurascens*) contributes to the formation of the blackish color of these marks.

DETERIORATION CAUSED BY LICHENS

Several lichens are capable of severe (albeit always superficial) deterioration of not only masonry joints but also bricks, without the structure necessarily having first suffered deterioration of another type (something of which few organisms are capable). However, this action is slow.

Lichens employ the same chemical mechanisms described earlier, which lead to the dissolution of crystalline or mineral cements (Brightman and Seaward 1977). They also make the surface of colonized materials more porous by penetration of their thalli (up to 10 mm from the surface in the case of crustose lichens) or their rhizins (in the case of the others) into the substrate. It should be noted that foliose lichens do not necessarily penetrate the substrate (Jaton 1985).

Many species of lichen are likely to colonize brick structures. The most damaging of these are the crustose lichens (particularly those in the *Verrucaria* genus) and encrusting lichens (*Caloplaca*) (Figure 8.2).

The secretions of endolithic lichens can cause discoloration of the material around the thalli. This phenomenon has been observed on bricks. The agent responsible was *Verrucaria calciseda* (Ciarello et al. 1985).

Finally, lichens leave very garish marks of uniform or mosaic colors. The most common marks are gray (e.g., *Physcia* spp., *Lecanora muralis* and *Parmelia saxatilis*), orange (e.g., *Xanthoria* spp. and *Caloploca* spp.), blackish (*Lecidea fuscoatra*) or greenish (*Lepraria incana*). The coloration remains obvious for a long time after the lichen has died, in contrast to what happens with algae. The marks left by lichen (particularly by foliose and, above all, fruticose types) stand out much more clearly than those produced by algae.

DETERIORATION CAUSED BY MOSSES

The chemolytic effect of mosses is less obvious than that of lichen. However, their rhizoids behave in a similar way to that of the rhizins of lichen and can therefore cause a certain amount of physical deterioration on the surface of colonized materials (Segal 1969).

The most obvious damage caused by mosses is the marks they leave behind. The most common mosses (e.g., *Tortula muralis, Grimmia pulvinata, Ceratodon purpureus, Bryum capillare* and *Funaria hygrometrica*) leave green marks in a vegetative state and when they are well moistened (Rückert 1974; Gérard 1978). In a dry state or on fructification, a large number of shades can appear (grayish, reddish, yellowish). *Bryum argenteum*, a moss which is common on brick structures, forms very typical shiny grayish pads. The marks left by mosses are generally rougher than those caused by lichen and more typically confined to masonry joints than lichen and algae.

DETERIORATION CAUSED BY VASCULAR PLANTS

Ferns and phanerogamia are capable of exerting a weak chemolytic effect, particularly via the microbial flora which constitutes the rhizosphere. However, this type of deterioration is secondary to the physical damage caused by the development of the roots or sometimes the stems through the colonized structure (Kieslinger 1932; Segal 1969; Govi 1991). This development causes microfissures (especially between the mortar joint and the brick), disjointing, large cracks and finally the collapse of some or all of the structure in conjunction with frost damage, which is accelerated under these conditions. It should be noted that in order for this type of damage to occur, it has to be preceded by deterioration allowing the roots or "subterranean" organs to infiltrate the structure.

The most damaging plants are the woody Angiospermae (e.g., *Salix* spp., *Sambucus* spp., *Buddleia davidii* and *Hedera helix*). In order to be completely exhaustive, trees located in the vicinity of a brick structure can also cause mechanical pressure which is continuous (upthrust by the root system, or crushing by the aerial system), discontinuous (friction from branches due to the wind) or accidental (branches or the whole tree falling) and is capable of causing severe damage.

Vascular plants form spots or mats varying greatly in color and size on brick structures. This phenomenon could be likened to that of other types of marks of biological origin. However, the unsightliness of these plant formations is not immediately obvious due to their spatial and temporal diversities which give colonized structures a certain aesthetic charm.

The decomposition products of vascular plants (e.g., humic matter and fulvic acids) or the leaching of mineral particles which have been intercepted by the foliage may also produce grayish trails in the vicinity of plants.

Finally, when this vegetation is plentiful (particularly in the case of climbing plants such as ivy, Virginia creeper, and wisteria), it alters the microclimate inside the construction appreciably but does not necessarily increase the humidity, as is commonly believed (in fact, vegetation acts as a temperature buffer and can prevent excess humidity if there is no severe root penetration of the masonry).

DETERIORATION FOLLOWING THE DISAPPEARANCE OF ORGANISMS

Problems may arise after the removal of vegetation which had been considered undesirable. This phenomenon can be attributed to three causes:

1. The treatment used alters the surface of the material and allows it to be recolonized more readily (this could be the case during mechanical brushing or raking);
2. Despite their damaging effect, plants provide a biological matrix (e.g., mucilage, mycelial network, and root system), which retains the decomposition products. Disintegration becomes apparent only when this matrix has been removed (Jaton et al. 1985; Nimis et al. 1992).
3. Vegetation provides protection against other damaging agents, particularly pollution (Lallemant and Deruelle 1983). Surfaces from which vegetation has been removed may be just as unattractive as surfaces on which there has never been any vegetation. Finally, these cleaned surfaces are rendered more sensitive to

attacks from other damaging agents and ultimately their deterioration could be more severe than that previously caused by the vegetation.

CONCLUSIONS

A wide diversity of organisms can potentially occur on brick structures. In most cases, however, only a few of them are actually colonize these structures, provided that they are regularly protected from the physical and chemical deterioration caused by the environment. The colonization is generally superficial and takes place mainly on pointing mortar. However, differences were observed which are attributable mainly to the presence or absence of microcracks in the structures or in their components.

The damage caused directly by the colonizing organisms is generally moderate, even under high bioreceptivity. Most of these organisms usually cause aesthetic damage that involves a change in the color or appearance of the surface. However, the appearance of these marks is relatively characteristic of each category of plants and varies greatly depending on the environmental conditions and the physiological state of the plants. Some of these marks or the traces of these marks may persist for a long time after the plants have died.

The chemolytic activity of the majority of plants (apart from crustose lichen) is weak on brick structures and remains very superficial.

The destructive effect of this vegetation mechanically is much greater but also remains very superficial, with the exception of the action of vascular plants on damaged masonry.

Finally, the severe damage caused to brick structures in the presence of colonizing flora is rarely the direct result of this flora but rather of other agents, the appearance of some of which has been favored by this vegetation which, in turn, is involved in the damage either directly or indirectly by encouraging another damaging agent (frost). This chain of events can take place only on structures that have been abandoned and not maintained for a long time.

Apart from these extreme cases, damage caused by vegetation on brick structures can be regarded as limited and easily avoidable by controlling the sources of humidity in these structures.

REFERENCES

Albertano, P., L. Luongo, and M. Grilli Caiola. 1991. Ultrastructural investigations on algal species deteriorating roman frescoes. In: Science, Technology and European Cultural Heritage, ed. N.S. Baer, C. Sabbioni, and A.I. Sors, pp. 501–504. Oxford: Butterworth-Heinemann.
Barcellona Vero, L., and M. Montesila, 1978. Mise en évidence de l'activité des thiobacilles dans l'altération des pierres à Rome – Identification de certaines souches. In: Symp. Deterioration and Protection of Stone Monuments, 4.1, 1–13. Paris: UNESCO-RILEM.

Bouly de Lesdain, M. 1951. Remarques sur la végétation lichénique des substratums variés, disséminés dans les dunes à l'est et à l'ouest de Dunkerque, de Mardyck (Nord), à la frontière belge. *Revue bryol. lichén.* **20**:289–296.

Brightman, F.H. 1965. The lichens of Cambridge walls. *Nature Cambs.* **8**:45–50.

Brightman, F.H., and M.R.D. Seaward. 1977. Lichens of man-made substrates. In: Lichen Ecology, ed. M.R.D. Seaward, pp. 253–293. New York: Academic Press.

Ciarello, A., L. Festa, C. Piccioli, and M. Raniello. 1985. Microflora action in the decay of stone monuments. In: Proc. 5th Intl. Congress on Deterioration and Conservation of Stone, pp. 607–616. Lausanne: Presses Polytechniques Romandes.

Coggins, C.R. 1980. Decay of Timber in Buildings. Dry Rot, Wet Rot and Other Fungi. East Grinstead: Rentokil Ltd.

De Ridder, M. 1971–1974. La végétation des murs. *Nat. belg.* **52(9)**:453–467; **53(10)**:495–507; **54(6)**:255–266; and **55(5)**:213–233.

Eckhardt, F.E.W. 1985. Mechanisms of the microbial degradation of minerals in sandstone monuments, medieval frescoes and plaster. In: Proc. 5th Intl. Congress on Deterioration and Conservation of Stone, pp. 643–652. Lausanne: Presses Polytechniques Romandes.

Gallé, L. 1973. Kryptogam növénytarsulasok a szegedi körtöltès téglaburkolatan. *Studia Bot. Hung.* **VIII**:25–32.

Gérard, C. 1978. Les bryophytes dans l'agglomération bruxelloise. *Nat. belg.* **59(6–7)**: 177–186.

Govi, G. 1991. Root penetration of solid porous medium. In: Science, Technology and European Cultural Heritage, ed. N.S. Baer, C. Sabbioni, and A.I. Sors, pp. 493–496. Oxford: Butterworth-Heinemann.

Grant, C., and A.F. Bravery. 1985. A new method of assessing the resistance of stone to algal disfigurement and the efficacy of chemical inhibitors. In: Proc. 5th Intl. Congress on Deterioration and Conservation of Stone, pp. 663–674. Lausanne: Presses Polytechniques Romandes.

Grossin, F., and P. Dupuy. 1978. Méthode simplifiée de détermination des constituants des salissures. In: Symp. on Deterioration and Protection of Stone Monuments. Paris, June 5–9, 1978: 4.4, 1–41.

Guillitte, O. 1993. Kinetics of plant colonization of composite materials. Ph.D. thesis, Faculty of Agriculture, Gembloux, Belgium: 249 pp (in French, summary in English).

Guillitte, O. 1994. Bioreceptivity: A new concept for building ecology studies. *Sci. Total Environ.* **167**:215–250.

Guillitte, O., and R. Dreesen. 1994. Laboratory chamber studies and petrographical analysis as bioreceptivity assessment tools of building materials. *Sci. Total Environ.* **167**:356–374.

Guillitte, O., and R. Dreesen. 1995. Bioreceptivity and biodeterioration of building stones colonized by cyanobacteria, algae and mosses. Laboratory chamber exposures and petrography. In: Interactive Physical Weathering and Bioreceptivity on Building Stones, Monitored by Computerized X-Ray Tomography (CT) as a Potential Non-destructive Research Tool, ed. M. De Cleene. European Commission, DG-XII, Protection and Conservation of the European Cultural Heritage, Research Report Nr. 2: 171–198.

Hruska Dell'Uomo, K., 1979. Sur la végétation de la classe *Parietarietea muralis* Riv.- Mart. 1955 dans les Marches (Italie centrale). *Doc. Phytosociologiques N.S.* **IV**:433–441.

Jaton, C., G. Orial, and A. Brunet. 1985. Actions des végétaux sur les matériaux pierreux. In: Proc. 5th Intl. Congress on Deterioration and Conservation of Stone, pp. 577–586. Lausanne: Presses Polytechniques Romandes.

Kieslinger, A. 1932. Zerstörungen an Steinbauten. Leipzig, Wien: Franz Deuticke.

Krumbein, W.E. 1972. Rôle des microorganismes dans la genèse, la diagenèse et la dégradation des roches en place. *Rev. Ecol. Biol. Sol* **9**:283–319.

Krumbein, W.E., and K. Jens. 1981. Biogenic rock varnishes of the Negev Desert (Israel) an ecological study of iron and manganese transformation cyanobacteria and fungi. *Oecologia* **50**:25–38.

Krumbein, W.E., and E. Schönborn-Krumbein. 1986. Biogene Bauschäden. Anamnese, Diagnose und Therapie in Bautenschutz und Denkmalpflege. *Bautenschutz + Bausanierung* **10**:14–23.

Lallemant, R., and S. Deruelle. 1983. Présence de lichens sur les monuments en pierre: Nuisance ou protection? In: Symp. on Deterioration and Protection of Stone Monuments, vol. 4, pp. 1–6. Paris: UNESCO-RILEM.

Leclerq, A., and E. Seutin. 1989. Les ennemis naturels du bois d'oeuvre. Gembloux: Les Presses Agronomiques.

Nimis, P.L., M. Monte, and M. Tretiach. 1987. Flora e vegetazione lichenica di aree archeologiche del Lazio. *Studia Geobotanica* 7:3–161.

Nimis, P.L., D. Pinna, and O. Salvadori. 1992. Licheni e conservazione dei monumenti. Bologna: CLUEB.

Palmer, R.J. 1991. Microbial communities involved in the weathering of three historic buildings in northern Germany. In: Science, Technology and European Cultural Heritage, ed. N.S. Baer, C. Sabbioni, and A.I. Sors, pp. 478–480. Oxford: Butterworth-Heinemann.

Pochon, J. 1968. Facteurs biologiques de l'altération des pierres. Monumentum, vol. 2, pp. 40–51. ICOMS.

Rammeloo, J., O. Guillitte, G. Draye, M. Van Leemput, F. De Roy, and S. Roland. 1992. La Mérule et autres champignons nuisibles dans les bâtiments (2nd edition). Meise: Jardin Botanique national de Belgique.

Rückert, G. 1974. Bryologische Studien an Ziegeldächern. *Beitr. naturk. Forsch. SüdwDtl.* **33**:55–57.

Saiz-Jimenez, C., X. Arino, and J.J. Ortega-Calvo. 1995. Mechanisms of stone deterioration by photosynthesis-based epilithic biofilms. In: Interactive Physical Weathering and Bioreceptivity on Building Stones, Monitored by Computerized X-Ray Tomography (CT) as a Potential Non-destructive Research Tool, ed. M. De Cleene. European Commission, DG-XII, Protection and Conservation of the European Cultural Heritage, Research Report Nr. 2: 25–62.

Sand, W., B. Ahlers, and E. Bock. 1991. The impact of microorganisms – especially nitric acid producing bacteria – on the deterioration of natural stone. In: Science, Technology and European Cultural Heritage, ed. N.S. Baer, C. Sabbioni, and A.I. Sors, pp. 481–484. Oxford: Butterworth-Heinemann.

Segal, S. 1969. Ecological Notes on Wall Vegetation. The Hague: Dr. W. Junk.

Trotet, G., P. Dupuy, and F. Grossin. 1973. Etude écologique des Cyanophycées des parois calcaires: Cas particulier des abris. *Bull. Soc. Bot. Fr.* **120**:407–434.

9

Application of NDE to Masonry Structures
Current Technology and Future Needs

R.H. ATKINSON[†], J.L. NOLAND[†], and G.R. KINGSLEY

Atkinson-Noland & Associates, Inc., 2619 Spruce Street, Boulder, CO 80302, U.S.A.

ABSTRACT

Nondestructive techniques for the assessment of condition, the progress of repair and the assessment of the conserved structure are presented. The techniques of ultrasonic pulse, mechanical pulse, Schmidt Hammer hardness, neutron probe, flatjack *in situ* stress, flatjack *in situ* deformability and in-place shear (Shove test) are introduced and their results are compared to commonly used destructive tests based on core or prism samples subjected to laboratory tests.

INTRODUCTION

A large number of unreinforced masonry buildings exist in the United States, many of which may be structurally marginal or inadequate for their present or proposed use. Recent advances in seismic hazard mapping have resulted in more stringent design requirements in many parts of the country. Changed functional use of masonry structures can also impose increased design loadings.

A critical element in any repair or upgrading project is the need to assess the condition of the structure. This assessment is needed to establish the existing condition of the structure and to plan for its repair. Secondly, means to assess in real time the progress of the repair are required, especially when techniques such as grouting are being used. Finally, an assessment of the modified structure is required to assure that the repairs have provided the needed upgrade in structural capacity.

Current practice is to determine masonry condition by cutting prisms or cores from the building for destructive laboratory tests. For statistical significance, a large number of specimens must be tested. The removal of a large number of test specimens from the structure will significantly disfigure the structure and in cases of historic structures may not be allowed. The development of nondestructive test methods for masonry structure evaluation is clearly needed.

[†] Deceased.

EVALUATION FACTORS

A structural engineer faced with the problem of evaluating the condition of an existing masonry structure requires quantitative material data in terms of peak strength, strain at peak strength, and modulus of rupture. The engineer also needs to know the location and extent of all flaws in the structure including cracks, bed joint delaminations, zones of deterioration due to environmental effects and zones of internal voids and poor construction practices. Finally, the level of existing stress in the structure should be determined to assess overall margins of safety under present or future loadings.

REVIEW OF CURRENT EVALUATION METHODS

The development of NDE techniques for masonry has generally involved an application of methods used for the NDE of concrete (Devekey 1988; Zoldners 1984) or of rock (Noland 1982; Rossi 1985). A recent study (Noland 1991) has developed and evaluated a number of NDE techniques for application to masonry. Most of the techniques described here are used in practice to evaluate masonry materials (Suprenant and Schuller 1995).

Ultrasonic Pulse

Perhaps the most common application of nondestructive testing methods to masonry has been with ultrasonic pulse velocity (UPV) techniques similar to those used for concrete. Figure 9.1 presents a comparison of masonry prism strength versus wave

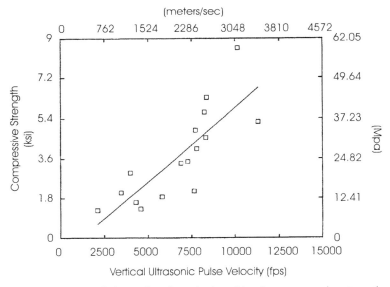

Figure 9.1   Correlation of ultrasonic pulse velocity with prism compressive strength.

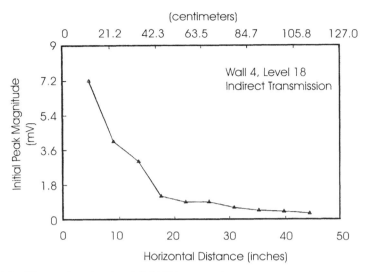

Figure 9.2 Ultrasonic pulse signal (54 kHz) attenuation.

velocity in which a reasonable correlation is seen. This correlation is, however, dependent on materials and test techniques and needs to be established for individual masonry constituents. Figure 9.2 shows the rapid attenuation in amplitude of a 54 kHz input signal with distance.

Previous work (Hobbs 1987; Calvi 1988; Berra 1987; Noland 1991) points to several conclusions. First, while UPV measurements can be correlated to masonry prism compressive strength for specific materials, a generalized relationship between masonry compressive strength and ultrasonic velocity is not anticipated. Second, UPV techniques are well suited to the detection of flaws, but signal strength deterioration limits their usefulness to modern materials and short transmission lengths. Third, studies to date have used the pulse velocity as the descriptive parameter. Attenuation or frequency analysis may reveal more about material condition than the velocity.

Mechanical Pulse

The mechanical pulse is generated by a surface impact and the pulse arrival is recorded with one or more accelerometers. There has been much development of this technique (including the "pulse-echo" technique) for concrete (Carino 1986). Because of the high amplitude and long wavelength of the input pulse, the technique is well suited to masonry field evaluations, and several researchers have used it for a variety of masonry applications (Forde 1984; Kingsley 1987). While mechanical pulse velocity has some correlation with masonry prism compressive strength, it is better suited to the detection of flaws and irregularities (Figure 9.3) (Noland 1991).

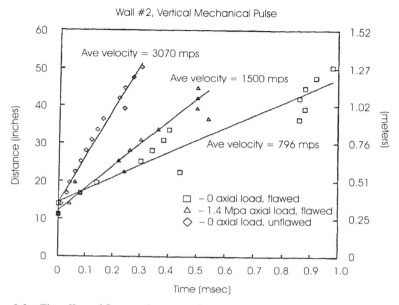

Figure 9.3   The effect of flaws and compressive stress on mechanical pulse velocity.

Hardness

The Schmidt Hammer Measurement of surface hardness (ASTM C 805-75) has been shown to have a reasonable correlation to masonry prism compressive strength (Noland 1982). While the quantitative prediction of masonry compressive strength based on Schmidt Hammer tests is not recommended without companion destructive tests, the method has good potential for the rapid and inexpensive evaluation of material uniformity in a structure.

Neutron Probe

The neutron probe (Livingston 1988; see also Chapter 14, this volume) uses prompt gamma/neutron activation to determine elemental composition of a target material. Elements are identified by characteristic gamma rays emitted from the material while it is being bombarded with neutrons. Neutron probe results can be useful in several types of building analysis: (a) determination of the composition of historic building materials, (b) location of contaminants such as water or soluble salts, and (c) location of voids. Although the neutron probe does not measure mechanical or structural properties, it can provide a useful complement to a structural evaluation (Kingsley 1988).

Flatjack *In Situ* Stress Measurement

A flatjack is a thin steel bladder that is pressurized with a fluid to apply a uniform stress over a small area (Figure 9.4). The use of large flatjacks to determine the *in situ* state of

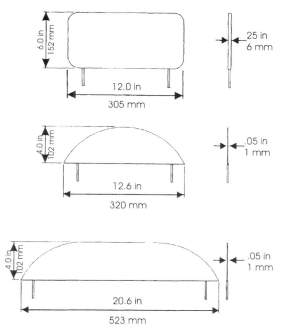

Figure 9.4   Typical flatjacks.

stress and deformability of rock was modified for use in masonry structures by Rossi (1985) and others (Kingsley 1988; Noland 1988).

Evaluation of *in situ* compressive stress is a simple process of stress-relief induced by the removal of a portion of a mortar joint, followed by restoration of the original state of stress by pressurizing a flatjack inserted in the slot (ASTM C 1196). When the mortar is removed from a horizontal joint, the release of the stress across the joint causes the slot to close by a small amount. The magnitude of this deformation is meas-ured using a removable dial gauge between two or more points located symmetrically on either side of the slot (Figure 9.5). A flatjack is then inserted in the slot and

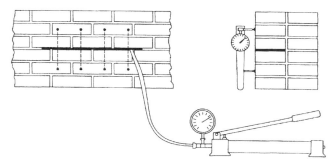

Figure 9.5   Single flatjack *in situ* stress test.

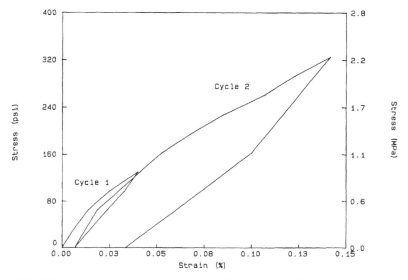

Figure 9.6   Masonry stress-strain curve obtained from a double flatjack test.

pressurized until the original position of the measuring points is restored. At this point, the pressure in the flatjack is equivalent to the vertical compressive stress in the masonry.

Flatjack *In Situ* Deformability Measurement

The deformation properties of masonry may be directly evaluated by inserting two parallel flatjacks, one directly above the other separated by several courses of masonry, and pressurizing them equally, thus imposing a compressive load on the intervening masonry (Rossi 1985; ASTM C 1197). The deformations of the masonry between the flatjacks are then measured for several increments of load, and used to calculate the masonry stress-strain curve (Figure 9.6) and deformability modulus. If some damage to the masonry is acceptable, the test may be carried out to ultimate stress. This technique is useful when a direct measure of material deformability is needed for stress analysis or deflection calculations. The double flatjack test, like the single flatjack test and the Shove test, may be considered nondestructive, because the mortar may be replaced leaving no evidence of testing.

In-place Shear (Shove) Test

The in-place shear test was designed to measure the *in situ* bed joint shear resistance of masonry walls (ABK 1981).This test is required for seismic hazard analysis in some parts of the U.S. by the Uniform Code for Building Conservation (ICBO 1994). It requires the removal of a masonry unit and a head joint on either side of a test unit. The

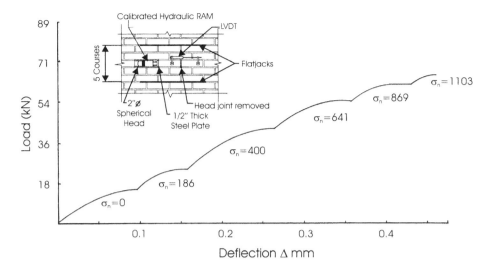

Figure 9.7 Typical results from a modified in-place shear test.

test unit is then displaced horizontally relative to the surrounding masonry using a hydraulic jack, and the horizontal force required to cause first movement of the test unit is recorded (Figure 9.7). The test procedure has been modified (Noland et al. 1991) using flatjacks above and below the test unit to control normal stress. The test is repeated for several levels of normal stress permitting friction angle determination (Figure 9.7).

Combination of Existing NDE Techniques

At the current level of development, the best application of NDE to masonry is to combine a number of complementary techniques. Rapid methods such as the Schmidt Hammer might be used to assess the condition of the entire structure, with pulse velocity methods used to map the variation in material condition in critical areas of the structure and direct measurements of material deformability and joint shear strength made using flatjack techniques in specific locations. Procedures and methods used would vary depending on individual building requirements. In all cases, experience and judgment in understanding the NDE techniques used and the nature of masonry is required for the accurate interpretation of results.

ASSESSMENT OF CURRENT METHODS

Of the varying methods described above, only those employing the use of flatjacks or the Shove test provide direct measures of the strength and stiffness of the masonry material in a quantitative form directly useful for detailed structural analysis. At present, these tests will only evaluate the outer layer of a masonry wall with the result that inner layers which typically are composed of poorer quality materials are overlooked.

Most applications using ultrasonic or mechanical pulse have been limited to using velocity as the evaluation parameter. While relationships with strength and the ability to find flaws have been demonstrated, use of velocity data alone is inadequate to determine material properties or to locate flaws to the accuracy required for detailed structural evaluation.

POTENTIAL FOR FUTURE ADVANCEMENT IN MASONRY NDE

Development of NDE techniques for masonry have to date adopted or modified techniques from the areas of concrete and rock evaluation. In the meantime, very considerable advances have been made in the application of quantitative NDE methods in the fields of medicine, aerospace structures, exploration seismology and manufacturing, among others.

Several avenues of opportunity exist for the application of these techniques to masonry. The ultrasonic and mechanical pulse methods can be advanced through the use of signal conditioning and use of frequency domain analysis of data now being recorded. Application of multiple sensor arrays as used in seismic surveys (Robinson 1986) or in medical imaging together with advanced data reduction and analysis algorithms may have the potential to improve mapping of structural flaws.

Recent developments in use of ground penetrating radar (Pittman 1984)) employing short pulse, video and synthetic pulse techniques together with time and frequency domain analysis may provide means for the rapid survey of masonry structures. Recent material developments in the aerospace industry (Dube 1988), which implant sensors in materials during construction to create so-called "smart materials," could have application to newly constructed or renovated masonry buildings to locate internal flaws and to provide warnings of excessive stress and strain conditions.

REFERENCES

ABK (a joint venture). Dec., 1981. Methodology for Mitigation of Seismic Hazards in Existing Unreinforced Masonry Buildings: Diaphragm Testing. Topical Report 03.
American Society for Testing Materials. Tentative Test Method for Rebound Number of Hardened Concrete. ASTM C 805-75.
Berra, M., et al. 1987. Ultrasonic pulse transmission: A proposal to evaluate the efficiency of masonry strengthening by grouting. In: Proc. 2nd Joint USA-Italy Workshop on Evaluation, pp. 93–109. Boulder: The Masonry Society.
Calvi, G.M. 1988. Correlation between ultrasonic and load tests on old masonry specimens. In: Proc. 8th Intl. Brick/Block Masonry Conf., pp. 1665–1672. New York: Elsevier.

Carino, N.J., M. Sansalone, and N.N. Hsu. 1986. A Point Source Point Receiver, Pulse-Echo Technique for Flaw Detection in Concrete. ACI Jour. Farmington Hills, MI: American Concrete Institute.

DeVekey, R.C. 1988. Non-destructive test methods for masonry structures. In: Proc. 8th Intl. Brick/Block Conf., pp. 1665–1672. New York: Elsevier.

Dube, C.M., et. al. 1988. Laboratory Feasibility Study of a Composite Embedded Fiber Optic Sensor for Measurement of Structural Vibrations. Dynamics Technology, Inc. Report DT 8723-01.

Forde, M.C., and A.J. Batchelor. 1984. Low frequency NDR testing of historic structures. In: 3rd Eur.Conf. on NDT Testing, pp. 1–6. Florence.

Hobbs, B., and S.J. Wright. July, 1987. Ultrasonic testing for fault detection in brickwork and blockwork. In: Proc. Intl. Conf. on Struct. Faults and Repair, vol. 1, pp. 169–174. London: Engineering Technics Press.

Intl. Conf. of Building Officials. 1994. Uniform Code for Building Conservation.

Kingsley, G.R. 1989. Nondestructive evaluation of a nineteenth century brick smokehouse in colonial Williamsburg, VA. In: Proc 1st Intl. Conf. on Structural Studies, Repairs and Maint. of Historical Bldgs. Florence.

Kingsley, G.R., and J.L. Noland. 1988. A note on obtaining *in-situ* load-deformation properties of unreinforced brick masonry in the United States using flatjacks. Final Report of the Joint USA-Italy Workshop on Evaluation and Retrofit of Masonry Structures, pp. 215–223. Boulder: The Masonry Society.

Kingsley, G.R., J.L. Noland, and R.H. Atkinson. Aug., 1987. Nondestructive evaluation of masonry structures using sonic and ultrasonic pulse velocity techniques. In: Proc. 4th N. Am. Conf., pp. 67.1–67.16. Boulder: The Masonry Society.

Livingston, R.A. et al. 1988. The application of neutron probe to the nondestructive evaluation of building condition. In: Proc Intl. Workshop on NDE for Performance of Civil Struct., pp. 1–6. Reno: Materials Research Society.

Noland, J.L., R.H. Atkinson, and J.C. Baur. 1982. An Investigation into Methods of Nondestructive Evaluation of Masonry Structures. Report to the Natl. Science Foundation, Atkinson-Noland and Assoc., Boulder. National Technical Information Service, Washington, D.C., Report Nr. PB 82218074.

Noland, J.L., R.H. Atkinson, G.R. Kingsley, and M.P. Schuller. 1991. Nondestructive Evaluation of Masonry Structures, Final Report, NSF Grant ECE-8315924.

Noland J.L., G.R. Kingsley, and R.H. Atkinson. 1988. Utilization of nondestructive techniques in the evaluation of masonry. In: Proc. 8th Intl. Brick/Block Masonry Conf., pp. 1–10. Dublin.

Pittman, W.E., R.H. Church, W.E. Webb, and W. McLendon. 1984. Ground Penetrating Radar – A Review of its Application in the Mining Industry, U.S. Bur. of Mines, IC-8964.

Robinson, E.A., and T.S. Durrani. 1986. Geophysical Signal Processing. New York: Prentice-Hall.

Rossi, P.P. 1985. Flatjack test for the analysis of mechanical behavior of brick masonry structures. In: Proc. 7th Intl. Brick Masonry Conf., vol. 1, pp. 137–148. Melbourne: Frank Daniels Pty. Ltd.

Suprenant, B.A., and M.P. Schuller. 1995. Nondestructive Evaluation and Testing of Masonry Structures. Addison, IL: The Aberdeen Group.

Zoldners, N.G., and J.A. Soles. 1984. An annotated bibliography on nondestructive testing of concrete, 1975–1983. ACI SP 82-39. *In-Situ* Nondestructive Testing of Concrete, p. 745.

10

Development and Application of Acoustic Tomography to Masonry

R.H. ATKINSON[†] and M. SCHULLER

Atkinson-Noland & Associates, Inc., 2619 Spruce Street, Boulder, CO 80302, U.S.A.

ABSTRACT

A research project was conducted to investigate repair of masonry structures using injection grouting. As part of this work, several nondestructive evaluation techniques were used to investigate masonry quality before repair and also to qualify the effects of the repair. This paper describes the use of acoustic tomography, an analytical procedure for interpreting large data bases of pulse velocity information, to reconstruct a velocity distribution through the masonry element being tested. Results of laboratory tests, conducted on a masonry pier prior to and following injection, show the utility of the technique. Also presented are results from a tomographic investigation conducted on a section of a historic masonry building on the campus of the University of Wisconsin, Madison.

INTRODUCTION

Atkinson-Noland & Associates conducted a research project to investigate the use of injectable cementitious grouts for repair and retrofit of old masonry structures (Manzouri et al. 1995). One of the tasks of this project was to determine techniques for evaluation of the efficacy of the injection grouting process. The evaluation technique should preferably be nondestructive and able to locate voids in masonry and to determine those areas which have been penetrated by grout following injection.

One approach that showed promise was tomographic imaging using sonic and ultrasound wave transmission velocities (Schuller et al. 1994). Tomography is a computational technique that calculates the distribution of some parameter of interest within an interior region using measurements taken on the edges of the region. For the work described in this paper, ultrasonic stress wave travel time measurements between points on the exterior of a slice through a masonry pier were used to determine the distribution of acoustic velocities over the interior portion of the slice. Zones of low velocity are assumed to represent masonry of low quality or containing voids whereas high velocity is associated with good quality material.

Figure 10.1   Test pier under construction.

MASONRY LABORATORY SPECIMENS

A series of masonry piers were constructed as part of the research project for the purpose of investigating the effect of injection grouting on compressive behavior of masonry. The piers were constructed using solid pressed clay units reclaimed from a circa 1915 structure. Mortar with proportions of cement:lime:sand of 1:2:9 was used to simulate old, deteriorated mortar. The piers were 14 courses tall, 2 1/2 units wide, and 3 wythes thick. Figures 10.1 and 10.2 show a pier under construction and when completed.

Several of the test piers were constructed with a quality reflecting typical construction practices of the early 1900s. These piers have furrowed bed joints and partially filled head joints. The interior wythe often consists of broken, uneven units, with typically empty collar joints. A tomographic survey was performed on the completed pier after which the pier was repaired by injection grouting. After the grout had obtained an age of 28 days, a second tomographic survey was made which allowed an estimation of the efficiency of the grouting process.

INJECTION GROUT FOR MASONRY PIER REPAIR

A grout consisting of Type I Portland cement, lime, fly ash, #70 sand, and 2% superplasticizer (ProKrete PSP) with a water/cement ratio of 1.0, was chosen for injection of this specimen. This mix is suitable for injection into the typically large (> 3 mm) voids found in the interior of old masonry construction. Injection ports were located at

Figure 10.2   Completed test pier.

mid-height of the head joints in every other course and spaced approximately 40 cm on center horizontally. The specimen was fully saturated immediately prior to injection, and grout was injected at a pressure of 0.8 atm. The majority of the internal voids appeared to be interconnected, with grout flows of 60 cm horizontally and 4 to 5 courses vertically being noted.

ULTRASONIC PULSE VELOCITY READINGS

A horizontal "slice" consisting of one course of masonry was chosen for study using tomographic imaging. A large number of ultrasonic (54 kHz) pulse velocity readings were taken both prior to and following injection. A typical set of wave transmission paths is shown in Figure 10.3, in which the transmitting transducer is located at the position "B." The receiver was moved successively from point to point. Following each set of readings, the transmitter was moved to the next point and the process repeated around the entire perimeter of the pier. Thus 94 separate readings of ultrasonic pulse velocity were acquired to image a single course of masonry.

Tomographic Imaging Software

The use of acoustic waves for imaging materials used for building construction presents a number of problems not present with medical imaging. For example, masonry and concrete are dispersive, refracting media in which sound waves may reflect or refract as they encounter boundaries of material having different sonic velocities. As a result, the wave will not travel in a straight line but may follow a curved path depending on the nature of the material and structure. The frequency of the acoustic wave will determine the rate of energy attenuation with travel distance. High frequency waves, such as those employed by ultrasonic devices, attenuate rapidly in a material such as masonry. Low frequency waves, such as those produced by an impact, suffer much less attenuation but are unable to detect the presence of very small flaws.

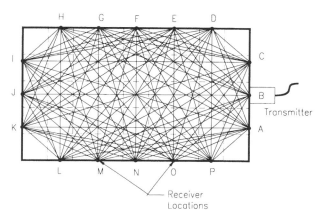

Figure 10.3   Plan view of signal ray paths for transducer located at point "B." Grid pattern shows division of horizontal slice into 5 × 9 pixels.

The software used for tomographic imaging in this study was originally developed by the mining industry for use in assessing underground conditions from exploratory boreholes using seismic techniques (Jackson and Tweeton 1995). The programs are based on the use of acoustic waves and are scale independent, thus permitting their application to masonry buildings.

Input to the program is the form of transmitter and receiver locations and pulse travel time between selected transmitter/receiver pairs. The nature of the technique requires that readings be taken through the medium being investigated, with transmitter and receiver located at the very least along two opposite sides of the area of interest. Positioning transducers along three sides will give better solution; a four-sided investigation will provide the most accurate results. Access to all four sides of the pier was possible and, in this case, transducers were located along each of the four sides.

The area being investigated is first divided into a number of elements termed pixels. The horizontal slice under study here has been divided into a set of 14 × 14 pixels. It is necessary to choose the pixel distribution and distribution of measurements such that each pixel is crossed by a number of ray paths. The algorithm then utilizes an iterative process to determine the velocity through each pixel in the set based upon the velocity as measured over each ray path. Results are provided in the form of a two-dimensional contour plot of velocity distribution throughout the slice. This procedure provides results which are easily interpreted. The accuracy with which the contour plot represents the actual structure depends on several factors, including the number of sides on which measurements are made, the linear spacing of measurement points, the frequency of the wave employed, and the size of the pixel grid.

The initial version of the tomographic software employed straight wave paths between transmitter and receiver. This assumption is only satisfactory when the velocity differences between materials in the object under test are less than 20%. Figure 10.4 presents results from the test pier using this assumption. An improvement in accuracy can be obtained by permitting the stress waves to travel curved, nonlinear paths. Results obtained making this assumption are illustrated in Figure 10.5. One drawback with this assumption is that regions of low velocity may not be transversed by any of the calculated wave paths, creating shadow zones. To overcome this problem the third version of the tomography program uses an advancing wave front assumption based on

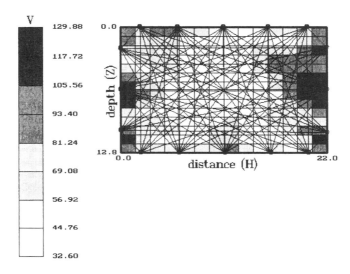

Figure 10.4 Straight-ray analysis minimizes path length between each transmitter/receiver pair. The method is good for analysis where velocity variations are less than about 20%.

Huygens' principle to model the stress wave transmission in the object. This provides a more accurate and realistic determination of the velocity distribution throughout the masonry as shown in Figure 10.6.

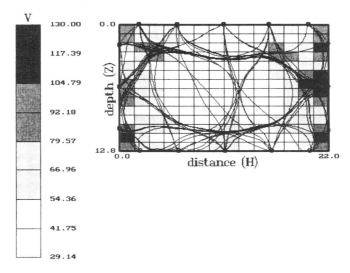

Figure 10.5 Curved-ray analysis accounts for bending of waves due to large velocity gradients. The problem with this method is that shadow zones are created at areas of low velocity and the program can become unstable in such cases.

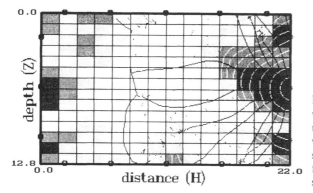

Figure 10.6 Migrating wavefront analysis, based upon Huygens' principle for wave propagation, eliminates shadow zones while allowing for diffraction and scattering of stress waves.

Several improved velocity-based reconstruction methods have been developed over the past several years and incorporated into the current tomographic software (Woodham and Schuller 1997). In general, these methods are designed to reduce the effects of anomalous data or to increase the contrast between high or low velocity regions contained in a uniform-velocity background material. The techniques improve visualization of internal anomalies in nonhomogeneous materials, such as concrete and masonry.

LABORATORY SPECIMEN RESULTS

The program outputs for the two cases are shown in Figures 10.7 and 10.8 as plots of the velocity distribution in the interior of the masonry. Figure 10.7 is for the original,

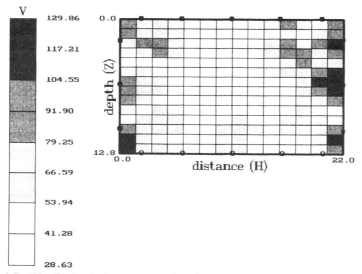

Figure 10.7   The final velocity reconstruction for an ungrouted pier, as constructed with a relatively sound exterior but with significant voids on the masonry interior.

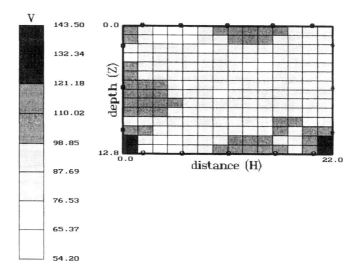

Figure 10.8 Velocity reconstruction for pier repaired by grout injection shows that significant voids are filled, velocities are more consistent throughout, and the average velocity is increased.

as-built case, and shows a large variation in wave velocity throughout the interior at this course. Velocities range from less than 30 inches/millisecond (760 m/s) to about 130 inches/millisecond (3300 m/s) for this case, with an indication of a large area in the interior of the pier with reduced velocity. High test velocity readings are evident around the perimeter of the pier. These results are consistent with the pier construction which had interior voids surrounded by a solid wythe of masonry.

The plot of Figure 10.8 shows the velocity distribution for the grouted case. Immediately obvious is that the velocity is much more consistent throughout the masonry, with no significant areas of reduced velocity. Also evident is the fact that the pulse velocity ranges in a narrow band from approximately 30 to 130 inches/millisecond (760–3300 m/s). The results appear to indicate that the injection grouting process was successful in filling all significant voids in the masonry interior.

CASE STUDY: UNIVERSITY OF WISCONSIN

A tomographic evaluation was conducted on the exterior masonry walls of the Red Armory and Gymnasium (Figure 10.9) located on the campus of the University of Wisconsin in Madison. The structure was built in 1894 and has seen several different uses during its life. Current proposals to change the usage of the gym to administrative space warranted the need for structural assessment, including the condition and as-built details of the exterior masonry walls. Because of the historic classification of this structure, all evaluation work had to be done without damaging any of the masonry.

Figure 10.9   The Red Armory and Gymnasium as viewed from the southwest corner.

The tomographic reconstruction technique was used to analyze a large pulse velocity data base to generate a velocity map of one masonry section. Mechanical pulse velocity (MPV) testing was conducted on a horizontal section of a pilaster to provide data for tomographic analysis. The pilaster has dimensions of approximately 0.9 m wide by 1.4 m long in plan view. Thirty-three transmitter and receiver locations were used to collect 412 different velocity readings for analysis.

At the pilaster, a grid was laid out with a 100 mm spacing (2 sender/receiver points per brick) on both interior and exterior faces with soapstone. At each point on the grid, a low-frequency stress wave was generated by tapping the wall with an instrumented rubber-faced hammer. The wave propagated through the masonry and was recorded on the opposite side of the wall by a piezoelectric accelerometer for determination of through-wall wave velocity.

Several different analyses were considered, with different boundary conditions, constraints, and numbers of iterations. The velocity profile shown in Figure 10.10 represents the final analysis and shows the calculated velocity distribution as a velocity contour plot. In this case, the higher velocities are representative of solid, dense masonry, whereas lower velocities indicate the presence of voids or cracks in the mortar and bricks.

Results from tomographic analysis are interesting and show that the pilaster section at the inside face has greater velocities than that of the rest of the wall. The velocity range here of 1400 to 2000 m/sec is representative of sound masonry with solidly filled joints and little or no deterioration.

The velocity at the middle of the wall and the exterior face is lower, with a range of 250 to 750 m/sec. This is representative of masonry with partially filled joints and internal voids. The lower velocities at the exterior may be due, in part, to weathering of

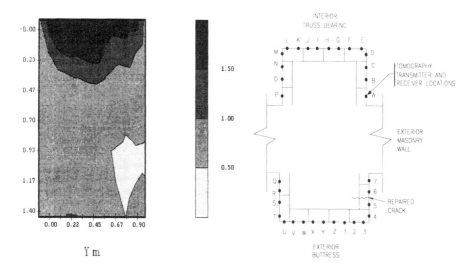

Figure 10.10   Results of tomographic analysis on pier section at the University of Wisconsin Armory and Gymnasium. Shading represents velocity (km/s, as indicated by the scale at to the right of the tomogram), where a greater velocity indicates well-built masonry with full mortar joints. Interior masonry (top of picture) has a higher velocity, whereas exterior masonry (bottom of figure) is of lower quality. The source and receiver locations are shown on a cross-section of the pier in the right half of the figure.

mortar and brick. Significant environmental deterioration was not noted, however a crack (patched with mortar) was observed on the exterior. The effect of this crack is evident as a low velocity zone and extends through at least half of the pier (lower right Figure 10.8). This could be evidence of separation of the buttress from the main wall.

CONCLUSIONS

The main advantage of tomographic imaging is that the results are easily interpreted and provide a complete two-dimensional picture of the interior masonry condition. All necessary data is acquired nondestructively using readily available equipment and the software requires only moderate computer power for solution of the velocity distribution. However, the technique is currently very labor intensive in terms of data collection, data reduction, and input of data into the tomographic imaging software. This process would be greatly aided by a multi-channel system capable of taking a large number of readings at each instant and automatically entering the appropriate parameter in the input file for the tomographic program.

Tomographic imaging is a useful analytical technique for determining masonry quality and also qualifying the effect of grout injection repair procedures. Subsequent research using advanced analytical algorithms and visualization software increases resolution and accuracy for use with historic masonry construction (Woodham and Schuller 1997).

ACKNOWLEDGEMENTS

This paper reports preliminary results of a study on the feasibility of using acoustic tomography for diagnosis of masonry structures. This study was funded by the National Science Foundation and was conducted in collaboration with the Politecnico di Milano. Development of the tomographic imaging technique was supported by the United States Nuclear Regulatory Commission under contract number NRC-04-94-081. The authors wish to thank Bill Foulks and Peter Wrenn of John G. Waite Associates, Albany, New York for their technical assistance at the University of Wisconsin.

REFERENCES

Jackson, M.J., and D.R. Tweeton. 1995. 3DTOM: Three-Dimensional Geophysical Tomography. U.S. Bureau of Mines.

Manzouri, T., P.B. Shing, B. Amadei, M.P. Schuller, and R.H. Atkinson. 1995. Repair and Retrofit of Unreinforced Masonry Walls: Experimental Evaluation and Finite Element Analysis. Report to the National Science Foundation, No. CU/SR-95/2, Boulder: Univ. Colorado.

Schuller, M.P., M. Berra, A. Fatticcioni, R.H. Atkinson, and L. Binda. 1994. Use of tomography for diagnosis and control of masonry repairs. In: Proc. 10th Intl. Brick/Block Masonry Conf., ed. N.G. Shrive and A. Huizer, pp. 1539–1549. Calgary: Univ. of Calgary.

Woodham, D.B., and M.P. Schuller. 1997. Characterization of Concrete Condition Using Acoustic Tomographic Imaging. U.S. Nuclear Regulatory Commission NUREG/CR-6518.

11

Quantitative X-ray Diffraction Analysis of Hand-molded Brick

R.A. LIVINGSTON[1], P.E. STUTZMAN[2], and I. SCHUMANN[3]

[1]Office of Highway Engineering R&D, Federal Highway Administration,
6300 Georgetown Pike, McLean, VA 22101, U.S.A.
[2]Building Materials Division, Div. 862, National Institute of Standards and Technology,
Gaithersburg, MD 20899, U.S.A.
[3]Lehr- und Forschungsbereich Bauphysik Werkstoffe im Bauwesen,
Technische Universität Hamburg-Harburg, Eißendorfer Str. 42, 2100 Hamburg, Germany

ABSTRACT

The durability of brick is related to its microstructure and mineralogy. It has been proposed that the ratio of cristobalite to quartz would be a reliable predictor of durability. To test this theory, quantitative X-ray diffraction analysis was applied to samples of historic brick from the United States and Europe. The quantitative method was based on finding the reference intensity ratios (RIR) for cristobalite and for quartz relative to an internal standard of corundum (Al_2O_3). Known amounts of corundum were added to the ground brick samples, and replicate X-ray diffraction patterns were taken. The intensities of the cristobalite, quartz, and corundum peaks were calculated after correcting for background. The cristobalite/quartz ratio agreed with the relative durability of bricks from Colonial Williamsburg in the United States. However, cristobalite was not detected in brick samples from Germany. Among other mineralogical differences observed, the German brick contained plagioclase feldspars while the American bricks did not. Also, one set of less durable bricks from Germany had detectable amounts of illite or mica. This suggests that the mineralogy of bricks made in Germany was fundamentally different as a result of either the raw materials used or the firing procedure. Consequently, the cristobalite index may be usable only for bricks with chemical compositions similar to those of Colonial Williamsburg. This study also revealed that corundum may not be the most suitable choice for the internal standard because of overlaps with quartz and feldspar peaks.

INTRODUCTION

The conservation of historic brick buildings requires the ability to predict the durability of the brick itself. The durability of historic brick can vary significantly, depending both on the material itself and on the local environment. However, even for modern brick, the available methods for predicting durability leave much to be desired (Bortz et al. 1990). These test methods rely on empirical durability functions rather than on a fundamental knowledge of the chemistry and physics of brick manufacture. Consequently, durability relationships developed for one particular type of brick may not apply to others.

A possible materials science approach to the problem of historic brick durability was suggested by an undergraduate researcher, R.E. Lindsley, at the College of William and Mary in Williamsburg, Virginia, who was studying the durability of bricks in the historic Colonial Williamsburg area (Lindsley 1982). She found that the durability of the brick, based on a visual assessment of distress, seemed related to the amount of cristobalite present. Cristobalite is a high-temperature polymorph of quartz. It has been established in experiments on the melting of potassium-rich clay minerals that the amount of cristobalite formed is a function of firing temperature (Brindley and Maroney 1960). As a general rule, bricks fired to a high temperature, around 1000 °C, are more durable than those fired at lower temperatures (Robinson1982).

One explanation for this effect may be found in the melting relationships. Brick-making clay consists of a mixture of clay minerals, either potassium-rich (illite) or sodium and calcium-rich (smectite) and quartz sand (Grim 1974). The composition of the clays in the Williamsburg area is illitic and thus can be displayed in the phase diagram shown in Figure 11.1 (Schairer and Bowen 1947). This phase diagram also applies to porcelain ceramics. This system has a eutectic point at 985°C at the intersection of the potassium feldspar, tridymite, and mullite fields. This suggest that to melt the clay, and thus to form a strong ceramic bond between the quartz grains, it is necessary to achieve at least this temperature.

The equilibrium silica phase at the eutectic is predicted to be tridymite (Schairer and Bowen 1947), but cristobalite is usually seen instead. The amount of cristobalite is associated with the kaolinite content of the clay rather than the amount of quartz that is melted (Brindley and Udagawa 1960).

It is an inconvenient fact that none of the three minerals associated with the eutectic point are usually detected in hand-molded brick after firing. Aside from the formation of cristobalite rather than tridymite, crystalline feldspar is not observed, but a glassy phase generally is (Livingston, unpublished). This is consistent with the experimental results of Brindley and Maroney (1960), in which a feldspathic glass rather than feldspar was produced under these conditions. These investigators also found that mullite could not be detected in samples fired at less than 1100°C. This temperature is rarely achieved in brick making, partly for reasons of fuel economy, but also because of the technology of the kiln, which operates under natural draft. In contrast, forced draft kilns, which produce higher temperatures, have been used to make porcelain, which consequently has a large mullite content.

Finally, cristobalite theoretically ought not to be found in the bricks after cooling to room temperature, but its persistence can be explained by the fact that aluminum is

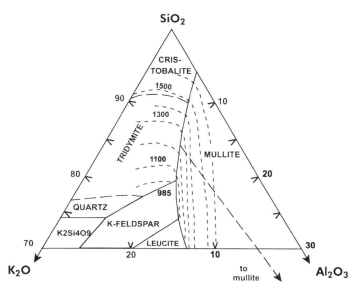

Figure 11.1   Part of the phase diagram of system K_2O-Al_2O_3-SiO_2 (after Schairer and Bowen 1947).

known to enter into the cristobalite crystal structure, thereby stabilizing it (Perotta et al. 1989).

The results of Lindsley led to the concept of a cristobalite index that could be used as the basis for durability prediction. The cristobalite index, η, is defined as:

$$\eta = \frac{X_{Cr}}{X_{Qz} + X_{Cr}},\qquad(11.1)$$

where X_{Cr} and X_{Qz} are the weight percentages of cristobalite and quartz, respectively. This ratio was chosen as a measure rather than the absolute amount of cristobalite in order to compensate for the variability of the constituents among bricks.

To determine the cristobalite index of a brick specimen, it is necessary to analyze the minerals present. The most practical method is X-ray diffraction (XRD). While the peak intensities in an XRD pattern should be proportional to the abundance of a phase in a mixture, this is in reality only a semi-quantitative measurement because the peak intensity-concentration relationship is not exactly linear. The departures from linearity arise from differential absorption of X-rays by the mineral phases in the sample itself. However, Klug and Alexander (1974) show that an absorption correction can be made by the use of an internal standard and associated calibration procedures. The internal standard is a mineral phase, absent in the original sample, that is added to the mixture in a known proportion. Given a known amount of internal standard, the concentration of the unknown phase can then be found from the peak intensity ratio of the unknown and internal standard. This approach to quantitative XRD has been successfully applied at the National Institute of Standards and Technology to determine the mineralogical composition of Portland cement clinker reference materials (Stutzman 1992).

An initial trial of the cristobalite index was undertaken as part of the NATO-CCMS Pilot Study on the Conservation of Historic Brick. As outlined in Appendix I (this volume), this was an international program for cooperation in research in the deterioration and conservation of historic brick. The pilot study provided a convenient means to obtain samples of historic bricks from different geographical regions, as well facilitating the cooperative analyses.

QUANTITATIVE XRD USING THE REFERENCE INTENSITY RATIO METHOD

The reference intensity ratio (RIR) method is a specific application of the internal standard method for quantitative XRD. The RIR is a constant relating the X-ray scattering power of a phase to that of the internal standard (Klug and Alexander 1974; Stutzman 1992). The RIR is defined as the ratio of the strongest peak of the unknown phase to that of an internal standard in a one-to-one mixture (Chung 1974; Hubbard and Snyder 1988).

The RIR values are calculated from a standard composite sample, consisting of a mixture of the pure phase and the internal standard phase, as follows:

$$RIR_{i\alpha} = \frac{I_{i\alpha}}{I_{jCo}} \times \frac{X_{Co}}{X_\alpha} , \qquad (11.2)$$

where: $RIR_{i\alpha}$ = RIR for peak i of mineral phase α,

$I_{i\alpha}$ = intensity of peak i of mineral phase α,

I_{jCo} = intensity of peak j of the internal standard, i.e., corundum,

X_{Co} = concentration of internal standard in the standard composite sample,

X_α = concentration of mineral phase α in the standard composite sample.

Then Y'_α, the concentration of mineral phase α in an unknown composite sample, is:

$$Y'_\alpha = \frac{I_{i\alpha}}{I_{jCo}} \times \frac{Y_{Co}}{RIR_{i,\alpha}} . \qquad (11.3)$$

Finally, the concentration of the mineral phase in the original sample is obtained by correcting for the dilution caused by the addition of the reference phase:

$$Y_\alpha = \frac{Y'_\alpha}{1 - Y_{Co}} . \qquad (11.4)$$

The precision of this technique can be affected by the heterogeneity of the composite sample and by preferred orientation. The sample heterogeneity is dealt with by grinding the sample to a very fine size, < 10 μm, and thorough homogenization. The effect of particle orientation is minimized by making replicate scans of each sample, rehomogenizing and repacking the sample in the sample holder between each scan.

SAMPLE COLLECTION

German Historic Brick

Nine samples of historic brick were obtained from several buildings in the North German cities of Lübeck and Hamburg, and some historic churches on the sea coast along the North Sea, as described in Chapter 4 (this volume). The dates of the buildings ranged from the 14th to 19th centuries. Individual bricks were removed by cutting out the mortar joints with an electric chisel. This method of sampling was chosen instead of drilling out cores in order to make the replacement less obtrusive. However, only very small quantities, on the order of 1 gram, were required for XRD. The bulk of each brick was used for other types of tests.

Colonial Williamsburg Modern Hand-molded Brick

Although brick samples are available from historic buildings in Colonial Williamsburg, it was decided instead to perform the XRD on some contemporary samples from the brick-making exhibition area. The brickmakers use a clay and sand mixture that is consistent from one batch to another. However, a particular batch was not fired at sufficiently high temperatures, producing poor quality bricks that failed the standard durability tests. Therefore, a sample of these failed bricks was obtained along with a sound brick from another properly fired batch. This was intended to provide a rough test of the ability of the cristobalite index to discriminate between good and poor quality brick.

PROCEDURE

X-Ray Equipment

An automated Philips X-ray powder diffractometer with sample changer was used for data collection. The system operates at 45 kV and 35 mA using copper Kα radiation, a variable divergence slit, 0.02° receiving slit, diffracted beam monochromater, and a scintillation detector. The diffraction patterns are recorded in the form of electronic digital data files rather than on paper strip charts. This makes it possible to process them on a personal computer for phase identification, peak profile fitting, and quantitative analysis.

Cristobalite and Quartz RIRs

A pair of RIRs for cristobalite and for quartz were prepared for the diffractometer using standards of pure cristobalite (NIST SRM 1879) and quartz from clean quartz crystal fragments selected under a stereomicroscope. The ideal internal standard should not produce diffraction peaks that interfere with peaks from phases being measured in the sample. It should be an easily obtainable, stable, pure material with a fine (1–10 μm) particle size, and low susceptibility to orientation (Klug and Alexander 1974). This study used corundum (α-alumina) as the internal standard, specifically the standard reference material provided by the United States National Institute for Standards & Technology, NIST SRM 674a. Mixtures of 50% corundum and 50% cristobalite or quartz were prepared. Each composite sample was then wetted with ethanol to make a slurry and blended with the assistance of a high-power ultrasonic probe. It should be noted that standard RIR mixtures need not be restricted to equally proportioned binary mixtures. Chung (1974) demonstrated that multi-phase mixtures of known phase abundance composition can be used. Snyder and Bish (1989) found that multiple standard mixtures using different phase-to-standard ratios provided more accurate RIRs, while the use of multiple peaks for each phase minimized effects of preferred orientation.

   The composite standard samples for RIR development were then packed into standard 16 mm × 20 mm cavity mount sample holders. To ensure that the scanned surface was as smooth as possible, the powders were backloaded against a glass plate. Data scans encompassed a 2θ range to include all peaks of interest at a scan rate of 2 seconds per 0.02° (2θ) step. Peak intensity ratios from four replicate scans, with the sample repacked for each scan, were averaged to establish the RIR.

Sample Preparation and Analysis

Each sample was first crushed by hand in a mortar and pestle. It was then reduced to final size by grinding in a orbital grinding mill with corundum cylinders to a particle size <10 μm. The next step consisted of adding 10% corundum internal standard. The composite sample was then homogenized by mixing the powder with ethanol and sonicating the resulting slurry with an ultrasonic probe. Each sample was scanned three times, with repacking of the powder between each scan. Diffraction scans were made from 10 to 54° (2θ) with a two second count time per 0.02° (2θ) step.

Data Reduction

The quantitative XRD method uses the integrated intensity, i.e., the total number of counts under each peak, rather the intensity of the peak channel alone. The calculation of the integrated intensity requires fitting the raw data to a specified profile shape, eliminating the contribution of overlapping peaks, and subtracting background. In this study, this was done using the commercially available software SHADOW[1]. The pseudo-Voight function provided the best fit as the profile shape to the diffraction

---

[1] Materials Data, Inc., Livermore

SOUND WILLIAMSBURG BRICK

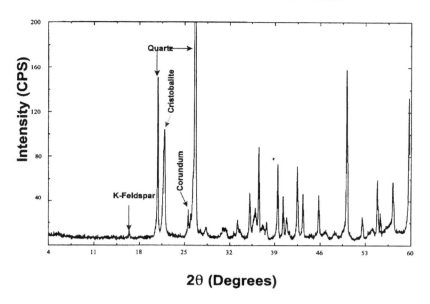

2θ (Degrees)

Figure 11.2   X-ray diffraction pattern for Colonial Williamsburg good brick.

peaks. The ability to run SHADOW in batch mode facilitated rapid and reproducible peak area measurements.

RESULTS

Quartz was found in all samples. However, cristobalite was detected only in the brick samples for Colonial Williamsburg (Figure 11.2). The quartz and cristobalite mass percentages and the cristobalite indices for these two samples are summarized in Table 11.1. The uncertainties were computed solely from the counting statistics. It can be seen that the cristobalite index for the sound brick is significantly higher than for the failed brick. The comparison of the data among the replicates show very good repeatability, indicating that the procedure is not very sensitive to the procedure for packing individual powder samples for XRD. However, the sum of quartz and cristobalite typically falls in the 70%–80% range. This is somewhat higher than the total SiO_2 content of these bricks, roughly 65% ± 1.3%, as measured by X-ray fluorescence. Conversely, the quartz content measured in the German historic bricks falls in the range of 20%–50%, Table 11.2, which is lower than would be expected. This suggests that the measurements may have a bias.

Regarding some qualitative results of the XRD patterns, the German bricks all contained plagioclase feldspar. The sound brick from Colonial Williamsburg also showed traces of feldspar, but of a more potassium-rich type (Figure 11.1).   However, no

Table 11.1   Quartz and cristobalite mass percentages in Colonial Williamsburg brick.

SOUND WILLIAMSBURG BRICK				
Scan #	Quartz	Cristobalite	Quartz + Cristobalite	Cristobalite Index
1	67.3% ± 12.1%	15.8% ± 3.0%	83.1% ± 12.5%	0.19 ± 0.046
2	53.2% ± 8.8%	13.3% ± 2.3%	66.5% ± 9.1%	0.20 ± 0.044
3	51.4% ± 8.4%	15.8% ± 2.2%	67.2% ± 8.7%	0.24 ± 0.045
Mean	57.3% ± 9.9%	15.0% ± 2.5%	72.3% ± 10.2%	0.24 ± 0.045
FAILED WILLIAMSBURG BRICK				
Scan #	Quartz	Cristobalite	Quartz + Cristobalite	Cristobalite Index
1	71.5% ± 10.8%	5.57% ± 0.95%	77.1% ± 10.8%	0.07 ± 0.016
2	74.2% ± 11.3%	5.75% ± 0.99%	80.0% ± 11.4%	0.07 ± 0.016
3	73.2% ± 11.2%	5.69% ± 0.99%	78.9% ± 11.3%	0.07 ± 0.016
Mean	73.0% ± 11.0%	5.67% ± 0.98%	78.7% ± 11.2%	0.07 ± 0.016

Note: The error terms are one standard deviation in mass percentage, calculated from X-ray counting statistics.

feldspar was observed in the failed brick. Some phyllosilicate minerals, illites, and micas appeared in the diffraction patterns for the bricks from Garding, Germany. These bricks had displayed a tendency toward sanding or granular disintegration. The presence of the illite and mica indicates either that these bricks were not fired at high enough temperatures, or that over time the glassy phase in the bricks had reacted with water. Finally, bassanite, $CaSO_4 \cdot \frac{1}{2}H_2O$, was detected in a sample from Hamburg. This is associated with gypsum, $CaSO_4 \cdot 2H_2O$, created in the brick by reaction with sulfur dioxide air pollution. It occurs in the less hydrated form of bassanite because the bricks samples were heated for other analyses prior to the XRD studies.

DISCUSSION

Sources of Bias

There seems to be a bias in concentrations found for the individual mineral phases. This bias is less of a problem for the cristobalite index since it is a ratio rather than an absolute value, and the individual biases may cancel each other out to a certain extent.

Nevertheless, before proceeding further, it is extremely desirable to identify the source of the bias so that it can be eliminated. Inspection of Equation 11.3 suggests three possible sources of bias. One possibility is the RIR, which is derived from a simple binary mixture of quartz and corundum, rather than a multicomponent mixture that more closely reflects the composition of bricks.

Table 11.2   Quartz contents of German historic brick.

Sample ID#	Sample Name	Mean	Std. Dev.
RL1	Dankwart	22.26%	1.52%
RL2	Marles	38.60%	3.53%
RL3	Hiobs luh	38.80%	9.78%
RL4	Garding 4	43.70%	3.79%
RL5	Garding 3H	31.20%	6.89%
RL6	Garding 3V	156.10%	38.33%
RL7	Hiobs 4uv	51.50%	5.09%
RL8	Hiobs 14g	33.10%	1.84%
RL9	Hiobs 14h	26.70%	0.49%

Another possibility lies in the measured corundum intensity, I_{jCo}. As can be seen in Figure 11.1, this is calculated from a small peak at 25.6° that lies on the shoulder of the major quartz peak at 26.7°. It also overlaps with a feldspar peak at 25.5°–25.8°. Moreover, the feldspathic glass phase normally found in bricks produces a broad diffuse background in the region of roughly 25°–35°. All of these factors complicate the determination of the background in the vicinity of the corundum peak and so could all affect the computation of the the corundum intensity.

This suggests that corundum may not be the most suitable internal standard for quantitative XRD of bricks. Other internal reference minerals should be evaluated, using a control sample consisting of specified amounts of quartz, cristobalite, and an appropriate feldspathic glass.

Quantitative Durability Functions Based on the Cristobalite Index

The ranking of the Colonial Williamsburg brick by the cristobalite index corresponds to their durabilities. This is at least consistent with Lindsley's earlier results and suggests that it would be worthwhile to investigate this concept further. To develop a statistically significant correlation between durability and the cristobalite index would require a much larger number of samples. It may be difficult to obtain a sufficient number of samples from a standing historic structure.

A more fundamental problem concerns an appropriate quantitative durability measurement for correlation with the cristobalite index. The method used here was essentially a visual assessment of distress, which involves a subjective judgement. The standard quantitative measurements of durability involve cycling by freezing and thawing; however, this method is not always reliable (Ritchie 1982). Other methods of quantifying durability using sulfate tests, sonic modulus measurements, or SEM image analysis have been suggested, but these have not yet been standardized (Bortz et al. 1990). Nevertheless, some quantitative measurement of durability must be made consistently on the brick samples in order to have data to correlate with the cristobalite content.

Such a correlation would be an improvement over the existing state of knowledge. Nevertheless, it would still be a statistical relationship, rather than one based directly on materials science.

Ultimately it will be necessary to determine the role that cristobalite plays in the brick's durability. Does it in itself contribute to the durability? Or is it merely a surrogate for other phenomena that occur during the firing of the brick?

Absence of Cristobalite in German Bricks

Since cristobalite was not detected in the samples from Germany, it is obviously impossible to apply the cristobalite index to these bricks. The absence of cristobalite could be due to several causes: low firing temperatures, different clay chemistry, or reversion of cristobalite to quartz over long time periods. Given the abundance of aluminum to stabilize the cristobalite, it is unlikely that reversion to quartz has occurred. Low firing temperatures are a possibility, but it is difficult to determine this. Thus, the most likely possibility is different clay chemistry.

The chemical compositions of the German and Colonial Williamsburg samples are tabulated in Table 11.3. For ease of comparison, only the major fluxes (Na_2O, K_2O, CaO, and Fe_2O_3) are presented. These are the elements that affect the melting process of the clays in the brick. These have also been normalized by dividing each concentration by the sum of the fluxes in each sample. The German bricks were analyzed by X-ray fluorescence and the Colonial Williamsburg bricks by prompt-gamma neutron activation.

It can be seen that the Fe_2O_3 content of the fluxes is roughly comparable among the samples. The major difference lies in the amounts of K_2O and Na_2O relative to CaO. The CaO proportion of the German bricks is roughly six times greater than that of Colonial Williamsburg bricks, while the K_2O content is only about one-half. It is known that such significant variations will affect the type of feldspar that is formed, and also the melting temperatures (Deer et al. 1966). In a study of bricks made with calcium-rich Canadian clay, Grattan-Bellew and Litvan (1978) found a linear relationship between the firing temperature and the amount of laboradorite, a plagioclase feldspar, in the fired brick. As noted above, firing temperature appears to be a good predictor of durability. Franke and Schumann (Chapter 3, this volume) present a method for measuring temperature using hematite crystallinity. This is based on the same set of samples used in this study.

Consequently, the chemistry of the brick must be known to apply the cristobalite index successfully. Alternatively, a durability function based on feldspar formation may be applicable to bricks like those from Germany.

Table 11.3   Flux constituents in brick samples.

Sample ID#	Sample Name	Oxide as Percent of Total Fluxes				Total Fluxes (mass %)
		Na$_2$O	K$_2$O	CaO	Fe$_2$O$_3$	
Germany						
RL1	Dankwart	5.2	20.1	30.7	44.0	18.9
RL2	Marles	16.0	18.5	35.7	29.8	23.8
RL3	Hiobs 1uh	2.1	18.3	37.2	42.4	15.3
RL4	Garding 4	6.8	22.5	18.6	52.0	12.9
RL5	Garding 3H	10.2	16.1	38.0	35.6	20.5
RL6	Garding 3V	10.2	16.1	38.0	35.6	20.5
RL7	Hiobs 4uv	2.1	18.3	37.2	42.4	15.3
RL8	Hiobs 14g	2.6	16.0	40.3	41.0	14.4
RL9	Hiobs 14h	2.6	16.0	40.3	41.0	14.4
Colonial Williamsburg						
CWGB	Sound brick	13.1	35.3	5.8	45.8	17.3
CWBB	Failed brick	16.0	34.7	4.9	44.3	16.8

CONCLUSIONS

This study has shown that quantitative XRD can be applied to measure cristobalite and quartz in historic bricks. However, corundum may not be the best internal standard for this application. The cristobalite index seems to be useful as a predictor of durability for Colonial Williamsburg-type bricks, i.e., those with a high K/Ca ratio. However, it is universally not applicable, as shown by the German bricks. Perhaps a two-dimensional index that also takes into account the formation of feldspar would cover a wider variety of brick types.

REFERENCES

Bortz, S.A., S.L. Marusin, and C.B. Monk, Jr. 1990. A critical review of masonry durability standards. In: Proc. of the 5th North American Masonry Conference, ed. D.P. Abrams, pp. 1523–1536. Boulder, CO: The Masonry Society.

Brindley, G.W., and D.M. Maroney. 1960. High-temperature reactions of clay mineral mixtures and their ceramic properties. II. Reactions of kaolinite-mica-quartz mixtures compared with the K$_2$O-Al$_2$O$_3$-SiO$_2$ equilibrium diagram. *J. Am. Ceramic Soc.* **43(10)**:511–516.

Brindley, G.W., and S. Udagawa. 1960. High temperature reactions of clay mineral mixtures and their ceramic properties: I. Kaolinite-mica-quartz mixtures with 25 weight % quartz. *J. Am. Ceramic Soc.* **43(2)**:59–65.

Chung, F.H. 1974. Quantitative interpretation of X-ray diffraction patterns of mixtures: I. Matrix-flushing method for quantitative multicomponent analysis. *J. Appl. Crystallography* 7:519–525.

Deer, W.A., R.A. Howie, and G. Zussman. 1966. An Introduction to the Rock-forming Minerals. London: Longman.

Grattan-Bellew, P.E., and G.G. Litvan. 1978. X-ray diffraction method for determining the firing temperature of clay bricks. *Ceramic Bull.* **57(5)**:493–495.

Grim, R.E. 1974. Applied Clay Mineralogy. New York: McGraw-Hill.

Hubbard, C.R., and R.L. Synder. 1988. RIR – measurement and use in quantitative XRD. *Powder Diffraction* **3(2)**:74–77.

Klug, H.P., and L.E. Alexander. 1974. X-ray diffraction procedures. New York: J. Wiley.

Lindsley, R.E. 1982. Mineral causes for deterioration patterns in brick structures at Colonial Williamsburg VA. Unpublished report. Geology Dept., College of William and Mary, Williamsburg VA.

Perotta, A.J., D.K. Grubbs, E.S. Martin, N.R. Dando, H.A. McKinstry, and C-Y Huang. 1989. Chemical stabilization of β-cristobalite. *J. Am. Ceramic Soc.* **72(3)**:441–3447.

Ritchie, T. 1982. Brick durability tests and the method of freezing. In: Proc. 5th Intl. Brick Masonry Conf., II.1. Rome.

Robinson, G.C. 1982. Characterization of bricks and their resistance to deterioration mechanisms. Conservation of Historic Stone Buildings and Monuments, pp. 145–162. Washington, D.C.: National Academy Press.

Schairer, J.F., and N.L. Bowen. 1947. Melting relations in the systems $Na_2O-Al_2O_3-SiO_2$ and $K_2O-Al_2O_3-SiO_2$. *Am. J. Sci.* **245(4)**:193–204.

Synder, R.L., and D.L. Bish. 1989. Quantitative analysis. *Rev. Mineral.* **20**:101–144.

Stutzman, P.E. 1992. X-ray powder diffraction analysis of three Portland cement reference material clinkers: NISTIR 4785. Gaithersburg, MD: NIST.

12

A Damage Atlas and Questionnaire for Evaluation of Deterioration of Ancient Brick Masonry Structures

K. Van Balen

R. Lemaire Center for Conservation, K.U.Leuven, De Croylaan 2,
3001 Leuven (Heverlee), Belgium

ABSTRACT

The aim of the research on brick masonry degradation is presented. The project is comprised of the following:

- Atlas of Damages to ancient brick masonry, a book with a description of the types of damage and their possible causes, in ancient brick masonry structures;
- Masonry Damage Diagnostic (expert) System (MDDS), an expert computer system allowing the user to define damage types and damage causes in ancient brick masonry structures.

The scientific methodology used for the development of both documents is given. Expert systems and their relation to expertise are discussed as experienced with the Masonry Damage Diagnostic System. The outcome of the project in relation to ongoing research on brick masonry is discussed.

INTRODUCTION

According to the decision taken at the 5th meeting of the NATO-CCMS Pilot Study in Berlin in 1991, an attempt was made to find the necessary framework to execute the idea of a damage atlas for historic brick structures. As decided at that meeting, attempts were to be made to look within European research programs to see if such an effort could be proposed to different partners with considerable experience in studying the deterioration of brick masonry structures. Independent of the Centre for Conservation of Historic Towns and Buildings (CCHTB), the University of Hamburg had developed the questionnaire discussed within the NATO-CCMS Pilot Study during the previous years, it was decided to collaborate with T.N.O.-Bouw (the building research station of the Netherlands) and the University of Milan. With those partners, the final proposal was worked out. It soon became clear that the limitation to an atlas would constrain the possible outcome and use of this "tool." Therefore the total project aimed to create an expert system to allow less-skilled persons to analyze, using the expertise collected in the system, different types of damage to historic brick structures. Thus the "expert system for evaluation of deterioration of ancient brick masonry structures" project was born.

A research group coordinated by the author developed the "Masonry Damage Diagnostic System (MDDS)" and a "Atlas of Damages of Historic Brick Structures," which aimed at improving the diagnosis before intervention, but which also can be used to evaluate previous interventions. Both are in fact similar actions in a circular approach of the loop: analysis → diagnosis → therapy → control (→ analysis) (Searls et al. 1997; Van Balen 1988).

After having explained the basis of the construction of the MDDS and the Atlas of Damages, discussions will be focused on the use of it, in view of multidisciplinary exchange of opinions to prepare the diagnosis of brick masonry monuments. The effect of the use of these instruments by a broader group of professionals with a lower technical background than the usually called expert, for which those instruments are meant, has to be considered. The reason for this is obvious if the presumption is accepted that conservation is improved by the regular control and regular maintenance of buildings more than by a "heavy" intervention every fifty years.

GENERAL APPROACH

A systematic questionnaire was developed that allows the collection of expertise from different sources in relation to damage to historic brick masonry structures. The main initial sources are literature, data from *in situ* investigation carried out on historic brick masonry buildings, and laboratory simulation tests. This information is collected in an "Atlas of Damage to Historic Brick Structures," containing uniform terminology and a uniform description of damage types and damage origins. This information is schematized into relations between damage types, causes, and the physical phenomena related to a set of deterioration processes. Particular attention is paid to the interaction between the different materials of which ancient brick masonry is composed and the effects of environmental factors. The deterioration causes can only be understood with a knowledge of the different historic brick masonry construction types and the historic, climatic, and geographic context in which those masonries have been built, used, and eventually restored. An MDDS is developed which, through systematization of this knowledge and relations, will guide the person using this expertise toward the assessment of damage type and damage causes. It also provides information on the type of investigation that has to be carried out on the masonry to be diagnosed, in order to improve the quality of the information about the damage type and damage origin. Therefore, appropriate (monument-friendly nondestructive) testing techniques are evaluated on their likelihood of increasing the precision of the diagnosis. For the creation of the expert system an expert's system shell is used based on decision tables.

Objective of the Study

The objective of the project is to improve our knowledge of the effects of environmental factors on damage to Europe's cultural heritage and to guarantee better treatment and protection of our heritage, by providing the professionals who work on the analysis of ancient buildings with an expert system including a damage atlas.

Scientific Approach

The durability of the masonry depends not only on the behavior of one material but on a complex interaction of different materials and different boundary conditions (e.g., traffic, pollution, precipitation, orientation). The approach takes into account different dimensions of the problem from material sciences, environmental sciences, biological sciences, historic sciences, architecture and urban development.

Thus far, the evaluation of damage and its subsequent interpretation have not included a proposal for treatment, but has concentrated on diagnosis. Precise descriptions of damage types and the process responsible for this damage are described under given circumstances.

Damage Approach

The relationship between damage definition (type) and damage cause (mechanism) is based on a thermodynamic approach: resistance against stress defines the damage (function). Thus, in terms of visible damage, the process of decay is the appropriate way to make tools that can be used for monitoring.

Definitions and terminology are based on maximum use of visual analysis techniques and maximum collection of relevant data on site. Additional guidance is given through testing techniques from nondestructive to destructive techniques if necessary.

The aim of the project was to create an instrument based on scientific information that could increase the number of persons able to execute general monitoring of historic buildings. By increasing their number, there should be a shift toward maintenance-type interventions on historic buildings instead of more "heavy" restoration interventions. Therefore, groups of technicians, architects, and engineers should be helped in executing a correct analysis of the major part of (more simple) damage cases, leaving the more difficult and special cases to the smaller group of leading professionals. The latter will thus be only involved in those cases where high specialization is required. Such instruments could also guide specialists when they have to deal with fields in which they do not have specialized knowledge. To define the group of the less specialized professional, who nevertheless has a broad background, the profile of

K. Van Balen

the "Monumentenwachters" (Monument Watchers) of the Netherlands or in Flanders has been taken as a reference.

Methodology

The methodology used is based on the scientific principles of research. In the stated problem, damage to historic brick structures and the development of the MDDS, defined the scientific description and deductions of the physical mechanisms causing the damage. Inherent choices were made in relation to the order of input taken into account for deduction; it started with the easiest way of identification, which is visual analysis (this also explains the usefulness of the damage atlas), and then included, in order, the *in situ* and laboratory tests. A thermodynamic model of decay of materials, as developed in the project, defines damage as a result of stresses and resistance, and allowed damage types and damage causes to be linked. This was then developed in terms of processes within the MDDS. The development of the MDDS allowed us in many cases to limit the problem to only those parameters which are described as really necessary (goal oriented), thus omitting irrelevant elements while the link with practice remains guaranteed. This approach is unique in this field and the experience of the project demonstrated the scientific interest of this engineering approach for the evaluation of deterioration of ancient brick structures. It is an applied scientific approach producing practical results for the conservation of historic brick monuments.

RESEARCH RESULTS

Terminology

In the first stage of the work, common definitions had to be set up which should be useful within the different instruments of the project. A first set of damage types has therefore been defined which is useful for the questionnaire but which could be developed within the MDDS. The hierarchic concept allows the user to narrow his definitions gradually. This approach was based on the assumption in the project that defining goes hand in hand with increasing knowledge. Vague knowledge needs broader terms while added information has to narrow the set of terms. In the questionnaire, the group of damage types is given with the subset of more precise terms. The logic in the definition was based on the visual discrimination. It has been defined so that in the order of the analysis, visual appreciation was the first "instrument" used. As the questionnaire and the related damage atlas are related to this first analysis, it was logical that the definition of damage types should use visual criteria. Within the MDDS the same terminology has been used while the "instrument" itself allows the user to check his interpretation of the terminology by answering questions defined by the conditions contained in the definition of the term. The structure of the terms of the damage types and definitions given in terms of conditions will be illustrated later.

QUESTIONNAIRE

Concept

The original questionnaire with which the project was started and which stemmed from the collaboration of the experts of the NATO-CCMS Pilot Study on Conservation of Historic Brick Structures has been modified considerably, as described in one of the project reports (Van Balen and Mateus 1994). The main reasons for this development are found in the interaction with the setup of the terminology, which was developed in relation to the MDDS, and in the subdivision of the questionnaire according to the order of investigation of the damage type into its possible cause. The first type of analysis is based on visual analysis and on-site measurements while the second has been made for the integration of laboratory results leading, in the third part, to a synthesis and an interpretation.

We found that even experts are hesitant to formalize the collection of information in a questionnaire if they perceive no direct interest or reply leading them to the diagnosis. As a monitoring instrument, the questionnaire seems to have the disadvantage of being too lengthy, too imprecise, and not synthetic. At first this seemed very discouraging, but we later realized that this actually demonstrated the advantages of the MDDS. We therefore concluded that the questionnaire should be developed electronically. The user, after giving some basic information on the building and according to the previous answers he has given, is requested to answer only those questions relevant to the problem, which is what the MDDS does. The latest version of the questionnaire itself was simplified and developed to allow the rapid collection of necessary data related to pictures for the damage atlas. We also found that in practice very few professionals and owners are willing to deepen a diagnosis with laboratory or *in situ* tests. Yet in the experience of most of the partners in the project, only those types of analyses can provide the necessary information for a full diagnosis. There is evidence that the analyses of the pore structure of the mortars and bricks as well as the chemical composition of the different mortars used are necessary to define whether the damage to the brick was due to the mortar or to the composition of the bricks (e.g., Van Gemert 1988). Here, the project has the task of proving the interest of different types of analysis for the diagnosis of damage and to stimulate proper diagnostic methods in that respect.

Applications

The questionnaire has been used to collect information on different examples of damage on historic brick structures. The major test group was composed of postgraduate students at the Center for Conservation of Historic Towns and Buildings, K.U.Leuven, and very satisfactory results were obtained. Data from 17 case studies were collected in which some nondestructive tests as well as laboratory tests were conducted. The members of the test group were positive in their evaluation as they − according to their comments − were forced to think through the problem while filling in the questionnaire. Within the project the questionnaire is also used as a structured way of collecting documentation on different cases from all the partners. Examples from Belgium, Germany, Italy, and the Netherlands have also been documented in this way. The full-scale masonry models of the Politecnico di Milano set up for monitoring damage processes have been included to check the possibility of evaluating the effectiveness of the questionnaire from a dynamic viewpoint, i.e., to see whether the questionnaire can inform us about the speed of the degradation process (Binda and Baronio 1993). An example of such a completed questionnaire is given in the appendix to this chapter.

Damage Atlas

A classification of damage patterns found in brick masonry was set up (Schumann 1993). The terminology used follows the same structure and setup as the questionnaire and the MDDS. The definitions are more extensive than the definitions presented in decision table form in the MDDS and possible damage causes are also given. A complete set of illustrations of the different damage types is provided in the atlas with an explanation about the possible causes of the damage. Consistency with the MDDS was guaranteed as they were developed to be used together.

Masonry Damage Diagnostic System

The MDDS (Van Hees 1995a) is a knowledge-based system (KBS). It is a database with information and additional knowledge to create relations according to given answers and questions. It is the translation of expertise into a system computers can handle. The knowledge is structured and can be consulted using a Decision Table System Shell (DTSS) developed by T.N.O.-Bouw. It is actually a Macintosh-based software program but a Windows version is being developed. The MDDS is a prototype and is not for sale. It is the aim of the partners of the project to create links with organizations that would like to develop the existing system for their use and co-finance in this way the updating and extension of the system. The knowledge is translated into a large set of decision tables which contain sets of conditions and actions. The set of condition tables is structured hierarchically way and can be presented as a decision table tree (Van Hees and Naldini 1995). For further details on the MDDS, see van Balen (1997).

Consultation Procedure

The computer program aims to make the consultation of the MDDS user-friendly. In contrast to the questionnaire, the MDDS adapts its questioning to previous answers given. Comparative data in the form of pictures and comparative results of test trends are supplied for consultative purposes in the event of uncertainty.

The output of the MDDS is given immediately on the screen, but a printed report of the consultation is also generated. This document can be used as a report by the user. The results of a consultation can be stored in a file to allow progressive, step-by-step consultation at different stages. As the project progressed, the usefulness of collecting examples of damage via MDDS became apparent. The structure of the KBS within the MDDS obliged users to work in a very systematic way while developing the system and using it afterwards.

CONCLUSIONS

The description of the damage types on historic brick structures has been improved. The link between terminology, questionnaire, damage atlas and MDDS is guaranteed by accurate definitions and the hierarchic concept of the damage types descriptions. In the same way the description of possible damage causes and the processes leading toward the above-mentioned damage types have improved. The increase in systematization that was sought by the project is a necessary and interesting by-product of the creation of KBS. The DTSS has proved to be a very interesting tool for the development of the KBS. The collection of different types of information using the questionnaire and other related summary sheets has allowed research teams to make an interesting collection of various degradation types. These examples are useful for the elaboration of the damage atlas. Reactions to the complexity of the questionnaire and uncertainty on the part of the user about which information should be mentioned in this document prove the advantage of the MDDS. It is certain that in the dialogue between the expert system and the user, the latter will feel more comfortable as he perceives that the questions asked are relevant to the problem while, on the other hand, the expert system limits questioning to only that information which it can consider in its reasoning. Further development of the MDDS could be guaranteed by the integration of research results from other projects and by the inclusion of data available on the degree and effects of pollution. Let us not forget, however, that no expert system will ever be as competent in each of the domains of expertise as real experts. Nevertheless, the MDDS will be of great interest for many routine operations where leading professionals are now wasting their time and could be replaced by low-profile professionals if they are helped by a system such as the MDDS, provided that a disclaimer is contained within the system: "For this (difficult and complex) case I have no answer. Please call an expert."

The MDDS is waiting to be expanded, as more topics are available than could be covered during the past project. The outcome of research on re-treatment of masonry with water repellents and a project that will soon begin on the conservation of pointing both aim to improve the KBS and expand the field it covers, so that it becomes more useful in practice. During the past few years, it has become clear that there is great interest in this approach. Its ability to combine different types of information, taking into account the complexity of scientific understanding of the degradation of brick masonry and translating this into a workable instrument in the field, has been appreciated by many field specialists and scientists. Scientific researchers are now requesting this type of approach to expand understanding of degradation in this and other fields concerned with the conservation of the built heritage. However, a synthesis of the huge amount of work done in the field of environmental degradation of architectural heritage building materials, as worked out in the MDDS, remains a long-term goal.

ACKNOWLEDGEMENTS

Acknowledgment is expressed to D.G. XII of the E.C., which supported the Environment R&D project EV5V-CT92-0108, and to the partners in the project: Politecnico di Milano, Milan (Italy), (Prof. G. Baronio, Prof. L. Binda) Building Research Institute (T.N.O.-Bouw), Rijswijk (The Netherlands), (ir. R. Van Hees, Dr.ir. L. Lucardie, Drs. S. Naldini, ing. L. Van der Klugt) Technische Universität Hamburg-Harburg, Hamburg (Germany), (Prof. L. Franke, Drs. geol. min. I. Schumann) K.U.Leuven, R.Lemaire Center for Conservation, Leuven (Belgium), (ir. J. Mateus).

REFERENCES

Binda, L., and G. Baronio. 1993. Presentation of the full-scale masonry models and the monitoring of damage process, unpublished paper presented at NATO-CCMS Pilot Study "Conservation of Historic Brick Structures," Venice, Nov. 1993.

Schumann, I. 1993. Classification of damage pattern found in brick masonry. Project Report, TUH-Harburg, Sept., 1993.

Searls, C.L., L. Binda, J.F. Henriksen, P.W. Mirwald, A. Nappi, C.A. Price, K. Van Balen, V. Vergès-Belmin, E. Wendler, and F. Wittmann. 1997. Group report: How can we diagnose the condition of stone monuments and arrive at suitable treatment programs. In: Saving Our Architectural Heritage: The Conservation of Historic Stone Structures, ed. N.S. Baer and R. Snethlage, pp. 199–221, Dahlem Workshop Report. Chichester: J. Wiley & Sons.

Van Balen, K. 1988. Stabiliteitsherstel in monumentenzorg. In: Stable-Unstable, Structural Consolidation of Ancient Buildings, ed. R. Lemaire and K. Van Balen, pp. 15–27. Leuven: Leuven Univ. Press.

Van Balen, K. 1995. Expertensystem für die Beurteilung von Verfallserscheinungen an historischem Ziegel-Mauerwerk. In: Instandsetzen von Mauerwerk, ed. E.G. Niël, WTA-Schriftenreihe, Heft 6, pp. 1–11. Aedification Verlag.

Van Balen, K. 1997. Monitoring of degradation: Selection of treatment strategies. In: Saving Our Architectural Heritage: The Conservation of Historic Stone Structures, ed. N.S. Baer and R. Snethlage, pp. 167–180, Dahlem Workshop Report. Chichester: J. Wiley & Sons.

Van Balen, K., and G. Mateus. 1994. What damage can we see and how? Unpublished Project Rep. 1.2.4., Feb., 1994, Leuven.

Van Gemert, D., and K. Van Balen. 1988. The influence of pointing mortar on the alteration of brick and masonry. In: Proc. of the 8th Intl. Brick, Block Masonry Conference, pp. 1751–1758, New York: Elsevier.

Van Hees, R. 1995. Entwicklung eines Systems für die Diagnose von Schäden an historischem Ziegel-Mauerwerk auf der Grundlage eines Knowledge Based System. In: Instandsetzen von Mauerwerk, ed. E.G. Niël, WTA-Schriftenreihe, Heft 6, pp. 12–18. Aedification Verlag.

Van Hees, R., and S. Naldini. 1995. The masonry damage diagnostic system. *Intl. J. Restor. Build. Mon.* **1(6)**:461–474.

APPENDIX

QUESTIONNAIRE

Table of contents

Part I

1. Object. General Description
2. Visual analysis
3. Environmental analysis
4. Background information
5. Technology and detailing
6. Non destructive tests in situ
7. Causes/agents based on non laboratory analysis
8. Sampling for laboratory analysis

Part II

8. Laboratory analysis on sampling

Part III

9. Final and integrated conclusions
after analysis of Part I and Part II

Ir.J.Mascarenhas Mateus , Prof.Dr.ir.arch.K.van Balen
Center for the Conservation of Historic Towns and Buildings, R.Lemaire

1	Object						
1.1	Address	*Bethaniaschuur*					
		Stationstraat / Bethaniastraat					
		Zoutleeuw					
1.2	General Description	(add ground plan and prospects= appendix 1.2)					

1.2.1 — Type of building / Construction:

Building:	dwelling ☐	church ☐	tower ☐	other	*Barn* ☒	
Wall:	defensive wall ☐		retaining wall ☐		other......................	☐
Bridge ☐	Ruins ☐	Other construction......................				☐

1.2.2 — Dimensions of the Construction:

	Max. (m)	Min.(m)	Average (m)		
Width					Radius (m)					
Width	|_|_8!_6|	|_|_|_!_|	|_|_|_!_|	Radius (m)	|_|_|_!_|
Length	|_|_2|_8!_0|	|_|_|_!_|	|_|_|_!_|		
Height	|_|_|_7!_7|	|_|_|_4!_6|	|_|_|_!_|		

1.2.3 — Year and phases of construction   (add description to the ground plan)

N. of phases	|_|_|	1st phase years |_1|_8|_6|_3|-|_|_|_|_| + 4 small repairings
		2st phase years |_|_|_|_|-|_|_|_|_|

1.2.4 — Damaged area   (add prospects = appendix 1.2)

structural wall	☒	nonbearing wall	☐	exterior wall	☒	vault	☐
foundation wall	☐	column ☐	arch	☐	partition	☐	
building frame	☐	stairs ☐	floor	☐	ornamental panel	☐	
Other part of the building:							☐
Bridge: ☐	structural arch		in-fill masonry ☐		Other:........................		☐
Other part of a construction:...							☐

1.2.5 — Use (previous and present)

Barn until some years ago, no use for the moment

1.2.6 — Historical data and accidental phenomena

Notice about seismic occurence (dates, intensity, epicentre):...

Notice about accidental impacts, explosions, war figths in relation with the building:

Natural disasters (storms, flood,...):................................

1.2.7 — General view of the building

2	**Visual Analysis of Damage** Date: | | |- |0|5|-|9|4|
	Orientation of the analysed area: S, N,E Heigth above ground level:S: 0.15m to 1.6m
	(Please use one set of forms for each analysed area of the construction) N: 0.0m to 1.7m

2.1	Characteristics of the original material

2.1.1

Masonry as whole:

Bonding (add picture(s)= appendix 2.1)

Distribution or mapping of different kinds of textures (add map if possible - appendix =2.1)

	Type of masonry	Wall tickness (m)	Nr. leaves in a section	Nr. of courses per meter	Heigth of brick courses (cm)	Tickness of joints (cm)	Phase/date of construction
Masonry 1(S,E)		|_|_0!_5|_2|	|_|_|	|1|3|	|_6!_0|	|_2!_0|	|_1|_8|_6|_3|
Masonry 2 (N)		|_|_0!_5|_2|	|_|_|	|1|4|	|_5!_5|	|_1!_5|	|_1|_9|_3|_8|

Bonding description: *No Regular Bond*

2.1.2

Plastering and Rendering:	*Two layers of withe wash at south facade*	
Thickness (cm) |_|_|	Number of layers |_2|	Finishing: *joints with white color*
Color: *1st- red; 2nd - white*	Consistency and roughness:............................	

2.1.3

Brick:

Type:	solid	☒	hollow	☐	soft-mud	☐	wire-cut	☐	salmon	☐	perforated	☐
malm		☐	molded		Other type:..............................	☐	Color:	*red and dark red*				

Most representative dimensions (cm) : S-(15x11x6;22x11x5.5;22x 11x 6);N(23x12x5.5);E(24x12x6)

Roughness of external surface:		glazed	☐	rough	☒	smooth	☐	....	☐

2.1.4

Masonry mortar:

Type:	smooth	☐	high porous	☐	haired	☐	other:........	☐	Color:	*Beige*

Pointing description:................   *irregular pointing*

Aggregates:(N)	lime knobs	☒	organic mat.	☐	other.......................		☐	size (cm) |_0!_5	Color: withe

2.2	Affected Material

2.2.1

Materials involved:							
Brick	☒	Mortar	☒	Interface brick/mortar	☒	Plaster	☐	Wall as whole	☒

2.2.2

Extension of the Damage:	Single brick(s) ☐	Zone with 1 material	☐	Zone with 2 materials	☐

2.2.3

Type of Damage: (for each type of damage add one photo = appendix 2.2)

2.2.4 Surface Changes ☒   2.2.5 Disintegration ☒   2.2.6 Cracks ☒

2.2.7 Deformation ☒   2.2.8 Biological Growth ☒

2.2.4

Surface Changes:

Discoloration:	fading	☐	staining	☐				
Transformation:	patina	☐	crust	☐				
Deposit:	soiling	☐	encrustation	☒	staining	☒	efflorescence	☒
Others:	scratch	☐	cut	☐	puncture	☐		

2.2.5

Disintegration of Building Materials:

Layering:	delamination/exfoliation	☒	flaking	☐	scaling	☐	blistering	☐
Loss of cohesion:	crumbling	☒	pulverization	☐	sanding off	☒	chalking	☐	erosion	☐
Loss of adhesion:	peeling	☐	blistering	☐				

2.2.6

Cracking:

crack	☒	hair crack	☒	crazing	☐	fracture	☒	rupture	☐

2.2.7

Deformation:

bulging	☒	bending	☐	bulking	☐	other	☐

2.2.8

Biological Growth:

higher plants	☒	mosses	☒	lichens	☒	algae	☒	fungi	☒

3	Technology and Detailing. Defects observed		
	Bonding(Y/N) |_N|	Jointing and Pointing (Y/N) |_Y|	Detailing (Y/N) |_N|
	Insulation materials (Y/N) |_Y|	Thickness of the walls (Y/N) |_N|	Number of leaves (Y/N) |_N|
	Other defects:..		

4	Environmental Analysis
4.1	Surroundings in relation with the construction as whole

Rural area ☒	City / Town ☐	Indust.area ☐	Isolat.house ☐	Marine envir ☐	Exposed ☐	Other: Swamp
Construction protected by:....................................			Protected facades (N/S/W/E)		|_|	
Facades the most exposed (N/S/W/E)			|_S| and |_W|			
Isolation against rising damp (Y/N)			|_N| Type of isolation:..			

4.2	Climate

Most frequent wind direction |_S|_W|	Average of rain fall (per year in mm) |_|_|_|

Days of frost / ice (per year) |_6|_5|			
Values for Relative Humidity cycle	Minimum	Maximum	Average
Temperature (°C/year)	|_-|_1|	|_2|_2|	|_|_|
Relative humidity (% / year)	|_7|_3|	|_8|_7|	|_|_|

Air Pollution (average values in ppm):						
Period	SO$_2$	NO$_x$	CO$_2$	O$_3$	Aerosols	Acid rain
	|_|_|_|	|_|_|_|	|_|_|_|	|_|_|_|	|_|_|_|	|_|ph___
	|_|_|_|	|_|_|_|	|_|_|_|	|_|_|_|	|_|_|_|	|_|ph___

4.3	Circumstances of the representative damages

Frequency:	each winter ☐	each summer☐	other frequency:...........		when heated ☐	irregular ☐
Location:		sheltered areas		exposed areas ☒	☒	
low areas (<2m high) ☐	imed.under terraces/roofs ☐		free edges ☐	other location.............. ☐		
near water transported elements☐	near protruding elements ☐		near chemical agressive products ☐			
uniform ocurrence ☐	irregular ocurrence ☒					
Presence of: urine ☒	guano ☐	leaching agents ☐				
Orientation of the affected area : *East side sheltered from rain - crusts*						
facing (N/S/W/E): |_S|	facing the seaside ☐	Other: South *Structural damage*				

5	Background Information about
5.1	The material itself (if some information is already known)

	Brick	Mortar	Rendering	Masonry
Nature of the clay used		■■■	■■■	■■■
Type of sand (calcareous, siliceous...)				■■■
Percentage of sand content				■■■
Type of binder	■■■			■■■
Percentage of binder content	■■■			
Percentage of salts content				
W / B ratio	■■■			■■■

5.2	The original manufacture (if some information is known)
	Conditions of firing:..
	Conditions of drying:...
	Conditions of shaping:...
	Environmental conditions during construction:..

5.3	Latter applied materials

Type and date of surface treatment:				
hydrophobic agents ☐	painting ☐	coating ☐	plaster ☐	Other:painting of joints ☒
Renewal of: bricks ☐	joints ☐	pointing ☐	rendering ☐	cleaning ☐
Consolidation: ☐	backfill with inj.mortar ☐		Other........................ ☐	
Reduction of moisture ☐	Water proof membrane ☐		Other........................ ☐	

6	Non Destructive Tests in Situ Results of Analysis						

6.1 Pointing hardness tester (add plan with observed zone=apx.6.1)

Zone	Period	Pointing Hardness	

Conclusions:..
Conclusions:..

6.2 Sonic Survey (add schematic plan = appendix 6.2)

Type of measure		Direction	Time(μs)	Path Length(m)	Velocity (m/s)	Variation coef.
Surface	(h≈1.22 m)	North	5500 - 12150	0.39		
Surface	(h≈1.67 m)	North	4138	0.39		

Frequency / Equipment

Conclusions: (average velocity, map of velocities, standard deviation...)   **Results with great variance.**
Great heterogeneity in the constitution of the wall.

6.3 Water absorption test. Tubes of Karsten technique (add plan = apdx.6.3)

Zone	Level	Time	Volume(ml)	
South	1.15 m	5 min.	4.6 ml	
South	1.15 m	10 min.	8.5 ml	
South	1.15 m	15 min.	all	

Conclusions: **Bricks with high porosity**

6.4 Neutron Probe (add plan - appendix 6.4)

Zone bomb.	Period	Gamma ray characteristics	

Conclusions:..

6.5 Measurement of loss of thickness (add schematic plan = appendix 6.5)

Zone	Period 1	Thickness 1(mm)	Period 2	Thickness 2 (mm	Ratio	

Conclusions:..

6.6 Other ND Tests used. Moisture content (South wall)

Level	Depth	Gann meter	Carbide bottle	El.resist.(mV)		Remarks
1.8 m	5 cm		7%			Brick
1.8 m	5 cm		7.50%			Mortar

Conclusions: **Brick and mortar with relative high water content**

6.7 ND Tests Final Conclusions. Combined results
....

7	**Causes / Agents of Damage without laboratory analysis (Area)**
7.1	Damage(s) due to the material itself and/or to fabrication process:........

7.1.1 Wrong selection of building materials:

nature of the clay used ☐   percent. of sand content ☐   percent. of lime content ☐

percentage of salts ☐   Arguments:......................

7.1.2 Manufacture: conditions of firing ☐   conditions of drying ☒   conditions of moulding ☐

Arguments: *Light red bricks more damaged than darker ones*

7.2	Damage(s) due to the fabrication of masonry (composite):....................

7.2.1 Problems and defects of the original technology:

conditions of construction ☐   wrong detailing ☐   bonding ☐   jointing and pointing ☐

isolation materials ☐   insufficient thickness of walls ☐   **other: not enough bond between phases of const.**

Arguments:.....................

7.3	Damage(s) due to the interaction with Environment:........................

7.3.1 General climate and environmental conditions:

Natural disasters: earthquake ☐   flood ☐   fire ☐   explosion ☐   hurricane ☐

Climate: rain ☒   hail ☐   frost ☐   snow ☒   wind ☐

relative humidity too high ☒   too low ☐   sun/radiation too much ☐   too less ☐

temperature - thermal charges ☐   Arguments: *Water penetration - roof in very bed condition*

7.3.2 Use of the construction of which material or masonry forms part and use of environment:

vibrations ☐   mechanical impact ☐   chemical aggressive products ☐

Arguments:.....................

7.3.3 Ground / Interaction with the soil foundation: natural consolidation of the soil ☐

changes in the soil nature ☐   % and nature of salt content ☐   soil rupture resistance ☒   ☐

other:.................. ☐   Arguments: **used as barn - great concentration of horse detritus**

7.3.4 Water: motion of water ☐   containing salts ☐   other: ☒   ....

Arguments: *Water from the ground, swamp area*

7.3.5 Air & Rain: physical, chemical, biological emissions ☐   air content (SO2, CO2, NaCl,...) ☐

Arguments:..

7.3.6 Biodeterioration:

insects ☐   germ number ☐   bio corrosion ☐   biogenic mineral acids ☐   micro-organisms ☐

organic acids ☐   Arguments:......................

7.4	Damage due to the interaction of material(s)with other material(s)in contact with it

7.4.1 Original or original like material:

brick and mortar ☐   brick and plaster ☐   metal and brick/plaster ☐

anchors and masonry ☐   steel reinforcement ☐   cement and masonry ☐

limestone and brick ☐   accumulation of salts ☐   other:.......................... ☐

Arguments:......................

7.4.2 Latter applied materials:

exchanging of single bricks or parts of masonry ☐   backfill with injection concrete/mortar ☐

Wrong surface treatment: plaster ☐   outdoor wall-cover ☐   painting ☐   cleaning ☐

hydrophobing ☐   consolidation ☐   repointing ☐   other............................ ☐

Arguments:......................

8	Sampling for laboratory Analysis (Area of construction_____)						
8.1	Sampling by		Name of the Institution:			KULeuven - Laboratory Reyntjens	
8.1.1	Type of sample: (add picture with masonry and sample before and after sampling=apdx.7.1)						
	Number of samples	Internally cored	Cored on surface	Full-size bricks	Powder	Parts	Masonry cored as whole
	On damaged bricks			1		3	
	Undamaged bricks						

8.1.2	Sample number	Dimensions (cm)	Weight (g)	Place of removal (m)		Type of precognized laboratory analysis (see classification part II)
				Height above ground level	Depth in the masonry	
	1			1.8		Physical tests
	2			1.9		Chemical tests
	3			2,0		Shrinkage test
	4			2,0		Frost test
	5			1,8		Chemical & Physical tests

8.1.3	Description of sampling and conditions of removal:
	Sample n. 1 Part of brick removed from south wall
	Sample n. 2 Part of brick removed from south wall
	Sample n. 3 & 4 Full brick from south wall
	Sample n. 5 Mortar removed from south wall

SAMPLE N. 5

9	Laboratory Analysis on sampling Area of construction:				Mortar - South	

9.1	Chemical Analysis	*Insoluble residue - 69,62 %*				

9.1.1	Composition of Building Material in %					
	Zone	Sample	SiO_2	Al_2O_3	Fe_2O_3	MgO	Na_2O
						0,7	*0,49*
	Zone	Sample	K_2O	SO_3	CO_2	CaO	H_2O
			2,05	*0,48*	5,9	*9,36*	

9.1.2	Soluble Ions (wt.-%) (water soluble contents)					
	Na^+	K^+	Ca^{+2}	SO_3^{-2}	Cl^-	NO_3^-

9.1.3	Calculated salt contents:					

9.1.4	Composition of the binder:..

9.1.5	Composition of the aggregate: *Soluble SiO2 - 0,73%*

9.1.6	Binder-Aggregate ratio of the mortar..

9.1.7	Calcium-carbonate content (wt-%) ⌴⌴⌴⌴

9.1.8	PFM microscopy description *Grey mortar with spots of lime and many quartz crystals*

9.1.9	Discoloring test results:...

9.1.10	Diffratometric analysis of sampled salts (XRay Test):			
	Sample	Depth of sampling (cm)	Salt name	Salt Formula

9.1.11	Efflorescence rate:		
	no effloresced ☐	slightly effloresced ☐	effloresced ☐

9.2	Physico-mechanical tests	*Loss on ignition (105 °C) : 9,81 %*

9.2.1	Gravimetric measurement:			(gann meter, carbon carbide,...)			
	Sample	Zone	Dimensions Volume (cm)	Weight after sampling (g)	Apparent density(kg/m3)	Water cont. on removal(g)	Moisture cont.(wt%)
			_x__x_		1959,78		

9.2.2	Porosity: *Loss on ignition at 1050 °C: 11,67 %*					
		Porosity			Hygroscopic behavior		
	Sample	Percentage in volume	TIV (ml/g)	Absol.density (kg/m3)	Coef.of water saturation	Capillary rise coeff.(kg/m2/t)	Init.rate of absorption Kg/m3/min
		46,8 - 52 %					

9.2.3	Granullometric analysis (add obtained curves). Conclusions for:
	Brick..
	....
	Mortar..
	....
	Binder...
	Plaster / rendering..
	....

10	Causes / Agents of Damages. Final Conclusions confirmed by Labo. Analysis
10.1	Damage(s) due to the material itself and/or to fabrication process:.........
10.1.1	Wrong selection of building materials: nature of the clay used ☐ percent. of sand content ☐ percent. of lime content ☐ percentage of salts ☐ Arguments:..
10.1.2	Manufacture: conditions of firing ☒ conditions of drying ☐ conditions of moulding ☐ Arguments: **Light red bricks more damaged than darker ones. Bricks with high porosity**
10.2	Damage(s) due to the fabrication of masonry (composite):...............
10.2.1	Problems and defects of the original technology: conditions of construction ☒ wrong detailing ☒ bonding ☒ jointing and pointing ☐ isolation materials ☐ insufficient thickness of walls ☐ **other: not enough bond** Arguments: **not enough bond between different phases of construction**
10.3	Damage(s) due to the interaction with Environment:...............
10.3.1	General climate and environmental conditions: Natural disasters: earthquake ☐ flood ☐ fire ☐ explosion ☐ hurricane ☐ Climate: rain ☒ hail ☐ frost ☐ snow ☐ wind ☐ relative humidity too high ☒ too low ☐ sun/radiation too much ☐ too less ☐ temperature - thermal charges Arguments: **water penetration (rain, dampness)**
10.3.2	Use of the construction of which material or masonry forms part and use of environment: vibrations ☐ mechanical impact ☐ chemical agressive products ☐ Arguments:..................
10.3.3	Ground / Interaction with the soil foundation: natural consolidation of the soil ☒ changes in the soil nature ☒ % and nature of salt content ☒ soil rupture resistance ☐ other:.................. ☐ Arguments: **probable high concentration of NO3 (used for horses)** Crack pa Herr
10.3.4	Water: motion of water ☐ containing salts ☒ other:.................. ☐ Arguments: **Water coming from the ground, high moisture level on bricks and mortars**
10.3.5	Air & Rain: physical, chemical, biological emissions ☐ air content (SO2, CO2, NaCl,...) ☐ Arguments:..................
10.3.6	Biodeterioration: insects ☐ germ number ☐ bio corrosion ☐ biogenic mineral acids ☐ micro-organisms ☐ organic acids ☐ Arguments: **roots of plants included on joints**
10.4	Damage due to the interaction of material(s)with other material(s)in contact with it
10.4.1	Original or original like material: brick and mortar ☐ brick and plaster ☐ metal and brick/plaster ☐ anchors and masonry ☐ steel reinforcement ☐ cement and masonry ☐ limestone and brick ☐ accumulation of salts ☐ other:.................. ☐ Arguments:..................
10.4.2	Latter applied materials: exchanging of single bricks or parts of masonry ☐ backfill with injection concrete/mortar ☐ Wrong surface treatment: plaster ☐ outdoor wall-cover ☐ painting ☐ cleaning ☐ hydrophobing ☐ consolidation ☐ repointing ☐ other.................. ☐ Arguments:..................

13

Decay of Brickwork Surfaces

Laboratory Tests and Studies on Outdoor Full-scale Models

L. BINDA, G. BARONIO, and T. SQUARCINA

Dip. Ing. Strutt., Politecnico di Milano, Piazza L. da Vinci 32, Milano, Italy

ABSTRACT

A systematic approach to the study of durability of wall surface treatments previously based on accelerated aging tests has now been extended to full-scale facades. Three small structures designed by the authors with modular facades made of sandstone and/or soft mud-facing bricks were built in an open field. A continuous content of water in the subsoil can be provided so that the capillary rise of water into the masonry is assured; soluble salts can also be provided from the soil. Besides, the collection of data concerning the environment, the moisture and salt movements in the walls, the deterioration of the external surfaces, and the interaction between masonry materials are considered. Since the process of decay is time dependent, the durability of the materials can only be measured if a parameter continuously evaluating the deterioration is used. A procedure is proposed for *in situ* and laboratory measurements, based on a laser sensor moving on a special frame and connected to a data acquisition system. Data are collected as profiles of the deteriorating surfaces at defined times.

Some facades of the full-scale models were treated with protective materials, while others, previously deteriorated, were treated with consolidants. The deterioration is measured *in situ*.

Comparison between the *in situ* and laboratory results are carried out to adjust the aging tests to the natural environment.

INTRODUCTION

Decorative elements, stone and brick facades, and plasters found in historic town centers have deteriorated so much over the past decades that repair and protection of their external surfaces is necessary. Unfortunately, knowledge of the techniques and the materials to be used is often lacking. Aging tests, even if already codified, are frequently unable to reproduce the real mechanisms of decay; in fact, they often rely upon comparison between accelerated decay of different materials without taking into account the different levels of environmental aggressivity. Furthermore, adequate measurement of the decay of the surfaces as a function of time has not yet been achieved. To set up adequate performance tests, a comparison has to be made between laboratory and natural decay. As stressed earlier (CIBW80/RILEM 71), existing buildings cannot be used successfully for data collection. Therefore, the authors propose that full-scale models be used to detect the rate of deterioration in real time and under natural environmental conditions.

Capillary rise of water and salt solutions are still among the principal causes of deterioration; special attention was given to create the condition of continuous and controlled feeding of water from the subsoil.

When dealing with the decay of external surfaces, which seems to have increased with industrial development, efforts have to be made to state whether cleaning, substitution, and/or protection are needed. All of these operations have an economic and aesthetic impact but can also lead to negative results. To make the right choice, the alternatives have to be carefully studied; in addition, one must take into account the future performance of the materials. Durability tests are welcome if they can help predict this performance; nevertheless the effects of aggressive agents are often only visually detected and aging tests are stopped when the first cracks or delaminations appear.

The degree of deterioration is sometimes detected by measuring loss of strength after a certain number of cycles; other parameters can be the loss of weight or the dimensional variation of the specimen. In the case of crystallization tests, both strength and weight can be highly influenced by the presence of salts, so that these parameters can be meaningless as a measure of deterioration. Furthermore, mechanical tests destroy the specimens. The authors propose a parameter that is not influenced by the salts contained in the specimens and which can be measured continuously during the test with a nondestructive technique; this measurement can also be made *in situ*. Obviously, the measure has to be carried out at defined intervals of time, quickly and with reliable and repeatable results. Special equipment allowing for easy monitoring based on a laser sensor is described. The parameter considered is the loss of thickness of the specimen, i.e., the variation of the roughness of the external deteriorated surface. The measurement procedure has proved to be repeatable, reliable, and able to give a quantitative value to the rate of deterioration of the external surface itself (Berra et al. 1993).

CRYSTALLIZATION TEST

Baronio and Binda (1983) proposed a salt crystallization aging test obtained as a modification of the Brard test; based on wet-dry cycles, it can be performed for total immersion as well as for capillary rise. The influence of different salts and different concentrations was detected as was the behavior of the material under different hygrometric conditions and cycle duration (Binda et al. 1985). The test was also carried out on masonry prisms, and the influence of the mortar and brick properties on the rate of decay was evaluated (Binda and Baronio 1985).

To test the durability of surface treatments, the proposed full immersion test was modified as follows: the lateral surfaces of the specimens are tightly wrapped with rubber to prevent evaporation except from the top surface; the specimens are then subjected to the following crystallization cycles:

- immersion of the side opposite to the upper surface to a depth of 10 mm in a saturated solution of Na_2SO_4 for 4 h;
- drying for 44 h in a climatic chamber at 20°C and 50% relative humidity (RH).

The thermohygrometric conditions and cycle duration were chosen as a result of previous experimental research and of a survey of the environmental conditions in the northern part of Italy (Binda and Baronio 1987). Different ways of quantifying the decay of the material were subsequently adopted: destructive mechanical tests, sonic tests, evaluation of weight, and volume loss.

Recently, the authors have proposed a procedure for measuring the rate of deterioration of the surfaces applied to the case of protection and consolidant treatments (Binda et al. 1992). A probabilistic model was also implemented to predict the decay of the material based on the laboratory data (Binda and Molina 1990). Finally, the authors feel that the studies on full-scale models built in a polluted environment should be continued in order to compare the results obtained in the laboratory to the natural environment (Baronio et al. 1992).

In the following sections, a brief description of the models is given. The first thermohygrometric data collected *in situ* is shown and an attempt to calculate the number, duration, etc. of the frost-defrost and salt crystallization cycles is presented. The rate of capillary rise of water and salt solution was detected with visual and destructive inspections. The surface treatment procedure is also described, and first comments on the type of decay shown from the untreated and treated walls are presented (Baronio et al. 1993). A nondestructive evaluation of the time-dependent surface decay is also proposed for *in situ* and laboratory experimental survey.

FULL-SCALE MODEL DESCRIPTION

At the end of 1990, three models were intentionally built in a polluted area of Milan; they are one-floor structures whose principal facades are divided into modular orthogonal panels exposed to the south and west (Figure 13.1a,b,c). This was done in order to obtain both conditions for the maximum evaporation and crystallization of soluble salts. Complete structures were built in order to have a thermal-hygrometric gradient inside the walls as in a normal residential building.

To study the effects of salt crystallization, artificial decay was caused in some areas of the walls by introducing a salt solution (Na_2SO_4) into small containers placed at chosen positions at the bottom of the walls (Figure 13.1a). The subsoil of the structures was excavated up to a certain level and coated with a layer of bentonite (Figure 13.1b). This operation was done to assure the capillary rise of water into the masonry. The presence of water in the subsoil is controlled by 5 piezometers. In two models – one with a stone facade, one with a brick facade – there are five pairs of orthogonal panels;

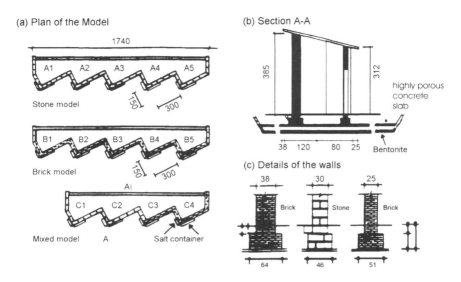

Figure 13.1   (a) Plan of the models, (b) section A-A, (c) details of walls and foundations. All dimensions are given in cm.

the third model – mixed stone and brick – has only four pairs of orthogonal panels. A view of the full-scale models is shown in Figure 13.2.

Figure 13.2   View of the full-scale models.

ENVIRONMENTAL DATA

The air temperature and RH have been continuously monitored since January, 1991, inside and outside the models, allowing for control of the microclimate.

Data for the Milan environment have been collected both from the Brera Astronomic Observatory (in the center of the city) and the Metereological National Service (at Linate Airport not far from the site) for the past ten years. The climate data have been collected and compared for some years. As an example, temperatures and RHs from Brera Observatory and from *in situ* measurements in 1991 are presented in Figures 13.3 and 13.4.

Figure 13.3 shows the *in situ* temperatures plotted against Brera temperatures. A linear correlation was attempted to interpret the relationship between the two climates: the *in situ* temperatures are approximately 1.5 °C lower than the Brera ones with much scatter in the data. In Figure 13.4 the RHs for the 1991 are compared for both sites; the scattering shown by the data suggests that the knowledge of the site microclimate characteristics is very important. In fact, an aim of the research was to characterize the thermohygrometric conditions of the environment with a special interest in freeze-thaw and salt crystallization actions. This information can be useful not only for adjusting the thermohygrometric condition of durability tests according to the environment, but also for defining the limit values of strengths and stresses to be used for the implementation of probabilistic models (Binda and Molina 1990).

Data collected *in situ* are processed to: (a) define number, duration, minimum and maximum temperatures, and the rate of their variation; (b) control the wet-dry cycles as well as the frost-defrost and crystallization cycles. In the period January 18, 1991, to February, 1993, there were only seven months that were affected by freeze-thaw

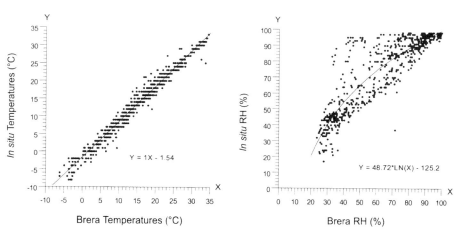

Figure 13.3 *In situ* temperatures plotted against Brera temperatures in 1991.

Figure 13.4 RH collected *in situ* during 1991 versus RH from Brera Observatory.

Table 13.1 Maximum and minimum temperatures during frost months, from January 18, 1991, to February, 1993.

	T_{max} [°C]	T_{min} [°C]	Nr. of cycles (below/above 0°C)
January, 1991 (from 18th)	+1	−2	6
February, 1991	+15	−8	17
December, 1991	+13	−6	22
January, 1992	+15	−6	20
February, 1992	+11	−1	11
December, 1992	+13	−6	8
January, 1993	+12	−4	7
February, 1993	+14	−3	14

cycles. The maximum and minimum temperatures registered for these months are given in Table 13.1, together with the number of cycles from above to below zero.

Possible crystallization phases of Na_2SO_4 (thenardite and mirabilite) are presented in Figure 13.5a,b. Temperatures and RHs measured in open air during the summer of 1991 are plotted and compared to the equilibrium curve of Na_2SO_4 in contact with air (Gmelins Handbuch 1957; Arnold 1977). Figures 13.5a,b and 13.6a,b show the temperature and humidities measured inside the model B4 for the same period. It is clear that in the external part of the models, both phases of Na_2SO_4 can be realized several times monthly and daily, while internally there is a very low probability of crystallization for Na_2SO_4 as thenardite.

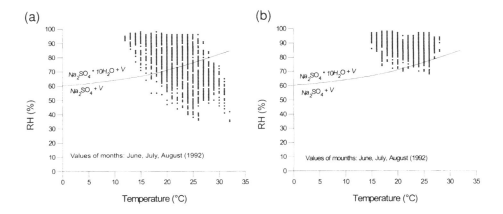

Figure 13.5 RH versus temperature compared to the equilibrium curve of Na_2SO_4 for 1992 (a: open air, b: interior model B4).

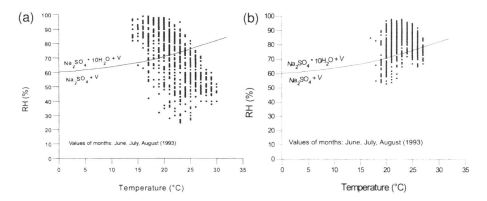

Figure 13.6   RH versus temperature compared to the equilibrium curve of Na_2SO_4 for 1993 (a: open air, b: interior model B4).

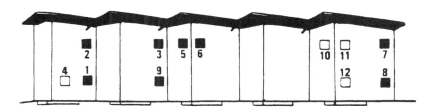

Figure 13.7   Position of thermocouples.

It is apparent that surface conditions and gradients from both surfaces influence decay much more than the conditions realized in the open air. To understand better the possibility of real cycling at external and internal surfaces of the walls, a series of thermocouples was applied at different strategic points of model A (Figure 13.7). The system was applied at the beginning of October, 1992, and some initial comments can be made on the usefulness of the results. Figure 13.8 shows the differences in temperature between open air and thermocouple 7 during October, 1992, and July, 1993.

In Figure 13.9, a correlation is attempted between the temperature of thermocouple 7 and 8 during October, 1992, January, 1993, and July, 1993. It can be seen that thermocouple 7 measures higher temperatures than 8 during the cold months.

To explain these results, it should be remembered that thermocouple 8 is positioned on a saturated area of the panel where evaporation plays an important role in lowering the temperatures. The values of the temperature on external and internal surfaces measured using thermocouples at two hours interval during January, 1993, are shown in Figure 13.10 as an example.

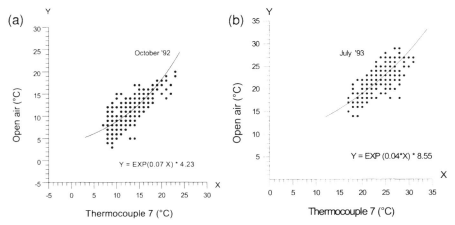

Figure 13.8a,b Correlation between open air and thermocouple 7 temperature during (a) October, 1992, and (b) July, 1993.

The differences in temperature detected between the open air and the surfaces of the walls, and between the external and internal surfaces, have to be considered as important environmental information that can be useful in explaining the decay phenomena in the material.

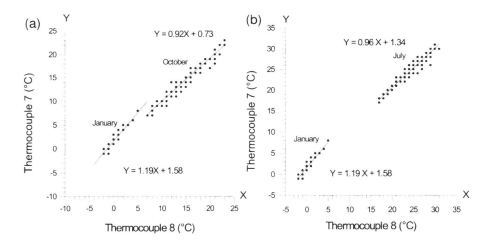

Figure 13.9a,b Correlation between temperatures of thermocouples 7 and 8 during October, 1992, January, 1993, and July, 1993.

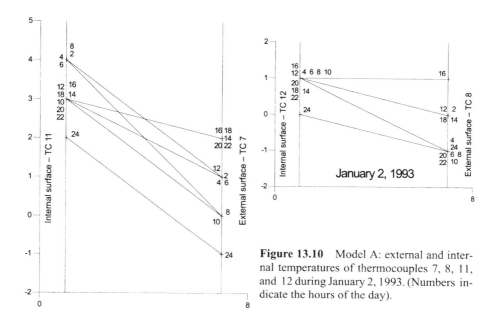

Figure 13.10   Model A: external and internal temperatures of thermocouples 7, 8, 11, and 12 during January 2, 1993. (Numbers indicate the hours of the day).

MOISTURE AND SALT MOVEMENT

Since February, 1991, the capillary rise of water has been controlled by measuring the apparent height of the water level on the facades at chosen points (Baronio et al. 1992), while waiting for a better procedure for monitoring moisture content. Important information was obtained on the level of maximum evaporation in the conditions of presence and absence of Na_2SO_4: it was evident from the first weeks of the experiment that the rate of capillary rise was higher in the areas where the Na_2SO_4 solution was absorbed. As an example of the *in situ* data, Figure 13.11 shows the height of capillary rise, measured each week for 22 months on panel B4 (brick with Na_2SO_4) and C3 (brick).

Bricks and stone were sampled during February, 1992 (indoor and outdoor), from the bottom of the walls, and their moisture content was measured. The data compared to the previously measured absorption data of the materials show that bricks and stones were probably saturated (Baronio et al. 1992).

The presence of Na_2SO_4 accelerates the rise of water and salt solution (B4). The difference (30 cm approximately) is maintained even after 22 months in comparison to the masonry where Na_2SO_4 is absent (panel C3). A lower level of rise means that there was an interruption in feed water.

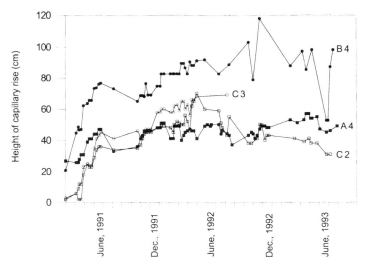

Figure 13.11   Height of capillary rise in panels into the brick wall (panels A4, B4, C2, C3).

TREATMENT OF THE STONE AND BRICK PANELS

Two types of epoxy systems especially studied for durable consolidation and protection of brick and stone surfaces were used to treat the external surfaces of panels A1, A2, B1, and B2 (Binda et al. 1992). Prior to their use, the treatments were successfully tested in the laboratory, applied to the materials used in the models.

The first is a cycloaliphatic epoxy resin (EP 150/203) synthesized by STAC (Italy), with a rather low compressive modulus (1000 N/mm^2 at 20°C) and a high glass transition temperature (55°C). The second is an aliphatic epoxy-based system (LITOTEX A-EP 222/19), with a modulus of 1350 N/mm^2 and glass transition temperature of 5°C.

For the laboratory tests, two different ratios resin/solvent were used. Glycolether was the solvent and the ratios were: 1/5, 1/7.7 for EP 222/19 and 1/5, 1/12.5 for EP 150/203. After durability tests the two ratios 1/7.7 for EP 222/19 and 1/12.5 for EP 150/203 were chosen for the full-scale models.

The applications of the two treatments *in situ* were realized by pumping the liquid through a plastic pipe into a special bag formed with a geotextile against the walls. The operation lasted two days.

The A3 and B3 models were treated with an acrylic resin (PARALOID B72) mixed with fine quartz, to avoid the glossy effect of the Paraloid. This treatment was performed as a protective film with a brush.

The deterioration of brick, stone, and mortars was surveyed since the first signs appeared on the surfaces. Decay is evident only on panels that were subjected to the rise of Na$_2$SO$_4$ solution. Model C shows only a few signs of deterioration of bricks,

Figure 13.12 Deterioration of a brick course.

Figure 13.13 Detatchment of a 1.5 mm layer due to fatigue.

probably due to freeze-thaw action. Models A and B were subjected to the most aggressive action of Na_2SO_4. The first signs appeared around December, 1991, on panels B4, B5.

Maximum decay showed up at the highest level of capillary rise, i.e., the maximum evaporation level (10th to 11th course). Distribution and amount of deterioration are different according to the type of material and treatment, as can be described below:

- Panels B1, B2 (epoxy): after the treatment, changes in the moisture level could be detected. The level stopped apparently at the second course.
- Panel B3 (acrylic): soon after the treatment, a whitish powder material covered the entire surface of the panel. Decay of the material appeared at the 10th and 11th course in six months (Figure 13.12).
- Panel B4, B5 (untreated): the deterioration is mostly evident at the level of the 10th course where the moisture rise reaches a peak.

PENETRATION OF DECAY

During the long experience of research, the authors have studied several cases of decay as a results of salt crystallization. The decay has been referred to as a continuous delamination of the exterior surface (Binda and Baronio 1987). This phenomenon is caused by fatigue effects of the wet-dry cycles especially when soluble sulfates are present inside the material (Figure 13.13).

The thickness of the layer that is delaminated is strongly dependent on (a) the thermohygrometric conditions of the microenvironment, (b) the porosity and the mechanical strength of the material (Arnold 1976), and (c) the duration of wet-dry cyles (Lewin 1981). Nevertheless, whatever the thickness of the layer is, the material properties are modified only in a narrow millimetric area underneath the detached layer. We have

Figure 13.14   Penetration of decay below   **Figure 13.15**   Reduction of cross-section
the deteriorated surface.   of a wall due to environmental actions.

observed this phenomenon several times and can account for it according to the
mechanism of decay (Binda and Baronio 1987; Larsen and Nielsen 1990). Figure
13.14 shows the deteriorated layer below the delaminated surface of a brick sampled
with its mortar joint from a badly decayed wall (Figure 13.15). The thickness of this
layer is no more than 1.5 mm. This same phenomenon extended to the mortar joint.
The surface of the mortar, apparently composed of loose material, appeared in very
bad condition but, after cutting and cleaning, the decayed area was clearly only few
millimeters.

Once the same mechanism of failure is detected in both cases, the same principle
can be applied *in situ* if a measurement procedure is set up for the laboratory test. The
use of a nondestructive evaluation method is then needed to give the rate of deterioration as a function of time.

MEASURE OF DAMAGE AS A FUNCTION OF TIME

Decrease of surface properties cannot be represented by mechanical tests that are destructive and also misleading when the pores of the material contain soluble salts.
From a structural point of view, surface decay can be well represented as a decrease of
the thickness of an element (load-bearing wall, column, pier, arch, etc.), leading to a
lower carrying capacity of the element itself (Figure 13.16).

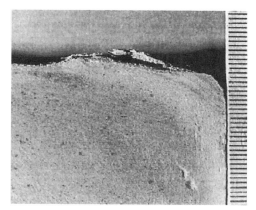 

Figure 13.16   Penetration of decay into a brick   **Figure 13.17**   Measurement device.
specimen submitted to crystallization cycles.

This dimensional variation (more precisely, the reduction of the cross-section of the structural element) could hence be considered as a parameter to measure the deterioration (Binda et al. 1992). This parameter can also describe the surface roughness of the element.

The measurement procedure we propose has been used up to now mainly during laboratory aging tests and is described below.

To measure degradation at each cycle, a simple device is used, consisting of a dial gauge fixed to a plate through a rigid support (Figure 13.17) (Binda et al. 1992). The gauge has a resolution of 10 microns, and its point has a diameter of 5.6 mm. A rigid grid is applied to the specimen after each cycle, which allows for a certain number (m) of measurements to be made on the specimen surface (9 for stone specimens, 15 for brick specimens).

Before the first cycle, the specimen height δ_{0j} ($j = 1,...,m$) is recorded to define the original position of the m points. The measurement is repeated at every cycle and indicated as δ_{ij} ($i=1,...,n, j = 1,...,m$), where n is the number of cycles.

Data are recorded at every cycle as $\Delta_j = \delta_{ij} - \delta_{0j}$, variation of the height with respect to the initial value δ_{0j} considered as zero, and reported in a graph versus the number of cycles, c.

Figure 13.18 represents the nine curves obtained for a specimen of Serena stone, a sandstone coming from the quarries of Fiorenzuola (central part of Italy). Local height losses represent the thicknesses of the layers that are being detatched in the area around the nine points. Several peaks clearly appear in the diagram. They have a precise meaning: every bulge of the surface represents the formation of a new layer, which will be detatched in subsequent cycles. Thus the real onset of the decay can be recorded.

Since 1981, an attempt has also been made to measure approximately the rate of decay *in situ*. This was done with the aim of controlling: (a) the behavior of the materials,

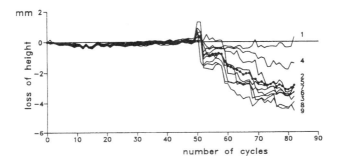

Figure 13.18   Data recorded in 9 points of a stone specimen relative to the undamaged starting position.

(b) the effectivness of surface treatments, and (c) the real times of natural decay to be compared with the laboratory decay.

Details of the facades were photographed approximately four times a year, and damage was calculated as a percentage of the original area. An example is shown in Figure 13.19. In all cases, decay was observed to have followed similar paths: after an initial high rate of deterioration, a steady state was reached, followed by a quick increase of decay; then another steady state is detected, and so on. The steady state certainly represents the time that cryptoefflorescence needs to find its way through the material.

Performance of Consolidants and Protectives

The dial gauge measure has also been applied to study the durability of treated surfaces to crystallization of salts.

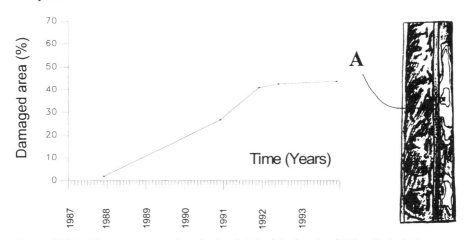

Figure 13.19   Damage measured on the detail (A) of the facade of Milan Cathedral.

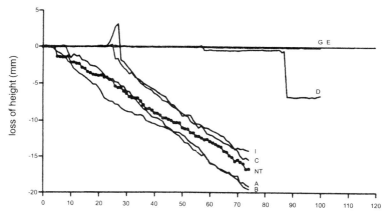

Figure 13.20 Loss of height curves for pink Angera stone specimens, treated and untreated (NT).

The specimens are treated on the upper surface before wrapping the lateral surfaces (see section on **CRYSTALLIZATION TEST**). The loss of height is then measured at every cycle. As an example (Figure 13.20), the damage curves of a pink Angera stone (a limestone from Lake Maggiore, Italy) with and without treatment are presented. NT corresponds to the untreated specimens.

The specimens were sampled from a deposit in the cellar of Ca' Granda (15th century) in Milan, where they were put after partial destruction due to bombing in the second world war. They were treated with ten different types of products (called A, B, C, E, F, G, H, I) and subjected to crystallization cycles.

Figure 13.20 shows the average curves for the treated and untreated specimens; it is clear that only three treatments – D, E, and G – were successful.

Nevertheless, the meaning of "average" has to be defined. In fact, as it can be seen from Figure 13.18, the loss of height for the single points of measure is not so much different for the first cycles when the damage is low. Subsequently, there is a great scattering, when damage is very high. An even higher scattering can be detected for treated specimens, when very thick layers are detatched. This problem will be dealt with in the future.

USE OF A LASER SENSOR AS A PROFILE RECORDING DEVICE

The usual techniques adopted to detect the profile and roughness of material surfaces in rock mechanics are based on a point-by-point measure performed through dial gauges or displacement transducers that require direct contact with the surface. Such techniques, however, have the drawback of consuming time for both measurement and processing and risk surface damage, especially for soft and very deteriorated materials. The laser sensor, as a noncontact means of obtaining reliable information on the

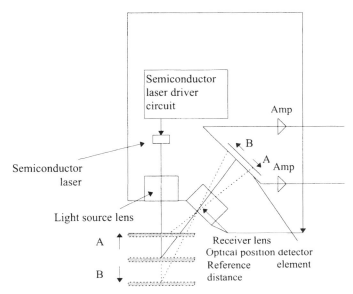

Figure 13.21   Operating layout of the laser sensor.

surface characteristics within a short period of time, is a relatively new technique. Some applications have already been reported on rock joints (ENEL/CRIS 1989), undertaken to evaluate the joint roughness coefficient (JRC) and on stone aggregates (Peroni et al. 1991) used to ascertain the average roughness, profile, and undulation depth. The laser sensor is generally based on a semiconductor laser driver circuit emitting a laser beam, thrown perpendicularly to the surface to be examined. The reflected light is converged by the receiver lens and cast on the detector element of the optical position as a small spot (Figure 13.21). If the distance is changed, the light spot is moved accordingly. The optical element in turn encodes the amount of movement into an electric signal. An arithmetic circuit, provided in the laser unit controller, outputs the electric signal that indicates the displacement of the surface. Some profile measurements have been carried out using a laser sensor with a spot of 1.0×2.0 mm, a resolution of 40 microns, and a linearity of 0.8% for a measurement range of 80 mm. The standard distance of the sensor from the surface is 100 mm, with a measurement range of ± 40 mm. The sensor is connected to a vertical steel frame through a dragging trolley, which moves on a linear support beam by means of a step-by-step electric motor (Figure 13.22).

Preliminary trials carried out on the frame with a centimeter-scale comparator led to the evaluation of the mechanical oscillations of the trolley within a range of ± 0.01 mm. The profiles are automatically measured, plotted and recorded through a suitable data acquisition system. A layout is presented in Figure 13.23. Based on the acquired experience, it has been ascertained that environmental light variation does not affect the measurements.

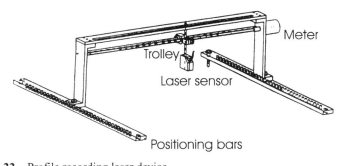

Figure 13.22   Profile recording laser device.

Some problems arise when surfaces have crystals with reflecting cleavage planes that can direct the emitted ray out of the sensor receiver lens. Black spots on the surfaces can also cause measurement variations. These problems can, however, be solved by applying removable opaque coatings or gypsum on the surfaces. Two frames of different sizes are used for measurements on specimens in laboratory and on walls *in situ*, respectively.

Laboratory Measurements

In the laboratory, the maximum length of the detectable profile is 300 mm. The laser sensor is positioned at a distance of about 70 mm above the surface of the specimens, and the velocity of the trolley is 2 mm/s. The surface of some specimens has been evaluated both with the dial gauge and with the laser device. Figures 13.24–13.26 compare respectively two measurements in new brick, a deteriorated brick, and a badly deteriorated stone cored *in situ*. In addition to a good agreement between the two types of measurements, the figures show the advantages of the laser device.

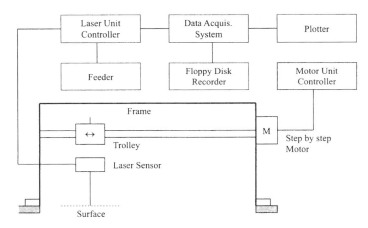

Figure 13.23   Layout of the instrumentation system for the laser measures.

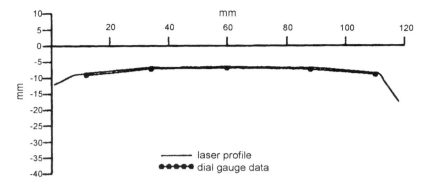

Figure 13.24   Profile of a new brick specimen.

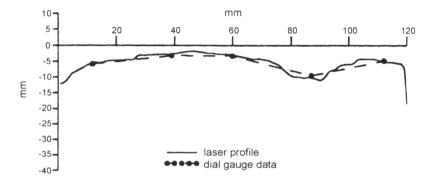

Figure 13.25   Profile of a deteriorated brick specimen.

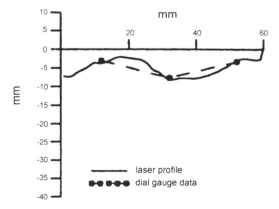

Figure 13.26   Profile of badly deteriorated stone specimen.

Figure 13.27 Frame applied to the a wall of the full-scale models.

In Situ **Measurements**

For *in situ* measurements, the vertical frame is initially fixed on two steel bars with a series of 36 holes, which enables the frame to move in increments of 20 mm and to detect parallel profiles (Figure 13.22). The frame and bars have been in turn fixed on the walls through steel supports, suitably inserted in the walls themselves (Figure 13.27). This allows accurate repetition of the profile measurements of the deteriorated surfaces at defined times. The maximum length of detectable profile is 620 mm. The laser sensor is positioned at a distance of about 100 mm above the surface of the walls, and the velocity of the trolley is 4 mm/s.

The equipment was proposed and set up at ENEL-CRIS (Milan) by M. Berra and A. Fatticcioni (Berra et al. 1993).

Figure 13.28 is an example two typical horizontal profiles. The first is a recording of a profile of a brick course; the second, a profile of a mortar bed. In Figure 13.28a, the presence of heading joints is clearly visible.

Figure 13.29 shows a vertical profile of a stone wall in the deteriorated areas. The profiles will be recorded at least four times every year.

CONCLUSIONS

The following comments can be made at this time:

- The data collected *in situ* on thermohygrometric conditions can be used to define the environmental conditions in a detailed way.
- Moisture and salt movements inside the wall are very important in explaining the decay process.

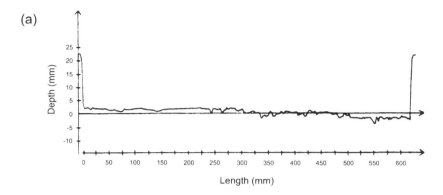

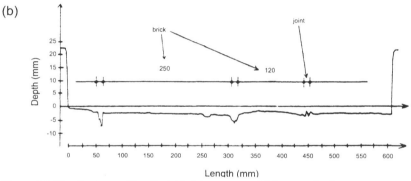

Figure 13.28   *In situ* profile of a (a) brick course and (b) mortar bed.

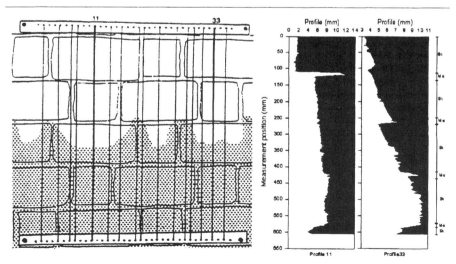

Figure 13.29   Vertical profiles of a stone wall obtained by laser scanning.

- The moisture and salt maximum level is higher for brick panels than for stone panels. Decay seems to be equally distributed and more superficial on the stone surfaces, but deeper and more concentrated on the brick surface.
- Special care must be given to the technique of application of protective and consolidant materials.
- Aging tests should be designed to reproduce failure mechanisms that actually occur in different natural environments.
- Attempts have to be made to calculate the differences between the rate of decay *in situ* and in laboratory.
- When the decay of the surface appears as delamination and crumbling and the material properties underneath the deteriorated surface are not deeply changed, dimensional variation (e.g., loss of thickness) versus time can be used as a suitable parameter to define the damage.
- The measure of this parameter is a nondestructive evaluation of the decay, hence of the performance of the material.
- The profile recording laser device is a successful tool for these measurements both *in situ* and in laboratory. Complete and reliable profiles can be obtained in a very short time without any contact with the deteriorated surface.

ACKNOWLEDGEMENTS

The authors wish to thank ESEM and ICITE-CNR for providing respectively the site and construction of the models, and E. Dagheti, C. Fumerio, B. Lubelli, C. Tatti, C. Arcadi, M. Antico, A. Vai, A. Fantucci, R. Borsotti for their help in the laboratory. F. Cantoni and P. Rocca from ICITE-CNR have worked with us in the construction and continual monitoring of the models. In addition, several students of the Faculty of Architecture have based their degree thesis on the models and subsequent laboratory findings (Baronio et al. 1992, 1993).

REFERENCES

Arnold, A. 1977. Behaviour of some soluble salts in stone deterioration. In: 2nd Intl. Symp. on the Deterioration of Building Stones, pp. 27–36. Athens: Universite technique nationale.
Baronio, G., and L. Binda. 1983. Essais de cristallisation du sulphate de sodium dans des conditions de temperature et d'humidité relative connues. In: Proc. Sem. Dur. des Betons et Pierres, CISCO, Saint Rémy Les Chevreuse, pp. 233–242. Paris: CISCO.
Baronio, G., L. Binda, F. Cantoni, and P. Rocca. 1992. Durability of preservative treatments of brick and stone masonry surfaces: Use of outdoor physical models. The Response of Masonry to the Environment, BMS, vol. 6, nr. 2, pp. 50–53. London: Masonry Intl.
Baronio, G., L. Binda, F. Cantoni, and P. Rocca. 1993. Durability of stone and brickwork protectives and consolidants: Experimental research on full-scale models. In: 6th Intl. Conf. on Durability of Building Materials and Components, Omiya, vol. 2, pp. 824–833. Omiya: E&FN SPON.
Binda, L., and G. Baronio. 1984. Measurement of the resistance to deterioration of old and new bricks by means of accelerated aging tests. *J. Durability of Building Materials* 2:139–154.

Binda, L., and G. Baronio. 1985. Alteration of the mechanical properties of masonry prisms due to aging. In: 7th IBMaC, vol.1, pp. 605–616. Melbourne: IBMaC.

Binda, L., and G. Baronio. 1987. Mechanisms of masonry decay due to salt crystallization. *J. Durability of Buildings Materials* 4:227–240.

Binda, L., G. Baronio, and T. Squarcina. 1992. Evaluation of the durability of bricks and stones and of preservation treatments. In: 7th Intl. Congress on Deter. and Conservation of Stone, pp. 753–761. Lisbon: Laboratorio Nacional de Engenharia Civil.

Binda, L., A.E. Charola, and G. Baronio. 1985. Deterioration of porous materials due to salt crystallization under different thermohygrometric conditions. I. Brick, pp. 279–288. Lausanne: Presses polytechniques romande.

Binda, L., and C. Molina. 1990. Building materials durability: Semi-markov approach. *J. Mat. Civ. Eng.* **12(4)**: 223–239.

Berra, M., A. Fatticcioni, L. Binda, and T. Squarcina. 1993. Laboratory and *in situ* measurement procedure of the decay of masonry surfaces, 6th Intl. Conf. on Durability of Building Materials and Components, vol. 2, pp. 834–843. Omiya: E&FN SPON.

CIBW80/RILEM 71. 1987. Prediction of Service Life of Building Materials and Components, Final Rep. CIBW80/RILEM 71-PSL *Mat. & Struct.* **115**:55–77.

ENEL/CRIS. 1989. Profilografo a laser per il rilievo della rugosità dei giunti in roccia. ENEL/CRIS Internal Report No. 3788.

Gmelins Handbuch der anorganischen Chemie. 1957. 8 Auflage, Band 7. Weinheim: Verlag Chemie.

Larsen, E.S., and Nielsen, C.B. 1990. Decay of bricks due to salt. *Mat. & Struct.* **23**:16–25.

Lewin, S.Z. 1982. The Mechanism of Masonry Decay through Crystallization, pp. 110–144. Conservation of Historic Stone Buildings and Monuments, Washington, D.C.: Natl. Academy of Sciences.

Peroni, G., F.M. Fraschetti, and R. Lanucara. 1991. Studio sugli inerti impiegati nella manutenzione delle pavimentazioni. Indagine eseguita con l'uso di rugosimetro a laser. *Autostrade* 3:66–73.

14

Application of Neutron Scattering Techniques to the Investigation of Brick and Mortar

R.A. LIVINGSTON

Office of Highway Engineering R&D, Federal Highway Administration,
6300 Georgetown Pike, McLean, VA 22101, U.S.A.

ABSTRACT

Neutron scattering methods measure the exchanges in momentum and energy in collisions between neutrons and the nuclei of materials. This provides an array of analytical techniques for studying the chemistry and microstructure of historic bricks and mortars. The information they provide can be used to obtain a better understanding of the processes that create the initial microstructure and also how the microstructure changes over time with exposure to environmental factors, which can then be used to develop improved durability tests or to provide a better match of physical properties between the original masonry and replacement materials.

INTRODUCTION

A major obstacle to applying the materials science approach to the study of bricks and mortar has been the nature of the materials themselves. Many of the important phases in these materials are usually amorphous or poorly crystallized, which makes them difficult to analyze with conventional methods of X-ray diffraction and optical microscropy. Moreover, the phases in the mortar are very sensitive to environmental conditions, particularly water vapor pressure and carbon dioxide. Consequently, they tend to break down under the vacuum of scanning electron microscopes and also will change over time when exposed to the atmosphere.

However, methods based on neutron scattering have proven to be very well-suited for this kind of problem in a number of fields including glasses, ceramics, and polymers (Axe 1991). One reason for this success is that neutrons scatter very efficiently off the hydrogen nucleus. This property can be used in a number of ways to examine hydrogenous materials like colloids, clay minerals and biological materials, the study of which is sometimes known as "sludge science" (Lindner 1992).

Since most building materials also fit into the category of sludge science, neutron scattering ought to be a very useful tool in this field. The purpose of this paper is to provide an introduction to the method, or group of methods, together with some examples of how they can be applied to study various problems concerning brick and mortar. These include the identification of hydrous materials in mortar by neutron diffraction, the measurement of the state of water in mortar by quasi-elastic neutron scattering, and the characterization of microstructure by small angle neutron scattering. Some additional methods involving neutrons in the analysis of brick structures are described in other papers in this volume. Livingston and Taylor (see Chapter 37) report on the application of the neutron capture method to measure chloride and water concentrations in a brick building in Colonial Williamsburg. Visser et al. (Chapter 32) describe the use of neutron thermalization to measure moisture in the Rathaus of Lübeck. This is also a type of neutron scattering, but it involves much higher energies (1 electronvolt to 1 Mega electronvolt) than the neutron scattering methods covered here, which use neutron energies in the range of 0.001 to 1 electronvolts. Consequently, neutron thermalization cannot measure the same physical phenomenon as neutron scattering.

NEUTRON SCATTERING THEORY

Neutron scattering can be described simply in terms of the fundamental laws of motion of physics. Figure 14.1 shows the process of the scattering of the neutron off the nucleus of a target material.

Before the collision, the neutron has an incident velocity, represented by the vector **v**. After the collision, the scattered velocity **v′** has a different direction. The angle through which the vector is rotated is given as 2θ. Since in this illustration the magnitude of both of the velocity vectors is the same, the neutron has the same energy before and after the collision. This is known as elastic scattering. If the neutron gives up or gains energy in the collision, it is known as inelastic or quasi-elastic scattering. The basic principle of neutron scattering is simply to select neutrons with a specific velocity, scatter them off a target material, and measure the velocity of the scattered neutron as a

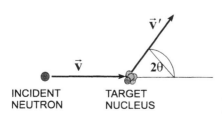

function of the scattering angle. However, for various reasons having to do with quantum mechanics, neutron scattering data are generally not reported in terms of velocities and scattering angles. Instead, the neutron is described in terms of its wave function $\psi(\mathbf{x},\omega,t)$ as shown in Figure 14.2. In this formalism, the key parameters are the wavevector, **k**, which is proportional to the momentum, and the neutrons frequency, ω. In this case, the

Figure 14.1 Schematic diagram of momentum transfer during neutron scattering.

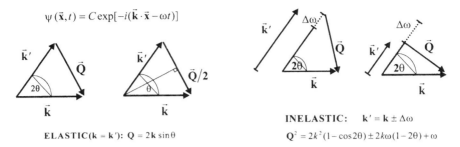

$$\psi(\bar{\mathbf{x}},t) = C\exp[-i(\bar{\mathbf{k}}\cdot\bar{\mathbf{x}} - \omega t)]$$

ELASTIC($\mathbf{k} = \mathbf{k}'$): $Q = 2\mathbf{k}\sin\theta$

INELASTIC: $\mathbf{k}' = \mathbf{k} \pm \Delta\omega$

$$Q^2 = 2k^2(1-\cos 2\theta) \pm 2k\omega(1-2\theta) + \omega$$

Figure 14.2   Vector diagram of elastic neutron scattering in reciprocal space.

Figure 14.3   Vector diagram of inelastic neutron scattering in reciprocal space.

incident wavevector is **k**, and the scattered wavevector is **k'**. The vector difference between the two is symbolized as **Q**. As shown in Figure 14.2, for elastic scattering, where **k** = **k'**, there is a simple formula for converting the magnitude of Q into the scattering angle, θ. Therefore, neutron scattering data are usually given as I(Q), the intensity of neutrons scattered into at a specific Q. Since the process is described in reciprocal space, the dimension of Q is inverse angstroms ($\mathring{A}^{-1}$) or inverse nanometers (nm^{-1}).

In the case of inelastic scattering, the incident and scattered wavevectors differ in magnitude, as shown in Figure 14.3. The difference in magnitude represents a gain or loss of energy by the neutron during the interaction. This energy exchange is on the order of the thermal fluctuations of the nucleus, or $0.025 < E < 1$ electronvolts. It is usual to denote this energy shift as a change in the neutron's frequency, as indicated in Figure 14.3 by $\pm\Delta\omega$, where $\Delta\omega = \Delta\omega = \hbar E$. It is still possible to relate Q to θ in this situation, provided that $\Delta\omega$ is measured. Consequently, neutron scattering data for experiments involving inelastic scattering are reported in the two-dimensional intensity, I(Q,ω).

There is actually a family of methods based on neutron scattering. Depending on the experimental arrangements, the methods can be used to obtain information on either the spatial distribution of the microstructure (diffraction, small-angle scattering), or the dynamics of the constituents of the material (quasi-elastic).

NEUTRON DIFFRACTION

Considered as waves rather than particles, neutrons have typical wavelengths of 0.16 nm (1.6 Å) at room temperatures. This is on the order of the distance between of atoms in a crystal lattice. Since Bragg's Law also applies to elastic scattering of neutrons, it is possible to use them for diffraction studies of crystal structures. With its high sensitivity to hydrogen, neutron diffraction is used to measure the positions of water molecules or OH⁻ groups in the structure of cementitious materials such as pozzolanic mortars.

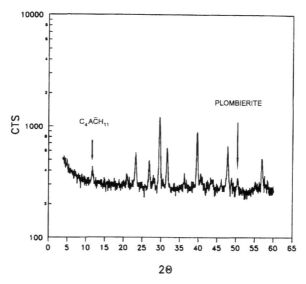

Figure 14.4 Neutron diffraction spectrum of historic mortar specimen from the Hagia Sophia in Istanbul. The symbol $C_4A\bar{C}H_{11}$ stands for tetra calcium aluminum carbonate hydrate.

In practice, the neutron wavelength is usually selected to be 0.154 nm (1.54 Å), which is the same as the Cu K_α X-ray peak used in X-ray diffraction. The neutron diffraction pattern can thus be directly overlaid on an X-ray diffraction pattern of a sample. The spacing of peaks will be the same for both kinds of diffraction patterns. However, relative intensities of peaks for a given crystal may be very different because of differences in scattering cross-sections between the two types of radiation. Thus comparison between the two kinds of diffraction patterns can yield information that is not possible to obtain from either one alone.

With this method, it has also been possible to identify C-S-H gel in the unusual form of plombierite, along with a carbonated tetra calcium aluminum hydrate phase in historic Byzantine mortar made with brick dust (Livingston et al. 1992), as shown in Figure 14.4.

Moreover, neutron diffraction can be done on comparatively large specimens, on the order of 1 cm in diameter, and under a wide range of environmental conditions. It is thus possible to measure nondestructively the hydration and pozzolanic reactions *in situ* and follow the reactions over time (Christensen et al. 1986). However, to avoid the large background produced by quasi-elastic scattering from hydrogen, described in the next section, it may be necessary to mix the samples with deuterated water rather than ordinary water. This does not affect the crystal structure, but it can significantly slow down the rate of reaction.

QUASI-ELASTIC NEUTRON SCATTERING

Another neutron method involves the quasi-elastic scattering of neutrons off moving water molecules. This is a special case of inelastic scattering. Since the mass of the H_2O is relatively low, it can transfer or gain kinetic energy from collisions with neutrons. Thus by measuring the two-dimensional neutron scattering intensity, $I(Q,\omega)$, it is possible to determine the amount water with significant kinetic energy. Water molecules that are bound in the hydrated cement phases as interlayer water or OH groups do not have translational motion and thus no appreciable kinetic energy. Consequently, this can be used to determine the percentage of bound or free water in mortar as a function of time (Livingston et al. 1996). The time evolution of the bound water index is shown in Figure 14.5 for a Portland cement mortar.

It should be emphasized that this information is based directly on first principles of physics. The only parameter that is required is the diffusion constant of water. With additional measurements, even this parameter can be obtained from quasi-elastic scattering data. Figure 14.6 is a plot of the Lorentzian width of the $I(Q,\omega)$ function of the mortar at an early age. From this the diffusion constant of water, D, is calculated. The value that is found, 3.1×10^{-9} m^2/s, agrees very well with that of free water.

The capability of quasi-elastic neutron scattering to monitor the reaction of water with Portland cement has been used to study the kinetics of the reaction in detail (FitzGerald et al. 1998). This has revealed at different stages that the hydration reaction involves at least three different rate-limiting processes. The initial stage is a slow reaction, which is still not well understood. It known as the induction period. This is followed by the peak reaction period, in which the rate constant has an Arrhenius-type temperature dependence that indicates a surface reaction limiting step. Finally, the reaction rate follows a square-root dependence with time, which suggests a diffusion limited reaction. This research has focused initially on the reactions of pure tricalcium

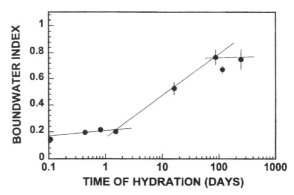

Figure 14.5 Quasi-electric measurement of the consumption of water in the Portland cement hydration reaction. The bound water index is the ratio of water incorporated in the hydrated cement phases to the total amount of water in the mix.

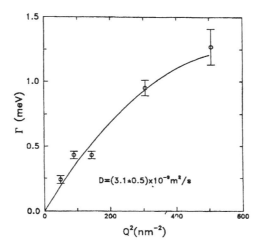

Figure 14.6 Plot of Lorentzian function width vs. Q^2 for Portland cement mortar (D = diffusion constant of water).

silicate, but it can be readily extended to the pozzolanic materials found in some historic mortars (FitzGerald et al. 1998).

SMALL ANGLE NEUTRON SCATTERING (SANS)

A third neutron scattering method measures the angular distribution of cold neutrons scattered at very small angles from materials. Cold neutrons have been chilled down to roughly 40°K by scattering through a block of heavy water (D_2O) ice. At this temperature, the typical neutron wavelength is around 1.6 nm (16 Å). This length provides information on the development of the microstructure, including the typical particle size and the fractal dimensions of the structure, which in turn gives information on the processes by which the microstructure and hence the strength of the concrete develop (Allen 1991).

The SANS data represent the spatial Fourier transform of the pair correlation function of the material (Teixiera 1986). The pair correlation function, in turn, can be used to quantify the microstructure. Figure 14.7 presents an idealized plot of the logarithm of I(Q) vs Q for typical SANS data (Kriechbaum et al. 1994). The slope of this curve is the fractal dimension. Two different fractal dimensions have been identified in this plot. At smaller Q, the fractal dimension D_v concerns the density. At higher Q, the fractal dimension D_f is related to the distribution of surface elements. The limiting value of the slope of the curve in the Porod region as Q→ ∞ yields an estimate of the total surface area. From the plateau in Guinier regime at very small Q, the characteristic particle size can also extracted. Also shown are two important lengths. The raduim of

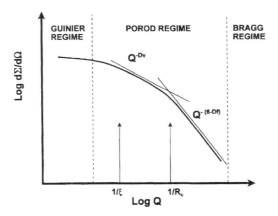

Figure 14.7 Idealized SANS data plot illustrating significant features used for microstructure characterization. See text for explanation.

gyration, Rg, provides an estimate of the characteristic particle size. The correlation length, $1/\xi$, defines the limit for the fractal region.

Allen and Livingston (1998) have shown how these microstructural parameters can be derived using an appropriate mathematical model of the scattering process. It is then possible to use the parameters to quantify changes in microstructure as a result of modifications such as the addition of varying amounts of silica fume to Portland cement mixtures.

In Figure 14.8, SANS data have been combined with small angle X-ray scattering (SAXS) measurements for several materials of interest in the conservation of historic masonry. The methods are actually complementary since SANS works over the length scales of 1–1,000 nm, while SAXS operates at 100–10,000 nm. The samples include historic mortar from the Hagia Sophia, as described by Cakmak et al. (Chapter 35, this volume), historic brick subjected to varying numbers of salt cycles (Franke and Schumann, Chapter 5, this volume), and a typical Portland cement concrete specimen.

In the case of the brick specimen, the difference appears to be associated with a change in the slope at higher Q. In other words, there is a difference in the surface fractal. This presumably reflects an increased number of microcracks as a result of salt cycles. The curve for the Portland cement mortar is very typical of this kind of gel-like material, concave upward and with a large amount of the scattering at high Q values. On the other hand, the curve for the Hagia Sophia mortar, differs greatly from the Portland cement. This mortar, which is 1,500 years old, has been identified as a pozzolanic, rather than a pure lime mortar (Livingston et al. 1992). Therefore, it must have originally shared some characteristics with the Portland cement mortar, but now after aging and carbonation, its curve is more like natural rock, convex upward and with less detail at high Q.

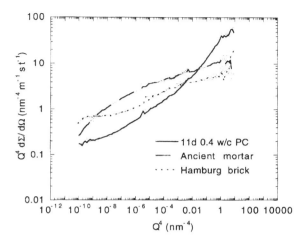

Figure 14.8   Small angle scattering plots for several masonry materials. "Ancient mortar" is a sample from the Hagia Sophia (see Cakmak et al., this volume). "Hamburg brick" is from samples provided by Franke and Schumann. The ordinary Portland cement paste is eleven days old, 0.4 water/cement ratio, is indicated by "11 d 0.4 w/c PC."

Finally, the fractal dimensions of the material can also yield insights on the processes by which the microstructure develops during curing. In mortar materials based on Portland cement or pozzolanic reactions, the microstructure grows through the accumulation of very fine particles into a framework that provides the strength. The details of this growth process are not completely understood. Computer simulations using different assumptions of how particles aggregate and reaction kinetics produce structures with characteristic fractal dimensions (Witten 1986). It could then be possible to compare the fractal dimensions of materials measured by SAXS and SANS against these computer simulations to determine which growth model is most realistic.

CONCLUSIONS

Neutron scattering methods provide a array of analytical techniques for studying the chemistry and microstructure of historic bricks and mortars. The information they provide can be used to obtain a better understanding of the processes that create the initial microstructure and also how the microstructure changes over time with exposure to environmental factors. This can then be used to develop improved durability tests or to provide a better match of physical properties between the original masonry and replacement materials.

REFERENCES

Axe, J.D. 1991. Neutron scattering: Progress and prospects. *Science* **252**:795–802.

Allen, A.J. 1991. Time-resolved phenomena in cements, clays and porous rocks. *J. Appl. Crystall.* **24**:24–634.

Allen, A.J., and R.A. Livingston. 1998. The relationship between differences in silica fume additives and the fine scale microstructural evolution in cement-based materials. *J. Adv. Cement-based Materials*, in press.

Christensen, A.N., H. Fjellvag, and S. Lehmann. 1986. Time-resolved powder neutron diffraction investigations of reactions of solids with water. *Cement Concrete Res.* **16**:871–874.

FitzGerald, S., D. Neumann, J. Rush, D. Bentz, and R. Livingston. 1998. *In situ* quasi-elastic neutron scattering study of the hydration of tricalcium silicate. *Chem. Mater.* **10**:397–402.

Kriechbaum, M., G. Degovics, P. Laggner, and J. Tritthart. 1994. Investigations of cement pastes by small-angle X-ray scattering and BET: The relevance of fractal geometry. *Adv. Cement Res.* **6(23)**:93–102.

Lindner, P. 1992. Neutrons tackle 'Sludge Science'. *New Scientist* **Jan. 25**:38–41.

Livingston, R., and A. Allen. 1995. Application of small-angle neutron scattering method to the study of the durability of historic brick and mortar. In: Ceramics in Architecture, ed. P. Vincenzoni, pp. 573–580. Faenza, Italy: CIMTEC.

Livingston, R.A., D. Neumann, A. Allen, and J. Rush. 1996. Application of neutron scattering methods to cementitious materials In: Materials Res. Soc. Symp. Proc., vol. 376, ed. D. Neumann, T. Russell, and B. Wuensch, pp. 459–469. Pittsburgh: Materials Research Society.

Livingston, R.A., P.E. Stutzman, R. Mark, and M. Erdik. 1992. Preliminary analysis of the masonry of the Hagia Sophia Basilica, Istanbul. In: Materials Issues in Art and Archaeology III, Materials Res. Soc. Symp. Proc., vol. 267, ed. P. Vandiver et al., pp. 721–736. Pittsburgh: Materials Research Society.

Teixiera, J. 1986. Experimental methods for studying fractal aggregates. In: On Growth and Form: Fractal and Non-fractal Patterns in Physics, ed. H.E. Stanley and N. Ostrowsky, pp. 145–162. Dordrecht: Martinus Nijhoff.

Witten, T.A. 1986. Scale-invariant Diffusive Growth. In: On Growth and Form: Fractal and Non-fractal Patterns in Physics, ed. H.E. Stanley and N. Ostrowsky, pp. 54–68. Dordrecht: Martinus Nijhoff.

15

Transport of Salt Solutions in Brickwork

L. FRANKE and J. GRABAU

Technische Universität Hamburg-Harburg, Arbeitsbereich Bauphysik und Werkstoffe im Bauwesen, Eißendorfer Straße 42, 21071 Hamburg, Germany

ABSTRACT

Examination of historic brick buildings showed gypsum enrichment beneath the brick surface. Experiments were done to determine whether these salt concentrations were due to dry sulfate deposition or the result of sulfate uptake from acid rain. Drying tests by evaporation from brick prisms with a calcite content of 0.8% set into a solution of sulfuric acid clearly showed that the resulting gypsum is deposited almost exclusively within the first 2 mm beneath the brick surface.

INTRODUCTION

During our examination of some 15 historic brick buildings in northern Germany, salt efflorescence composed mainly of gypsum was observed to be the primary cause of damage in all but a few buildings (cf. Chapter 5, this volume). This raises the question of the source of the sulfates.

Unlike limestone or marble that are composed of calcium carbonate, which readily reacts with SO_2 to form gypsum, bricks are silcate-based materials that would seem unlikely to undergo such reactions.

We examined whether the required sulfates could originally have been present in the mortar joints, as would be the case if gypsum-based mortars were used or sometimes was the practice in northern Germany (see Chapter 2, this volume). As these sources could generally be excluded, it was concluded that the damage must have been the result of air pollution, in this case sulfur dioxide. Therefore, the reactions as shown in Figure 15.1 can be assumed.

Calcium-rich solutions migrate from the lime mortar into the brick pore space leading to precipitation of calcium carbonate in the pores. Subsequently, acid pollutants penetrate the brick and react with the calcium carbonate and possibly the calcium feldspars. The salts formed by these reactions are transported in solution and are either

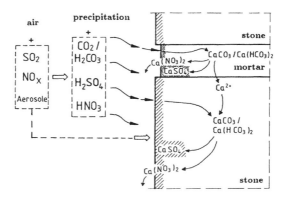

Figure 15.1 Sources of sulfates in masonry.

precipitated nearby or on the surface (if they are slightly soluble, e.g., gypsum) or are washed off by rain if they are soluble.

RESULTS

This mechanism of gypsum formation has been widely accepted as one major cause of the decay of natural carbonate stone buildings. A preliminary experiment suggests that it is justified to apply this same mechanism to fired brick as well. Brick prisms with a calcite content of 0.8 % were set into a diluted solution of sulfurous acid. Evaporation of water could only occur through the surface of the samples. Efflorescence was formed on the samples with no firing skin, which was identified as gypsum by IR and XRF analysis. If the samples still had their original firing skin, salt crystallization took place beneath this skin as shown in Figure 15.2. The calcite content decreased from 0.8 to 0.1 wt.%.

Figure 15.2 Brick prism in sulfurous acid.

Given the interest in understanding the mechanism of decay better, attempts were made to enrich the salt content by absorption of gypsum solutions. The results of these experiments are presented here.

The experimental set-up was the same as for the experiments with sulfurous acid. The objective was an enrichment of gypsum beneath the sample's surface followed by an examination of the pore-size dependence of salt crystallization. However, after a few weeks time, it was observed that no salt had appeared on the surface.

Thus, systematic experiments were conducted on the mechanism of gypsum transport within the brick. These consisted of evaporation tests with bricks of the type "Neuenfelder Klinker." The properties of this brick are:

- apparent density : 2.04 kg/dm^3,
- skeletal density : 2.63 kg/dm^3,
- water adsorption coefficient[1] : 13.0 kg/m$^2 \cdot$ h$^{0.5}$,
- porosity : 22.0 vol.%.

The samples were sealed with a watertight sealant (cf. Chapter 5, this volume) and then put in one of the following three solutions:

- deionized water,
- magnesium sulfate solution (concentration: 0.012 mol/l),
- gypsum solution (same concentration, saturated solution).

The amount of evaporated water was determined gravimetrically. The results are shown in Figure 15.3a (with firing skin) and Figure 15.3b (without firing skin).

RESULTS FOR SAMPLES WITH FIRING SKIN

The results for water are given as a control. A dynamic equilibrium was found here. After an initial saturation period, the evaporation rate remains nearly constant.

In the case of the soluble $MgSO_4$, there is a minor difference compared with water evaporation only after a long experiment period. The salt crystallizes on surface and does not influence the evaporation rate very strongly.

There is a big difference with the gypsum solution: after about three days, there is no further evaporation. In this period, about 15 kg/m^2 of solution have evaporated; therefore, the amount of gypsum deposited in the brick is about 30–40 g/m^2.

A similar result was obtained for samples with no firing skin (Figure 15.3b). There is a larger influence of $MgSO_4$, compared to the impact on samples with original firing skin. Again there is a significant effect on the evaporation rate in the case of the gypsum solution.

---

1   DIN 52617

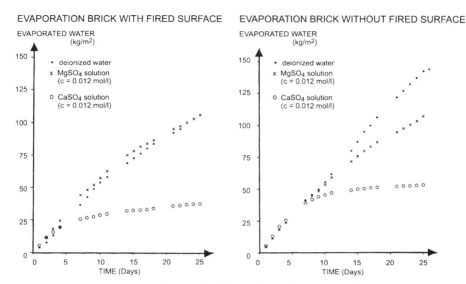

Figure 15.3 Evaporation results (a) with firing skin and (b) without firing skin.

After the evaporation experiments were finished, the samples were cut in thin slices of about 2 mm thickness as shown in Figure 15.4. The soluble sulfate in each skin was determined by leaching followed by spectrophotometry of the leachate. The results of sulfate distribution after transport of the solutions are shown in Figure 15.5.

The salt is deposited nearly completely within the first two mm beneath the surface, as can be seen in Figure 15.5. The same result was obtained for samples with or

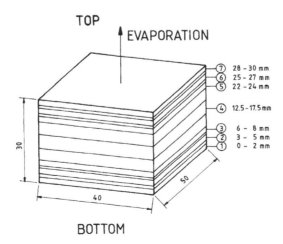

Figure 15.4   Sample preparation for analysis.

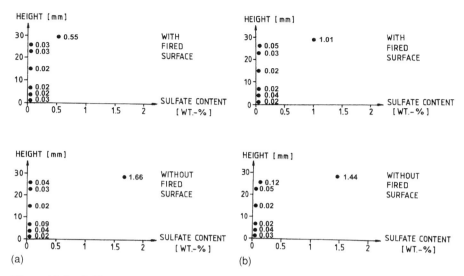

Figure 15.5 Sulfate distribution on evaporation of (a) saturated gypsum and (b) $MgSO_4$ solution (c = 0.012 mol/l).

without firing skin. The same result was also obtained when $MgSO_4$ was added to the transported solution. Some of the salt crystallized on the surface of the samples, and so was not taken into consideration with these analyses.

DISCUSSION AND CONCLUSIONS

What are possible explanations for the behavior after the transport of gypsum solutions and crystallization?

1. There may be a decrease of partial water vapor pressure, but according to Raoult's Law, this effect is very small for these dilute solutions (for ideal solutions the vapor pressure will decrease from p to 0.9998p). This effect should also influence the processes during the transport of the magnesium sulfate solution which had the same concentration as the gypsum solution.
2. The pores can be blocked by salt, or there may be a change of surface energies of the pores. However, if the pores are closed by salts there must also be en effect on capillary water adsorption (cpw) which was not detected thus far. There is still a need for further examination of the influence of cpw.
3. Formation of a fine porous structure of the salt which has a higher equilibrium water content than the pure brick can take place. Therefore evaporation at relative humidity of 50% (which is the laboratory atmosphere) may not be possible. Some experiments relating to this hypothesis are still in progress.

It is important to note that even small amounts of insoluble salts are able to nearly stop evaporation, as Niesel and Hoffmann (1990) and Künzel (1991) have demonstrated.

This evidence confirms our hypothesis on decay of bricks. A retarded drying of the brick causes a longer dwelling time of the acid pollutants. As the dissolution of calcite is rather slow, the decay process can be accelerated by this effect.

FURTHER RESEARCH ISSUES

Additional work has to be done on the effect of salt incrustations on capillary water adsorption. The effect of cycling between water sorption and drying must also be examined. Thus far, experiments were only carried out with one type of brick. Bricks with other pore-size distributions have to be examined.

Further work has to be done on the effects of H_2SO_3 and H_2SO_4 to confirm our hypothesis on brickwork decay. The influence of pore-size distribution on salt crystallization and vice versa is currently under study at our institute (K. Eickemeier, unpublished results).

REFERENCES

Hoffmann, D., and K. Niesel. 1990. Vorgänge des kapillaren Feuchtigkeitsaufstiegs und der Verdunstung in porösen Baustoffen. *Schriftenreihe der Sektion Architektur TU Dresden* **30**:110–115.

Künzel, H. 1991. Trocknungsblockade durch Mauerversalzung. *Bautenschutz + Bausanierung* **14**:63–66.

16

Influence of Brick Microstructure on the Characteristics of Cement Mortars

J. ELSEN

Division Building Materials, Belgian Building Research Institute (WTCB-CSTC),
Avenue P. Holoffe 21, 1342 Limelette, Belgium

ABSTRACT

The results presented are part of a research program designed to evaluate the frost sensitivity of brick-mortar combinations carried out at the Belgian Building Research Institute. Thin-sections of a large series of masonry samples were prepared before and after frost-thaw cycles. These thin-sections were examined with polarization and fluorescence microscopy to study the physico-chemical phenomena occuring at the interface between brick and mortar. The pore structure was characterized with automated image analysis techniques.

It was found that the effective water/cement (W/C) ratio in masonry mortars is relatively independent of its initial W/C ratio. Masonry mortars made with a fine to average sand and masoned with bricks with a high initial rate of absorption (IRA) have an effective W/C ratio greater than 0.7, making them frost sensitive. Those made with a coarse sand and masoned with bricks with a low IRA have an effective W/C ratio less than 0.25 and hydrate incompletely.

INTRODUCTION

Following numerous cases of damage to cladding masonry mortar of mostly single-family dwellings built after 1975, BBRI (Belgian Building Research Institute, WTCB-CSTC) began a large research program. The first damage was observed after the 1981–1982 winter. When damage was rather significant, the cladding wall curved in such a way that it had to be shored up pending its demolition and reconstruction. Research concentrated primarily on facades exposed to rain, especially unprotected areas (absence of overhanging wall copings and eaves overhangs). In an initial research project, BBRI studied the water transfer from fresh mortar to brick during construction as well as the mechanical and physical characteristics of the mortar after a certain setting time, using bricks with different pore structures. The results of this research show that the pore structure of bricks has a considerable influence on the quality of the mortar (Gérard 1987).

Consequently, a mortar should always be studied in combination with the material with which it is to be used. One of the most significant results of this study is that bricks with a high Haller number, i.e., with a high suction power towards free water, absorb the water in the fresh mortar only moderately and so do not dehydrate the latter, which was a generally accepted idea in the construction world (the Haller number gives the quantity of water, expressed in g per dm^3, that is absorbed in 1 minute when in contact with 5 mm water, norm NBN B24-202).

The final objective of the present research is to develop a model that will enable us to assess the frost resistance of any brick-mortar combination. This has to be possible both for masonry brick-mortar combinations (microscopic and physical tests) and for a hypothetical combination on the basis of the characteristics both of a brick and of the various components of a mortar. In this respect, the physical and chemical phenomena occurring in the brick-mortar interface have been studied with the help of an optical polarizing and fluorescent microscopy. Therefore, we use petrographic techniques.

MASONRY WORK

For microscopic investigation and the frost tests, a series of samples were masoned according to the Belgian standard NBN B24-401, with 300 kg of cement per m^3 of dry sand. The masonry work consists of combinations of two bricks masoned with different mortars. This way 36 different combinations were made (B0-B1-B2-B3-B4-B5) × (S1-S2-S3-S4-S5-S6): B represents brick and the numbering of the bricks correspond to an increasing water suction capacity, the so-called Haller number (B0 is a PVC sheet with a Haller number equal to 0 and B5 with a Haller number equal to 100); S stands for the sand type and the numbering of the different sand types correspond to a coarser grading.

RESULTS OF THE MICROSCOPIC EXAMINATION
AND IMAGE ANALYSIS

Thin-sections were made for the different samples at 28 days and after 20 frost-thaw cycles. These thin-sections were fully described: first qualitatively, using a polarizing microscope (ASTM 1983) with fluorescence, and then quantitatively using an automatic image analysis system (Wilk et al. 1984; Gudmundsson et al. 1981).

Qualitative and Quantitative Characterization of the Pores

The total porosity of the different masonry mortars differs only slightly, in contrast to the porosity determined by means of the image analysis of thin-sections, i.e., the porosity of pores larger than 7 μm. Here a thin-section is automatically scanned and a

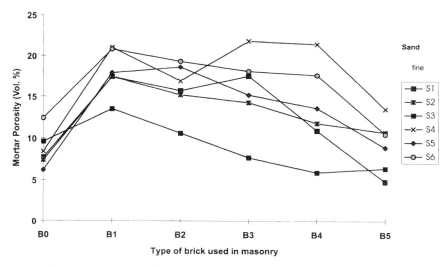

Figure 16.1   The pore content (in vol. %) of masonry mortars made with different sand types (S1…S6) and different bricks (B0…B5), determined by means of automatic image analysis on thin-sections prepared after 28 days. B0: PVC; B1: extruded clay brick; B2: calcium silicate brick; B3-B5: machine-molded clay brick.

large number of images digitalized and further filtered, in order to select the pores as a singular phase. A digitalized image consists of 512×512 pixels, each pixel having a gray scale of between 0 and 255. The so determined pore content is shown in Figure 16.1 for the different masonry mortars. We can see that the pore contents after masoning with a PVC plate (B0) show little difference for the different masonry mortars and that these differences are rather small. A similar pattern, albeit in a smaller degree, is noticeable when masoning a B5 brick. The pore content of the other samples is quite a bit higher. The mortars made with the finer sands generally show a smaller pore content, especially the S3.

Capillary Porosity

In a first phase, the capillary porosity (W/C ratio) was determined for the samples described in the section on **MASONRY WORK**. The capillary porosity is visually determined on thin-sections by comparing the sample with those of reference concrete mixtures with a known W/C ratio. These results are shown in Figure 16.2. What is remarkable is the high values for all the combinations with the brick B5, with the exception of the B5-S6, for the combinations B4-S1 and B4-S3, the combinations B3-S3 and B1-S3 and for all the combinations with B0. These combinations are part of the samples which showed the most damage during the frost tests.

J. Elsen

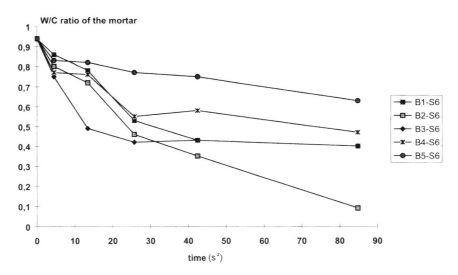

Figure 16.2 The W/C ratio of masonry mortars made with different sand types (S1…S6) and masoned with different brick types (B0…B5), microscopically determined on thin-sections.

The values of the capillary porosity are clearly related to the pore content (Figure 16.2). Masonry mortars with a higher capillary porosity have a low pore content and vice versa. The W/C ratio was determined afterwards by means of image analysis.

During the second phase, the capillary porosity was determined for a series of samples masoned with a Portland cement P40 (300 kg/m^3 dry sand). Three different brick types (B1, B3 and B5) were combined with two sand types (S1 and S5). For each combination, three mortars were made, each with a different W/C ratio. The results of this series were quite remarkable. We noticed no gradation at all of the capillary porosity related to the distance to the contact face brick-mortar. The microscopically determined W/C ratio remains constant for each combination, independent of the original W/C ratio.

WATER TRANSFER FROM FRESH MORTAR TO BRICK

To explain the hydration that was microscopically described from the thin-sections, the research program was extended to the study of the water transfer from fresh mortar to brick, during the first hours after masoning. In the first phase the same combinations as described above (see section on **MASONRY WORK**) were used. First, mortars were made with 300 kg cement PPz30 per m^3 dry sand. Water retention was determined according to the standard NBN B14-212, which allowed us to calculate the water loss by a conventional suction force. The fresh mortar was placed between bricks and removed at fixed intervals: after 20 seconds, 3 minutes, 11 minutes, 30 minutes, and 120 minutes. These mortar samples were weighed and then immediately dried at 105°C.

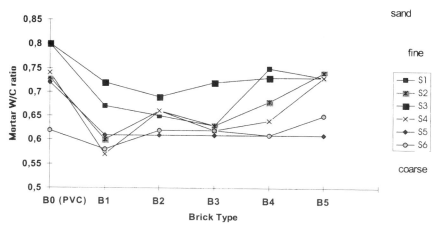

Figure 16.3   Effective W/C ratio of a masonry mortar made with sand S6, determined at different times after masoning with different bricks (B1...B5).

This allowed us to calculate the water volume (in mass % of the dry mass of the components) still remaining in the mortar after different time intervals. The results allow us to calculate the effective W/C ratio of these mortars related to the time that elapsed from the masoning onward. The results of these calculations are given in Figure 16.3 for the bricks B1 to B5 masoned with a mortar made with the sand S6. After two hours the curves in this figure are nearly horizontal, with the exception of the brick B2. The differences between them are rather large. The combination B5-S6 has an effective W/C ratio of 0.63 and the combination B2-S6 one of 0.09. The results can be summarized as follows:

- Masonry mortars made with a fine to average sand and combined with a brick with a high Haller number have an effective W/C ratio greater than 0.70, which makes them frost sensitive.
- Masonry mortars made with an average or coarse sand and combined with a brick with a very low Haller number have an effective W/C ratio less than 0.25. These mortars do not contain enough water to be able to hydrate the cement sufficiently and thus are insufficiently strong, i.e., these mortars are "burnt."

In a second phase, this test method was also applied on the series of samples described in the section on **Capillary Porosity**. The results fully confirm the findings of the microscopic investigation of the thin-sections.

CONCLUSIONS

For mortars, and for concrete in general, the W/C ratio is one of the most important factors determining the frost sensitivity and durability of a masonry mortar. The difficulty with masonry mortars lies in that the effective W/C ratio does not correspond with the initial ratio, the reason being that a part of the water is absorbed by the brick. This effective W/C ratio can be determined on existing masonry work by means of fluorescence microscopy on thin-sections. For masonry work, a simple test method was developed that enables the determination of the effective W/C ratio, thus allowing the prediction of the frost sensitivity of masonry mortars.

- A gradation of the capillary porosity in a masonry mortar related to the distance of the interface brick-mortar was barely detectable.
- The effective W/C ratio in masonry mortars is independent of the initial W/C ratio.
- Masonry mortars made with a fine to average sand and masoned with bricks with a high Haller number have an effective W/C ratio greater than 0.70, making them frost sensitive.
- Masonry mortars made with a coarse sand and masoned with bricks with a low Haller number have an effective W/C ratio less than 0.25 and hydrate incompletely. These mortars are "burnt"; however, they can absorb water when they come into contact with water (through rain), thus allowing the hydration to be continued. In this case, these mortars become frost resistant.

ACKNOWLEDGEMENTS

This research has been carried out at the Belgian Building Research Institute (CSTC-WTCB) in collaboration with N.V. GEOS (B-Wellen). The research has been funded by the Belgian national and regional governments.

REFERENCES

ASTM C856-83. 1983. Petrographic Examination of Hardened Concrete. Philadelphia.
Gérard, R. 1987. Proc. of the 1st Intl. Congress from Materials Science to Construction Materials Engineering, vol. 2, ed. J.C. Maso, pp. 387–395. Versailles: RILEM, AFREM.
Gudmundsson, H., S. Chatterji, A.D. Jensen, N. Thaulow, and P. Cristensen. 1981. Quantitative Microscopy as a Tool for the Quality Control of Concrete. In: Proc. 3th Intl. Conf. on Cement Microscopy, pp. 228–237. Houston: ICMA
Wilk, W., G. Dobrolubov, and B. Romer. 1984. The development of quantitative and qualitative microscopic control of concrete quality and durability and of frost-salt resistance test with rapid cycles, pp. 309–239. Proc. 6th Intl. Conf. On Cement Microscopy. Albuquerque: ICMA.

17

Characterization of Historic Mortars from Buildings in Germany and The Netherlands

B. MIDDENDORF[1, 2] and D. KNÖFEL[1]

[1]University of Siegen, Laboratory for Chemistry of Construction Materials (BCS),
Paul-Bonatz-Str. 9–11, 57068 Siegen, Germany
[2]Present address: University of Kassel, Department of Structural Materials,
Mönchebergstr. 7, 34109 Kassel, Germany

ABSTRACT

The mortars of heavily damaged portions of historic brick buildings were examined to determine the type of binder and aggregates used. The methods of working and different areas of application of these mortars during different periods were also derived from these results.

The results of analyses of mortars from northern Germany and from Utrecht in The Netherlands are presented with emphasis on chemical and mineralogical results. Along with lime, gypsum-anhydrite mortars were also used in northern Germany, the latter mainly used for religious buildings. Because of the higher initial strength of the gypsum-anhydrite mortars, compared to lime mortars, complicated parts of a building like brick arches or vaults could be built with these mortars.

The analytical results of chemical and mineralogical investigations of the mortars are presented and discussed (see Appendix 17.I) together with photographs of thin-sections (Appendix 17.II). Projects still in progress and those planned for the future are described.

INTRODUCTION

At the 4th NATO-CCMS meeting in Amersfoort (NL) we presented the way we analyze historic mortars containing different kinds of binder and aggregates (Appendix 17.I). In this paper, the results of the chemical and mineralogical investigation of mortars are presented and discussed. In Appendix 17.II, examples of thin-sections of historic mortars investigated are shown.

DESCRIPTION OF SAMPLED BUILDINGS

The designations of the sampled masonry mortars are given in Tables 17.1–17.4 in abbreviated form and are explained below. The art historical age of the sampled mortars is also given.

The samples listed in Table 17.1 are from secular and religious buildings in Lübeck, Germany, as well as from the Bardowick Cathedral. The cathedral was begun in 1146. Its compact towers are typical of the Romanesque period. A part of the masonry is shown in Figure 17.1. It is built with small bricks and the joints are thin and made of gypsum mortar.

The results listed in Table 17.2 are from mortars of the St. Georgenkirche in Wismar, Germany. In 1230, construction of the church was begun; the choir was finished in 1340–1360. This Basilica belongs to early Gothic architecture. Figure 17.2 shows the west side of the building. Plans exist to restore or reconstruct the monument in the near future. For restoration work, we recommend a mortar mixture based on hydraulic lime as binder and sand and shells as aggregate, class 2 mortar (Scholz 1984).

Figure 17.1   Part of the masonry from the Bardowick Cathedral.

Table 17.3 shows the results from different buildings from the town Utrecht in The Netherlands. The abbreviations used for the samples are also listed in Table 17.3. Some of the samples (U2–U8) were taken from the secular building complex called the German

Figure 17.2   West side of the St. Georgenkirche in Wismar.

Table 17.1 Results of analyses of historic mortars from monuments from Lübeck and Bardowick (Germany).

Sample	Masonry built in:	Binder content [wt.%]			Binder/aggregate value
		lime	gypsum	anhydrite	
HLMG40-1	1278	26.4	0.8	–	1/2.1
HLMG40-2	1300	30.7	–	–	1/2.0
HLMG40-10	1300–1320	35.4	–	–	1/1.6
HLMG42	13th–14th century	17.8	–	–	1/4.1
HLMG40-3	14th–15th century	31.6	–	–	1/1.8
HLMG40-4	1600	24.4	2.1	–	1/2.1
HLMG40-7	17th century	42.6	–	–	1/1.1
HLMG40-5	1720–1740	31.0	6.6	7.0	1/0.9
HLMG40-9	1720–1740	48.4	–	–	1/0.9
HLMG40-6	1840	17.2	2.5	–	1/3.8
HLJAK 1	1260	31.2	1.3	–	1/1.6
HLJAK 2	1270–1280	33.6	1.2	–	1/1.7
HLJAK 3	1290	29.9	–	–	1/2.1
HLJAK 4	1300	2.8	90.3	4.7	1/0.01
HLPET 1	1898 (?)	15.9	59.7	–	1/0.3
HLPET 2	1898	17.6	13.5	–	1/2.0
HLPET 4	1420	6.8	81.2	8.1	1/0.01
HLMAK 1	1275	3.0	72.5	13.4	1/0.04
HLMAK 2	1285	7.5	53.2	21.6	1/0.1
BA I	1194	7.7	60.5	3.2	1/0.4
BA II	1840	13.9	61.4	2.9	1/0.3
BA III	1900	12.8	37.6	2.6	1/0.9
BA IV	1404–1405	6.0	79.8	2.3	1/0.1
BA V	1792	5.1	82.5	–	1/0.1

HLMG40-1–HLMG40-10, HLMG42: samples form the secular building Mengstraße 40–42 in Lübeck.
HLJAK 1–HLJAK 4: samples from the Jakobikirche in Lübeck.
HLPET 1–HLPET 4: samples form the St. Petrikirche in Lübeck.
HLMAK 1 and HLMAK 2: mortars form the Marienkirche in Lübeck.
BAI–BAV: samples from the Bardowick Cathedral in Bardowick.
– : <0.01 wt.% .

House, which was at one time used as a military hospital. In Figure 17.3, a general overview of the whole complex is given.

The results from different secular buildings from Stralsund are given in Table 17.4. Stralsund is situated on the coast of the Baltic Sea vis-à-vis Rügen Island. Different secular buildings were sampled and the results are described in Table 17.4.

Table 17.2 Results of analyses of historic mortars from the St. Georgenkirche in Wismar (Germany).

Sample	Masonry built in:	Lime content [wt.%]	Soluble SiO_2 [wt.%] *	Content of important ions [wt.%] [**]						b/a value
				SO_4^{2-}	NO_3	Cl^-	Al^{3+}	Na^+	K^+	
WSG IVa	1230–1250	20.9	1.01	0.06	0.57	0.17	0.40	0.11	0.04	1/3.4
WSG IVb	1230–1250	45.5	0.76	0.08	1.76	0.55	0.46	0.32	0.11	1/1.2
WSG IVc	1230–1250	48.1	0.58	0.16	0.04	0.02	0.39	0.46	0.02	1/1.0
WSG VI B	1250–1260	45.0	0.94	0.06	1.62	0.48	0.80	0.32	0.15	1/1.2
WSG VII	1250–1260	63.4	1.20	0.10	3.92	1.62	0.48	1.05	0.42	1/0.6
WSG Ia	1290–1320	23.9	0.42	0.11	0.06	0.05	0.28	0.02	0.03	1/3.0
WSG Ib	1290–1320	48.3	0.43	0.07	0.08	0.10	0.35	0.04	0.02	1/1.0
WSG VIII	1290–1320	40.3	1.28	0.18	1.63	0.50	0.53	0.23	0.25	1/1.3
WSG X	1350–1360	40.7	1.47	0.04	0.07	0.05	0.48	0.04	0.02	1/1.5
WSG IIa	1404–1450	55.8	1.25	0.06	0.08	0.09	0.40	0.04	0.02	1/0.7
WSG IIb	1404–1450	77.1	2.05	0.45	3.88	0.86	0.68	0.78	0.28	1/0.3
WSG III B	1450–1500	30.2	2.85	0.39	0.52	0.18	0.92	0.26	0.14	1/2.3
WSG IX B	1460	39.1	0.80	0.03	0.18	0.26	0.49	0.18	0.05	1/1.6
WSG V	1500–1594	43.2	0.84	0.05	0.02	0.02	0.39	0.01	0.02	1/1.2

* treated with HCl and Na_2CO_3.
** cations were measured from the HCl-soluble portions and anions from the water-soluble portions of the mortars.
WSG: St. Georgenkirche, Wismar; WSG B: St. Georgenkkirche, Wismar, drilled sample.

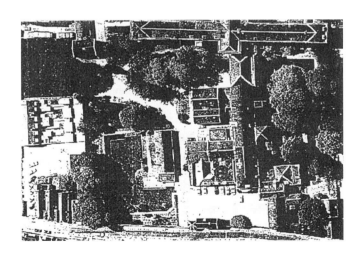

Figure 17.3 General view of the German House in Utrecht (The Netherlands).

Table 17.3   Results of analyses of historic mortars from Utrecht (NL).

Sample	Masonry built in:	Lime content [wt.%]	Soluble SiO$_2$ [wt.%] *	Content of important ions [wt.%] [**]						b/a value
				SO$_4^{2-}$	NO$_3^-$	Cl$^-$	Al^{3+}	Na$^+$	K$^+$	
U 2	15th century	22.9	0.46	0.04	0.01	0.01	0.06	0.01	0.01	1/3.2
U 3	1550	62.4	1.78	0.06	0.14	0.07	0.08	0.06	0.02	1/0.6
U 4	1525 ± 5a	36.2	0.71	0.03	0.01	0.04	0.13	0.05	0.03	1/1.7
U 5	14th century	26.7	0.57	0.02	0.23	0.07	0.08	0.05	0.02	1/2.6
U 6	16th century	45.9	0.68	0.04	0.41	0.16	0.10	0.13	0.04	1/1.1
U 7	18th century	41.8	0.46	0.10	0.04	0.14	0.04	0.08	0.02	1/1.3
U 8	15th century	28.9	0.40	0.10	0.38	0.13	0.06	0.17	0.04	1/2.3
U 9	1080	25.3	0.77	0.01	0.01	0.01	0.11	0.02	0.01	1/2.8
U 10	13th century	37.1	0.81	0.05	0.12	0.09	0.11	0.04	0.02	1/1.6
U 11	1414	33.6	0.66	1.21	0.94	0.49	0.11	0.33	0.11	1/1.7
U 18	1414	34.1	1.82	0.01	1.09	0.43	0.09	0.30	0.12	1/1.6
U 13	1756	39.2	1.74	0.12	0.61	0.46	0.79	0.39	0.06	1/1.2
U 15	1756	49.2	0.73	0.04	0.02	0.01	0.12	0.01	0.01	1/1.0
U 16	1756	46.2	0.76	0.13	0.02	0.05	0.12	0.21	0.02	1/1.1
U 14	1844–1845	44.8	2.10	0.34	0.07	0.09	1.18	0.20	0.04	1/1.0
U 17	1620	43.8	0.72	0.12	0.02	0.04	0.14	0.03	0.02	1/1.2
U 22	1620	35.5	0.93	0.04	0.01	0.02	0.07	0.05	0.01	1/1.7
U 19	1640	42.6	0.97	0.03	0.01	0.02	0.11	0.03	0.01	1/1.3
U 12	ca. 1300	28.6	0.64	0.04	0.55	0.11	0.08	0.05	0.04	1/2.3
U 24	ca. 1300	29.8	0.64	0.03	0.12	0.05	0.07	0.42	0.02	1/2.2
U 20	14th century	20.2	0.58	0.05	0.45	0.18	0.07	0.11	0.05	1/3.6

*   treated with HCl and Na$_2$CO$_3$.

** cations were measured from the HCl-soluble portions and anions from the water-soluble portions of the mortars.

U 2–U 8: samples from the secular building complex German House, which was used as a military hospital in former times; construction began in 1348.

U 9: mortar sample from the Marienkirche.

U 10: mortar from the secular building Oude Gracht 129.

U 11 and U 18: samples from the secular building Servestraat 8; both mortars were taken from the same building part.

U 13–U 16: mortars from the secular building Agnietenstraat 5; samples are from different parts of the building.

U 14: mortar sample from the secular building Mariaplaats 27.

U 17 and U 22: samples from the secular building Nieuwe Gracht 5; samples are from different parts of the building.

U 19: taken from the building Nieuwe Gracht 161.

U 12 and U 24: taken from the secular building Ganzemaarkt 24; mortars are from different parts of the building.

U 20: mortar sample from the secular building Markahoeck 10.

Table 17.4 Results of analyses of historic mortars from Stralsund (Germany).

Sample	Masonry built in:	Lime content [wt.%]	Soluble SiO$_2$ [wt.%] *	Content of important ions [wt.%] [**]						b/a value
				SO$_4^{2-}$	NO$_3^-$	Cl$^-$	Al^{3+}	Na$^+$	K$^+$	
ST 1	13th century	41.9	1.13	0.45	0.79	0.64	0.20	0.37	0.19	1/1.1
ST 2	14th century	39.6 (17.7)	n.m.	n.m.	0.24	0.22	0.75	0.01	0.01	1/0.8
ST 3	14th century	46.0	2.05	0.09	0.17	0.11	0.28	0.04	0.03	1/0.9
ST 4	16th–17th century	39.2	0.68	0.12	0.47	0.52	0.15	0.23	0.13	1/1.3
ST 5	1300–1350	26.5	0.55	0.07	1.33	0.41	0.10	0.25	0.18	1/2.3
ST 6	1300–1350	29.0	0.40	0.05	0.41	0.43	0.04	0.21	0.12	1/2.1
ST 7	1300–1350	24.7	0.35	0.06	1.11	0.31	0.04	0.13	0.10	1/2.6
ST 8	1300–1350	26.9	0.85	0.05	0.95	0.66	0.13	0.31	0.18	1/2.3
ST 9	1300–1350	30.1	0.37	–	0.63	0.55	0.05	0.23	0.15	1/2.0
ST 10	1300–1350	24.5	0.57	–	0.41	0.37	0.06	0.14	0.11	1/2.7
ST 11	1300–1350	32.0	0.59	0.04	0.74	0.33	0.10	0.11	0.14	1/1.8
ST 12	1300	37.5	1.14	0.12	0.26	0.10	0.59	0.03	0.02	1/1.4
ST 13	1300/1400	35.7	0.97	0.41	0.43	0.14	0.19	0.05	0.04	1/1.5
ST 14	1400	44.9	1.55	0.07	1.32	0.43	0.14	0.15	0.13	1/1.0
ST 15	14th century	47.5	0.52	0.07	0.02	0.01	0.16	0.02	0.04	1/1.0
ST 16	1354 d	35.1	0.46	0.01	0.04	0.12	0.18	0.04	0.03	1/1.7
ST 17	17th century	47.0	0.35	0.02	0.03	0.14	0.08	0.06	0.05	1/1.1
ST 18	17th century	73.9	0.38	0.03	0.10	0.31	0.14	0.04	0.08	1/0.3
ST 19	18th century	23.5	0.65	0.07	0.12	0.05	0.11	0.03	0.01	1/3.1
ST 20	1760/80	37.1	0.35	–	0.03	0.05	0.10	0.02	0.02	1/1.6
ST 21	18th century	31.2	0.68	–	0.04	0.06	0.20	0.02	0.02	1/2.1
ST 22	1354 d	37.9	0.76	0.05	0.22	0.13	0.20	0.06	0.04	1/1.5
ST 23	18th century	23.4	0.59	0.01	0.04	0.06	0.18	0.02	0.02	1/3.0
ST 24	1350	38.7	0.47	0.04	0.07	0.10	0.13	0.05	0.02	1/1.6

*   dissolved in HCl and Na$_2$CO$_3$.
** cations were measured from the HCl-soluble portion and anions from the water-soluble portion of the mortars.
– : <0.01 wt.%
d: dendrochronological age dating;
n.m.: not measured.
ST 1: sample from the townhall of Stralsund.
ST 2–ST 4: mortars from the secular building Mühlenstraße 5; the samples are from different parts of the building. (ST 2 contains 17.7 wt.% gypsum)
ST 5–ST 10: mortars taken from different parts of the secular building Schillstraße 37.
ST 11: taken from the secular building Papenstraße 10.
ST 11–ST 15: samples from the buildings Filterstraße 3a/2b.
ST 16–ST 24: samples from the secular building Mönchstraße 45; mortars were taken from different parts of the building.

RESULTS

Table 17.1 shows the results of analyses of historic mortars from buildings in Lübeck and Bardowick. The measured values listed in Tables 17.1–17.4 are not normalized to 100%.

A comparison of the analyses of the mortars from secular and religious buildings shows that mortars used for religious buildings often consist of gypsum, anhydrite, and lime. There is only one mortar (HLMG-40-5) from a secular building that contains a higher amount of gypsum and anhydrite. In the other mortars from secular buildings, only a small amount of gypsum was determined (HLMG40-1, HLMG40-4, HLMG40-6). In our opinion, this must be a secondary formation that could be a result of the enriched SO_2 content of the atmosphere.

The binder/aggregate values (b/a) of mortars, which contain gypsum and/or anhydrite as binder, are much higher than those for pure lime mortars, which means that the content of aggregate in gypsum/anhydrite mortars is much smaller (cf. HLJAK4, HLPET 4, HLMAK 1 and BA I to BA V).

In our opinion, the reason for using gypsum mortar for religious buildings is the initial strength that was needed for the construction of complicated parts of buildings, such as brick vaults or brick arches. Researchers in Italy have also found gypsum mortars in vaults of churches that are normally built up of lime mortar (Cioni 1991).

Another point of interest is that cracks in gypsum/anhydrite mortars mostly heal through crystallization of $CaCO_3$. Petrographic examinations frequently revealed this, especially in this type of mortar. An explanation cannot be offered at the moment. A modest atlas of photomicrographs of thin-sections of mortar samples including laboratory specimens and field specimens is presented in the Appendix 17.II.

Table 17.2 gives the results of the chemical and mineralogical analyses of the mortars from the St. Georgenkirche in Wismar. In general it can be said that all analyzed mortars from this building were made of lime; no gypsum or anhydrite was used as binder. These lime mortars contain different kinds of aggregates, i.e., quartz, feldspars, glauconite and sometimes shells. The b/a value differs from 1/0.3 to 1/3.4. If the mortars contain a high amount of lime (b/a =1/0.5 to 1/2.0) usually dry-slaked lime was used (Kraus et al. 1989). The results of microscopic investigations prove this. In Appendix 17.II, photomicrographs of mortars prepared with dry slaked lime as binder are shown.

A comparison of the analyses of samples WSG IIa and WSG IIb shows that these mortars are completely different, although both mortars were taken from the same part of the building. WSG IIa is an original joint mortar and WSG IIb is a restoration mortar that was used to fasten a wooden peg in the masonry. The biological decomposition of this wooden peg can be a possible explanation for the high amount of nitrate in the mortar. Some other samples from this building also show high amounts of nitrate (WSG IVb, WSG VI, WSG VII, WSG VIII), even in the absence of wooden pegs. An explanation for these high nitrate amounts can be that architects in former times used special kinds of nitrate-containing additives to optimize the properties of the material.

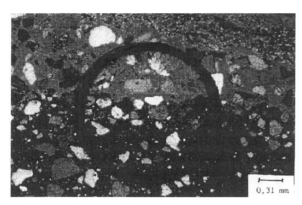

Figure 17.4   Marked contact mortar/brick (sample U 7; crossed nicols).

Another possibility is that this nitrate resulted from nitrate-producing bacteria. A contamination with bird droppings is a further explanation.

Table 17.3 shows the results of the analyzed mortars from secular buildings in Utrecht, Netherlands. Lime was used as binder for all mortars. The b/a values varied from 1/0.5 to 1/3.6 and the soluble SiO_2 content vary from 0.4 to 2.1. The SiO_2 content give hints of the degree of the purity of the lime used. If a mortar contains a high content of SiO_2 (U3, U 13, U 14 and U 18), the raw material may have contained hydraulic components.

A comparison of the samples U 15 and U 16 shows that both mortars consist of the same materials, because all values are very similar. This example shows that our analytical method works quite well (Appendix 17.I; Middendorf and Knöfel 1991).

Microscopic investigations have shown that the bonding between mortar and brick is not always satisfactory. On Figure 17.4, which was taken with a petrographic microscope using crossed nicols, the contact brick/mortar looks quite perfect, but using a SEM with a BSE detector (Figure 17.5) bonding failures are detectable. The pores and cracks that are seen on the contact mortar/brick will decrease the adhesion strength of the masonry.

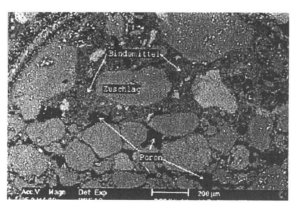

Figure 17.5   SEM photograph of the marked thin-section from Figure 17.4; sample U 7 (Bindemittel = binder; Zuschlag = aggregate; Poren = pores).

In Table 17.4 the results of the analyses of the mortars from secular buildings of Stralsund are listed. In general it can be said that all mortars, apart from ST 2, were mixed with lime. The aggregates used are quartz and feldspars, which partly differ in size and form. Sometimes glauconites and shells (see Appendix 17.II) are found. Generally, all mortars, apart from ST 3 and ST 12, have a lower SiO_2 content than the samples listed in Table 17.2 and Table 17.3. That means that the original material used had high purity. The higher degree of purity is also seen in the relative low contents of SO_4^{2-}, NO_3^- and Cl^- anions, because the measured values are in general lower than the values which we determined from all other samples. The mortars of Stralsund also have a higher content of aggregate than the other mortars determined in Utrecht, Wismar, Bardowick, and Lübeck.

Mortar sample ST 2 is the only one which contains gypsum in form of binder, but there is no explanation for the use of gypsum in this secular building. It is interesting that this mortar has a low content of aggregate. Mortar sample ST 3 has a high content of Mg^{2+} (not listed in Table 17.4), but the content of anions is very low. The Mg^{2+} content can be explained by a certain amount of dolomite in the limestone. Because dolomite is changed to MgO and CaO during the burning procedure, $MgCa(CO_3)_2$ is not detectable by using X-ray powder diffraction methods.

A comparison of the analyses of the mortars ST5 and ST 8 show that these mortars were made of the same raw materials. Microscopic investigations support this argumentation.

CONCLUSIONS

Mortar mixtures with gypsum and/or anhydrite were mostly used for construction of complex building parts of religious buildings, because a high initial strength of the mortars was needed there. Secular buildings were mostly constructed by using lime mortars.

The mortars used for religious buildings contain a higher amount of binder than those used for secular buildings. Microscopic investigations demonstrate that mortars containing a high amount of lime (b/a = 1/0.5 − 1/2.0) were usually made with dry slaked lime.

The analytical results suggest that it is possible that the raw materials for mixing the mortars were taken directly from the area around the building site. In Table 17.5 some possible raw material deposits and the analyzed buildings are listed.

To support our interpretations, we are analyzing mortars from the Nikolaikirche and St. Johanniskirche. Both buildings are situated in Lüneburg (Germany), a town 30 km southeast of Hamburg. The mortar samples taken from these religious buildings were mostly made of gypsum without any aggregate.

Table 17.5   Possible raw material deposits for buildings where mortar samples were taken.

Buildings	Possible raw material deposit
St. Georgenkirche, Wismar	limestone from Gotland
Cathedral of Bardowick, Bardowick	gypsum/lime raw material from Lüneburg
Stralsund	limestone from Rügen Island
Lübeck	gypsum/lime raw materials from Bad Segeberg

Our research has shown, that it is necessary to determine the compressive strength and the porosity of the historic mortars which were analyzed. These values are important for the preparation and investigation of laboratory-made mortars. Moreover, we would like to measure the adhesion strength between mortar and brick. Drilling cores from the masonry are needed for these measurements.

Given the analytical results, we shall be able to prepare laboratory-made mortars to restore the damaged parts of monuments. For this purpose we are developing mortar mixtures similar to historic ones for the restoration of masonry formerly made of gypsum mortar (see Chapter 27, this volume). In a further project, we have determined the age of lime mortars by using the radiocarbon method (Malone et al. 1980; Folk and Valastro 1976). The measurements were taken in 1992 in the laboratory of Prof. Dr. Geyh at the Bundesanstalt für Bodenforschung in Hannover (Germany), and the results are published in Middendorf (1994, 1996).

ACKNOWLEDGEMENTS

We wish to thank Dr. W. Duttlinger for critical and helpful comments as well as Mrs. Hof for her cooperation throughout the laboratory investigations. We are especially grateful to the curators of monuments from Lower Saxony, Lübeck, Stralsund, Wismar and Utrecht (NL), their help is giving us the opportunity to take mortar samples from historic monuments. We are grateful to the Umweltbundesamt Berlin for kindly giving financial support.

REFERENCES

Cioni, P. 1991. Volte bottili in Laterizio in Toscana: Loro Caratteristiche e Consoldidamento. In: Proc. 9th Intl. Brick/Block Masonry Conf., vol. 8, pp. 1523–1530. Berlin: Deutsche Gesellschaft für Mazerweksbau e.V.

Folk, R.L., and S Valastro. 1976. Successful technique for dating of lime mortar by carbon-14. *J. Field Archaeology* **3(2)**:203–208.

Kraus, K., S. Wisser, and D. Knöfel. 1989. Über das Löschen von Kalk vor der Mitte des 18. Jahrhunderts: Literaturauswertung und Laborversuche. *Arbeitsblätter für Restauratoren* **6(1)**:206–221.

Malone, C., S. Valastro, and A.G. Varel. 1980. Carbon-14 chronology of mortar from excavations in the medieval church of Saint-Benique, Dijon, France. *J. Field Archaeology* **7(3)**:329–343.

Middendorf, B. 1994. Charakterisierung historischer Mörtel aus Ziegelmauerwerk und Entwicklung von wasserresistenten Fugenmörtel auf Gipsbasis. Diss. zur Erlangung des Grades eines Doktors der Naturwissenschaften. Univ. Siegen.

Middendorf, B. 1996. Altersbestimmung historischer Kalkmörtel mittels der ^{14}C-Methode. In: Bauchemie Heute: Fakten, Modelle, Anwendungen. Festschrift zum 60. Geburtstag von Prof. Dr. D. Knöfel, ed. K.G. Böttger et al., pp. 165–172. Darmstadt: Diss.-Dr. Darmstadt (ISBN 3-931713-15-6).

Middendorf, B., and D. Knöfel. 1991. Investigations of mortars from medieval brick buildings in Germany. In: Proc. 13th Intl. Conf. on Cement Microscopy, pp. 304–323. Duncanville, TX: Intl. Cement Microscopy Association.

Scholz, W. 1984. Baustoffkenntnis, 10. Auflage, pp. 347–350. Düsseldorf: Werner Verlag.

APPENDIX 17.I: Method for the Chemical–Mineralogical Characterization of Mortars

General

The aim is to describe a simplified chemical and mineralogical analysis of historic mortars, using flow charts. The term "historic mortars" refers to all mortars used before the fabrication of Portland cement. Several attempts have been made to overcome difficulties in finding suitable ways of analyzing historic mortars and of obtaining relevant information from them (Dupas and Charola 1986; Jedrezejewska 1960; Wisser 1989).

Description of Method

The flow chart for the analytical method to characterize ancient mortars (Figure I.0) begins with "sampling." It is very important for successful work that the sampling of the mortars is done very carefully and exactly. Therefore, the location of the object must be recorded and photographs have to be taken. A description of the method should explain how the mortar was sampled; for example, in the form of drilling cores or if a hammer and a chisel were used. Moreover, the state of the mortar (in a good or bad condition; what kind of damage) must be recorded. After sampling, the mortar must be stored in plastic bags, or something equivalent, to restore the moisture.

The next steps take place in the laboratory, where the samples must be prepared for analysis. Normally, 150 g of mortar are used; however, if possible, one should try to work with more material, depending on the size of the aggregate. Preparation work is necessary, because any contamination by dirt or parts of brick or natural stone will invalidate the analysis. Usually a brush is used for the cleaning procedure of the mortar.

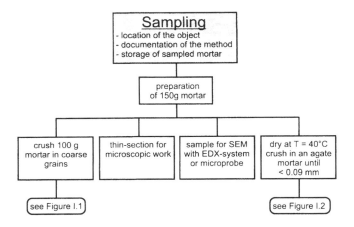

Figure I.0   Flow chart of the analytical method to characterize historic mortars.

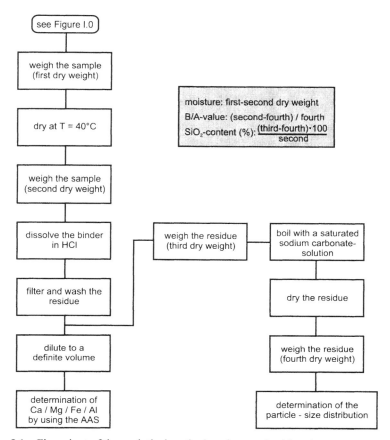

Figure I.1   Flow chart of the analytical method to characterize historic mortars.

From the 150 g of prepared mortar, ca. 100 g are crushed into coarse grains and the sample weighed (Figure I.2). This weight reflects the weight of the laboratory stored mortar. After this, the mortar has to be dried at a temperature of 40°C to constant weight. It is very important, that the temperature is less than 40°C, because at higher temperature gypsum will dehydrate to $CaSO_4 \cdot \frac{1}{2} H_2O$. When the mortar is dried it has to be weighed again and the difference between the first and second weight is the moisture content of the mortar.

From the dried mortar, the binder has to be dissolved in HCl or other solvents, depending on the aggregate. The residue must be filtered and washed, and the filtrate must be diluted to a definite volume. This filtrate is used for determination of cations, e.g., Ca^{2+}, Mg^{2+}, $Fe^{+2/+3}$ and or Al^{+3}, for which atomic adsorption spectroscopy (AAS) is used. The residue must be dried (third dry weight) and later boiled with a saturated, i.e., sodium carbonate solution. This procedure is used for the determination

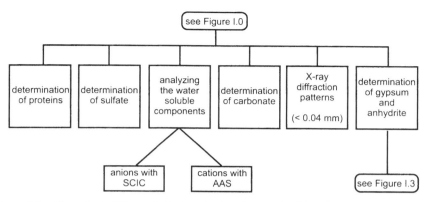

Figure I.2   Flow chart of the analytical method to characterize historic mortars.

of the soluble SiO_2 content. After this step, the sample has to be dried again and must be weighed for the fourth time. The residue is used for the determination of the particle-size distribution. To calculate the binder/aggregate value (b/a) and the content of soluble SiO_2 (wt.%), the equations in Figure I.1 have to be used.

In Figure I.0, three boxes have not yet been explained. For further determinations, ca. 50 g mortar are necessary. One piece of mortar is used for SEM analyses, normally in combination with an EDX system. Another possibility to get information about the microstructure of the binder, or of the reaction products of binder and bricks or natural stone, is to use an electron microprobe. A very powerful method to determine the origin of binder and aggregate is the use of a petrographic microscope. For the preparation of thin-sections, a mortar piece of 10 g is needed. In Appendix II, examples are shown. For the determination of CO_2, proteins, etc., ca. 30 g of mortar have to be dried at 40°C and then crushed in an agate mortar until the grain size is smaller than 0.09 mm. This powder is used for the determination of proteins (Figure I.2), sulfate, carbonate and the water soluble components, e.g., efflorescence. For X-ray diffraction patterns the powder has to be crushed into an agate mortar again, until the grain size is smaller than 0.04 mm. If there is not much material available, only a small amount of sample can be measured on a Si sample holder and X-rayed afterwards. X-ray diffraction patterns in combination with the information obtained from a petrographic microscope are very powerful for the identification of binder and/or aggregate. If the historic mortar was made of hydrated lime or dolomite, the analysis can be stopped here. For the determination of gypsum and/or anhydrite mortar, further investigations have to be made (Figure I.3).

Exactly 3 g of dried mortar will be burnt at a temperature of 350°C to constant weight. The burnt sample has to be weighed and the weight difference can be calculated as the water of crystallization for gypsum. The first branching of Figure I.3 shows that 5 g mortar must be dissolved in 80 ml of HCl and afterwards must be boiled for nearly two minutes. To this volume, 200 ml hot distilled water must be added and then

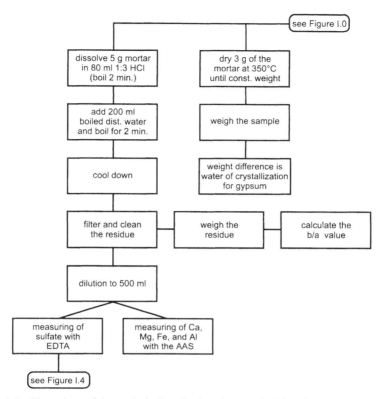

Figure 1.3 Flow chart of the analytical method to characterize historic mortars.

boiled afterwards for two minutes again. The hot solution has to cool down and must be filtered. It is possible to calculate the b/a value for a second time. The filtrate has to be diluted to a volume of 500 ml. For this filtrate, which contains the binder, the cations will be measured by using the AAS. EDTA is used to determine the sulfate content. This procedure is described in Figure I.4.

From the diluted volume, 5 ml have to be taken to dilute them with distilled water. The pH value has to be adjusted with KOH solution to 12. A small amount of indicator (1 g Calceine and 99 g KNO_3) must be put in and, by using an UV lamp, it should be titrated with EDTA until the color changes from green to orange. To precipitate the sulfate as $BaSO_4$, the pH value has to change to 1 or 2. Add a measured volume of a known $BaCl_2$ solution form to the sample and warm it up. The sulfate anions react with the barium cations to barium sulfate which has to be filtered. For further investigations, the filtrate is used. First the pH value has to be changed from acid to 12 by using a concentrated KOH solution. Now the content of barium can measured in the filtrate. If the barium content is known, the sulfate value can be calculated.

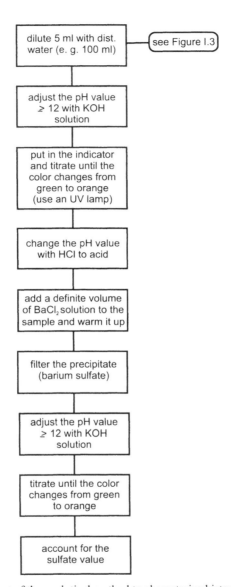

Figure I.4   Flow chart of the analytical method to characterize historic mortars.

If all determinations have been carried out as described in the flow charts, the mortar has been very well characterized. Generally it can be said that this method works quite well if the aggregate is not soluble in the solvent used, but if the binder and aggregate are of the same material, e.g., lime mortar with carbonate stones as aggregate, another way to determine the b/a value has to be found.

References

Dupas, M., and A.E. Charola. 1986. A simplified chemical analysis system for the characterisation of mortars. In: Proc. 2nd Intl. Kolloquium: Werkstoffwissenschaften und Bausanierung, pp. 309–312. Esslingen: Technischen Akademie.

Jedrezejewska, H. 1960. Old mortars in Poland: A new method of investigation. *Studies in Conservation* **5**:132–137.

Wisser, S. 1989. Historische und moderne Mörtel im Verbund mit Naturstein: Chemisch-mineralogische und mörteltechnische Eigenschaften. Freiburg (Breisgau): Hochschulverlag.

APPENDIX 17.II: Examples of Photomicrographs of Thin-Sections of Mortars

General

By using the petrographic microscope, mortars and aggregates can be characterized quite well. Some examples are given in the following microphotographs.

Part I: Historic Mortars

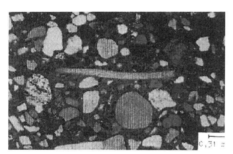

Figure II.1 Different kinds of aggregates in a lime mortar. In the middle of the photo is a small piece of a shell. Sample: WSG Ia.

Figure II.2 Residue of a dry-slaked lime in a lime mortar. Sample: WSG VII.

Figure II.3 Healed crack through crystallization of calcium carbonate in a gypsum/anhydrite mortar. Sample: Ba III.

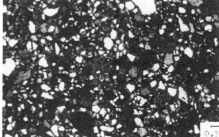

Figure 11.4 General view of mortar sample with fine-grained aggregate. Sample: ST5.

Part II: Different Aggregates Used in Historic Mortars

Figure II.5 Limestone from Öland with fossils.

Figure II.6 Limestone form Estland with fossils.

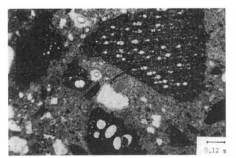

Figure II.7 Charcoal pieces used to darken the mortar.

Figure II.8 Piece of anhydrite in a gypsum matrix.

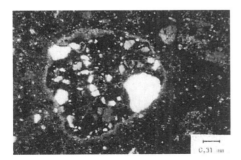

Figure II.9 Piece of brick in a gypsum mortar, with a reaction border.

Part III: Laboratory-made Mortars

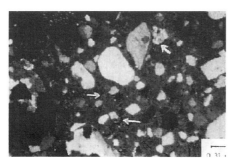

Figure II.10   Hydrated white lime with small cracks in the same binder (arrows).

Figure II.11   Gypsum mortar (binder is marked with arrow).

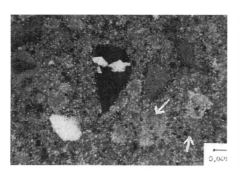

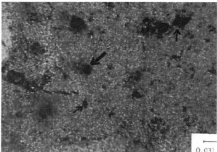

Figure II.12   Mixture of hydrated white lime and gypsum.

Figure II.13   Mixture of hydrated white lime and Portland cement with the typical interference color of calcite and residues of cement clinker (arrow).

18

Gypsum and Lime Mortars of Historic German Brick Buildings

Analytical Results and Restoration Material Requirements

B. MIDDENDORF [1, 2] and D. KNÖFEL [1]

[1]University of Siegen, Laboratory for Chemistry of Construction Materials (BCS),
Paul-Bonatz-Str. 9–11, 57068 Siegen, Germany
[2]Present address: University of Kassel, Department of Structural Materials,
Mönchebergstr. 7, 34109 Kassel, Germany

ABSTRACT

The chemical and mineralogical results of analyses of mortars from buildings in northern Germany are presented. Along with lime, gypsum-anhydrite-lime mortars have been used on the exterior walls of brick buildings for ca. 500 years and are still in good condition. Since gypsum has a non-negligible solubility in water (2.6 g/l), it is astonishing that these materials are still present in masonry joints. Mineralogical investigations are needed to determine the type of binder mixtures and which additives or retarders were used.

The reproduction method of mortars for restoration work, which in this case is restricted to joint mortar, is also discussed. The test results for selected hardened laboratory mortar mixtures, based on α- and/or β-hemihydrate and hydraulic or latent hydraulic additives, partly mixed with lime hydrate and retarders, are presented. The properties of hardened mortars studied are dynamic modulus of elasticity, hygric swelling and shrinking, compressive strength and bending tension strength as well as solubility in water.

INTRODUCTION

The use of gypsum as a building material has a long history. It was mostly used as a building or a statuary stone but was also used for the production of mortars, renderings, and undercoats. Recently, this traditional building material has been increasingly rejected in favor of hydraulic binders. Nevertheless, gypsum has considerable advantages over cement: a favorable production method with regard to energy, much quicker solidification, good adhesion to plaster supports, and simple workability. Its solubility in water is a disadvantage, which makes it very difficult to use for the exterior of a building. Within the framework of the NATO-CCMS project, investigations were carried out a great number of mortars partially taken medieval brick buildings. These were mainly used for the exterior of a building as joint and masonry mortar and are still well preserved. From a preservation point of view, these buildings should be restored with traditional building material; however, the main problem is to produce a gypsum mortar mixture with enough resistance to water to use on the exterior. For this reason, gypsum mortars are currently being investigated, since they have the necessary technological properties (Knöfel and Schubert 1990) and only a small degree of solubility in water. An effort is made to produce adequate mortar mixtures with the help of modern binder components. These have the necessary technological properties and can also be used for preservation purposes, since materials were used in former times are no longer available in the same quality. Another property to be considered when producing these mortars is the setting time, which can be influenced by adding different retarders.

CHARACTERIZATION OF HISTORIC MORTARS

Results and Discussion

All masonry or joint mortars investigated here are from nonsecular buildings in northern Germany and have been taken primarily from the exterior walls. In Tables 18.1–18.3, the age of the samples, the content of binder, the binder/aggregate ratio (b/a), and the compressive strength are listed, if it was possible to measure it. The chemical-mineralogical methods of investigation that were carried out have been described in detail elsewhere (Wisser and Knöfel 1987; Middendorf and Knöfel 1991), the determination of compressive strength of historical mortar samples has been done according to the method which has been developed by *ibac* at the Technical University of Aachen, Germany (Schubert and Schmidt 1990). The age given always refers to details from art historical evidence.

Table 18.1 gives part of the results of the chemical-mineralogical analyses as well as the compressive strength of the mortars from the St. Georgenkirche, Wismar (WSG). In general, it can be said that all analyzed mortars from this building were made of lime; neither gypsum nor anhydrite was used as a binder. These lime mortars contain different kinds of aggregates, e.g., quartz, feldspars, glauconite, and sometimes shells. The b/a value varies from 1/0.3 to 1/3.4. If the mortars contain a high amount of lime (b/a ≈ 1/0.5 to 1/2.0), then dry-slaked lime was usually used (Kraus et al. 1989), as shown by microscopic investigations. In all probability, lime for the production of these mortars was imported from Sweden, as microscopic investigations of gothlandic limes with unburnt pieces of lime from sampled mortars showed identical

Table 18.1 Characterization of historic lime mortars from the St. Georgenkirche in Wismar (Germany).

Sample	Masonry built in:	Lime [wt.%]	Soluble SiO$_2$ Content [wt.%]*	b/a value	β_{ST} [N/mm^2]
WSG Ia	1290–1320	23.9	0.42	1/3.0	n.m.
WSG Ib	1290–1320	48.3	0.43	1/1.0	7.4 ± 0.5
WSG IIa	1404–1450	55.8	1.25	1/0.7	n.m.
WSG IIb	1404–1450	77.1	2.05	1/0.3	7.6 ± 1.1
WSG IVa	1230–1250	20.9	1.01	1/3.4	6.5 ± 1.2
WSG IVb	1230–1250	45.5	0.76	1/1.2	6.5 ± 1.3
WSG IVc	1230–1250	48.1	0.58	1/1.0	8.0 ± 1.1
WSG V	1500–1594	43.2	0.84	1/1.2	3.1 ± 1.4
WSG VII	1250–1260	63.4	1.20	1/0.6	4.4 ± 0.8
WSG VIII	1290–1320	40.3	1.28	1/1.3	n.m.
WSG X	1350–1360	40.7	1.47	1/1.5	5.7 ± 0.6
WSG III B	1450–1500	30.2	2.85	1/2.3	n.m.
WSG VI B	1250–1260	45.0	0.94	1/1.2	n.m.
WSG IX B	1460	35.1	0.80	1/1.6	7.8 ± 1.5

WSG: St. Georgenkirche, Wismar   B: drilled sample
β_{ST}:   average compressive strength [N/mm^2]   *:   dissolved in HCl and Na$_2$CO$_3$
n.m.:   not measurable   b/a: binder/aggregate value (analyzed
                                                         values are not standardized to 100%)

results (Middendorf, unpublished). The content of SiO$_2$ opened with HCl and Na$_2$CO$_3$, an indicator for hydraulic components, varies between 0.42 wt.% and 2.85 wt.%. For a SiO$_2$ content greater than 1.5 wt.%, it can be assumed that marled limes were used as basic materials. A correlation of these values with the b/a values determined and the compressive strength measured cannot be carried out. The values for compressive strength are between 3.1 and 8.0 N/mm^2, which makes it possible to put them into mortar group II (DIN 1053). With regard to the results of porosity measurements (Table 18.4), total porosity varies between 32 and 42 vol.% and the average pore radius, with the exception of sample WSG IVa, is on a scale of about 0.5 μm. The main portion of pores can be found among the capillary pores (Romberg 1978); for the lime mortars investigated here, it is generally greater by factor of 2 than for the gypsum-anhydrite-lime mortars investigated. The content of air voids of lime mortars is distinctly smaller than for gypsum-anhydrite-lime mortars, which can explain different technological properties, e.g., the freeze-thaw resistance.

Table 18.2 Characterization of historic mortars from monuments in Lübeck and Bardowick (Germany).

Sample	Masonry built in:	Binder content [wt.%]			b/a value	β_{ST} [N/mm²]
		lime	gypsum	anhydrite		
HLJAK 1	1260	31.2	1.3	–	1/1.6	6.5 ± 1.6
HLJAK 2	1270–1280	33.6	1.2	–	1/1.7	6.7 ± 0.7
HLJAK 3	1290	29.9	–	–	1/2.1	8.0 ± 1.6
HLJAK 4	1300	2.8	90.3	4.7	1/0.01	20.7 ± 6.5
HLPET 1	1898 (?)	15.9	59.7	–	1/0.3	n.m.
HLPET 2	1898	17.6	13.5	–	1/2.0	n.m.
HLPET 4	1420	6.8	81.2	8.1	1/0.01	13.0 ± 3.3
HLMAK 1	1275	3.0	72.5	13.4	1/0.04	19.1 ± 0.7
HLMAK 2	1285	7.5	53.2	21.6	1/0.1	38.9 ± 14.5
BA I	1194	7.7	60.5	3.2	1/0.4	n.m.
BA II	1840	13.9	61.4	2.9	1/0.3	n.m.
BA III	1900	12.8	37.6	2.6	1/0.9	n.m.
BA IV	1404–1405	6.0	79.8	2.3	1/0.1	n.m.

HLJAK: Jakobikirche, Lübeck; HLPET: St. Petrikirche, Lübeck
HLMAK: Marienkirche, Lübeck; BA: Bardowick Cathedral, Bardowick
β_{ST}: average compressive strength [N/mm²]
–: content ≤ 0.01 wt.%
n.m.: not measurable
b/a: binder/aggregate value (analyzed values are not standardized to 100%)

Table 18.2 shows the results of analyses of historic mortars from religious buildings in Lübeck (HLJAK, HLPET, HLMAK) and Bardowick (BA). The b/a values of mortars containing gypsum, anhydrite, and lime as binder are much higher than those of pure lime mortars, which means that the content of aggregate in gypsum-based mortars is much smaller. Also, the small amounts of aggregate in the gypsum-based mortars must be "impurities" of the raw material, because these amounts of aggregates are too small to modify the technological properties of the mortars. No craftsman would use such small quantities of aggregate to modify the technological properties of mortar.

In our opinion, the reason for using gypsum mortar in nonsecular buildings involved the initial strength needed for the construction of complicated parts of buildings, i.e., vaults or arches.

With regard to compressive strength, the gypsum-based mortars have distinctly higher values than lime mortars. In general, one can claim that the higher the content of gypsum and/or anhydrite of the binder, the higher the compressive strength. However,

Table 18.3   Characterization of historic mortars from religious buildings in Lüneburg (Germany).

Sample	Masonry built in:	Binder content [wt.%]			b/a value	β_{ST} [N/mm²]
		lime	gypsum	anhydrite		
LN 1	1400–1447	4.0	88.7	1.2	1/0.05	12.8 ± 1.7
LN 2	19th century	10.6	–	–	1/6.5	5.4 ± 2.6
LN 3	1400–1447	2.8	94.6	0.5	1/0.01	5.0 ± 1.6
LN 4	1400–1447	8.3	86.7	2.8	1/0.01	45.4 ± 4.1
LN 5	19th century	11.7	–	–	1/6.3	n.m.
LN 6	1400–1447	3.1	94.2	0.9	1/0.005	28.7 ± 7.9
LN 7	1400–1447	7.9	88.9	2.0	1/0.002	31.9 ± 7.4
LJ 1	before 1450	4.6	91.3	1.6	1/0.009	19.0 ± 5.2
LJ 2	before 1450	4.1	83.7	2.9	1/0.008	27.0 ± 4.8
LJ 3	after 1430	6.9	89.5	0.6	1/0.01	15.5 ± 3.5
LJ 4	before 1450	4.9	86.5	0.6	1/0.08	12.1 ± 3.5
LJ 5	before 1450	4.8	81.4	2.4	1/0.115	n.m.
LJ 6	before 1450	2.8	84.9	4.0	1/0.08	15.8 ± 5.0
LJ 7	before 1450	5.7	77.6	3.6	1/0.13	16.7 ± 3.7
LJ 8	1850 (?)	10.8	31.3	–	1/1.3	19.0 ± 5.2
LJ 9	before 1450	5.4	88.1	4.8	1/0.002	25.4 ± 6.0

LN: Nikolaikirche, Lüneburg;   LJ: St. Johanniskirche, Lüneburg
β_{ST}:   average compressive strength [N/mm²]
-- :   content ≤ 0.01 wt.%
n.m.:   not measurable
b/a: binder/aggregate value (analyzed values are not standardized to 100%)

one has to consider that measurements of compressive strength for historic mortars usually prove rather faulty owing to the leveling of surfaces. Compressive strength could not be measured for the samples from Bardowick, because the pieces of mortar were too small for such measurements.

The results of the investigations for the historic mortar samples from Lüneburg are listed in Table 18.3. Samples labeled LN are from Nikolaikirche; LJ stands for samples taken from St. Johanniskirche. Interestingly, the results can be summarized in three groups. Mortars from the 15th century (LN 1, LN 3, LN 4, LN 6, LN 7, LJ 1-LJ 7, LJ 9) are nearly free of aggregates, and the binder was mainly produced of gypsum. The small content of anhydrite and lime certainly existed already in the basic material. The samples BA I and BA IV (see Table 18.2) show nearly identical results. One can claim that the same basic materials were used since the town of Bardowick is in the direct vicinity of Lüneburg. The mortars of the samples LJ 8, LJ 10, and LJ 11 have a higher content of aggregates and the binder was made of lime and gypsum. Parallels to the samples BA II and BA III (see Table 18.2) from Bardowick are also evident. Samples

Table 18.4 Results of mercury porosimetry data of historic mortars.

Sample	Total porosity [vol.%]	Content of air voids [vol.%]	Content of capillary pores [vol.%]	Content of gel pores [vol.%]	Average pore radius [µm]
WSG Ib	38.92	3.90 (10)*	33.84 (87)	1.18 (3)	0.4814
WSG IIa	34.27	4.18 (12)	29.12 (85)	0.97 (3)	0.4381
WSG IIb	38.24	4.53 (12)	32.64 (85)	1.07 (3)	0.4538
WSG IVa	32.27	4.63 (14)	26.66 (83)	0.98 (3)	1.0387
WSG IVb	41.74	4.14 (10)	36.91 (88)	0.69 (2)	0.5480
WSG IVc	40.54	3.27 (8)	35.86 (88)	1.41 (3)	0.4611
WSG V	38.10	4.29 (11)	32.70 (86)	1.11 (3)	0.4173
WSG VII	39.05	4.63 (12)	33.92 (87)	0.49 (1)	0.4013
WSG X	37.11	4.61 (12)	31.54 (85)	0.95 (3)	0.5692
HLJAK 4	35.02	5.61 (16)	27.69 (79)	1.73 (5)	2.0117
HLMAK 1	23.12	5.88 (25)	15.91 (69)	1.33 (6)	1.2264
HLMAK 2	27.81	4.37 (16)	22.96 (83)	0.48 (2)	1.6368
HLPET 4	27.31	5.61 (21)	20.84 (76)	0.86 (3)	1.1852
BA I	13.86	4.39 (32)	8.54 (62)	0.93 (7)	1.4238
BA II	23.54	5.40 (23)	17.48 (74)	0.67 (3)	0.7591
BA III	16.38	4.34 (26)	11.03 (67)	1.00 (6)	0.4117
BA IV	24.95	6.55 (26)	17.89 (72)	0.51 (2)	1.5816
BA V	23.27	4.91 (21)	17.69 (76)	0.67 (3)	1.1702
LN 1	24.76	6.69 (27)	17.55 (71)	0.52 (2)	2.3617
LN 2	27.42	5.46 (20)	16.79 (61)	5.17 (19)	0.4245
LN 3	36.81	5.64 (15)	30.94 (84)	0.23 (1)	2.6804
LN 4	18.68	5.51 (29)	11.89 (64)	1.28 (7)	1.1822
LN 6	26.87	6.16 (23)	19.70 (73)	1.01 (4)	1.6610
LN 7	20.93	5.49 (26)	14.44 (69)	1.00 (5)	1.8119
LJ 1	35.04	7.36 (21)	27.41 (78)	0.26 (1)	2.6060
LJ 2	21.62	6.12 (28)	14.85 (69)	0.64 (3)	2.4765
LJ 3	25.13	5.38 (21)	19.03 (76)	0.73 (3)	0.4175
LJ 4	29.36	6.54 (22)	22.39 (76)	0.43 (1)	2.8014
LJ 6	19.08	6.17 (32)	12.21 (64)	0.70 (4)	1.8265
LJ 7	24.47	7.99 (33)	15.40 (63)	1.08 (4)	3.9739
LJ 8	35.14	6.21 (18)	28.01 (80)	0.92 (3)	1.9174
LJ 9	30.76	6.87 (22)	23.40 (76)	0.50 (2)	2.6938
LJ 10	37.44	4.33 (12)	31.85 (85)	1.25 (3)	1.1885

WSG: St. Georgenkirche, Wismar   HLJAK: Jakobikirche, Lübeck
HLMAK: Marienkirche, Lübeck   HLPET: St. Petrikirche, Lübeck
BA: Bardowick Cathedral, Bardowick   LJ: St. Johanniskirche, Lüneburg
* Numbers in parentheses indicate % of total porosity.

LN 2 and LN 5 are identical lime mortars, which can be proved by chemical analysis and microscopic investigations.

The compressive strengths (see Tables 18.2, 18.3) depend on the binder used and on the b/a value. The corresponding measured values are on the same level as the compressive strengths of historic bricks (see Franke and Schumann, Chapter 4, this volume).

A comparison of the results of mercury porosimetry shows that the average pore radius is larger in gypsum-anhydrite-lime mortars than in pure lime mortars (see Table 18.4) due to the higher content of air voids (by a factor 1.5). The content of capillary pores is smaller in gypsum-anhydrite-lime mortars than in pure lime mortars. Individual interpretations of samples are impossible, since the conditions for the mortars during the period of time between working and sampling are unknown, i.e., one does not know, for example, the extent to which the mortar structure was altered by rising moisture or if the binder of the joint mortars was washed out by precipitation. However, some results show that the structure of historic gypsum-based mortars has become more compact over time, owing to a recrystallizing process, which in our opinion results in a higher resistance to solubility caused by moisture, as the surface open to attack is reduced by these processes. Observations of thin-sections and with a scanning electron microscope for selected mortar samples also show that a healing of cracks can occur in gypsum mortars and that surfaces can protect themselves against harmful influence of penetrating water by crystallization of sinter incrustation. In Figure 18.1, a laboratory-made pure gypsum mortar is shown. The shape of the gypsum crystals is monoclinic prismatic and, in general, the crystals are small. In comparison, Figure 18.2 shows a historic gypsum mortar. It can be seen that the crystals are much more compact than those of the laboratory-made gypsum mortar and that the crystals have rounded edges caused by the attack of water.

Radiocarbon determinations of the lime mortars age have shown that this method cannot be taken as a standard (Geyh 1991; van Strydonck et al. 1983; Middendorf 1996). From the point of view of preservatation, the measurements lack exactitude, and the preparation of samples is time consuming as well as expensive. The age of the samples we used had already been characterized extremely well by curators of historical monuments, and these were used to study the applicability of the measuring method in the field of building chemistry. Ages determined by nuclear chemistry turned out to be slightly younger than the ones given by the curators, which can be explained by the slow carbonatization of the lime.

REQUIREMENTS FOR ADAPTED RESTORATION MATERIALS

We are trying to produce gypsum mortar mixtures resistant to water, based on the chemical, mineralogical, and technological test results described above. These mixtures are to be used as joint mortars for the preservation of monuments, especially for restoration measures on the exteriors of damaged buildings. These mortars produced

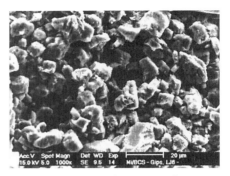

Figure 18.1 Set and hardened gypsum, prepared from pure β-hemihydrate. The crystals are fine grained with a needle-like monocline prismatic shape. Width of the figure is 123 µm.

Figure 18.2   SEM photograph of a historic gypsum-lime-anhydrite mortar. The gypsum crystals are much more compact than those shown in Figure 18.1 because of the recrystallization processes caused by attacks of water.

with gypsum must have properties compatible with the historic mortars, which can never be completely removed from the joints, and must be adapted to the masonry.

Basic Materials

As can be seen from Table 18.5, α- and β-hemihydrate were mainly used for the production of gypsum mortar mixtures. Blastfurnace slag sand (BSS) and powdered trass (TRP) have been added as latent hydraulic binders, and ordinary Portland cement (OPC) was added as hydraulic binder. Furthermore, tests were done for hydrated white lime (HWL), hydrated hydraulic lime (HHL) and anhydrite (AN). Citric acid (cit) or L(+)-tartaric acid (tart) were added as retarders, each with 0.1 wt.%, to the α- or β-hemihydrate in order to optimize the workability time. Furthermore, gypsum mixtures with tartaric acid and a hydrophobic agent (hyd) were prepared to decrease the water solubility of the mortars. The prepared mixtures can be found in Table18.5 ; the figures in brackets give the percentage of each binder.

Results and Discussion

The mortar mixtures in Table 18.5 have been investigated thoroughly. For present purposes, investigations were restricted to the measurements of compressive strength, swelling and shrinking while setting, water solubility and the dynamic modulus of elasticity.

As can be seen in Table 18.5, gypsum mortars produced with α-hemihydrates (α-HH), obtained in an autoclave procedure, have the highest compressive strength, the highest modulus of elasticity, and a water solubility which is lower by nearly 40% than a mortar made of pure β-hemihydrate (β-HH). The compact structure between individual gypsum crystals made of α-HH, which are quite coarse, prismatic or flat, is most likely responsible for this. Moreover, α-HH mortars show less porosity than

Table 18.5 Technological properties and resistance to water of selected gypsum mortar mixtures.

Trial Mixture	E-modulus after 28 d [kN/mm²]	β_{ST} after 28 d [N/mm²]	Swelling / shrinking [mm/m]		Water solubility standardized to β-HH [%]
α-HH	21.35	43.25	+0.60	−0.60	60.3
β-HH	9.26	15.55	+0.27	−0.15	100.0
β-HH+cit	7.55	6.69	+0.17	−0.21	85.3
β-HH+tart	10.29	22.95	+0.13	−0.20	79.8
β-HH+1.0 wt.% hyd+tart	6.58	12.25	+0.12	−0.15	55.6
β-HH+2.0 wt.% hyd+tart	6.43	11.98	+0.10	−0.16	47.0
β-HH/AN(80/20)	11.06	23.40	+0.98	−0.22	164.8
β-HH/AN(80/20)+tart	12.78	29.63	+0.15	−0.20	87.5
β-HH/HHL(80/20)+tart	4.53	7.89	+0.07	−0.14	49.7
β-HH/HHL(70/30)+tart	3.62	5.84	+0.07	−0.19	32.3
β-HH/α-HH/HHL(40/40/20)+tart	10.15	19.97	+0.02	−0.16	34.2
β-HH/BSS/HHL(70/25/5)+tart	9.85	21.35	+0.08	−0.26	28.9
β-HH/BSS/HHL(60/35/5)+tart	11.41	23.29	+0.24	−0.29	23.9
β-HH/TRP/HHL(70/25/5)+tart	5.97	10.16	+0.07	−0.16	101.7
β-HH/TRP/HHL(60/35/5)+tart	7.04	12.20	+0.22	−0.50	59.5
β-HH/OPC/HWL(70/25/5)+tart	8.46	17.38	+0.09	−0.55	32.5
β-HH/OPC/HWL(60/35/5)+tart	8.91	19.89	+0.18	−0.79	13.8

α-HH: α-hemihydrate
BSS: blastfurnace slag sand
AN: anhydrite
HWL: hydrated white lime
hyd: hydrophobic agent
β_{ST}: average compressive strength
E-modulus: dynamic modulus of elasticity

β-HH: β-hemihydrate
TRP: powdered trass
HHL: hydrated hydraulic lime
OPC: Portland cement PC 35 L NW/HS (DIN 1164)
cit: citric acid (0.1 wt.% to β-HH)
tart: tartaric acid (0.1 wt.% to β-HH)

those made of β-HH, which also indicates a growing density of the structure, causing a reduction of the surface, which explains the better water resistance.

The addition of 0.1 wt.% citric acid to β-HH in order to slow down the setting process causes a distinct coarsening of the structure of the dihydrate crystals that were formed. This explains a decrease in the modulus of elasticity and compressive strength, compared to mortars made of pure β-HH (see Figure 18.3). Water resistance is only slightly better than in mortars made of pure β-HH. The degree of swelling and shrinking is also a little smaller than in mortars made of pure β-HH, which can also be explained by a coarsening of the structure.

Figure 18.3   Set and hardened gypsum, prepared of β-hemihydrate containing 0.1 wt.% citric acid. The crystals are much larger than those prepared from pure β-hemihydrate (see Figure 18.1). Width of figure is 123 μm.

Figure 18.4   Set gypsum, prepared of pure β-hemihydrate containing 0.1 wt.% tartaric acid. The characteristic features are determined by small and flat gypsum crystals. The porosity is much smaller than those of mortars prepared from pure β-hemihydrate.

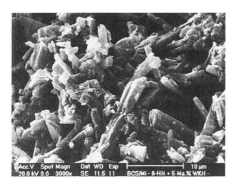

Figure 18.5   Set and hardened gypsum-lime mixture, prepared of 95 wt.% β-hemihydrate and 5 wt.% hydrated white lime. This SEM photo shows that many interstices are filled with lime.

Figure 18.6   Gypsum mixture, prepared from β-hemihydrate, 0.1 wt.% tartaric acid, and 2 wt.% of a hydrophobic agent. The gypsum crystals lost their typical needle-like shapes and their size increased. This hydrophobic protection is only temporary, because of the many cracks.

The addition of 0.1 wt.% tartaric acid as a retarder to β-HH causes a slight coarsening of the structure (see Figure 18.3). The simple addition of tartaric acid increases the compressive strength, the modulus of elasticity, and the water resistance of the mortar. A comparison of the samples β-HH/AN(80/20) and β-HH/AN(80/20)+tart shows this very distinctly. The value for the swelling of gypsum mortar also decreases when tartaric acid is added. A slower setting, indicating an orderly growth of crystals, could be a reason for this. The same effect can also be seen for the addition of citric acid.

Mixtures of β-HH and hydrated hydraulic lime (HHL) have a smaller modulus of elasticity and a smaller compressive strength. The more HHL is added to the mixtures, the better the water resistance of the set mortar will be, which is demonstrated by the comparison of the mixtures β-HH/HHL(80/20)+tart and β-HH/HHL (70/30)+tart. The lime gets into the interstices of the dihydrate crystals and reduces the surface, which can be made partly soluble (see Figure 18.5). When comparing the mixtures β-HH/HHL(80/20)+tart to β-HH/α-HH/HHL(40/40/20)+tart, the sample with α-HH distinctly shows a better resistance to water. A combined addition of BSS and HHL considerably increases the modulus of elasticity, the compressive strength as well as the resistance to water of the mortars. Results for swelling and shrinking are also sufficient for use as masonry mortar. Comparisons with gypsum mortar mixtures containing TRP show that they have a distinctly smaller modulus of elasticity and compressive strengths as well as a high solubility in water; thus, they are not suitable for use on outside parts of a building. A slight increase of compressive strength and of resistance to water as well as a slight reduction of the modulus of elasticity with regard to mortars made of β-HH has to be noted for the combined use of OPC, HWL, and tartaric acid. These mortars show only a little swelling; however, shrinkage is distinctly higher than for other mortars investigated. The stronger shrinking might result from adding of OPC, the hydration of which starts again owing to storage in a damp atmosphere (20°C, 95% RH).

Mixtures of β-HH, tartaric acid, and a hydrophobic agent have a slightly smaller modulus of elasticity and a smaller compressive strength than mortars prepared from pure β-HH. The more hydrophobic agent has been added to the mixture, the better the water resistance of the set mortar will be, which is demonstrated by the comparison of the mixtures β-HH+1.0 wt.% hyd+tart and β-HH+2.0 wt.% hyd+tart. The hydrophobic agent forms a thin coating over the dihydrate crystals and prevents the solution of these crystals in water. This is, however, only a temporary coating because the coating gets cracked during the setting period. Through these cracks water can attack the dihydrate crystals and dissolve the mortar (see Figure 18.6).

SUMMARY

One can say that lime and/or gypsum-anhydrite-lime mortars, which differ distinctly in their technological properties, were used for the nonsecular brick buildings in northern Germany, depending on the available raw material deposits. The question remains: which additives were used in former times to make the gypsum-based mortar more workable and more resistant to water. Investigations of mortars produced in the laboratory are attempting to solve this problem.

We think that further optimizing water-resistant gypsum mortar mixtures, based on β-HH and α-HH with the agents blast furnace slag sand, ordinary Portland cement and hydrated hydraulic lime, holds the most promise for use on the exterior of buildings. Mixtures of different additives and also aggregates are used to optimize technological properties such as compressive and flexural strength, modulus of elasticity, hygric swelling, and shrinking.

ACKNOWLEDGEMENTS

We wish to thank Mrs. I. Hommel and Mr. Dipl.-Labchem. A. Zöller for their support during the experimental investigations. Moreover, we are indebted to the Umweltbundesamt in Berlin for kindly giving financial support to this research project.

REFERENCES

Geyh, M.A. 1991. Die ^{14}C-Methode – Altersbestimmung mit Problemen. In: Berichte zur Denkmalpflege in Niedersachsen, 4/91, pp. 135–138.

Knöfel, D., and P. Schubert. 1990. Zur Beurteilung von Mörteln für die Instandsetzung von Mauerwerk. *Bautenschutz + Bausanierung* 13:10–14, 15–20.

Kraus, K., S. Wisser, and D. Knöfel. 1989. Über das Löschen von Kalk vor der Mitte des 18.Jahrhunderts-Literaturauswertung und Laborversuche. In: Arbeitsblätter für Restauratoren, pp. 206–221, Heft 1, Gruppe 6.

Middendorf, B. 1996. Altersbestimmung historischer Kalkmörtel mittels der ^{14}C-Methode. In: Bauchemie heute: Fakten, Modelle, Anwendungen; Festschrift zum 60. Geburtstag von Prof. Dr. D. Knöfel, ed. K.G. Böttger et al., pp.165–172. Darmsadt: DDD, Diss.-Dr. ISBN 3-931713-15-6.

Middendorf, B., and D. Knöfel. 1991. Investigations of mortars from medieval brick buildings in Germany. In: Proc. 13th Intl. Conf. on Cement Microscopy, pp. 304–323. Duncanville, TX: Intl. Cement Microscopy Association.

Romberg, H. 1978. Cement Steinporen und Betoneigenschaften. *Beton-Information* 5:50–55.

Schubert, P., and S. Schmidt. 1990. Bestimmung der Druckfestigkeit des Mörtels im Mauerwerk. *ibac* Kurzbericht 28, 3/90. Aachen: Technical University.

van Strydonck, M., M. Dupas, and M. Dauchot-Dehon. 1983. Radiocarbon dating of old mortars. In: Council of European Study Group on Physical, Chemical and Mathematical Techniques – Applied to Archaeology, vol., 8, pp. 337–843. Rixensart, Belgium: PACT.

Wisser, S., and D. Knöfel. 1987. Untersuchungen an historischen Putz- und Mauermörteln, Teil 1: Analysengang. *Bautenschutz + Bausanierung* 10:124–126.

19

Characterization of Mortars and Plasters from Historic Monuments in Turkey

A. GÜLEÇ

Central Laboratory for Restoration and Conservation, Eski Darphane,
Sultanahmet, Istanbul, Turkey

ABSTRACT

The chemical, physical, and petrographic properties of mortars and plasters of three historic monuments in Turkey – a Roman Bath at Ulnus (Ankara), Tahtakale Bath (Istanbul), and Esekapý Madrasa at Koca Mustafa Paþa (Istanbul) – were characterized to provide necessary data to determine the criteria for the requirements of mortars and plasters for restoration of these monuments.

INTRODUCTION

Mortars and plasters are important components of historic monuments. In addition to their structural functions, they also give information about the historic development of a building.

The conservation and restoration of historical monuments require detailed information about the original materials and the materials used in repairs. A correct characterization of mortars and plasters can only be accomplished through interdiciplinary studies, which should include chemical, physical, petrographical, and mineralogical examination of the samples.

Although there is no standard method of analysis, chemical characterization of the original mortars and plasters has been made possible, to an appreciable extent, by analytical techniques. The techniques to determine the amounts of major components of mortars and plasters have been discussed by Jedrezjewska (1960, 1967, 1981), Cliver (1974), and Stewart and Moore (1981). Binding fraction, to calculate the degree of hydrolic properties of mortars and plasters, has been studied by Dupas (1981). In addition, quantitative and qualitative analyses of mineralogical species and soluble salts in the mortars and plasters have been studied with instrumental (XRD, SEM, IR, AA, etc.) and petrographic methods (Charola 1984; Arnold 1984; Tabasso and Sammuri 1984).

Characterization of the physical properties of mortars and plasters is influenced by the total porosity, pore-size distribution and density, and can be studied using several methods (Fitzner 1988; ASTM 1980).

However, physico-mechanical characterization of old mortars and plasters has been restricted due to the difficulty of obtaining samples of adequate size from the monuments (Stewart and Moore 1981). Therefore, mechanical strength measurement of old mortars and plasters is very rare. Massazza and Pezzuoli (1981) reported that the measurement of hardness also gives some idea about mechanical strength. Flexibility and adhesion are important physico-mechanical properties for restorers who want to prepare suitable mortars and plasters for historic monuments (TS 24 1985).

Since a wide range of analytical techniques and testing methods are available for the examination of mortars and plasters, it is difficult to compare the data from different researchers. Several attempts have been made to standardize the methods. The available standard methods are designed for modern mortars and plasters (Scott 1956; ASTM 1980) and neglect information required to characterize older ones.

The present study deals with the identification of mortars and plasters from three historical monuments: a Roman Bath at Ulnus, Tahtakale Bath, and Esekapý Madrasa (ancient school), both in Istanbul.

The Roman Bath (RB) at Ulus, in Ankara was first excavated by Prof. Mahmut Akok, between 1940–1952. The ruins are from the Frigian and Roman periods with a few repairs from the Byzantine and Seljuk periods. After excavation, the ruins were restored by strengthening and capping the wall with mortar and plaster. Since then it has been used as an open air museum.

Tahtakale Bath (TB) is located at Eminönü, in Istanbul. Although it does not have an inscription, it was registered in the Waqfiyya (foundation deed) of Mehmet the Conqueror in 1489, and therefore it was probably constructed between 1453–1489 in the Byzantine harbor of Nerion, near the sea walls (Konuþur 1985). In 1660 and 1688 it was partially burnt. The fire of 1926 was hazardous for the frigidarium of the men's division and for the caldarium of the ladies division. After the first decade of the 19th century, it was no longer used as a bath and was converted to a warehouse. The original plan of the building was altered due to the new functions. The ladies division was especially changed; parts of its walls and domes were dismantled. The men's division, however, was not altered and remained well conserved. The domes were one or two bricks thick with respect to the span. The mortar found on the domes and sawtooth frieze of the drums gives evidence that the original domes were covered with roof tiles.

Esekapý Madrasa (EKM) is located at Koca Mustafa Paþa, in Istanbul. It was registered in the Waqfiyya of the Ýbrahim Pasha, who was the Vizier (minister) to Süleyman the Magnificent in 1560 (Ahunbay 1988). It was constructed after 1560 near the Ýsa Gate of the land walls. Orignally, EKM was an old Byzantine church. It was, however, later converted to a mosque, and the madrasa was added by the famous architect Sinan. After its destruction in the 1894 earthquake (Müller-Wiener 1977), the madrasa was not restored. The porticoes, present up until 1930, were completely lost through lack of maintenance. The classrooms with domes and the mosque without any roof are still present.

Sampling and Visual Examinations

The sampling of mortars and plasters was carried out at different points of the monument to show the similarities and differences in the characteristics of the materials. Using these samples, a statistical analysis of the materials of a monument can be performed and the relationship of the material properties and building technology can be established.

The number and size of the samples depend on the condition of the monument. If the monument is in the process of being restored, many as well as quite large-sized samples can be taken, as, e.g., in TB. In the other cases, e.g., EKM and RB, the number and size of the samples are limited. All total, 79 samples were taken from TB, 47 samples from EKM, and 19 samples from RB. Locations of all samples were listed on-site.

Before exposing the samples to chemical, mineralogical, or other analytical investigation, they were examined for color, presence of vegetable fibers or any other visible organic materials, and nature of the aggregates (color, size, amount). Representative results of visual properties of 40 samples of TB, 30 samples of EKM, and all samples of RB are given in Tables 19.1, 19.2, and 19.3.

Petrographical Examinations

Thin-section studies were carried out by using a "James Swift" polarizing microscope to identify the minerals. Photographs were taken with an "Olympus OM-1" camera.

Chemical Examinations

Calcium carbonate content, ignition loss, and moisture absorption capacity of the samples were determined by calcination. Approximately 500 mg (with 0.10 mg precision) of finely ground sample was heated at 105°C, 550°C, and 1050°C for 2, 1, and 0.5 hours, respectively; after cooling, they were weighed for each case. From the weight differences, percent of moisture absorption, ignition loss at 550°C and carbonate content of the sample were calculated. The results are given Tables 19.1, 19.2, and 19.3.

The quantitative analyses of some ions of the selected samples were carried out with "GBC-903" model single beam AA spectrophotometer. Two samples of each, finely ground and dried at 105°C, were weighed between 50 to 150 mg, up to 0.10 mg precision. The first series of these samples was treated with distilled water and kept in a water bath for an hour. The second series was treated with a few milliliters of concentrated hydrochloric acid. After completion of the reactions, distilled water was added, and they were kept in a water bath for an hour. Both series were filtered, washed, and distilled water was added to bring the volume to 100 ml.

Table 19.1 Visual and calcination analyses of Roman Bath samples.

No	Sample Type	Color	Size	Aggregate Type	Amount	Organic Material	Binder Strength	% CaCO$_3$
1	P	R	F	B	VL	–	W	31.86
2	M	Pi	C	S+B	VL	–	VW	31.45
3	M	R-Pi	F	B+S	VL	–	W	26.05
4	P	R-Pi	F	B+S	VL	–	St	29.07
5	M	DG	VF	S	VL	–	VSt	21.82
6	M	Wh	F	S	VL	–	VSt	18.18
7	P	Pi	C	S+B	L	–	W	36.10
8	P	G	C	S	L	–	W	46.94
9	M	G	F	S	VL	–	St	19.84
10	P	Pi	C	S+B	VL	–	W	28.13
11	M	Pi	C	S+B	VL	–	W	21.27
12	P	Y-Wh	C	S	VL	–	St	18.36
13	M	Y-Wh	C	S	VL	–	St	25.04
14	M	R-Pi	F	B+S	VL	–	St	23.67
15	M	Y-Wh	C	S	VL	–	St	30.27
16	M	Y-Wh	C	S	VL	–	St	22.46
17	M	G	F	S	VL	–	W	26.85
18	P	G	F	S	VL	–	VSt	26.09
19	P	G	C	S	VL	–	VSt	18.33

Note: P: plaster; M: mortar; Pi: pink; R: red; G: grey; Wh: white; Y: yellow; D: dark; C: coarse; F: fine; B: brick; S: sand; L: large; Sm: small; W: weak; St: strong; T: vegetable fibers; V: very; w: wall; b: basement; d: dome.

The first series was examined qualitatively for soluble salts. The quantitative analysis of Na$^+$, K$^+$, and Mg^{2+} for both series was carried out by AA spectrophotometry.

Tests for proteins and saponifying oil materials have been made on untreated samples, but none of these organic materials were found. The only organic materials found were visible vegetable fibers in various lengths and amounts.

PHYSICAL EXAMINATION

Porosity of selected samples was measured with high pressure mercury porosimetry, after the samples were dried at 50°C. The samples were not large enough to conduct mechanical tests, such as compressive strength or adhesion.

Table 19.2 Visual and calcination analyses of Esekapý Madrasa samples.

No	Sample Type	Color	Size	Aggregate Type	Amount	Organic Material	Binder Strength	% CaCO$_3$
1	Mw	R	F	B+S	VL	–	W	22.89
2	Mw	Pi	F	B+S	VL	–	W	29.50
3	Mw	Pi	F	B+S	L	–	W	43.66
4	Mw	R-Pi	F	B+S	L	–	W	32.47
5	Mw	Wh	F	S	Sm	–	VW	43.69
6	Mw	Y-Wh	C	S	L	–	W	42.46
7	Mw	R	C	B	L	T	W	49.64
8	P	Wh	F	S	VSm	–	W	81.23
9	P	R	C	B+S	L	T	W	32.57
10	Mw	Pi	VF	S+B	L	–	VW	47.08
11	Mw	Pi	VF	S+B	L	–	VW	53.30
12	Mw	Wh	F	S	L	–	VW	37.29
13	Mw	Pi-Wh	F	S+B	L	–	VW	49.02
14	Mw	R	C	B+S	L	–	W	40.52
15	Mw	Wh	C	S	L	–	VW	43.44
16	P	Wh	VF	S	VSm	–	W	82.88
17	P	Pi	C	S+B	L	–	VW	42.66
18	Mw	Wh	C	S	L	–	VW	53.21
19	Md	Pi-Wh	C	S	L	–	St	37.65
20	Md	Pi-Wh	C	S	L	–	St	43.07
21	Md	Pi-Wh	C	S	L	–	St	42.83
22	P	Wh	VF	S	VSm	–	W	82.08
23	P	R	C	B	L	–	W	38.82
24	Mw	R	C	B	L	–	VSt	38.89
25	P	Wh	F	S	VSm	T	W	80.85
26	P	Pi-Wh	C	S	L	–	W	42.01
27	Mw	Wh	F	S	L	–	W	46.08
28	P	Wh	VF	S	VSm	T	W	83.17
29	P	R	F	B	L	T	W	31.29
30	Mw	R	F	B	L	–	W	33.68

Note: P: plaster; M: mortar; Pi: pink; R: red; G: grey; Wh: white; Y: yellow; D: dark; C: coarse; F: fine; B: brick; S: sand; L: large; Sm: small; W: weak; St: strong; T: vegetable fibers; V: very; w: wall; b: basement; d: dome.

Table 19.3 Visual and calcination analyses of Tahtakale Bath samples.

No	Sample Type	Color	Size	Aggregate Type	Amount	Organic Material	Binder Strength	% CaCO$_3$
1	P	Wh	VF	S	VSm	T	St	87.75
2	P	Pi	C	B+S	L	T	St	37.98
3	Mw	Pi	C	B+S	L	–	VSt	22.77
4	P	R	F	B	Sm	T	St	43.26
5	P	Wh	F	S	VSm	–	W	85.08
6	P	R	C	B	L	T	W	36.54
7	P	Wh	F	S	VSm	–	St	83.46
8	Mw	Wh	C	S	Sm	–	St	30.72
9	P	Pi	F	B	L	–	St	66.97
10	P	Wh	F	S	VSm	–	W	82.05
11	Mw	Pi	F	S+B	L	–	W	42.35
12	P	Pi	F	B	L	T	W	38.29
13	P	Wh	VF	S	VSm	–	St	75.69
14	P	R	C	B	L	T	St	36.70
15	P	Wh	VF	S	VSm	–	St	80.28
16	Mb	Pi	F	S+B	Sm	–	W	60.43
17	Mb	Pi	C	B+S	L	–	St	47.04
18	Mb	Pi-Wh	C	B+S	L	–	St	48.54
19	Mb	R	C	B	L	–	St	51.39
20	Mb	Wh	C	S	L	–	St	47.80

(continued)

Results and Discussion

The mortar samples of TB and EKM consisted of uniformly distributed binder, fine and coarse aggregates of various colors and textures. Crushed and partly ground bricks were mostly used as aggregates and artificial pozzolanic materials. Color varied from red to whitish cream. A few of the mortar samples contained short cut vegetable fibers as organic material. There were two layers of plaster. The inner layer resembled mortars in composition, color, and texture. However, it contained more lime than some of the mortar samples. The outer layer was whitish cream colored. This rather thin layer consisted of a very large quantity of lime (around 80%) and very fine aggregates of ground stones. Most of the plaster samples contained large amounts of short cut vegetable fibers.

The mortar samples from RB, with few exceptions, showed very different characteristics from those of TB and EKM. They consisted primarily of randomly distributed limeless binder, fine and coarse pebble-like aggregates of various textures, which

Table 19.3   *(continued)*

No	Sample Type	Color	Size	Aggregate Type	Amount	Organic Material	Binder Strength	% CaCO$_3$
21	Mw	Pi	C	B+S	L	–	St	41.31
22	Mb	Pi	C	B+S	L	–	St	44.02
23	Mb	R-Pi	F	B+S	VL	T	W	24.64
24	Mw	Pi	C	S+B	Sm	–	W	63.95
25	Mw	Pi	F	S+B	L	–	W	34.00
26	Mw	Pi-Wh	C	S+B	L	–	St	44.28
27	Mb	Wh	F	S	Sm	–	W	41.18
28	Mw	Pi-Wh	C	S	L	–	W	46.47
29	Mb	R-Pi	C	B+S	L	T	St	43.01
30	Mw	Pi	F	S+B	Sm	–	W	59.11
31	Mw	Wh-Pi	C	S+B	L	–	W	42.70
32	Mw	Pi	C	S+B	L	–	St	37.97
33	Mw	R	C	B	Sm	–	St	60.36
34	Mw	R	C	B	L	–	St	45.41
35	Mw	R-Pi	C	B+S	L	T	St	36.68
36	Mw	R	C	B	L	–	St	53.52
37	Mw	Pi	C	S+B	L	–	VSt	41.94
38	Mw	R	C	B	L	–	VSt	35.13
39	Mw	Pi	C	S+B	L	–	W	33.92
40	Mw	R-Pi	F	B+S	L	T	W	49.59

Note: P: plaster; M: mortar; Pi: pink; R: red; G: grey; Wh: white; Y: yellow; D: dark; C: coarse; F: fine; B: brick; S: sand; L: large; Sm: small; W: weak; St: strong; T: vegetable fibers; V: very; w: wall; b: basement; d: dome.

showed modern mortar characteristics. Their color changed from dark grey to light grey. The plaster samples of RB showed almost the same composition, color, and texture as the mortar samples. Only a few samples, which were taken deeper than the others, were similar to these from TB and EKM.

The results of visual and calcination analyses clearly showed that most mortar samples of TB and EKM were lime mortars that were supported by crushed and ground bricks as artificial pozzolanic materials. These kind of mortars were generally called "Khorosany mortars," if they were from Seljuk or Ottoman periods, or "Roman mortars," if they were earlier than those periods.

The lime content of wall and basement mortars of TB totaled ca. 40% by weight. While the lime content of the basement mortar samples extends to 50%, the lime content of wall mortar samples varied from 30% to 50%. These results show that the binder used for the construction of walls was more or less similar to that of the basement construction materials.

The lime content of mortar samples of EKM, which were taken from walls, was quite similar to those of the wall mortar samples of TB. The mortar samples, used for construction of domes, contained 30% lime. Since the basement of EKM was underground, no sample was examined.

The different layers of plaster samples showed very different lime contents. Inner pink layers had around 35% while outer white layers had about 80% lime.

The lime content of mortar and plaster samples of RB totaled around 20% and 30%, respectively. Plaster samples 7 and 8 showed larger amounts of lime than the others. These samples were taken from the water storage of the bath, where carbonates dissolved in water should have precipitated over the surfaces. Therefore, the calcium carbonate found in these samples should be the total of the lime and precipitate.

Thin-section analyses of mortar and plaster samples of RB showed that they were quite homogeneous with most of mass made up of quartz, calcite and very little plagioclase and feldspar. The quartz content was rather high (Figure 19.1). The aggregate content was over 65%, and the aggregates were very close to each other (Figure 19.2). Quartz and calcite grain sizes varied in size from 0.1mm to several millimeters, and their shapes were angular with low spherical property. Just a few samples of RB had crushed and ground brick pieces (Figure 19.3).

Thin-section analyses of TB and EKM mortar and plaster samples showed very different characteristics from those of RB samples. Mortar samples were mostly made up of crushed brick pieces (Figure 19.4), a small amount of quartz, carbonates, calcites (Figure 19.5), a very little plagioclase, and feldspars. The appearance of carbonate and broken shells indicated that these aggregates were prepared by crushing the "Küfeki" stone, which is a kind of local calcareous sedimentary rock.

The mortar samples of domes (outside) of EKM were different from the wall samples. They did not contain any crushed bricks and stone pieces but rather large amounts (over 65%) of pebble-like aggregates (Figure 19.6) whose size varied from 0.3–3 mm. Their moisture absorption capacities are lower than even those of RB samples. Although vegetable fibers were included mostly in inner plaster samples from TB and EKM (Figures 19.7, 19.8), some of mortar samples had also these kind of additives.

The inner layers of plaster samples were very similar to the mortar samples. The only difference was the size of aggregates, which changed from very fine to 2 mm. The outer white layer was soft and very homogeneous. The amount of aggregates totaled no more than 15% and the diameters were less than 0.1 mm (Figure 19.11, 19.12). The lines between inner (pink) and outer (white) plaster layers of TB and EKM showed different characteristics under the microscope. Although the lines of TB were straight (Figure 19.9), the lines of EKM were uneven (Figure 19.10). The different characteristics of these lines could have been caused by different application of plaster layers. The outer layer of TB should have been applied after the inner layer was set, while the opposite was true in the EKM case.

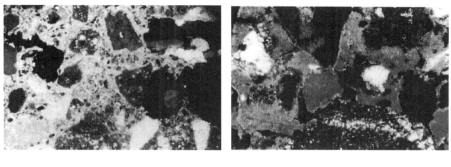

Figure 19.1   The quartz minerals in RB 6.   **Figure 19.2**   Very close aggregates in RB 9.

0 ⊢━━━━━━━━━━━┥ 1mm

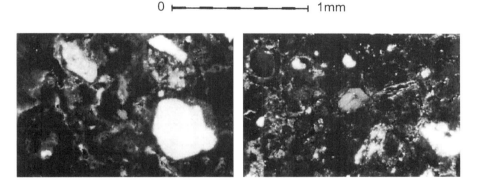

Figure 19.3   The brick pieces in RB 7.   **Figure 19.4**   The brick pieces in TB 22.

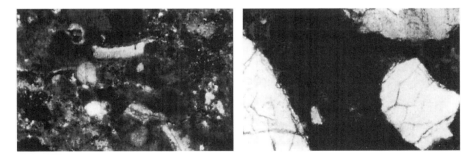

Figure 19.5   The quartz, carbonate, and calcite minerals in EKM 13.   **Figure 19.6**   The pebble-like aggregates in EKM 6.

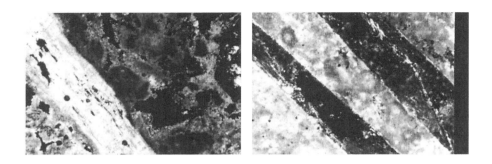

Figure 19.7 The vegetable fibers in TB 12.　　**Figure 19.8** The vegetable fibers in EKM 17.

0 ⊢━━━━━━━━━━━⊣ 1mm

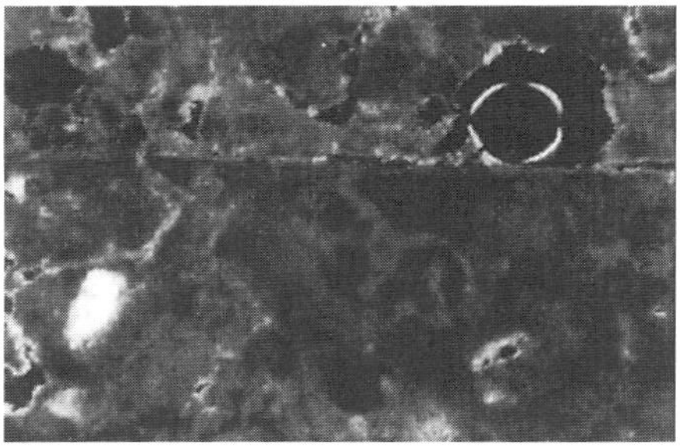

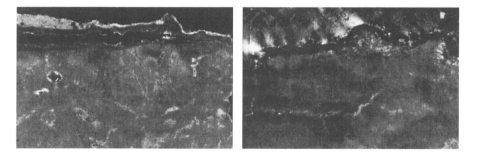

Figure 19.9 The straight line between white (7) and pink (6) layers of TB plasters.

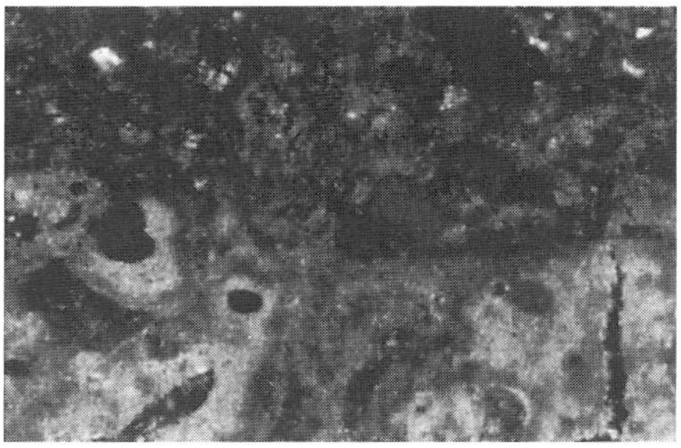

Figure 19.10 The uneven line between white (22) and pink (23) layers of EKM plasters.

Figure 19.11 The crust and flake on the surface of white plaster (7) layer of TB.

Figure 19.12 The crust and flake on the surface of white plaster (16) layer of EKM.

Table 19.4   The porosity properties of selected samples.

Sample Place and No	Specific Pore Volume (cm³/g)	Density (cm³/g)	Microporosity (%)
RB 6	0.092	0.082	89.2
RB 14	0.350	0.310	83.6
TB 10	0.477	0.338	88.4
TB 24	0.228	0.210	92.4
EKM 4	0.235	0.169	71.8
EKM 17	0.300	0.248	82.7
EKM 22	0.480	0.398	82.8
EKM 23	0.345	0.283	81.9

The white outer layer plasters were highly affected by the environmental conditions. Flakes and crusts, composed of gypsum, soot and dust, that formed were caused by air pollution. These effects were observed at both TB and EKM white plaster samples (Figures 19.11, 19.12).

Porosimetric measurements of mortar and plaster samples of RB indicated that these materials are denser and the specific pore volume (SPV) is lower (0.08–0.09 cm³/g) (Table 19.4) (Figure 19.13a). Only a few RB samples (Figure 19.13b) have similar SPV values to the samples of TB and EKM. While the SPVs and pore-size distributions of TB and EKM mortar samples were similar (Figures 19.13c, 19.13d), the inner (pink) layer of the plaster samples showed different characteristics due to placement inside or outside the monuments. The pink layer of plaster samples, from the inside, showed homogeneous pore-size distribution (Figure 19.13e) while those from outside did not (Figure 19.13f). The SPV of white plaster layer of TB and EKM showed similarity to each other. These layers showed rather homogeneous pore-size distribution (Figures 19.13g, 19.13h). The mortar samples from domes are different from all other samples. Although their pore-size distribution is homogeneous, SPV's are lower (0.16–0.26 cm³/g) than the mortar and pink plaster samples.

CONCLUSION

Chemical analyses as well as microscopic and porosimetric examinations have demonstrated that the mortar samples of TB and EK are basically "Khorosany" mortars with a homogeneous matrix, mostly made of crushed brick, calcite, quartz and very little plagioclase and feldspars. The lime was very well ground. The quality of workmanship used seems to be of high order. The mortar and plaster samples of RB were simple modern cement mortars, which probably were used in previous restorations of the monument.

The plasters of TB and EKM were made up with two distinct layers. The inner pink layers are quite similar to the mortar samples, while the outer white layers were a

A. Güleç

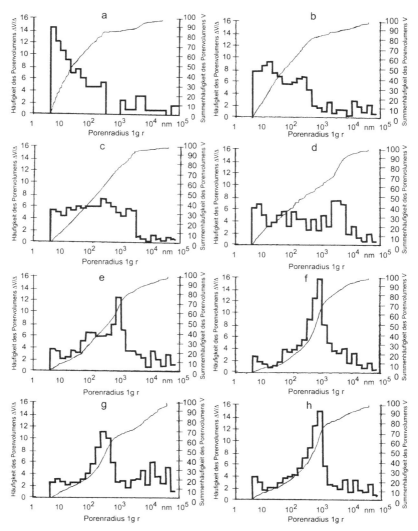

Figure 19.13 The porosimetric measurements of (a) RB 6, (b) RB 14, (c) TB 24, (d) EKM 4, (e) EKM 17, (f) EKM 23, (G) EKM 22, (h) TB 10 samples.

finishing layer composed of lime and little very fine aggregate. Most of the plaster samples contain vegetable fibers to increase strength, and they were in sound state.

The porosity measurements of mortar and plaster samples of TB and EKM were similar and they have higher SPV than RB samples.

There were no remarkable amounts of soluble salts and no evidence of dolomite. Only the white layer of plasters showed gypsum formation at the exposed surfaces, this caused by air pollution.

ACKNOWLEDGEMENT

I wish to thank Dr. Konrad Niesel for providing the porosimetric measurements.

REFERENCES

Ahunbay, Z. 1988. Mimarbaþý Koca Sinan, Yaþadýðý Çað ve Eserleri. Ýstanbul: Ayrý Basým.
Akok, M. 1968. Ankara Roma Hamamý. *Türk Arkeoloji Dergisi* **17**:5–33
Arnold, A. 1984. Determination of mineral salts from monuments. *Studies in Conservation* **29**:129–138.
ASTM. 1980. Standard Method of Test for Cement Content of Hardened Portland Cement Concrete. C 85-66, part 14.
Charola, A.E., et al. 1984. Characterization of ancient mortars, chemical and instrumental methods. In: Intl. Symposium on Scientific Methodologies Applied to Works of Arts, pp. 28–33. Milan: Arcadia.
Cliver, E.B. 1974. Test for analysis of mortar samples. *Bull. Assoc. Preserv. Technol.* **6(1)**:68–73.
Dupas, M.1981. L'analyse des Mortiers et Enduits des Peintures Murales et des Batiments Anciens. Symp. on Mortars, Cements and Grouts Used in the Conservation of Historic Buildings, pp. 281–295. Rome: ICCROM.
Fitzner, B. 1988. Porosity properties of naturally or artificially weathered stone. In: Intl. Congress on Deterioration and Conservation of Stone, pp. 236–245, ed. J. Ciabach. Torun, Poland: Nicholas Copernicus Univ.
Jedrzejewska, H. 1960. Old mortars in Poland, a new method of investigation. *Studies in Conservation* **5(4)**:132–138.
Jedrzejewska, H. 1967. Investigation of ancient mortars. In: Archeological Chemistry, pp. 147–166. Philadelphia: Univ. of Pennsylvania Press.
Jedrzejewska, H. 1981. Ancient mortars as criterion in analysis of old architecture. In: Symp. on Mortars, Cements and Grouts Used in the Conservation of Historic Buildings, pp. 311–329. Rome: ICCROM.
Konuþur, B. 1985. Tahtakale Hamamý. Ýstanbul: ÝTÜ Sosyal Bilimler Enstitütsü, Yüksek Lisans Tezi.
Massazza, P., and M. Pezzuoli. 1981. Some teachings of Roman concrete. In: Symp. on Mortars, Cements and Grouts Used in the Conservation of Historic Buildings, pp. 219–245. Rome: ICCROM.
Müller-Wiener, W. 1977. Bildlexikon zur Topographie Ýstanbul, p. 119. Tübingen: Verlag Ernst Wosmuth.
Scott, W.W. 1956. Standard Methods of Chemical Analysis, vol. 2. London.
Stewart, J., and J. Moore. 1981. Chemical techniques of historic mortar analysis. In: Symp. on Mortars, Cements and Grouts Used in the Conservation of Historic Buildings, pp. 297–310. Rome: ICCROM.
Tabasso, M.L., and P. Sammuri. 1984. Evaluation of Mortars for Use in Conservation from the Standpoint of Release of Soluble Salts. ICOM Committee for Conservation, 7th Triennial Meeting, pp. 84.10–84.11. Copenhagen: ICOM.
TS (Turkish Standards) 24. 1985. Physical and Mechanical Testing Methods of Cement.

20

Air Pollution Trends in Germany

S. FITZ

Umweltbundesamt, Bismarckplatz 1, 14193 Berlin, Germany

ABSTRACT

Trends in air pollution levels in Germany over the last twenty years for sulfur dioxide, nitrogen dioxide, ozone, and particulate matter are reviewed. Continuous measurements of sulfur dioxide, available since the early 1970s, indicate that levels have dropped significantly, even in industrial areas. In contrast, only a slight reduction in nitrogen dioxide, whose main source is vehicular traffic, has been detected. Ozone levels have remained constant, with occasional slight increases observed. Particle deposition has been reduced to levels comparable to SO_2.

AIR AND ITS POLLUTION

For many centuries – based on the premises of the Greek philosopher Empedokles – air was considered to be one of the four basic elements. Its importance for all earthly things was stressed by this idea, as well as the concept of its indivisibility. With the birth of modern chemistry, more precisely, with the discovery of oxygen and nitrogen at the end of the 18th century and the first experiments of air analysis performed by Cavendish in 1789 (Walden 1947), air became known as a mixture of gases that can also contain liquid droplets (aerosols) and/or solid particles.

Today we know that the composition of air may fluctuate according to natural influences and may vary regionally. We also know that humans, animals, and plants are the result of long-lasting evolutionary processes that have, among other things, adapted to changing environments, including those of the air. The natural environment is part of this process and arises from the interaction with the environmental situation as well.

Change occurs – as the genesis of minerals, stone materials, and their formation shows – over extremely slow, geological time scales.

Because nitrogen, oxygen, and argon represent more than 99.9% of the composition of air, in the past it was not evident that trace components could also yield substantial effects. However, studies of historical sources (Herrmann 1972; Brimblecombe and Rohde 1988) reveal that even in antiquity, "smoke effects" were known and measures were taken to minimize damage, as for instance by removing certain industries emitting high amounts of "smoke" from the cities. Nevertheless, there was a common understanding that polluted air only presented a local problem, and thus abatement measures were only undertaken locally. Answers to general problems were not strategies to reduce the level of air pollutants, rather to distribute them more evenly. Even into the mid-1970s, with the policy mandating "tall stacks," point sources of pollutants (e.g., power plants) remained the main emittants. This policy did not reduce emission levels, rather it lessened the local load through "dilution," which resulted in a general increase of regional pollution levels. A change in policy occurred when it was recognized that pollutants are transported from one country to another, causing damage beyond the emitting country. In 1979, the Convention on Long-Range Transboundary Air Pollution of the United Nations Economic Commission for Europe was signed and came into force after ratification by 32 signatories in March, 1983. The contracting states (including all of Europe and North America) have agreed to reduce air pollution and to develop strategies for combating emissions.

MONITORING AIR POLLUTANTS

Prior to the 1950s, investigations of air quality were sporadic, regionally based, and complicated by the lack of adequate measuring equipment. The first systematic and continuous measurements began in the 1950s in the U.S. and were later taken up in Germany in the early 1960s. Still, measurement devices for the detection of trace gases (or air pollutants) were extremely limited. The detection of SO_2 was the most advanced, while comparable methods for detecting nitrogen oxides or ozone were lacking. Economically feasible devices for continuously measuring the most aggressive pollutants, e.g., nitric acid, which occur in very low concentrations, have only recently been developed.

Which compounds affect material surfaces the most? To date it is known that sulfur dioxide, nitrogen dioxide, ozone, and particulate matter are present in the atmosphere in relatively high concentrations. Their relevance to deterioration processes has been demonstrated and is substantiated by available measurements, which date back 20–30 years. The following discussion considers SO_2, NO_x, ozone, and particulates. Other pollutants, e.g., ammonia, chlorides, fluorides, and nitric acids, may play a major role in weathering processes; however, they cannot be discussed in the context of trends due to of the lack of sufficient data.

SULFUR DIOXIDE

The primary source for SO_2 is almost exclusively the combustion of fossil energy sources, principally coal. Natural gas and refined oil burn nearly sulfur free. Natural SO_2 emitted from volcanic sources can be omitted in this context, because of its regional insignificance. The main emission sources are power plants (ca. 75% of the total emissions), industrial processes (15%) and domestic heating systems (10%). In

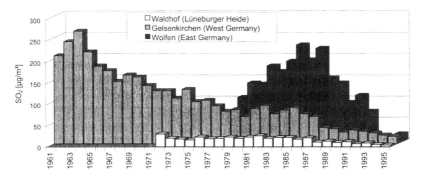

Figure 20.1 Development of SO_2 concentration (annual mean values) at industrial sites in West Germany (Gelsekirchen, 1961–1995) and East Germany (Wolfen, 1979–1995) compared to background levels (Waldhof/Lüneberger Heide, 1972–1995).

industrial areas, SO_2 concentrations reached an annual mean value of approximately 200 µg/m^3 in the 1960s.

With the beginning of systematic control of air quality, efforts were taken to reduce levels of pollution in West Germany to lessen the load on the environment (e.g., Verordnung über Großfeuerungsanlagen vom June 6, 1983 [statutory regulation for large combustion sources of June 6, 1983]). In the former East Germany, however, no systematic efforts were taken to improve air quality until after the reunification of Germany in 1989. On the contrary, during the 1980s, the average concentration of SO_2 levels increased over 1960 levels. Since reunification, an improvement in air quality has been observed in the former East Germany due to the closure of numerous industrial plants and the subsequent reconstruction of those which survived the economic change (Figure 20.1, Table 20.1).

Table 20.1 Emissions of sulfur dioxide and nitrogen oxides, calculated as nitrogen dioxide in (kt) in Germany differentiated between the areas of former West Germany and East Germany. Source: Umweltbundesamt.

State	1975	1980	1985	1990	1992
Sulfur dioxide					
West Germany	3,308	3,166	2,369	878	875
East Germany	4,111	4,320	5,385	3,534	3,021
Nitrogen oxides					
West Germany	2,511	2,926	2,908	2,460	2,426
East Germany	501	514	568	573	478

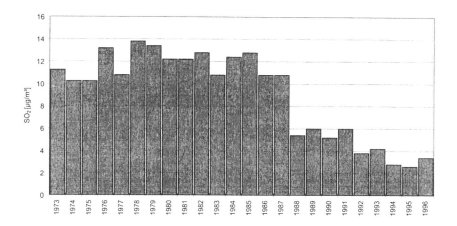

Figure 20.2   Time series of sulfur dioxide background concentrations (annual mean values 1973–1996). Data averaged from five sites and obtained from the Umweltbundesamt network in West Germany).

Since 1973, measurements of "background concentrations" in regions far from pollutant sources have been made and are available from the German Federal Environmental Agency's Network. Using an average value from five sites (all situated in the former West Germany), the annual mean level of SO_2 was, until 1987, approximately 12 μg/m^3 SO_2. This value has now dropped to a marginal level of 3 μg/m^3 SO_2 (Figure 20.2).

In dense urban areas, a similar trend in the reduction of SO_2 levels is observable. For comparison, let us consider (a) Berlin-Wedding and (b) Munich-Pasing (Figure 20.3). In the 1970s, the concentration of SO_2 in Berlin-Wedding was about 140 μg/m^3. By 1987 it had decreased slightly to a level of ca. 100 μg/m^3 SO_2. Over the past 10 years, levels have been reduced to 20 μg/m^3 SO_2. This site suffered particularly from "transboundary" air pollution transport over the Berlin Wall from the former East Germany.

In Munich (as well as in many urban sites in West Germany), the average concentration of SO_2 was at a level of approximately 35 μg/m^3 in the beginning of the 1980s. Since 1988 a clear reduction of the SO_2 load has been observed. Today, in Munich, Hamburg, or other large German cities, the average concentration of SO_2 is about 10 μg/m^3.

In terms of weathering processes of materials, annual averages of pollutant concentrations are primarily used for calculation purposes. The present state-of-the-art for quantitative calculations of deterioration processes do not need finer time resolution of the pollution parameters to expain observed effects. However, some additional information is needed: the existing circumstances plus any episodic extremes and/or seasonal variations. These will fluctuate according to energy consumption, i.e., during the colder parts of the year, more energy is consumed and thus more pollutants are emitted

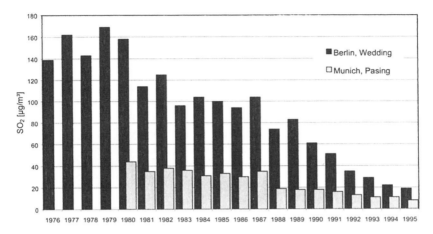

Figure 20.3 Comparison of sulfur dioxide concentrations (annual mean value, 1976–1995) at urban sites in Munich-Pasing and Berlin-Wedding.

through burning processes. Comparison of two Berlin at sites in 1989 shows an annual variation in the high levels of sulfur dioxide pollution in winter and illustrates further the local differences within one city (Figure 20.4). At the East Berlin site (Parochial-straße), the concentration of SO_2 is much higher than at the West Berlin site (Wedding). The main difference between the sites is the different heating systems used in the surrounding areas: in West Berlin, sulfur-free gas is used almost exclusively in most households, whereas in East Berlin the heating systems are based almost completely on high sulfur-containing lignite.

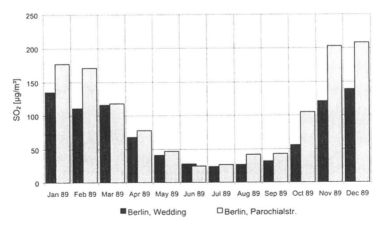

Figure 20.4 Monthly variation of sulfur dioxide concentrations at the Berlin sites of Wedding (West Berlin) and Parochialstraße (East Berlin) in 1989.

NITROGEN DIOXIDE

Nitrogen dioxide is formed in very high temperature firing processes. Its only natural occurrence is lightning, and thus natural sources do not play a major role. The main sources for the formation of nitrogen oxides are industrial power plants and internal combustion engines (vehicular traffic). The primary oxidation product – nitrogen monoxide (NO) – is oxidized relatively quickly by ozone (or by oxygen) to form nitrogen dioxide (NO_2). This reaction is responsible for the reduction of ozone concentrations at sites with high NO_2 emissions. During air transport, NO_2 is exposed to UV(b) radiation (effective only in daytime) and decomposes to form extremely reactive radicals, which help to form ozone again at places removed from the original pollutant source.

For automobiles with gasoline engines, as one of the main sources of nitrogen oxides, it was hoped that the introduction of abatement technologies, such as catalyzers, would decrease the level of NO_2 pollution. The effectiveness of this measure, however, has been almost completely counterbalanced by the increase in the number of automobiles (Table 20.1).

Looking at the NO_2 levels from the "background" station of the Umweltbundesamt network, an average value of ca. 11 µg/m³ NO_2 was determined, while at sites distant from traffic, levels were ca. 5 µg/m³ (Figure 20.5). Trends are not recognizable from 1968 to the present. Also, regional differences and patterns cannot be detected.

In urban areas, a slight reduction in NO_2 levels can be detected from an average annual mean of 50 µg/m³ in 1982 to approximately 40 µg/m³ in 1995. A closer view of specific sites shows different trends: in Berlin, a reduction of NO_2 was observed

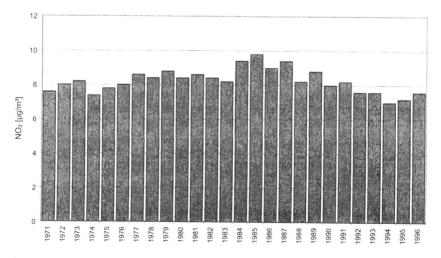

Figure 20.5 Development of nitrogen dioxide background concentrations (average from five sites of the Umweltbundesamt network in West Germany); annual mean values 1971–1996.

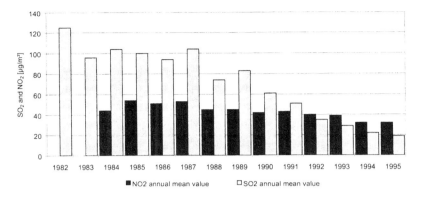

Figure 20.6   Comparison of time series (1982–1995) for sulfur dioxide and nitrogen dioxide at the urban site Berlin-Wedding.

(Figure 20.6); in Munich-Pasing, the reduction of SO_2 was offset by an increase of NO_2 concentrations (Figure 20.7).

OZONE

Air, in general, contains a considerable amount of naturally produced ozone, formed under the influence of UV(b) radiation. Depending on the formation mechanism, ozone levels can be greater at higher altitudes. For example, at the measuring site of Schauinsland in the Schwarzwald region (Black Forest, SW Germany), the year-long average is about 81 $\mu g/m^3$ O_3 while at a low altitude site in the Lüneburger Heide (northern Germany), 51 $\mu g/m^3$ O_3 is the measured average.

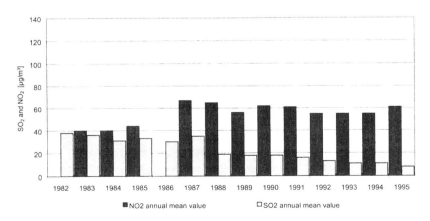

Figure 20.7   Comparison of time series (1982–1995) for sulfur dioxide and nitrogen dioxide at the urban site München-Pasing.

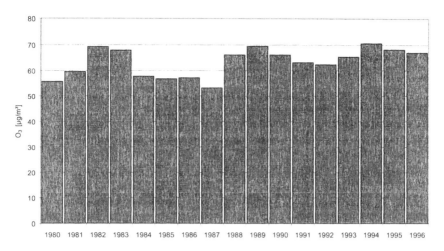

Figure 20.8   Time series for ozone concentrations (annual mean value) as an average from five sites of the Umweltbundesamt network in West Germany.

In addition to the naturally formed ozone that underlies some variations, depending on hours of daylight and radiation intensity, an anthropogenetically formed component must be considered. This component is a result of complicated air chemistry transformations and reactions, as mentioned briefly above.

Systematic measurements of ozone in dense urban areas do not extend back many years. Nevertheless, a trend towards higher levels of ozone can be observed (Figure 20.8). For sites affected directly by vehicular traffic, however, this trend is not detectable. The reaction of NO with O_3 and the formation of other reactive species leads to a reduction of O_3 levels at those sites; however, this results in an increase of ozone levels at sites located a few kilometers from the source NO_2 (Figure 20.9).

PARTICULATES

Direct effects of particulates through a chemical reaction with surfaces can almost be excluded. Nevertheless, particulate matter deposited on surfaces acts as a highly aggressive material. It can affect an extremely large surface area and is loaded with a variety of compounds – salts and acids – which, in turn, interact with the surface areas. Furthermore, soiling of surfaces is not only an aesthetic problem. Physical properties of porous surface areas change radically when the pore structure is altered as a result of particle deposition. From this point of view, it is important to study the trends of particulate deposition. Long-term trends are comparable to those of SO_2 emissions (Figure 20.10). This may indicate that the same sources of pollutants are involved, i.e., the burning of fossil fuels. However, a differentiation should be made between the types of soot and dust particles, as they clearly have different sources and thus will also vary in regional distribution.

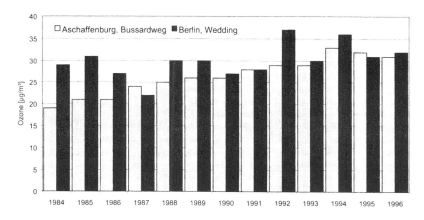

Figure 20.9 Comparison of time series for ozone (annual mean value) at the sites Aschaffenburg-Bussardweg and Berlin-Wedding for 1984–1996.

LIMITS AND TOLERANCE VALUES FOR AIR POLLUTANTS

Compared to a few years ago, a substantial decrease of SO_2 concentrations in ambient air can be observed currently. NO_2 levels have leveled off while ozone levels have slightly increased during the same time period. Does this mean that weathering processes have stopped, slowed down, or are they continuing with undiminished speed?

To evaluate concentration limits, a reference point is needed and the effects on human health are often used. Different limits have been given, depending on the

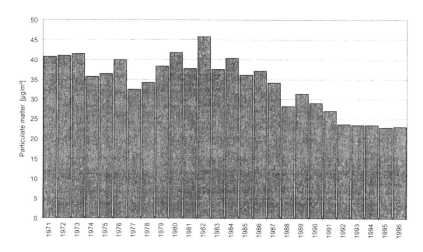

Figure 20.10 Development of particulate matter concentration (annual mean value) for 1971–1995; average from five sites of the Umweltbundesamt network in West Germany.

Table 20.2 Concentration limits of air pollutants as regulated by different organizations within guidelines and ordinances of Germany.

Guideline	Variable	Concentration Limit ($\mu g/m^3$)		
		SO_2	NO_2	sst
22. BImSchV	annual median of daily averages (when sst >150 $\mu g/m^3$)	80		150
22. BImSchV	annual median of daily averages (when sst <150 $\mu g/m^3$)	120		150
TA-Luft (Technical Guidance Air)	annual arithmetic average of half-hour averages	140	80	150
EU-Guideline 80/779/EWG, Annex II	annual arithmetic average	40–60	50	150
WHO	annual average	50	40	

sst = suspended particulate matter

regulating organization (TA Luft 1986; 22. BImSchV; EU-Guideline 80/779/EWG, Annex II and IV). An overview is given in Table 20.2.

The levels listed in Table 20.2 are much higher than actual measured concentrations. Likewise, the critical levels of SO_2 for crops (30 $\mu g/m^3$ SO_2) and forest ecosystems (20 $\mu g/m^3$ SO_2), and NO_2 for all plants (30 $\mu g/m^3$ NO_2) are higher than measured concentrations.

Materials are not able to regenerate themselves as biological systems can, once the stress source is removed. Thus the issue of critical levels for materials has to be treated in a different way. Measurable effects occur at lower concentrations than those mentioned above. The question posed must therefore be: can a situation for objects exist in the environment where further weathering is excluded? For many materials, the answer is no. We know, for example, that all porous materials change their surface structure near areas of pollutant deposition; yet when deposition ceases, those structural changes that have already taken effect, still remain.

It will never be possible to define a level of pollution that can exclude material changes, even when pollution is kept below this level, for deterioration and weathering processes take place even in the absence of pollutants. It thus seems appropriate to identify target levels for pollutants that could be accepted as "tolerable." Expert discussions over recent years have led to a proposal to find a connection of acceptable levels of pollution with some "background weathering" (UN ECE 1993). Within the UN ECE material exposure program (Stöckle 1998), the observed lower 10 percentile of corrosion rates from all test sites included within the representative network (Europe and North America) was taken as a basis. The 1.2- to 2-fold background corrosion rate could then be taken as an accepted corrosion rate (Gregor et al. 1996). This methodology starts with real effects and also takes into account the local and regional climatic conditions. Then, with this very valuable approach, it may be possible to draw up regional maps showing where the acceptable levels of air pollutants for different materials are exceeded.

REFERENCES

22. BImSchV-22. Verordnung zum Bundesimmissionsschutzgesetz.

Brimblecombe, P., and H. Rohde. 1988. Air pollution – Historical trends. *Durability of Building Materials* **5**:291–308.

EU-Guideline 80/779/EWG, Annex II and IV.

Gregor, H.-D., B. Werner, and T. Spranger, eds. 1996. Manual on Methodologies and Criteria for Mapping Critical Levels/Loads and Geographical Areas Where They Are Exceeded. Berlin: Umweltbudesamt.

Herrmann, G. 1972. Beiträge zur Bestimmung von Schwefeldioxid in der Atmosphäre und Herstellung von Schwefeldioxid-Luft-Gemischen, p. 11. Berlin: Akademie-Verlag.

Stöckle, B. 1998. Ergebnisse aus dem UN/ECE-Bewitterungsprogramm. In: Arbeitsheft Bayerisches Landesamt für Denkmalpflege. München, in press.

TA Luft. 1986. Technische Anleitung zur Reinhaltung der Luft, Erste Allgemeine Verwaltungsvorschrift zum Bundesimmisionsschutzgesetz vom 27.2.1986. GMBl. **37**:95–144

UN ECE 1993. Internal Workshop Report: Critical Levels for Buildings and Materials, including Cultural Heritage. Bath, March 24–26, 1993.

Verordnung über Großfeuerungsanlagen vom 22.6, 1983.

Walden, P. 1947. Geschichte der Chemie. Bonn: Universitäts-Verlag.

21

Effects of Air Pollutants on Renderings
Experimental Protocols and Background

D. HOFFMANN, K. NIESEL, and H. ROOSS

Federal Institute for Materials Research and Testing (BAM), Unter den Eichen 87,
12205 Berlin, Germany

ABSTRACT

Results of a study on outdoor exposure tests for diverse renderings are presented. The main objective of the program was to gain information on dose-response relations for diverse renderings from outdoor exposure tests, which were conducted at six locations in the Berlin area, with different SO_2 concentrations, over the course of several years. To ensure a comparison of results, the composition of the renderings was standardized (sand was used as the aggregate and predominantly aerial nonhydraulic lime as a binder) and pollution levels were monitored by the Berlin air quality monitoring network. Apart from analysis of water-soluble secondary constituents enriched during exposure and from determination of their phase composition in different depth positions, several physico-technical properties and characteristics relevant during a weathering process were investigated. Improved and newly developed methods are presented. The reunification of Germany occurred during the test period and greatly impacted the immission[1]-dependent reactions, which were observed to decrease drastically due to the imposition of stringent pollution controls on industry and the subsequent shutdown of plants in former East Germany.

Test plates were produced with a scraped finish and mounted on specially constructed racks, which exposed them to SO_2 attack but not to direct rainfall; they faced south and were arranged perpendicularly, as on a building. Thus, a swift reaction process could not be expected in the time available. It proved necessary to extend the time intervals between samplings and to shift the focus of the original program to building samples, which represented results over a longer stress period. This introduced deviation from homogeneity and comparability.

---

[1] "Immission" is the deposition defined as the reverse of emission of pollution.

INTRODUCTION

The main objective of this research program was to determine whether there exists a connection between the immission rate of air pollutants and the degree of damage to a building material, thus establishing dose-response relationships. We also wanted to know to what extent a rendering's physico-technical properties and structural characteristics will be subjected to a change as a result of differing pollutant concentrations, and whether one could determine quantitatively the corresponding influences, e.g., by SO_2 and NO_x. Test conditions were obtained by using outdoor exposure racks erected at various locations, each of which had different microclimatic conditions. At nearby measuring stations, continuous measurements were made of immission, temperature, and relative ambient humidity, etc. Rendering was the principal test material, the surface of which was roughened (scraped finish) to prevent local formation of thin-sealing films of hardened paste. A sandy limestone (Baumberger "sandstone") was included in the test program.

The starting materials were characterized to recognize as many irregularities of a material as possible, analogous to work on natural stone (Niesel and Schimmelwitz 1982) (see Table 21.1). This is extremely important when considering additional difficulties that can arise from a material having a relatively small thickness and being quite friable. In addition, there are inhomogeneities specific to production runs which are not limited to plastering.

Since some measures were promoted to reduce air pollution by a factor of two, our main interest in choosing exposure sites was directed to regions of considerable immission levels, with SO_2 and NO_x sources in the vicinity. Exposure racks were erected close to several stations of the Berlin air quality measuring network. These sites are indicated on a schematic map of Berlin (West) (Figure 21.1), also marked with SO_2 concentration isolines.

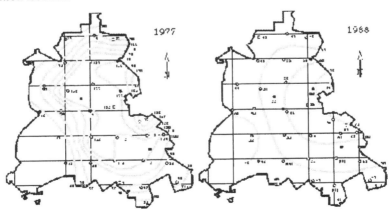

Figure 21.1   Air quality monitoring network of Berlin (West): Comparison of yearly average of the SO_2 concentration in mg/m^3 for 1977 and 1988 as well as (black) points of exposure racks established.

Table 21.1 Characteristics and test methods for assessing behavior of porous building materials.

Concept	Characteristic Values	Methods
Simulating weathering	Scale factor p_1 of the mass loss curve, described by the Weibull relation as a function of cycle number	Sodium sulfate crystallization test (various methods)
Degree of filling of pores	Saturation coefficient, S_1; "relative degree of impregnation," S_i; critical saturation degree, S_{cr}	Water absorption at normal atmospheric pressure and at 15 Mpa, capillary liquid rise, relative dimensional change while frosting
Pore-size distribution	Specific pore volume, discrete values (e.g., microporosity d_{10m} value, interval according to Ravaglioli, field capacity), specific surface area, Σ_m	Mercury porosimeter test, relationship in matrix suction/water content, physiosorption
Moisture content	Water capacity Ψ_k; open porosity, ε_0	Capillary liquid rise, water absorption, underwater weighing
Moisture transport	Water absorption coefficient, w_0; length-related water penetration coefficient, b	Capillary liquid rise
Permeable porosity	Specific gas permeability, D_s; water vapor diffusion resistance index, μ	Fluid transport at defined pressure and concentration gradients
Evaporation	Mass loss as a function of time	Evaporation development, monitored by weighing
Mechanical characteristics	Compressive and bending strength at "dry" and "wet" states, modulus of elasticity, surface hardness ("macrohardness"), surface abrasion, thermal expansion coefficient	Compression test, bending test, vibratory behavior, ball indentation, grinding abrasion, relative length change

The reason for concentrating on older facades was the closure of several industrial plants in central Germany, i.e., the former GDR, where strongly emitting flue gas sources were situated; they were the principal source of SO_2 for Berlin, even at the program's start. In recent years, one has seen increasing improvement in air quality due to reduced SO_2 emissions in this region. The yearly average was reported to have decreased by 50%, from 1977 to 1988 (Hanus and Niesel 1990). Thus differences found between exposure locations established near monitoring stations were also remarkably reduced. This tendency has continued over the past few years (cf. Figure 21.2). The same is true for the NO_x emitters. Of course, this positive trend in air quality improvement reduces the chance of finding distinct effects within a reasonable time period, thus necessitating a shift from freshly prepared samples to research-directed instead to

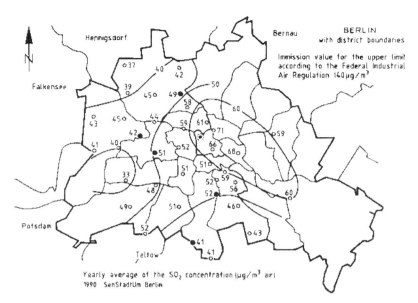

Yearly average of the SO₂ concentration (µg/m³ air)
1990 SenStadtUm Berlin

Figure 21.2 Air quality monitoring network of greater Berlin: Yearly average of the SO$_2$ concentration in µg/m^3 for 1990.

in situ findings on older buildings. Research was directed towards analyzing rendering samples from facades erected many years ago, which over time have formed a weathering profile. The results are complemented by a determination of SO$_2$ uptake under defined conditions by various rendering types, each having a planned composition and field behavior over 1.5 years.

Since concentrations were reduced by half, relative variations between monitoring stations also needed to be adjusted. At Lerschpfad, an area very close to the city's highway (Stadtautobahn) and normally a region of medium immission levels, the highest SO$_2$ concentrations measured were 59 µg/m^3 air,

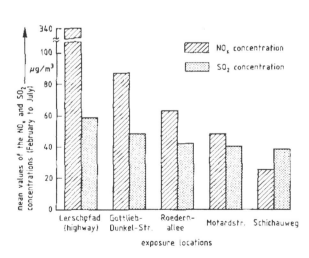

Figure 21.3 Comparison of NO$_X$ and SO$_2$ concentrations in µg/m^3 air as an average monitored at different exposure locations in Berlin from February to July, 1991.

as shown in Figure 21.3. In contrast, for Schichauweg at the southern boundary, the lowest value of 38 $\mu g/m^3$ was found. Levels decreased in 1992 to 49 $\mu g/m^3$ and 23 $\mu g/m^3$, respectively. It is doubtful whether one can clearly pinpoint the corresponding influences on renderings, distinguishing between locations, and whether there exists a corresponding factor not exceeding 2. This situation is much better for NO_x concentrations and their possible influence on material behavior. Corresponding values show a maximum at Lerschpfad of 340 $\mu g/m^3$ air and at Schichauweg a minimum of 25 $\mu g/m^3$. In addition to this data, it would be of interest to know how often and how long wetting by dew occurred. However, such quantitative monitoring was not conducted. Therefore, immission of pollutants measured by the monitoring stations may over time give a rough indication for classifying five out of six exposure locations, as shown in Figure 21.2.

Specimen Preparation

Experimental

In contrast to a free-standing column, materials exposed outdoors (representing the contours of a building) are not uniformly affected by atmospheric influences in all directions. Weathering, such as that by SO_2 attack which takes place mainly in rain, can be excluded by using an exposure rack, as shown in Figure 21.4. This approach was tested in a former program (Schimmelwitz and Hoffmann 1977). The rack faced south to avoid the effect of the principal rain and wind directions. Although such a design cannot be considered more than a compromise, because it does not present a large, closed surface as in a building, it may nevertheless be taken as the basis for comparing results.

Figure 21.4 Rack facing south for exposing rendering specimens to ambient atmosphere (air monitoring station shown at left in background).

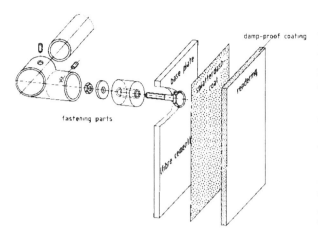

Figure 21.5 Clamping device to mount rendering plates on an outdoor rack for atmospheric exposure (SO_2), shown in an enlarged view (see also Figure 21.4).

As shown in detail in Figure 21.5, clamping devices established on the racks consisted of different metal parts, the fastening of which can be seen in an enlarged view of the single base plates. In addition, the function of a splatterdash coat, which allows the rendering system to adhere to the fiber cement plate, is fulfilled by coarse sand spread over the surface after having been first coated with an epoxy film. Afterwards, a fresh mix was applied, whereby the format of the plates was created with the aid of appropriate stencils. One day after application, the fresh surfaces were scratched in order to avoid the effects of a thin layer containing fines that could block the penetration of polluting gases. They were then stored in a climatized chamber at a constant relative humidity of 90%. This procedure served to expedite carbonation prior to exposure in an atmosphere containing SO_2. To support this process, the specimen surface was periodically moistened by spraying water, so that the material underwent the most favorable conditions spatially and temporally for the carbonating reaction several times. Thereafter, lateral margins of specimens, now hardened and in position to be transported elsewhere, were sealed by applying a bituminous emulsion to make them watertight. Thus, a common starting condition for specimen plates was achieved before they were mounted on racks. After the pre-treatment, the zonal succession of the concentration profile markings increased in quality the longer the test continued.

Starting Material

Binding Agent

To simulate the historical composition of renderings, which contain fewer hydraulic components than modern renderings, and to avoid the local formation of thin films of hardened paste, lime hydrate or relatively pure dolomitic hydrate was initally chosen for plastering. Thus, starting conditions could be simplified but also modified. In order to compare the response of different rendering types to the attack of gaseous effusion, we needed to guarantee that their surfaces offered the same volume content of calcium hydroxide when exposed to the atmosphere. One has to take into account three

Table 21.2 Chemical analyses of model renderings.

Constituents		Lime Hydrate	% by Mass Lime Putty (dried state)	Dolomitic Hydrate
Portions insoluble in hydrochhloric acid		0.60	0.31	3.57
Soluble silica	SiO_2	1.66	0.70	1.88
Total oxides [1]		0.74	0.64	1.64
Calcium oxide	CaO	96.12	97.43	54.41
Magnesium oxide	MgO	0.58	0.71	38.27
Potassium oxide	K_2O	0.04	0.01	0.09
Sodium oxide	Na_2O	0.05	0.05	0.11
Total sulfur expressed as	SO_3	0.08	0.05	0.03
Total		99.87	99.90	100.00
Chloride	Cl^-	<0.01	<0.01	0.07
Nitrate	NO_3^-	n.d.	n.d.	n.d.
Nitrite	NO_2^-	n.d.	n.d.	n.d.
Residue (calculated)		0.12	0.09	—

[1]Aluminum oxide, Al_2O_3; iron (III) oxide, Fe_2O_3; and titanium oxide, TiO_2
n.d.: nondetectable
— : no data

differing binding agents – a hydrated lime produced by industrial slaking of calcined limestone and a lime putty, the raw materials for both which originate from the same geological stage, and an industrially (completely) calcined and hydrated dolomite – as well as where each cementing component should be matched to the others in order to get comparable $Ca(OH)_2$ portions per volume. In the case of dolomitic hydrate, it was necessary to equate its MgO and $Mg(OH)_2$ calcium hydroxide equivalent according to its stoichiometric proportions. For this, $Mg(OH)_2$ was translated to MgO, and $CaCO_3$ into $Ca(OH)_2$ prior to calculation. In this way and in consideration of the impurities of each product, weight proportions resulted that relate to the aggregate quantity as 1 to 3.1 (or 1.0 for the dried equivalent) to 1.1 (lime hydrate:lime putty:dolomitic hydrate). Material data as well as further characteristics, e.g., concerning the origin of binding agents, can be obtained from Table 21.2.

In addition, one can obtain details on chemical analyses (Table 21.3) and on the mineral composition of these calculated nonhydraulic binders, as shown in the histogram presentation of Figure 21.6.

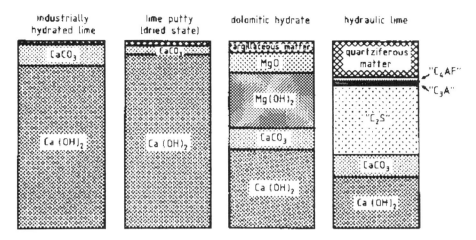

Figure 21.6 Mineral composition calculated for rendering types concerned C$_2$S, C$_4$AF, and C$_3$A represent dicalcium silicate (belite), tetracalcium aluminate ferrite, and tricalcium aluminate, respectively.

Rendering

Rendering data as well as additional data concerning, e.g., the origin of binding agents are shown in Table 21.4. In addition to materials cited, a lime plaster with cement admixture and a corresponding mix with hydrated dolomite were used. Mix proportions (lime:cement:aggregate by mass) amounted to 1:0.6:16.3 or 1:0.6:18.3 while having a spread value of 18 cm and showing water-retention values of 86.3% or 88.3%.

After having placed the fresh rendering on base plates, the hardening process began immediately. In an early stage, drying is the decisive factor, leading to shrinkage and consolidation of cryptocrystalline Ca(OH)$_2$ by approach of lime-hydrate particles. Subsequently, or running parallel to it, is carbonate hardening. This is a rather complex process, since actual strength development takes place only by repeated dissolution and precipitation associated with recrystallization (Hoffmann and Rooß 1977). When a rendering predominantly contains lime, its hardening is based upon the chemically rather simple reaction of a transfer of lime hydrate into carbonate under water release, whereupon crystal coarsening (Ney 1967) follows by contributing CO$_2$-loaded water to the dissolution process. However, the determining factors for the initial formation of binder/aggregate agglomeration, and thus its geometric configuration (including the structure of the later significant pore system), are aided by the processes of transport and evaporation of the water portion, in which Ca(OH)$_2$ was originally found in suspension or solution.

From a chemical viewpoint, preparation should be carried out by following exactly a given mix proportion formula tested before fabrication. This, however, does not ensure uniformity in local distribution of sand and binding agent, dispersion of lime, wetting of aggregate grains, and subsequent compaction after laying, so that the

Table 21.3 Chemical analyses of Billerbeck lime and Baumberger sandstone.

Constituents		Hydraulic lime ("Billerbeck lime") % by mass	Baumberger "sandstone" % by mass
Ignition loss at 1000°C		—	—
Portions insoluble in hydrochloric acid		20.72	53.26
Soluble silica	SiO_2	13.59	2.11

Total oxides
    aluminum oxide
    iron(III) oxide
    titanium oxide
	R_2O_3
	Al_2O_3
	Fe_2O_3
	TiO_2
		3.35	1.83

Calcium oxide	CaO	59.49	42.27
Magnesium oxide	MgO	1.07	0.37
Potassium oxide	K_2O	0.12	
Sodium oxide	Na_2O	0.07	
Total sulfur expressed as SO_3	S	1.44	0.10
Total		99.85	99.94
Sulfite	SO_3^{2-}	n.d.	n.d.
Sulfide	S^{2-}	n.d.	n.d.
Chloride	Cl^-	<0.01	<0.01
Nitrate	NO_3^-	n.d.	n.d.
Nitrite	NO_2^-	n.d.	n.d.
Residue (not detected)		—	—

n.d.: nondetectable
—: no data

reproducibility of a rendering is not guaranteed. Of course it is not possible to postulate a strict comparability in renderings because artefacts are caused by manufacturing, and long-term effects, such as carbonation, also produce heterogeneous areas in this type of two-component system. Plaster hardening is a most complex process. Thus differences in the respective state of the binding agent give rise to distinguishing features in material cohesion which, however, have to be disregarded. Graf (1934) described numerous possibilities for modifying lime mortar and renderings with regard to their properties or characteristics by applying different proportions of starting materials and the following treatment in the course of production and storage. He may be credited with having introduced tests on building lime to a standardized protocol. A lack of

Table 21.4 Characteristic data of rendering types used in this project.

Binding Agent	Raw Material						Rendering Mix		
	Type	Occurrence	Geological origin	Mineral phases [1]	Bulk density ρ (kg/dm^3)	Specific surface Σm (m^2/kg)	Proportion by mass	Spread value (cm)	Water retention value (%)
Industrially hydrated lime	Massive limestone	Painten near Kelheim, on Danube, Bavaria	Malm series, stage ε–ζ	$Ca(OH)_2$ $CaCO_3$	0.42	16,230	1:16.3 [3]	17.0 [4]	84.1 [5]
Lime putty (stored more than 2 years with an excess of water [57%])	Massive limestone	Altmannstein near Kelheim, on Danube, Bavaria	Malm series, stage ε–ζ	Highly disperse $Ca(OH)_2$ $CaCO_3$	1.32	31,400 [2]	1:7.2 [3]	16.5 [4]	89.3 [5]
Industrially (completely) calcined and hydrated dolomite	Dolomite	Scharzfeld, Harz Mountains, Lower Saxony	Middle Zechstein, main dolomite stage	$Ca(OH)_2$ MgO $Mg(OH)_2$ $CaCO_3$ quartz	0.55	12,310	1:18.7 [3]	17.2 [4]	87.0 [5]
Hydraulic lime	Lime	Billerbeck near Munster, Westphalia	Upper Cretaceous	Ca_2SiO_4 $Ca(OH)_2$ $CaCO_3$ quartz	0.65	4,780	1:7.8 [3]	18.2 [4]	84.7 [5]

(1) after calcining and slaking
(2) for the dried sample
(3) standards according to DIN EN 196-1
(4) according to DIN 18 555
(5) according to ASTM C 91, however, at a residual pressure of 8.16 Pa (= 60 mm Hg) instead of 50.8 mm Hg.

suitability concerning mix proportion and homogenization of the components, water addition, and pre-wetting of adjacent building stone (including mistakes during application of rendering and its subsequent treatment during hardening) affect the final product. Therefore, it may be worth all the effort to trace this back by means of "fingerprints" taken afterwards, provided that no admixtures for changing workability properties were introduced to complicate the picture unnecessarily.

Many factors may influence test results, yet it is possible to deduce general trends. In any case, homogeneity provides the starting point required for exposure studies. In addition, results recently obtained in characterizing salt distribution in porous brickwork after penetration by sulfate and chloride solutions, which lasted over months, may suffice to give an idea of the problems met during preparation of samples for depth profiles (Hoffmann and Niesel 1990). One who is content with the customary mode of expression that a fresh mortar or rendering "clenches up" to its substrate should clearly realize that the actual running processes may of course seldom fulfil this idealized conception, even though a plaster sludge saturated in calcium hydroxide can penetrate unhindered. How laborious it is, in any case, to detect interfaces microscopically with corresponding nonpoint contact becomes evident when one searches, e.g., in a polished section, for suitable regions at the boundary between plaster and brick (Niesel 1989; Niesel and Rooss 1983).

With the beginning of the industrial age, a further development occurred in plaster technology, which allowed counteractive measures against, e.g., the presence of residues of burnt lime caused by incomplete slaking during a soaking process with the aid of an industrial slaking procedure. In this way, a more uniform usable mix results, sometimes, leading to lower strength values of the final product. Based on recent knowledge concerning the use of methods to characterize fresh and solid mixes (cf. RILEM 1982), tools have been developed that enable the materials scientist to advance research that had been mainly determined empirically until now. However, indications of uncertainty are still encountered, even when dealing with the flow diagram shown in Figure 21.7. How far we are still from the acquisition of defined characteristics relevant to plaster production is discussed in another paper (Niesel 1994), which reviews the need for basic research in this field.

SAMPLING AND PREPARATION

For sampling material to establish corresponding depth profiles, a milling cutter was used that allows defined portions to be removed from the specimen's height, millimeter by millimeter. A precondition for this is that a rigid drilling frame is used on which the milling head is fastened so that it practically has no chance of giving way when aggregate grains of that brittle matrix are grasped by its cutting edges. However, first one should bring the rendering's surface into such a position that its main parts run parallel to the cutting plane. This way it is impossible to spread over the whole surface at the same level. Thus, one should only sample the most projected regions to establish the first layer of the profile and should confine further sampling to these regions.

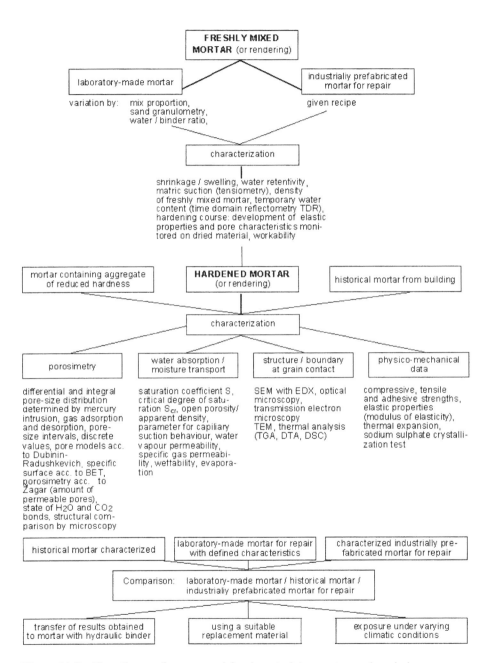

Figure 21.7 Flow diagram for a protocol for characterizing mortars and renderings.

It should be noted that much effort is necessary to obtain the planned results. In the case of weathered rendering, this begins with the selection of a building. For example, when finally a facade is located with scaffolding in place, one often finds that the old external rendering has already been chiseled away. Or, as has recently become the rule, it simply concerns an attic expansion for living space, or the rendering is overcoated with paint. When a suitable location has been found, however, one must act immediately by taking samples, simply because this may not be possible the next day. Sampling should yield flat fragments – as large as possible – of that brittle and sometimes crumbly material which often adheres tenaciously to its plastering subsurface. Patience and persistence are necessary. When carrying samples from the building to a vehicle, and later to the laboratory, one needs to exercise extreme caution to avoid damaging the samples. In the case of two-coat work, the weather-exposed outer layer must be carefully separated from the layer underneath without causing damage.

To sample by abrasion, large-sized rendering plates were used, embedded in a plastic frame by means of epoxy resin to even out the differences in thickness and to facilitate sampling parallel to the original surface, where precision is necessary to the millimeter. Epoxy resin requires 24 hours to harden, during which the sample must remain immobile. For the actual work, a machine equipped with rotating, grinding, and cutting tools is available to assure that – as far as allowed by the material – layer fragments of defined thicknesses are obtained with sufficient accuracy.

Problems exist with the scraped finish because of (a) its unevenness in certain cases, and (b) it contains coarse quartz grains which should be removed prior to use with tweezers to avoid pulling out the matrix from the actual surface at the same time. If such a procedure is not followed, controlled abrasion is not satisfactory. During abrasion of defined material portions, millimeter by millimeter, an additional problem may arise: since the milling shaft is rigid in terms of torsional action, it cannot deviate under load and the tool mills easily through the material, and sometimes brittle parts situated below the level just abraded are grasped by its cutting edges and break away; consequently one has to dispose of these unwanted fragments. In an earlier contribution (Hanus and Niesel 1990), the principles of preparatory measures concerning specimens for the determination of water vapor diffusion are described. Material used for the present study was occasionally in a friable state, since it succumbs to weathering processes. It was also available in limited quantity. Preparation of specimens is very time-consuming, especially since they have to be reduced to uniform thickness and separated from adjacent material, such as undercoat or even splatterdash coat, to remove heterogeneous parts containing voids or wood inclusions. To guarantee tightness between sample and mounting despite irregular contours of rendering surfaces, an additional sealant was used, which was applied by melting wax. This was found necessary to close shrinking cracks produced during the first embedding phase. To avoid intrusion of molten wax into the rendering and to favor recovery of specimens already tested without damaging them, a supplementary mask of adhesive tape was applied below the wax mass.

Preparation of climate-stored rendering plates, especially those exposed outdoors over years and originating from a former test series, is quite difficult because of their reduced thickness and friability. Since one cannot separate them from their substrate by sawing that thin and rather crumbly material, one is obliged to strike it off cautiously with a plastic hammer. The same is true for the relatively brittle specimens of the present series, which have not yet had sufficient time for consolidation by hardening and alteration during their 6-month storage period. On one hand, it is necessary to provide good adherence of rendering on the fiber-reinforced cement plate. This is desirable so that the sandwiches can endure the whole exposure duration without separation and fall of their upper layer. On the other hand, it is rather difficult to shear it off for preparation purposes in a nondestructive way near the interface marked by the splatter-dash coat. However, it cannot be separated without damaging the surface, for instance by hammer blows. Therefore, it is necessary to remove the carrier plate from behind in slender strips after sawing them perpendicularly to this bearing plane. Although this is a time-consuming procedure, it is nevertheless considered to be the only successful method.

ACKNOWLEDGEMENTS

We thank the Federal Environmental Agency (Umweltbundesamt) for allocating funds, without which it would not have been possible to carry through the project in its present form, and our colleagues from the laboratories of Chemical and Electro-Chemical Methods, Physical and Chemical Characteristics, and Technology of Building Materials.

Special mention is made of the contributions of Mrs. Gabriele Müller, Mrs. Elgin Rother, Mrs. Edith Tessmann and Mr. Jürgen Götze, which exceeded their normal workloads. The preparation of drawings was accomplished by Mrs. Gudrun Blamberg, Mrs. Karin Glöckner. Mr. Christian Kowalec devoted his close attention to the mathematical aspects of the project, especially in computer graphics and the application of his own software development. Dr. Detlef Hanus also participated in the realization of this project.

Appreciation is expressed to Dr. Stephan Fitz of the Bundesumweltamt for generous support and the international cooperation he made possible within the framework of the NATO-CCMS Pilot Study "Conservation of Historic Brick Structures."

REFERENCES

ASTM C 91-87a. 1987. Standard specification for masonry cement, March.
DIN 18 555. 1982. Part 1. Prüfung von Mörteln mit mineralischen Bindemitteln, Frischmörtel; Bestimmung des Wasserrückhaltevermögens nach dem Filterplattenverfahren.
DIN EN 196-1. 1990. Prüfverfahren für Zement; Bestimmung der Festigkeit.
Graf, O. 1934. Über die Prüfung der Baukalke. *Der Bautenschutz* **5(11)**:121–135; **5(12)**: 137–143.
Hanus, D., and K. Niesel. 1990. Influence of air pollutants on rendering. In: Proc. 3rd Expert Meeting NATO-CCMS Pilot Study "Conservation of Historic Brick Structures," ed. S. Fitz, pp. 104–131. Berlin: Umweltbundesamt.

Hoffmann D., and K. Niesel. 1990. Vorgänge des kapillaren Feuchtigkeitsaufstiegs und Verdunstung in porösen Baustoffen. *AID Schriftenreihe der Sektion Architektur, TU Dresden* **30**:110–115.

Hoffmann, D., and H. Rooß. 1977. Wechselwirkung zwischen Schwefeldioxid und Kalkmörteln. *Materialprüfung* **19(8)**:300–304.

Ney, P. 1967. Die Erhärtung von Luftkalkmörteln als Kristallisationsvorgang. *Zement-Kalk-Gips* **20**:429–434.

Niesel, K. 1989. Quelques aspects expérimentaux de l'étude du transfert d'humidité en maçonnerie.

Niesel, K. 1994. Zum Problem des Nachstellens von Kalkmörteln. *Bautenschutz + Bausanierung* **17(2)**:65–68.

Niesel, K., and H. Rooss. 1983. Aspekte der Untersuchung von Porenraumveränderungen in feuchtem Mauerwerk–Aspects of the testing of pore volume changes in damp masonry. *Ziegelindustrie International* **36(7)**:339–349.

Niesel, K., and P. Schimmelwitz. 1982. Zur quantitativen Kennzeichnung des Verwitterungsverhaltens von Naturwerksteinen anhand ihrer Gefügemerkmale. BAM Research Report No. 86, Berlin (West): Bundesanst. Materialprüf. (Abridged English version: Niesel, K. 1983. The weathering behavior of natural building stone. *Stone Industries* **10**:30–31.)

RILEM 1982. Recommendations MR 1–21, 1982 (E). Testing methods of mortars and renderings. 1st Edition, December, 24 pp.

Schimmelwitz, P., and D. Hoffmann. 1977. Untersuchung über die Erhärtung von Außenputzen aus Luftkalkmörtel und ihre Verwitterung unter besonderer Berücksichtigung der Einwirkung von Luftverunreinigungen. ERP-Forschungsbericht, Az. 2222. *Silicates Industriels* **54(3–4)**:47–54.

Spohn, E. 1955. Das Wasserhaltevermögen von Putz- und Mauermörteln. *Zement-Kalk-Gips* **8(9)**:299–301.

22

Effects of Air Pollutants on Renderings

Exposure Tests

D. HOFFMANN and K. NIESEL

Federal Institute for Materials Research and Testing (BAM), Unter den Eichen 87, 12205 Berlin, Germany

ABSTRACT

Test results obtained from 1.5-year-old exposed samples show only a slight sulfate absorption to a depth of about 1 mm. Pores coarsened in comparison to unweathered reserve samples, and the water absorption coefficient was reduced, as is typical in a reaction with sulfur oxide air pollutants. The same is also true for material of the same age but under elevated SO_2 concentration at an exposure site. Further insights into the field conditions permit measurements of deposition velocity and uptake rate of sulfur dioxide. Cement-containing products show their highest values in the dry state. Plaster made with lime putty has a fourfold higher adsorption velocity and a doubled uptake compared to one made with industrially hydrated lime. After capillary water saturation, a similar sulfate content can be determined in all material types having been exposed for the same time period. However, another ranking order exists in terms of deposition velocity, emphasizing the prominent importance of exposure conditions for a weathering process.

INTRODUCTION

Exposure of defined rendered surfaces is indispensable for gaining insight into the rate of atmospheric attack, especially that by SO_2. The change in physico-technical and chemical parameters during a formation of depth profiles is of interest. In this chapter, results of natural and artificial weathering tests are presented. Information on the principles and objectives of test procedures are available elsewhere (Hoffmann and Niesel 1998b).

CHARACTERIZING STARTING MATERIAL FOR EXPOSURE

Physico-technical Features

For atmospheric exposure tests, plasters were made with lime putty, industrially hydrated lime, industrially (completely) calcined and hydrated dolomite, hydraulic lime,

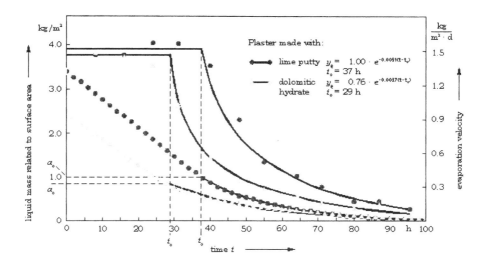

Figure 22.1 Evaporative course and velocity of two selected laboratory-prepared renderings before exposure.

and sand standardized according to EN 196 (DIN EN 196-1 1990) as an aggregate. To one lime and one dolomitic plaster, small portions of white Portland cement were added to each.

Table 22.1 lists data determined prior to exposure. Based on coulometric test results, we assumed that lime plasters were carbonated uniformly and thoroughly, whereas the cement admixture, because of its tightening effect (increase of fine pore portion impeding CO_2 diffusion), allowed only an unsatisfactory carbonating reaction. Additionally, it is possible to characterize plaster plates by their evaporation behavior. Because of reduced thickness (2 cm), problems could result when the inflection point between both evaporative phases is established. Nevertheless, in individual cases, reasonable accuracy can be achieved, as presented in Figure 22.1. Having an almost identical geometry, both specimens show different values for a_o, which are also transferable to residual water content. Thus, evaporation parameters b reflect material-specific differences in this part of the curve.

By considering their abrasion behavior (Figure 22.2), it is obvious that renderings with lime putty and industrially hydrated lime have the lowest strength, followed by those with a cement admixture. Plaster made with dolomitic hydrate shows the highest resistance and is known to furnish an elevated early strength comparable to that of hydraulic rendering.

Quantifying this behavior, Table 22.2 presents the values obtained for renderings made with various materials.

The cumulative curves of amounts of wear show nearly a linear course for the relevant material. This points to the fact that there is a comparable abrasion resistance at

Table 22.1 Characteric values of room-stored but precarbonated renderings with a scraped surface, calculated from their pore-size distribution and other parameters (0–5 mm depth).

Rendering Types	Specific pore volume (cm^3/g)	d_{10m} μm	Ravaglioli interval (%)	Micro-porosity (%)	Specific surface area (m^2/g)	Sulfate content (% by mass)	Carbonate content (% by mass)	Vapor diffusion resistance index μ	Water absorption coefficient w_0 (kg/($m^2 \cdot h^{0.5}$))
Plaster made with lime putty	0.125	–	6.3	45.7	0.53	0.02	3.15	9.5	25.7
Plaster made with industrially hydrated lime	0.135	–	16.9	48.6	0.63	n.d.	2.76	11.0	13.9
Plaster made with industrially calcined and hydrated dolomite	0.126	–	9.6	39.2	0.52	n.d.	1.34	10.9	26.7
Lime plaster mixed with Portland cement	0.143	9.79	44.9	80.7	1.48	0.02	4.32	11.5	21.1
Dolomitic plaster mixed with Portland cement	0.123	16.33	34.8	82.4	1.37	0.04	3.24	12.7	11.9
Hydraulic plaster	0.117	–	19.3	53.9	1.11	n.m.	3.72	13.7	9.5

– : exceeding upper limit method's working range
n.d.: not detectable
n.m.: not measured

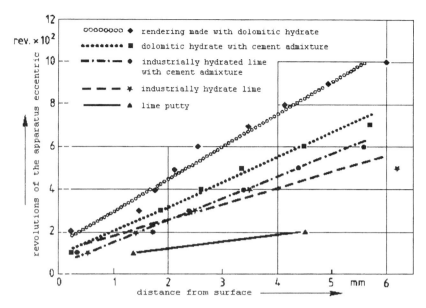

Figure 22.2   Abrasion behavior of laboratory-prepared renderings before exposure, depending upon their composition.

each depth position, which make it possible to detect changes due to the influence of atmospheric pollutants.

Table 22.2   Values obtained for renderings made with various materials.*

Lime putty	ca. 50 rev./mm of depth
Lime hydrate	ca. 70 rev./mm of depth
Lime hydrate and cement admixture	ca. 110 rev./mm of depth
Dolomitic hydrate and cement admixture	ca. 130 rev./mm of depth
Dolomitic hydrate	ca. 180 rev./mm of depth

* For details of the abrasion test, refer to the web site:
http://www.bam.de/a_vii/moisture/ transport.html.

Deposition Velocity and Uptake of SO_2 for Plasters According to the Chamber Method

There is currently no method available to quantify SO_2 uptake by a building material. Samples from a facade can indeed deliver data as, e.g., the rate of uptake of a gas related to a time unit, even though defined environmental conditions are lacking. Different processes, such as dissolution of neo-formed phases by rain or dew water, their reprecipitation at another place, recrystallization and frost action, can modify the

Table 22.3 Deposition velocity, V_{d20}, and uptake, Φ_{20}, for SO_2 after 20 h, determined on specimen plates made of different renderings (SO_2 concentration 405 µg/m³).

Binder Type	V_{d20} in cm/s	Φ_{20} in mg/m²
Dolomitic hydrate with cement admixture	1.71	74.8
Industrially hydrated lime with admixture	0.54	59.5
Lime putty	0.45	54.6
Baumberger "sandstone"	0.40	51.0
Hydraulic lime	0.20	32.1
Industrially hydrated lime	0.11	29.1
Dolomitic hydrate	0.09	24.6

material to an unknown degree and reinforce weathering effects. Exposure height and direction are additional variables. Such data, therefore, represent no more than a stage of deterioration arbitrarily selected. Problems arise when comparing building materials with each other. An experimental device developed by the Institute for Inorganic and Applied Chemistry, at the University of Hamburg, enables determination of deposition velocity or uptake of SO_2. Across the reaction chamber of this device flows a gas of known concentration. From its reduction in concentration, one can calculate the deposition velocity and the uptake, by considering the surface area available for reaction.

Corresponding to the load or stress during a smog situation or a moderate pollution in winter, SO_2 concentrations of 150 ppb (405 µg/m³) and 37 ppb (100 µg/m³) were respectively chosen to simulate an average stress during winter months. Tests were carried out at a temperature 20°–22° C and 50%–60% relative humidity (RH) over a period of 20 hours. The specimens consisted of five different renderings taken from outdoor exposure plates after a 90-day pre-storage at 20°C and 90% RH; Baumberger "sandstone" was used as well. The calculation formulas are reported elsewhere (Wittenburg 1994). In Figure 22.3, both absorbing features of a plaster made with lime putty are plotted versus time. The test results obtained give a

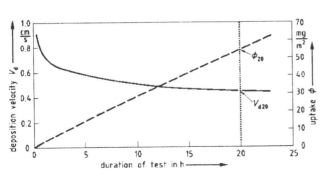

Figure 22.3 Time course of SO_2 deposition velocity, V_d, and uptake, ϕ, monitored on a plaster made with lime putty.

Table 22.4 Deposition velocity, V_{d20}, und uptake, Φ_{20}, for SO_2 after 20 h, determined on water-saturated specimen plates made of different renderings.

Binder Type	V_{d20} in cm/s	Φ_{20} in mg/m^2
Dolomitic hydrate with cement admixture	6.9	81.1
Industrially hydrated lime with admixture	9.3	81.2
Lime putty	5.1	79.8
Industrially hydrated lime	9.3	81.3
Dolomitic hydrate	7.5	81.1

ranking order shown in Table 22.4.

As can readily be seen, the cement admixture increases deposition velocity, V_{d20}, and uptake, Φ_{20}, as well. Therefore, renderings with dolomitic hydrate or hydrated lime would be least sensitive towards an SO_2 effect, whereas their equivalents with cement admixture show an almost doubled uptake. Plaster made with lime putty takes an intermediate position. A decrease of gas concentration to 100 $\mu g/m^3$ leads to a higher velocity and a correspondingly lower uptake. In this sequence, plasters with hydrated lime alone indicate lowest values. Dispersivity of the binding agent possibly exerts a significant influence on this behavior. In any case, one cannot definitely deduce the ranking order from the pore-related data.

Reserve samples corresponding to those used here show that values for specific pore volume lie close to one another. However, in the case of both cement-containing renderings, the values for R interval and microporosity are obviously higher and for the median many times smaller than in batches without admixture.

When comparing these data as material parameters with those obtained from lime-bond sandstones, we noticed that under the effect of the elevated gas concentration, none shows a higher velocity or uptake than the cement-containing plasters. Nevertheless, the values for lime renderings are on the same order of magnitude as the sandstones. Tests were also carried out on plates saturated with distilled water by capillary rise at the high gas concentration. Table 22.4 lists the results obtained. It turns out that V_{d20} of wet specimens is considerably higher than those in a dry stage (cf. Table 22.3).

Whereas SO_2 uptake of all plaster types is nearly the same, small differences in deposition velocity appear – a result influencing their ranking order. Under these circumstances, lime plaster shows the highest values. Thus, only the SO_2 absorption data obtained in dry stages represent material parameters, while wetted samples absorb the admitted SO_2 quantity almost quantitatively. Transferring such a finding to conditions of a building, one can realize that the absorptive ability of SO_2 depends mainly on a material's moisture content, i.e., conditions of exposure determine a rendering's behavior towards SO_2.

OUTDOOR EXPOSURE OF BUILDING MATERIALS AT
LOCATIONS WITH DIFFERENT LEVELS OF POLLUTANT STRESS

Time-dependent Modifications

Until mid-1992, five different rendering types had been stored on racks outdoors over 1.5 years. The sixth sample, a hydraulic lime plaster, was mounted at a later date. Three stages can be compared: initial state, exposure after 0.5 years, and after 1.5 years. For the materials that used dolomitic hydrate as a binder, the cement-containing mix showed no change in sulfate content of its uppermost millimeter layer after 1.5 years at any location. In samples without admixture, slightly elevated amounts were found compared to the starting material, and this remained constant over the course of time. Only lime renderings with and without cement took up measurable quantities of SO_2 (Figure 22.4).

This means, using samples from Gottlieb-Dunkel-Strasse as an example, that material made of lime putty and having a starting SO_4^{2-} content of 0.06% by mass, contains 0.09% after six months and 0.12% after 1.5 years. This value correspondingly increases in plaster with industrially hydrated lime from 0% to 0.04% to about 0.33%, respectively. Material from other exposure locations furnishes similar values. One can find a plausible ranking order in their reaction with the air pollutant, because the maximum SO_4^{2-} content in samples was also found as far as at Lerschpfad (highest air pollutant concentration near the highway). Since such results are always related to the outermost rendering layer, a subsequent diminution occurs when penetrating to a greater depth. Apparently only the first millimeter is directly influenced by

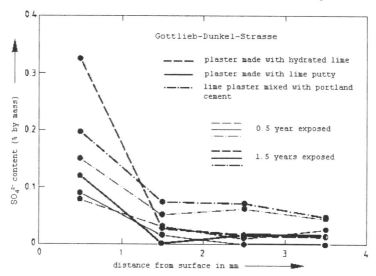

Figure 22.4   Sulfate enrichment in the uppermost layer of various rendering types after different exposure periods.

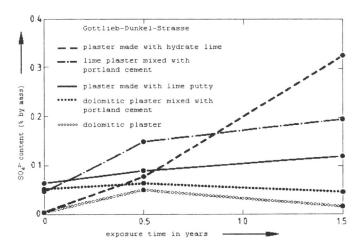

Figure 22.5 Comparison of sulfate concentration profiles in renderings after 0.5- and 1.5-year exposure periods.

atmospheric SO_2, since values at 2 mm depth are situated insignificantly above those present at the start of the test (Figure 22.5). It should be noted that differences of 0.02% are within the scattering range where even preparation of a 1 mm thick layer (accuracy in abrading, mass of the test portion, extraction, etc.) still yields the 0.02% difference in sulfate content related to mass. Therefore, the chemical reactions are obviously extremely weak, so structural modifications can be expected to take place on a limited scale. Only the outer 5 mm of rendering could be affected: this corresponds to the layer used for comparisons.

Both plaster mixes with dolomitic hydrate are those with the smallest change in chemical composition and therefore show no trends in structural data related to exposure duration. The water absorption coefficient of the dolomitic plaster merely rises with time at all locations (Figure 22.6).

After 1.5 years of exposure at the location with the lowest noxious gas concentration, the greatest value was found ($w_0 = 26.1$ kg/(m^2·h$^{0.5}$)), while at the location with the highest concentration, the smallest value was determined: 19.6. In the case of lime plaster with cement admixture, there are no pertinent systematic changes in w_0 or μ. One can perhaps find an extremely small decrease of specific pore volume but not at all locations, suggesting subsequent hydration or carbonation and consequently showing structural compaction. The same is true for pure lime plaster, whereas that made with lime putty points to clear dependencies. Thus the median of pore sizes increases to coarser pores and microporosity decreases at three of five locations. Slightly fluctuating w_0 values increase with time at all locations.

In Figure 22.7, these parameters are plotted for both extreme conditions of samples taken from Schichauweg (with the lowest SO_2 concentration) and Lerschpfad (with the maximum value). For this part of the program, one can summarize that at given

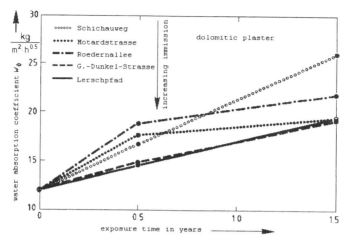

Figure 22.6 Increase in water absorption coefficient, w_0, of a dolomitic plaster referring to locations and exposure time.

exposure conditions, 0.5 (compare Hoffmann 1992) and even 1.5 years are simply too short to produce systematic structural modifications, even in renderings. Therefore, results obtained should be considered with utmost caution, since the trends found could partially lie within a scatter range of the results, visible only by a corresponding spread of the coordinate system.

Due to slight chemical modifications, renderings made with lime putty or industrially hydrated lime show nearly identical abrasion depth profiles after 0.5 as well as 1.5 years (Figure 22.8), in contrast to their nonexposed equivalents. This is valid for exposure locations with high (Lerschpfad) and also low air pollution levels (Schichauweg).

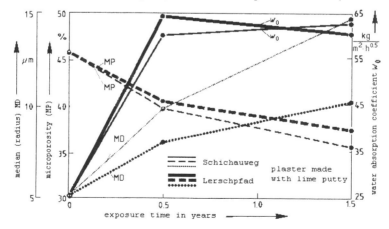

Figure 22.7 Variations on pore-related parameters in a plaster made with lime putty after different exposure times.

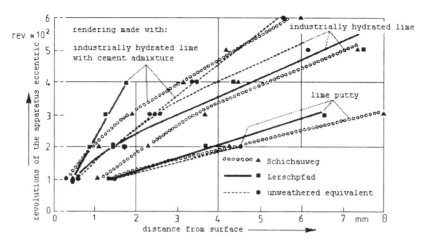

Figure 22.8   Abrasion profiles of lime renderings after a 1.5-year exposure: cumulative curves of single amounts of wear.

Lime plaster with cement admixture displays an increased strength only near the highway (Lerschpfad). There, all sample surfaces have become dark-colored, probably as a result of deposition of such pollutants as abraded tire rubber and other grime originating from traffic. Only tiny modifications appear in dolomitic materials within the first 0.5 years, and are solely recognized by a faint surface consolidation. After 1.5 years, however, drastic differences can be observed in comparison to rendered lime material, which is also evident in the case of a cement admixture (cf. Figure 22.9).

Although the behavior of materials from Lerschpfad is quite similar to those stored indoors, corresponding samples from Schichauweg exposed to low NO_x and SO_2 concentrations show a very high abrasion resistance (about 1800 rev. per mm depth progress). This result cannot be explained merely by their higher carbonate content. Other influences may have been responsible, e.g., a higher average RH or increased dew formation at this location.

Such material (initially such slightly soluble phases as $Mg(OH)_2$ and MgO besides amorphous Mg carbonates, and of course the calcium component are present) requires an increased moisture content for optimal strength development, more than is required by lime rendering (cf. Hoffmann and Rooss 1994). This may also explain the similarities in abrasion characteristics among the unweathered samples, although they contain twice the carbonate content. Pore data can be considered as well for an explanation. Thus, pore volumes differ remarkably down to 5 mm profile depth: material from Schichauweg shows 0.106 cm³/g while that from Lerschpfad 0.121 cm³/g, which indicates a higher density for the former. In comparison, we found no remarkable differences in the discrete values of pore-size distribution.

Renderings with dolomitic hydrate and admixed cement show a completely different abrasion behavior than an equivalent rendering without a hydraulic portion. Here conditions are obviously reversed (Figure 22.10), so that samples from Schichauweg

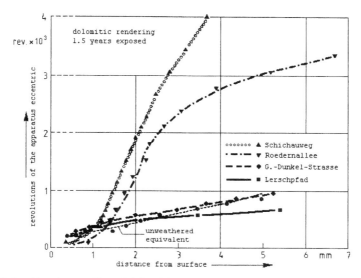

Figure 22.9 Abrasion profiles of dolomitic rendering at different locations after a 1.5-year exposure: cumulative curves of single amounts of wear.

correspond to those that are unweathered, whereas those from Lerschpfad are distinctly stronger despite more intense SO_2 immission. The cumulative curve of amounts of wear has an almost linear course, indicating a comparable structural cohesion at each depth position. The pore characteristics can also explain the different abrasion curves, whereby only pore volume exhibits definite tendencies (0.122 cm^3/g in Lerschpfad material and 0.138 cm^3/g in such from Schichauweg). Therefore, this type is closely similar to that made with hydrated lime and cement; the sample of the latter, however, allowed an abrasion test only to 2 mm distant from its surface (cf. Figure 22.8).

At Lerschpfad, better hardening conditions prevail for cement-containing material, since drizzle presumably occurs by spray from the highway during and after rainfall. At Lerschpfad, one additionally finds the highest fraction of suspended particulates. At Schichauweg, the supply of such media was apparently insufficient for intensified hydration. Here dolomitic hydrate with admixed cement did not become so hard, and a high moisture level is present which requires plausible interpretation.

Influence of Exposure Conditions on Material Behavior

As already pointed out, load or stress by pollutant gases was reduced over time at single exposure locations. It seems probable that in the urban area of Berlin, different climatic factors other than atmospheric SO_2 attack can strongly affect building materials. Nevertheless, despite all of the rather small, time-related dependencies, one rendering made with lime hydrate was apparently subjected to systematic variations proportional to immission intensity.

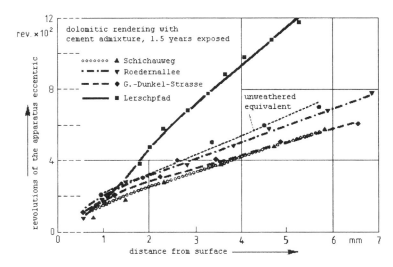

Figure 22.10   Comparison of abrasion profiles in a dolomitic rendering with cement admixture after 1.5 years of exposure: cumulative curves of single amounts of wear.

Figure 22.11 shows several structural parameters, such as the median and microporosity of pore-size distribution as well as the water absorption coefficient of test samples exposed over 0.5 and 1.5 years, plotted for the respective locations which were ranked in the order of atmospheric SO_2 concentration. It turns out that an increasing level of SO_2 and NO_x immissions causes a decreasing portion of micropores and a shifting of the median towards coarser pores, being in such way coupled with a reduction of w_0. The time influence may be expressed such that a portion of micropores after 1.5 years exposure is noticeably more strongly developed in proportion to that of a 0.5 yr exposure, whereby the 50% fractile of pore-size distribution is correspondingly decreased. The water absorption coefficient is apparently not significantly affected by these structural changes.

Despite the small SO_2 absorption, it seems amazing that abrasion behavior also reveals systematic modifications in the direction of increasing or decreasing immission (cf. Figures 22.9, 22.10). However, not all materials are involved: lime renderings are not subjected to these influences as much, although their pore-related parameters did change. Above all, mixes that were placed on racks in an incompletely hardened state show this phenomenon, i.e., those with cement admixture and those containing a magnesian component. In the direction of decreasing SO_2 and NO_x immissions – namely from Lerschpfad over Gottlieb-Dunkel-Strasse to Roedernallee and Schichauweg – deeper regions of rendering made with dolomitic hydrate are subjected to a consolidation process (cf. Figure 22.9), and this is not reflected in the CO_2 contents. Thus samples down to about 4 mm depth taken from Schichauweg show a mean value of 2.11%; Roedernallee shows 2.97%; whereas at Lerschpfad, 2.35% was measured. Further

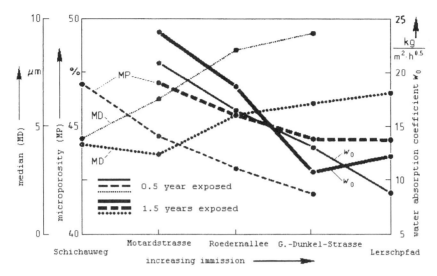

Figure 22.11 Some structural variations of pore-related parameters, determined on plaster made with lime hydrate and referring to locations and exposure time.

information is furnished by a CO_2 distribution for three locations compared to CO_2 concentration prior to exposure (Table 22.5).

It should be noted that carbonation alone cannot be responsible for increased strength of a dolomitic rendering; more favorable conditions at Schichauweg might be a factor. For an explanation of such differences, the "time of wetness" concept could account for countercurrent gradients of mean temperature and RH from the city's center to its outlying areas, as has been discussed by Fitz (1994). Another reason could be the low supply of moisture within this location area. At low levels, residual MgO internally extracts water from originated $Mg(OH)_2$, in such a way as to increase strength (Würzner 1919). The volume augmentation of binder particles thus produced leads to

Table 22.5 CO_2 concentration profiles in dolomitic rendering at three locations and prior to exposure.

Distance from Surface (mm)	CO₂ Content (% by mass)			
	Prior to exposure	After 1.5 years of exposure		
		Schichauweg	Roedernallee	Lerschpfad
1	On average 1.34	2.58	3.85	2.57
2		2.36	3.27	2.20
3		2.23	2.30	–
4		1.28	2.47	2.28

a diminution of pore volume. Because of subsequent consolidation of plaster through drying and cementing of $Mg(OH)_2$ gel, a high final strength will be attained. Over time, this gel becomes crystalline (Nacken 1927), i.e., it "ages" and forms products thermodynamically that are more resistant with an ordered crystalline structure and elevated grain size (Calyj 1963), thus contributing to a further densification of the rendering.

Dolomitic plasters with cement admixture also show an inverted succession of structural strength, so that the most favorable hardening conditions must have occurred at Lerschpfad, with the most unfavorable ones at Schichauweg (cf. Figure 22.10). Probable reasons for this have already been discussed.

Finally, with respect to weathering progress, it should be noted that recent results of a 5-year outdoor exposure study show, in principle, comparable trends (Hoffmann and Niesel 1998a).

REFERENCES

Calyj, V. P. 1963. The aging mechanisms of single metal hydroxides and their systems (orig. Russ.). *Z. neorg. Chim.* **8(2)**:269–273.

DIN EN 196-1. 1990. Prüfverfahren für Zement; Bestimmung der Festigkeit. Edition March 1990, 16 pp.

Fitz, S. 1994. Conservation of historic brick structures. How many open questions were left after seven years of joint efforts within the NATO CCMS Pilot Study? In: Proc. EC Workshop Research on Conservation of Brick Masonry Monuments, Heverlee/Leuven.

Hoffmann, D. 1992. The Federal Institute for Materials Research and Testing: Study on lime mortar and rendering.In: Contrib. EUROLIME Colloquium Karlsruhe, 26/05–28/05/1991, ed. German EUROCARE Secretariat, Karlsruhe, Newsletter **1**:32–35.

Hoffmann, D., and K. Niesel. 1998a. Parameters of lime rendering as modified by atmospheric influence. UN ECE Convention on Long-Range Transboundary Air Pollution: Workshop on Quantification of Effections of Air Pollutants on Materials. Berlin, in press.

Hoffmann, D., and K. Niesel. 1998b. Quantifying the effect of air pollutants on rendering and also moisture-transport phenomena in masonry including its constituents. http://www.bam.de/a_vii/moisture/transport.html.

Hoffmann, D., and H. Rooss. 1994. Zur Erhärtung von Purpasten aus Kalk. *Bautenschutz u. Bausanierung* **17(3)**:48–51; **17(4)**:57–63.

Nacken, R. 1927. Über den Abbinde- und Erhärtungsvorgang der Zemente. *Zement* **16(43)**:1017–1023; **16(44)**:1047–1051.

Wittenburg, C. 1994. Trockene Schadgas- und Partikeldeposition auf verschiedene Sandsteinvarietäten unter besonderer Berücksichtigung atmosphärischer Einflußgrößen. Diss. Fachbereich Chemie, Univ. Hamburg, 14/03/1994. Publ. series: Angewandte Analytik, Univ. Hamburg, No. 22, 137 pp.

Würzner, K. 1919. Die physikalischen Grundlagen des Abbindens und Erhärtens. *Zement* **8(46)**:559–562; **8(47)**:571–574.

23

Effects of Air Pollutants on Renderings

Reaction Zones on Buildings vs. Orientation

D. Hoffmann and K. Niesel

Federal Institute for Materials Research and Testing (BAM), Unter den Eichen 87,
12205 Berlin, Germany

ABSTRACT

Tests carried out for this part of our program suggest that with respect to SO_2, for the same exposure time, the rendered building surface area at the same height position represents a uniform reaction face independent of the cardinal point. At this face, differing concentration profiles develop only later under conditions of the prevailing microclimate and with the aid of cycles of dissolution, transport, and reprecipitation. Compared with this, nitrate and chloride show clear dependence of the facade orientation relative to an emission source. This is the origin of systematic changes in pore structure caused by varying solar irradiation, temperature changes, and dew formation. A much greater influence on a pore system of the same age material is its exposure height. On a building whose lower facade is located near trees and shrubs, one can recognize a remarkable rise of the water absorption coefficient and specific pore volume determined by mercury intrusion porosimetry, increasing in elevation from ground level. One also observes a decrease in coarse and fine pores. This leads to a formation of a preferential diameter between 2 μm and 100 μm, which is practically congruent with the region of capillary activity. Connected with this is a decrease in vapor diffusion resistance. In this way, without reference to the cardinal point, height patterns on a building develop, which are expressed in an increasing weathering intensity at the same exposure duration. Therefore, sulfate formation is determined by quantity and chemistry of binding agent, but is extensively influenced by location on a building.

INTRODUCTION

The formation of strata is not only an associated phenomenon up to the final stage of weathering but also one of main causes for its occurrence (Niesel 1986). During long-term outdoor exposure of a construction material, this is the vehicle as well as the target of the stresses being expressed by changes in structure and chemistry. In the material or in its open pore space, new geometric proportions are gradually produced, which ultimately control penetration and permeation of fluids. During moisture transport one can repeatedly observe how soluble salts precipitate near an evaporation surface, at the interface of a building material with the ambient atmosphere, or close behind it. In the case of rendering, this is true for chemical compounds formed only by reaction of a component with external influences and also for those compounds already present. As a renewable weather-protective coat for a building, such a material is subject to chemical and physical attacks. As in most investigations of this kind, individual findings may not be too important, whereas observed trends require close consideration.

The aggressive media, especially those which react with binding-agent phases, do not exercise their influence uniformly over the entire material volume. This finding does not seem unusual if one considers that the rendering geometry contributes a diminishing efficiency because of a concentration decrease in the substrate direction. In the same way, local conditions ultimately give rise to a gradient caused by the possibility of dew formation or the dispersivity and coating of the crystal surfaces by various reaction products. In this way a heterogeneity perpendicular to a surface can be produced, if it has not already been caused by texturing in the process of manufacture and carbonation. The basis for this is not only gas permeability but also capillary behavior, which is indeed directly related to pore sizes. Under such conditions, a depth profile develops whereby dissolution, local solution transport, and re-precipitation are responsible for its formation. Of course, most of the weathering deterioration does not originate from a single stress factor, rather it is the result of a combination of different causes – an important fact when selective statements on the main deleterious factors are required. This is obviously true for SO_2 attack, since physical processes besides chemical conversion also participate. This has the disadvantage that apparently secondary influences can unexpectedly turn out to be principal causes. Among others, one objective of this research program consisted of analyzing these conditions.

MATERIAL ON A BUILDING: MODIFICATION OF A RENDERING DEPENDING UPON ORIENTATION TO CARDINAL POINTS

It is not easy to pinpoint the causes of the distribution of soluble constituents within the pore system. It is even more difficult to detect their influence on structural characteristics of a building material. Changes at boundaries between aggregate grains and agglomerates of the binding agent caused by local reactions and enrichments as well as by physical processes are not always significant, and sometimes are even superimposed by the scattering of measured values.

Pore space composed mainly of open and permeable cavities causes changes in chemistry, principally parallel to the rendering profile faces. It represents after all the voids between different-size aggregate grains and the local enrichments of binding agent. As a consequence of hardening, both form together a kind of framework granting mechanical strength to the rendering layer, which enables buildings to withstand weathering.

Samples were taken at nearly the same height from several parts of a free-standing three-story house near the Federal Institute, representing its four facades. Because the samples originated from sides of a building diversely oriented and also somewhat varying in their composition, one cannot assume a systematic sequence of properties. The essential similarities would be their common existence for more than about 30 years. Nevertheless, it should be considered that when producing a scraped finish at a building, gravel grains of about 2–5 mm diameter are usually introduced into the raw mix, which then gives the decorative effect intended. This admixture, sometime constituting a volume of up to 20%, was removed by sieving before starting the chemical analysis to assure comparability of the mass of its binding substance with, e.g., that of any smooth finish.

Table 23.1 shows the mix proportions for the rendered finish sampled from four sides of a house nearly at the same height. By subtracting sulfate contents originating from atmospheric SO_2 reaction, one obtains the composition of a lime plaster with cement admixture in all cases.

For mercury porosimetry, the samples were divided into layers of the outer 5 mm and the portion below. Roughness and irregular appearance of the finish layer led to difficulties in preparation as well as to influences on the results obtained. Data determined and values calculated therefrom are given in Table 23.2 (cf. Figure 23.1).

Use has been made of the Ravaglioli interval (R interval) and the microporosity. Leaving aside the mean critical diameter, d_{10m}, which was found to be too near the outer border of the range tested, a variation of discrete values occurs with a tendency from one to the next layer abraded that is independent of cardinal point. Thus, specific

Table 23.1   Composition of ca. 30-year-old external wall rendering samples taken from all sides of the building.

Rendered Finish	M = proportions by mass V = proportions by volume	Ratio of Components		
		Lime	Cement	Sand
ENE facade	M	1.0	0.2	9.7
	V	2.0	0.2	7.4
SSE facade	M	1.0	0.6	12.6
	V	2.0	0.5	9.7
WSW facade	M	1.0	0.6	11.2
	V	2.0	0.5	8.6
NNW facade	M	1.0	0.6	12.4
	V	2.0	0.5	9.6

D. Hoffmann and K. Niesel

Table 23.2 Characteristic values for pore-size distribution determined in a ca. 30-year-old rendering and their change due to differing exposure conditions being dependent on cardinal points.

Sampling Place	Facade (rough and irregular surface)								Gable (smooth surface)			
Orientation	ENE		SSE		WSW		NNW		SSE		NNW	
Height in m	4–6		6–8		6–8		6–8		8–12		8–12	
Depth in mm	0–5	>5	0–5	>5	0–5	>5	0–5	>5	0–5	>5	0–5	>5
Specific pore volume in cm^3/g	0.16	0.16	0.13	0.18	0.17	0.20	0.16	0.17	0.17	0.16	0.19	0.20
d_{10m} in μm	(1)	62.0	(1)	52.5	(1)	68.3	(1)	70.0	(1)	(1)	37.5	(1)
R interval in %	14.6	29.7	20.2	30.0	14.6	18.6	15.7	22.1	20.2	23.0	23.8	16.4
Microporosity in %	49.0	68.5	61.9	75.0	53.2	67.9	53.2	59.8	58.4	62.7	75.0	66.0
Median (radius) in μm	2.7	0.6	0.6	0.5	1.6	0.50	1.0	0.8	1.0	0.8	0.4	0.6

(1) Achieving or exceeding upper limit of method's working range at 75.0 μm pore diameter.

pore volume, R interval, and microporosity increase systematically with depth, whereas the median or 50% fractile decreases. This means a decreasing porosity and a prevalence of coarser pores in the outer layer than in a rendering's interior. A likely explanation may be the clogging of fine pores by neoformation of mineral phases from reaction or by recrystallization. Influences according to respective cardinal points can be possibly expressed by differences in or amount of corresponding values.

Since concentration profiles prove a weathering process occurs in the outer 4 to 5 millimeters, a comparison of surface layers requires special attention (Figure 23.1).

Structural data of the SSE facade vary substantially from those of other sides. Besides the filling of pore space with reaction products, orientation to one of the busiest Berlin streets, "Unter den Eichen," and also greater exposure to sunlight, temperature differences and dew probably play an important role here.

Moreover, one can also satisfactorily estimate available pore space by the water absorption coefficient, w_0, or water vapor diffusion resistance index, μ. Provided that heterogeneity and irregular cross-section are taken into account, both of which determine capillary liquid absorption of the specimen concerned, the fitted model obtained includes some parameters with sufficient accuracy. Although practically dominating the measuring problems for renderings, difficulties result in clarifying such a brittle and crumbly material to specimens that have fairly rectangular contours. Thus, for

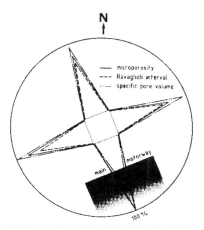

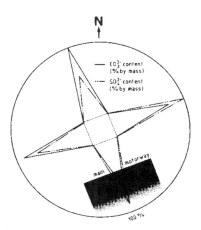

Figure 23.1 Pore-size distribution of surface layers (0–5 mm depth) in external wall renderings: discrete values whose maxima were set to 100%, as represented for the facades of a building.

Figure 23. 2 Sulfate and carbonate concentrations at the surface (1 mm depth) in external wall renderings: contents whose maxima were set to 100%, as represented for the facades of a building.

capillary behavior, integrated average values are obtained. Though one can only perform capillarity measurements on plaster fragments over a total cross-section – corresponding to their absorption surface – and after a relatively short but material-specific time period of about six hours to one day, the curve's validity is not yet satisfactorily guaranteed. However, one can gain information on the important water absorption coefficient. This gives insight into dynamics of rain-water movement penetrating from outside and is one of the driving forces for redistribution of migrating salts within the profile. By automatically recording gravimetric values in this way, plausible curve plots were obtained.

From samples taken, circular-shaped slices with a uniform thickness were examined to determine water vapor diffusion. The low resistance of plaster against deformation during mechanical stress as a result of temperature cycles can be explained by the fact that its open structure accompanies a relatively high porosity. Among other things, this promotes a high permeability for fluids, bringing in reactive constituents. The water absorption coefficient and water vapor diffusion resistance index are highest in samples from the ENE facade; they decrease in those from SSE and NNW; and achieve their minimum at a building's side pointing towards WSW. When plotting both characteristic values against each other, a linear dependence results.

In all samples, chemical analysis indicates a continuous decrease of sulfate content towards the rendering interior. Maximum enrichment of more than 2% relative to the mass of the dried substance was found at the surface of the scraped finish, especially at ENE and SSE facades of the building (see Figure 23.2). In contrast, the lowest amount was detected at its NNW side, which may be ascribed to partial leaching caused by elevated rain incidence. As can be expected, the calcium fraction in an aqueous extract

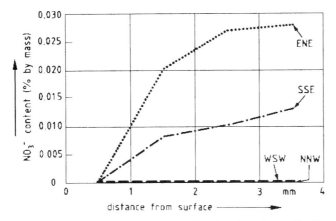

Figure 23.3 Comparative depth profiles showing nitrate distribution in ca. 30-year-old external wall rendering samples taken from all sides of the building.

decreases with increasing depth of the profile. Therefore, in the upper layer of a rough finish from ENE and SSE facades, one can certainly expect a maximum of water-soluble calcium and sulfate fractions, whereas the lowest amount was met at the NNW side. Generally found at traces of 0.03% down to less than 0.01%, nitrate was not detected in all outer layers of a profile but appeared distinctly in the scraped finish of ENE and SSE sides (see Figure 23.3). This nitrate occurrence may obviously be attributed to the proximity to a busy street in Berlin, whereas the smooth finish shows, at both gable-sides, small amounts of nitrate at SSE facade. Nitrite could not be detected. Chloride concentrations – here ranging from 0.02% to less than 0.01% – did not seem to be distributed as systematically as usual for the other anions already cited. In some circumstances there exists a prevailing orientation to SSE and ENE as being the main direction to the source of pollution. Measured pH values in aqueous extracts were always situated above the neutral point, with their maximum at 10.9. They increase with diminishing calcium sulfate content, especially in deeper layers from material of SSE and ENE facades. In aqueous extracts of experimental rendering exposed outdoors, lower pH values have been observed than in their indoor equivalents. This is evidently due to intense carbonation and sulfation at an unobstructed contact with the atmosphere.

There is a steep decline of sulfate content within the first millimeters of depth profile of a lime-containing porous building. It is also not surprising that its absolute value in the same material can be variable with the cardinal point (cf. Figures 23.2, 23.4). However, the systematic change in the sequence of amounts over the entire profile should be considered as the low values for the abraded first millimeter accordingly go hand in hand with relatively elevated values of the fourth millimeter, while conversely high sulfate contents at the surface are associated with low ones in the profile depth. The calculated mean of the four contents belonging to each profile was uniformly close to 0.8% by mass. If one assumes comparable material at all building sides at the same height and a satisfactory moisture supply for solution transport, a unilateral immission does not have to be taken into account as a possible explanation for the mutual intersection of the individual concentration curves, as conditioned by the

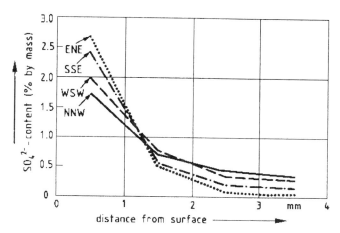

Figure 23.4   Sulfate distribution in ca. 30-year-old external wall renderings sampled from all sides of a house at the same height.

orientation of a building towards its source. To the contrary, one can imagine that – proceeding from a nearly homogeneous distribution in the first four millimeters of the profile – a supplementary enrichment of this salt would merely have taken place, in the long run, in the sense of neoprecipitation originating by a more or less intense evaporation. If this result can be confirmed by additional analytical data obtained at other buildings sampled at all their facades, we will be able to dispell a long-standing misconception. This would mean that, at least in the case of sulfate, one has to understand the entire building rendering surface at one and the same height as a practically uniform reaction face, at which – depending upon microclimate – the formation of different concentration gradients would have taken place afterwards as a consequence of the cycles of dissolution, transport, and re-precipitation.

Unfortunately chemistry only permits the determination of concentration profiles caused by different air pollutants and graded in millimeters for the powdered material or aqueous extracts that are needed. Structural changes can be detected integrally in ranges between 0–5 mm distance from a sample's surface or from a depth greater than 5 mm, since for mercury porosimetry a certain quantity of material in solid pieces must be available, which can only be arduously obtained from the friable sample. The abrasion behavior, which indirectly yielded information on structural changes in this range, also shows considerable differences related to the direction of outdoor exposure (Figure 23.5).

Plainly visible is a distinct hardening in the scraped finish layer down to about 2 cm depth at the SSE facade; such a layer occurs much less at the NNW side and does not appear at all on the ENE side. In the latter, one observes a comparable resistance near the surface and also in a 3 to 5 mm depth, corresponding to an almost linear increase of the cumulative curve. This behavior can also be deduced from structure: the SSE side simultaneously presents the highest number of fine pores and the lowest pore volume, whereas the conditions of the ENE side are reversed (high specific pore volume, low portion of micropores). In light of this, the influence of carbonation or sulfation, which took place at its expense, does not seem to be so significant.

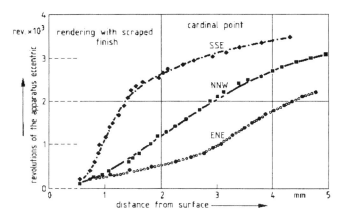

Figure 23.5   Abrasion behavior of a wall rendering, depending upon the respective cardinal point: cumulative curves of single amounts of wear of specimens taken from the same height.

A smooth finish (rubbed surface) present at the gable region of this building shows, on the other hand, a comparable abrasivity on the SSE and NNW facades down to a depth of about 2 cm (Figure 23.6). At a greater distance from the surface, the rendering of the NNW side is stronger, which also reflects a higher amount of fine pores and a shift of the median to smaller pore radii in contrast to material of the opposite exposure direction (cf. Table 23.2). Generally, however, differences between scraped and smooth renderings can be determined with regard to structure and other data, which are clearly expressed by abrasion behavior and sulfate absorption. The surface layer rich in binder is always found in this type of finish, which is inevitably obtained by a rubbing procedure. Although largely remote in this case, it has possibly exerted a kind of protective function for underlying material and offered resistance to hardening by carbonation, sulfation, and recrystallization. Weathering intensity of rendered facades at a certain height, caused by air pollutants such as SO_2, is not determined to such a degree by the direction of the emission source, but rather by the microclimatic circumstances at the exposure site, whereas pollution by nitrate or chloride show clear dependence. This can also be deduced from results of a survey on facades with limestone called "Caen stone" from Caen, France, where sulfates from traffic and industry as well as

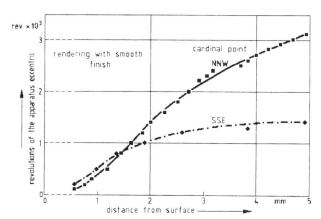

Figure 23.6   Abrasion behavior of a wall rendering, depending upon the respective cardinal point: cumulative curves of single amounts of wear of specimens taken from the same height.

chlorides from the marine environment of the nearby Atlantic coast are causing corresponding deterioration (Samson-Gombert 1991).

It should be emphasized that only water-soluble constituents are captured this way; those already fixed by precipitation and having formerly participated in profile formation are not. Although this instantaneous view of a continuing evolution is subjected to the seeming disadvantage that monitoring of former stages is no longer possible, it yields information of material behavior with regard to present absorption and solution transport. Previous depositions and conversions characterized merely by a summarizing effect can be investigated by an acid digest or, better directly with a scanning electron microscope combined, for instance, with an energy-dispersive X-ray analyzer.

MATERIAL ON A BUILDING: HEIGHT-DEPENDENT MODIFICATIONS

During visual evaluation, care was taken to sample rendering fragments from regions situated as far as possible perpendicularly from one another. For structural characterization, the water absorption coefficient as well as discrete values of pore-size distribution and vapor diffusion resistance index were utilized. Figure 23.7 shows curves for the flat fragments sampled from different heights of a house on a rendered external wall facing west at the yard side. Here, trees and shrubs were planted around the building. With increasing elevation from ground level, we found a considerable rise in the water absorption coefficient, which could indicate that the degree of weathering or

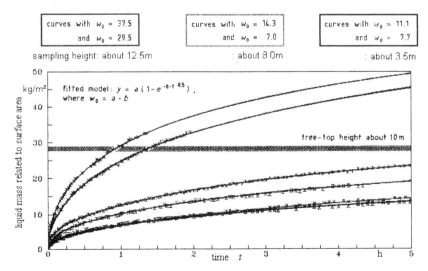

Figure 23.7   Capillary absorption behavior of six ca. 40-year-old rendering fragments (lime plaster with cement admixture) taken from western facade of a dwelling house at different heights.

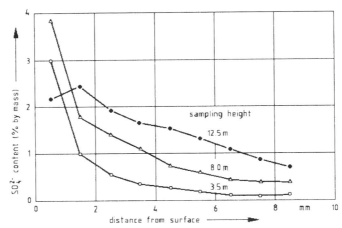

Figure 23.8 Sulfate distribution in ca. 40-year-old external wall renderings sampled from different heights of a dwelling house.

structural damage due to corresponding attack was augmented. In addition, the sulfate content increases with building height, as seen in Figure 23.8. Plotting average sulfate content across the whole profile versus elevation from ground level, we found an almost linear increase with height. The distribution in samples taken from 12.5 m height further indicates leaching in the first millimeter.

Nitrate and chloride appear only in the lower parts of the building, i.e., they are detected only at 3.5 m. As previously found, the distribution is characterized by a gradual increase with depth, where these ions are missing in the outer 2 to 3 mm. It remains doubtful, however, whether maximum values of 0.018% for nitrate and 0.012% for chloride could exert significant influence on weathering progress. Calcium runs parallel to sulfate, potassium probably does also; however, at 0.01% it cannot be taken into account. From this building, samples were taken at different heights for determining porosimetry by mercury intrusion.

Integrating results across the whole thickness of the plaster, we deduced the influence of exposure height upon the discrete values of porosimetric data already mentioned (Figure 23.9). For this purpose, the same parameters as before were used, as well as the water absorption coefficient and water vapor diffusion resistance index, which were plotted against the sampling heights on the building. We observed that the specific pore volume and w_0 grow with increasing distance from ground level, whereas microporosity, R interval, and μ decrease, meaning that the small pores will be shifted to larger diameters.

This finding can even be expanded, considering for example a change of d_{10m} value for the single plaster courses with increasing elevation. One can monitor how weathering, starting from the surface, affects increasingly deeper layers of rendering, so that at 12.5 m fitting of this parameter was almost fully attained over the whole plaster cross-section. Specific pore volume shows a corresponding behavior (cf. Table 23.3). From

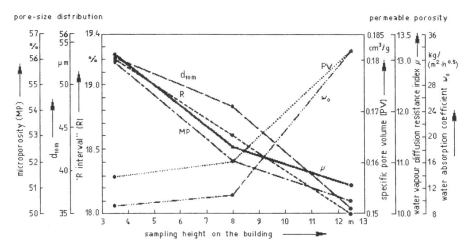

Figure 23.9 Pore characteristics of a ca. 40-year-old rendering and their change by means of differing exposure height, western facade, yard-side.

these results, we concluded that a diminution of coarse pores will first be caused, for example, by filling with reaction products from sulfuric air pollutants. Such a conversion leads to a narrowing of the pore channels to about a third and consequently a lowering of d_{10m} to a smaller diameter. Fine pores are also subject to systematic change, i.e.,

Table 23.3 Characteristic values for pore-size distribution determined in a ca. 40-year-old rendering and their change by means of differeing exposure conditions dependent on building height.

Sampling Place	Facade (smooth surface)					
Orientation	W		W		W	
Height in m	2–4		6–8		12–16	
Depth in mm	0–5	>5	0–5	>5	0–5	>5
Specific pore volume in cm³/g	0.15	0.17	0.15	0.16	0.18	0.19
d_{10m} (diameter) in μm	52.7	53.7	37.4	57.7	35.1	37.8
R interval in %	20	18	20	17	18	17
Microporosity in %	57	54	54	50	51	48
Median (radius) in μm	1.2	1.5	1.7	2.5	2.2	2.8
Water absorption coefficient, w_0, in kg/(m² · h⁰·⁵)	9.4		10.8		33.4	
Water vapor diffusion resistance index, μ	13.1		11.3		10.6	

here a decrease of the micropore portion of the whole profile is found with increasing height, but differences between both layers (from 0 to 5 mm and greater than 5 mm in depth) are not remarkably reduced. From this follows a pore-size distribution characterized by a steeper development of the cumulative curve, which corresponds to a pronounced maximum of pores during simultaneous narrowing of their range. Pores between 2–100 μm diameter are principally concerned, whereby the distribution curve shows a distinct maximum at 10 μm.

Since capillary effects occur in pores between about 0.1 μm and 100 μm diameter (Lutz et al. 1985), the water absorption coefficient (as a representation of this behavior of a material) will be also influenced by this convergence. Vapor diffusion takes place in pores larger than 0.1 μm in diameter. According to the results obtained, the resistance to water vapor diffusion decreases with sampling height. The corresponding process is practically not influenced by coarser pores but more by finer pores, since once their fraction decreases, the specific pore volume simultaneously increases. This could mean that through a weathering process, fine pores were enlarged and coarser pores narrowed by recrystallization and neoformation of mineral phases (Figure 23.9). This is in accordance with changes of d_{10m} (cf. Figure 23.8). Together with the corresponding findings, this causes an elevated porosity and results in the vapor diffusion behavior. Therefore one can, at least in the case of samples tested, amplify the statement in such a way that this phenomenon is not essentially affected by more intense weather attack on the higher situated parts of a building. Another factor for structural change could be plant growth, especially when it is found at a greater building height and seen as traces in coarser pores of surface samples taken there.

The influence of sampling height at a building is also evident, as shown by the grinding abrasion curves determined on rendering fragments (Figure 23.10). With an increasing height position, strength decreases in accordance with pore data being equal to a smaller portion of micropores, shift of median to coarser pores, and increase of pore volume.

Here, an elevated intensity of weathering at upper building parts compared to lower ones clearly emerges. It is obvious since the abrasion behavior of a sample from 3.5 m height assumes a tripartite curve course. The first part – down to about 1 mm depth (I) – is characterized by a steep slope of the cumulative curve (about 1700 revolutions of the eccentric per mm of depth; crust indication). It is followed by a second section (II), with about 600 rev./mm ranging between 1 and 3 mm distance

Figure 23.10   A coarse pore in a rendering, filled with sulfate reaction products causing size reduction (SEM micrograph).

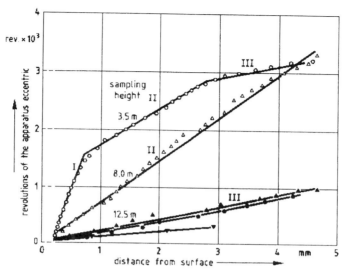

Figure 23.11 Modification of abrasion behavior of rendering fragments with sampling height: cumulative curves of single amounts of wear (Roman numerals indicate layers of same strength).

from the specimen's surface. The next part (III) finally shows no more than 200 rev./mm. A similar slope, as in section III, is found in material from a greater height. Thus, rendering obtained at an 8 m height reflects approximately curve section II at 3.5 m, whereas rendering at 12.5 m height corresponds to that of section III of the same materials. Thus with increasing building height, an impression emerges not only of a

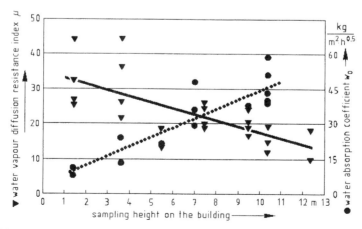

Figure 23.12 Capillary absorption and water vapor diffusion behaviors of rendering fragments taken from the facade of a ca. 50-year-old dwelling house at different heights.

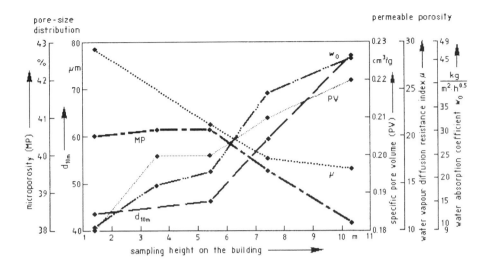

Figure 23.13 Pore characteristics of a ca. 50-year-old rendering with hydrated lime and cement admixture and their modification by means of differing exposure height.

structural breakup but also of erosion, and the original rendering surface is no longer visible – a suspicion which increases by visual assessment of corresponding samples.

If vegetation is absent around a building, nearly the same behavior is observed. Thus an elevation of w_0 is found with increasing distance from ground level, whereas the μ value shows a countercurrent behavior (Figure 23.11). If a diagram analogous to Figure 23.9 is developed for such a building from discrete values of the mercury porosimeter test, w_0, and μ value, the same course is indicated with one exception: as values plotted against sampling height (Figure 23.12). Because of intense degradation of the surface and its roughness, only characteristics that represent results of material sampled at least at a depth of more than 5 mm could be taken into consideration. Together with w_0, they demonstrate a dependence upon building height. Based on the weathering degree, both specific pore volume and w_0 increase, while microporosity as well as μ simultaneously decrease. However, contrary to previous experiences (Hoffmann 1992), the d_{10m} value expresses an inverse tendency. Showing a clear displacement, this parameter behaves as a measure for modification of the coarse pore range.

This can be seen by comparing test results at the heights of 1.4 and 10.5 m. Such remarkable phenomenon, exhibiting a narrowing and then widening of pore space, can be explained by the countercurrent dependence of sulfate content (Figure 23.13). If diminishing of pores with increasing building height could be formerly ascribed to a neoformation of clogging salt precipitates, then here it is the result of decreasing sulfate with height attributable to leaching and thinning of the profile during erosion, which left the original surface unavailable for analysis. In the previous case, protective

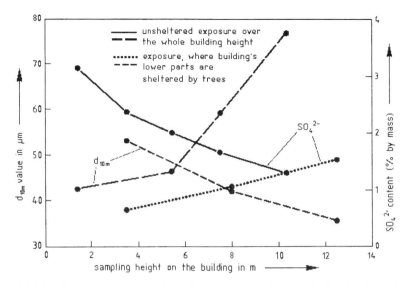

Figure 23.14 Countercurrent dependence in each case of sulfate content and portion of coarse pores d_{10m} in external rendering from two walls facing west (ca. 40–50 years old), plotted versus building height.

and absorptive behavior by plant growth (e.g., trees) at lower levels could have the opposite effect. On the present plant-free site, however, total sulfate amount originating from the external 5 mm abraded layer of greater than 3% by mass at a height of 1.4 m diminishes to 1.7% at the 7.4 m level; however, the d_{10m} value taken from samples at a deeper layer shifts simultaneously from 40 μm to 80 μm. This assumption is permissible since the observed tendency also remains constant in deeper parts of a rendering profile. Thus at a distance from the surface of >5 mm, a sulfate content of >1% still exists at 1.5 m height, whereas 7.4 m samples show no more than 0.5% at a corresponding depth. As mentioned, contrary to earlier work, we note a decrease of total averaged sulfate content with building height, which corresponding depth profiles may reflect (Figure 23.14). Therefore a common feature is the diminishing of sulfate with increasing depth.

In this way a zonal formation on a building takes shape and finds its expression in a different weathering intensity after the same exposure duration, either as a sulfate enrichment (as reported by Grün 1933) or in an elevated immission by air pollutant precipitation (Barcellona et al. 1972; Efes and Luckat 1977; Luckat 1974).

Statements that nitrate and chloride are enriched in the rendering's interior could be confirmed. The NO_x reaction was conspicuously linked to the cardinal-point orientation and the close proximity to an emission source of a main motorway; this finding can be transferred to a building's height (Figure 23.15). As has been shown (Hoffmann 1992), detectable quantities appear predominantly in the building's lower parts, up to 4 or 5 m.

280   *D. Hoffmann and K. Niesel*

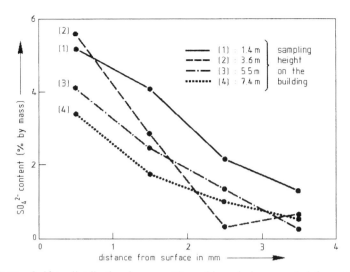

Figure 23.15 Sulfate distribution in a ca. 50-yr-old rendering sampled from the western facade of a dwelling house at different heights.

REFERENCES

Barcellona, S., L. Barcellona Vero, and F. Guidobaldi. 1972. The front of S. Giacomo degli Incurabili Church in Rome: Biological and chemical surface analyses. Istituto di Fisica Tecnica – Consiglio Nazionale delle Ricerche. Roma: Centro di Studio Cause de Deperimento e Metodi di Conservazione delle Opere d'Arte, No. 15.

Efes, Y., and S. Luckat. 1977. Relations between corrosion of sandstones and uptake rates of air pollutants at the Cologne cathedral. In: 2nd Intl. Symp. on the Deterioration of Building Stones, pp. 193–200. Athens: The Chair of Physical Chemistry of the National Technical University of Athens.

Grün, R. 1933. Die Verwitterung der Bausteine vom chemischen Standpunkt. *Chemiker-Ztg.* **57(41)**:401–404.

Hoffmann, D. 1992. The Federal Institute for Materials Research and Testing: Study on lime mortar and rendering. In: Contrib. EUROLIME Colloquium Karlsruhe, 26/05–28/05/1991, ed. German EUROCARE Secretariat, Karlsruhe, Newsletter **1**:32–35.

Luckat, S. 1974. Die Einwirkung von Luftverunreinigungen auf die Bausubstanz des Kölner Domes. II. *Kölner Domblatt* **38/39**:95–106.

Lutz, P., R. Jenisch, H. Klopfer, H. Freymuth, and L. Kampf. 1985. Lehrbuch der Bauphysik, Schall, Wärme, Feuchte, Licht, Brand; Teil 1 einer Baukonstruktionslehre, Stuttgart: B.G.H. Teubner.

Niesel, K. 1986. Aspekte der Natursteinverwitterung aus der Sicht eines Materialprüfers. *Bautenschutz + Bausanierung* **9(1)**:16–23; **9(2)**:60–66.

Samson-Gombert, C. 1991. Relations entre les altérations d'un calcaire en oeuvre et les paramètres de l'environnement, principaux résultats et applications. In: Actes du Colloque International ASESMO/LCCM sur la Détérioration des Matériaux de Construction, La Rochelle 12/06–14/06/1991, ed. F. Auger, pp. 185–194. La Rochelle: Univ. de Poitiers, Institut Universitaire Technique (IUT).

24

Salt-induced Gypsum Formation on Renderings

P. FRIESE and A. PROTZ

FEAD-GmbH, Research and Development Laboratory for Rehabilitation of Old Buildings
and Ancient Monuments, Rudower Chaussee 5, 12526 Berlin, Germany

ABSTRACT

The appearance of dark areas on the surface of calcitic materials exposed to air pollution is usually caused by uptake of sulfur dioxide and the subsequent reaction to form gypsum. When liquid water is present, e.g., rain, rising damp, and condensation, the velocity of gypsum formation is 1–2 orders of magnitude higher than in the absence of liquid water. The presence of hygroscopic salts is shown to have a similar effect; the growth of dark areas on facades is explained by an autocatalytic reaction of calcite with sulfur dioxide and oxides of nitrogen from the air. Finally, a mechanism for the growth of gypsum crusts is proposed.

INTRODUCTION

In the streets of old cities and towns, we very often see dark-colored bands and spots on renderings or other calcite-containing facades (see Figure 24.1). These bands seem to grow slowly from the ground upwards and sometimes reach heights of several meters above ground level. Remarkable are the comparatively sharp boundaries between the dark spots and their surroundings.

Most homeowners and other concerned people interpret the appearance of these disfiguring dark areas as a sign of rising damp and very often undertake extensive measures to stop the supposed ascending water. However, water and salt analyses of the masonry carried out on many of these buildings showed that there was no significant rising damp and that only a moderate amount of water (2%–5%) was found adjacent to the ground level (Künzel 1991).

To study the origin of the described dark areas and bands, chemical analyses were carried out on samples from the surface layer (depth 1 mm), which were taken along a vertical axis of the facade shown in Figure 24.1. According to the results of these

Figure 24.1 Formation of dark areas and bands at the surface of renderings.

chemical analyses, which are shown in Figure 24.2, the dark spots are caused by formation of a gypsum layer at the surface. At the lower part of the wall, nearly all of the original calcite is converted into gypsum through reaction with atmospheric sulfur dioxide:

$$CaCO_3 + SO_2 + 1/2 \, O_2 + 2 \, H_2O \quad \rightarrow \quad CaSO_4 \cdot 2 \, H_2O + CO_2 \,. \quad (24.1)$$

In the intermediate region between the dark spots and surroundings, a sharp decrease of the gypsum concentration and an increase of calcite concentration is observable.

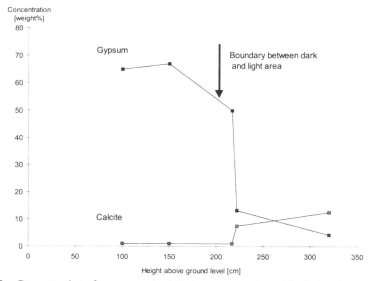

Figure 24.2 Concentration of gypsum and calcite in the surface layer (depth 1mm) vs. height above ground level.

It is well known that gypsum crusts may incorporate dust particles, which darken the material, and that sometimes the crusts on marble and other pure calcitic materials are nearly black. The partial solution in water and the recrystallization of gypsum crystals leads to a strong adhesion of the dust particles to the gypsum crust.

Reaction 24.1 needs water for the formation of gypsum, and it is well known that the absorption of sulfur dioxide is enhanced by increasing relative air humidity (RH) (Künzel and Walther 1991; Spicer 1992; Spedding 1969). When liquid water is present (e.g., rain, rising damp, or condensation), the reaction velocity is 1–2 orders of magnitude higher than in the absence of liquid water.

SALT-INDUCED GYPSUM FORMATION

Reaction velocity depends on the concentration of the reactants, and it can be assumed that one has homogeneous gypsum formation over the entire area of a facade, provided there is a uniform distribution of atmospheric sulfur dioxide and water. Splashing rainwater, rising damp, and hygroscopic salts may accelerate gypsum formation in the surrounding ground, and thus the appearance of dark areas. However, the growth of these areas to heights of several meters on dry masonry and the formation of the sharp boundaries still need to be explained.

The concentrations of some ions of soluble salts in the dark gypsum layer and in the lighter surface layer of the rendering are shown in Figure 24.3. The samples were taken at a distance of 5 cm (below and above the boundary of the dark area), at 1 mm depth.

After extraction with water, the ion concentration was determined by ion chromatography. Remarkable is the approximate tenfold higher nitrate concentration in the gypsum layer. The absence of corresponding sodium, potassium, and magnesium ions suggests that calcium nitrate was formed by reaction of the calcite with the nitric oxides (NO_x) polluting the air:

$$CaCO_3 + 2\,NO_2 + 1/2\,O_2 + nH_2O \quad \rightarrow \quad Ca(NO_3)_2 \cdot nH_2O + CO_2\,. \quad (24.2)$$

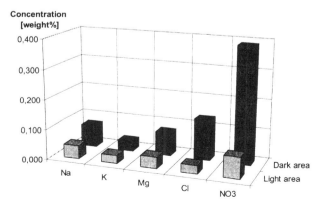

Figure 24.3 Concentration of selected anions and cations in the surface layer (depth 1 mm) from the same facade shown in Figure 24.1. Height above ground level: 217 cm and 222 cm.

Calcium nitrate is very hygroscopic, and at RHs >50% it forms liquid hydrates. Under normal weather conditions (in middle Europe), this means that the calcium nitrate in the surface layer of the rendering forms a liquid salt solution that is distributed in the surface layer. This solution enhances the uptake of sulfur dioxide as well as nitrogen oxides from the air; new gypsum and calcium nitrate are formed, accelerating the reaction, which is limited only by the concentration of the pollutants in the air. In chemical kinetics, these "feedback" mechanisms are known as autocatalytic reactions. Some of these reactions may form reaction fronts or waves (see Figure 24.4) and there is an obvious similarity to the formation and growth of dark areas on renderings.

Taking into account the action of calcium nitrate as a catalyst, the following simple explanation for the growth of the described dark areas on renderings can be given. In the area surrounding the immediate ground, enough water is available (rain, rising damp) to accelerate gypsum and calcium nitrate formation. The reaction ceases after the main portion of calcite is converted into gypsum. The resulting gypsum crust has a lower average pore-size diameter (see Figure 24.5) than the undisturbed mortar. Thus, in the periodic change of wetting and drying of the rendering, the liquid calcium nitrate solution remains in the gypsum crust because of higher capillary forces.

The uptake of sulfur dioxide and nitric oxides into the rendering that is dry and not covered with a salt-containing gypsum crust is comparatively low, because there is not enough water available.

The preconditions for an enhanced reaction of the air pollutants with the rendering materials are given at the boundary between the gypsum crust and the nearly undisturbed rendering. Enough calcite and calcium nitrate solution are available to act as a catalyst, which leads to an accelerated reaction velocity. Thus, the dark gypsum crust grows into areas that are not yet covered with gypsum.

Figure 24.4 Chemical waves of the Belousow-Zhapotinski reaction (Field and Schneider 1988); view of a liquid surface of the reaction system (above) and formation of dark spots on renderings (Künzel 1991) (right).

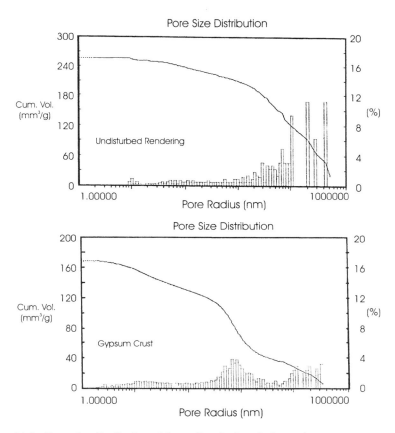

Figure 24.5 Pore-size distribution of the undisturbed rendering and gypsum crust.

CONCLUSION

The described dark areas and bands on renderings are observable, especially in geographic regions with a high incidence of air pollution. The growth mechanism of gypsum crusts described in this paper is only a hypothesis, based on analytical results at damaged renderings of several buildings. To verify this hypothesis, it is necessary to carry out further experiments and observations over a period of several years.

REFERENCES

Field, R.J., und F.W. Schneider. 1988. Oszillierende chemische Reaktionen und nichtlineare Dynamik. *Chemie in unserer Zeit* **22**:17–29.

Künzel, H. 1991. Trocknungsblockade durch Mauerversalzung. *Bautenschutz + Bausanierung* **14**:63.

Künzel, H.M., und W. Walther. 1991. Einflüsse von Feuchte und Konservierungsmaßnahmen auf die Schwefeldioxidaufnahme von Natursteinen. *Bautenschutz + Bausanierung* **14**:93.

Spedding, D.J. 1969. Sulphur dioxide uptake by limestone. *Atmosph. Environ.* **3**:683.

Spicer, E.C. 1992. Dry deposition of SO_2 on limestone and marble: Role of humidity. In: Proc. 7th Intl. Congr. on Deterioration and Conservation of Stone, ed. G. Delagdo Rodrigues et al., p. 397. Lisbon: Laboratório Nacional de Engenharia Civil.

25

Adobe Brick of an Ancient City Wall in Reggio Calabria

G. BORTOLASO

Syremont S.p.A. (Montedison Group), via Fauser 4, 28100 Novara, Italy

ABSTRACT

Sun-dried bricks from an ancient city wall in Reggio Calabria (Italy) have been analyzed. Since their unearthing in the 1960s, they have badly decayed and a documented restoration was carried out in 1968, which involved a partial replacement with new bricks. The physical, mineralogical, and chemical composition of the original and new bricks was ascertained in order to plan a proper conservation intervention, eventually using the same 1968 "recipe." The results show a very close similarity between the recent bricks and the original ones, suggesting adoption of the same fabrication for the new material to be used for the replacement. Other recommendations for the maintenance of the remains are given in the conclusions.

INTRODUCTION

In this study, 20-meter-long relics of an ancient Greek wall surrounding the town of Reggio Calabria, in Southern Italy, in the area known to archaeologists as Magna Graecia, were examined. Remnants of Greek civilization abound in Southern Italy, particularly in Calabria and Sicily.

Around 1968, in the urban area of the so-called "Angels' Hill" in Reggio Calabria, the remains of a thick wall were unearthed. It comprised two adobe brick curtain walls, 4 meters apart, with a rubble filling (Figures 25.1 and 25.2).

The new atmospheric conditions soon necessitated a conservation intervention, which included a partial replacement of the bricks. Following the advice of Professors Gullini and Chiari of Turin University (unpublished report at Soprintendenza ai beni archeologici della Calabria, Reggio Calabria), the original brick composition was identified and imitated for the manufacture of new pieces of adobe, following the traditional sun-baking procedure.

Figure 25.1 View of the original wall (lower part) integrated with new bricks (upper part). Maximum height, 2.30 m.

Figure 25.2 Cross-section of the brick curtain walls filled with rubble.

By 1990, the state of conservation of the wall was again at issue, and the institution in charge of the archaeological site commissioned a thorough study to plan for the treatment and protection of the whole structure.

SAMPLING

From the curtain wall facing the street, three brick samples were taken. Samples No. 1 and 2 were determined to be "new," while No. 3 was original. Two more samples, 4 and 5, were taken from the curtain wall facing the hill's slope. Both were found to be original brick material. A final sample, No. 6, was taken from the southeastern part of the wall, which also faces the street, and determined to be original material.

ANALYTICAL PROCEDURES AND RESULTS

All samples were oven dried at 65°C to constant weight and sieved through a 0.1 mm mesh sieve. The grain-size screening allowed for a basic differentiation between varied compositions. As seen in Table 25.1, the original adobe bricks show a tendency toward a coarser grain size, although fewer samples of new brick were examined.

Table 25.1   Residual fraction with grain size > 0.10 mm.

Sample Number	%
1 new	56.4
2 new	57.1
3 original	57.2
4 original	71.4
5 original	81.6
6 original	73.2

Two samples (No. 1 and 6) were chosen as representative of the newly made and original bricks. According to the ASTM standards (D 4318-84), their plastic limit was calculated.

A water capillary absorption test was also carried out on four samples, representatives of both modern and ancient manufacture. As seen in Table 25.2, the plastic limit is twice as high in new brick than in the ancient one, whereas the percentage of water absorbed by capillarity is unvaried in the paired samples.

Table 25.2   Plastic limit (on grain size < 0.10 mm) and capillary water absorption.

Sample Number	Plastic Limit%	Water Absorption %
1 new	35.6	29.1
2 new	–	29.3
4 original	–	20.9
6 original	17.3	21.5

Table 25.3   Chemical composition (fraction with grain size < 0.10 mm).

Sample Number	SiO$_2$ %	TiO$_2$ %	Al$_2$O$_3$ %	Fe$_2$O$_3$ (Fe^{2+}+ Fe^{3+}) %	MnO %	MgO %
1 new	44.8	1.8	17.4	7.6	0.2	1.7
2 new	39.6	1.6	15.3	6.4	0.2	1.2
3 original	49.2	1.9	16.6	6.8	0.3	0.8
4 original	53.8	2.3	15.9	6.8	0.2	0.8
5 original	47.6	2.3	19.8	7.7	0.2	1.0
6 original	55.7	2.3	16.8	6.8	0.3	1.0

Sample Number	CaO %	Na$_2$O %	K$_2$O %	CO$_2$ %	SO$_3$ %	N$_2$O$_5$ %	Cl %	WL* %
1 new	7.3	2.0	2.4	3.1	0.03	<0.01	0.01	7.7
2 new	10.6	1.5	2.4	6.2	0.08	<0.01	0.03	8.8
3 original	2.9	2.0	2.5	0.15	0.18	1.00	1.00	9.7
4 original	2.4	2.1	2.9	0.4	0.07	0.17	0.34	7.0
5 original	2.4	2.2	3.0	0.7	0.30	0.82	0.73	9.65
6 original	1.9	2.2	2.9	0.4	0.21	0.02	0.05	6.2

* Weight loss at 1,000 °C.

The chemical composition of the fraction featuring a grain size finer than 0.1 mm was analyzed after drying in oven at 105°C. On the same material, the ignition loss at 1,000°C was also calculated: this decrease accounts for the water of hydration and organic carbon present in the brick powder (see Table 25.3).

The silicon and aluminum oxide (SiO$_2$ and Al$_2$O$_3$) contents, along with the iron content (Fe$_2$O$_3$), show very limited variations. This confirms the similarity of the main components of the new and ancient adobe. The accessory components, however, reported as calcium, carbon, magnesium, sulfur, nitrogen oxides (CaO, CO$_2$, MgO, SO$_3$, N$_2$O$_5$), and chlorine (Cl) are more differentiated.

The mineralogical composition of the fraction with grain size smaller than 0.10 mm was analyzed by X-ray diffractometry, thus allowing a partial identification of the sandy portion and a complete identification of the clay portion.

According to the Udden-Wentworth scale, the classification of the clastic material is the following:

sand $\geq$ 0.0625 mm; silt $\geq$ 0.0039 mm < 0.0625 mm; clay < 0.0039 mm.

Table 25.4 shows the approximate occurrences of the minerals belonging to both the clastic and fine fractions. After gentle grinding without water and after sieving to separate the material with particles diameter smaller than 124 μ, the analytical procedure for identifying the clay material followed these steps:

- X-ray diffractogram of the untreated material,
- X-ray diffractogram of the material treated with ethylene-glycol (complete expansion of smectite and partial expansion of vermiculite),
- X-ray diffractogram of the material heated at 550°C for two hours (differentiation between caolinite and halloysite structures, collapse of smectite and vermiculite).

The differences in mineralogical composition of the four samples further underline the different manufacture of the adobe group of bricks. Illite, which is the only clay mineral found in the examined samples, is remarkably abundant in the original Greek bricks, whereas it is scarce in the newly made ones. Although it cannot be proven positively, one could also suppose that the original source for the raw clay is coincident or very similar to the one chosen for the modern intervention.

Though a petrographical analysis on the thin-sections was not carried out, a partial evaluation of the mineralogical composition, which included the larger grain size fraction, was performed on polished sections examined under reflected light.

In Figures 25.3 and 25.4 one can see the higher content of large grain size minerals in the new brick, compared to the finer grain size present in the ancient one.

The identification of the minerals was hampered by the use of reflected light, instead of transmitted light, and could only confirm the occurrences of quartz and plagioclase in both types of bricks. Crystals of calcite were noted in the new ones.

Table 25.4 Mineralogical composition.

Sample Number	Calcite	Quartz	Plagioclase	Illite
1 new	+	++	+	+
2 new	+	++	–	+
4 original	–	++	+	+++
6 original	–	++	+	+++

Legend: – absent + scarce
++ abundant +++ very abundant

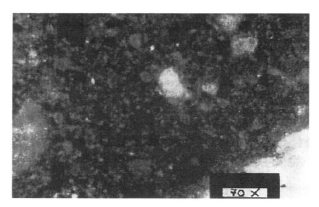

Figure 25.3   Mean grain size of a modern brick (70×, reflected light).

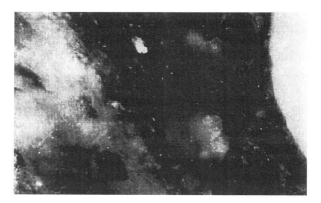

Figure 25.4   Mean grain size of an original brick (70×, reflected light).

CONCLUSIONS

Results obtained through the chemical, physical, and mineralogical analyses of the adobe bricks could differentiate the bricks manufactured in ancient and modern times. No remarkable difference was ascertained and the 1968 restoration can be considered highly successful.

A serious threat to the wall is posed by the new environmental conditions to which it is exposed following excavation. Although the basal part of the brick curtains were reburied to prevent collapse, the upper part, which was the object of our study, underwent new and severe stresses.

Climatological changes, which occurred after the Greek period, have transformed the environmental context in such a way that unfired clay material in this area cannot nowadays last without adequate protection.

During the last conservation intervention, ethyl-silicate was applied as a consolidant on the archaeological brick curtains, but its effectiveness is no longer apparent. Present conditions are so severe that even gentle pressure causes the bricks, ancient and new, to crumble.

To provide for the prevention and care of the archaeological remains, I suggest that the following steps be taken:

- integration with bricks having the same composition as the original ones,
- monitoring of the microclimatological conditions, with special regard to wind direction,
- installation over, and eventually around, the wall of an effective architectural shield capable of keeping the structure dry,
- maintenance of the archaeological site, with eradication of the plants growing on the structure.

Once all of these requirements are met, a further consolidation would be recommended to improve the physico-mechanical characteristics of the material.

Archaeologists and maintenance operators should be aware that any intervention would prove unsuccessful if, as in the case of all outdoor works of art, continuous care of the remains is not taken.

ACKNOWLEDGEMENTS

I am indebted to Ms. Andronico and Mr. Ascenti from the Soprintendenza ai beni archeologici della Calabria for their efficient and extensive aid.

REFERENCES

Accardo, A., S. Massa, P. Rossi-Doria, and M. Tabasso. 1978. Measures of porosity and mechanical resistance in order to evaluate the state of deterioration of some stones. In: Deterioration and Protection of Stone Monuments Intl. Symp., pp. 115–122. Paris: RILEM-UNESCO.

Albini, A., 1979. Sulla manifattura del mattone. Un po' di storia. In: Il mattone di Venezia, pp. 24–28. Venice: Cummne de Venezia.

Berner, R.A., 1981. Kinetics of weathering and diagenesis. In: Kinetics of Geochemical Processes, pp. 11–134, ed. Lasaga and Kirkpatrick. Washington, D.C.: Mineralogical Soc. of America.

Binda, L., G. Baronio, and A.E. Charola, 1988. Deterioration of porous materials due to salt crystallization under different thermohygrometric conditions. In: 6th Intl. Congress on Deterioration and Conservation of Stone, pp. 279–287, ed. J. Ciabach. Torun, Poland: Nicholas Copernicus Univ.

Bonora, F., 1979. Proposte metodologiche per uno studio storico dei mattoni. In: Il mattone di Venezia, pp. 57–64. Venice: Cummne de Venezia.

Dibble, W.E., and W.A. Tiller, 1981. Non-equilibrium water/rock interactions. Model for interface-controlled reactions. *Geochimic. Cosmochim. Acta* **45**:79–92.

Holdren, G.R., and R.A. Berner. 1979. Mechanism of feldspar weathering: Experimental studies. *Geochimic. Cosmochim. Acta* **43**:1161–1171.

Lindsay, W.L. 1979. Chemical Equilibria in Soils. New York: Wiley.

Robinson, G.C. 1984. The relationship between pore structure and durability of brick. *Ceramic Bull.* **63**:295–300.

Torraca, G., 1979. Physico-chemical deterioration of porous rigid building materials. Notes for a general model. In: Il mattone di Venezia, pp. 95–144. Venice: Cummune di Venezia.

26

Water-repellent Treatment on the Brick Wall of the External Facade of the Scrovegni Chapel in Padua

V. Fassina[1], S. Borsella,[2] A. Naccari[3], and M. Favaro[3]

[1]Laboratorio Scientifico-Soprintendenza per i Beni Artistici e Storici di Venezia,
Cannaregio 3553, Venice, Italy
[2]Comune di Padova-Settore Edilizia Monumentale, Padua, Italy
[3]Istituto Veneto per i Beni Culturali, San Polo 2454/a, Venice, Italy

ABSTRACT

On the right side of the fresco depicting the Last Judgement in the Scrovegni Chapel in Padua, salt efflorescences formed on the surface. This convinced us to survey the origin of these salts, as they could be very harmful to the fresco surfaces. The analyses carried out on joint mortars have shown the presence of sulfates, which have been ascribed to the reaction between calcium carbonate and sulfuric acid. This, in turn, is formed by the oxidation of sulfur dioxide emitted by fuel combustion (domestic or industrial).

The sulfation process caused a decohesion of the mortars, resulting in a strong decrease in binding and allowing water to penetrate the brick masonry. To prevent water penetration, it was decided that the sulfated mortars be removed and replaced by hydraulic lime mortars.

As the facade was not plastered, it was further proposed that the surface be protected by applying a synthetic polymeric substance, one which presents good water-repellent properties without significantly altering the water vapor permeability. To select the best protection, laboratory tests were carried out on different polymeric water-repellent materials. Taking into account the tests conducted, Wacker VP 1311 demonstrated the best performance of high degree of protection against water and low reduction of water vapor permeability.

INTRODUCTION

The Scrovegni Chapel is a small building erected at the beginning of 14th century in Padua. The wall masonry made of bricks is not plastered. Its great reknown is due to the extraordinary cycle of frescoes preserved in its interior, which was painted by the mature Giotto. The paintings run through the life of Jesus according to the Gospel and conclude with the great scene of the Last Judgement.

During a survey carried out some twenty years ago, we found that the frescoes were decaying as a result of sulfation processes provoked by sulfur dioxide entering through the entrance door (Biscontin et al. 1979).

Ten years ago, those charged with the conservation of the Chapel observed the formation of salt efflorescences on the Last Judgement, which were primarily located on the righthand side of the internal facade. The localized distribution of the efflorescences suggested that the migration of water and soluble salts from the external onto the internal facade may be responsible for this phenomenon. To verify this hypothesis, samples of brick and mortar from the main facade were taken during an inspection carried out on the external walls.

SALT EFFLORESCENCES

When water moves inside a brick wall, it transports salts into the pores. When the critical water content is reached, crystallization of salts occurs (Charola and Koestler 1982). This phenomenon can take place at different points in the pores depending on the solubility of the salts and the rate of water evaporation, which in turn depends on the moisture supply from the interior and the rate of ventilation at the surface. For this reason, we can distinguish the following two phenomena:

1. *Evaporation of water on the surface: Efflorescence.* Crystallization of soluble salts on the surface is due to the low rate of ventilation, which causes an evaporation rate lower than the rate of replenishment of water by capillary migration from inside the wall. Salt crystals are formed mainly outside the pores and consequently the disruptive effect is smaller. When efflorescences take place, salts are brought to the surface in solution during the wetting phase; most of the evaporation from the surface takes place during the drying phase, forming salt crystals on the surface.

2. *Evaporation of water in the pores: Subflorescence.* When crystallization takes place within the pores, the surface becomes dry, since the rate of escape of water vapor from the exposed surface is faster than the rate of replenishment by capillary migration from the interior. Crystals will form and grow in the pores, channels, and crevices along the plane at a certain distance below the exterior surface. As these crystals grow, they exert forces on the capillary walls, causing crumbling of thin surface layers.

To study the decay processes taking place in the brick masonry, it is very important to know the type of salts migrating in the brick wall.

Sampling was carried out on the left side of the external facade corresponding to the position of the salt efflorescences occuring on the fresco surfaces and also on other part of the external facade presenting brick exfoliation phenomena. X-ray diffraction analyses showed the presence of calcite, dolomite, and quartz and sometimes gypsum.

As a first step, quantitative determinations of soluble anions were carried out on drilling cores of bricks. Sulfate concentrations in bricks were found to be very low, less

Table 26.1   Anion concentrations in bricks determined by ion chromatography analyses during the first measurement campaign (Spring, 1988).

Sample	Depth		Depth		Depth	
	0–15mm	15–30 mm	0–15 mm	15–30 mm	0–15 mm	15–30 mm
	sulfates (%)		nitrates (%)		chlorides (%)	
18-19	0.16	0.02	0.01	0.02	–	–
16-17	0.60	0.09	0.23	0.06	0.03	0.03
10-12	0.67	0.05	0.97	0.39	0.23	0.06
14-15	0.27	0.05	0.09	0.02	0.02	0.01

– : no data

than 1%, and they showed a decrease from the exterior to the inner part of the brick (Table 26.1). In contrast, sulfate concentrations in mortars are very high, generally between 1% and 5%, with a peak of 11% in sample No. 5 (Table 26.2).

The different decay observed on bricks and mortars is ascribed to the different reactivity to atmospheric sulfur dioxide. The calcium carbonate of the mortar is transformed by sulfuric acid into gypsum. The sulfation process caused a decohesion of the joint mortars and their binding action is very strongly decreased allowing water penetration in the brick masonry. Water migration causes dissolution of salts present inside the wall, and when evaporation takes place, their crystallization occurs on the fresco surface.

In contrast, a direct attack of sulfuric acid on bricks cannot occur because the silicates contained in brick are chemically inert with respect to sulfuric acid. To explain the presence of the small amount of sulfate in bricks and the phenomenon of exfoliation taking place on some bricks, it is necessary to consider the migration of gypsum from the nearby sulfated mortars.

Regarding salt formation, we can affirm that on mortars they originate by a direct attack of sulfuric acid, while on bricks they are due to migration of gypsum previously formed in nearby mortars. In the second measurement campaign, we further investigated the amount of sulfates at different depths of mortars. (Table 26.3)

Table 26.2   Anion concentrations in mortars determined by ion chromatography analyses during the first measurement campaign (Spring, 1988).

Sample No.	Sulfates (%)	Nitrates (%)	Chlorides (%)
2	4.54	–	–
3	2.27	–	–
20	1.01	–	–
5	11.03	0.01	–
7	4.52	–	–
13	2.03	0.03	0.01

– : no data

Table 26.3   Sulfate concentrations in mortars at different depth (Spring, 1990).

	Depth				
Sample	Surface	0–15 mm	15–30 mm	30–50 mm	50–100 mm
	Sulfate (%)				
A	18.99	3.12	–	–	–
B	10.08	1.49	0.40	0.27	0.37
C	5.64	1.58	0.53	0.36	0.26
D	4.54	0.27	–	–	–
E	2.48	0.12	–	–	–
F	10.38	1.42	0.60	0.53	0.25
G	11.88	1.74	0.30	0.19	0.23

– : no data

In four samples, the sulfate concentrations on the surface is above 10%. The sulfate concentration profile decreases from the exterior to the interior of the mortars. The high sulfation degree on the surface is maintained until 15 mm at a discrete concentration, and lies between 1.4% and 3.1% in the depth 0–15 mm. In the inner portion of the brick, sulfate concentrations decrease to low concentrations, < 0.5% (Figure 26.1).

The presence of sulfate in mortars is harmful for their conservation and consequently the removal of the sulfated mortars and the replacement of them with hydraulic lime mortars was proposed.

As the the facade was unplastered, it was necessary to protect the surface to prevent water penetration during rain events.

For this reason, the application of some synthetic polymers having good water-repellent properties and high water vapor permeability was proposed. It is important to stress that any interventions on the external facade can strongly influence the state of conservation of the frescoes.

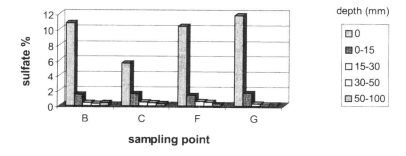

Figure 26.1   Sulfate concentrations in mortars at different depths (Spring, 1990).

EXPERIMENTAL

To find the most suitable product for our requirements, the following experimental tests on brick samples, taken from the facade, were carried out in laboratory:

- measurement of water absorption by capillarity, according to NORMAL 11/85,
- measurement of water vapor permeability, according to NORMAL 21/85.

Each test was repeated after treating the original samples with three different products according to the NORMAL Commission (1995). The test materials were:

- an alkyl-alkoxy-siloxane: Rhodorsil 224-Rhone Poulenc, diluted 1:10 in white spirit,
- a water soluble micro emulsion of alkyl-alkoxy-siloxane: Wacker VP 1311, diluted 1:7 in water,
- a water soluble alkyl-alkoxy-silane: Dynasilan BSM100 W, diluted 1:10 in water.

To evaluate the behavior of the products under real environmental conditions, some *in situ* tests were also conducted. The following two parameters were considered:

- the degree of water absorption at low pressure, by means of pipe method, according to NORMAL 44/93,
- the color change of the treated surface, according to NORMAL 43/93.

Before treatment, brick samples were conditioned for 24 hours at 25 °C and 50% RH. The adopted treatment methodology, reported earlier (NORMAL Commission 1993, 1995), is in summary: on a multilayer filter paper of 1 cm of thickness soaked up almost to its top with protective solution, the samples were laid in contact with the face on which the parameters had been measured before treatment. After the chosen time, samples were turned and then dried still in this upside down position resting on small glass beads for 30 days in the laboratory.

CAPILLARY WATER ABSORPTION AND WATER VAPOR PERMEABILITY MEASUREMENTS

Capillary Water Absorption versus Time and Degree of Protection

Measurement of water absorption by capillarity allows us to evaluate the kinetics of water absorption and the amount of water absorbed by means of the capillary rising damp process. Capillarity Protection Degree ($PDc\%$) is defined as the ratio percentage between the difference of the amount of water absorbed by capillarity at time t by a sample before (Wun) and after (Wt) treatment and the amount of water absorbed at the same time before treatment (Wun):

$$PDc\% = \frac{Wun - Wt}{Wun} \times 100 , \qquad (26.1)$$

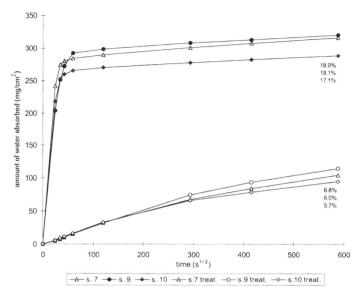

Figure 26.2 Water capillary absorption vs. time: comparison before and after treatment 1 with Rhodorsil 224 H.

where *Wun* is the amount of water absorbed by the untreated sample, *Wt* is the amount of water absorbed by the treated sample, and *PDc*% is the degree of capillarity protection. Generally, this ratio refers to capillary absorption carried out for short time (30–60 minutes). In our case, to study the behavior of protective substances over time, the degree of protection was calculated at 1, 4, and 24 hours.

Treatment 1   Rhodorsil 224

On the right end of the water capillary absorption curves (Figure 26.2), the percentage of water for each sample is reported. Before treatment, water absorption is very rapid and almost reaches the maximum value after 1 hour. The asymptotic value lies in the range of 17.1% and 18.9%.

After treatment, water absorption is strongly reduced. After four hours the amount of water absorbed on treated samples is 10% in comparison with the untreated samples. With reference to the degree of protection, it is quite good until 4 hours (average value 89%), but it decreases in the range 71%–76% after 24 hours (Table 26.4).

Treatment 2   Wacker VP 1311

Before treatment, water absorption is very rapid (Figure 26.3). Only sample No.15 shows a slow absorption, probably ascribable to a different pore-size distribution. The asymptotic value is in the range 15.8% and 18.6%.

Table 26.4 Protection degree (%).

Treatment	Rh 224			VP 1311					Dynasilan	
Sample No.	7	9	10	15	17	18	19	20	23	25
1 h	94	95	94	96	95	97	96	97	93	96
4 h	89	89	88	93	90	92	92	93	90	90
24 h	77	76	76	80	75	79	79	83	68	75

After treatment, water absorption is strongly reduced. After four hours the amount of water absorbed is 10% in comparison to the untreated samples.

The degree of protection is higher than 95% until one hour and it decreases more slowly during the time in comparison with the treatment with Rhodorsil 224 H. After 24 hours its average value is 79% (Table 26.4).

Treatment 3   Dynasilan BSM 100 W

Before treatment, water absorption is very rapid and reaches almost the maximum value after 1 hour. The asymptotic value lies between 17.8% and 18.2% (Figure 26.4).

After treatment, water absorption is strongly reduced. In comparison to the untreated samples, after 4 hours the amount of water absorbed is 10%

The degree of protection is less than Wacker VP 1311 and similar to Rhodorsil 224 H at 1 and 4 hours, while at 24 hours shows the lowest values of the three products (68% and 71%) (Table 26.4).

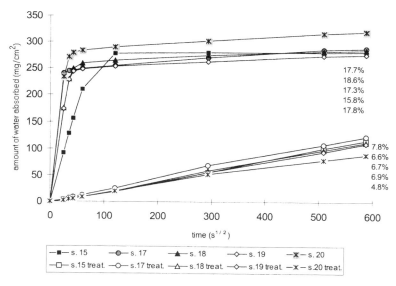

Figure 26.3 Capillary water absorption: comparison before and after Treatment 2 with Wacker VP1311.

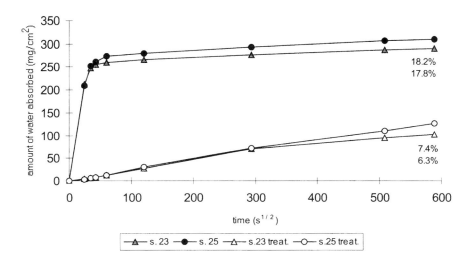

Figure 26.4 Capillary water absorption: comparison before and after Treatment 3 with Dynasylan BSM 100W.

Water Vapor Permeability

Measurement of water vapor permeability shows us the amount of water vapor passing through the brick over time in static conditions. A flux of water vapor through the sample occurs when there is a difference in the partial pressure between the two opposite surfaces of the brick sample. To reach this condition, each sample was fitted like a "plug" into a suitable box with a small amount of distilled water at its bottom; then the box was placed into a desiccator containing silica gel in sufficient quantity to absorb water vapor during the test. As air temperature strongly influences the difference in vapor partial pressure between sample surfaces, it was strictly controlled. When stationary conditions were reached, the water vapor flux (in g/m^2 for 24 hours) was calculated by measuring the weight loss of the box every 24 hours.

The comparison between the flux of water vapor before and after each treatment allows us to evaluate the reduction of water vapor permeability, $(P\%)$,

$$P\% = \frac{\Phi un - \Phi t}{\Phi un} \times 100 , \qquad (26.2)$$

where Φun is the flux of water vapor of the untreated sample in stationary conditions; Φt is the flux of water vapor of the treated sample in stationary conditions; and $P\%$ is the reduction of water vapor permeability due to a protective substance.

Low value of P (%) indicates that the applied product gives a minimun interference to water vapor flux. The knowledge of this parameter is very important in order to evaluate the properties of each product. In fact, the reduction of gaseous transport

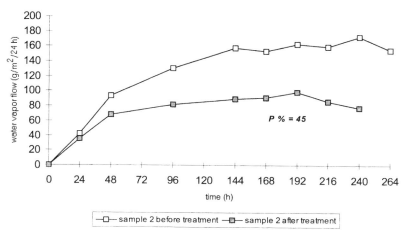

Figure 26.5   Water vapor permeability: comparison before and after Treatment 1 with Rhodorsil 224H.

through a brick wall can cause water condensation and accumulation of harmful salts inside, as well as stresses resulting from temperature changes, increasing the speed of deterioration processes.

The stationary conditions were generally reached after four days, while only six days were necessary for samples 2 and 4. Untreated samples have a permeability that lies between 160 and 250 g/m² for 24 hours (Figures 26.5–26.7). The treatment produces a permeability decrease which is about 45% for sample 2, treated with Rhodorsil 224 H and between 20% and 30% in the samples treated with VP 1311. Samples 4 and

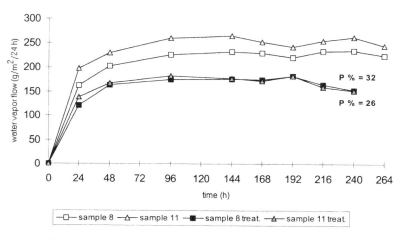

Figure 26.6   Water vapor permeability: comparison before and after Treatment 2 with Wacker VP 1311.

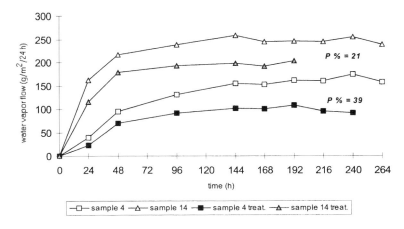

Figure 26.7   Water vapor permeability: comparison before and after Treatment 2 with Dynasilan BSM 100W.

14 treated with Dynasilan BSM 100 W show a different behavior, with a decrease of 39% and 21% in comparison with the original values.

BEHAVIOR OF THE PROTECTIVE SUBSTANCES ON SITE

To evaluate the properties of the behavior of chemical substances in environmental conditions, some tests were carried out *in situ*.

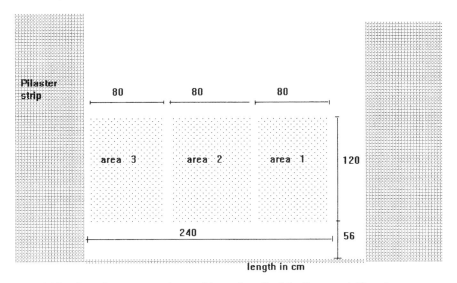

Figure 26.8   Sampling areas on the outside north wall of the Scrovegni Chapel.

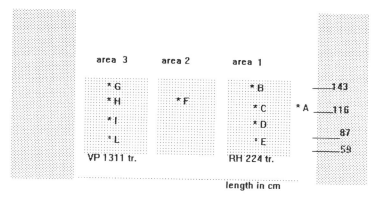

color measurement   * color and water absorption measurement

Figure 26.9   Color and water absorption measurement sampling points on the north wall of the Scrovegni Chapel.

On the north wall surface, three areas showing similar decay conditions were chosen for the on-site experiment (Figure 26.8). Only two of them were treated, leaving untreated the area in between. Among the chemical products tested in laboratory, Rhodorsil 224 H and Wacker VP 1311, both alkyl-alkoxy-siloxane products, were chosen.

The water absorption at low pressure, by means of pipe method, and the color change of the treated surface were measured (Figure 26.9).

Water Absorption at Low Pressure

The cylindrical box was fixed to the wall at its open side (11.4 cm^2 wide) with a rubber gasket. Before the beginning of the test, the apparatus was rapidly filled with water until the meniscus in the pipe stood at zero, then the flow was stopped. After five minutes, the water absorption was measured by looking the level in the pipe. Afterwards the absorption values were read every five minutes for half an hour.

The water absorption degree (*AD*) in ml/cm^2 was calculated by using the following formula:

$$AD = \frac{W_{30'} - W_{5'}}{A},$$ (26.3)

where $W_{5'}$ is the water absorbed after 5 minutes; $W_{30'}$ is the water absorbed after 30 minutes; and A is the contact area between sample and pipe set.

AD was calculated before the treatment using a 10 ml pipe and after the treatment using a 1 ml pipe. To evaluate the behavior of protectives after a certain time the test was repeated ten months after the treatment (see Table 26.5).

As in the laboratory tests, we calculated the protection degree (*PDp%*), comparing the absorption degree before and after treatment:

Table 26.5 Water absorption degree by pipe method.

Point	Before treatment (July 8, 1992) $AD_1(ml/cm^2)$	After treatment (July 31, 1992) $AD_2(ml/cm^2)$	After treatment (May 7, 1993) $AD_3(ml/cm^2)$
A	2.09	–	–
B	1.06	0.02	0.002
C	3.12	0.02	0.040
D	1.82	0.02	0.020
F	1.08	–	–
G	0.99	0.03	0.002
H	0.28	0.00	0.010
I	0.56	0.02	0.001

– : no data

$$PDp\% = \frac{AD_{before} - AD_{after}}{AD_{before}} \times 100 . \tag{26.4}$$

The results obtained showed a high degree of protection which is maintained during time (Table 26.6)

Table 26.6 Protection degree after treatment.

	Treatment with Rhodorsil 224			Treatment with Wacker Vp1311	
	PDp % (after 15 days)	PDp % (after 10 months)		PDp % (after 15 days)	PDp % (after 10 months)
B point	98	100	G point	97	100
C point	99	99	E point	100	96
D point	99	100	I point	96	100

Color Change of the Surface after Treatment

The instrument used to measure the color coordinates of selected surface areas was a Minolta Chroma meter CR-200 portable tristimulus color analyzer. It features an 8-mm-diameter measuring area diffusely lit by a pulsed xenon arc lamp. Detection is achieved with silica photocells filtered to match the CIE Standard Observer Response.

Replicate measurements of the color coordinates of selected areas of the wall surface were recorded as L*,a*,b*, using CIE illuminant C. Color difference (ΔE) in CIE-LAB units was calculated according the following equation:

$$\Delta E' = [(L_1{}^* - L_2{}^*)^2 + (a_1{}^* - a_2{}^*)^2 + (b_1{}^* - b_2{}^*)^2]^{1/2}$$
$$\Delta E'' = [(L_1{}^* - L_3{}^*)^2 + (a_1{}^* - a_3{}^*)^2 + (b_1{}^* - b_3{}^*)^2]^{1/2} \qquad (26.5)$$

where $L_1{}^*, a_1{}^*, b_1{}^*$ =   values before treatment;
      $L_2{}^*, a_2{}^*, b_2{}^*$ =   values after treatment;
      $L_3{}^*, a_3{}^*, b_3{}^*$ =   values after treatment;
      L^* =   lightness-darkness difference;
      a^* =   redness-greeness difference;
      b^* =   yellowness-blueness difference;

and ΔE is the the calculated total color difference; $\Delta E'$ between values before and just after the treatment; and $\Delta E''$ between values before and after 10 months of the treatment.

The ΔE value is higher as color change is greater (see Tables 26.7 and 26.8). The data obtained show an $\Delta E'$ quite high, probably because comparative measurements were carried out before a complete drying of the wall surface. $\Delta E''$, which refers to our last measurements, is lower than previous ones, pointing out a considerable decrease of color change.

Table 26.7   Color brightness and chromatic coordinates.

Sampling points	8/7/92 $L_1{}^*$	31/7/92 $L_2{}^*$	5/5/93 $L_3{}^*$	8/7/92 $a_1{}^*$	31/7/92 $a_2{}^*$	5/5/93 $a_3{}^*$	8/7/92 $b_1{}^*$	31/7/92 $b_2{}^*$	5/5/93 $b_3{}^*$
A	52.7	n.e.	51.7	12.9	n.e.	12.9	21.7	n.e.	22.3
B	63.4	58.5	64.1	3.4	3.8	3.0	16.1	17.6	16.9
C	57.2	49.0	51.0	10.1	10.7	10.6	16.0	17.0	17.0
D	55.2	52.5	53.7	11.8	11.1	11.1	18.4	18.8	19.0
E	56.3	52.6	57.4	7.3	8.1	6.9	13.8	14.8	13.6
F	56.3	n.e.	56.2	3.0	n.e	3.0	15.9	n.e.	16.2
G	53.7	49.9	50.9	1.8	2.3	2.1	13.3	15.4	15.1
H	55.5	57.9	58.2	15.9	15.1	14.4	23.2	22.9	22.6
I	58.8	54.6	56.9	4.1	4.5	4.2	17.0	17.4	17.5
L	52.4	51.7	52.9	10.1	10.4	9.5	18.0	18.2	18.1

n.e., not evaluated

CONCLUSIONS

Comparison of capillary water absorption curves before and after the treatment shows generally a degree of protection higher than 90% for all the products and for short times (until 4 hours). In the case of prolonged contact with water, the degree of protection decreases further.

Table 26.8   Color change.

Sampling Points	$\Delta E'$	$\Delta E'''$
A	not calculated	1.17
B	5.14	1.14
C	8.28	6.30
D	2.82	1.76
E	3.92	1.19
F	not calculated	0.32
G	4.37	3.34
H	2.55	3.15
I	4.24	1.97
L	0.79	0.97

In any case, by considering the duration of an usual precipitation event, it is possible to affirm that the degree of protection is satisfactory for all the products; however, Wacker VP 1311 and Rhodorsil 224 H show the best performances (Figure 26.10).

With reference to the reduction of water vapor permeability after treatment, it is more evident for Rhodorsil 224 H in which the time for drying is expected to be double. In reality this value becomes lower because treated samples tend to absorb a smaller quantity of water in comparison to the untreated ones, and consequently the drying process needs a shorter time.

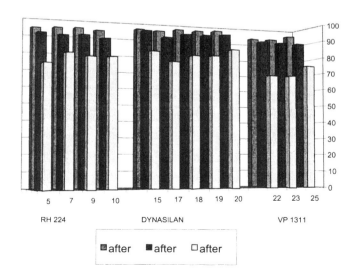

Figure 26.10   Protection degree for Rhodorsil 224H, Wacker VP1311, and Dynasilan BSM 100W at different times.

The reduction of water vapor permeability gives the best results for Wacker VP 1311 and Dynasilan BSM 100W.

In general, all the tests carried out in the laboratory show that the protective substances applied have both good water-repellent properties and a low reduction of the water vapor permeability.

With reference to *in situ* experiments, the degree of protection against water absorption measured by the pipe method is very high for both Rhodorsil 224 H and Wacker VP 1311.

Color changes after a short time were high, but successively decreased to value similar to the initial stage.

Considering the laboratory and on-site measurements carried out, it seems that Wacker VP 1311 shows the best performances. What it is very important is the increase in degree of protection that takes place 10 months after the application.

The amount of product used in laboratory was 0.8 kg/m^2.

ACKNOWLEDGEMENTS

We wish to thank arch. G.F. Martinoni, former head of the Monuments technical office of the Municipality of Padua, for assistance in the field work and Dr. R. Arbizzani for some of the laboratory measurements.

REFERENCES

Biscontin G., S. Diana, V. Fassina, and M. Marabelli. 1979. A survey on atmospheric pollutants inside and outside of Scrovegni's Chapel in Padua. In: Proc. of the 3rd Intl. Symp. on Deterioration and Preservation of Stones, Venice, Oct. 24–27, 1979, pp. 677–688. Padua: La Photograph.

Charola, A.E., and R.J. Koestler. 1982. The action of salt water solutions of the silico-alluminate matrix of bricks. In: Il mattone di Venezia, Ateneo Veneto 29 ottobre 1982, Venezia pp. 67–76. Venezia: Istituto per lo Studio delle Dinamica delle Grandi Masse, CNR.

Fassina, V., and A. Naccari. 1995. Studio del comportamento della struttura muraria della Cappella degli Scrovegni sottoposta a trattamento con sostanze protettive. In: 1st Intl. Congr. On Science and Technology for the Safeguard of Cultural Heritage in the Mediterranean Basin. Catania: Cousorzio Catania Ricerche.

Fassina, V., and A. Naccari. 1996. Evaluation of the protective treatment of the external facade of the Scrovegni Chapel in Padova. In: 8th Intl. Congr. on Deterioration and Conservation of Stone, pp. 523–534. Berlin: Rathgen Forschungslabor.

NORMAL 11/85. Assorbimento d'acqua per capillarità – Coefficiente di assorbimento capillare. NORMAL Commission Recommendation, 1985.

NORMAL 21/85. Permeabilità al vapor d'acqua. NORMAL Commission Recommendation, 1985.

NORMAL 43/93. Misure colorimetriche di superfici opache. NORMAL Commission Recommendation, 1993.

NORMAL 44/93. Assorbimento d'acqua a bassa pressione. NORMAL Commission Recommendation, 1993.

NORMAL Commission. 1993. Protectives Experimentation Subgroup of NORMAL Commission 1993: Metodologia per la valutazione di prodotti impiegati come protettivi per materiale lapideo. Parte I: tests e trattamento dei campioni. *L'EDILIZIA* 7:57–71.

NORMAL Commission. 1995. Protectives Experimentation Subgroup of NORMAL Commission 1995. Methodology for the evaluation of the protective products for stone materials. Part II: Experimental tests on treated samples. In Intl. Coll. on Methods of Evaluation of Protective Products for the Conservation of Porous Building Materials in Monuments, pp. 19–21. Rome: ICCROM.

27

Water-resistant Gypsum-Lime Mortars for the Restoration of Historic Brick Buildings

B. MIDDENDORF[1,2] and D. KNÖFEL[1]

[1]University of Siegen, Laboratory for Chemistry of Construction Materials (BCS), Paul-Bonatz-Str. 9–11, 57068 Siegen, Germany
[2]Present address: University of Kassel, Department of Structural Materials, Mönchebergstr. 7, 34109 Kassel, Germany

ABSTRACT

The use of gypsum as a building material can be traced back over 4500 years. Gypsum-anhydrite-lime mortars as well as pure lime mortars were used for the joints on the outside brick walls of religious buildings in northern Germany. These gypsum mortar mixtures are about 500 years old and still in good condition. The solubility of gypsum in water is a disadvantage that makes it very difficult to use gypsum externally. Since the end of the 19th century, this traditional building material has been increasingly rejected in favor of hydraulic binders. An effort has been made to produce adequate mortar mixtures with the help of modern binder components that have the necessary technological properties and can also be used for preservation purposes. Water-resistant gypsum mortar mixtures based on β-hemihydrate, α-hemihydrate and added hydrated hydraulic lime are suitable building materials for external use as joint mortars. Mixtures of different additives and aggregates are used to optimize technological properties. Results of analyses of selected mortar mixtures are presented. Criteria for the assessment of mortars intended for the repair of masonry are considered in some detail in the Appendix to this chapter.

INTRODUCTION

The use of gypsum as a building material with its different properties was already known in ancient Egypt 2500 B.C. when the Cheops pyramid was built. The oldest description of the mineral gypsum was given by Theophrastus in 314 B.C. (Schwiete and Knauf 1969). In Germany, the 12th century was the height of the use of gypsum for terrazzo floors and mortar. After the first half of the 19th century, knowledge of the production, preparation and properties of different gypsum-based materials was lost when hydraulic binder was introduced (Steinbrecher 1992).

Modern gypsum building materials are almost always intended for internal use, due to the special properties of this building material. General advantages are: favorable production methods with regard to energy, quick and controllable setting behavior, good adhesion to plaster, and the ease of working. However, its high solubility in water (2.6 g/l) and a low wet strength does restrict its use to the interior of a building. Nevertheless, chemical-mineralogical investigations of historic joint mortars from brick buildings in northern Germany have shown that gypsum-anhydrite mortars with a small content of lime have been used externally for religious buildings (Middendorf and Knöfel 1994). A great part of these joint or masonry mortars is still well preserved.

According to Steinbrecher (1992), this durability is due to its composition (binder and aggregates with the same kind of substance) as well as to its preparation with extremely small quantities of water. A water/binder value of less than 0.4 and a bulk density of 2.0 g/cm^3 is given for a historic gypsum mortar.

The reproduction of medieval recipes differed to a great extent in terms of the deposits of natural raw gypsum and the regionally different traditions of the craft.

This chapter discusses information on the development of water-resistant mortars for the restoration of joints based on gypsum and lime, which meet both physical and preservation requirements for a building.

For use in historical religious brick buildings, joint mortars should meet the following criteria (only water resistance was assessed here)[1]:

- Based on gypsum and lime
- Water resistant
- Compatible with historic materials
- Dynamic modulus of elasticity (after 28 d) $\leq 10 \text{ kN/mm}^2$
- Compressive strength (after 28 d)   10–15 N/mm^2
- Low shrinkage   < 0.5 mm/m
- Sufficient time of workability ≥ 1 h
- Good workability properties
- Resistance to frost
- No efflorescence.

MATERIALS USED

Production of water-resistant joint mortar mixtures based on gypsum and lime has been tested. Commercially available binders, aggregates, and additives have been used for these tests. The binders used were: β-hemihydrate (β-HH), produced with natural

---

[1] Criteria for the assessment of mortars intended for the repair of masonry are considered in some detail in the Appendix.

gypsum stone; α-hemihydrate (α-HH), a so-called flue-gas gypsum obtained from the desulfurization of combustion gases of fossil fuels; hydrated hydraulic lime (HHL), produced with marled limestone. Powdered limestone (PLS), with a specific surface of 4100 cm^2/g, and a quartz sand (QS), with grain sizes from 0.125 to 1.0 mm, were used as inert aggregates. Tartaric acid (tart) was used to optimize setting behavior. Tests with hydrophobing additives (hyd.) were also done; calcium siliconate was used.

EXPERIMENTAL INVESTIGATIONS

All fresh mortar mixtures were prepared for a spreading area of 16 ± 0.5 cm according to DIN 1168, part 2. This consistency proved to be suitable for practical use. According to DIN 1164, part 7, sample pieces (size 40×40×160 mm) were formed from the mixtures to be investigated.

At the same time, sample pieces sized 15×15×60 mm were produced to determine water resistance via leaching tests. For this, the sample pieces were stored in flowing water for several weeks to get results quickly. Moreover, the solubility in water was determined with leaching tests and by wet-chemical measures for the determination of sulfate and calcium content. Table 27.1 shows some of the mortar mixtures produced; abbreviations are listed below. As all mixtures contain 0.1 wt.% tartaric acid (tart), with regard to the hemihydrate used, the tartaric acid has not been listed separately among the abbreviations. The values in brackets for the abbreviations give the content of binder components in wt.%.

Measured values in Table 27.2 refer to laboratory tests. In addition, sample pieces were exposed to outdoor weathering for at least 180 days. After termination of laboratory tests, the most suitable mixtures of the investigation program were inserted into historic masonry.

Hygric swelling and shrinking were measured at least up to the 28th day. After this period no substantial changes could be observed.

The bigger the dynamic modulus of elasticity (E-modulus), the smaller the "elasticity," i.e., a high E-modulus only allows a slight elastic change of form which can cause cracks in the masonry. The values for the dynamic modulus of elasticity and for the compressive strength (β_{ST}) should be distinctly smaller for mortars than for the stone used in the masonry, as, otherwise, cracks and other damage can be the result (Knöfel and Schubert 1990). The test methods to determine workability time, the freeze-thaw cycling behavior, the capillary water absorption and water emission as well as liability to efflorescence are given in the "Handbuch für Mörtel und Steinergänzungsstoffe" (Knöfel and Schubert 1993). Moreover, the set mortars have been characterized with the help of a scanning electron microscope (SEM) and mercury porosimetry to quantify the causes of higher water resistance.

Table 27.1 Mortar mixtures produced and their abbreviations.

Basic Mixture	Abbreviation
α-HH/β-HH/HHL(50/30/20)+tart	abH(532)
α-HH/β-HH/HHL(20/60/20)+tart	abH(262)
α-HH/β-HH/HHL(50/20/30)+tart	abH(523)
α-HH/β-HH/HHL(20/50/30)+tart	abH(253)
α-HH/β-HH/HHL(50/30/20)+tart+0.5% hyd	abH(532)+hyd
α-HH/β-HH/HHL(20/60/20)+tart+0.5% hyd	abH(262)+hyd
α-HH/β-HH/HHL(50/20/30)+tart+0.5% hyd	abH(523)+hyd
α-HH/β-HH/HHL(20/50/30)+tart+0.5% hyd	abH(253)+hyd
α-HH/β-HH/HHL(50/20/30)+tart+20% PLS	abH(523)+20P
α-HH/β-HH/HHL(20/50/30)+tart+20% PLS	abH(253)+20P
α-HH/β-HH/HHL(50/20/30)+tart+20% QS	abH(523)+20Q
α-HH/β-HH/HHL(20/50/30)+tart+20% QS	abH(253)+20Q
α-HH/β-HH/HHL(50/30/20)+tart+25% QS+25% PLS	abH(532)+25Q+25P
α-HH/β-HH/HHL(20/60/20)+tart+25% QS+25% PLS	abH(262)+25Q+25P
α-HH/β-HH-HH/HHL(50/20/30)+tart+25% QS+25% PLS	abH(523)+25Q+25P
α-HH/β-HH/HHL(20/50/30)+tart+25% QS+25% PLS	abH(253)+25Q+25P

α-HH: α-hemihydrate; β-HH: β-hemihydrate; HHL: hydrated hydraulic lime; tart: L(+)-tartaric acid (0.1 wt.% to the hemihydrate); hyd: hydrophobic agent; PLS: powdered limestone; QS: quartz sand (0.125–1.0 mm diameter).

RESULTS AND DISCUSSION

As can be seen in Table 27.2, gypsum mortars produced with α-hemihydrate have the highest value for E-modulus and a compressive strength of 43 N/mm^2 as well as a water solubility that is 40% less than for mortars produced from pure β-hemihydrate. Both forms of hemihydrate crystallize rhomboidally, but show different application/technical and energetic properties. Their method of production is also different. While α-HH is produced by an autoclave procedure, β-HH is formed at atmospheric pressure and temperatures of about 45°–200°C; during setting it forms needle-shaped, monoclinic-prismatic dihydrate crystals which become felted. The compact structure of gypsum crystals formed of α-HH may be the reason for the high E-modulus values and mechanical strength values.

Moreover, mortars made of α-HH have a lower porosity than those based on β-HH, which also indicates that the structure must be more dense and therefore results in a reduced surface. This causes lower water solubility.

Table 27.2 Technological properties and resistance to water of selected gypsum mortar mixtures.

Basic Mixture	E-modulus after 28 d [kN/mm²]	β_{ST} after 28d [N/mm²]	Swelling/ shrinking [mm/m]		Resistance to water standardized to β-HH [%]
β-HH	9.26	15.55	+0.27	−0.15	100
α-HH	21.35	43.25	+0.60	−0.60	60
β-HH+tart	10.29	22.95	+0.13	−0.20	80
abH(532)	11.16	26.09	+0.12	−0.22	65
abH(262)	8.88	17.15	+0.15	−0.23	65
abH(523)	9.65	18.46	+0.12	−0.26	60
abH(253)	7.58	14.75	+0.10	−0.27	73
abH(532)+hyd	11.08	23.74	+0.12	−0.18	79
abH(262)+hyd	9.11	20.65	+0.12	−0.21	62
abH(523)+hyd	9.82	22.68	+0.10	−0.28	60
abH(253)+hyd	7.28	17.49	+0.11	−0.33	60
abH(523)+20P	9.45	17.73	+0.11	−0.23	56
abH(253)+20P	6.79	11.86	+0.11	−0.24	65
abH(523)+20Q	12.20	23.16	+0.13	−0.17	54
abH(253)+20Q	7.97	13.91	+0.14	−0.17	54
abH(523)+50Q	17.37	25.77	+0.10	−0.15	67
abH(253)+50Q	12.73	16.11	+0.12	−0.15	82
abH(532)+25Q+25P	15.13	24.77	+0.07	−0.11	44
abH(262)+25Q+25P	11.05	16.64	+0.04	−0.11	33
abH(523)+25Q+25P	13.11	21.05	+0.05	−0.13	40
abH(253)+25Q+25P	10.23	13.42	+0.06	−0.14	39

E-modulus: dynamic modulus of elasticity, β_{ST}: average compressive strength, See Table 27.1 for list of abbreviations.

The addition of 0.1 wt.% tartaric acid to β-HH as a retarder, in order to optimize workability, causes a slight coarsening of structure, while at the same time the needle-shaped character of the dihydrate crystals is nearly lost. The simple addition of tartaric acid increases the compressive strength, the E-modulus, and reduces the water solubility of the mortars. The value of the mortar swelling behavior also decreases when tartaric acid is added. A slower setting, indicating an ordered crystal growth and resulting in bigger crystals, could be a reason for this. The same effect can also be seen when organic acids are added.

E-moduli and compressive strengths can be controlled by combining both dihy-drate forms (α-HH, β-HH). Since these mixtures have a high water solubility, hydrated hydraulic lime was added, because during preliminary tests, the latter turned out to be the most suitable binder with hydraulic properties owing to its improving properties for the set mortar mixtures. A comparison of the samples abH (532) and abH(523) with the mortar made of pure β-HH shows that compressive strength and the value for E-modulus decrease while the lime content rises.

Water resistance is about 40 % higher than for mortars based on pure β-HH. If the ratio between α-HH/β-HH is reduced, this also causes a decrease of mechanical strength and of elasticity. If 0.5 wt.% of a hydrophobic agent (hyd) are added to the mortar mixture, the properties are only negligibly influenced. Owing to the hydropho-bic agent the individual dihydrate crystals have a thin "protective coating," which is initially water-repellent (see Figure 27.1). However, as SEM investigations have shown, this coating has small cracks through which water can reach the crystals, and partly dissolve them. Thus, the protective coating loses its effect, a fact which further explains the relatively low water resistance.

An addition of powdered limestone (compare abH(523) with abH(523)+20P) to the gypsum mortar mixtures increases water resistance and slightly decreases mechanical strength and the E-modulus, as the inert powdered limestone aggregate deposits be-tween the gypsum crystals formed during the setting process and consequently influ-ences the microscopic formation of the structure of the binder matrix (see Figure 27.2). Compared with mixtures without aggregates, quartz sand as an aggregate causes a slight increase of mechanical strength values and of the E-modulus. Quartz grains are embedded in an undisturbed binder matrix (see Figure 27.3), which results in the fact that the set mortar has a small porosity, especially concerning capillary porosity. Be-cause of this, it offers only a small surface to the solving attack of water, which is also shown by the results for water resistance. The addition of quartz sand also has a posi-tive impact on the shrinking behavior of mortars so that they can also be described as having low shrinkage.

The binder has been weakened with 50 wt.%, which reduces the water solubility even further. A combination of powdered limestone and quartz sand has been chosen deliberately, to be able to fix the properties of the set mortars according to the require-ment scheme. It became obvious that mixtures with a binder content of α-HH, 20 wt.% exhibit the most favorable properties for use in historic brick walls.

Figures 27.4–27.7 show the test pieces (15×15×60 mm) of the total series of experi-ments, which have been stored hanging freely in flowing water for 28 days. These ex-treme conditions do not simulate the real weathering influences to which a building is generally exposed, but they show results for an effective assessment of binder mixtures after a short period of time. The results of these survey tests can be correlated with the solubility measurements done in the laboratory.

In Figures 27.4–27.7 one can see that the mortar pieces have dissolved slightly, but they have a distinctly higher water resistance than the sample based on pure β-HH

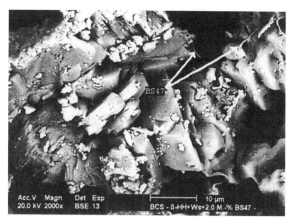

Figure 27.1 SEM photograph of set and hardened gypsum mixture prepared from β-HH, 0.1 wt.% tartaric acid (tart) and 2.0 wt.% of a hydrophobic agent (hyd). Because of hyd, the gypsum crystals are covered with a thin coating which protects the material against water attack. This protection is only temporary, because it has a lot of cracks; see arrows.

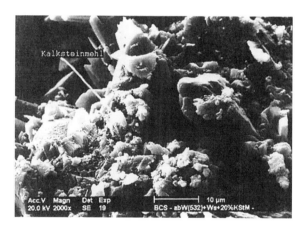

Figure 27.2 SEM photograph of the set and hardened α-HH/β-HH/HHL(50/30/20) +0.1% tart+20% PLS (powdered limestone) mixture. The inert aggregate of PLS (Kalksteinmehl) between the gypsum crystals can be seen.

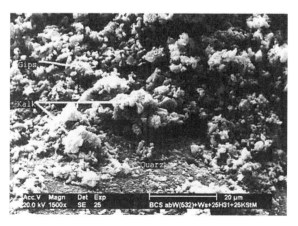

Figure 27.3 SEM photograph of the set and hardened α-HH/β-HH/HHL(50/30/20) +0.1% tart + 25% QS (quartz sand) mixture + 25%PLS. The good bonding of the QS grains and the binder can be seen. The sample stands out as it has only a small porosity, which can be basically seen in the photograph.

Figures 27.4–27.7 Sample pieces (15×15×60 mm) after 28 days storage in flowing water. As a comparison, Figure 27.4 also shows the sample, which was produced of pure β-HH (in the up-permost figure). WaKH: hydrated hydraulic lime (HHL); KStM: powdered limestome (PLS); H31: quartz sand (QS), Ws: tartaric acid (tart); BS47: hydrophobic agent (hyd).

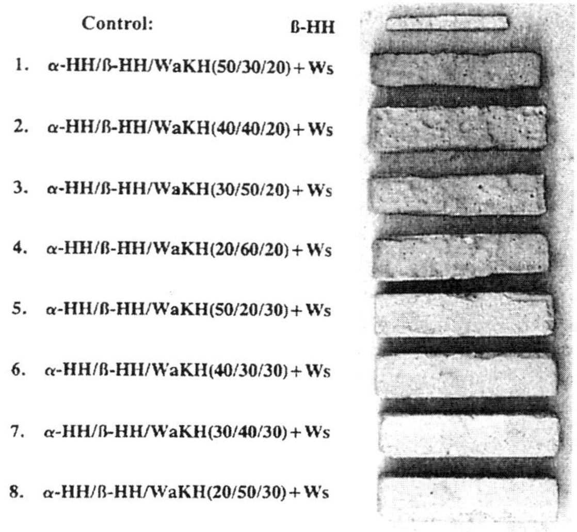

Control: ß-HH

1. α-HH/ß-HH/WaKH(50/30/20)+Ws

2. α-HH/ß-HH/WaKH(40/40/20)+Ws

3. α-HH/ß-HH/WaKH(30/50/20)+Ws

4. α-HH/ß-HH/WaKH(20/60/20)+Ws

5. α-HH/ß-HH/WaKH(50/20/30)+Ws

6. α-HH/ß-HH/WaKH(40/30/30)+Ws

7. α-HH/ß-HH/WaKH(30/40/30)+Ws

8. α-HH/ß-HH/WaKH(20/50/30)+Ws

Figure 27.4 Samples (15×15 × 60 mm) after 28 days in flowing water.

9. α-HH/ß-HH/WaKH(50/30/20)+Ws+BS47

10. α-HH/ß-HH/WaKH(40/40/20)+Ws+BS47

11. α-HH/ß-HH/WaKH(30/50/20)+Ws+BS47

12. α-HH/ß-HH/WaKH(20/60/20)+Ws+BS47

13. α-HH/ß-HH/WaKH(50/20/30)+Ws+BS47

14. α-HH/ß-HH/WaKH(40/30/30)+Ws+BS47

15. α-HH/ß-HH/WaKH(30/40/30)+Ws+BS47

16. α-HH/ß-HH/WaKH(20/50/30)+Ws+BS47

Figure 27.5 Samples (15×15 × 60 mm) after 28 days in flowing water.

(Figure 27.4, uppermost sample). The samples' color nearly corresponds to historic joint mortars (samples 29–32 on Figure 27.7 were moist when the photograph was taken) so that one can talk about an optical adaptation.

17. α-HH/ß-HH/WaKH(50/30/20) + Ws + 20%KstM

18. α-HH/ß-HH/WaKH(20/60/20) + Ws + 20%KstM

19. α-HH/ß-HH/WaKH(50/20/30) + Ws + 20%KstM

20. α-HH/ß-HH/WaKH(20/50/30) + Ws + 20%KstM

21. α-HH/ß-HH/WaKH(50/30/20) + Ws + 20%H31

22. α-HH/ß-HH/WaKH(20/60/20) + Ws + 20%H31

23. α-HH/ß-HH/WaKH(50/20/30) + Ws + 20%H31

24. α-HH/ß-HH/WaKH(20/50/30) + Ws + 20%H31

Figure 27.6 Sample pieces (15×15×60 mm) after 28 days of storage in flowing water.

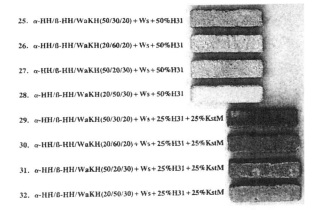

25. α-HH/ß-HH/WaKH(50/30/20) + Ws + 50%H31

26. α-HH/ß-HH/WaKH(20/60/20) + Ws + 50%H31

27. α-HH/ß-HH/WaKH(50/20/30) + Ws + 50%H31

28. α-HH/ß-HH/WaKH(20/50/30) + Ws + 50%H31

29. α-HH/ß-HH/WaKH(50/30/20) + Ws + 25%H31 + 25%KstM

30. α-HH/ß-HH/WaKH(20/60/20) + Ws + 25%H31 + 25%KstM

31. α-HH/ß-HH/WaKH(50/20/30) + Ws + 25%H31 + 25%KstM

32. α-HH/ß-HH/WaKH(20/50/30) + Ws + 25%H31 + 25%KstM

Figure 27.7 Sample pieces (15×15×60 mm) after 28 days of storage in flowing water.

All mortars investigated were highly resistant to freeze-thaw cycling and did not show any efflorescence. The workability time lay within the range of an hour, but it can be lengthened with an increased addition of tartaric acid.

SUMMARY

Investigations have shown that it is possible to produce water-resistant joint mortars based on gypsum and lime whose properties are compatible with historic brick walls. They can be produced with commercially available binders. Thus, the outside walls of brick buildings that were built with gypsum mortar can be restored with a gypsum-based mortar. Damage, such as formation of ettringite when C_3A-containing cement mortar is used, can be avoided. Properties of set mortars can be adapted to a criteria owing to a combination of individual mortar components used.

The mixtures:

α-HH/β-HH/HHL (20/50/30)+0.1%tart+20%PLS

α-HH/β-HH/HHL (20/50/30)+0.1%tart+20%QS

α-HH/β-HH/HHL (20/50/30)+0.1%tart+25%PLS+25%QS

turned out to be most suitable. Test walls were built with these mortars and subsequently they were inserted into the southern facade of St. Wilhadikirche in Stade (northern Germany). These test surfaces are continuously monitored. After five years, they still do not show any damages.

ACKNOWLEDGEMENTS

An earlier version of this paper was published in the Proc. of the 10th Intl. Brick and Block Masonry Conference, Calgary, Canada, 1994, pp. 1571–1580.

We wish to thank Mrs. I. Hommel and Dipl.-Chem. A. Zöller for their support during experimental investigations and Dr.-Ing. K.G. Böttger for critical and helpful comments. Moreover, we are indebted to the Umweltbundesamt in Berlin for kindly giving financial support to this research project.

REFERENCES

Knöfel, D., and P. Schubert. 1990. Zur Beurteilung von Mörteln für die Instandsetzung von Mauerwerk. *Bautenschutz + Bausanierung* **13**:10–20.

Knöfel, D., and P. Schubert. 1993. Handbuch – Mörtel und Steinergänzungsstoffe in der Denkmalpflege. Berlin: Verlag Ernst & Sohn.

Middendorf, B., and D. Knöfel. 1994. Characterization of Mortars from Historic German Brick Buildings and Requirements for Restoration Material. In: Proc. 3rd Intl. Masonry Conf., No. 6, pp. 24–30, ed, H.W.H. West. Stoke-on-Trent, UK: British Masonry Society.

Schwiete, H.E., and A.N. Knauf. 1969. Alte und neue Erkenntnisse in der Herstellung und Anwendung der Gipse. Merziger Druckerei und Verlags GmbH.

Steinbrecher, M. 1992. Gipsestrich und -mörtel: Alte Techniken wiederbeleben. *Bausubstanz* **10**:59–61.

APPENDIX: Assessment of Mortars Intended for the Repair of Masonry

General

For repair work using mortars, it is often of interest to know other quality characteristics in addition to those stipulated by standards. Therefore a working group including research workers and practical professionals undertook the task of describing other important qualities and corresponding test procedures for mortars, especially for the repair of masonry, going beyond those stipulated by the standards. These additional qualities concern, in particular, the durability of masonry, especially fair-faced masonry. Questions concerning structural stability were not considered in this connection. These statements do not in any way affect the applicability of standards DIN 1053, part 1, DIN 1855 and DIN 18557.

A list of relevant qualities has been drawn up. The appropriate test methods are contained in Knöfel and Schubert (1990). For the assessment of the test results, characteristics and/or requirements have been set up which will be weighted individually in accordance with their significance.

Qualities and Requirements

To begin, mortars intended for the repair of masonry are subject to wet and hardened mortar tests and properties that go beyond what is stipulated by the applicable standards. The purpose of these tests is to achieve a more complete knowledge of the qualities of the mortar (see Table A.1). The tests are divided into two groups, of which the first includes the "necessary" and the second the "desirable" tests. For the assessment of the mortar, recourse should be had at least to Group A ("necessary"). This group includes, in addition to wet mortar tests, hardened mortar tests both of the actual mortar and of the stone-mortar masonry structure.

For the production of the stone-mortar masonry structure to be tested, the same type of masonry stone or stones having the same properties should be used. If necessary, evidence of the same properties can be obtained by corresponding tests or expert opinion. The extent of the tests should be related to the significance of the building measure. It goes without saying that the tests should cover only mortars which are known (or proved by tests) to be permanently, chemically compatible with the other building materials contained in the masonry.

Guiding values or requirements for assessing the tests results are given in Table A.2. These guiding values are, in part, absolute data (e.g., shrinkage, adhesive strength). This is appropriate where assessments of the mortar (e.g., shrinkage) or minimum values of the stone-mortar masonry structure are made irrespective of the stone qualities. Other guiding values are the quality relationships between the mortar and the stone material. This is appropriate where for increased durability the qualities of the mortar are to be adjusted to those of the stone material (e.g., E-modulus). Other guiding values or requirements contain only indications such as "similar to stone" or "as low as possible" as characteristics. Such general statements are sufficient for many qualities (e.g., tendency to segregate). Some qualities are not subject to any requirements at all (e.g., volume weight) because they are irrelevant for the durability of the masonry despite their importance for characterizing mortars.

Assessment

Since the qualities mentioned are of varying significance for the durability of masonry, their weighting must vary accordingly. A weighting of the quality characteristics is contained in Table A.3 for the tests of group "necessary."

Table A.1 Mortar tests.

GROUP A	(Test is necessary):	
Wet mortar:	*characteristic*	*method*
	1. Consistency	A 1
	2. Workability period	A 2
	3. Water retention	A 3
Hardened mortar:		
a: not bonded with stone	1. Dynamic E-modulus	A 4
	2. Coefficient of thermal expansion	A 5
	3. Swelling and shrinkage	A 6
	4. Resistance to freezing and thawing cycle	A 7
	5. Water absorption coefficient	A 8
b: bonded with stone	1. Adhesive tensile strength	A 9
	2. Adhesive shearing strength	A 10
	3. Compressive strength of the joint	A 11
	4. Reaction to atmospheric influences	A 12
GROUP B	(Test is desirable)	
Wet mortar:	1. Tendency to segregate	B 1
	2. Volume weight	B 2
	3. Air content	B 3
Hardened mortar:		
a: not bonded	1. Permeability to steam	B 4
	2. Absorbed moisture	B 5
	3. Efflorescence	B 6
	4. Rate of saturation	B 7
	5. Overall porosity	B 8
	6. Compressive and bending strength	B 9

The extension of the mortar characteristics beyond those stipulated by the applicable standards, which is provided for by this test schedule in connection with the mentioned guiding values and requirements, with due consideration being given to the weighting of the test results, is meant to enable the expert to assess the suitability of a mortar for a given masonry with greater certainty. Any quantitative assessment of the suitability of a mortar for given masonry structure that would go even further by using "value ratings" from quality tests which could be assessed and weighted may easily give a false impression of accuracy.

Table A.2 Guiding values or requirements.

Group	Mortar	Quality	Test Method[1]	Base Value / Requirement — Mortar	Base Value / Requirement — Mortar/Stone[2]
A necessary	wet mortar	- consistency	A 1	slump: (17 ± 0.5) cm unless otherwise required	
		- workability time	A 2	$\geq$ 1h	
		- water retention	A 3	great with highly absorbing stones, small with little adsorbing stones	
	hardened mortar not bonded with stones	- dynamic E-modulus	A 4		0.1 ... 1.0, as little as possible
		- coefficient of thermal expansion	A 5		0.5 ... 1.5, as close to 1.0 as possible
		- swelling, shrinkage	A 6	$\leq$ 2mm/m	as close to 1 as possible
		- freeze-thaw cycle resistance	A 7	minor spallings, no major or continuous cracks	
		- water absorption coefficient	A 8		
	hardened mortar bonded with stones	- adhesive tensile strength	A 9	$\geq$ 0.1 N/mm^2 adhesive tensile strength	
		- adhesive shearing strength	A 10	$\geq$ 0.1 N/mm^2 adhesive shearing strength	
		- compressive strength	A 11	$\geq$ 2 N/mm^2 as a rule [3] preferably without cracks, spallings	
		- reaction to atmospheric influences	A 12		
B desirable	wet mortar	- tendency to segregate	B 1	as low as possible	
		- volume weight	B 2	no requirement	
		- air content	B 3	no requirement	
	hardened mortar not bonded with stones	- permeability to steam	B 4		roughly the same as for stone
		- absorbed moisture	B 5		roughly the same as for stone
		- efflorescence	B 6		as little as possible
		- total porosity	B 7		as low as possible
		- compressive and bending tension strength	B 8		no requirement
			B 9		no requirement

(1) See Knöfel and Schubert (1990).
(2) Relationship of qualities of mortar and stone, e.g., $\beta_{ST\ mortar}$ / $\beta_{ST\ stone}$.
(3) Greater if necessary, depending on static requirements.

Table A.3 Weighting of mortar qualities for the Group A, necessary tests.

GROUP A	Necessary Tests:	Weight Factor
Wet mortar:	Weighting is omitted for the time being	
Hardened mortar:		
a: not bonded with stone	1. Dynamic E-modulus	3
	2. Coefficient of thermal expansion	1
	3. Swelling and shrinkage	3
	4. Resistance to freeze-thaw cycle	x
	5. Water absorption coefficient	1
b: bonded with stone	1. Adhesive tensile strength	2
	2. Adhesive shearing strength	2
	3. Compressive strength of the joint	1
	4. Reaction to atmospheric influences	x

x: For the time being, these criteria are not considered because there is insufficient experience with the proposed testing method.

Such accuracy is unrealistic for several reasons, e.g., some test methods lead to widely scattered results, certain criteria may have to be defined more precisely in the future and even the weighting of the qualities could be altered in some details.

Nevertheless, the working group is convinced that this paper will be able to help the expert in assessing with greater precision a mortar that is to be used for the repair of masonry. More experience will have to be gained.

References

Knöfel, D., and P. Schubert. 1990. Zur Beurteilung von Mörteln für die Instandsetzung von Mauerwerk. *Bautenschutz + Bausanierung* **13**:10–20.
Knöfel, D., and S. Wisser. 1988. Microscopical Investigations of Some Historic Mortars. In: Proc. 10th Intl. Conf. Cement Microscopy. Duncanville, TX: Texas Intl. Cement Microscopy Association.
Wisser, S., and D. Knöfel. 1987. Untersuchungen an historischen Putz- und Mauermörteln; Teil 1: Analysengang. *Bautenschutz + Bausanierung* **10**:124–126.
Wisser, S., and D. Knöfel. 1988. Untersuchungen an historischen Putz- und Mauermörteln; Teil 2: Untersuchungen und Ergebnisse. *Bautenschutz + Bausanierung* **12**:163–173.
Wisser, S., K. Kraus, and D. Knöfel. 1988. Composition and properties of historic lime mortars. In: Proc. 6th Intl. Cong. On Deterioration and Conservation of Stone, ed. J. Ciabach. Torun, Poland: Nicholas Copernicus Univ.

28

Injection Grouting for the Repair of Brick Masonry

R.H. ATKINSON† and M.P. SCHULLER

Atkinson-Noland & Associates, Inc., 2619 Spruce Street, Boulder, CO 80302, U.S.A.

ABSTRACT

A research project investigated injection grouting as a means to repair and strengthen unreinforced brick masonry buildings. A series of cement-based grouts was evaluated to optimize properties such as fluidity, injectability, mix stability, and bond strength. Laboratory trials showed that a properly formulated grout, when injected at low pressures through small-diameter holes drilled into mortar joints, can be effective for filling voids and repairing cracks caused by structural overloading. In addition, nondestructive pulse velocity testing was demonstrated to be useful for qualifying the effect of the repair process.

INTRODUCTION

Unreinforced masonry buildings comprise a significant portion of the building inventory in the United States including many historic monuments. The effects of environmental deterioration, settlements, excess loading and seismic loadings have rendered many of these buildings structurally marginal or inadequate. In addition, seismic regulations are requiring strengthening of many of these buildings.

Although injection grouting is used in the United States for masonry repair, no scientific studies exist to characterize the grout mixes used or to evaluate the structural efficiency of grout-injected brick masonry. In Europe, Paillere (Paillere 1989) has conducted an extensive study of grout mixtures for masonry injection, Binda (Binda 1989) has used the grout mixes developed by Paillere to inject laboratory piers, and Tomazevic (Tomazevic 1989) has tested a limited number of full-scale walls which were repaired by injection grouting.

The research project had the following components:

- development of grout mixes,
- injection of laboratory piers,

- development of nondestructive evaluation methods,
- injection and testing of full-scale masonry shear walls.

GROUT MIX DEVELOPMENT

Cementitous materials were evaluated as the basis for the injection grout. Because existing clay masonry is often highly absorptive and can contain both very fine cracks and large internal voids, injection grouts for masonry should possess the following properties:

- water retentivy to resist absorption of water by the brick,
- low viscosity to penetrate fine cracks,
- stability of solid components to resist segregation in the mixing tank and injection lines,
- low shrinkage,
- adequate bond strength to brick units and mortar.

Grout Mix Components

Cementitious Material. Portland cement served as the main binding agent for all mixes. Materials studied included normal Type I Portland cement, high early strength Type III Portland cement, and a proprietary cement sold in the United States for use in masonry mortar (MC). The Blaine fineness values for these materials are: Type I, 4000 cm^2/g; Type III, 5000 cm^2/g; and masonry cement, 8000 cm^2/g.

Pozzolans. A Type F pozzolanic fly ash and microsilica formulation (MS) produced by W.R. Grace were evaluated as partial cement replacements.

Aggregate. Some grout mixes designed for masonry containing large cracks or voids contained a silica sand having maximum particle size of 0.212 mm.

Admixtures. A modified naphthalene sulfonate formaldehyde base superplasticizer (SP) produced by ProKrete was used in most mixtures as a fluidifier. Several mixtures also evaluated a proprietary admixture for reinforced masonry grout manufactured by Sika Corporation (Grout-Aid) having expansive properties.

Evaluation of Trial Grout Mixtures

A standard program was developed and used to provide a quantitative evaluation of over 30 trial grout mixtures. The following tests (Figure 28.1) were employed in this evaluation:

- Marsh Funnel Viscometer – A grout funnel test employed in the oil drilling industry was used to evaluate viscosity (American Petroleum Institute).
- Inclined Plate Test – This test, adapted from the geotechnical grouting industry, uses an inclined glass plate against a smooth surface of the host

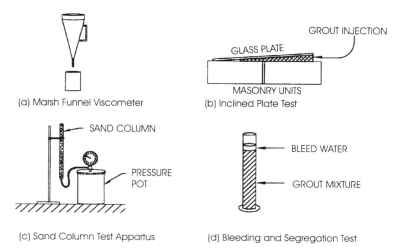

(a) Marsh Funnel Viscometer

(b) Inclined Plate Test

(c) Sand Column Test Appartus

(d) Bleeding and Segregation Test

Figure 28.1 Test methods for the evaluation of trial grout mixtures: (a) Marsh funnel viscometer; (b) inclined plate test; (c) sand column test apparatus; (d) bleeding and segregation test.

material to simulate a crack of decreasing width. Grout is injected at the thicker end of the opening and the minimum width of the injected crack can be determined from the distance the grout travels.
- Sand Column Test – The time of penetration of grout through a standardized sand column evaluates the injectability of the grout. For our tests, the grain size of the sand was selected to simulate an average void size of 0.2 to 0.4 mm (L'Association Francaise de Normalisation (AFNOR), NF P 18-891).
- Stability – Settlement, segregation and expansion (if any) were evaluated by observations of the grout mixture in a graduated cylinder (ASTM C 940C-87).
- Strength, Tensile – The grouted sand column was allowed to cure for 28 days and then was sectioned into cylinders which were loaded in diametrical compression to measure a tensile splitting strength. This strength provides a relative measure of grout tensile strength among the various grout mixtures.
- Strength, Tensile Bond – The bond wrench test (ASTM C 1072-86) was used to determine the flexural tensile bond strength of the grout mixture to a standard masonry unit. Test specimens were fabricated by injecting the trial grout mixture into a 0.9 mm opening between two brick units.

Results from Grout Mixture Evaluation

Over 30 different grout mixtures have been evaluated in the program. Selected results are presented to illustrate the change of grout properties as components and proportions change. A simple cement-water grout mixture containing Type I cement at a water/cement (w/c) ratio of 0.75 is used as a baseline in comparing various properties.

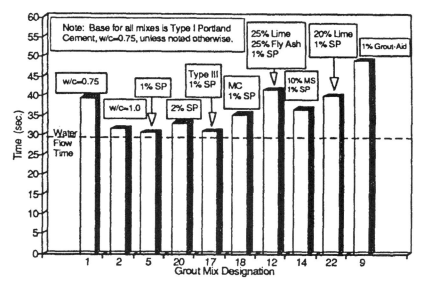

Figure 28.2   Effect of grout composition on marsh funnel time (SP denotes superplasticizer, MS denotes microsilica, and MC denotes a proprietary masonry cement).

Measurements of relative viscosity, as measured by the Marsh funnel test, are shown in Figure 28.2. Increases in the water/cement ratio and additions of superplasticizer decreased viscosity. Additions of ultrafine materials such as fly ash, lime or microsilica increased viscosity. When these materials were used in the mixture, use of a superplasticizer was essential to achieve flow through the Marsh funnel. Mixtures containing sand did not flow through the Marsh funnel.

Another measure of viscosity obtained using the sand column test is presented in Figure 28.3. Where the trial grout could not penetrate the 36 cm of sand, the maximum height of the grout penetration in the sand is listed. Mixtures containing ultrafine materials had very poor performance whereas cement-water grouts and grouts with superplasticizers had low sand column transit times.

Figure 28.4 presents results from the ASTM C 940 test which show that addition of ultrafine materials to the grout mixture significantly decreased bleeding and segregation. Mixture with ultrafine materials experienced only about 1% bleeding whereas materials without the fine material components had bleeding rates of above 3%. Stability of the grout mixture is important to assure that all components of the mixture are delivered in the correct proportion to the area being injected.

Results from the bond strength tests are presented in Figure 28.5, where the flexural bond tensile strength of the cement-water grout with a w/c ratio of 0.75 is used as a reference base. Grout mixtures containing lime or masonry cement are shown to significantly reduce strength. Use of a superplasticizer and higher water/cement ratios increase bond strength which results from the greater injectability of the grout mixture.

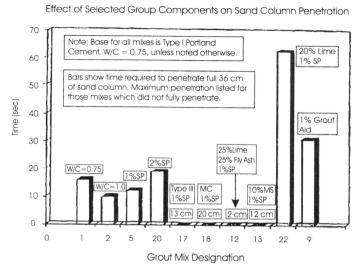

Figure 28.3   Effect of grout composition on sand column penetration (SP denotes superplasticizer, MS denotes microsilica, and MC denotes a proprietary masonry cement).

Use of a Type III cement with smaller particle sizes also significantly increased the tensile bond strength. For comparison, the tensile bond strength of a modern Type S mortar is also shown.

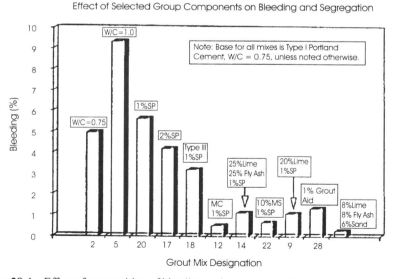

Figure 28.4   Effect of composition of bleeding and segregation (SP denotes superplasticizer, MS denotes microsilica, and MC denotes a proprietary masonry cement).

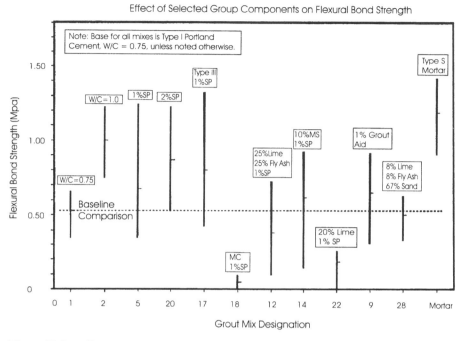

Figure 28.5 Effect of grout composition on flexural tensile strength (SP denotes superplasticizer, MS denotes microsilica, and MC denotes a proprietary masonry cement).

MASONRY WALL TEST

A preliminary evaluation of the efficiency of injection grouting for the repair and strengthening of damaged masonry was conducted using a three-wythe brick masonry wall section 1.5 m by 1.25 m in size. The wall had been built and tested in a previous program to evaluate *in situ* test methods and contained internal voids and extensive cracking (Noland et al. 1991). Prior to any testing, the vertical stress-strain response and a map of through-wall ultrasonic wave travel times had been obtained. At the conclusion of the *in situ* test program, a similar set of measurements were obtained for the damaged state. The damaged wall was treated by injection grouting using a grout mixture containing Type I cement, microsilica, superplasticizer and an expansive admixture. After a 28-day curing period, the vertical stress-strain and through-wall ultrasonic travel time measurements were repeated.

The stress-strain results, Figure 28.6, indicate that the damaged wall had a significantly lower stiffness, especially in the lower stress levels associated with service loading levels. The injection grouting repair of this wall restored the initial tangent modulus of the wall to its original value and increased the stiffness of the wall over the full loading range.

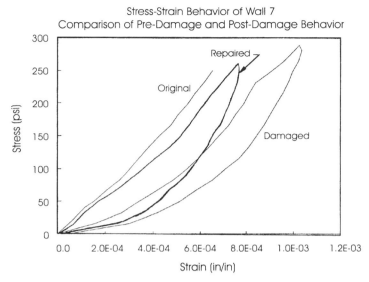

Figure 28.6 Masonry test wall compressive behavior (145 psi = 1.0 MPa).

The through-wall ultrasonic technique provides a means to visualize measure of grouting efficiency. Component masonry containing few or no cracks and voids will possess a high wave velocity leading to low travel times through the wall (Figure 28.7a). Damage to the wall in the form of cracks will produce longer wave travel times as cracks interrupt the direct wave travel paths (Figure 28.7b). The effectiveness of the injection grouting method in filling the cracks is illustrated in Figure 28.7c, where the wave travel time has been reduced to slightly better than the original undamaged wall. This indicates that in addition to filling cracks induced by wall overloading, the injection grout also filled void areas present in the undamaged wall. These most likely were partially filled mortar cracks.

SUMMARY

Results from this research program have shown that grout mixtures for injection grouting of brick masonry can be formulated to provide good injectability and bond strength. High water/cement ratios, the use of a superplasticizer, and use of finely ground cement provide good injectability. Use of ultrafine materials such as fly ash and microsilica add stability to the mixture but increase viscosity. The use of lime and masonry cement in the mix was shown to reduce the tensile bond strength.

The results from a trial grout mixture injected in a laboratory test wall provides a very convincing demonstration of the effectiveness of injection grouting as a method to restore the original structural capacity to a damaged wall. Full wall stress-strain measurements showed that the initial tangent modulus of the wall was restored by

(a)

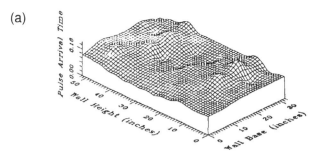

Wall 7, Through—Wall UPV, Original Condition

(b)

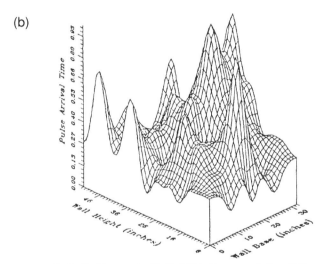

Wall 7, Through—Wall UPV, Damaged Condition

(c)

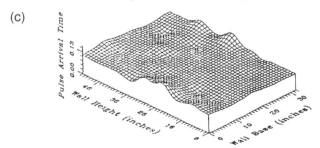

Wall 7, Through—Wall UPV, Repaired Condition

Figure 28.7   Three-dimensional surface plot of through-wall ultrasonic pulse arrival time: (a) original, as-built condition; (b) damaged condition; (c) following repair by injection of cementitious grout (1 inch = 25.4 mm).

injection grouting. Through-wall ultrasonic measurements provided a means to verify that the extent of crack and void filling was close to 100 percent.

ACKNOWLEDGEMENTS

This paper presents results from a program to investigate the efficiency of injection grouting techniques for the structural repair and strengthening of old brick masonry buildings. This program is part of a three-year collaborative study between the authors and Prof. B. Shing (University of Colorado), Prof. L. Binda (Politecnico di Milano), and P.P. Rossi (ISMES-Bergamo). The United States portion of the study was supported by the National Science Foundation under Grant No. MSS-9114511. Results of the research project can be found in Manzouri et al. (1995).

REFERENCES

American Petroleum Institute. Recommended Practice 13(b), Standard Procedure for Field Testing of Drilling Fluids.

ASTM C 940C-87. Standard Test Method for Expansion and Bleeding of Freshly Mixed Grouts for Preplaced-Aggregate Concrete in the Laboratory. American Society for Testing and Materials.

ASTM C 1072-86. Standard Method for Measurement of Masonry Flexural Bond Strength. American Society for Testing and Materials.

Binda, L., and G. Baronio. 1989. Performance of masonry prisms repaired by grouting under various environmental conditions. *Masonry Intl.* **3(2)**:74–79.

L'Association Francaise de Normalisation (AFNOR), NF P 18-891. Special materials for hydraulic concrete structures, materials for grouting concrete structures, sand column grouting test in wet and dry media.

Manzouri, T., P.B. Shing, B. Amadei, M.P. Schuller, and R.H. Atkinson. 1995. Repair and Retrofit of Unreinforced Masonry Walls: Experimental Evaluation and Finite Element Analysis. Report to the National Science Foundation, No. CU/SR-95/2. Boulder: Univ. of Colorado.

Noland, J.L., R.H. Atkinson, G.R. Kingsley, and M.P. Schuller. 1991. Nondestructive evaluation of masonry structures. Final Report, NSF Grant ECE 831 5924.

Paillere, A.M., M. Buil, A. Miltiadou, R. Guinez, and J.J. Serrano. 1989. Use of silica fume in cement grouts for injection of fine cracks. In: 3rd Intl. Conf. on Fly Ash, Silica Fume, Slag and Natural Pozzolans in Concrete. ACI SP 114, vol. 2.

Tomazevic, M., and D. Anicic. 1995. Research, technology and practice in evaluating, strengthening and retrofitting masonry buildings: Some Yugoslavian experiences. In: Proc. Intl. Seminar on Evaluating, Strengthening and Retrofitting Masonry Buildings. Boulder: The Masonry Society.

29

Desalination of Brickwork and Other Porous Media

P. FRIESE and A. PROTZ

FEAD GmbH, Research and Developement Laboratory for Rehabilitation of Old Buildings and Ancient Monuments, Rudower Chaussee 5, 12489 Berlin, Germany

ABSTRACT

Contamination of historic brickwork with soluble salts is often responsible for progressive decay; thus it is necessary to develop efficient techniques for desalination. The basic mechanisms of salt transport in porous media, i.e., diffusion, convective transport, and electromigration, are described and some new techniques for desalination of brickwork are introduced with examples of practical applications.

INTRODUCTION

It is well known that, in many cases, the decay of stones and bricks is caused by the presence of soluble salts. Therefore, it is imperative that we develop new techniques for the desalination of brickwork. Especially historical brickwork with wall paintings and architectural elements of cultural value need desalination to protect them from further decay.

Desalination of brickwork and other porous materials means the transportation of soluble salts into another medium. If the salts are dissolved in water, three mechanisms are available for this purpose: diffusion, convective transport, and electromigration (Figure 29.1).

An example of salt transportation through diffusion is shown in Figure 29.1a. A porous body contaminated with soluble salts is dipped into distilled water. Salt molecules migrate into the surrounding water until the equilibrium concentration is reached. One disadvantage is that diffusion proceeds slowly; without repeated renewal of the water, complete desalination is not possible.

Another mechanism is the convective transport of soluble salts, which requires pressure gradients as the driving force (Figure 29.1b). A porous plate (e.g., an element of brickwork) containing soluble salts is placed in a water source. The upper surface is

Mechanism of Salt Transportation

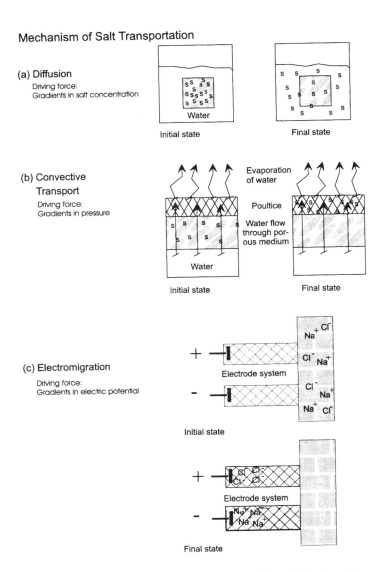

(a) Diffusion

Driving force:
Gradients in salt concentration

(b) Convective Transport

Driving force:
Gradients in pressure

(c) Electromigration

Driving force:
Gradients in electric potential

Figure 29.1 Mechanism of salt transportation in porous media: (a) diffusion, (b) convective transport, (c) electromigration.

covered with a poultice material. With the water stream, the salts are washed out into the poultice. The required pressure difference is caused by capillary pressure:

$$p = \frac{2\sigma \cos q}{r} \qquad (29.1)$$

where σ is the surface tension of the liquid, q is the wetting angle, and r is the pore radius. In contact with a water reservoir, most of the pores of the plate and the poultice are at first filled with water (capillary suction). Evaporation of water in the outer layers of the poultice leads to a steady water flow through the plate. The velocity of the liquid flow depends on the pore-size distribution and the evaporation rate at the surface of the poultice. In practical application, normal evaporation rates at 10°C are sufficient to induce a water flow for desalination. Heating and additional air convection enhances the desalination velocity.

The third mechanism of salt transportation is the migration of ions in an electric field to the corresponding electrodes. Electrode systems can be inserted into the porous medium or placed at the surface with an electrochemical contact to avoid destruction of the medium. In both cases it is possible to remove the reaction products at the electrodes containing the cations and anions of the salts. Following Faraday's law, the amount of removed salts depends on the current charge.

DESALINATION OF MASONRY WITH THE AID OF REPEATED APPLICATION OF POULTICES

Presently, the use of wetted poultices – which are fixed at the surface and removed after drying – is the most frequently applied technique for the desalination of masonry (Fassina and Costa 1986). In Figure 29.2, the transport of salts from the masonry into the poultice is shown schematically. The spatial distribution of salts in the unwetted masonry is usually determined by an exponential decrease from the surface into the inner layers (Friese and Pohlmann 1986). This means that the salts are mainly concentrated in the outer layers. By fixing (putting on) the wetted poultice at the surface, a part of the water is sucked up into the porous building material at the initial stage. This liquid flow induced by capillary forces shifts the salts into deeper regions of the masonry, which hinders the removal of salts as the average distance of the salts to the poultice increases. Evaporation of water at the surface of the poultice leads to a capillary water flow from the bulk to the surface and therefore to convective transport of salts into the poultice. This transport is supported by diffusion of salts in the same direction induced by the spatial differences of salt concentration. Simultaneously, a part of the water is sucked up into deeper regions of the masonry. To obtain a satisfactory degree of desalination, repeated application of poultices is necessary (Fassina and Costa 1986).

Generally, the transport of salts during humidification of the porous masonry from the surface decreases the efficiency of desalination with the aid of poultices. Using different poultice materials, such as cellulose, bentonite, and mixtures of both, under realistic conditions, we found no significant amounts of salts in the poultice. This means that the soluble salts are shifted with the water flow into other regions of the porous body only. Satisfactory results of desalination with poultice techniques have been obtained by applying a special compress rendering, containing calcitic minerals with

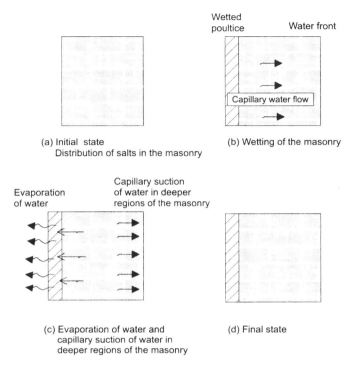

Figure 29.2 Application of a poultice for desalination water flow and change of salt distribution.

very small pores (pore-size diameter < 0.1 μm) at the surface of a historical facade over a period of two years (Friese et al. 1997).

DESALINATION OF BRICKWORK WITH INJECTION POULTICE TECHNIQUES

Convective transport is used for desalination of brickwork according to a technique developed by Friese and Hermoneit (1993). The principle of this technique is shown in Figure 29.3. Small holes are drilled into the joints, and needles, which keep a poultice pressed at the surface, are inserted. The poultice material is a sponge-like cellulose. The addition of water at a distance from the surface and the evaporation of water in the poultice leads to a steady water flow through the salt-containing layers of the masonry into the poultice. Treatment over 1 and 4 weeks completely washes the salts out into the poultice.

Figure 29.4 shows an arrangement of the injection poultice technique at a wall of the St. Nikolaikirche in the center of Berlin. This area was strongly contaminated with soluble salts (approximately 6%–8% mass in the layer 0–3 cm). The salts originated

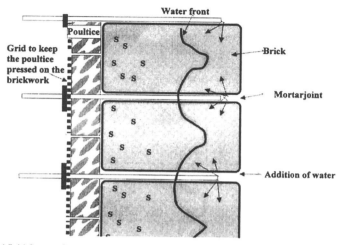

a) Initial state of salt distribution. Beginning of water addition.

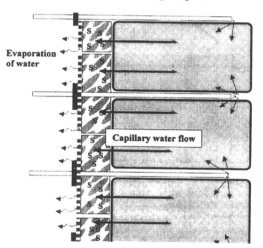

b) Final state of salt distribution. The salts are washed out of the brickwork into the poultice.

Figure 29.3   Desalination of brickwork with the injection poultice technique. The water is added behind the salt-containing layers of the masonry. With the capillary water flow to the surface, the salts are washed out into the poultice.

from the excrement of pigeons. St. Nikolai, one of the oldest churches in Berlin, was heavily damaged in World War II, and the ruins were favorite breeding places for pigeons for several decades. This led to the strong salt contamination at different areas of the brick masonry. In Figure 29.4, salt efflorescences in the neighborhood of the

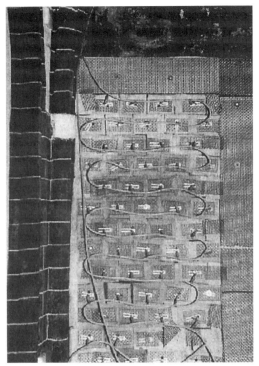

Figure 29.4   Application of injection poultice technique in brickwork of the St. Nikolaikirche in Berlin.

poultice are visible; the salt-induced decay of old bricks is observable in many parts of the church. Complete desalination of the area shown in Figure 29.4 took ten days.

Another example of the application of the injection poultice technique is the desalination of the facade of the "Jan Bouman Haus" in the Dutch Quarter of Potsdam, built up in the 18th century (Friese and Protz 1997). Rising damp as well as the influence of wastewater and bird excrement provided strong enrichment of soluble salts up to a height of 2.5 m above ground level. Figure 29.5 gives an impression of the state of the building in 1995, before desalination, and the results achieved after restoration. Table 29.1 presents the corresponding values of water and soluble salts for the facade before desalination. For desalination, the injection poultice technique described above was used with some variation. Water was added in the middle, and poultices were located at both sides of the masonry (see Figure 29.6a). The arrangement of the poultices inside and outside of the building is shown in Figure 29.6b, c. The maximum salt capacity of the poultice is on the order of 4–5 kg salt/m^2. During the desalination of the upper region, it was necessary to change the poultice twice because of salt saturation. After desalination of the upper region, the positions of the poultices were changed to lower parts of the brickwork. The total amount of soluble salts removed from the facade shown in Figure 29.6 was approximately 60 kg.

A disadvantage of the injection poultice technique lies in the fact that small drill-holes (diameter approximately 6 mm) are necessary to insert the needles to add the water and to keep the poultice pressed against the wall. In brickwork, the holes are drilled into the joints, and after desalination they can be repaired without difficulty. For desalination of wall paintings or sheets of sandstone, however, nondestructive techniques must be used.

Figure 29.5 The facade of the "Jan Bouman Haus" in the center of Potsdam (Germany) before and after desalination and restoration.

DESALINATION WITH THE AID OF ELECTROMIGRATION

On a larger scale, a technique for electrochemical desalination has been used (Friese 1988a, b). Electrodes were inserted into the masonry and a potential of 50–60 volts was applied against an earth connection system. Part of the anodic reaction products (primarily liquid chloride and nitrate hydrates) flowed into a container. Another part was enriched around the metallic anode core and could be removed mechanically. Figure 29.7 shows the electrode system for electrochemical desalination of masonry.

Table 29.1 Water and salt concentrations at different heights over the ground level (average values over the whole thickness of the brickwork) for the "Jan Bouman Haus," Potsdam, before desalination.

Height above ground level (cm)	Content of water (weight %)	Content of soluble salts (weight %)
30	11.1	0.17
60	9.5	0.39
85	3.4	0.86
140	3.4	1.70
200	6.0	4.20

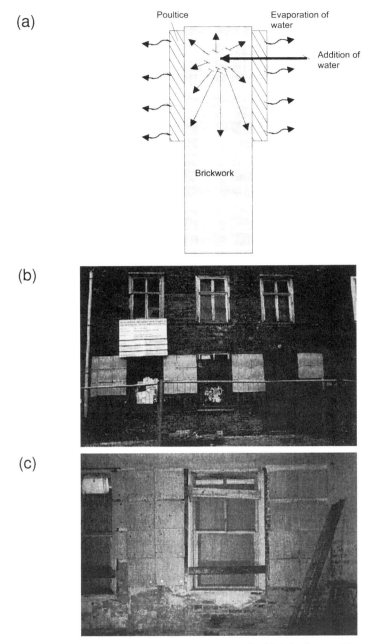

Figure 29.6   Desalination of the "Jan Bouman Haus" with injection poultice technique. Schematic view (a) and practical application (b, c). Poultices are located on both sides of the brickwork (b: exterior; c: interior).

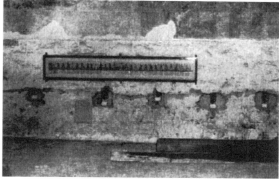

Figure 29.7 Single electrode system (anode) for electrochemical desalination of masonry. The anions migrate in the electric field to the anode. Some of the anodic reaction products are liquid and flow into a container. Other reaction products form efflorescence and can be removed mechanically. The cations migrate to the cathode, which is usually formed by an earth connection rod (top). Arrangement of electrode systems below the wall painting "Totentanz" in the St. Marienkirche in Berlin (bottom).

An outstanding example for the successful application of this techniques is the St. Marienkirche located in the center of Berlin. This church has a very famous wall painting from the 15th century that has shown a very rapid decay over recent decades. After installing an electrochemical desalination arrangement below the wall painting in 1987, no further decay was observable until now. From 1985 to 1997, approximately 35 kg of soluble salts were removed, mainly in a region of masonry with a length of 3–5 m that was extremely contaminated with soluble salts. We estimate that complete desalination of the masonry will require a further 10–20 years.

The direct desalination of wall paintings and architectural elements of cultural value (e.g., terracotta) requires nondestructive techniques. For this purpose, special electrode systems have been developed (Figure 29.8), which are located at the surface with a soft electrochemical contact to the porous, salt-containing media (Friese and Protz 1994). A moderate wetting of the porous media is necessary for an efficient electrochemical desalination. In practice, an alternating arrangement of cathode and anode systems is applied with a slow addition of water between the systems. Figure 29.8c shows the results of electrochemical desalination over a period of one week.

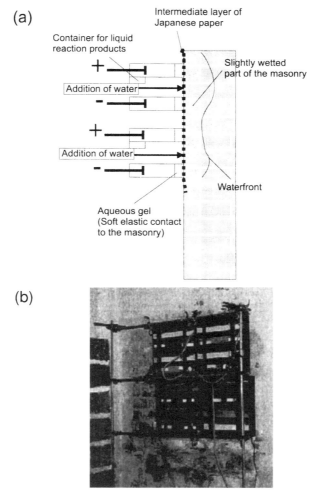

Figure 29.8 (a) Schematic view of electrode systems for nondestructive desalination and (b) their practical application.

REFERENCES

Fassina,V., and F. Costa. 1986. Preliminary results of desalination of *Ca Pesaro* brick masonry, p. 36. Esslingen: WTA Colloquium Materials Science and Restoration.

Friese, P. 1988a. Ein neues Verfahren zur Sanierung salzverseuchter Wände mit aufsteigender Feuchtigkeit, *Bautenschutz + Bausanierung* **11**:122.

Friese, P. 1988b. Removing of soluble salts and drying of masonry by means of electrochemical techniques, Proc. 6th Intl. Congr. Deterioration and Conservation of Stone, pp. 624–632, ed. J. Ciabach. Torun, Poland: Nicholas Copernicus Univ.

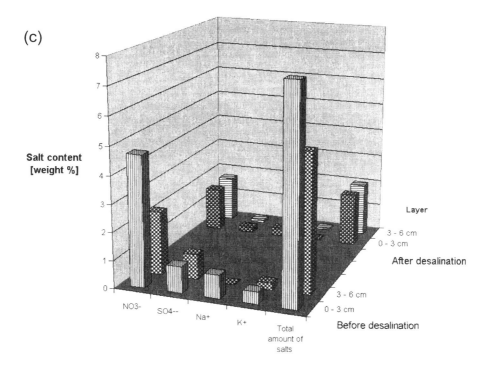

Figure 29.8 *(continued)*   (c) Change of salt contamination after one week.

Friese, P., and B. Hermoneit. 1993. Entsalzung von Ziegelmauerwerk mit dem Injektionskompressenverfahren. *Bautenschutz + Bausanierung* **16**:27.

Friese, P., and L. Pohlmann. 1986. Zustandsanalyse von Mauerwerk mit aufsteigender Feuchtigkeit. *Bauphysik* **8**:7.

Friese, P., and A. Protz. 1994. Salzschäden an Ziegelmauerwerk und praktische Erfahrungen mit Entsalzungsverfahren. *Bautenschutz + Bausanierung* **17(8)**:39–45.

Friese, P., and A. Protz. 1997. Entsalzung mit zweiseitiger Kompresse. *Bautenschutz + Bausanierung* **20(8)**:10–13.

Friese, P., A. Protz, and D. Peschel. 1997. Kompressenputz mit passenden Porenradien. *Bautenschutz + Bausanierung* **20**:26–30.

30

Weathering and Conservation of North German Terracotta
Schwerin Castle as a Case Study

S. WALLASCH[1], F. SCHLÜTTER[2], H. JULING[2], and R. BLASCHKE[2]

[1]German Center for Crafts and the Preservation of Historic Monuments,
Propstei Johannesberg, 36041 Fulda, Germany
[2]Amtliche Materialprüfungsanstalt, Abteilung Analytische Baustoffmikroskopie,
Paul-Feller-Str. 1, 28199 Bremen, Germany

ABSTRACT

The historic terracotta ornament (plaques and tiles) of the Schwerin Castle represent an early example of the industrial production of terracotta in northern Germany. This case study reports on a key monument in the research report entitled, "Preservation of North German Terracotta," which covered the castles of Schwerin, Gadebusch, and Basedow. The goal of the study was to identify both the causes and development of the various types of damage to terracotta, both where their cause is environmental and where it lies in the manufacturing process. A further stage involved problems encountered on-site during conservation.

An overview of the methods and main subjects of our work, which was carried out through interdisciplinary cooperation, is given, along with the initial results of the chemical investigations, in particular, ceramic tests and protective material tests. Attempts were also made to correlate the primary surface blackening with the subsequent scaling off through analytical microscopy installed in a mobile SEM laboratory.

Blackening can be explained as the result of normal weathering under constantly changing conditions, with frequent, very dry conditions. Alternating algae layer growth and drying of slime deposits forms a waterproof hydrophobic black skin that collects fly ash and other compounds. In addition to the formation of black gypsum crusts, other thin dense films observed on the samples are the result of an earlier conservation treatment with waterglass. Once the surface of the terracotta is sealed by the waterproof black skin, subsurface frost cracks can occur if moisture is supplied from the backside of the terracotta. These can be observed on the corresponding details from the palace. Crystals of gypsum growing from outside into the space of subsurface cracks intensify the scaling process by changing the conditions for contraction and expansion within the surface zone.

INTRODUCTION

The goal of this study was to identify both the causes and development of the various types of damage to terracotta, both when the cause is environmental and when it lies in the manufacturing process. The following stage involved the problems of on-site conservation. In this paper, the term "conservation" does not refer to the protective material complex but to the materials and techniques necessary for preservation, e.g., adhesive mortars (to fill blistered areas), battering mortars (to secure the transitional areas of intact surfaces and deteriorated surfaces), and filler masses.

The main subject of this study was the Schwerin Castle (Figure 30.1). Parts of the building date back to the 12th century. Between 1845 and 1850, it was converted and extended to form the residence of the Grand Duke. The 16th century lunette gable with large surface terracotta facing was completely removed from the building in 1845, even down to the terracotta tablets bearing the original motif. The terracotta elements of the castle can thus be seen as an early example of industrial, or rather serial, production.

Figure 30.1 Terracotta facing of the Schwerin Castle, from 1845.

Figure 30.2 illustrates the various forms of decay as well as different, partially superimposed damage views that were typical for this period. The following categories of damage may be established:

1. Large-scale bubbling, which to a certain extent is recognizable through its effects on the surface. In places, blisters have already burst and the core body is exposed. The fineness of the blisters as well as their variation in coloring, which shows no transitional phase between the surface and the underlying body, supports the theory that the material was built up in two layers. The result of the firing seems to have been explicitly connected with the terracotta's form due to an as yet unidentified difference in the thermic and hydroponic behavior of basic mass and surface.

Figure 30.2   Map of damage and original photograph.

2. The phenomenon of surface sections turning black or crust formation. Forms of deterioration, which are familiar from tiles, also follow.
3. Scaling: this involves a deterioration parallel to the surface where scaly particles break away.
4. Sandy disintegration, a frequent problem whereby the object loses material in the form of sandy grains.

In comparison to the placques from northern Germany in the 19th century, a special feature is the fact that these old pieces show remains of an original building period coloring.[1]

COOPERATING INSTITUTIONS AND WORK PLAN

The Department of Analytical Microscopy on Building Materials, which is associated with the Civic Center of Testing Materials in the Institute of Materials Science in Bremen, was involved in the microscopic investigations of samples taken from the Schwerin Castle. Specializing in optical and electron microscopy investigations of building structures, it has contributed to various preservation research projects by concentrating on stonework decay and preservation, in particular to problems involving historic half-timbered buildings and historic wall paintings.

---

[1] The existence of the castle in Gadebusch offers very useful possibilities to define both original and new elements using the same analytical methods. It can be established in advance that the tendency toward deterioration in the Renaissance placques as exemplified in Gadebusch is much smaller, with the exception of cases of critical exposure. The extent to which an original 16th century surface treatment or the boiling in oil had any effect still needs to be explained.

Figure 30.3   Mobile SEM laboratory.

Figure 30.4   Interior of the mobile SEM laboratory. The SEM equipped with EDX and image analyzer are located on the right-hand side. The polarizing microscopes are installed behind the viewpoint of the photographer.

Within the interdisciplinary research program delineated below, this department was responsible for carrying out microscopic analysis of the terracotta structures, which were in part badly damaged. An initial investigation of the black surfaces and the mechanism of deterioration of the surface on the upper gable was necessary. Most of the investigations were carried out in Schwerin within one week in a mobile laboratory designed by R. Blaschke and funded by the BMFT (Federal Ministry of Research and Technology). This mobile laboratory was used to carry out on-site analysis of samples (Figure 30.3). It contained optical microscopes, video equipment, a SEM with EDX microanalysis, a sputter coating unit, and wet chemistry (Figure 30.4). It proved itself to be a powerful tool for conservation for the following reasons:

- Common inspection and preparation of the sample by both scientist and restorer, from extraction to analysis, allowed a direct exchange of experiences and promoted useful on-site discussions.
- Confusion through the interchange of extracted samples and deterioration due to lengthy storage periods could be avoided. This is especially valuable when working with soluble salts or microbiological agents.
- The number of samples collected could be minimized.

Sampling was limited to loose material obtained from the outer surfaces, since authorities required the use of nondestructive testing methods. From the approximately 1 cm^2-sized samples, sections were embedded in epoxy resin for light microscopic inspection; other parts were prepared for SEM investigation of the upper and lower surfaces as well as cross section.

The individual test steps are summarized below. They were realized to varying degrees at the individual locations by institutes belonging to the BMFT.

Individual Test Steps

- Mapping of damage (restorers).
- Emission measurements to identify particle and gaseous pollutants in the air; this began in Schwerin because the castle's location on the island has given rise to extreme local conditions; at the time, a massive gypsum burden was found exclusively in surface areas (University of Hamburg).
- Technical testing of ceramics (School of Architecture and Building, Weimar).
- Technical testing of mortars to define adapted mortars (University of Siegen).
- Electromicroscopic scanning and X-ray analyses on site in mobile laboratories (Department of Analytical Microscopy).
- Infrared spectroscopic and chromatographic tests to conform organic treatment (Wilhelm-Klauditz-Institut, Braunschweig).
- Investigation into remains of coloring (binders, pigments).

Laboratory Tests to Adapt and Develop Conservation Methods

- Adapting and developing liquid stone protective agents (Institute for Building Research, Aachen).
- Blister-fixing mortar (University of Siegen).
- Bonding (battering) mortar to secure the transitional layer of the surface, which is not suffering from deterioration to the deteriorated material (University of Siegen).
- Filler masses (University of Siegen).
- Colored jointing mortar (University of Siegen).

PRELIMINARY RESULTS

Table 30.1 presents the chemical analyses for several terracotta types. The compiled characteristic analyses draw attention to interesting differences in materials. The following may be assumed: (a) when one looks at test samples 1–3, i.e., terracotta from Schwerin and Gadebusch (from the 16th and 19th centuries), the differences in silicon, iron, and aluminium content become clear. The materials from the 19th century have a

Table 30.1   Compilation of full chemical analyses of different terracotta types.

Test samples	Al_2O_3	SiO_2	FeO	TiO_2	CaO	MgO	Na_2O	K_2O	Heat loss
1	10.4	78.1	4.8	0.4	1.4	1.0	0.9	2.7	0.46
2	8.9	79.1	4.4	0.4	1.4	1.0	1.4	2.1	1.25
3	12.4	69.0	9.9	0.4	2.5	1.8	0.5	2.4	0.73
4	10.6	71.7	6.7	0.6	3.0	0.8	1.1	3.1	2.0
5	16.7	64.6	5.1	–	3.2	3.4	0.7	2.6	2.20
6	24.1	57.0	12.7	–	2.6	0.5	0.1	2.0	0.50

Test Samples 1–6:

1. Terracotta relief Schwerin, ca. 1850, analysis HAB Weimar
2. Terracotta relief Gadebusch, ca. 1904, analysis HAB Weimar
3. Terracotta relief Gadebusch, ca. 1570, analysis HAB Weimar
4. Medieval tile, Stralsund, analysis HAB Weimar
5. Terracotta relief Schallaburg, Austria, 1906, analysis Koller (Bundesdenk-malamt, Vienna)
6. Medieval tile, Stralsund, 1573, analysis HAB Weimar

Compilation of Physical Values:

Density, in the medium:	2.7 g/cm^3
Raw density:	1.85 g/cm^3
Overall porosity as a result:	30%
Natural water assimilation:	15% mass
Maximum water assimilation:	27% mass
Mercury porosity:	25%–30% volume

markedly higher SiO_2 content, which points to an enhanced dilution of the raw material and thus an increase quartz content. The reverse is true of the iron and aluminum oxide values.

Koller and Prandstetten (in Zotti 1975) came to the same conclusions of similarly low iron oxide and aluminum oxide values when testing terracotta from Schallaburg, Austria.

Despite the characteristic nature of these first examples, this means that the Renaissance terracottas were manufactured with a markedly fatter clay. At this point, the question as to the composition of the original raw material is of great importance. Because one of the deposits in the Schwerin area, which provided a good clay for heating to red-hot temperatures, was used both in the 16th and 19th centuries, it makes sense to investigate these deposits with respect to their mineral content. Attempts were made to reproduce the materials, to show stages in the composition of the mass and the firing process.

Figure 30.5 shows the pore-size distribution of terracotta materials from the Schwerin Castle. Maximum pore radius is subject to remarkably narrow limits at approximately 0.1 to 1 μm, forming about 70% of the measurable pore space. The 0.01 to 0.1 μm pore radius interval represents an additional 20% of the pore space.

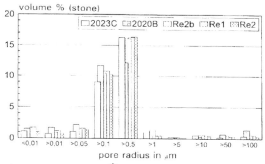

Figure 30.5 Pore-size distribution of 19th century terracotta.

The following estimates in respect of the hydroponic behavior were made: the pore space of the terracotta under investigation is characterized as inhabiting the borderline areas of micropores and capillary pores. Because the main proportion of the pores develops on the capillary pores, the material can be characterized as being capillary active, i.e., relatively strongly absorbent. These characteristic dimensions are of great importance, especially for questions concerning absorption of conservation media.

MICROSCOPIC INVESTIGATIONS

Black Skins on Terracotta Surfaces

One reason for surface blackening is the formation of gypsum crusts, as shown in Figure 30.6. SEM analysis reveals the morphology of this black incrustation, which consists largely of gypsum crystals (Figure 30.7). An EDX microanalyzer was adapted to the SEM to allow elemental analysis within the microstructured surface of the sample

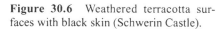

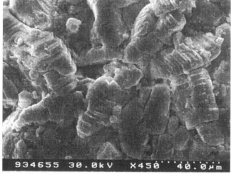

Figure 30.7 Black skin areas from Figure 30.5 consist mainly of twinned crystals (below 50 μm). Spherical particles identified as fly ash.

Figure 30.6 Weathered terracotta surfaces with black skin (Schwerin Castle).

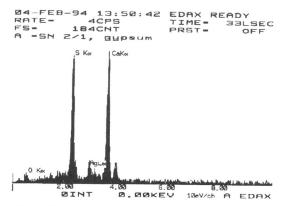

Figure 30.8 EDX spectrum (gypsum) crystals of Figure 30.6 shows equal peaks of S and Ca (Ag coating).

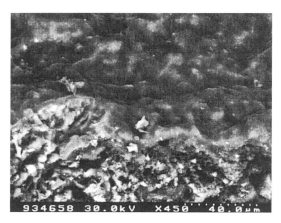

Figure 30.9 Oblique view of the smooth surface coating layer (upper part) and the fractured plane through the depth of the specimen (bottom). The thickness of the dense coating is about 5 μm.

(Figure 30.8). Inorganic particulates, such as fly ash, may contribute to the black discoloration of the outer surface. Microscopic analyses gave no indication of organic material in this case.

On three samples immediately adjacent to the sample shown, the terracotta surfaces were found to be covered by a partially fissured black film, approximately 5 microns in depth (Figure 30.9). The EDX spectrum shows the comparison between the terracotta material and the thin layer covering the surface (Figure 30.10). The elemental ratios and the morphology indicate that these are the residues of a former surface treatment by waterglass.

On a further sample, a thin black film was also found (Figure 30.11). The polarized light microscope image (Figure 30.12) indicated gypsum layer formation parallel to the surface. Back scatter electron (BSE) imaging allows the various compositions of the sample to be differentiated in accordance to the atomic number of the elements contained. On the surface of this sample, we found a film with a thickness of less than 10 microns and a surprisingly high back scatter intensity (Figure 30.13 and 30.14). The brightness in this area indicates a different composition of the black skin compared with the terracotta material. By EDX measurements, we found a very high iron content in the surface-covering thin black film (Figure 30.15).

The Role of Gypsum Crystallization in Deterioration of the Upper Surface

Independent from the different characters of the surfaces, all samples taken from the upper gable area exhibit the following similarities: (a) they displayed strong gypsum

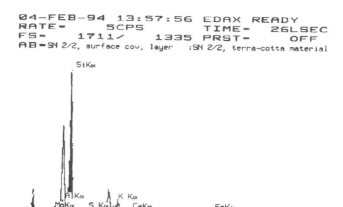

```
04-FEB-94 13:57:56 EDAX READY
RATE-      5CPS              TIME-    26LSEC
FS=     1711/    1335 PRST-          OFF
AB=SN 2/2, surface cov. layer   :SN 2/2, terra-cotta material
```

Figure 30.10   Comparing the EDX spectra of the Al-rich terracotta material (white curve) with that of the thin coating layer (black curve), we can estimate an earlier treatment with water-glass sealing the pores in the terracotta.

Figure 30.11   Terracotta with relics of black skin with efflorescing gypsum (white).

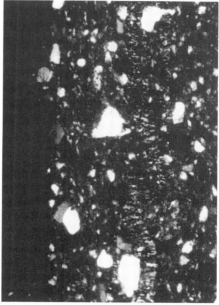

Figure 30.12   Cross-section of a specimen from the area shown in Figure 30.10. Between crossed polars, the cracks appear filled up by crystals of gypsum (PolMi, brightfield, # polars, height of photo about 1 mm).

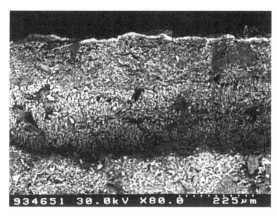

Figure 30.13 Fractured plane corresponding to the thin-section in Figure 30.11. In the middle is a 0.2 mm thick layer of gypsum. On the top, a trace of a bright layer with a high coefficient of back-scattered electrons (BSE); this indicates the content of an element with a high Z number (SEM-BSE micrograph).

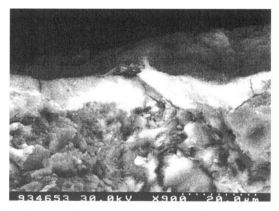

Figure 30.14 Selected area of Figure 30.12 (SEM-BSE micrograph).

crystallization in cracks underneath the surface, up to a depth of 800 microns; (b) numerous crystallized layers were to be seen.

The observed skins have formed waterproof hydrophobic surfaces. After sealing the plates of terracotta, now subsurface frost cracks can occur if dampness is supplied from the backside of the plate, which can be observed on the corresponding details of the palace (upper gable area).

On fractured planes one can see that the gypsum crystals grow from the outer wall of the subsurface crack inwards (Figure 30.16). Such features seem to indicate their appearance *after* crack generation. The growing of gypsum crystals intensifies the scaling process by changing the conditions for contraction and expansion within the subsurface zone (Figure 30.17).

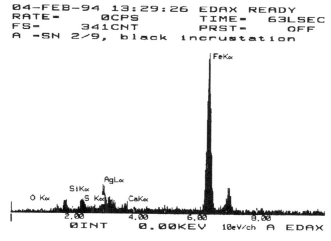

Figure 30.15 The EDX spectra of the bright dense layer seen in Figure 30.13 indicates a high content of Fe.

Some of the examined samples clearly exhibit a tendency towards a buildup of exfoliation structures. The smallest cracks are mostly free of gypsum (Figure 30.18). Gypsum formation is restricted to the outer millimeter of the terracotta plates and ornaments.

Parts of the lower gable area also show evidence of enhanced black skins; however, there are no indications of the onset of decay. Removed terracotta material taken from comparable areas in the 1970s have also been investigated. The microscopic analyses have shown a very thin black film, which consists largely of organic material containing amounts of inorganic particles. The thickness of that film is up to 10 microns.

Figure 30.16 Selected area from Figure 30.12. The palisade-shaped layer of gypsum indicates their nucleation on the outer wall of the subsurface tract (SEM-BSE micrograph).

Figure 30.17   Asymmetric features of the gypsum layer (middle) seem to indicate their appearance after crack generation (SEM-BSE micrograph).

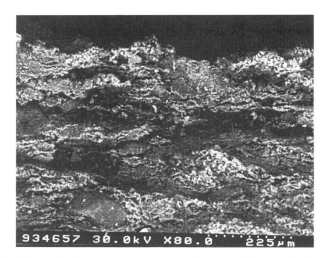

Figure 30.18   The smallest cracks are mostly free of gypsum. (On samples free of cracks, we sometimes observed pores filled up by gypsum but also no indication of beginning decay.)

The surfaces of the examined terracotta ornaments also exhibit a waterproof behavior. Alternating layers of algae growth and drying out slime deposits may form such hydrophobic skins by collecting fly ashes and compounds and its local enrichment. In laboratory tests, it was impossible to remove this material from the surface by organic solvents or acids and bases. Only hydrofluoric acid was able to remove this superficial layer chemically.

CONSERVATION

To address the question of conservation media for this ceramic material, a preliminary estimate of the investigation under laboratory conditions of the capacity of the terracotta is given. In the next phase of our project, we will carry out tests to establish the basic suitability of polyurethane (used as prepolymers in the solvent butyl acetate), elasticated fluosilic acid ester watery micro-emulsions (mixture of silane and siloxane), and normal commercially available fluosilic acid ethyl ester (diluted).

A major problem with respect to the application of the protective material, which is the absorbent capability of the terracotta surfaces, is subject to wide variations in the case of small pieces on the plaque surface. As can be seen, the unweathered surfaces, i.e., grooved areas from drill cores, are extremely absorbent. The surfaces appear to be intact (blackened surfaces under which blistering due to crystallization of gypsum is present) are as good as sealed. This means that for deteriorating sections, where the upper surface has already come adrift, the results are promising, although not all characteristic profile values are in. While a partial securing of these areas should be avoided, we must be prepared to dilute these blackening seals. In this area, laboratory tests will be carried out on dry-acting particle rotation processes.

In regard to the penetration processes of protective agents or of terracotta that do not have a sealed surface, in polyurethane prepolymers, a particular, special pore radius interval crops up and dominates the whole spectrum. The penetration depth of approximately 8 cm is remarkable: this is a result that is hardly possible even with sandstone. It should be emphasized that the depth of penetration cannot be the only selection criterion for adhesive agents. Ongoing laboratory tests will provide results on identifying the deep profile-related values after the application (pore size, flexibility under stress, elasticity module, simulation of weathering, etc.).

In 1994, application tests for different liquid conservation media types (elasticated fluosilic acid ester and polyurethane prepolymer), adhesive mortars, and dry-cleaning processes were begun on sample areas of the Schwerin castle. Further sample areas to investigate the suitability and durability of all methods, techniques, and materials followed until the end of 1994. In addition, on-site tests were conducted from 1995–1997 to describe the profile-related effects of the conservation media on terracotta and their further adaptation to special cases.

REFERENCE

Zotti, W. 1975. Die Restaurierung der Schallaburg: Eine Dokumentation. St. Pölten: Verlag Niederösterreichisches Pressehaus.

31

Change in Physico-technical Characteristics in Brick Masonry Effected by Modified Composition

D. HOFFMANN and K. NIESEL

Federal Institute for Materials Research and Testing (BAM), Unter den Eichen 87,
12205 Berlin, Germany

ABSTRACT

Granulometry of sand, mixing water content of lime plaster, as well as mix proportion are parameters that determine structural characteristics and properties such as pore volume, capillary water absorption, and water vapor diffusion resistance. Corresponding information is essential for buildings worthy of being preserved. One can deduce that granulometric composition and elevation of mixing water content together effect a considerable structural modification in hardened plaster, which is also reflected in masonry by capillary and evaporation behavior. So bricks of a dry-pressed type, with decreasing apparent density, cause an increase of maximum liquid absorption reached by capillary action. This is related to surface area a being equivalent to maximum absorption height. In the case of a bond applied to this brickwork, since mortar covers about 20% of an external surface, it influences water rise as well evaporation. When fine sand, which has been sifted at 0.5 mm, is used in mortar production instead of sand standardized according to EN 196-1, characteristic values such as a and w_0 shift in the same direction. Similarly effective is an increase of surface tension, e.g., when using a saturated solution of calcium sulfate as a test liquid, whereas conditions reverse in the case of denser bricks. This is also the case when using coarser standard sand. Nevertheless, such a solution, in comparison to water, likewise prevents evaporation on a moisture-saturated masonry section, whereby differences in density, because of different absorption heights, find their expression in the size of evaporation surface, which finally leads to differing starting points of curves. Brickwork made with standard sand shows this phenomenon only after several repetitions of this solution rise. From these findings it turns out that the general behavior of masonry during moisture transport decisively depends on pore volume and pore-size distribution of brick and mortar, especially in the region of capillary activity, and above all on grain-size distribution of a mortar's aggregate, whereby the water demand increases with decreasing particle diameter.

INTRODUCTION

In another work concerning the influence of mix proportion of plasters on their structure and sulfate absorption (Hoffmann and Niesel 1998, section 5.4), it was shown that in the outer surface layer of 1 mm thickness, leaner mixes absorbed more sulfate than did richer ones. This was the starting point for suggestions on how to modify a rendering's structure by varying its components (grain-size distribution, portion of sand and binder, and water demand) and how this procedure would affect physico-technical properties and characteristics. Thus moisture transport and weathering behavior are directly interrelated, and that way one comes a bit nearer to the objective of explaining physical properties of a material from its microstructure.

The basic concept is that the system is a complex mixture of hardened binding agent, aggregate sand, as well as pores whose portion, size, and distribution are mainly determined by mix proportion, granulometry of sand, and quantity of mixing water (ASTM 1987). It is common knowledge that an increase in binder content makes a mortar mechanically more resistant, while its tendency to crack formation increases. With regard to workability of fresh mortar, a fine sand demands an increased quantity of water for mixing. This in turn, however, increases porosity in comparison to another mortar of the same composition and aggregate granulometry and also decreases strength at the same time. In samples taken from a building, one can determine mix proportion and granulometry without difficulty but not the original content of mixing water which strongly influences structure. Because no additional data were generally obtained by the usual mortar analyses and, nevertheless, transport and storage of moisture occur through open pore space, further criteria for assessing pore structure will be necessary. Therefore, when attempts are made to reproduce historical renderings (cf. Niesel 1994), it is necessary to quantify pore volume, distribution of pore radii and physico-technical characteristics as, e.g., capillary water absorption and vapor diffusion, and to identify the influence of these parameters by systematically varying the portions of binder, aggregate, and water.

SAND AS AN AGGREGATE

Given this objective, the following procedure was chosen: for all tests, a sand standardized according to DIN EN 196 (1990) was used. When the coarse portion is removed by sieving, one obtains fractions with particle sizes ≤ 1.0 mm, ≤ 0.5 mm, ≤ 0.25 mm, and ≤ 0.16 mm. Figure 31.1 illustrates the grain-size distributions of the sands used. Next, a procedure which is long familiar in soil science – the measuring of matric suction or potential (Croney et al. 1952) – also allows determination of pore radii in loose granular materials.

Since water serves as a test medium, one can reliably determine processes arising in practice. By exerting a defined pressure, a certain part of water under tension is removed from pores. This way one can predict how much water remains in the sample at a particular suction or corresponding pressure potential. By gradual pressure variation,

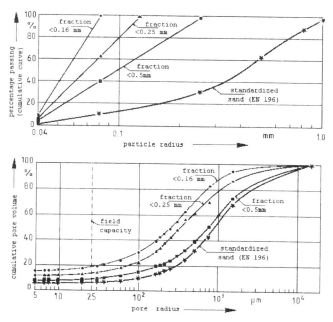

Figure 31.1   Grain- and pore-size distributions of the sands used.

a decreasing moisture content in a building material is similarly produced. To each pressure a particular pore radius can be associated. For water, the following approximate equation is valid:

$$r = \frac{1500}{P},$$ (31.1)

where r corresponds to pore radius in nm and P to pressure applied in 10^5 Pa. One thereby obtains information on pore volume and distribution of pore sizes (Hoffmann et al. 1995; Krus and Kiessl 1991; Tombers 1991). Such curves are shown in the lower part of Figure 31.2. There one can find the pore spectrum being shifted to smaller radii with decreasing grain-size of sand. In this figure, the respective pore volumes of each were set to 100%. In an interval below a diameter of 50 μm, referred to as field capacity in soil science, water can only be retained by capillary forces, whereas with larger pores gravitational draining is predominant. The volume portion of pores of this size could therefore be consulted as a criterion for capillarity.

As reported elsewhere, a regression function for describing capillary liquid rise has been established at the Umweltbundesamt (Hoffmann and Niesel 1988):

$$y_s = a\left(1 - e^{-b \cdot t^{0.5}}\right).$$ (31.2)

This equation is valid for most bricks, mortars, renderings, some concretes, and numerous natural stones but not for all sands. The curves in Figure 31.2 show capillary

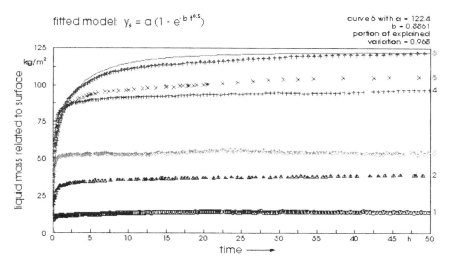

$$\text{fitted model: } y_s = a (1 - e^{-b\, t^{0.5}})$$

curve 6 with a = 122.4
b = 0.8861
portion of explained
variation = 0.968

Figure 31.2 Liquid rise in sand: (1) > 0.5 mm fraction of sand standardized according to EN 196; (2) standard sand; (3) fraction ≤ 1.0 mm; (4) ≤ 0.5 mm; (5) ≤ 0.25 mm; (6) ≤ 0.16 mm.

transport of six sand fractions with different grain size (cf. Niesel 1994a, b). Only the absorption curve for the fraction smaller than 0.16 mm in diameter can be fitted to the function with a relatively good measure of precision. From these data, the validity range of the above-mentioned relation is determined. In the case of sand, genuine capillary transport begins only when the amount of pores smaller than 50 μm in diameter occupies ca. 20% by volume.

One should note that capillarity data obtained, especially on loose granular matter packing, could, apart from results on building stone and other solid material, furnish suggestions for local intensifications of moisture rise as would be of interest, e.g., in desert regions. There are also other characteristics to be determined as, e.g., bulk density, pore volume (porosity), field capacity (amount of pores < 50 μm in diameter) and filling degree after capillary suction. This was possible because an equal sand volume after defined compaction is always used for these tests. Figure 31.3 represents relationships between these parameters and grain size of sand. Bulk density (apparent density of dry material) decreases with increasingly finer sand, whereas pore volume and filling degree correspondingly increase, because more pores occur in the range of capillary activity. This is shown by the increase of pore volume below the field capacity.

While it was not our objective to study sand intensely, it is absolutely necessary to define it before mixing it with thebinding agent and water.

LIME PLASTER

One can regard a mortar or rendering as a cement hardened in an adequate time between or on building blocks where a minimal strength is required at grain boundaries

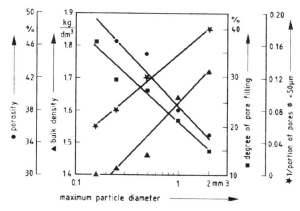

Figure 31.3   Changes of structural parameters when using sand with different grain sizes.

and at the interface to neighboring materials. Therefore, aggregate grains have to be bound into the whole, and the interstitial spaces in such agglomerate must be at least partially filled by a binding agent. In this connection, the phenomenon known as "leaning," which has been poorly defined up until now, plays a crucial role. The principle is that binder or mortar matrix material more or less surrounds aggregate grains and lines pore walls in such a way that stress relief can take place and crack formation can be avoided.

Everyone who has prepared mortars or renderings can attest to the difficulty in obtaining good reproducibility, even when constant starting conditions such as mix proportion and water demand are maintained, and despite performance by the same person with an identical mix having the same characteristics. Figure 31.4 shows the scattering of corresponding structural data in which pore-size distribution for lime

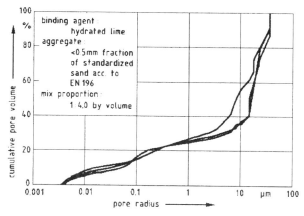

Figure 31.4   Comparing pore-size distribution of lime mortar batches while using the same recipe.

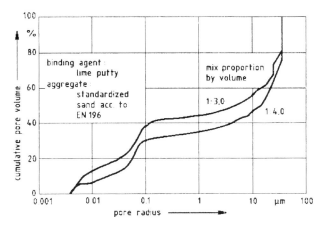

Figure 31.5 Shifting pore-size distribution of lime mortar: influence of mix proportion.

mortar batches of the same recipe is plotted. These results can only be obtained when the necessary conditions are strictly maintained (e.g., mixing time).

By increasing the binder portion in a mix, one can generally shift the pore spectrum of the hardened mortar formed from this mix to finer pores (Figure 31.5).

The portion of fine pores smaller than 5 μm in diameter (the so-called microporosity according to Honeyborne and Harris (1958)) increases here to about 5%, whereas the median (the 50% fractile of pore-size distribution) drops from 12 μm to 8 μm. At the same time, one can observe an elevation of pore volume measurable by mercury intrusion. The mixing water content for both renderings was comparable (21.3% and 21.6% by mass). Since the water absorption coefficient, w_0, could not be determined for the majority of samples due to geometric deficiencies, only limited information was obtained. An increasing binder portion obviously causes a rise in this characteristic.

This tendency is still more distinct (Figure 31.6) when one compares this mix to a historical mortar that has a mix proportion of lime hydrate to sand of 1 to 0.9 by volume. Caution should be taken, however, with respect to an interpretation since it is probable that other techniques (e.g., soaking of quicklime together with sand and also another content of mixing water) were used during the mortar's preparation. Likewise, a pore-size distribution similar to

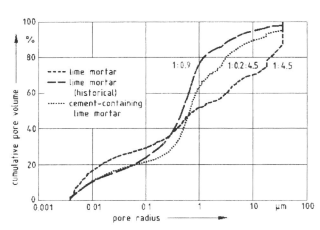

Figure 31.6 Shifting pore-size distribution of lime mortar: influence of the mix proportion and a Portland cement admixture.

that of the historical material can be obtained by additing small amounts of Portland cement (Figure 31.6). Since a suitable substitute mortar has to fulfil criteria other than this (e.g., similar pore volume and low modulus of elasticity), a reduced quantity of Portland cement-containing mortar is out of consideration, at least when lime was used as binding agent for historical material. To attain comparable behavior and structure and to produce mortar that is free of cracks and will remain so, one must utilize older techniques.

Results on the influence of an aggregate's grain-size composition on physico-technical properties and characteristics are also available. They are based upon mortars with the same mix proportion, 1:4.0 by volume. This differed considerably in mass depending on the binding-agent aggregate batch, because of the applied standardized sand used and with its fraction smaller than 0.5 mm. Consistency was regulated by he spread value (18 cm was selected), thus producing an increased water demand of about one third, namely from 18% to 29%, when using a mortar manufactured with fine sand. Figure 31.7 represents respective pore-size distributions for corresponding samples. The specific pore volumes were set to 100% again. However, we did not expect that mortar containing a fine fraction would show such a very small amount of fine pores, namely a microporosity of 28% in contrast to one of 55%. It should be emphasized that the pore volume is nearly double, which cannot be recognized by this type of representation. A behavior occurs here analogous to that observed on sand whereby with increasingly finer fractions, the pore volume (expressed as porosity), the pore filling degree, as well as the w_0 increase. Does this mean that one can just transfer these conditions to mortars? It does not appear quite so simple, because similar to the grain-size effect, an increase of mixing water content is followed by a higher w_0 in hardened mortar. From this, we can conclude that both parameters uniquely influence structural changes observed and operate in the same direction. Only systematic tests may help to quantify their contribution to the entire event.

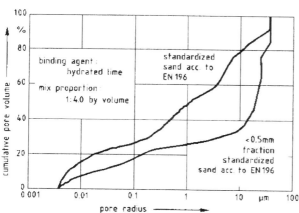

Figure 31.7 Shifting pore-size distribution of lime mortar: influence of sand fraction.

Some additional, interesting trends can be elucidated by combining of single characteristic values. Due to the lack of sufficient data, only tendencies valid for both kinds of granular matter should be shown. Existing gaps still have to be closed. In such lime mortars, an elevated pore volume always runs parallel to a diminished portion of micropores. However, the fewer the

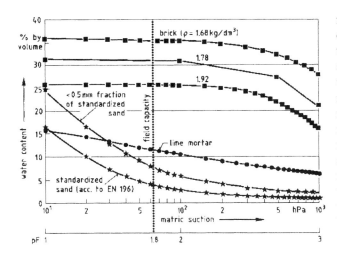

Figure 31.8   Water content depending upon matric suction, determined on dry-pressed bricks, lime mortar and aggregate sands.

number of micropores — or inversely expressed, the more coarse pores such materials possess — the higher the values are reached for w_0. This means that microporosity may provide information on frost sensitivity of building materials, but is less involved in capillary transport. According to Weber et al. (1984, p. 17), at a diameter smaller than 0.08 μm, capillary transport should completely come to a standstill. Of course, the kind of behavior of such a building material will be further influenced by the base on which the plastering was applied as well as by the bricks or natural stones situated in between the mortar. Their absorbing behavior still exerts an additional effect on drying mortar during hardening in its structural development. Therefore, from Figure 31.8, the matric suctions of sand, the lime mortar produced thereof, and typical bricks of different density demonstrate that it is neither permissible to view a mortar in isolation nor to lose sight of the complexity of the process.

According to our experience, several correlations can be established between pore-related characteristics for bricks, mortar prisms, rendering fragments, and accumulations of aggregate sand. A total survey on capillary and evaporative behaviors will be ultimately furnished only by the brickwork itself, in which a geometrically complicated scaffold of bed and head joints runs through a regularly stacked brick pile. Current findings represent the first steps towards this goal. By varying test conditions in a way directed towards an objective, one can appreciably reduce the sample number and test duration, which would otherwise necessarily increase excessively. Thus, one has not only to select measures carefully but to consider that preparative uncertainties may initially restrict the significance of the results obtained.

INVESTIGATION OF CAPILLARY ABSORPTION IN MASONRY SECTIONS

After considering the relationships of aggregate sands and mortars, one can obtain information on the transport event in an entire masonry structure by including bricks. In addition to properties determined by firing conditions, such as a decrease of pore

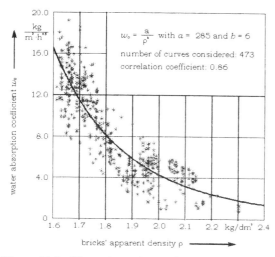

$$w_o = \frac{a}{\rho^b} \text{ with } a = 285 \text{ and } b = 6$$

number of curves considered: 473

correlation coefficient: 0.86

Figure 31.9   Water absorption coefficient, w_0, as a function of apparent density, ρ, determined on brick stacks from different production runs. In addition, data for some sedimentary stone specimens are plotted.

volume and an increase of apparent density, such a view of the pore parameters of a satisfactorily characterized ceramic material also shows a reduction in the fraction of fine pores as a result of the sintering process. Correspondingly, w_0 diminishes with density (Figure 31.9). The curve represents a type of hyperbola for which 473 values were available. At the same time, a higher brick density is associated with a smaller pore volume. Further details can be found in the literature on this subject (Niesel 1994b; Hoffmann and Niesel 1996; Niesel 1993; Niesel and Hoffmann 1992; Niesel and Rooss 1983).

Regarding the experiments with masonry sections, the relationships are not quite distinct; the schematic presentation shown in Figures 31.10 should aid in clarification. Dry-pressed facing bricks of similar apparent density and specifically from the same production run were used in their setup. Pure lime mortar with a mix proportion of lime hydrate to sand of 1:4.0 by volume was taken initially to avoid a barely detectable blocking effect, e.g., caused by cement grout on the bricks' boundary faces. Standardized sand according to DIN EN 196-1 served as the aggregate in addition to a sieve passing plain ≤0.5 mm diameter, with which one can almost fit the absorption behavior of mortar to that of brick.

For two masonry sections, lime putty was also used as a binder. Furthermore, in several cases the mortar mix proportion and brick density were modified as well. Consistency was adjusted by the spread value according to DIN EN 459-2 (1995). The test specimens were situated in water-containing troughs on balances, whereby one could monitor mass change during moisture rise and evaporation events. For determining capillary absorption by weighing the whole specimen, one also has to hold the liquid level constant while running the required test setup. Thus the validity of the above-mentioned regression function can be demonstrated for wall sections of ca. 63 to 36 cm base area (transversal cross-section) and 125 cm height brick courses laid in a cross bond with pure lime mortar. After the experiment, the moisture content of porous bricks freed from mortar is gravimetrically stated. In the same way, one can remonitor the capillary rise in its various stages and afterwards recalibrate, using a method based on measurement of a dielectric constant (Figure 31.11).

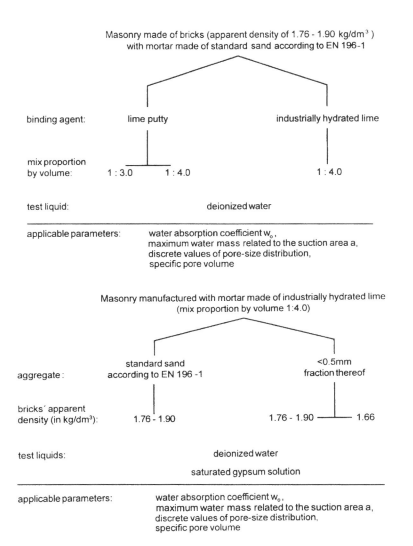

Figure 31.10   Schematic presentation of experiments with masonry sections.

In another enlarged view of such a masonry section, the moisture distribution can be seen in Figure 31.12. Here, soaking has reached the upper brick layer. However, the carbonation of the mortar joints was not as uniform as had been expected. Therefore, the tests were started after a one-year cure, corresponding to a periodic moistening with the objective of an utmost uniform carbonation.

Figure 31.13 shows a test setup for determining capillary liquid absorption and evaporative behavior of masonry sections.

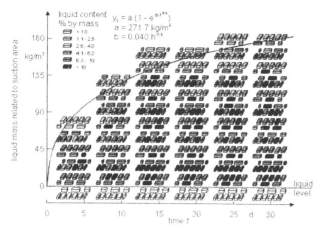

Figure 31.11   Enlarged view showing moisture distribution within 10 courses of a brickwork section participating in capillary water rise.

Within dry brickwork, which is a system of two components with respect to material – and accordingly to matric suction, but also to morphology of evaporation surface – a permanent water change takes place between both components during the water supply from below. Of course, this depends upon whether brick or mortar is better able to conduct moisture, i.e., to transport it quickly or with a higher flow through the cross-sectional area. Moreover, this event is decisively dependent on each volume portion – here about 20% for mortar.

First, mix proportion and its influence on the capillary behavior of brickwork is of interest. Mixes with standard sand as aggregate and lime putty as binder were produced in the proportion 1:4.0 and 1:3.0 by volume. The water demand of fresh mortar was at 21.8% and 20.6%, being comparable with each other. In the curves of water absorption for corresponding masonry sections, the participation of mortar in the overall event is clearly evident (Figure 31.14). Richer mixes result in an elevated moisture rise. The w_0 also slightly increases from 4.1 to 5.4 $kg/(m^2 \cdot h^{0.5})$, caused by the higher content of fine pores as well as a larger pore volume, already found in comparable mortar prisms. If one uses industrially slaked lime hydrate instead of lime putty, with the same mix proportion of 1:4.0 and comparable water demand, then

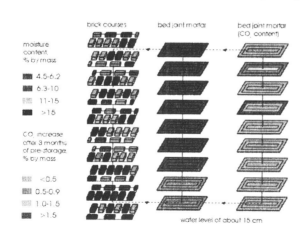

Figure 31.12   Enlarged view of a two-year-old masonry section stored in a constant climate without curing: moisture and carbonate distribution.

Figure 31.13 Masonry section for tests on capillary behavior and moisture release, placed upon a scale in a tank for the water supply.

masonry using this mortar shows an appreciably higher moisture rise with a similar w_0. Compared with lime putty, mortar with this binder shows a higher pore volume and an increased fraction of fine pores, whereby this behavior is explained. Every change of mortar composition, therefore, also exerts a distinct influence on a wall's entire behavior. When increasing the apparent density of brick from about 1.66 to 1.76 and up to 1.90 kg/dm^3, while holding the same mix proportion and using standard sand fraction ≤ 0.5 mm, this leads to a decrease of the capillary head and thus of its practically equivalent maximal value for water absorption related to the surface of a material column a from ca. 200 to ca. 183 kg/m^2. Also, w_0 shows only insignificantly lower values (ca. 10 as against 9 kg/(m$^2 \cdot$ h$^{0.5}$)). Nevertheless, in such a way, one can quantify the bricks contribution to water rise.

Since granulometry of aggregate sands exerts an appreciable effect on a mortar's

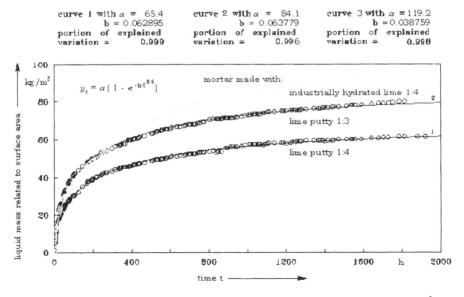

Figure 31.14 Capillary liquid rise in masonry (brick apparent density 1.76–1.90 kg/dm^3, standard sand as a mortar aggregate): influence of mix proportion and binder type.

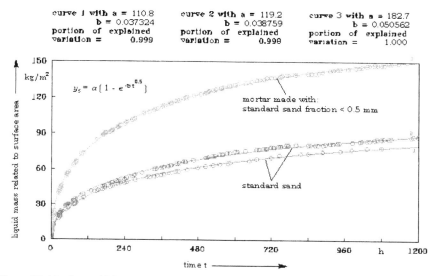

Figure 31.15 Intensifying capillary liquid rise in masonry by using sand 0.5 mm diameter as a mortar's aggregate (apparent brick density 1.76–1.90 kg/dm³, industrially hydrated lime, mix proportion 1:4.0).

structure, a corresponding behavior on masonry sections was also found. Using the fraction ≤ 0.5 mm as an aggregate, moisture rises considerably higher and likewise finds its expression in the a value (i.e., 183 as opposed to 111 or 119 kg/m², while employing standard sand). In the same direction, w_0 increases from ca. 4 to 9 kg/(m² · h⁰·⁵) (see Figure 31.15). On brick it can be shown that a increases, e.g., in the presence of calcium sulfate or sodium sulfate solutions – a phenomenon explainable by their surface tension. Such events are comparable in brickwork when using low-density brick and fine sand ≤ 0.5 mm as a mortar's aggregate, where a increases from ca. 200 to 278 kg/m² when a saturated gypsum solution serves for a test (Figure 31.16).

The w_0 thereby only increases insignificantly from 9.8 to 10.3 kg/(m² · h⁰·⁵). Nevertheless, conditions reverse when using bricks with an apparent density between 1.76 and 1.90 kg/dm³ (Figure 31.16). In other words, water rises higher (a = 182.7 kg/m²) than a gypsum solution does (a = 174.2 kg/m²). Simultaneously w_0 drops from 9.2 to 7.7 kg/(m² · h⁰·⁵). In the first case, capillary action of brick apparently dominates, whereas in the second instance the mortar's capillarity becomes more significant. Mortar with standard sand and dense brick behaves similarly. Water absorption diminishes in comparison to the test result with water from 119 to 72 kg/m² and w_0 has a lowered value, i.e., 3.9 as against 4.7 kg/(m² · h⁰·⁵), which indicates that a change in the mortar's structure might have occurred. According to mercury porosimetry tests, a gypsum solution obviously induces a distinct reduction of specific pore volume from 0.117 to 0.108 cm³/g at a nearly uniform pore-size distribution. Similar events presumably also happen in mortars made with fine sand. However, in

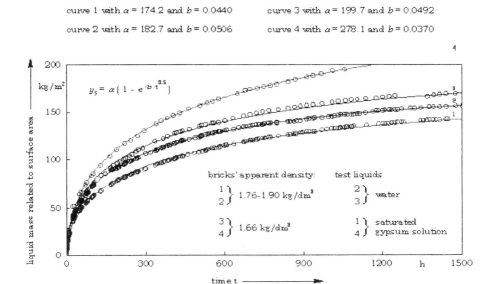

curve 1 with α = 174.2 and b = 0.0440   curve 3 with α = 199.7 and b = 0.0492

curve 2 with α = 182.7 and b = 0.0506   curve 4 with α = 278.1 and b = 0.0370

Figure 31.16   Elevated capillary liquid absorption of masonry by using a saturated solution of calcium sulfate instead of water (sand $\leq$ 0.5 mm diameter as a mortar aggregate, industrially hydrated lime, mix proportion 1:4.0).

the case of "favorable" brick (low apparent density, high pore volume, large portion of pores showing capillary activity), this effect does not appears to be that distinct. When repeating the soaking process with gypsum several times, one can increase the reduction of a and w_0, which will probably results in further structural changes.

The effect of air circulation on capillary absorption at comparable climatic conditions is shown in Figure 31.17. In ambient air practically without any circulation, a liquid mass related to surface area of 182.5 kg/m^2 was absorbed (curve 2), whereas a masonry section exposed to this circulation shows no more than 86 kg/m^2. In the interest of reproducibility and comparability, one needs therefore to ascertain a high constancy of all factors which influence climate.

INVESTIGATION OF EVAPORATIVE BEHAVIOR IN MASONRY SECTIONS

Besides moisture absorption, liquid release during an evaporation process represents an essential specific behavior. After having reached an equilibrium state at the end of the absorption test, water was drained from the tanks where sections were placed, and the course of evaporation related to visually recognizable surfaces was gravimetrically monitored. Of this, about 20% is assignable to the mortar's face. The masonry section dries, whereby capillary transport initially plays a role, followed later by diffusion

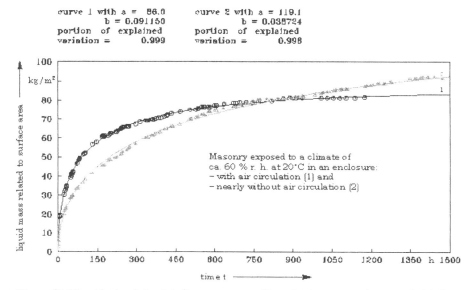

Figure 31.17 Air circulation's influence upon capillary rise in masonry (apparent brick density 1.76–1.90 kg/dm^3, sand 0.5 mm diameter as a mortar's aggregate, industrially hydrated lime, mix proportion 1:4.0).

connected with an immobilization of solute salts. The appropriate model used to describe the material-specific section of this process is:

$$y_e = a \cdot e^{-b(t-t_0)}.\qquad(31.3)$$

When comparing mortar from both of the masonry section, of which lime putty was used as a binder (Figure 31.18), one finds a nearly parallel course of curves, whereby that with the richer mix (curve 3) is found above the mix containing more aggregate (curve 2). This is also true when looking at the remaining moisture content related to total capillary absorption. Industrially hydrated lime in a comparable mix proportion behaves slightly differently (curve 1). At any time in this brickwork, a greater liquid content remains than in its equivalent made with lime putty.

Concerning the influence of apparent brick density, one obtains curves with distinct starting points because of different evaporation surfaces being smaller in the case of denser brick, which makes a comparison difficult (Figure 31.19). When considering the course of an evaporative curve, one can clearly realize parallelism of their linear sections, each in such way characterizing a constant evaporation velocity.

Starting from inflection points of both curves, which for low-density brick run at 44% of total capillary absorption and for high-density brick at 42%, courses according to the evaporation formula result (Hoffmann et al. 1996). Observing arbitrarily moisture content after 2000 h, the masonry section with low-density brick contains 8.4% while the high-density equivalent has only 2.4%. This means that the masonry section

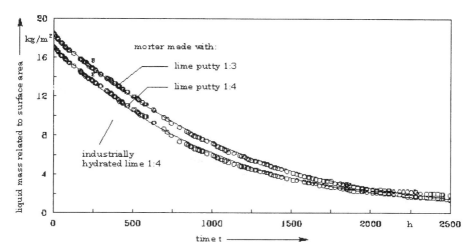

Figure 31.18   Evaporation behavior of masonry sections as shown in Figure 31.13 (apparent brick density 1.76–1.90 kg/dm³, standard sand as a mortar's aggregate): influence of mix proportion and binder type.

with low-density brick shows, at all times, an elevated water content or, in other words: a material that has the highest absorption, and thus contains the most water, achieves a final state, or its equilibrium moisture content, after a longer period of time. This is a truly remarkable result.

Curves with dissimilar starting points are reached when tests are performed using gypsum solution instead of water (Figure 31.20), because of differing rise or

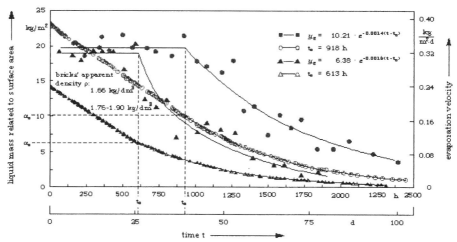

Figure 31.19   Modifying evaporation behavior of masonry by using bricks with different density: determination of corresponding inflection-point moisture, a_0, and evaporation parameter, b.

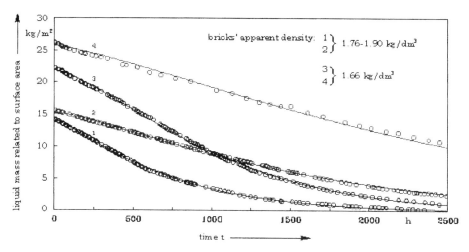

Figure 31.20   Modifying evaporation behavior of same masonry sections, as shown in Figure 31.15, by using bricks with different apparent density and additionally a saturated solution of calcium sulfate (curves 2 and 4) instead of water (sand ≤5 mm diameter as a mortar's aggregate, industrially hydrated lime, mix proportion 1:4.0).

evaporation surface, respectively. Although during a capillarity test performed on masonry made with sand ≤ 0.5 mm diameter, performed while using a calcium sulfate solution, the same w_0 was found despite a higher capillary head. This corresponds to an unchanged pore structure; evaporation behavior was influenced so much that a clear reduction of evaporation velocity resulted. Sections having bricks of different density here also show the same velocity down to the end of this linear portion. In both cases, however, remaining moisture content is always higher than when water is used as a test liquid. After 2000 h, low-density brickwork shows a considerably higher moisture percentage (about 67%) than is the case for dense brick (only 27%). This means that the influence of the kind of solution on this process is effectively increased by low-density bricks and so possibly caused by clogging of fine pores with reprecipitated gypsum crystals. Similar findings are also described by Franke and Grabau (Franke and Grabau 1990).

A shift of grain-size spectrum to smaller diameters leads to a higher water rise and to a larger evaporation surface to an increased liquid mass related to it. The slope of both types of evaporation curves is different (Figure 31.21).

From 0 to ca. 600 hours on a brickwork section made from fine sand as a mortar aggregate (curve 3), a decrease of 14 to ca. 6 kg/m^2 and from 100% to 43% relative to total capillary absorption can be observed. Over the same time period, in the latter mortar, it still shows 66% as opposed to ca. 52% after 500 hours and 37% as opposed to 23% of its original moisture content after 1000 hours, whereby the dry state is reached correspondingly later. Similar results can be found when using curve 2 for interpretation. Expressed another way, this means that a brickwork with fine sand mortar, but

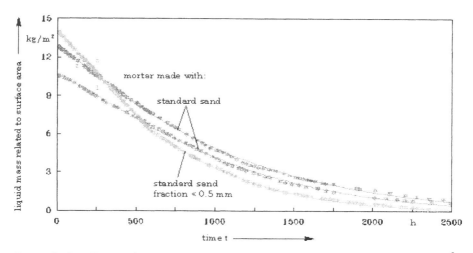

Figure 31.21 Evaporation behavior of masonry (apparent brick density 1.76–1.90 kg/dm³, industrially hydrated lime, mix proportion 1:4.0): influence of grain-size distribution of sands used as a mortar aggregate.

otherwise the same brick material, releases its moisture more rapidly – despite the higher water absorption – than brickwork with a mortar containing standardized sand. Hence, one can conclude that a large pore volume and a high number of pores contributing to capillary activitiy influences evaporation positively, i.e., accelerates it. Since no important changes occurred in the capillary behavior of brickwork with standard sand as an aggregate, it would not be surprising if this is also not the case during evaporation. Only after the third repetition of a soaking process by a gypsum solution was a deceleration of moisture release found, compared to the test using water. In the case of fine-sand mortar, a remarkable influence is caused even after the first soaking process, as indicated in Figure 31.20. Pore geometry and surface tension seem to participate in this. During tests, the question arose regarding climatic influence on an evaporative course. Therefore, behavior was determined on one and the same masonry section at the same temperature and relative humidity, but with different air circulation. In agreement, e.g., with Kamei, who reported about a Kibushi alumina (cf. Krischer and Kast 1978, p. 314), air movement produces a considerably elevated evaporation velocity (Figure 31.22).

Having a comparable starting moisture in both cases – capillary absorption taking place under air circulation – differing amounts have been presented for a_0 and b values as well. During moisture rise and evaporation under the same climatic conditions, i.e., when equally taking into account water fillings with and without air circulation (cf. Figure 31.17) and in this way also evaporation surfaces, it is surprising to note that the evaporation parameter, b, shows each time almost identical values (0.0016 or 0.0015), thus confirming its material-specific character; a_0, in turn, adopts different amounts. At this time, however, further interpretations are not yet possible.

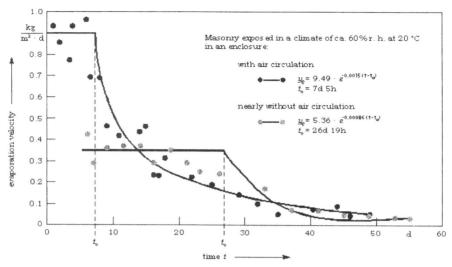

Figure 31.22 Modifying evaporation velocity of masonry by air circulation (apparent brick density 1.76–1.90 kg/dm^3, standard sand, industrially hydrated lime, mix proportion 1:4.0).

REFERENCES

ASTM C 91-87a. 1987. Standard specification for masonry cement. Edition March, 198, 5 pp.

Croney, D., J.D. Coleman, and P.M. Bridge. 1952. The suction of moisture held in soil and other porous materials. *Road Res. Techn.* No. 24 (Dept. Sci. Ind. Res., Road Res. Lab.). London: H.M.S.O., 42 pp.

DIN EN 196-1. 1990. Prüfverfahren für Zement; Bestimmung der Festigkeit. Edition March 1990, 16 pp.

DIN EN 459-2. 1995. Baukalk; Teil 2: Prüfverfahren. Edition March, 1995, 19 pp.

Franke, L., and J. Grabau. 1990. The influence of salt content on the drying behavior of bricks. In: Proc. 7th Expert Meeting Nato-CCMS Pilot Study Conservation of Historic Brick Structures, Venezia, Italy 22/11–24/11/1993, ed. S. Fitz, pp. 132–141. Berlin: Umweltbundesamt. (Also: Bauphysikalische Folgen von Gipshautbildungen an Mauerwerksoberflächen. 1995. *Bautenschutz + Bausanierung* **18(7)**:83–84; **18(8)**:27–30.)

Hoffmann, D., M. Niedack-Nad, and K. Niesel. 1996. Evaporation as a feature of characterizing stone. In: Proc. 8th Intl. Congr. on Deterioration and Conservation of Stone, Berlin, 30/09–04/10/1996, ed. J. Riederer, vol. 1, pp. 453–460.

Hoffmann, D., and K. Niesel. 1988. Quantifying capillary rise in columns of porous material. *Amer. Ceram. Soc. Bull.* **67(8)**:1418.

Hoffmann, D., and K. Niesel. 1996. Relationship between mechanical characteristics and the pore structure of building materials. *Silicates Industriels* **61(11/12)**:253–261.

Hoffmann, D., and K. Niesel. 1998. Quantifying the effect of air pollutants on rendering and also moisture-transport phenomena in masonry including its constituents. http://www.bam.de/a_vii/moisture/transport.html.

Hoffmann, D., K. Niesel, and R. Plagge. 1995. Water retention characteristics and conductivity of porous media. *Am. Ceram. Soc. Bull.* **74(11)**:48–50.

Honeyborne, D.B., and P.B. Harris. 1958. The structure of porous building stone and its relation to weathering behavior. The structure and properties of porous materials. In: Proc. 10th Symp. Colston Research Society, pp. 343–365. London: Butterworths.

Krischer, O., and W. Kast. 1978. Die wissenschaftlichen Grundlagen der Trocknungstechnik, 3rd edition; Berlin, Heidelberg, New York: Springer-Verlag, 489 pp.

Krus, M., and K. Kiessl. 1991. Vergleichende Untersuchungen zur Bestimmung der Porenradienverteilung von Natursandsteinen mittels Saugspannungsmessung und Quecksilber-Druckporosimetrie. IBP (Fraunhofer-Inst. f. Bauphysik) Bericht FtB-11/1991, 14 pp., 6 pp. Appendix.

Niesel, K. 1993. Porositätsdaten zur Kennzeichnung des Feuchtigkeitstransports in Ziegelmauerwerk. In: Werkstoffwissenschaften und Bausanierung, Tagungsber. 3. Intl.. Kolloquium zum Thema Werkstoffwissenschaften und Bausanierung, Techn. Akad. Esslingen, Ostfildern, 15/12/1992, ed. F. H. Wittmann, part 1, pp. 67–80. Ehningen bei Böblingen: Expert-Verlag.

Niesel, K. 1994. Zum Problem des Nachstellens von Kalkmörteln. *Bautenschutz + Bausanierung* **17(2)**:65–68.

Niesel, K. 1994a. Détermination de l'ascension capillaire de liquide dans des matériaux poreux de construction. In: Actes de la journée ICOMOS/Direction du Patrimoine "Les remontées d'eau du sol dans les maçonneries," Paris: Musée des Monuments Français 25/01/1994, Paris, 21 pp.

Niesel, K. 1994b. Feuchtigkeitsaufstieg in porösen Baustoffen. *Materialprüfung* **36(10)**: 432–437.

Niesel, K., and D. Hoffmann. 1992. Pore characteristics and moisture in brick masonry. In: Proc. 7th Intl. Congress on Deterioration and Conservation of Stone, vol. 2, ed. J. Delgado Rodrigues et al., pp. 735–743. Lisboa: Laboratório Nacional de Engenharia Civil.

Niesel, K., and H. Rooss. 1983. Aspekte der Untersuchung von Porenraumveränderungen in feuchtem Mauerwerk-Aspects of the testing of pore volume changes in damp masonry. *Ziegelindustrie Intl.* **36(7)**:339–349.

Tombers, J. 1991. Untersuchungen zur Salzverteilung in verbautem Naturstein. Diss. Univ. Saarland., Saarbrücken, 188 pp.

Weber, H., K. Iversen, H. Klock, H. Schoer, and H. Winkler. 1984. In: Mauerfeuchtigkeit, Ursache und Gegenmaßnahmen. Grafenau/Württemburg: Expert-Verlag, 143 pp.

32

Measuring Moisture Content in the Gothic Brick Masonry of the Lübecker Ratsbierkeller
Comparison of Neutron, Radar, Microwave, and Gravimetric Methods

H. VISSER and A. GERVAIS

Norddeutsches Zentrum für Materialkunde von Kulturgut (ZMK) am Niedersächsichen Landesamt für Denkmalpflege, Scharnhorststr.1, 30175 Hannover, Germany

ABSTRACT

Moisture was measured in brick masonry of the "Lübecker Ratsbierkeller" using neutron probe, radar transmission, microwave, and gravimetric methods, the latter applied to drilling powder, used as a supplementary method.

The neutron probe method was used for depth profiles along drilling holes. It yielded reliable results with depth in the masonry in areas where no additional hydrogen was found. Additional hydrogen, for example in gypsum mortar, led to values that were too high. These deviations can be detected by comparison with the gravimetric method and can be calculated by chemical analysis of the material (solid core or drilling powder). Radar has been shown to be reliable in salt-free masonry but not in material with high amounts of ions in solution. The microwave method was reliable in both salt-free and salt-rich masonry if frequencies > 10 GHz are used.

Used on its own, the gravimetric method might not be very reliable when it is applied to drilling powder. As a supplementary method, however, it is useful for checking the neutron probe method and for identifying deviations. These can be calculated by chemical analysis of the drilling powder, and the values obtained with the neutron method can be corrected.

INTRODUCTION

Situated in northern Germany, the medieval town of Lübeck has a Gothic town hall that was built in the 13th century, with annexes from the 14th and 15th centuries. Famous for its Gothic rib vaults (Figure 32.1) is the part called the "Ratsbierkeller," which is situated below the annexes and was built in two parts during the years 1298–1308 and

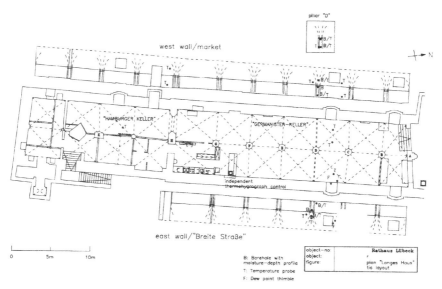

Figure 32.1   Cellar floor plan and schematic layout of the "Langes Haus" (Long House). B: borehole with moisture-depth profile; T: temperature probe; F: dew point thimble.

1442–1444. The older part (situated underneath the "Long House") is also called "Germanist's Cellar," the younger part is named "Hamburg Cellar" after historical meetings of a former society.

BUILDING MATERIAL, MOISTURE, AND SALT PROBLEMS

The building material is medieval brick, which was made from local Pleistocene clays. The few wall bricks that have been spot-checked were found to be well-burnt (at temperatures of 920°–1000°C) with a relatively high total porosity of 31%–35% (see Franke 1993; Freyburg and Starke 1993). The walls and vaults are covered with plaster, the Gothic ribs remaining uncovered.

The cellars below the town hall annexes, the so-called "Ratsbierkeller," have acute moisture and salt problems. Moisture problems have existed from the beginning (1308) since the walls were never insulated from the adjacent wet soil. This was the reason for later corrective measures, such as elevation of the floor level (decided on in 1875). It is important to note, however, that these measures were undertaken not because the moisture affected the stability of the brick masonry construction but because of the troublesome effect moisture had on the usage of the cellars.

The moisture is enriched in nitrate and chloride ions; at least part of them originate from the surrounding groundwater, which has been polluted by human activity close to the surface since medieval times. These ions, remaining in solution, did not cause damage until 1900.

A change took place in 1900, when a cellar restaurant was opened which needed a heated, comfortable atmosphere. Attempts were made to eradicate the troublesome dampness by internally insulating the vaults. For this reason the vaults were covered with a historic insulating plaster, the first layer of which consisted of cement plaster armed with a second layer of overlapping pieces of glass sheets. However, the picturesque ribs remained uncovered. As the air in the restaurant is undersaturated with water, especially during the long heating period, evaporation of moisture takes place at the surface of the uncovered brick material of the ribs. Ions transported in the moisture were left behind, so that a huge enrichment of salt took place in the ribs and in adjacent brick masonry areas. This process still continues today. The salt crystallizes in the pores of the ceramic material, cracking them by crystallization pressure. Parts of the ribs have already been destroyed by this process and adjacent areas are at risk. The annex parts of the restaurant were closed for public use in 1995. Since then, the rate of destruction has slowed down, after cutting off the heating, leaving behind damaged the gothic rib vaults (Figure 32.2).

MOISTURE MEASUREMENTS IN THE WALLS

To analyze this damage process quantitatively and to find ways of halting it, salt and moisture contents in the walls were measured. Moisture was measured for distribution in depth in the masonry, along drilling profiles (neutron probe method and gravimetric method using the drilling powder), and by nondestructive transmission methods (radar and microwave). The methods were chosen to minimize the loss of original material or to test nondestructive methods.

COMPARISON OF METHODS

The methods used for measuring moisture are shown in Table 32.1. Below we summarize our experience using these methods in Gothic brick masonry (see also Table 32.2). In the first run, the standard gravimetric method was not used for the Gothic material, as it was thought that less-destructive methods would provide similar results (see CONCLUSIONS). To obtain depth profiles by this method, drilling cores of at least 5 cm diameter are necessary. Smaller diameters are said to cause deviations due to loss of moisture (Wendler et al., pers. comm.).

Neutron Probe Method

A neutron source was introduced into the drilling hole (12 mm diameter) so that neutrons interact with the surrounding material. The neutrons spread into the tested material, where they are scattered and decelerated. As the deceleration effect of hydrogen atoms on neutrons is much higher than the effect of any other atoms in the wall material, the percentage of backscattered and decelerated neutrons is a direct measure of the hydrogen concentration in the masonry. The special measuring technique applied here

Figure 32.2 (a) Overview in the dining room of the Ratsbierkeller; (b) rib vaulting detail marked with little black points with a diameter of 1 cm (right part of the photo) for photogrammetry of the Ratsbierkeller; (c) detail of rib vaulting with salt incrustation; little black points on the left and right hand are the "little helpers" for photogrammetry.

Table 32.1   Applied moisture measuring methods: advantages and disadvantages.

Methods	Advantages	Disadvantages
Standard Gravimetric Method	• Greatest accuracy	• Greatest loss of original substance. • Measurements cannot be repeated at the same point.
Gravimetric Method with Drilling Powder	• Reduced loss of original subsance	• Less accurate than standard gravimetric method. • Measurements cannot be repeated at the same point.

Neutron Probe	• Less loss of original substance
	• Further measurements can be repeated as required at the same point.
		• Low radioactivity
		• Variation of the analysis volume:
		  − masonry drier = analysis volume greater,
		  − masonry wetter = analysis volume smaller.
		• Additional hydrogen in gypsum, cement, etc., can cause deviations

Georadar	• Nondestructive (apart from calibration samples)	• Deviation in salt-rich masonry. • Metallic components can cause extreme deviations.
Microwave with 10 GHz	• Nondestructive (apart from calibration samples)	• Less depth of penetration. • Metallic components can cause extreme deviations.

was developed by Ganß and Rönicke (1993). Measurement took place when the restaurant was still operating and open to public access.

Measuring integrates over a large volume of different materials, for example brick and mortar together. In the middle of normal masonry, about 66% of the registered backscattered neutrons are derived from a volume which corresponds approximately to a supposed bowl with a diameter of 10 cm. Higher moisture causes a smaller analyzed volume; less moisture a larger volume. With the neutron probe, moisture content is measured in this volume unit in the first step. To compare these data with those obtained by the gravimetric method, they have to be recalculated to weight. In the "Ratsbierkeller," an average brick density of 1.7 was used as a recalculation factor.

The drilling powder obtained was used to determine moisture contents by the gravimetric method (see below) and also for chemical analysis. Measuring moisture by neutron probe can be repeated at any time in the existing drill holes. The holes are protected with a gum tapon to prevent desiccation.

Possible Deviations

The neutron probe method measures concentration of H atoms, which is dependent on water content. Many building materials have additional H contents: organic bound, hydroxides, crystal-bound water. For example, the gypsum frequently found contains

Table 32.2   Comparison of the applied methods.

Methods	Analyzed Volume	Depth of Penetration	Causes of Deviation	Effect of Deviation	Minimizing Deviation
Standard Gravimetric Method	Cylinder 5 × 5 cm	According to the borehole depth	–	–	–
Gravimetric Method with Drilling Powder	Boreholes with a diameter ≥1.2 cm	According to the borehole depth	• Mixing of drilling powder of different depth in the borehole • Losses of moisture due to dessication during the drilling process	• Inexact values • Values too low	–
Neutron Probe	Supposed corresponding bowls with actived neutron activity, with a diameter of ca. 10 cm (boreholes with a diameter of 1.2 cm)	According to the borehole depth and the corresponding bowl diameter	• The additional hydrogen in bitumen, gypsum, cement, etc., is measured and leads to calculated moisture values that are too high.	• Values too high	• Measurements are corrected by determination of hydrogen in gypsum, cement, bitumen, etc. • Comparison with the moisture measurements obtained by the gravimetric method with drilling powder.
Georadar	Depth of penetration (cm) × 20 cm × 30 cm	• Some dm in wet masonry • Up to more than 1 m in dry masonry	• Measurements are influenced by ions in solution. • Dependent on material. • Metallic components can cause extreme deviations.	• Ions in solution cause higher values (caution with measurements in masonry with acute salt problems).	• Calibration with the original material improves the accuracy.

20.9 wt.% water. This additional hydrogen is measured by the neutron probe and leads to calculated moisture values which are too high. Therefore, in general, neutron probe moisture values may be either correct or could be too high.

Common building materials containing additional hydrogen are:

- gypsum mortar,
- salts with water of crystallization,
- cement (with up to 30% water),
- organics, such as bitumen (used as an insulating material in the "Ratsbierkeller") organic paint, bacteria, algae, etc.,
- water of crystallization in argillaceous materials (of importance in adobe or in low burnt bricks).

Application of the Neutron Probe Method

Moisture was measured with the neutron probe in a cross-section of the Ratsbierkeller (Figure 32.3). The results are shown in Figures 32.4 and 32.5, where they are compared with results of the gravimetric method. As neutron probe values are either too high or correct and gravimetric data are either too low or correct, the true moisture values are found either on one of the measuring curves or in the space between the two curves. In cases where the two curves plot together (Figure 32.5, upper part, 40–80 cm drilling depth), true values are ensured on the curve lines.

In the lower part of Figure 32.5, one can see that gravimetric data might be more eccentric. This is due to large changes between mortar and brick moisture values, whereas neutron data are a more smooth interpolation of brick and mortar together.

In general, neutron and gravimetric data plot together better in the inner part of the masonry than close to the surface.

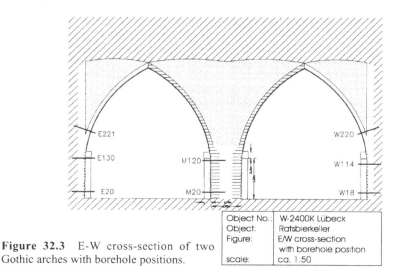

Object No.:	W-2400K Lübeck
Object:	Ratsbierkeller
Figure:	E/W cross-section with borehole position
scale:	ca. 1:50

Figure 32.3   E-W cross-section of two Gothic arches with borehole positions.

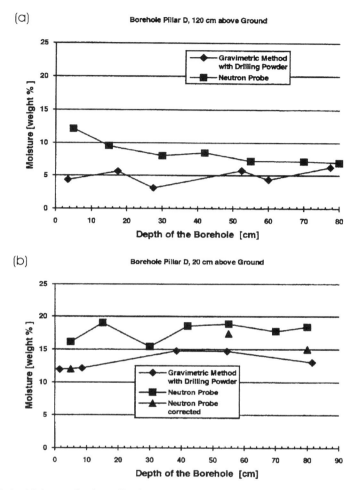

Figure 32.4 Moisture-depth profiles in central pillar D: (a) 120 cm; (b) 20 cm above ground.

Figure 32.4 shows moisture values of the lower part of a pillar with gypsum mortar. The gypsum content of the drilling powder was analyzed and the calculated deviation caused by gypsum crystal-bound water amounts to between 1–4 wt.%, average 3 wt.%. The corrected neutron moisture values are marked with triangles, which in part lie directly on the gravimetric moisture curve and in part between the two curves.

Radar and Microwave Methods

Electromagnetic waves of radar and microwave frequencies can be used as a nonde-structive method to determine the moisture content of building materials. When these

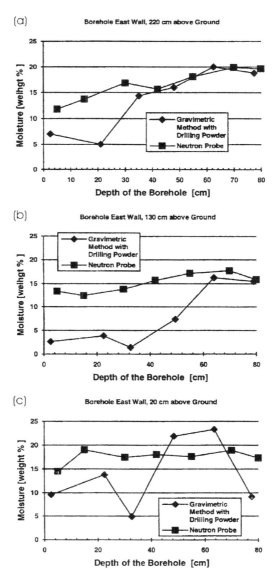

Figure 32.5 Moisture-depth profiles in the east wall located on the Breitestraße: (a) 220 cm; (b) 130 cm; (c) 20 cm above ground.

waves transmit the material, the water dipoles swing in the alternating field and have a decelerating effect. Thus the velocity of the waves (or the dielectricity constant calculated from the velocity) can support the calculation of moisture content, based on calibration series with building materials in laboratory tests. Ions of soluble salts in water

have an additional decelerating effect, as the ions swing in the same way. This alteration is high at low frequencies but decreases to higher frequencies, as larger ions cannot follow rapid electric field alternations in the same way that the smaller water
dipoles do (R. Blum, pers. comm.).

Possible Deviations

(a) Deviations can be caused by soluble salts, which affect radar and low-
     frequency microwave measurements more than high-frequency measurements
     (see above). Through laboratory tests, Blum and Rahm (1993) showed that de-
     viation effects can be neglected if they are caused by ions and if measured using
     (high frequency) microwaves of 10 GHz.
(b) Mineral composition of building materials: The velocity of the radar waves in
     masonry is determined by the dielectric constants of the minerals in mortar and
     bricks. Calibration in the laboratory is based on an uniform mineral composi-
     tion of masonry. Changing mineral compositions (change from calcite mortar
     to gypsum or cement mortar, changing Fe_2O_3 contents) are possible causes for
     deviation. Metallic components can make measurement impossible.

Application of Radar Transmission Method

Two pillars were checked with the radar transmission method, frequency 500 MHz.
The velocity (v) of the radar waves was used to calculate moisture (u), according to the
formula:

$$u(\text{vol}\%) = \frac{c^2 / v^2 - 3.9}{0.36}.$$

(32.1)

This formula was obtained by calibration with (salt-free) bricks in the laboratory.

Radar moisture values coincide with neutron probe and gravimetric moisture values in a part of the pillar with a low salt content (0.09% NO_3^-, 0.14% Cl^-). This is not
the case in parts with a high salt content (1.2% NO_3^-, 2% Cl^-), where moisture values
measured with radar were twice as high as the others.

Application of the Microwave Transmission Method

The Gothic ribs were checked by microwave transmission with 10 GHz (independent
of soluble salts). With this method, relative moisture values were obtained and relative
lateral changes could be found. Moisture values could not be calculated as no standard
samples were taken.

Penetration depth of 10 GHz microwaves depends very much on moisture content:
in dry stone material it might be 1 to 2 m, in totally wet material it is not more than 2 cm
(Blum, pers. comm.), Consequently, neither penetration of the pillars nor comparison
with the radar method was possible.

Application of the Microwave Reflection Method

The plastered vaults were checked using the microwave reflection method with 10 GHz (independent of soluble salts). Using this method, relative changes in humidity of the plaster could be observed. An observation of the brick material behind the plaster was not possible.

Gravimetric Method Using Drilling Powder as a Supplementary Check

The drilling powder was weighed before and after desiccation, the weight difference giving the moisture content in weight. This method was used here as a supplementary check of the other methods.

Possible deviations are derived from losses of moisture, especially during the drilling process, and/or mixing of drilling powder of different depth (also caused by lateral abrasion).

The first process always results in values that are too low. The second might produce values that are too low, if moisture increases in the drilling direction, or too high, if moisture decreases in the drilling direction. In the "Ratsbierkeller," moisture increased in the drilling direction. Thus, moisture values were either too low or correct (guaranteed lower limit).

CONCLUSIONS

- The neutron probe method shows reliable results by depth in the masonry, in parts where no additional hydrogen is found.
- Combination of the neutron probe method and the gravimetric method (drilling powder) can provide guaranteed results, drilling a core of 12 mm diameter. These results can achieve the same accuracy as the standard gravimetric method with cores of 5 cm diameter.
- Deviations due to additional hydrogen in gypsum, etc., can be calculated by chemical analysis. Neutron probe method data corrected in this way can achieve the same accuracy as the standard gravimetric method.
- If, at the surface of the material, radical changes of material or moisture content occur, the neutron probe method cannot analyze these thin layers correctly. This is due to the large volume (210 cm diameter) analyzed.
- None of the methods applied gave guaranteed calculated moisture values of these thin surface layers.
- Radar, as a nondestructive method, is reliable in salt-free masonry but not in material with high amounts of ions in solution.
- Using the microwave method as a nondestructive method, the ribs and the plaster could be analyzed. Deeper parts of the masonry, however, could not be reached by this method. Without standard calibration, only relative changes of moisture and no calculated moisture values are available.

- It was impossible to compare results that were obtained using the microwave method with the others due to (a) different analyzed volumes and (b) different depths of penetration.
- The expectation that results similar to those obtained with the standard gravimetric method could be obtained by less destructive methods was realized by success in depth in the masonry but *not* in many of the close to surface measurements.

ACKNOWLEDGEMENTS

We are most grateful to Dr. H.-J. Schwarz (Hannover) for discussion and help in correcting this paper and Dr. Ing. habil. R. Blum with Dipl.-Phys. U. Rahm (Leonberg) for discussion and information. We also thank V. Battersby (Hannover) and J. Lupp (Berlin) for correcting the English version. The Federal Minister for Research and Technology (Bundesminister für Forschung und Technologie) sponsored the investigation under the program "Investigation and Development for Conservation of Building Material and Care of Monuments."

REFERENCES

Blum, R., and U. Rahm. 1993. Bericht über Ultraschall- und Mikrowellenmessungen im Ratsbierkeller (Germanistenkeller) zu Lübeck. Leonberg: Laboratorium für Dynamik und Optik.

Franke, L. 1993. Untersuchung eines Ziegelbohrkerns vom Lübecker Ratsbierkeller. Bericht vom 17. Mai, 1993. Hamburg-Harburg: Technische Universität Hamburg-Harburg.

Freyburg, S., and J. Stark. 1993. Ermittlung von stoffkundlichen und technisch-physikalischen Ziegelkenndaten. BMFT-Pilotobjekt Ratsbierkeller Lübeck, Hochschule für Architektur und Bauwesen, Fakultät Bauingenieurwesen, Lehrstuhl Baustoffkunde. Weimar: Universität Weimar.

Ganß, E.-D., and H.-J. Rönicke. 1993. Feuchtetechnische Untersuchungen Rathaus Lübeck (Ratsbierkeller). KAI Projektgruppe Bauphysik, Materialforschungs- und Prüfanstalt an der Hochschule für Architektur und Bauwesen, Bericht Juni 1993 (Kurzfassung der Meßergebnisse). Weimar: Universität Weimar.

Kahle, M. 1992. Feuchteuntersuchung an zwei Pfeilern des Ratsbierkellers in Lübeck. Kurzbericht, Institut für Tragkonstruktionen, Forschungsgruppe Mauerwerk, Bericht vom 13. Nov., 1992. Karlsruhe: Universität Karlsruhe-West.

Kahle, M., and B. Illich. 1994. Bestimmung des Feuchtegehaltes historischen Mauerwerks mit Radar. *Bauphysik* **16(1)**: 6–13

Livingston,R.A. 1992. The nondestructive measurement of chlorides and moisture in historic masonry using the neutron probe. Intl. Conf. on Nondestructive Testing, Microanalytical Methods and Conservation of Works of Art. In: Proc. 3[a] Conf. Int. sulle Prove Non Distruttive Metodi Microanalitici e Indagini Ambientali per lo Studio e la Conservazione delle Opere d'Arte, pp. 377–386. Viterbo: Instituto Centrale del Restauro e Associazione Italiana Prove non Distruttive Monitoraggio Diagnostica.

Richter, U. 1993. Untersuchungsbericht, Ratskeller Lübeck. Abteilung Angewandte Analytik im Institut für Anorganische und Angewandte Chemie, Bericht Feb., 1993. Hamburg: Universität Hamburg.

33

Conservation of St. Pancras Chambers, Designed as the Midland Grand Hotel

M. DAVIES

Margaret & Richard Davies and Associates, Architects and Conservation Consultants,
20a, Hartington Road, London W4 3UA, U.K.

ABSTRACT

St. Pancras Chambers, the former Midland Grand Hotel, designed by Sir George Gilbert Scott, was partly opened in May, 1873. The remainder of the hotel was opened to guests in 1876. The hotel flourished until the turn of the century. Following the amalgamation of the Midland Railway Company with the London Scottish Railway in 1921 to form the London Midland Scottish Railway, the decline of the hotel continued until 1935, when the building was converted to offices for the use of the railway company.

St. Pancras Chambers is an outstanding example of the Gothic revival in English architecture. Although St. Pancras Chambers was protected by the British Historic Building Legislation and listed as Grade I in 1967, it has remained as a "Building at Risk" for almost 25 years. Following the surveys of "Safety and Condition," undertaken in 1991/2, recommendations for repair were accepted by the building owner, the British Railways Board. In 1992, with the support of the Department of Transport, British Railways Board made a commitment to repair the envelope of St. Pancras Chambers. The contract for the "Primary Safeguarding Works" was completed in March, 1995. This paper describes the survey and repair of the historic brickwork.

In 1996, following intensive and detailed negotiation, London & Continental Railways Limited, having been selected as the Development Team for the Channel Tunnel Rail link, assumed responsibility for St. Pancras Chambers. A competition for the reuse of the Chambers was launched in 1996. In September, 1997, two consortia teams were selected to move to the final stage of the competition. The final selection was made at the end of 1997.

INTRODUCTION

St. Pancras Chambers was designed by Sir George Gilbert Scott as a competition entry for the new London terminus hotel for the Midland Railway Company. The Midland

Grand Hotel was opened to visitors in May, 1873: it continued to function as a hotel until 1935, when the building was altered to provide office accommodation.

Following threat of demolition in 1960, St. Pancras Chambers was protected by Grade I listing. Over the last thirty years, however, it has been left empty and semi-derelict: by 1990 there were serious concerns about its condition.

In December, 1990, the Conservation Practice was appointed to undertake a detailed survey of the condition of the building, with particular emphasis on safety matters. Phase I, a period of five weeks, focused on safety, while the five-month long Phase II study included the detailed investigation of every element – from bricks and balustrades, to carpets and chimneys.

The first task was to establish a coherent base for survey information: no original drawings were available; the hotel had not been built to the successful competition design and "as built" drawings did not exist. A new dimensional survey of each floor was undertaken and plotted on AutoCAD (release 10) and elevations were prepared by reference to a collage of referenced photographs. (Figure 33.1)

Access to certain areas of the building was a major problem: the survey team had to work in accordance with a strict safety regime; the roof was accessible to two-person teams wearing body harnesses while the turrets and gables could only be inspected using binoculars. The teams made full use of "cherry pickers" whenever the opportunity arose (Figure 33.2).

One of the first observations was of the general quality of the design with fine attention to detail. Sir George Gilbert Scott introduced subtleties of color, texture, and surface finish in the quoins, window heads, and face work of the building so that chevron patterns and diaper work complement the modeling of carved and molded brickwork.

It was immediately clear that the brickwork had been subject to a range of problems, some of which were localized while others were of a general nature and occurred throughout the building. Typical problems included erosion of the entire brick, loss of

Figure 33.1   South elevation (AutoCAD drawing).

Figure 33.2   Inspection using a "cherry picker."

face, cracking, crazing, efflorescence, sulfate attack, and saturation, in addition to defects associated with the use of inappropriate mortars.

SURVEY

The survey of masonry faults and damage was undertaken by two-person teams working systematically around the building. The elevational drawings were printed at 1:50 to enable the surveyors to identify problems in individual bricks where appropriate. Each fault was numbered and scheduled (Figure 33.3a, b) against the elevation and zone, together with the specification for repair. The total number of masonry faults (brickwork and stone) was in the order of 4,800.

As the work progressed it became possible to identify "problem patterns" in the brickwork which were then divided into seven main categories on the basis of the cause of the problem:

1.   Congenital: problems which were designed/built into the building.
2.   Functional: problems which arose as a result of the use of the building.
3.   Environmental: climate, exposure, pollution.
4.   Biological: problems arising from the presence of organic matter.
5.   Incidental: fire, impact damage.
6.   Wilful: problems caused by insensitive or inappropriate repairs and maintenance regimes, neglect, etc.
7.   Material: the characteristics of the original brickwork.

Figure 33.3a   Brickwork faults – noted on elevation.

Congenital Brickwork Problems

Architectural Concept

The architectural form of the building – articulated, decorated high gothic design – has inevitably contributed to the localized deterioration of the fabric of the building. Exposed ornamental projections are more vulnerable to damage of all kinds; a

THE CONSERVATION PRACTICE — St. Pancras Chambers, Euston Road.				External Masonry; West Wing: West Elevation; Grandstair Bay		Sheet No. ·057 Date: 3/7/92 Dwg No 15/AL/02		
Fault location number	MATERIAL	ELEMENT	FAULT	ACTION	SPEC CLAUSE	QUANTITY	NOTES	COST
W 300	Stonework (LAH)	Window 3 mullia L/s jamb + above transome	Moderate area of erosion	Piece in new	C406 W300.0	225·350 ·50		
W 301	" (LAH)	Window 3 mullio General	Open joints	Repoint	C406 W480.0 or C406 W490.0	allow 4m		
W 302	" (LAH)	" R/h Head	Crack	Grout crack	C406 W460.0	0·3m		
W 303	" (LAH)	mullion low level	Area badly cracked	Piece in new	C406 W700.0	200·100 ×1000		
W 304	" (LAH)	r/h joint	Damaged area	Piece in new	C406 W700.0	125·100· 50		
W 305	" (LAH)	mullion top 2 stones	Cracks	Stitch cracks	C406 W490.0	0·8m		
W 306	(LAH)		Hairline cracks	Point crack	C406 W480.0	0·3m		
W 307	" (LAH)		Damaged area	Piece in new	C406 W700.0	200·25· 90		
W 308	" (LAH)	Window 3 mullion General	Open joint.	Repoint	C406 W480.0 or C406 W490.0	allow 4m		
W 309	(LAH)	" Label	Open joint			0·5m		
W 310	" (LAH)	" Head	Fracture	Stitch fracture	C406 W470.0	0·25m		
W 311	" (LAH)	" Mullion	Crack	Point crack	C406 W465.0	0·7m		

Figure 33.3b   Brickwork faults typical schedule.

convoluted roof form will lead to temperature differentials across zones of brickwork, which in turn will affect the ability of the brickwork to shed water and dry out; the hollows in carved or undercut work may be designed in such a way that they hold water or snow; the resulting frost damage will contribute to surface failure and fabric breakdown.

Types of Bricks

Three types of bricks predominate at St. Pancras Chambers: the core work in Grippers Patent bricks, facing work in Tucker bricks, and soft red rubbers for carved dressings. Edward Gripper, a Nottinghamshire farmer who found good brick clay – Keuper marl – on his land, was one of the first brickmakers in the area to use the continuous burning Hoffmann kiln. Grippers Patent bricks were known for both their strength and their high cost.

The facing work is largely in Tucker bricks, which are hand pressed from Etruria marl. They have smooth fine-grained faces and sharp arises. The face of the brick appears to have a thin veneer of darker color than the body of the brick: this may be attributed to the presence of coal gases in the kiln during firing. If the Tuckers were also fired in a Hoffmann kiln, the faces may have been influenced by coal gases from the green state.

Dressings, architraves, archivaults, and chimney stacks are of soft red rubbers, carved to shape, with fine joints in lime putty.

Construction Problems

It is also important to consider the way in which the building was built: it appears from the building records that the rate of construction of the masonry was so fast that the brickyard could not maintain an adequate supply of bricks. In the early days, Gripper may have tried to speed up the manufacturing process: the inclusion of many under-fired bricks suggests that he was unsuccessful and that other manufacturers were approached to make good the deficit. Similarly, a number of bricks can be found that are similar to the Tucker bricks in scale and surface finish but different in character and quality.

The detailed study of the brickwork also revealed differences in the work undertaken by different bricklaying teams. Daywork joints are hard to detect but the quality of jointing and pointing in the facework is variable, with discrepancies in bond, brick spacing, and size of joint.

Functional Brickwork Problems Resulting from the Use of the Building

Despite the separation of the hotel from the train shed, a significant amount of deterioration can be attributed to sulfur dioxide and sulfates produced by the steam trains. Damage to the brickwork on the north elevation may be due in part to local fumes and gases; however, there is also a significant buildup of soot and clinker which leads to further corrosion of the brick face. Use of diesel trains appears to have caused little damage, the effects being contained within the track zone. Electrification of the railways has contributed to local damage where anchor points for the high voltage cables have been fastened to the north elevation and adjacent walls.

The north wall of St. Pancras Chambers defines the edge of the station concourse. In this zone, damage to brickwork is broadly limited to local areas and included minor alterations such as blocking up of doors or windows and fixing of signs.

Brickwork Problems Associated with Microclimate, Exposure, and Pollution

Microclimate

The street layout allows the prevailing westerly winds to build up momentum along the Euston Road towards the west elevation of St. Pancras Chambers where the projecting entrance wing takes the full force (Figure 33.4). Similarly the height of the twin towers and the gable over the Grand Stair are perhaps the most exposed parts of the building. Wind erosion and subsequent damage to the masonry is most severe in this part of St. Pancras Chambers (Figure 33.5).

Pollution

Arising primarily from vehicular traffic along the Euston Road but also from city center conditions, pollution has contributed to a buildup of sooty deposits and surface damage. The slow evaporation of weak solutions of acid deposition on the leeward

745

Figure 33.4   View along roof top.

Figure 33.5   Erosion of soft brickwork against hard pointing.

side of surface projections and of the building itself has led to further deterioration of the brickwork, both locally and on the east elevation.

Biological Brickwork Problems

Problems are also generated by plant growth on the building. This may be sustained by deteriorating stonework (e.g., saturated Ketton stone [oolitic limestone] which is easily invaded by organic material) and also by other debris lying in gutters, hollows, valleys, balconies, etc.

The colonization of parts of the building by pigeons, nesting at the western end and perching at the eastern end, has led to the accumulation of guano, which decomposes into a toxic chemical cocktail that attacks the brickwork. Algae growth on saturated masonry, particularly adjacent to broken rainwater pipes, damages the fabric in two ways: (a) by preventing the surface from drying out and (b) by creating a weak acid which attacks the fabric.

Incidental Brickwork Problems

Most buildings are subject to incident damage. St. Pancras Chambers is no exception and in recent years was particularly vulnerable as a direct result of its redundant status. The north wing was damaged by a fire that broke out during a holiday weekend in May, 1988. Intense local heat caused damage to the brickwork, both that which was in a

Figure 33.6   Fire damaged brickwork.

stable state and especially that which was already deteriorating as a result of saturation. Sections of brickwork have had to be dismantled, and other areas required repair.
Although capable of fulfilling their original purpose, the brickwork was permanently
discolored (Figure 33.6) An additional cause of deterioration arises from impact damage. St. Pancras Chambers was slightly damaged by bomb and shrapnel in both world
wars, but of greater significance is damage caused to both carriageways by careless vehicle drivers.

Wilful: Avoidable Brickwork Problems

This category includes the range of problems that stem from well-meaning but unin-
formed repair work. The use of cement-rich, hard pointing is, perhaps, the single most
significant cause of the deterioration of historic brickwork in Europe. At St. Pancras
Chambers, the problem has been compounded by the extensive use of plastic repair
mortars, which create a hard casing to original (damaged) brickwork, behind which
deterioration of the soft clay body is accelerated (Figure 33.7a, b).

The repointing of zones of brickwork may lead to a patchy surface appearance, particularly where the material and the nature of the repointing differs from the original.
The selection of replacement bricks is another prime consideration and will affect both
the appearance of the building as a whole and the weathering qualities of adjacent historic material. New material must be selected to be compatible with the original material in terms of:

- appearance – color, texture, size,
- durability – porosity, hardness, density,
- composition.

Figure 33.7a Damaged, over-cleaned **Figure 33.7b** Local damage.
brickwork.

Failure to maintain a building allows comparatively minor matters to develop into major problems. At St. Pancras Chambers, the continued neglect of the rainwater disposal system has led to the saturation of the masonry. This, in turn, has activated salts within the masonry, including those present in the clay body, salts introduced by rising damp, sulfates originating both within the building flues and from trains entering the train shed, as well as the accumulation of calcium carbonate and calcium sulfate from limestone dressings, string courses, and cornices (Figure 33.8).

Figure 33.8 Salt migration indicated by pale brick headers.

Specification of Repair

Having identified the extent and causes of damage to the brickwork, the next stage of work was to agree on the approach to repair, i.e., to determine the best methods of repair, and to retain as much of the original material as practicable by defining the extent of replacement.

It was clearly necessary to clean the masonry as any dirt, particularly soot and clinker encrustation, obscures structural failures, material variation, and architectural detail. Further, it was essential that any new brickwork should match the original in color, texture, character, size, bond and mortar. Repairs designed to match soot-blackened face work (and on St. Pancras Chambers often pointed with black mortar) cannot be corrected subsequently to match the original color when this has been revealed by cleaning.

Trial cleaning operations were undertaken as part of the survey of condition. It was necessary to extend this work to evaluate a variety of cleaning techniques. The opportunity was taken to test the most common, commercially available methods of cleaning and the less well-known approaches of specialist firms. Six firms were invited to demonstrate their approaches to the task: each undertook cleaning work on similar parts of the building, working within "private" carrels, using both the preferred specification and, subject to the approval of the architect, their own proprietary method of work.

As a result of this pre-qualification exercise: (a) four specialist firms were selected as approved potential subcontractors; (b) the specifications for cleaning masonry (limestone, sandstone, granite, brick face work, carved brickwork, and rubbed brickwork) were confirmed; and (c) exemplar panels were clearly identified to show the standard of work that was required. A clause in the specification required the specialist subcontractor to prepare a further sample panel to confirm that available personnel and equipment could achieve the desired result.

The preferred specification for cleaning the brickwork was as follows:

1. Brush down with stiff bristle brush.
2. Carefully remove clinker using sharp chisels.
3. Low pressure air, water and granular abrasive system (permitted granulate: glass powder, particle size 0.1–0.5 mm, stone powder, particle size 0.005–0.3 mm).

Other specified methods of cleaning included fine pencil abrasive, using low pressure dry air microparticle system, for cleaning sandstone.

Brickwork repair included piecing-in individual bricks and rebuilding elements in those areas where the original material was no longer capable of doing the job for which it was intended or where the appearance of the brickwork was so disfigured that it detracted from the whole.

It was necessary not only to achieve a good "unit" match of individual bricks but also to match the color, grain, and plasticity of the mortar for bedding and pointing, in addition to ensuring that the work would be carried out by craftsmen who would work in sympathy with the original brickwork.

Three principal brick types were used in the construction of St. Pancras Chambers:

- *Gripper's* bricks – made from Keuper marl from Nottinghamshire – used in the core work. These bricks tolerated the damp conditions well and, despite releasing certain salts into interior plaster, did not deteriorate to any great extent. They are, therefore, outside the scope of this paper.
- *Tucker* bricks – made from Etruria marl – fine grain, smooth (worked) face being somewhat darker in color than the body clay; sharp arises, dimensionally accurate with subtle variation in color; laid with 2 mm joints in face work on the south elevation; used for face work and for molded specials. Tuckers were handmade, double-pressed bricks.
- *Rubbers* – soft, dark red bricks, extensively used in carved work, patterned face work (with Tuckers), and quoin decoration. Rubbers used in voussoirs are set in fine-jointed lime putty.

Both brick samples and mortar samples were analyzed. Mortar samples obtained from different parts of the building were found to have different characteristics. Specification for the new mortar had to be identified on a zone by zone basis.

It was noted that the sulfates found in the mortar samples, resulting from many years of pollution, had attacked and severely weakened the mortar, which had degraded in many areas to the extent that it could only be regarded as a plaster material. The use of an eminently natural hydraulic lime was recommended for the repair mortar, because of its greater resistance to future salt attack and pollution.

Gray Italian hydraulic lime was specified for general mortar while white French hydraulic lime was used for the gauged work to red rubbers in the voussoirs. Silver sand and coarse gardening sand was specified in various proportions to match local variations in pointing color. The character of the brickwork is varied. It is obvious that there were several teams of bricklayers involved in the construction of St. Pancras chambers and that each had its own "signature" or style, which may be recognized by joint width or rhythm in the brick bond. However, all original work was found to be true with consistent bedding lines and a smooth, even vertical face.

Repair work that had been undertaken over a period of 120 years was easily recognized by uneven bedding joints, poor selection of bricks which do not match the originals, and the use of black pointing (to blend with the soot-blackened face work). Damage to brick voussoirs was found to have been made good with plastic repairs, which in turn had cracked away from the body clay leaving the core to erode away behind the hard "carapace."

Specialist firms were required to pre-qualify for the brick repair work in a similar manner to that described for the masonry cleaning work. Examples of piecing-in, new work, and repointing were carried out in accordance with the specification. Once again, it became clear that it is the intelligent hands and sympathetic approach of the craftsman that is of prime importance in repair and conservation work.

Although a number of brick companies had expressed their interest and ability to remanufacture bricks to match the originals used in the construction of St. Pancras Chambers, many found that it was difficult to achieve the desired results within a commercially viable framework. Nonetheless, the project benefitted from their interest, involvement, and knowledge of brickmaking. One of the critical factors that made it difficult to match the original bricks was, in fact, the march of progress. The original bricks, made in the 1870s, had been made in a labor-intensive industry, which drew upon local supplies of materials and labor and relied upon traditional methods for firing the bricks. The variation in the quality of each of these components influenced the outcome of the brick manufacturing process.

The modern brickmaker has mechanized the production line and sought to eradicate variations in firing the processed material. This, in turn, has led to a standardized, entirely predictable product, which is rarely suited to the repair of historic buildings. Indeed, it is the variation inherent in historic brickwork that gives it character and interest. In undertaking conservation work, the aim is to match the subtle characteristics of the original material and its method of manufacture while accepting that the finished result may not meet modern performance criteria.

PROCUREMENT

It is always a challenge to achieve the correct balance between the conservation requirements of a Grade I listed building, the economic restraints of a limited budget, and commercial viability.

The cleaning and repair works to the masonry were procured through a main contractor who was instructed to select a specialist subcontractor from an approved list. The selected subcontractor was required to take over the Employer's agreement or registration with the brick supplier for the supply of sufficient bricks of the correct specification for the completion of the project.

This extended procurement route (main contractor − subcontractor − supplier) meant that it was difficult for the main contractor to ensure that the subcontractor met his obligations with regard to the supply of bricks within the variations (of color, size, and character) specified or agreed by the architect, within the constraints of time and cost.

The investment of time and effort on research and development prior to tendering the works meant that many problems had already been resolved . However, although the brick manufacturer succeeded in making bricks that closely matched the originals, a number of unforeseen problems arose in the production of the new Tucker bricks. It proved impractical and uneconomical to make standard Tuckers as pressed "specials"; the new bricks thus had to be molded, but on release from the oiled mold, the clay tended to cling or drag so that the shape of the green brick became distorted. Deformation in apparently "true" green bricks occurred during the initial drying cycle. Drying times had to be adjusted to reduce distortion damage. The manufacturer had to select carefully before sending any bricks to site and had to accept a higher wastage rate than expected.

It proved virtually impossible to match the sharp arises of the original bricks: the manufacturer attempted to finish each arise with a steel rule, but this resulted in misshapen bricks.

The specification required that the Tuckers should be supplied in four color variations. Rather than use four different mixes, the manufacturer sought to achieve variation by firing the common mix to four different temperature levels with the result that each color type differs in size. A variation of ±3 mm on each type could aggregate at a size variation of 12 mm. This, therefore, required a sensitivity in building the brickwork.

The specially shaped bricks, which were hand thrown, were subject to a variety of shrinkage and deformation problems as the brick passed through the molding, initial drying, heating, and firing sequence. The squint bricks, used on obtuse angles on the building and therefore required to be reversible, provided three arises and three faces, each of which might be subject to distortion in the manufacturing process. After much trial and error it was found that the introduction of a frog into the brick reduced the incidence of distortion.

Similar problems were encountered with the baluster pier bricks in which the relationship of fair face to unit mass is extreme. Again, the introduction of frogs into the "column" and the "pier" was found to reduce the dimensional variation and distortion.

The remanufacture of the decorative bricks to the chimney-tops, using handthrown molding techniques rather than on-site carving, also led to problems of shrinkage and distortion. The solution was to identify a "prime line" which took priority over all the others.

PROGRESS ON SITE

Cleaning was undertaken using the JOS system and Hodge Clemco Easy Blast system, using 3 mm and 6 mm nozzles at a pressure of 40 p.s.i. with olivine 90 grade abrasive.

It proved difficult for many of the subcontractor's personnel to match the quality and rhythm of the original brickwork. Where the bed joint has been matched, it was frequently impossible to achieve vertical joints of even width. Similarly, building face work to match the evenness of the original was difficult, particularly where limited piecing-in was specified (Figure 33.9). In some cases it was necessary for work to be taken down and done again.

Where entire elements have been rebuilt, it has clearly been easier for the bricklayer to achieve satisfactory results.

The apparently simple task of identifying bricks to be cut out for new bricks to be pieced-in was also more demanding and more critical than was anticipated. Marking bricks with chalk (Figure 33.10) proved unsatisfactory, and a policy of a drilling a marker hole in each defective brick was adopted.

Figure 33.9   Unacceptable repair (color, pointing) in low quality brickwork.

Repair work incorporating squint bricks had to be carefully pre-planned and equally carefully set out to ensure that distortion on the short face of the brick did not spoil the work.

CONCLUSION

Given the commercial pressure for competitive tendering at all levels, it is difficult to ensure that the experience gained on projects such as the primary safeguarding works is not lost. The team (manufacturer, subcontractor, contractor) is unlikely to come together again for a similar project unless the contracting world becomes even more specialized. This underlines the need for wide dissemination of project-related data on an international basis.

Figure 33.10   Bricks marked for removal using chalk marks.

34

Brick Masonry of the Crypt of San Marco Basilica

Evaluation of On-site Desalination Experiments and Laboratory Consolidation Treatments

V. FASSINA[1], R. ARBIZZANI[2], A. NACCARI[3], and M. FAVARO[3]

[1]Laboratorio Scientifico, Soprintendenza ai Beni Artistici e Storici di Venezia, Cannaregio 3553, Venice, Italy
[2]CNR-ICTMA, Padova, Italy
[3] Istituto Veneto per i Beni Culturali, Venezia, Italy

ABSTRACT

Water infiltration in the Crypt of the San Marco's Basilica is the main cause of brick decay due to salt crystallization. In the attempt to prevent water penetration, some measurements on moisture and salt content were performed. Subsequently, experimental removal of salts was carried out by controlling desalination during in-field trials. Water absorption by capillarity was tested in the laboratory on bricks of different porosity using different consolidant and protective agents. Rhone Poulenc proposed a system to stop water infiltration in the masonry of the Crypt by injecting as much silicate as possible inside the wall. Further experiments were also carried out to consolidate the decayed wall masonry by using a mixture of Rhodorsil RC90 and Rhodorsil 11309, which was subjected to extensive laboratory testing.

INTRODUCTION

Some years ago, those charged with the conservation of the St. Marco Basilica decided to use the crypt for celebration (Figure 34.1). As the crypt is below the average sea level, the crypt walls were completely saturated with saline water.

As the first step of the restoration work intended to stop water infiltration, it was necessary to make a preliminary survey on the moisture and salt content of the brick-wall and on environmental conditions (Fassina and Stevan 1991). Sharp changes in relative humidity and temperature can generate new processes of decay as, for example, the decrease in relative humidity in the crypt could cause crystallization of salts, mostly on the brick surface.

Figure 34.1   Crypt of S. Marco Basilica.

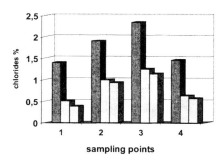

Figure 34.2   Chloride concentration in area P.

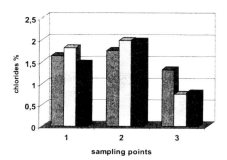

Figure 34.3   Chloride concentration in area S.

Also, the bricks of the vault were saturated with saline water due to the famous flooding of November 4, 1966, in which water reached a maximum level never before reached.

Among the causes of decay of the wall masonry of the crypt, the presence of large amounts of salts (Figures 34.2, 34.3) is without doubt the most important. For this reason, it was not only necessary to stop water infiltration, but to check the mechanism of decay during changes in relative humidity.

Water moving inside a brickwall transports salts in the pores, and when the critical water content is reached, the crystallization of salts takes place (Charola and Koestler 1982). This phenomenon can take place at different points in the pores, depending on the solubility of the salts and the rate of water evaporation, which in turn depends on the moisture supply from the interior and the rate of ventilation at the surface. For this reason we can distinguish the following two phenomena:

1. *Evaporation of water on the surface: Efflorescence.* The crystallization of soluble salts on the surface is due to the low rate of ventilation, which causes an evaporation rate lower than

Figure 34.4   Salt efflorescences on the brick's surfaces.

the rate of replenishment of water by capillary migration from inside the wall (Figure 34.4). The salt crystals are formed mainly outside the pores and consequently the disruptive effect is smaller. When efflorescence takes place, salts are brought to the surface in solution during the wetting phase, and most of the evaporation from the surface takes place during the drying phase, forming salt crystals on the surface.

2. *Evaporation of water in the pores: Subflorescence.* During crystallization within the pores, the surface becomes dry since the rate of escape of water vapor from the exposed surface is faster than the rate of replenishment by capillary migration from the interior. Crystals will form and grow in the pores, channels, and crevices along the plane at a certain distance below the exterior surface. As these crystals grow, they exert forces on the capillary walls causing crumbling of thin surface layers.

To study the decay processes taking place in the brick masonry of the crypt, it is important to know the type of salts migrating in the brickwall. For this reason, X-ray diffraction analyses on salt efflorescences from mortars and bricks were carried out.

The results obtained indicate the presence of the mineral constituents such as calcite, quartz, plagioclase, feldspars, dolomite and clorite, and newly formed minerals such as halite, sylvite, gypsum, and mirabilite. The latter are present only in one sample, and in a very small amount. In contrast, halite (NaCl) and sylvite (KCl) are generally present in all samples (Table 34.1).

Results obtained indicate without doubt that halite is the main newly formed compound and its origin is ascribed to capillary migration from seawater.

As regards crystallization pressure, it is evident that NaCl is far more dangerous than other salts, even when present in a very low amount (Table 34.2). Fortunately the high value of crystallization pressure of NaCl is balanced by its high water solubility. In fact, to reach the saturation conditions, a very great amount of NaCl must be dissolved. Consequently, one does not often have in-pore crystallization.

DESALINATION OF BRICK MASONRY

To avoid further decay processes caused by crystallization of salts on elimination of water infiltration, the removal of salts from the brickwall was proposed. In general, there is a tendency to remove all masonry affected by soluble salts and to replace it

V. Fassina et al.

Table 34.1 Minerals contained in salt efflorescensces identified by X-ray diffraction analyses.

Sample	Quartz	Calcite	Plagioclase Feldspars	Dolomite	Clorite	Halite	Sylvite	Mirabilite	Gypsum
crp2	–	–	–	–	–	xxxx	(x)	–	–
crp6	–	–	–	–	–	xxxx	x	–	–
crp7	–	–	–	–	–	xxxx	x		
crp8						xxxx	x		
crp13						xxxx	x		
crp14						xxxx	(x)		
crp1	xxx	xxxx	x	(x)	–	(x)	–	–	–
crp3	x	xxxx	x	–	–	–	–	–	–
crp4	(x)	xxxx	–	–	–	xx	–	–	–
crp5	xxx	–	xxxx	–	–	–	–	xx	–
crp9	xxx	xx	(x)	x	(x)	(x)	–	–	xx
crp10	xxxx	xx	x	x	(x)	x	–	–	–
crp11a	xxx	xxxx	xx	x	(x)	x	–	–	–
crp11b	xxxx	xxxx	(x)	(x)	–	x	–	–	–

xxxx = very abundant; xxx = abundant; xx = present; x = small amount; (x) = very small amount.

with fresh brick courses (Fassina and Costa 1986). Such a system is very costly, and it would be desirable to develop less costly salt extraction systems.

From a theoretical point of view, the removal of water soluble salts from a building masonry can be accomplished with the following systems (Fassina 1988):

1. Electrodialysis and electrolysis have been used occasionally in conservation intervention; however, difficulties are likely to be met in the practical application of these electrical systems to the case of building masonry.
2. Intensive washing with salt-free water. A drawback to this method is that the water added to the masonry may create a problem as bad as the one it is meant to cure, and its successive removal might be costly and difficult.

Table 34.2 Crystallization pressure for some salts.

Salt	pressure (N/mm²)			
	Css/Cs = 2		Css/Cs = 10	
	0°C	50°C	0°C	50°C
$CaSO_4 \cdot 1/2H_2O$	33.5	39.8	112	132.5
$CaSO_4 \cdot 2H_2O$	28.2	33.4	94.8	111.0
Na_2SO_4	7.2	8.3	23.4	27.7
$Na_2SO_4 \cdot 10H_2O$	29.2	35.5	97	115.0

Css/Cs = supersaturation concentration; Cs = saturation concentration.

3. A wet poultice is applied to the surface to be desalted and is left to dry. Salt crystals concentrate on the evaporation surfaces, which are in the poultice. When the poultice is dry, it can be brushed off carrying away the salts it contains.

The disadvantages described above for the first two systems convinced us to undertake experimental studies on the third method, which was first realized in a small-scale experiment.

Wet poultice formed by absorbent paper (Figure 34.5) applied on the brick surface has two important roles: it forces salt migration from inside the wall to the external surface and prevents crystallization of salts on the brick surface because it acts as a sacrificial surface, minimizing the disruptive effect caused by crystallization of salts in the brick pores.

To have good reproducibility of the desalination, experimental conditions were standardized as much as possible according to the following criteria:

- the same area of application was considered,
- the amount of poultice was weighed before application,
- the same thickness of poultice was considered.

The poultice was prepared in a small cement mixer. Water was added first, in contrast to normal concrete mixing practice. Mixing and adding clay was continued until a consistency rather like whipped cream was obtained. This paste was then applied to the wall to a thickness of 5 mm by pumping equipment. For absorbent desalination material, sepiolite was chosen instead of the absorbent paper used during a preliminary test, because of its greater practicality in yard works and its satisfying effectiveness in salt removal.

After a certain time, the poultice dried out due to the evaporation of water. This process causes the migration of water soluble salts from the wall to the poultice. Consequently, salt crystals concentrate in the evaporation surfaces. Drying of the poultice was extremely slow due to the thickness of the wall, the high relative humidity, and the low temperature of the air. To accelerate drying process a heating system was used inside the room. The poultice was left to dry for several days until the clay shrunk and lost contact with the masonry (Fassina and Rossetti 1992).

Figure 34.5 Absorbent paper applied on brick surface to remove salts from wall masonry.

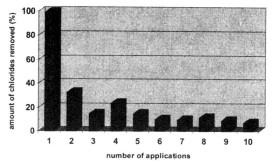

Figure 34.6 Amount of chloride removed after each application in area P.

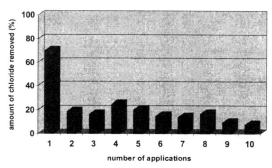

Figure 34.7 Amount of chloride removed after each application in area S.

Salt removal is at its maximum when the poultice is wet. In fact, shrinkage of the clay causes loss of contact with the masonry and migration of salts ceases. When the poultice dried, it was brushed off and analyzed to determine the salt content. Once the it had been removed, the cycle was repeated again.

Desalination experiments were carried out on two different areas previously characterized from a quantitative point of view in terms of chloride concentration.

As can be seen in Figures 34.2 and 34.3, the chloride concentration decreases from the surface to the inner part of the brick.

If we consider the amount of salt removed after each operation, we observe that the first application is much more efficient than the following ones (Figures 34.6, 34.7). To evaluate the efficiency of salt extraction, it is very important to compare the amount of salt present before extraction with the amount of salt removed after each operation.

From the analyses of core brick samples carried out before extraction (chloride concentration is between 1.4% and 2.4%), we made an approximate calculation that chloride in the wall was 2 kg per square meter calculated on a 7 cm depth. An approximate calculation of the total amount of salt removed during the experiment was 0.5 kg of chloride per square meter, which is about 25% of the initial amount. This means that chloride removal reached the thickness of 2 cm (Figures 34.8, 34.9). We can conclude that the method used to remove salts is efficient but, as predicted, it will present some practical difficulties to reach high efficiency.

To accelerate salt removal, the crypt was divided into different closed areas to create separate rooms in which it was possible to introduce heating. In this way, salt

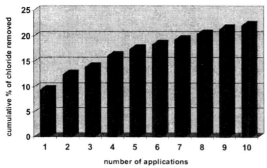

Figure 34.8   Efficiency of chloride removal in area P.

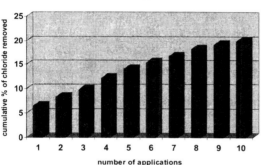

Figure 34.9   Efficiency of chloride removal in area S.

crystallization could take place on the sepiolite sacrificial surface. When the sepiolite layer dried, it was removed and a new wet poultice was applied (Fassina and Arbizzani 1993).

CHARACTERIZATION OF BRICKS AND CHOICE OF CONSOLIDATING MATERIALS

After water penetration was stopped and salt removal was carried out, it was necessary to undertake an appropriate treatment to improve the cohesion of bricks as well as to allow the evaporation of residual water and to produce a certain migration barrier to the salts remaining in the wall masonry.

The crypt, however, poses problems completely different from situations generally found. For example, it is usually necessary to prevent water penetration, while in the case of the crypt, an inverse protection needed to be created to allow residual water to escape from wall masonry as water vapor.

If we apply a water-repellent protection to the surface, saline solution can continue to migrate towards the surface, while water evaporation and crystallization of salts will occur in the subsurface. The best results can be obtained by making a protection in depth, through means of strongly migrating water soluble silanes, and successively impregnating the bricks with a consolidant substance.

We attempted to evaluate some consolidants of the ethyl silicate or siloxane-based polymer type by measuring capillary water absorption.

The criterion to select the consolidant was to find the one that was able to reduce water absorption strongly as a result of decreasing porosity. The main goal is to improve resistance to migration of water-soluble substances without preventing the escape of water vapor.

The following consolidant products were tested:

(A) Rhodorsil RC90+Rhodorsil 11309: mixture of ethyl silicate (RC 90) and poly-methyl-phenyl-siloxane (11309),
(B) Rhodorsil RC70: ethyl-silicate,
(C) Rhodorsil RC80+Tegosivin HS: mixture of poly-methyl-siloxane and ethyl-silicate (RC80)+ alkyl-alkoxy-silane (HS),
(D) Tegosivin HS: alkyl-alkoxy-silane.

Macroscopic observation of wall masonry showed three different types of bricks. Thus we decided to make the application of consolidant on the different types observed (Figure 34.10). The three types of bricks can be described as follows:

- Type 1 is a low porosity brick, pink-colored, compact and homogeneous with large yellow inclusions.
- Type 2 is a more porous brick, yellow-pink colored, with small red-brown inclusions.
- Type 3 is a very porous brick, yellow-green colored, with large cavities.

To evaluate the physical behavior of the bricks as a result of the consolidation intervention, laboratory tests were carried out on the three different types of bricks, each of which measured $5 \times 5 \times 2$ cm and was taken from the original wall. The following parameters were considered:

- capillary water absorption,
- protection degree in relation to capillary water absorption,

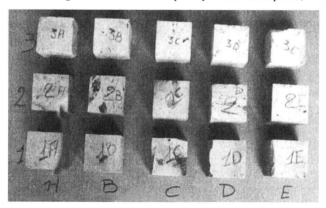

Figure 34.10 Three different types of bricks found on wall masonry.

- drying behavior of wet bricks,
- artificial aging tests.

The tests carried out were:

- Measurement of water absorption by capillarity (according to NORMAL 11/85),
- Measurement of the drying index (according to NORMAL 29/88).

Measurement of water absorption by capillarity allows an evaluation of the amount of water absorbed by means of capillary rise and kinetics of water absorption. Measurement of the drying index allows an evaluation of the drying process due to water release when the brick is at a low relative humidity. Tests were carried before and after the treatment.

CAPILLARY WATER ABSORPTION AND CAPILLARY PROTECTION DEGREE

Capillary water absorption is obtained when the sample comes in contact with an absorbent paper that is completely saturated with water. The amount of water taken from the sample is determined by weighing it at different times. At a certain point, the water content reaches an asymptotic value.

It is very interesting to introduce a parameter, termed *protection degree* (*PD*), which represents the ratio between the difference of the amount of absorbed water by capillarity before (W_{bt}) and after (W_{at}) the treatment and the amount of absorbed water before (W_{bt}) the treatment expressed in percentage:

$$PD = \frac{W_{bt} - W_{at}}{W_{bt}} \times 100 . \qquad (34.1)$$

Generally this ratio, referred to as capillary absorption, is carried out for a short time (1 hour). In our case, we considered three different times: 4 hours, 96 hours, and 264 hours (Fassina and Molteni 1994).The protection degree tested for a long time gives us an indication of the resistance to water penetration exerted by the consolidant. We consider now water capillary absorption before and after treatments (A), (B), (C), and (D).

Capillary Water Absorption before Treatment

The data obtained before the treatment are reported in Figure 34.11 and allow us to make the following observations:

- Type 1 bricks show a very rapid water absorption from the beginning of the test, and the asymptotic value (average maximum value 20.8%) is reached in the first hour.
- Type 2 bricks absorb water more gradually than others and the maximum amount is low, 19.3%. Water absorption kinetics are slower than other bricks probably due to different pore-size distribution.

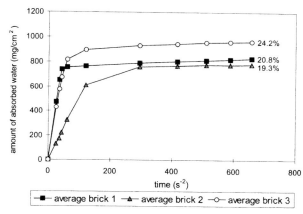

Figure 34.11 Capillary absorption of water for the three different types of bricks before treatment.

- Type 3 bricks show fast water absorption, very similar to the Type 1, and they reach the highest asymptotic value, 24.2%.

The comparison of the three types of bricks show us that Type 3 bricks are the most porous, with respect to the other two types. Type 1 and 2 bricks reach the same asymptotic value, more or less, but have a different curve trend because their pores are of different diameters.

Capillary Water Absorption after Treatment

Treatment A.   The amount of water absorbed after treatment is strongly reduced for the different types of bricks. After four hours, untreated samples have almost reached asymptotic value, while the treated ones show the beginning of absorption (Figure 34.12a, b, c). Protection degree maintains high values after a long time of contact with water: 90% after 96 hours (Figure 34.12d).

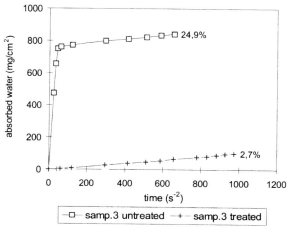

Figure 34.12a Capillary absorption of water for Type 1 brick treated with mixture of Rhodorsil RC90+Rhodorsil 11309.

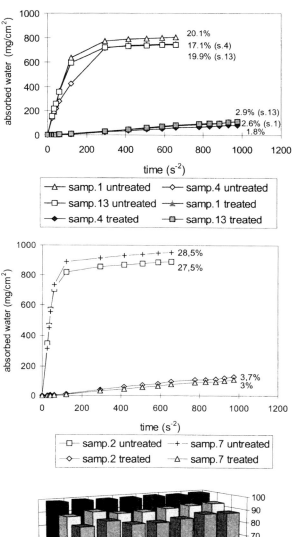

Figure 34.12b Capillary absorption of water for Type 2 brick treated with mixture of Rhodorsil RC90+Rhodorsil 11309.

Figure 34.12c Capillary absorption of water for Type 3 brick treated with mixture of Rhodorsil RC90+Rhodorsil 11309.

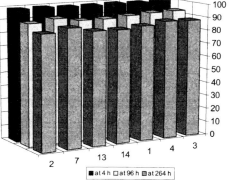

Figure 34.12d Protection degree for different kinds of bricks treated with mixture of Rhodorsil RC90+Rhodorsil 11309, at different times (4 h, 96 h, 264 h).

V. Fassina et al.

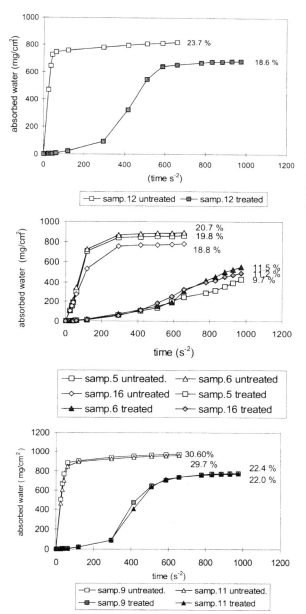

Figure 34.13a Capillary absorption of water for Type 1 brick treated with Rhodorsil RC70.

Figure 34.13b Capillary absorption of water for Type 2 brick treated with Rhodorsil RC70.

Figure 34.13c Capillary absorption of water for Type 3 brick treated with Rhodorsil RC70.

Treatment B. The amount of water absorbed after treatment is very low until 24 hours, but successively starts to increase continuously until it reaches 70%–80% of the amount of water absorbed before treatment (Figure 34.13a, b, c). In Type 2 bricks the

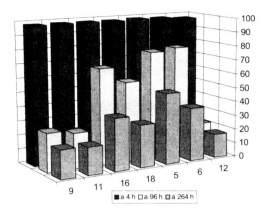

Figure 34.13d Protection degree for different kinds of bricks treated with Rhodorsil RC70, at different times (4 h, 96 h, 264 h).

amount of absorbed water increases more slowly than in the other two types due to different pore-size distribution; after four days it maintained a protection degree greater than the other two (Figure 34.13d). Protection degree is good after four hours, but decreases sharply after 96 h on Types 1 and 3 bricks while decreasing less sharply for Type 2.

Treatment C. This type of treatment is good both for short and long durations and was applied only on Type 2 and 3 bricks (Figures 34.14a, b, c). Type 3 bricks were better than Type 2 (Figure 34.14d).

Treatment D. This was carried out only on Type 2 bricks (Figure 34.15a). Tegosivin HS, when used alone (Figure 34.15b), is less effective in repelling water than when it is used together with RC80 (Figure 34.14d).

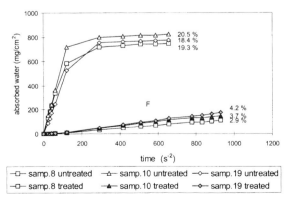

Figure 34.14a Capillary absorption of water for Type 2 brick treated with mixture of Rhodorsil RC80+Tegosivin HS.

420   *V. Fassina et al.*

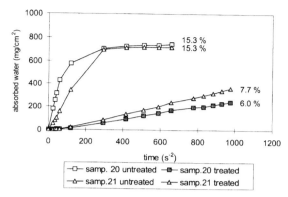

Figure 34.14b   Capillary absorption of water for Type 2 brick treated with mixture of Rhodorsil RC80+Tegosivin HS.

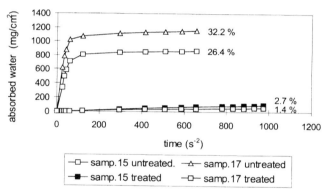

Figure 34.14c   Capillary absorption of water for Type 3 brick treated with mixture of Rhodorsil RC80+Tegosivin HS.

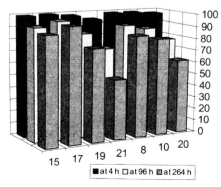

Figure 34.14d   Protection degree for different kinds of bricks treated with mixture of Rhodorsil RC80+Tegosivin HS.

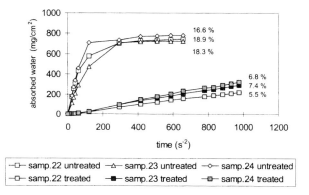

Figure 34.15a Capillary absorption of water for Type 2 brick treated with Tegosivin HS 20%.

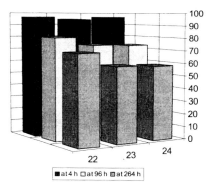

Figure 34.15b Protection degree for Type 2 brick treated with Tegosivin HS 20%, at different times (4 h, 96 h, 264 h).

DRYING INDEX

The sample, previously saturated with water, is placed into a box that contains silica gel to maintain a dry environment. It is weighed from time to time to determine the amount of evaporated water. Water evaporation occurs in controlled conditions and its amount is recorded in a graph. The experiment yields information about the velocity of water release and the amount of residual water remaining after a certain time.

As we expect from the maximum values in the water capillary absorption test, the amounts of absorbed water by total immersion are different for the three types of bricks (Figure 34.16).

Drying Index before Treatment

Types 1 and 3 bricks release water as quickly as they absorb it, and the amount of residual water is 1% and 3%, respectively. In contrast, Type 2 bricks release water more slowly than the other ones, and the amount of residual water is higher, 4%.

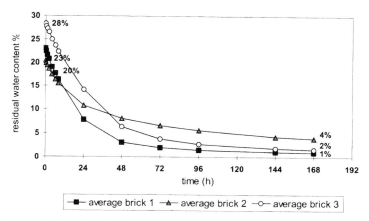

Figure 34.16   Drying index for the three different types of bricks before treatment.

Drying Index after Treatment

Treatment did not completely stop water evaporation, as can be see in the graphs (Figures 34.17–34.19). The consolidation treatments greatly reduced water absorption and consequently the initial amount released is very low. At the end of the test, residual water in treated samples is less than in the previous test with untreated ones.

TRIAL OF SALT CRYSTALLIZATION BY TOTAL IMMERSION: ARTIFICIAL AGING

Cubic samples 5 cm on a side were treated on all sides with the four types of consolidants (A, B, C, D) by means of capillarity and were left at room temperature for one month to allow the products to polymerize. One sample for each type of brick was left untreated as a control. During treatment, Type 2 bricks absorbed less consolidant than the others.

To estimate the efficacy of the treatments, cubic samples were subjected to accelerated aging tests of wetting and drying by using a 15% of sodium chloride solution. The sodium chloride solution was used instead of the usual $Na_2SO_4 \cdot 10H_2O$, as appropriate for experiments on the crystallization of salts, because it was the predominant salt that appeared in the efflorescences on the bricks of the crypt.

The wetting phase was carried out by total immersion in the solution followed by the drying phase carried out in an oven. During drying, crystallization of sodium chloride caused some stress in the capillaries of bricks.

Samples were put in five different vessels according to the different consolidant treatments. One vessel contained untreated samples as a control. After each cycle, the weight change was determined. After some cycles, untreated samples showed a large increase in weight, about 10% for all brick types, due to the presence of salts in the sample.

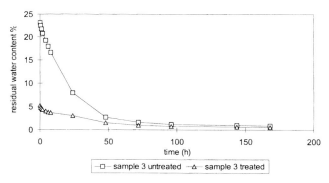

Figure 34.17a   Drying index for Type 1 brick treated with mixture of Rhodorsil RC90+Rhodorsil 11309.

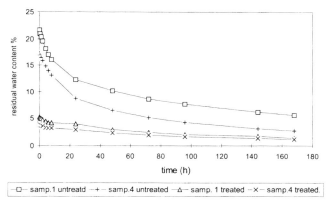

Figure 34.17b   Drying index for Type 2 brick treated with mixture of Rhodorsil RC90+Rhodorsil 11309.

The bottom of the vessel containing untreated samples showed the presence of brick powder and scales generated by the disintegration of the bricks. The amount of powder was increased continuously.

After some cycles, the vessel containing bricks treated with Rhodorsil RC70 also presented increased powdering.

After ten cycles, all vessels showed a certain amount of powdering material at the bottom; however, two of them (Treatments A and B) showed a very low amount.

CONCLUSIONS

Before *in situ* application, it was necessary to verify the degree of protection in the laboratory.

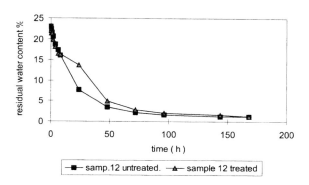

Figure 34.18a   Drying index for Type 1 brick treated with Rhodorsil RC70.

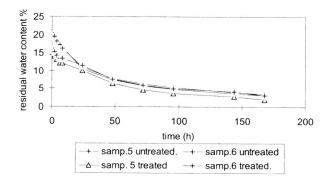

Figure 34.18b   Drying index for Type 2 brick treated with Rhodorsil RC70.

Type 3 bricks are the most porous, show the maximum amount of consolidant absorption for treatment with the mixture Rhodorsil RC90+Rhodorsil 11309 and with mixture of Rhodorsil RC80+Tegosivin HS, and exhibit the maximum degree of protection. Treatment with Rhodorsil RC70 showed a lesser amount of absorbed product and a very low protection degree.

Type 2 bricks have the lowest porosity and show consolidant absorption less than Type 1; however, the protection efficiency is very high, especially for the mixture Rhodorsil RC90+Rhodorsil 11309, while it decreases sharply in some samples treated with Rhodorsil RC80+Tegosivin HS. Treatment with Rhodorsil RC70, even in the presence of high amounts of consolidant, does not allow a good water resistance. In fact, protection degree is only 30%. Treatment with Tegosivin HS, which was carried out only on Type 2 bricks, shows performances that can be compared to those of mixture Rhodorsil RC80+Tegosivin HS, but is inferior to those of treatment Rhodorsil RC90+Rhodorsil 11309.

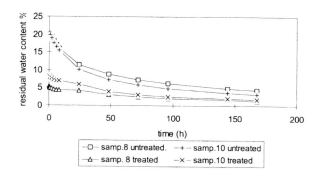

Figure 34.19a Drying index for Type 2 brick treated with mixture of Rhodorsil RC80+Tego-sivin HS.

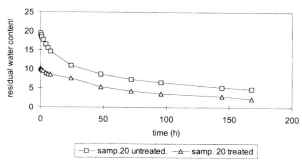

Figure 34.19b Drying index for Type 2 brick treated with mixture of Rhodorsil RC80+Tego-sivin HS.

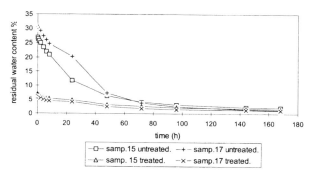

Figure 34.19c Drying index for Type 3 brick treated with mixture of Rhodorsil RC80+Tego-sivin HS.

On *Type 1 bricks* it is not possible to draw many conclusions because only two treatments – Rhodorsil RC90 and Rhodorsil RC70 – were carried out. The first gave the best results.

Comparison of different treatments in relation to the three types of bricks clearly shows that treatment with Rhodorsil RC90+ Rhodorsil 11309 yields the best results. Only in one case – treatment of Type 3 brick with Rhodorsil RC80+Tegosivin HS – were comparable results found. By contrast, treatment with Rhodorsil RC70 yielded the worst performance independent of brick type.

Results obtained in the laboratory show that a mixture of Rhodorsil RC90+Rhodorsil 11309, which is a mixture of ethyl silicate and poly-(methyl-phenyl-siloxane) performed best on all types of bricks.

ACKNOWLEDGEMENTS

The authors wish to thank Mrs. Alessandro Gaiani and Federico Vianello for the graphical support. A special thank to I.A.R. and Rhone Poulenc companies for the valuable support offered in field experiments.

REFERENCES

Charola A.E., and R.J. Koestler. 1982. The action of salt water solutions of the silico-aluminate matrix of bricks. In: Il mattone di Venezia, Ateneo Veneto, pp. 67–76. Venice, Oct. 29, 1982, Venice: Instituto per lo Studio della Dinamica delle Grandi Masse, CNR.

Fassina, V. 1988. Il risanamento delle murature. Un esperimento di desalinizzazione a Venezia. In: Recupero Edilizio **6**, a cura di Luisella Gelsomino, pp. 69–76. Bologna.

Fassina, V., and Arbizzani. 1993. Considerazioni sulla metodica di rimozione dei sali solubili dalle murature della cripta e sull'impiego di resine per rallentare i processi di assorbimento capillare dell'acqua connessi all'umidità delle strutture. In: Basilica Patriarcale in Venezia-San Marco-la cripta e il restauro, ed., pp. 113–130. Venice:Vallardi.

Fassina, V., and F. Costa. 1986. Preliminary results of desalination of Ca' Pesaro brick masonry. In: Proc. 2nd Intl. Symp. on Materials Science and Restoration, pp. 365–376. Esslingen: Technische Akademie Esslingen.

Fassina, V., and C. Molteni. 1994. Problemi di Conservazione connessi all'umidità delle murature: La diagnostica e le tecnologie conservative applicate al restauro della cripta di S. Marco in Venezia. In: Proc. 3rd Intl. Symp. on the Conservation of Monuments in the Mediterranean Basin, pp. 803–813. Venice, June 22–25, 1994. Padova: La Photograph.

Fassina, V., and M. Rossetti. 1992. Problemi di conservazione connessi all'umidità delle strutture. Diagnostica. In: Basilica Patriarcale in Venezia-San Marco-la cripta, la storia, la conservazione, pp. 87–112. Venice: Vallardi.

Fassina, V., and A.G. Stevan. 1991. The moisture behavior in Venetian building structures. In: Proc. 4th Expert Meeting on Conservation of Historic Brick Structures, pp. 61–74. NATO-CCMS Pilot Study, Amsterdam, Oct. 28–29, 1990. Berlin: UBA.

NORMAL 11/85. Assorbimento d'acqua per capillarità. Coefficiente di assorbimento capillare. NORMAL Commission Recommendation, 1986. Rome: ICR-CNR.

NORMAL 29/88. Misura dell'indice di asciugamento (drying index). NORMAL Commission Recommendation, 1988. Rome: ICR-CNR.

35

Influence of Effective Material Properties on Dynamic Analysis and Earthquake Response of Hagia Sophia

A.S. ÇAKMAK[1], M.N. NATSIS[1], C.L. MULLEN[1], R. MARK[2], and R.A. LIVINGSTON[2]

[1]Department of Civil Engineering and Operations Research, Princeton University, Princeton, NJ 08540, U.S.A.
[2]Office of Highway Engineering R&D, Federal Highway Administration, Washington, D.C. 22101–2296, U.S.A.

ABSTRACT

Finite element (FE) studies of the Hagia Sophia, a 6th century masonry edifice in Istanbul, Turkey, provide insight to the structure's response to dynamic loads. The church contains four great brick arches springing from stone piers that offer primary support for a 31-meter diameter central dome and two semidomes. Stone and brick masonry material properties for the numerical model are adjusted to match system mode shapes and frequencies identified from measured response to a recent low-intensity earthquake. The calibrated model is used to predict the measured responses, and the effect of soil-structure interaction is demonstrated. Stresses under simulated severe earthquake loading are estimated at the critical locations in the arches.

INTRODUCTION

Begun in 532 as the principal church of the Byzantine Empire (and converted to a royal mosque after the fall of the Empire in 1453), Hagia Sophia in Istanbul held the record as the world's largest domed building for some 800 years. In order to preserve this historical structure, it is necessary to understand the earthquake response in its present condition. This paper addresses aspects of the present-day effective dynamic material properties of the primary dome support structure under recorded and likely earthquake excitation. Early development of a numerical model for eigenvalue analysis of Hagia

Sophia has been discussed by Çakmak et al. (1993). A very good match was attained in the first three natural frequencies measured during an ambient vibration survey of the actual structure (see Erdik and Cakti 1990). A low-level event of magnitude 4.8 occurred on March 22, 1992, with the epicenter at Karabacey, Turkey, about 120 km south of Hagia Sophia. Strong motion acceleration time histories recorded for this event have been analyzed in both time and frequency domains. System identification performed on this data has been discussed by Çakmak et al. (1993). The first three mode shapes correspond to simple horizontal translation (modes 1 and 2) and a complex form of torsional rotation (mode 3) of the entire primary structure system. Here we compare the earthquake response of the numerical model and the identified system and extend the model to improve the predictions and provide estimates of severe earthquake responses.

EFFECTIVE DYNAMIC MATERIAL PROPERTIES AND MEASURED RESPONSE

The primary structure supporting the main dome of the Hagia Sophia and its orientation are illustrated in a cutaway view in Figure 35.1. The main dome is spherically shaped and rests on a square dome base. Major elements include the four main piers supporting the corners of the dome base and the four main arches that spring from these piers and support the edges of the dome base. The instrumentation array described by Erdik and Cakti (1993) has been designed to capture the motion of the major elements comprising the main dome support structure during earthquake events.

The main piers are comprised of stone masonry up to the springing level of the main arches. The stone blocks are almost rigid, whereas the mortar is relatively compliant. The main arches, dome, and portions of the main piers and buttresses above the

Figure 35.1 Main dome support structure and strong motion instrument array.

Table 35.1 Chemical analysis of Hagia Sophia mortar samples.

Constituent (%)	Sample Number (see location key)							
	1	2	3	4	5	6	7	8
Free Lime (CaO)	0.07	0.15	0.02	0.05	0.08	0.06	0.07	0.03
Insoluble Residue	58.9	53.9	53.4	59.3	29.8	51.6	60.9	59.5
Soluble Silica (SiO_2)	5.56	6.22	8.50	6.32	10.78	14.78	7.59	5.70
Total Lime (CaO)	15.4	17.9	17.0	13.8	25.2	14.4	13.7	15.9
Carbonate (CO_2)	11.8	13.8	12.1	9.36	17.5	7.80	10.5	11.9
Sulfate (SO_3)	0.23	0.01	0.10	0.15	1.82	0.10	0.05	0.23
Total Water (H_2O)	1.91	1.83	2.13	ND	ND	ND	ND	ND
Free/Total Lime	0.43	0.86	0.15	0.33	0.33	0.43	0.54	019

Location Key:
1. (A.D. 532–537) SE Buttress, Gallery West Hall
2. (A.D. 532–537) SE Pier (East Arch)
3. (A.D. 532–537) SW Exedra
4. (A.D. 532–537) Dome Rib
5. (A.D. 986–994) Dome
6. (A.D. 1346–1354) Dome
7. (A.D. 558–562) NE Buttress, Gallery Roof, Pier Wall
8. (A.D. 558–562) NE Buttress, Gallery Roof, East Wall

springing point of the main arches are comprised of brick masonry. Chemical analyses (Anon.) of the mortar are presented in Table 35.1.

Based on the cement chemistry definition (Taylor 1964), the Hagia Sophia brick mortar may be qualitatively classified as a pozzolanic material. Unlike a Portland cement, a pozzolanic material does not react by itself with water to yield cementitious phases. Pozzolans generally contain glassy phases that contribute soluble silica in the presence of lime. Burnt shale or brick dust could be considered as artificial pozzolans, and there is evidence for the use of crushed brick as a pozzolan in ancient Roman masonry called "coccio pesto" (Moropoulou et al. 1993).

Pozzolanic lime mortars have much higher tensile strengths than those of pure lime. Table 35.2 provides a comparison of strengths for various mortar materials (Lea 1979).

The mortar used in the Hagia Sophia brick masonry may be considered a form of concrete with tensile strength approaching 3.5 Mpa based on Table 35.2. The bricks may be thought of as providing stiffness rather than strength as is the case in present-day construction. The mass density of the composite is about 1500 kg/m^3, which is lighter than present-day concrete.

Figure 35.2 shows the earthquake induced N-S (Y), E-W (X), and vertical (V or Z) acceleration component time histories recorded during the 1992 Karacabey event. The three components for each response location are displayed in a plan arrangement oriented to the view seen from the entrance to the basilica. In all cases, the records indicate a nonstationary process acting with three approximately stationary time intervals. The first interval extends from 2 to 12 s and corresponds to the action of compressional waves; the second, from 15 to 25 s, corresponds to the arrival of shear waves; and the

Table 35.2 Comparison of strengths of mortar materials. Data from Lea (1979).

Binder	Time to Set (hr)	Time to Full Strength	Tensile Strength (MPa)	Compressive Strength (MPa)
Lime	24	100 days-years	0.3–0.7	9
Gypsum	0.5–1.0	0.5–1.0 hr	4.6–5.0	46–50
Portland cement	5–8	100–150 days	2–3	21–28
Pozzolanic	10–12	150 days–1 year	3.4–3.8	14–17

third, from 35 to 40 s, corresponds to a period of decay in the energy of the input motion and will not be emphasized here. N-S motion tends to dominate the response motion with particularly intense N-S motions at locations 4 and 6. The peak displacement at location 4 is estimated as 0.071 cm, which is double that of the locations 2, 3, and 5. Similarly, the peak displacement at location 6 is estimated to be 0.13 cm, which is almost double that at location 8.

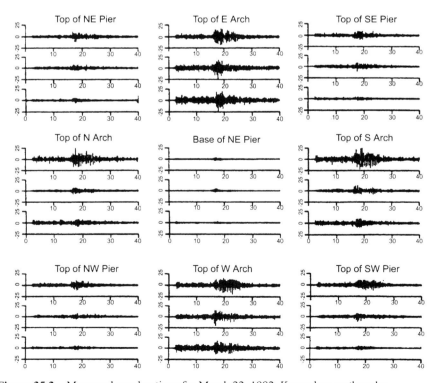

Figure 35.2 Measured accelerations for March 22, 1992, Karacabey earthquake.

Two characteristics of the measured response are not captured by the numerical models discussed in Çakmak et al. (1993). First, the system responds primarily at 1.85 Hz in the second interval, a 10% reduction in the mode 2 frequency relative to the ambient vibration frequency of 2.09 Hz. The first interval indicates mode 2 response at 2.00 Hz, a 5% reduction relative to the ambient vibration. Second, the SW main pier and the arches that spring from it respond at higher amplitudes in mode 2 motion than the other piers and arches. Similar behavior is also noted for mode 1 response.

SIMULATION

Two select attempts at matching the recorded response using linear FE models are discussed here with particular attention paid to accounting for the two characteristics described above. The first model, named *hsdyntc9*, has been constructed by Davidson (1993). It is similar to the linear FE model used by Çakmak et al. (1993) for eigenvalue analysis but has more refinement of the mesh in the region of the arches. The elastic properties have been adjusted to match the observed frequency during the second interval of the earthquake response motion. The elastic moduli and density used in this model are the same as those for the eigenvalue model, except the Young's moduli, E, in surcharge and tension areas were not reduced and a ratio of 1.00:0.68 was used for E values of stone and brick masonries, respectively. The second model, named *hsdynss*, has been constructed with the same geometry above the floor level as the *hsdyntc9* model. The effect of soil-structure interaction has been incorporated, however, by supporting the portions of the main piers below floor level with linear translational soil springs acting normal to the faces of the piers. Soil spring stiffnesses have been distributed in a manner reflective of expected variations in soil elastic moduli. Such patterns have been obtained from seismic tomography which measured compressional wave velocity of foundation material along a grid of horizontal and vertical planes in the area below and contained by the four main piers. The frequencies obtained by eigenvalue analysis of the *hsdyntc9* and *hsdynss* models are given in Table 35.3.

Simulated response of the *hsdynss* model to the earthquake was calculated using the mode superposition method with input acceleration at all soil spring locations in the model identical to that measured in the corresponding component direction at the Kandilli seismographic station, a nearby bedrock free-field location. A pseudo-nonlinear response has been estimated by selecting different moduli in the first and second time intervals of the earthquake response motion. Figure 35.3 shows a comparison of some of the measured and simulated acceleration time histories.

STRESS ANALYSIS

Static dead load stresses in a model named *10try6* have been calculated using a pseudo-nonlinear procedure described by Davidson (1993). The procedure attempts to capture intermediate selfweight deformations experienced during a number of major

Table 35.3   Earthquake calibration[1].

Mode	Observed	Simulation[2]		Dominant Motion
		Fixed Base	Soil Springs	
1	1.53	1.79	1.57	E-W (X-axis) translation
2	1.85	1.94	1.80	N-S (Y-axis) translation
3	2.15	2.16	2.02	Torsional (Z-axis) translation

[1] All frequencies are in Hz.
[2] Fixed Base = *hsdyntc9*, Soil Springs = *hsdynss*.

stages of construction. The FE mesh for the *10try6* is essentially the same as that used in the *hsdyntc9* model. Using magnitude M = 6.5 and M = 7.5 earthquake input accelerations generated at the site according to the procedure described by Findell et al. (1993), response time histories for the *hsdyntc9* model have been simulated. Maximum stresses in the critical crown region of the east and west arches corresponding to the static and dynamic loadings are summarized in Table 35.4. These results give benchmarks for severe response characteristics and highlight the important of dynamic response to past and potential failures of the primary support structure.

Table 35.4   Simulated stresses[1] for severe earthquakes.

Load Case	East Arch		West Arch	
	M=6.5	M=7.5	M=6.5	M=7.5
DL	0.80(3.30)		1.21(3.61)	
EQ	0.60(0.60)	1.72(1.72)	0.51(0.51)	1.48(1.48)
Total	1.40(3.90)	2.52(5.02)	1.72(4.12)	2.73(5.09)

[1] All stresses are in Mpa. Maximum tensions for *hsdyntc9* are listed with maximum compressions given in parentheses.

CONCLUSION

Numerical modeling of the Hagia Sophia has been performed using calibrated linear finite element analyses. System identification from a recent low-intensity earthquake indicates a nonlinear behavior for the masonry structure even at very low response levels. The linear models provide reasonable estimates of overall dynamic characteristics including frequency and primary modes of response. Incorporation of nonlinear behavior and soil-structure interaction may be achieved in an approximate way and improves the low-intensity predictions. Numerical modeling provides an important

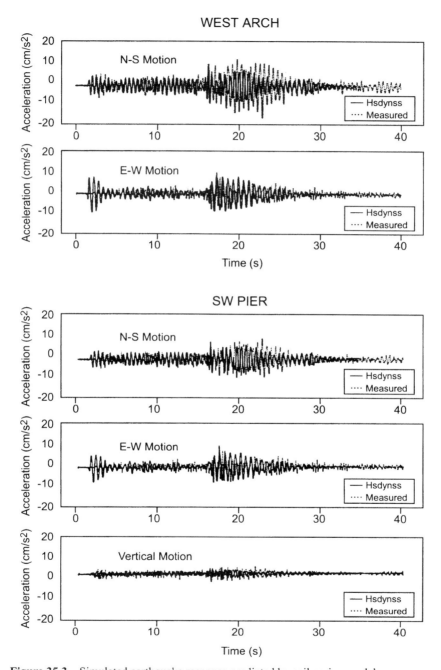

Figure 35.3   Simulated earthquake response predicted by soil-spring model.

means of monitoring the earthquake survivability of the Hagia Sophia. Seismic events with greater intensities than those observed in this study can be expected to occur in the future. This will produce larger deformations and/or cracking. To model these effects realistically will require taking into account the characteristic nonlinear behavior of the masonry construction.

REFERENCES

Anonymous. Mortars from Sancta Sophia. Unpublished manuscript, Van Nice Collection, Dunbarton Oaks, Washington, D.C.

Çakmak, A.S., R. Davidson, C.L. Mullen, and M. Erdik. 1993. Dynamic analysis and earthquake response of Hagia Sophia. In: Proc. of STREMA '93, 3rd Intl. Conference, Bath UK, June 16–18, pp. 67–84. Southampton: Computational Mechanics Publ.

Davidson, R.A. 1993. The Mother of All Churches: A Static and Dynamic Structural Analysis of Hagia Sophia. Unpublished senior thesis, Dept. of Civil Engineering and Operations Research. Princeton University.

Erdik, M., and E. Cakti. 1990. Istanbul Ayasofya Muzesi Yapisal Sisteminin ve Deprem Guvenliginin Saglanmasina Yonelik Tedbirlerin Tespiti. 2nd Research Report, Earthquake Research Institute, Bogazici University.

Erdik, M., and E. Cakti. 1993. Instrumentation of Hagia Sophia and the analysis of the response of the structure to an earthquake of 4.8 magnitude. In: Proc. of STREMA '93, 3rd Intl. Conference, Bath UK, June 16–18, pp. 99–114.

Findell, K., H.U. Köylüoglu, and A.S. Çakmak. 1993. Modeling and simulating earthquake accelerograms using strong motion data from the Istanbul, Turkey region. *Soil Dynamics and Earthquake Engineering* 12:51–59.

Lea, F.M. 1979. The Chemistry of Cement and Concrete, pp. 491–435. New York: Chemical Publishing Co.

Moropoulou, A., G. Biscontin, K. Bisbikou, A. Bakolas, P. Theoulakis, A. Theodoraki, and T. Tsiourva. 1993. Physico-chemical study of adhesion mechanisms among binding material and brick fragments in "coccio pesto." *Scienze Beni Culturali* IX.

Taylor, H.F.W. 1964. The Chemistry of Cements, pp. 221–223. London: Academic Press.

36

Deterioration and Restoration of Brickwork at the Octagon House, Washington, D.C.

J.G. WAITE

John G. Waite Associates, Architects, 384–386 Broadway,
Albany, New York 12207, U.S.A.

ABSTRACT

The Octagon House, constructed 1799–1801, is one of the most significant houses in Washington, D.C. Purchased by the American Institute of Architects as its headquarter in 1902, the house has become a symbol of the architecture profession in the United States. As part of the recent restoration campaign, the exterior brick masonry was completely restored. Over the years, the jack arches over the window openings had failed and the exterior walls were deteriorated from the effects of airborne pollutants and improper repointing methods. Removal of the original wood framing and replacement with a steel and concrete flooring system during a 1950s renovation had caused additional problems to the exterior bearing walls. As part of the recent restoration, the architects, using a grant from the Getty Grant Program, investigated the causes of the masonry deterioration and directed its restoration. Masonry restoration procedures included cleaning and repointing the brickwork, rebuilding the chimneys to their historic forms, stabilization of the jack arches, and replacement of the steel and concrete floor systems with wood framing.

INTRODUCTION

The Octagon (Figure 36.1) has been described as the most significant historic house in Washington, D.C., after the White House. Constructed between 1799 and 1801 for John Tayloe III, a wealthy Virginia planter, The Octagon was designed by Dr. William Thornton, the first architect of the United States Capitol. Intended as a winter townhouse, the Tayloe's country seat was Mount Airy in Richmond County. After the President's House was burned by the British in 1814, The Octagon was occupied by President and Mrs. Madison until 1815.

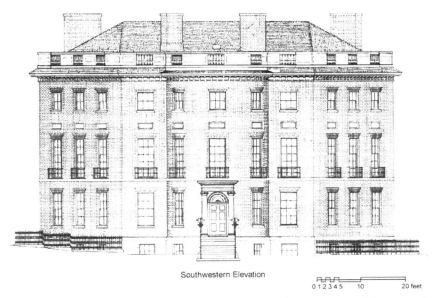

Southwestern Elevation

0 1 2 3 4 5   10   20 feet

Figure 36.1   Restored southwestern elevation drawing of The Octagon, Washington, D.C.

After the death of Mrs. Tayloe in 1855, the house was rented to various tenants over the course of the following forty-five years. In 1902, The Octagon was purchased by the American Institute of Architects for use as its headquarters. The rescue of the building by the American Institute of Architects (AIA) was a truly inspirational effort, and was led by the giants of the profession at the time in the United States. The preservation effort occurred when Charles Follen McKim, of McKim, Mead and White Architects, was president of the AIA. McKim, a strong advocate for The Octagon, was joined by Frank Miles Day, George B. Post, Cass Gilbert, Daniel H. Burnham, Henry Bacon, Ralph Adams Cram, and Thomas Hastings. The building has since become a symbol of the AIA. Over the span of nine decades that the AIA has controlled The Octagon, its treatment has mirrored the profession's attitude toward historic buildings. The house was extensively repaired by the AIA during its first decade of ownership. Major renovations of the building were carried out in 1945–1955 and again in 1968–1970.

Because of the deteriorating condition of the building, a thorough restoration was programmed for the building in 1990 by the American Architectural Foundation. Mesick-Cohen-Waite Architects (now John G. Waite Associates, Architects) of Albany, New York, were selected to direct the restoration. Directing the work for the architects was John G. Waite, Principal-in-Charge, and Michael Curcio, Project Manager. To begin the process, a historic structure report and restoration master plan were commissioned. While this study was being prepared, repairs were begun on the exterior of the building because of obvious structural problems. The first priority was the restoration of the brick jack arches.

JACK ARCH RESTORATION

For some time it has been apparent that the brick jack arches over the window openings of the front facade were in varying states of deterioration. The front elevation is constructed of face brick laid up in a lime and sand mortar. The jack arches are laid up with very narrow joints (approximately 1/8 inch wide) of lime paste (slaked lime without sand or cement).

Over the years, some of the lime paste pointing has been eroded from the joints and settlement had occurred in the wall resulting in vertical cracking in the joints in a number of the jack arches. The problems were compounded in the curved section of the facade where bricks were displaced both horizontally and vertically from their original positions. In the flat wall areas, many of the jack arch bricks had dropped vertically out of position. It was later determined that this displacement was in large measure caused by the removal of the original wood floor framing during the 1945–1955 and 1965–1970 renovation campaigns, and the installation of concrete and steel floor framing which drastically altered the loading pattern on the brick-bearing walls.

Past efforts to arrest this deterioration consisted of repointing deteriorated joints with a Portland cement and sand mortar and the replacement of damaged brick. These measures were largely unsuccessful because the Portland cement mortar not only did not match the appearance of the original paste but was incompatible physically as well. As movement of the wall continued, the deterioration of the partially repointed arches accelerated. The replacement brick did not match the appearance of the original brick; furthermore, they were set in Portland cement mortar.

ANALYSIS OF PROBLEM

In 1990, the architects examined the jack arches to determine their exact condition and to identify effective methods for their stabilization. Previously, it had been recommended that the jack arches be dismantled and rebuilt in place. Another proposal was for the arches somehow to be stabilized from their back by the removal of interior plaster. The examination indicated that the jack arches did not need to be dismantled. Generally, they could be repointed *in situ*. In several locations, mismatched replacement brick needed to be removed. Also, where severe brick displacement and replacement has occurred, portions of the arches needed to be rebuilt.

Although it previously was thought that four to six of the jack arches required urgent repairs, the examination indicated that fourteen arches needed immediate attention. Funding from the Getty Grant Program was used to undertake the stabilization of the most deteriorated arches, to determine the effectiveness of the proposed treatments and to ascertain the time and level of effort required.

September 26, 1990, a construction contract was awarded to Tidewater Restoration, Inc. of Dunnsville, Virginia, for this initial work. The work on the first arches was subject to detailed study and analysis which was utilized in guiding the stabilization and repair of the remaining arches.

STABILIZATION TECHNIQUES

The initial approach to the stabilization of the jack arches was the following:

1. The arches were temporarily supported with shoring so that work could be more safely and effectively executed. Run-off tarps were installed to protect the window glass and work in progress.
2. Old mortar was removed from the top and end vertical joints only. Broken bricks were removed for repair with epoxy when possible. If the existing brick was beyond repair or incompatible, an appropriate replacement was installed (Figure 36.2).
3. A masking barrier was formed with duct tape to protect the adjoining brick surfaces. Expanded polystyrene backer beads were wedged into joints and a lime/Portland cement paste was injected into the cracks and allowed to set (Figure 36.3).
4. Any paint located on the surface of the brick was removed with a paint stripper previously tested on site.
5. The arch face was cleaned with a restoration cleaner also previously tested on site.
6. Incised (nonstructural) horizontal joints were pointed with lime/Portland cement paste (Figure 36.4).
7. Supports were removed from arches.
8. Damaged brick was repaired with colored mortar where necessary.
9. Final cleaning.

Figure 36.2 Jack arch during restoration. Arch has been supported with wood and shoring and cement mortar has been raked out of joints.

Figure 36.3 Jack arch repointed with lime paste mortar, which was injected into joints.

After using this procedure and sequence initially, the conservation team discovered the following order of approach to be more satisfactory:

1. Support arch, mount run-off tarps.
2. Remove mortar top and end vertical joints only.
3. Wedge with expanded polystyrene backer bead into joints, masking barrier duct tape outer edges.
4. Paint removed with stripper.
5. Arch face cleaned with chemical cleaner.
6. Remaining vertical joint pointing.
7. Broken bricks removed and repaired with epoxies. Missing brick pieces were fabricated and installed.
8. Lime/Portland cement paste injected into joints. Replacement brick fabricated and installed where required.
9. Damaged brick patched with colored mortar where necessary.
10. Incise horizontal joints repointed.
11. Minor final cleaning.
12. All masking and supports removed.

Figure 36.4 Restored jack arch. Note incised horizontal joints.

Based on the results of the stabilization of the initial arch, the construction contract was amended on October 23, 1990, to provide for the complete stabilization of the fourteen most deteriorated jack arches. A second jack arch stabilization contract was awarded for the remaining twenty-seven arches in June, 1991. Work on this contract was completed in November, 1991.

BRICK CLEANING

As part of the initial jack arch contract, tests were carried out on October 24, 1990, on the north elevation of the building using the following masonry cleaning agents and concentrations. The weather was dry and the ambient temperature was ca. 70° F during the tests.

1. Hydroclean restoration cleaner at 1:10 concentration.
2. Sure Kleen Restoration Cleaner at 1:10 concentration.
3. Hydroclean restoration cleaner at 1:50 concentration.
4. Sure Kleen Restoration Cleaner at 1:50 concentration.

Previously, on October 22, 1990, dilutions of 1:20 of the same cleaning agents were used. All of the tests were carried out using a fifteen minute dwell time with a water wash at 500 psi pressure and a 40° nozzle. The pump used was a Norblast Power Washer, which used a Honda motor with a maximum pressure capacity of 3000 psi. The tests were administered by Fred Ecker, Greg Cowan, and E.J. Benedict of Tidewater Restorations, Inc. and observed by Nancy Davis and Lonnie Hovey of The Octagon staff, Norman Koonce of the American Architecture Foundation, and architects John G. Waite and Michael Curcio.

Based on observations during and subsequent to testing, it was found that the most effective and most dilute method for cleaning the masonry was either Sure Kleen Restoration Cleaner at a dilution of 1:20 or Hydroclean restoration cleaner at a dilution of 1:20. All of the jack arches were cleaned using the Sure Kleen Restoration Cleaner as part of the jack arch restoration contracts.

In July, 1991, a contract was awarded to RAMCO Technology, Inc., of Hartford, Connecticut, for the cleaning of the exterior walls of The Octagon. Hydroclean restoration cleaner at a dilution of 1:20 was used to clean the brickwork. The objective of the cleaning was to remove only the residue of surface pollutants from the brick surfaces and not to "overclean" the brick. Work on this contract was completed in October, 1991.

REPOINTING OF BRICKWORK

The exterior brick walls were generally in good condition. All of the walls exhibited evidence of having been repointed in at least half a dozen separate campaigns since the initial construction of the building. The only original pointing that had survived was at the top of the front wall, concealed by the wood cornice and fascia. The original tooling of the mortar was a convex "vee" joint. Samples of the original mortar were analyzed by Frank G. Matero, Architectural Conservator, in November, 1990. It was found that the original mortar consisted of lime and white sand and was quite bright in appearance. None of the recent mortar matched the original in color, texture, or tooling; much of it contained gray Portland cement, which is also much harder, denser, and more rigid than the original mortar. Because it is not as plastic, the cement mortar is harder than the brick, resulting in fracturing of the brick when settlement occurs. Since the cement mortar is harder and more impervious than the original pointing, moisture in the form of vapor that passes through the wall is forced to exit through the brick themselves, rather than the mortar joints. This results in the precipitation of dissolved salts within the face of the bricks, rather than in the mortar joints. Eventually this results in the spalling of the brick surfaces.

A related problem was the weathering away of both the arrises of the bricks and the pointing mortar, leaving open joints between the bricks. The joints had either remained open or had been repointed with gray Portland cement. Some of the repointing had been done sloppily and Portland cement had been smeared on the faces of the brick. In some cases, the arrises of the brick had been damaged by the past repointing, making the joints appear to be wider than they actually were.

A series of tests were undertaken to determine the most effective, and least damaging, method of removing the Portland cement mortar from the joints. The methods tested included hard chisels, penumatic chisels, and small electrical, hand-held masonry saws. It was apparent that the most appropriate method was clearly hand-held pneumatic chisels developed for the stone carving industry. Tools manufacturered by the Trow & Holden Co. of Barre, Vermont, with chisel points custom made for The Octagon's joints, were utilized by Tidewater Restoration, Inc. for the work.

Once the cement mortar was removed, all joints were repointed using a lime-rich mortar formulated to match the chemical and physical properties of the original mortar. The formula used for this new pointing mortar was 1 part white Portland cement, 1.5 parts hydrated high calcium lime, and 7 parts sand. A riverbank in Maryland yielded sand which closely matched the sand used in the original mortar. Before repointing, the old mortar joints were raked out to a depth of 3/4 to 1 inch. The new mortar was applied in three lifts, each of which was tooled. The joints were finished off with a convex vee joint that duplicated the tooling of the original mortar sample (Figure 36.5). The repointing work begun in July, 1991, was completed in December, 1992.

CHIMNEYS

While the walls were being repointed, the four chimneys were restored to their original configurations and heights. The two front chimneys had been rebuilt during previous restoration efforts with a mixture of old and new bricks laid in Portland cement mortar. These chimneys were dismantled to original brickwork at the roofline. They were then rebuilt using modern reproduction brick laid up in lime-rich mortar. The new bricks

Figure 36.5 Detail of corner showing restored brickwork at left which are original brick of main elevation, made by a professional brickmaker, while the brick on the right from the side and rear walls, which are also original, were burned on the site by Tayloe's slaves. Consequently, they are not as hard or regular as front elevation brick.

were manufactured by Old Carolina Brick Co. of Salisbury, North Carolina. They are identical in size, color, and texture to the original chimney bricks.

The two rear chimneys were largely original; they had not been removed or rebuilt during the twentieth century restorations. However, the tops of the chimneys needed to be rebuilt with reproduction brick to extend them to their original height.

Although the masonry work was a significant part of the restoration masonry work, there were other major components as well. These included the repair of the original windows, restoration of the wood cornice, replacement of the 1970 roof with old-growth cypress shingles which matched the original ca. 1815 shingles, and reproduction of the original ca. 1815 wood balustrade and Philadelphia gutter. After these elements were completed, in January, 1993, the exterior of The Octagon once again appeared as it did prior to the death of John Tayloe III in 1828.

INTERIOR FRAMING

During the 1950s, the original wood floor framing for the second floor was removed and a new concrete and steel floor structure was installed under the direction of architect Milton Grigg, who had done similar work at Monticello, the home of Thomas Jefferson. During the 1968–1970 renovation, The Octagon's original third floor wood framing was partially replaced with steel beams (Figure 36.6). As a result of the monitoring program begun in 1990 and subsequent structural investigations, it was found that much of the exterior wall cracking was caused by the 1950s concrete and steel wall construction acting as a diaphram that was too rigid for the rest of the building,

Figure 36.6 Steel and concrete floor structure added in 1950s. This structure loaded the exterior-bearing walls uniformly, replacing the point-loading pattern of the original wood framing.

especially the walls made up of handmade brick and soft lime mortar. The original wood framing consisted of joists that rested on heavy girts, which in turn were framed into the brick-bearing walls. This point-loading pattern of the floor framing into the exterior walls, which had existed for a century and a half, was replaced by the continuous concrete and steel floor membrane.

A photograph of the drawing room in the 1950s showed the extent of the work that occurred. It was possible to stand on the first floor and see all the way to the underside of the third floor structure. One reason this occurred was that the engineers at the time believed that the framing did not meet current design standards. Subsequent testing by the Forest Products Laboratory of the U.S. Department of Agriculture in Madison, WI, revealed that the properties of the old wood far exceeded the design properties of new wood of the same species. Specifically, the Forest Products Laboratory reported that "the timbers have ample strength for continued service for many years," and that in fact, "the material was so far superior to the kinds of woods that were being addressed in the 1950s tables it would be invalid to use those tables." Unfortunately, by the time this was ascertained, the original framing had been removed from the building.

As part of the recent restoration effort, all of the 1950s concrete and steel floor structural elements were removed. Using historic photographs and measured drawings, working drawings for a new timber framing system based on the original framing were prepared. The new framing members, which were installed in 1994, are of newly harvested Southern yellow pine, the same species as the original wood (Figure 36.7).

Figure 36.7 New wood framing that replicates original construction, including loading patterns on bearing walls.

Since the original loading pattern was reinstated and the brick-bearing walls repaired and repointed, the building returned to a structurally stable condition and with no further structural cracking evident in the walls. The restoration of the interior-bearing walls also included filling in large holes cut for the 1968–1970 HVAC system.

Once the exterior walls were stabilized and the wood framing reinstalled, the complete restoration of the building was able to progress. The interior work, including the restoration of all the original spaces, consisted of the replication of historic finishes were missing. New electrical, plumbing, and HVAC systems were installed throughout the building. In 1995, the restored building was reopened as a historic house museum (Figure 36.8).

Photo credits: John G. Waite Associates, Architects.

Figure 36.8 The Octagon House after restoration.

37

Diagnosis of Salt Damage at a Smokehouse in Colonial Williamsburg

R.A. LIVINGSTON[1] and T.H. TAYLOR, JR.[2]

[1]Office of Highway Engineering, R&D, HNR-2, Federal Highway Administration, 6300 Georgetown Pike, McLean VA 22101, U.S.A.
[2]Architectural Conservation Office, Colonial Williamsburg Foundation, Williamsburg, VA 23187–1776, U.S.A.

ABSTRACT

The diagnosis of a historic brick smokehouse in Colonial Williamsburg attacked by soluble salts has been carried out using a multidisciplinary approach that included nondestructive testing, materials science, and architectural history research. The nondestructive measurement of the distribution of sodium chloride and moisture in the brick was done with the neutron probe. The results were confirmed using cores drilled from the brick. Contrary to initial assumptions, the source of the salt was not rising damp but rather brine solution used in curing meat.

INTRODUCTION

To perform a complete diagnosis of deterioration of an historic structure requires a combination of architectural research, nondestructive testing, and materials science. The case of a small brick building suffering from severe salt deterioration is presented here as an example of this multidisciplinary approach.

The subject of this study is a smokehouse on the grounds of the Benjamin Powell House at Colonial Williamsburg, which was built around 1800. As described below, the structure has been significantly modified at various times in its history. In its present form, it is a simple, bare brick structure, square in plan, approximately 14 feet on a side, with a pyramidal wooden roof. The north elevation of the smokehouse is shown in Figure 37.1. The west wall is broken by a door, but otherwise the remaining three sides have the same appearance as that shown in Figure 37.1. The building was constructed with two different types of brick coursing. On the inside, an American bond (three

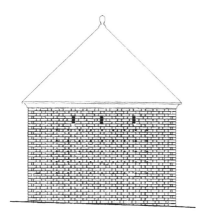

Figure 37.1 North elevation of the smokehouse, including neutron probe measurement grid.

rows of stretchers to one row of headers) was used. On the outside, Flemish bond (each course consisting of alternating headers and stretchers) was used. This mode of construction results in a complete separation of the interior from the exterior wythes, so that there must be a continuous vertical plane of mortar, or collar joint, running up the center of each wall.

Until 1981 the smokehouse was kept in use to demonstrate the process of curing and smoking meats. However, by 1981 it was evident that heavy deterioration of the brick and the mortar was occurring on all four sides of the structure, requiring repeated repointing and even replacement of brick. Preliminary investigations suggested that the damage was being caused by the action of soluble salts. The building was taken out of use and became the focus of intensive study by the Colonial Williamsburg Foundation's architectural conservator (Taylor 1983).

INITIAL MOISTURE MONITORING PROGRAM

The first monitoring program focused on determining the movement of moisture in and out of the walls. The temperature and humidity of the interior were monitored using a thermohygrograph. In addition, a square grid of points was laid out on the walls. At the grid points, moisture measurements were made periodically using an electrical resistivity-type moisture meter (Protimeter).

The Protimeter proved, however, to be unsatisfactory for this application. Replicate measurements showed poor repeatability, probably because electrical resistivity-type moisture meters were originally designed for use on wood, where the water content is on the order of 20%, and thus provides a continuous electrical pathway for the current. In contrast, brick have much lower moisture contents, on the order of 1% to 5%, which makes for much less reliable continuity. The presence of high concentrations of salt also affected the moisture measurements adversely, since it altered the conductivity of the solution.

NEUTRON PROBE INVESTIGATIONS

In view of the problems with the electrical resistivity method, it was then decided to try a nondestructive method of moisture measurement known as the neutron probe. This technique has the advantage of measuring moisture content directly, rather than by an indirect measurement used by the Protimeter. Simultaneously, the neutron probe

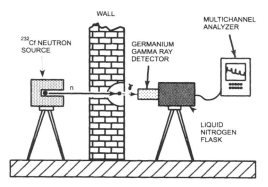

Figure 37.2 Schematic diagram of the neutron probe.

provides direct measurement of chlorides and several other constituents of the material. Finally, the neutron probe measures to a depth of 10–20 cm into the material, whereas the Protimeter is limited to surface measurements on masonry materials.

The neutron probe is a field application of the prompt gamma neutron activation method of elemental analysis (Evans et al. 1986). It consists of a small portable neutron source, either a radioisotope such as ^{252}Cf or a linear accelerator, a Ge(HP) gamma ray detector, and associated electronics. In operation, the neutron source is placed next to the target material under investigation. As shown in the schematic diagram in Figure 37.2, the neutrons penetrate the target and interact with nuclei of its constituent elements. These interactions can be either inelastic scattering of high-energy neutrons or capture of neutrons of thermal energy. In either case, the result is the production of gamma rays of specific energies characteristic of the target elements. These gamma rays are then detected, and the results are displayed as a gamma ray spectrum (Figure 37.3) in which peaks associated with a number of elements can be

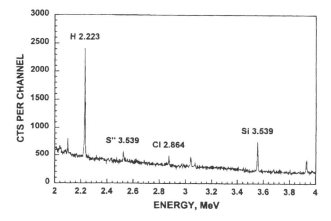

Figure 37.3 Portion of a typical gamma ray spectrum from Colonial Williamsburg brick wall.

identified. Interpretation of this data together with other knowledge about building materials can provide valuable insights into the condition of the structure.

It should be stressed that the neutron probe is not the same as the more familiar neutron activation analysis. In the latter, samples of the target material must be brought to a nuclear reactor and irradiated for some period of time in a very tightly controlled thermal neutron beam. After irradiation, gamma rays from radioactive decay of activated elements are measured over intervals of time ranging from hours to months. In addition to the lengthy counting period required, neutron activation analysis is also restricted to a relatively small set of minor or trace elements.

Although it is, among other things, a nuclear moisture measurement method, the neutron probe is also different from the well-known neutron moisture meter that is commercially available from such manufacturers as Troxler Electronic Laboratories. This method operates on the principle of neutron thermalization. An example of the application of the neutron thermalization method to brick masonry is given by Visser and Gervais (Chapter 32). This measures the change in the energy distribution of the neutron spectrum produced by scattering from hydrogen and other elements in the material. It is thus an indirect measurement of hydrogen content that must be calibrated for each application (ASTM 1978). Moreover, it is limited to relatively thin layers of material. In contrast, the neutron probe measures hydrogen directly. Moreover, if desired, its data can be processed to provide the neutron thermalization factor.

Two measurement campaigns were made with the neutron probe on the smokehouse, both with equipment and personnel loaned by NASA's Goddard Space Flight Center in Beltsville, Maryland. The first campaign took place in 1982 and was intended primarily to test the feasibility of applying the neutron probe to the assessment of building condition. In this campaign, a set of twelve points in a three-foot-by-four-foot grid was measured on the north wall. These measurements were doubled; that is, the grid of points was first measured with the neutron source on the outside of the building and the detector on the inside. Then the positions of the detector and source were reversed and measurements repeated over the grid. The results were encouraging. Both salt and hydrogen could easily be detected, along with a number of the major elements of the brick and mortar. Also, what appeared to be a void was detected in the wall (Evans et al. 1986). These results were later confirmed by drilling cores, as described below.

Based on the results from the first campaign, a more extensive effort was planned. This was carried out in 1987, using a more compact electronics system. A total of forty-five points were measured on the north wall in a rectangular grid on one-foot centers (Figure 37.1). This provided a sufficient amount of data to allow the application of geostatistical techniques and thus permitted the development of maps of elements within the wall.

NEUTRON PROBE RESULTS

The neutron probe is a point-by-point measurement technique. Each measured point actually represents a volume of about 10,000 cm^3 of the target material. However, with spatial contouring software, it is possible to interpolate values between the measurement points to provide contour maps of individual elements in the wall.

Figure 37.4 presents such a contour map based on the intensity of the chlorine gamma ray signal. For this map, the data have been converted into concentrations of sodium chloride using a calibration procedure based on laboratory experiments on a simulated brick wall containing known amounts of salt (Livingston 1992). The shading represents the weight percent of sodium chloride with the highest concentration shown as black and the lowest as white. The values of each contour are given in the key. From the map, it appears that the salt is localized in the upper lefthand (northeast) region of the wall. The salt content decreases sharply toward the ground level.

The contour map for water content, based on the hydrogen gamma ray signal, is presented in Figure 37.5. It shows a range of values from less than 2% to 11%, which is consistent with moisture contents typically found in a masonry wall. In contrast to the salt contour map, the water content is greatest at the ground level and declines with height, reaching background levels at roughly the four-foot level. Moreover, the contours are nearly horizontal. This pattern of water distribution is typical of rising damp.

CORES

To confirm the results from the neutron probe investigation, it was decided to remove some cores from the wall of the smokehouse by drilling. This was done using an

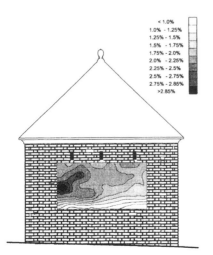

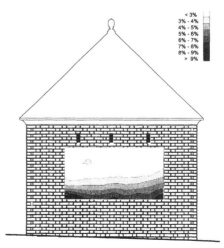

Figure 37.4   Contour map of chloride distribution.

Figure 37.5   Contour map of hydrogen distribution.

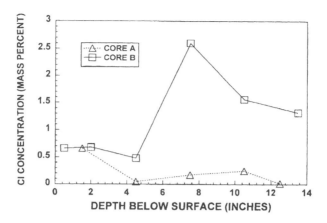

Figure 37.6 Chloride distributions in two cores from the north wall of the smokehouse, analyzed by X-ray fluorescence.

air-cooled, diamond-tipped bit, with a one-inch diameter. Two pairs of cores were taken, one from the inside of the wall and the other from the outside, at two points. One point, A, was chosen for its low Cl signal and the other, B, was selected because it has the highest Cl signal. This study is described in detail elsewhere (Livingston 1985).

The data from the cores is presented in Figure 37.6. As expected, the Cl content of core A was relatively low. The peak of the concentration was located near the surface. On the other hand, for core B, the concentration of Cl peaked at a greater depth into the wall. The overall concentration was also much higher, consistent with the neutron readings.

IMPLICATIONS OF SALT CONTENT FOR BRICK DETERIORATION

To put the contour map of salt distribution in Figure 37.4 in perspective, it is necessary to relate the salt content to risk of damage to the brick. There is very little quantitative information on this subject. The most relevant study was carried out by Larsen and Neilsen (1990) on historic brick structures in Denmark. They found that the brick remained apparently undamaged at salt contents below roughly 1.5%. In Figure 37.7, this contour has been plotted. In addition, the area of the wall that appears by visual inspection to be less damaged has been marked in heavy line. It is interesting that 1.5% contour coincides with the boundary between damaged and undamaged brick. However, as discussed below, the upper region where the damaged brick is found also seems to be of more recent construction.

The total amount of salt contained in this region of the wall can also be calculated from the contour map. It is estimated to be 44 kilograms (97 pounds) of salt. However, given the uncertainties involved in deriving the calibration factor, this value should be

Figure 37.7 Results of visual inspection of the north wall. Realtively good quality brick is indicated by heavy outline. For comparison, the contour for 1.5% Cl content is also presented

regarded as approximate within an error band of $\pm$ 10 kg (22 pounds). This gives a range of 75–120 pounds of salt. From this, the amount of effort required to desalinate the entire wall can be estimated.

VISUAL INSPECTION

The results of the neutron probe mapping the core analyses seemed to suggest that there was a difference in the construction of the wall between upper and lower parts. This led to a closer visual inspection of the walls themselves, and several interesting features were noticed.

Generally below the line indicated in Figure 37.7, the walls seem to be in much better condition. A thin translucent surface layer was noticed on these parts of the walls. Both the brick and the mortar joints seemed to be more uniform in workmanship than in the upper part. The mortar on the lower section appeared to be of a different composition, although this observation may have been complicated by the fact that the mortar joints on the upper section had been repointed in the last five years.

HISTORICAL DOCUMENTATION

The exact date of construction for the smokehouse and its companion structure, the dairy, is not known. If they had been constructed prior to 1782, they would have appeared on the Frenchman's Map, a plan of the town that depicted most of the structures including many outbuildings. Neither of the structures is shown on the map which is dated March 11, 1782. The owner of the property in 1782 was Benjamin Powell, a well-known carpenter and builder. Although unlikely, it is possible that he could have built the smokehouse and dairy sometime between the time the town was surveyed and June 17, 1782, when he sold the lot to Zachriah Rowland for 340 pounds. Rowland did

Figure 37.8   Historical photograph, date unknown, showing smokehouse with gable roof and stucco covering.

not live on the property and probably did not have time to build the structures, because he sold the property several months later to Patrick Robertson. Robertson may have been in possession of the property as early as July, 1783. Robertson, a resident of Portsmouth, was not closely associated with the property, and he, too, put the house up for sale shortly after he acquired it. However, he was not able to sell it until October, 1791, when he conveyed it to Benjamin Carter Waller. Waller bought the property for 150 pounds, less than half the price that Rowland paid for it in 1782. The decline in value suggests that Robertson did little to improve the property during the time he owned it. Benjamin Carter Waller died in 1820, leaving the property to one of his sons, Dr. Robert Page Waller. It is likely that both the smokehouse and the dairy were built after Waller acquired the property in 1791.

The best clue for dating the smokehouse is an updated pre-restoration photograph showing the structure with a gable roof and with exterior walls stuccoed and scored to look like stone (Figure 37.8). This Greek Revival style suggests that the building was modified during the 1830s or 1840s. It appears that the stucco was applied to conceal the deteriorated brick and/or the visual differences between the upper and lower portions of the wall. The stucco was probably applied when the gable roof was constructed. The original roof may have collapsed from neglect or burned in a fire.

When the Colonial Williamsburg Foundation restored the smokehouse in 1955–1956, the gable roof and the brick gable ends were removed. An interior photograph dated May 24, 1955, shows that the interior surfaces of the brick walls were already severely deteriorated. At that time a new door, door sill, and door frame were installed. In addition, severely deteriorated or missing bricks around the door, vents, and roof eaves were replaced with new bricks.

DIAGNOSIS

There are several different hypotheses for the origin of the salt in the walls. One is that the salt was deposited by rising damp. Another is that it was introduced during construction. A third is that it was deposited from brine used during the meat-curing process while the building was used as a smokehouse.

Based on the evidence acquired thus far, the first hypothesis, rising damp, seems to be ruled out on the basis of water and salt distributions. If the salt were deposited by rising groundwater, it would have been concentrated at the level where the water reaches its maximum height. However, in this case, the salt is found considerably above the water level as can be seen by comparing Figures 37.4 and 37.5. The horizontal distribution of salt is also inconsistent with that of rising damp. Along the wall at a given height, the concentration of the salt would be expected to be fairly constant if rising damp were the source. In this case, however, the salt is unevenly distributed horizontally. It is concentrated in the lefthand (northeast) upper quadrant of the wall. Finally, the depth profile is also abnormal for salt deposition by rising damp. In this process, evaporation of the groundwater leaves the salt concentrated at the surface. At the Powell smokehouse, the maximum salt concentration occurs near the center of the wall, with the greatest concentration occurring above the level of maximum ground water rise.

Thus the conclusion is that the salt was originally deposited in the interior of the wall. Subsequently, it has been diffusing outward and downward as a result of rainwater leaching. In fact, it almost appears as if the groundwater is leaching away the salt at lower levels. However, this could be due to lower permeability in the lower section of wall resulting from construction differences.

This leaves the other two hypotheses, which are more difficult to prove or disprove. Various pieces of evidence, discussed above, suggest that the upper sections of the walls were rebuilt sometime in the mid-nineteenth century. During this reconstruction, salt-contaminated materials may have been introduced. The sand used in the mortar may have contained salt if it came from beaches on the Chesapeake Bay. Another possibility is that salt may have been deliberately applied during construction to de-ice the brick or to slow down the setting of the mortar. One difficulty with this theory is that the salt is concentrated in one region.

The third hypothesis, the infiltration of salt from the curing process, would fit this highly localized pattern if the salt were introduced into the wall in solid form rather than in a brine solution. This situation could occur if a block of salt somehow fell into a crack in the wall, possibly at the leftmost vent.

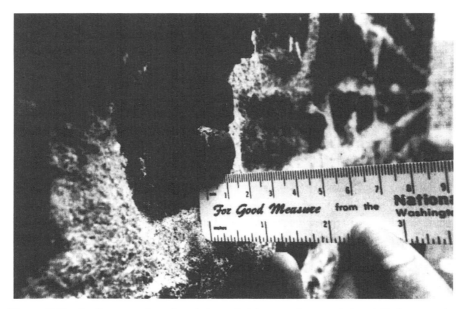

Figure 37.9   Surface recession of smokehouse brick over a five-year interval. Reference point is the original surface of an epoxy plug inserted in duell hole for core (see Figure 37.6).

PROGNOSIS

The diagnosis indicates the present condition of the structure and the possible causes of damage. However, in order to make decisions about the treatment of the smokehouse, it is necessary to make some estimates about the rate of deterioration in the future. The magnitude of the problem can be seen from the fact that the mortar joints must be repointed approximately every eighteen months. Another indicator of the rate of damage was provided as a result of the core drilling. After the cores were taken, the holes were patched using a mixture of ground-up brick in polyvinyl acetate. This plug proved to be much more durable than the brick. As shown in Figure 37.9, the surface individual brick had receded over one centimeter in the last four years. At these rates, the building could become structurally unsound in another five years.

TREATMENT ALTERNATIVES

A.   The first preservation option is to continue to replace the brick and mortar that has seriously or completely eroded away. However, the prognosis is that at the current rate of deterioration, most, if not all, of the surface areas will have to be replaced within five to seven years. In addition, considerable amounts of salt will remain in the interior portions of the walls. In time, the salts will leach out and destroy the new brick. It is conceivable that this process could go through several cycles resulting in considerable expense and, in the end, little, if any, of the original structure will be visible.

B. The second option is to prevent moisture from entering the brick walls. A damp-proof course consisting of overlapping sheets of lead, pieces of slate, or some other permanent impervious membrane would be inserted into the wall. A cut is made through the wall at the base of the structure to permit the course to be inserted. A damp-proof barrier may also be obtained by injecting chemical solutions usually containing silicone or aluminum stearate into the wall. Finally, the amount of water entering the building from the ground can be reduced through the installation of a foundation drain (Smith 1984).

All of the methods described above are designed to stop or reduce the migration of water from the ground into the walls. However, the diagnosis is that rising damp does not appear to be the principal source of the salts. In fact, as has been mentioned, rising damp may have even helped remove salts from the lower portions of the wall. In addition, most of these alternatives introduced visual intrusions onto the buildings.

C. Since the salts are the destructive element in the deterioration process, desalination of the brick walls is a third alternative. The traditional method of accomplishing this consists of the application and reapplication of clay poultices to the brick surfaces until the salt is removed. Poultices will work as long as there is moisture present in the brick. As each poultice is removed, the Cl content of the poultice should be monitored to determine how much salt is being removed from the wall.

D. A fourth alternative is to apply a sacrificial coating of stucco to the walls of the structure. This was done in the nineteenth century to both the smokehouse and the dairy. Instead of removing the salt, the location of the salt action would be shifted from the brick surface to the stucco surface. The drawback to this alternative is that the stucco must become a permanent coating. As soon as it is removed, the brick will continue to deteriorate.

E. The last and least desirable alternative is to demolish at least the upper parts of the structure and reconstruct them.

FUTURE RESEARCH

There are a number of additional research tasks that ought to be carried out in order to learn more about the condition of the structure and ways to treat it. The neutron probe data could be analyzed for elements such as aluminum, iron, titanium, boron, and samarium that are characteristic of the bricks. These data may be helpful in determining whether the upper and lower sections of the wall were built using different batches of materials.

Trial patches of poulticing should be carried out to provide estimates of the rate of removal of salt. Monitoring the salt content of the poultice as a function of time would give an idea of the most efficient time interval to leave the poultice in place. With this information and the knowledge of the total mass of salt in the wall, it would then be possible to estimate how long it would take to desalinate the building.

The migration pathways of rainwater through the walls need to be better understood. Preliminary observations indicate that the rain seeps from the roof tiles directly into the walls. Therefore, monitoring the water content of the wood during rain would be worthwhile. In this material, it would be appropriate to use the electrical resistivity method.

More research into the structural condition of the wall would also be justified. As a first step, the internal structure of the walls should be confirmed. This may require removal of several bricks in order to expose the interior wythes. A borescope inspection may also be possible.

Monitoring of the structural condition could also include applying strain gauges to record the differential expansion and contraction between the inner and outer sides of the wall. The rate of cracking can be evaluated with photogrammetry or by direct monitoring with linear voltage differential transformers (LVDT) or other such methods. Finally, cracking could also be monitored using the more advanced method of acoustic emissions, which makes it possible to locate regions of active microcracking within the walls.

REFERENCES

ASTM. 1978. Standard Test Method for Moisture Content of Soil and Soil-Aggregatre in Place by Nuclear Methods (Shallow Depth). ASTM Sandrad D-3017-78. Philadelphia: American Society for Testing of Materials.

Bowley, M.J. 1975. Desalination of stone: A case study. *Arch. J.* **162(29)**:149–152.

Evans, L.G., J.L. Trombka, R.A. Livingston, and T.H. Taylor. 1986. Neutron-gamma-ray techniques for investigating the deterioration of historic buildings. *Nuclear Instr. Meth. Physics Res.* **A242**:346–351.

Larsen, G.S., and C.B. Nielsen. 1990. Decay of bricks due to salt. *Material and Structures* **23**:16–25.

Livingston, R.A. 1985. X-ray analysis of brick cores from the Powell-Waller Smokehouse, colonial Eilliamsburg. In: Proc. 3rd N. American Masonry Conf., ed. J. Matthys and J. Borchelt, pp. 61–64. Resont, VA: The Masonry Society.

Livingston, R.A. 1992. Standardization of the neutron probe for the assessment of masonry deterioration. *J. Appl. Radiation Isotopes* **4(10/11)**:1285–1300.

Smith, B.M. 1984. Moisture Problems in Historic Masonry Wall: Diagnosis and Treatment, pp. 5–10, 37–44. Washington, D.C.: Natl. Park Service.

Taylor, T.H., Jr. 1983. Conservation of original brickwork at colonial Williamsburg. In: Proc. Intl. Colloq. on Materials and Restoration, pp. 385–390. Esslingen: Technical Academy of Esslingen.

38

Uppark: A Study in Fire
Damage to Brickwork

I.A. MCLAREN

The Conservation Practice, Knockhundred Row, Midhurst GU29 9DQ, U.K.

ABSTRACT

Uppark, a National Trust property, was severely damaged in a fire on August 30, 1989. The National Trust determined that the house should be rebuilt, incorporating as much of the salvaged material as was practicable. Protection of the structure during examination and restoration, description of damage to the interior and structure, and key restoration decisions are described and illustrated.

INTRODUCTION

Uppark was built in about 1690, high on the crest of the South Downs, facing the English Channel about 20 km distant to the south. It was then a four-story brick building, with a basement partially buried into the ground and an attic story contained within the roof space (Figure 38.1).

It changed hands in 1747 at which time various internal alterations were made and single-story extensions to the north were built. Further extensions were added to the north front in 1810 to form a new entrance.

The house was given to The National Trust in 1954. Since then the principal rooms on the ground and basement floors have been open to the public, while the upper two floors remained in residential use. The house is important principally for its 18th century interiors and furnishings.

The structure of the building consists of substantial brick walls supporting timber-framed suspended floors, and a timber-framed roof structure covered on the external faces with Cornish slate, and on the inner hidden slopes with plain clay tile. The internal load-bearing walls are built of a mixture of brick and clunch, or chalk, probably quarried locally.

The main four-story structure is approximately 30 m square and 13 m high, from basement floor to eaves. The external walls are approximately 915 mm thick at

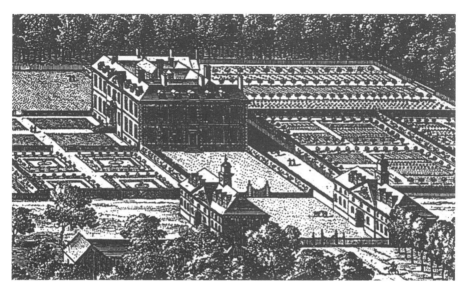

Figure 38.1   Uppark: 1715 engraving by Kip.

basement level and taper to 675 mm thick at eaves level. All masonry walls are built in lime mortar.

THE FIRE

On August 30, 1989, just after 3:30 p.m., a small fire broke out at roof level on the south front where workmen were carrying out roofing repairs. Despite efforts to extinguish the blaze, it soon took hold. The house was evacuated and nearly all of the movable items from the ground floor and basement showrooms were taken out. Eventually the fire consumed and destroyed most of the attic and first floor, and severely damaged the ground floor rooms. The basement, although relatively untouched by the fire, suffered major damage from water and falling masonry. The fire was not finally extinguished until the following day (Figure 38.2).

REBUILDING

Following an assessment of the remains, a decision was taken by The National Trust that the house should be rebuilt, incorporating as much of the salvaged material as would be practicable. Although at first sight the damage to the important ground floor showrooms seemed to be terminally severe, in fact there was a remarkably high survival rate of some important architectural features.

In the Red Drawing Room, for example, about half of the elaborately carved woodwork survived, and substantial quantities of wool flock wall hangings were rescued during the fire.

Figure 38.2   Aerial view of Uppark, August 31, 1989, the day following the fire.

STRUCTURAL DAMAGE

The brickwork structure suffered less damage than had first been thought. Structural failure was worst on the north elevation, where the fire had been at its fiercest, burning through the main staircase acting as a chimney. The timber lintel over the staircase window collapsed, bringing with it the masonry wall above (Figure 38.3).

Of eight main chimney stacks, only one collapsed during the fire, the remainder staying in place despite the loss of surrounding structural support (Figure 38.4). Even the Pediment, on the south elevation, remained intact, despite the fact that the roof behind, which would have previously provided lateral stability, was totally destroyed.

The conclusions to be drawn at that stage were that the ancient masonry had withstood high temperatures and the disruptive forces of collapsing timber floor extremely well.

PROTECTION

The immediate task was to stabilize the structure to make it safe and to cover the whole building with a temporary roof to protect the interior from the weather (Figure 38.5a). At the same time, the task of salvaging remnants of interior fixtures began.

Five months after the fire, when the salvage process was under way, the site was struck by storm-force winds which tore off the temporary roof, causing damage not only to the structure, but also allowing rain once more into the building (Figure 38.5b). A second protective cover was then erected, which was completed in August, 1990. The work of inspecting the brick structure in detail could finally begin (Figure 38.5c).

Figure 38.3 The north wall after the fire.

Figure 38.4 A chimney stack survived in place despite the loss of support. It was propped to prevent collapse.

(a)

(b)

(c)

Figure 35.5 (a) The protective covering seen from the north. (b) Collapsed scaffolding after the January, 1990, storm. (c) The second protective envelope.

BRICKWORK

The initial thought that the brickwork had survived the fire well was confirmed by close inspection. Except where walls had been disrupted by collapsing floors and timber lintels, the main walls were virtually intact.

STONEWORK

Although the brickwork showed little sign of damage, stone components within the structure did not fare so well. In many locations, the exposed faces of chalk blocks built into the walls had sheared off, although nowhere causing collapse. However, limestone lintels on the first floor were found, in almost every case, to have shattered into several fragments. It was thought, at the time, to have been caused by thermal stresses resulting from quenching stonework heated by the fire in cold water, although no scientific tests were done. The lintels were replaced in new stone.

BRICKWORK REPAIRS

In the main, brick repairs consisted of patching in or rebuilding small areas of brickwork, usually no more than 1 square meter in area. A decision was made to replace all burnt timber lintels by modern reinforced concrete, in the interests of achieving structural stability. In philosophical terms this has proved to be a controversial point, since some believed that this could and should be replaced in timber (oak) as before.

Mortar

An early decision was made to rebuild in lime mortar, to the original formula used in the building. This would ensure compatibility with the remaining elements of structure, and would thereby provide the same degree of flexibility in the structure as had existed before the fire. Analysis was carried out which established that the existing mortar formula was in accordance with traditional practice, with 1 part of binder (lime) to 3 parts of aggregate. In this instance the aggregate contained a high proportion of chalk. The new mix followed this formula, using HT1 powder (a furnace by-product) as a pozzalanic additive.

Bricks

In general, efforts were made to salvage as many bricks as possible, for both commercial and philosophical reasons. Bricks were made specially to match for work on the north elevation; for all repair work internally a mass produced brick, with approximately the same appearance, density and porosity characteristics as the originals, was selected. All new brickwork on the external elevations has been shaded, with a soot and water mix, to create a cohesive overall appearance.

Figure 38.6   Careful dismantling of brickwork showing individually numbered bricks.

The South East Corner

Major structural rebuilding was required in the south east corner of the building, where the one collapsing chimney falling on the first floor ruptured the external wall structure. The bricks themselves were largely undamaged, and, because of their historic value, as well as the high cost of replacements, they were all taken down and used in the reconstruction. In order to maintain the exact bonding pattern as before, each brick was individually identified prior to the wall being dismantled (Figure 38.6).

Lead Splatter

At the time of the fire, scaffolding was in place around the building. During the fire, lead from the perimeter eaves gutter melted, fell down on to this scaffolding and splashed back on to the brickwork, leaving a silvery gray line over both brick and stone. Consideration was given, at one time, to leaving this in place as a momento of the fire but eventually a decision was made to remove it.

Because there is an embargo on "hot work" on site – no flame-producing tools may be used – efforts were made to find a method of removal not employing heat. These ranged from chipping the particles off by hand, to dissolving them in nitric acid. In the end, however, no effective substitute for heat was found, and the brickwork was cleaned using a flame torch and wire brushes, which proved to be entirely successful. In order to allay fears of fire, the whole operation was very closely controlled, and included technicians standing by with fire extinguishers and elaborate protection arrangements. Work ceased three hours before the end of the working day so that the site could be closely inspected to ensure that no smoldering embers remained.

OTHER REPAIRS

Although the bulk of the brickwork repairs arose as a direct result of the fire, other defects were found during the course of the site inspections. In many locations, old ferrous straps were found to be severely rusted, causing, in the two northern chimneys, for example, major disruption of the brick structure. All such straps were replaced in grade 316 stainless steel.

In rebuilding the timber-suspended floors, the opportunity has been taken to form ventilated pockets to house the main beam bearing, thereby reducing the risk of decay (Figure 38.7).

Photogrammetry

Before repair work started, all the masonry walls were recorded on drawings by means of photogrammetric survey, which produces accurate scale drawings in great detail. These have been used to instruct brickwork repairs, and form a valuable tool in both the management and recording of the project.

This survey has been fed into the office computer graphics system and forms the basis for building up drawings of the finished work (Figure 38.8). An archive of the entire work was created as the work progressed.

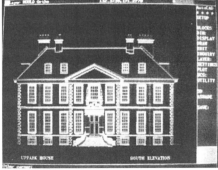

Figure 38.7 Repaired internal masonry with original brickwork and rubble chalk, new brickwork below, including ventilated beam pocket with reinforced concrete lintel over.

Figure 38.8 The south elevation built up from the post-fire photogrammetic survey by computer graphics.

Figure 38.9   The principal elevation facing south, before the fire. It has been rebuilt to match exactly, using salvaged remnants wherever possible.

PROGRAM

Work started on site in August, 1990, and was completed in the summer of 1994, with a further year for furnishing the interiors. By the end of 1991 the completion of the first stage of the work, the repair of the structure and the construction of the roof to form a weathertight enclosure, had been accomplished, making the building ready to receive interior finishes and fittings. Completion of the structural work produced settlement cracking in the masonry walls, due to loads being reimposed. These cracks were repaired as soon as loading was completed. There are no other signs of structural distress, and, it seems likely that the majority of the original brickwork structure will have survived the cataclysmic events of August, 1989.

ITEMS FOR FURTHER STUDY

Because of various pressures at the time of making major decisions for rebuilding Uppark, little was done in the way of scientific testing to back up those decisions. In general, assessments of the condition of elements of the structure were made on the basis of visual examination only.

39

Historic Plasters of Village Churches in Brandenburg

B. ARNOLD

Brandenburgisches Landesamt fhr Denkmalpflege, Brüderstr. 13,
10178 Berlin, Germany

ABSTRACT

A large variety of historic plasters and mortars from the Middle Ages can be found on village churches in Brandenburg. These buildings have been registered by a project group supported by the Deutsche Bundestiftung Umwelt. Investigations into the chemical, mineralogical, and physical properties of several types of plasters have been conducted. No significant differences in the physics of mortars and plasters of the involved regions and ages have been found. The use of gypsum binder is not typical. In many cases, historic plaster turned into gypsum, even though the surface appeared to be "healthy." The process of turning lime into gypsum is a result of air pollution and climate influences. Often a complicated system of tiny cracks can be found underneath the surface layer. These cracks spread primarily parallel to the surface and are filled with gypsum in different concentrations and in several types of crystallization.

INTRODUCTION

Village churches comprise an important part of the cultural heritage in Brandenburg. Churches built during the Middle Ages (12th–14th centuries) show high quality in construction material (Figure 39.1). Fieldstone was used as the main building material. In addition, a large variety of historic plasters and mortars (elevated joints with simple or double grooves, painted joints, friezes, ornaments on windows and doors) were employed. These are endangered not only by unprofessial conservation efforts, but also by air pollution. Research into historic mortars, plaster, and renderings is the subject of an ongoing interdisciplinary project among restorers, art historians, and scientists, and is supported by the Deutsche Bundestiftung Umwelt (German Federal Environmental Foundation).

The first step involved the registration of churches with historic renderings in Brandenburg. This provided an overview of the existence of historic renderings in the region and the current state of damage. Next we selected churches with the most

Figure 39.1   Lugau (county Elbe-Elster) village church from 13th century.

interesting findings, from the point of view of conservators and scientists, and conducted investigations into the mineralogical, chemical, and physical properties of the samples. Results were compared to gain insights into building, civilization, and art history of northeast Germany, and have been compiled into a database.

REGISTRATION AND VALUATION

Registration was necessary to get an overview of the stock of relevant mortars and plasters in medieval churches, of their kinds, volume and conditions, as well as their special types of ornamental decoration and coloring (Figure 39.2).

In Brandenburg, we have around 1400 churches. Nearly half are fieldstone churches while nearly a quarter show joints, friezes, grooves, ornaments, or colors from the Middle Ages.

Now, as ever, these valuable fragments on medieval buildings are threatened by environmental pollution. However, ignorance, improper assessment, and inaccurate conservation efforts are also to blame for important losses.

Until now, research concerning the exteriors of medieval village churches in our region has been limited. One reason may be the supposed humbleness of the objects. Another may be the difficulties in interpreting the findings without the cooperation of scientists, restorers, and art historians.

The current project has led to well-founded answers to essential questions of technology, age, outer influences, and principles of decoration. In addition, it has allowed concise questions to be posed to scientists and probes to be taken effectively in ways acceptable also for conservators.

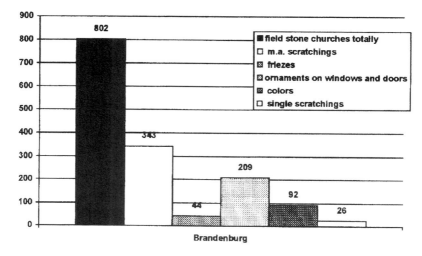

Figure 39.2 Plaster, colors, and ornaments on village churches.

There were also art historical assessments and a systematization of the findings. Traditional art history, with its typological view, was complemented by the observation of aspects such as the treatment of stones, joints, plaster, or coloring. Thus it was possible to create new hypotheses of the medieval organization of building, influences of workshops, clients, economical, and political structures. The usual criteria to determine the age of the buildings have been broadened, and our picture of the original appearance of the medieval village churches has become more precise.

Masonry

Churches built during the 12th–13th centuries have a regulary masonry, which was comprised of squared field stones (Figure 39.3). Later, in 14th–16th centuries, churches were not built as accurately. Split material was primarily used (Figure 39.4).

Mortar – Plaster

At first the masonry was built *in strata*. In the middle of the masonry, smaller, unsplit field stones were used. This masonry was then decorated, from top to bottom, with the double-scratched joint plaster. Thus the mortar must be not identical with the joint plaster and, as evidence shows, it is in fact not in most cases. From case to case, both mortars and plaster show higher and smaller content of binder. Sometimes we were able to find a "sinter skin" between the mortar and plaster. There were no significant differences to be found between the several counties and regions.

 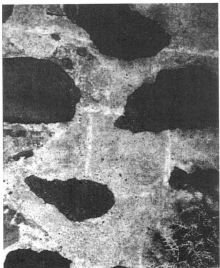

Figure 39.3 Groß Welle (county Prignitz) church, detail, north side.

Figure 39.4 Kleinow (county Prignitz) church, detail, north side.

Plaster or No Plaster

The accurately squared masonry of the older churches was not covered (Figures 39.3 and 39.5). This was only done for the joints and edges of the stones. Also, small areas without square stones (vaulted parts of the window openings, gable triangles on the east side, etc.) were covered with plaster. Later masonry was not as regular; however, the aesthetics of the old churches were obligatory. Thus, the plaster of later buildings (until the 16th century) shows double scratchings in order to imitate regular masonry.

Shape of Joints

Regular square masonry corresponded to "classic" joint-shaping. First, the smoothed joint plaster was double-scratched. Then it was roughened up with the trowel outside of the scratchings. The thusly created smooth plasterband stood in contrast to the rough edges. Later, when the masonry became irregular and the plaster covered the whole stones, the decoration with the plasterband became independent of the real joints and stones. Over time, the net of joint bands became coarser and more roughly scratched.

Coloring

The earler joint bands were evidently colored with lime. Only a few colors were used: white, red, and black (gray). In the Elster-Elbe region, good examples of simple or

 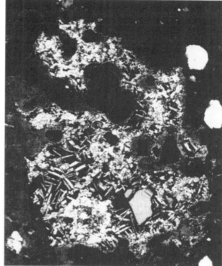

Figure 39.5   Schönwalde (country of Elbe-Elster), village church; 16th century plaster covered behind a vestry.

Figure 39.6   Sarnow (county Prignitz), village church, south, 50×.

double red strokes can be found. There is also evidence of decorations with alternating red-white plaster squares. Special architectural details, such as portals, windows, ledges, etc., were emphasized by decorative scratchings and coloring. Evidence of this technique can also be found in the Uckermark.

SCIENTIFIC INVESTIGATIONS

The goals of our scientific investigations were to (a) compare regional and chronological differences between types of plasters, (b) pinpoint the source of damage, (c) to find technologies for conservation and restoration.

We investigated the chemical composition of the plasters according to the analysis scheme of Knöfel (Knöfel and Schubert 1993). The mineralogical microfabric was determined using light and electron microscopes. Sieve lines and porosities were also determined.

Binder

The binder content of plasters from the Middle Ages lie between 25% and 70%. In the county of Prignitz, mortars have a higher content of lime than in the other regions. The hydraulic part in the mortars is small (1%–4%). Gypsum binder was not in use. We also could not find dolomite mortars or organic components in the motars.

Upon inspection, plasters of the Middle Ages, and sometimes Baroque plasters, show nuggets of lime. This refers to the dry slake of the lime. Microscopical investigations show an average of 4%, with a maximum of nearly 20%.

In mortars with a high content of binder (seen often in the county of Prignitz), we find calcium silicate phases (Figure 39.6). After chemical analysis, this content is estaminated to be the hydraulic part and is responsible for higher strength. However, the mineralogical microfabric shows that the calcium-silicate phases are stained and do not contribute to increased strength. The reasons for this phenomenon are the high content of binder and the strong recrystallization.

Aggregates

Aggregates are without exception unwashed sands. The muddy parts of the sands yield the typical color (ochre) of the mortars. The primary component of the aggregates is quartz (between 50% and 80%). Feldspars comprise between 3% and 10% of all aggregates. The carbonatic parts (limestone and lime sandstone) are most prevalent in the county of Uckermark (between 8% and 17%). In the other counties, it is under 5%.

After chemical analyses of aggregates from gravel pits in several regions in Brandenburg, the gravel and sand content of hydraulic parts was found to be under 1%.

Regional and Chronological Comparison

Whenever possible, samples of medieval and younger (e.g., Baroque) mortars from several regions of Brandenburg were compared. We analyzed mortars and plasters in the Elbe-Elster (southwest of Brandenburg), Uckermark (northeast), and Prignitz (northwest). In all cases, the plasters and mortars consisted of lime with small hydraulic parts. The use of a gypsum binder was not typical. The mixing proportion between binder and aggregates is very high. No significant differences in the chemical analyses of mortars and plasters were found in the regions and eras compared (Figure 39.7).

Damage

In the counties of Elbe-Elster, Uckermark, and Prignitz we analyzed plasters of two churches from their north, east, and south sides. An analysis of the west side was not possible because of weathering factors, which often resulted in the renovation of the plasters. In each case we analyzed a properly and badly preserved plaster.

The air pollution in the county of Elbe-Elster is high. The nearby industrial region of Halle and Leipzig is a major factor. Because of a lack of industrialization, air pollution is considerably less in Uckermark and Prignitz (Table 39.1).

The best preserved plasters are usually located on the south or east sides of the churches. In most cases involving historic plaster, lime turned into gypsum even though the surface did not seem to be damaged. We found gypsum in the first 2 mm of the plaster layer in Elbe-Elster, while in Uckermark and Prignitz only 0.5 mm was

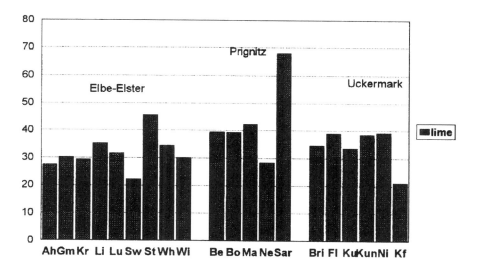

Figure 39.7 Comparison of lime of medieval mortars. Abbreviations identify individual churches.

affected. These results clearly show the dependence of the state preservation on air pollution.

Microscopic investigations using a polarization microscope showed a complicated system of thin cracks under the surface of the layer. The development of the crack system is characteristic over the whole cross-section of detached mortar parts. If the mortar is fixed on the underground substrate, the crack system does not run so deep. In this case the cracks spread mostly parallel to the surface.

In the counties with less air pollution, gypsum is only a film on the surface. In Elbe-Elster the cracks are filled with gypsum in several concentrations and in several types of crystallization. Apparently, gypsum has taken over the role of lime as binder. In some samples from Elbe-Elster, the gypsum replaces the calcareous binder and stabilizes the system. This effect works, however, for only a short time. The thermal expansion coefficient of gypsum is fivefold higher than that of lime, and the volume of gypsum is double. Thus the original structure of the plaster layer will be destroyed eventually.

Table 39.1 Air pollution levels in Elbe-Elster and Uckermark (1990): SO_2 and particulates.

	SO_2 ($\mu g/m^3$)	Particulates ($\mu g/m^3$)
Doberlug-Kirchhain (Elbe/Elster)	33 (1991)	52
Angermünde (Uckermark)	19	37

Figure 39.8 Schönewalde (county Elbe-Elster), village church, detail of the north side.

Medieval decorations have often been lost on the north sides of village churches. In effect, the deposited gypsum has been washed out. In fact, the microfabric of the plaster is not destroyed, but the surface shows a loss of calcareous binder; there are exceptions. If, for example, many trees are to be found on the north sides, this will influence the microclimate. Thus the north side of the village church of Schönewalde (Elbe-Elster) shows extreme damage due to weather conditions. The internal structure of the north side mortar consists of alternating zones of fragile and stable crusts (Figure 39.8). The extention of cracks reaches 800 µm.

The changes in microfabric details are described by Neumann et al. and Schlüter et al. in "Mittelalterliche Putze und Mörtel im Land Brandenburg" (1998).

RESTORATION

The first goal of the restorers was to stabilize the original surface, since aged mortars are often cracked to thin shells with little contact to the wall. Thus their first step was to introduce injection mortar behind the mortar shells. The aim was a stable connection between the fixed mortar and the loose mortar shells. The E-modulus of the injection material should be similar to the stabilized plaster. Many tests show the possibility of using commercial products like Ledan or Sulfadur. The problem, however, is to assimilate the E-modulus. Best results came out with microbubbles and marble powder.

In the next step, the fabric had to be stabilized. We tried to stabilize the plasters with polysilicic acid-ethyl esters; however, the depth of penetration was often not satisfactory. Commercial products and special developments like condensated polysilicic acid esters were used. The E-modulus and the mineralogical microfabric were checked with REM-DEX before and after stabilizing.

If the cracks were smaller than 200 µm, the stabilzation turned out to be successful. Cracks between 200 µm and 800 µm are still a problem as they must be "bridged" with an appropriate filling material.

The tests will be continued to gain more knowledge about the role gypsum plays in the structure of aged mortars.

ACKNOWLEDGEMENT

The author thanks the Deutsche Bundesstiftung Umwelt for their support during all phases of the work.

REFERENCES

Arnold, B, H. Burger, H.-H. Neumann, and R. Wens. 1996. Historical plaster on village churches in Brandenburg. In: Proc. of 8th Intl. Congress on Deterioration and Conservation of Stone. Berlin: Möller Druck und Verlag GmbH.

Arnold, B, H. Burger, H.-H. Neumann, C. Obermeier, and R. Wens. 1997. Erforschung und Erhaltung historischer Putze und Mörtel im Hinblick auf Umweltschäden. Tagungsbericht 13. IBAUSIL, ed. F.A. Finger, pp. 2-0939–2-0948. Weimar: Institut für Baustoffkunde, Bauhaus Universität.

Knöfel, D., and P. Schubert. 1993. Mörtel und Steinergänzungsstoffe in der Denkmalpflege. Berlin: Sonderheft BMFT-Verbundforschung Denkmalpflege.

Mittelalterliche Putze und Mörtel im Land Brandenburg. 1998. Arbeitsheft 9 des Brandenburgischen Landesamtes für Denkmalpflege. Potsdam: Potsdamer Verlags Buchhandlung.

Obermeier, C. 1996. A database for historic renderings in Brandenburg. In: Proc. of 8th Intl. Congress on Deterioration and Conservation of Stone. Berlin: Möller Druck und Verlag GmbH.

Bricks under the Influence of Huge Salt Immissions

Buildings of a Thuringian Potash Mine

S. HERPPICH

Zollern-Institut beim Deutschen Bergbau-Museum, DMT, Herner Str. 45,
44787 Bochum, Germany

ABSTRACT

The building materials used in the potash mine of Bleicherode show the effect of persistent salt immissions over a period of 90 years. The salts responsible for the strain on the brick masonry and also on the machinery were primarily chlorides (NaCl and KCl) and, in smaller amounts, sulfates. In succession, the bricks were severely damaged and the metal in the machinery corroded. Sometimes the chlorides penetrated the whole thickness of the walls, whereas the sulfates were primarily found in the outer parts of the masonry, directly on the facades.

HISTORICAL INTRODUCTION

The subject of this study is an industrial monument consisting of the buildings of a potash mine in Bleicherode, Thuringia, located in the southern Hartz Mountains. This site, where potash salts were mined, belongs geologically to the Upper Permian (225–240 million years ago) mid-German potash deposit. In Bleicherode, the potassium seam "Stassfurt" (Zechstein subdivision 2) was mined. The area of the mining district belonging to the potash mine of Bleicherode covers about 140 km^2. The salt was normally used for the production of fertilizer but during World War II it was used to produce explosives. The mined products here were carnallitite with carnallite ($KMgCl_3 \cdot 6H_2O$), halite (NaCl) and kieserite ($MgSO_4 \cdot H_2O$); anhydritic hardsalt containing halite, sylvinite (KCl), carnallite, anhydrite ($CaSO_4$); and kainite ($KCl \cdot MgSO_4 \cdot 3H_2O$). Table 40.1 shows the historical analysis of the crude salt.

Table 41.1   Historical analysis of 1931 (Archives Potash Mine Bleicherode, KB 227).

Analysis of Crude Potassium Salt in Weight-%		
	(a) Kainit	(b) Duengesalz
KCl	24.8	35.8
NaCl	49.4	45.0
$MgCl_2$	0.6	0.5
$CaSO_4$	4.6	4.7
$MgSO_4$	0.3	−
unsoluble	19.7	13.5 (anhydrite and clay)
H_2O	0.6	0.5

Representations of different samples:
(a) Kainit, Lösesalz (kainite, salt for dissolving process),
(b) 20er Düngesalz (fertilizing salt, about 20% potassium by weight).

The whole industrial facility was built between 1899 and 1911. Production began in 1902 and continued until 1991, when the reunification of Germany and the decreasing capacity of the deposit led to the end of production.

In the beginning, the mine was under direction of the Prussian state and was named "Salzbergwerk Bleicherode" (Schmidt and Theile 1989). In the first year of production, 30,000 tons of salt were mined (Ostmann et al. 1983). Production increased to 260,000 tons in 1912 (VEB Kaliwerk "KARL LIEBKNECHT" Bleicherode 1962). In 1903–1904, a potassium chloride plant was established in the southern part of the area (Figure 40.1) to process the mined products. In 1923 the administration changed. With the foundation of the "Preussische Bergwerks- und Hüttengesellschaft Berlin (PREUSSAG)," all mines under the direction of the Prussian state came together in the new company (Ostmann et al. 1983). Production rates increased; during 1936–1944 up to about 1,000,000 tons per year were mined (Festschrift 1949; Ostmann et al. 1983; VEB Kaliwerk "KARL LIEBKNECHT" Bleicherode 1962). In 1946, after World War II, the area was occupied by Russian troops and the mine came under Russian administration. For expropriation purposes, the proceeds from the production of potassium salts served as a payment of indemnities (Specht et al. 1994). At that time, the company was called "Staatliche Aktiengesellschaft (SAG) der UdSSR für Kalidüngemittel" (Ostmann et al. 1983). This period lasted until 1952. Thereafter, the mine was converted to state property. After 1954 the mine was called "VEB (Volkseigener Betrieb) Kaliwerk 'Karl Liebknecht' Bleicherode" (Ostmann et al. 1983).

Since its shutdown in 1991, the mine has been used as a depository for industrial waste. The potash mine Bleicherode is a technical monument of national importance. In general, the original structures and buildings as well as the machinery have been

Figure 40.1   Potash Mine Bleicherode, site plan of 1903.

Scale: ⊢──⊣ 50 m

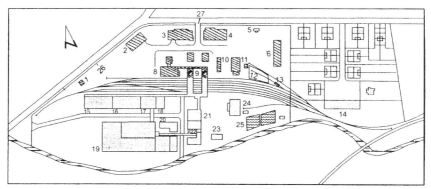

▨ Investigated and documented buildings belonging to the projected museum.

1,2	shed	11	boiler house
3,4	office space for management	12	coal store yard
5	fire station	13	engine shed
6	workshops	14	celebration place
7	machinery buildings	15-25	other buildings of the salt plant
8	grinder building	26	exterior wall
9	shafts Velsen I and II	27	main entrance
10	ventilation building		

preserved, though in varying states of conservation. They embody the architectural and technical characteristics typical for this kind of industry in that region for the period of the turn of the century. In 1986, most of the buildings and some machinery were classified as an ancient monument. Because of the historical, technical, and architectural importance, current plans are to conserve the whole industrial plant as a potash mining museum.

DOCUMENTATION OF BUILDINGS AND MACHINERY

The first step in this study was to document the 16 brick buildings and representative machinery. Figure 40.1 shows the documented area of the buildings belonging to the projected industrial museum. One of the main structures of the projected museum is the grinder building, where the salt was ground and sifted. In this article, examples of material investigation of this building are given.

The most important machinery includes a working steam engine constructed in 1909, which is located in one of the machinery buildings and is still functional, and also the whole system of grinding machines, sieves, and conveyor belts in the grinder building.

The crude potassium salt entered the grinder building through a shaft on a conveyor belt, fell into the grinding apparatus, was ground and then transported by elevator to the 4th floor. There it fell down over some sieves and another grinding roll. Finally, the fractional salt left the building on a second conveyor belt, which transported it into the factory for the solution procedure. This process caused huge salt dust emissions inside the building. The most important dust emissions took place near the incoming conveyor belt and the big grinder apparatus on the first floor. Since there was no machine for dedusting, water spraying was used inside for dust control.

INVESTIGATION OF BUILDING MATERIALS

The building materials, mostly bricks, were investigated mainly with regard to the soluble salts and moisture content. Preliminary results concerning the investigation of brick materials are presented below.

Different types of damage can be observed. In some buildings, large settlement cracks have occurred because of settlement movements induced by mining. The brick material of the grinder building was investigated intensively. At the north facade, the bricks are severely damaged. In some parts of the facade, mostly near the windows, loss of whole bricks as well as mortar is common. Other bricks show detaching scale and parts that are sanding and flaking. The most important damage types are flaking, sanding, scaling, and salt efflorescences. White salt efflorescences are often combined with thick grayish-brown crusts. They are underlayering the grayish crusts. The white salt efflorescences consist of sylvinite (KCl) and halite (NaCl), while the grayish crusts also contain gypsum and anhydrite. The grayish crust reaches a thickness up to 5 cm. Sometimes you can see a fluidal texture induced by the direction of the wind. Sometimes the gypsum crusts formed cauliflower-like structures.

The light red or orange bricks show the most damage, while the darker bricks are in better condition. This is due to the fact that the darker ones, with partly gray or violet colors, were burnt at higher temperatures; thus they have a higher density and less porosity. The analysis of the mineral assemblage (by X-ray diffraction analysis) showed that the darker ones must be burnt at temperatures above 1000°C whereas the others were burnt below 1000°C.

Brick damage has not only occurred outside, but also inside the building. Inside you can also find a huge amount of salt efflorescence, sometimes crystals (chlorides) in the form of whiskers up to 3 cm long, which can form up to several layers, and also loss of material by flaking and sanding. The salt efflorescences often occur between the bricks and plaster, which results in plaster detachment. Furthermore, in some parts of the building, mold is beginning to form because of the high relative humidity (RH).

To study the kind, distribution, and amount of salt and humidity, drill cores were taken from different levels of the building, outside and inside, as well as from different facades and analyzed. The locations of samples taken from the northern facade of the grinder building are shown in Figure 40.2.

Sample No.	Salt Content (weight-%)			
	Cl⁻		SO₄²⁻	
	outside → inside		outside → inside	
	1.08	→ 0.76	1.39	→ 0.46
	1.05	→ 1.41	0.97	→ 0.10
	1.87	→ 0.95	1.88	→ 0.58
	0.61	→ 0.95	2.61	→ 0.22
	0.69	→ 0.37	0.46	→ 0.05

Figure 40.2 North facade of the grinder building of the Potash Mine Bleicherode with the locations of sampling and the salt content. The samples MK 30, MK 31, and MK 33 are bricks; MK 29 is a triassic quartz sandstone.

The soluble salt content was analyzed at different depths of the drill core up to 25 cm. The main salts found were chlorides and sulfates. The amount of nitrates and fluorides in all the samples was negligible. Often the amount of chloride increases from outside to inside. The maximum value of about 2.6 weight-% in this profile was found in sample No. 31 (see Figure 40.2). This location was near the central grinder apparatus, where huge salt dust emissions occurred. During production, water spraying was used to control dust levels. The water enabled soluble chlorides to be readily transported into the wall. It is obvious that most of the chloride content came from the salt dust emissions inside. By contrast, the sulfate content decreases from outside to inside (Figure 40.2), the source of which was air pollution.

The other analyzed samples, which are not presented here in detail, showed that in most cases (73 drill cores consisting of bricks, sandstones, or mortars were analyzed) chlorides represent the main salt strain for the material. Sulfates are mostly concentrated in the outer 1 or 2 cm of the drill core, whereas the chlorides often penetrate the whole brick. The reason for this is the different solubility of chlorides and sulfates. In general, chlorides are more soluble than sulfates. The solubility of NaCl is 5.421 mol/l, of KCl 4.028 mol/l, and of gypsum ($CaSO_4 \cdot 2H_2O$) 0.015 mol/l at 20°C (Küster et al. 1958).

The visible decay phenomena correlate directly with the content of chloride. The crystallizing pressure of NaCl is 55–374 N/mm^2, depending on temperature and degree of supersaturation of the solution (Winkler 1973) and is with that higher than the compressive strength of the analyzed brick samples ranging between 13 and 45 N/mm^2. Thus, repeated crystallization and solution processes led to material destruction.

Humidity is one of the most important agents for the decay of building materials because water is the medium for salt transportation; it leads to swelling and shrinkage, and it strains the material by freezing and thawing processes. Different kinds of humidity have been investigated at different depths: sampling humidity, hygroscopic humidity, and saturation humidity (Figure 40.3). Sampling humidity is the real moisture content of the sample. Hygroscopic humidity is analyzed in the laboratory under defined climates; it describes the moisture a material can uptake from air humidity. The higher the content of soluble salts, the higher the hygroscopic humidity of the brick becomes (Arendt 1983). Saturation humidity is the maximum moisture content a material can have. That value depends on the porosity and permeability of the materials. In all samples there is nearly no difference in moisture content at different depths. Sample No. 30 is the lowest brick sample of the profile. Here you have more sampling humidity than hygroscopic humidity because here most of the humidity came from rising ground moisture. The others show more hygroscopic humidity, which is influenced by the chloride content. Hygroscopic humidity nearly reaches the saturation humidity (Figure 40.3), which means that the humidity of the masonry cannot be higher; it is the maximum value.

FUTURE PLANS

The next goal is to create a practical restoration plan. First, the masonry and machinery will need to be cleaned by dry-cleaning methods. Severely damaged bricks and mortars must be replaced. Desalination of the masonry would be cost prohibitive because the salinated area is too vast. It is important to maintain a constant climate inside such that salt migration can be stopped and the cycle of crystallization and solution be interrupted. The equilibrium moisture content of NaCl is at about 75% relative air humidity; for KCl, it is between 83% and 88% RH (depending on temperature). Above these values you have solution while below you have crystals (Klopfer 1974). To avoid a change of state, the climate must stabilize above or below these values. Higher RH values will negatively impact the machinery. The corrosion rate of metals increases

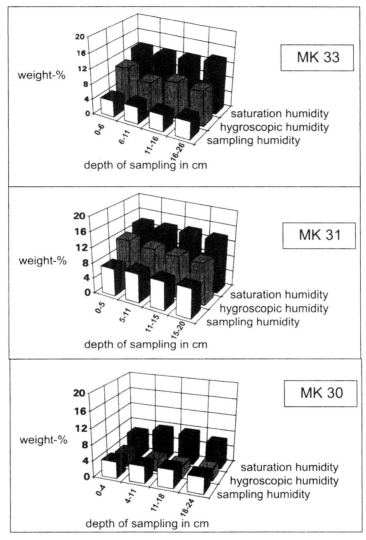

Figure 40.3   Comparison of different humidity contents in relation to the sampling depth. The location of the samples MK 30, MK 31, and MK 33 with the salt content are shown in Figure 41.2. All the samples are bricks.

rapidly above 60% RH in combination with the salt dust; thus a range below this value must be achieved.

After the building material is restored, the next step will be to create a plan for the utilization of this potash mine as a museum.

ACKNOWLEDGEMENT

This project was sponsored by Deutsche Bundesstiftung Umwelt, Osnabrück.

REFERENCES

Arendt, C. 1983. Trockenlegung: Leitfaden zur Sanierung feuchter Bauwerke. Stuttgart: Deutsche Verlagsanstalt.

Festschrift. 1949. Zum 50-jährigen Bestehen des Kaliwerks Bleicherode 1899–1949. Bleicherode.

Klopfer, H. 1974. Wassertransport durch Diffusion in Feststoffen. Wiesbaden, Berlin: Bauverlag GmbH.

Küster, F.W., A. Thiel, and K. Fischbeck. 1958. Logarithmische Rechentafeln. Berlin: de Gruyter.

Ostmann, F. et al. 1983. Bleicheröder Kalikumpel. Betriebsgeschichte des VEB Kalibetrieb "Südharz" Kaliwerk "Karl Liebknecht" Bleicherode im VEB Kombinat Kali 1899–1983. Berlin: Verlag Tribüne.

Schmidt, W., and W. Theile. 1989. Denkmale der Produktions- und Verkehrsgeschichte, Part 1. Berlin: VEB Verlag für Bauwesen.

Specht, S., E. Niedling, D. Fulda, and A. Heynke. 1994. 100 Jahre Kalirevier Südharz: Lagerstätte – Produktionsgeschichte – Sicherung und Nachnutzung. *Erzmetall* **47(1)**: 62–70.

VEB Kaliwerk "KARL LIEBKNECHT" Bleicherode. 1962. Betriebsgeschichte des VEB Kaliwerk "KARL LIEBKNECHT" Bleicherode 1899–1962.

Winkler, E.M. 1973. Stone. Properties, Durability in Man's Environment. New York: Springer.

Appendix I

Proposal for a Pilot Study on the Conservation of Historic Brick Structures

The Committee on the Challenges of Modern Society stated in its meeting held at the NATO Headquarters, Brussels, on May 11 and 12, 1987, in the Decision Sheet AC/274-DS/16 from June 22, 1987, Topic V (a):

> *The Committee . . . agreed to establish this study on the basis of the proposals in AC/274-D/228 . . .*

The revised version of NATO-CCMS document AC/274-D/228 was prepared at the Experts Meeting held in Berlin on March 30–31, 1987:

In this Pilot Study, Historic Brick Structures are meant to encompass both exposed brick surfaces, brick constructions, as well as rendered and plastered brick facades. The mortars and plasters to be studied include traditional and modern lime, dolomite, and lime-cement compositions. The types of damage of primary concern are those caused by water, air pollution, and salt working separately or in combination.

While individual studies may concentrate on one or more of these systems, it is the great goal of this Pilot Study to describe and understand all of the causes of damage that can be elaborated in an Atlas of Damage to Historic Brick Structures.

Further one seeks to simulate these damages in field tests and chamber studies leading to a fundamental understanding of the mechanical and physico-chemical mechanisms of decay.

To undertake an evaluation of the many conservation, restoration, consolidation, and cleaning procedures employed on damaged historic brick structures is considered to be essential. An aspect of the Pilot Study will be the development of a state-of-the-art review of current conservation/restoration methods.

1. Atlas of Damage to Historic Brick Structures

Methods for the description and characterization of the state of historic brick structures and of materials used within these objects as bricks, mortar and plaster should be developed as a basis for:

- the evaluation of the causes of the damages within the very complex system of various factors and their different effects,
- the evaluation of the extent of damages on historic brick structures,
- the finding of methods for the preservation of historic brick structures.

The methodology for the assessment of the degree and extent of deterioration and alteration makes use of phenomenological description and of analytical methods. This will include:

- characterization of the materials and structures in respect to their physical and chemical composition as well as to their alterations using geological, physical and chemical tests and analysis,
- characterization of environmental influences on the brick structures by gaseous and particulate pollutants, climatic factors, taking in consideration the microclimate,
- description and characterization of the constructive situation of the structure (exposure to rain, wind, sun, emission, conditions due to design, level, etc.),
- documentation of the history of the brick structure, especially in respect to former use, repairs, conservation and other treatments, time of exposure, etc.,
- mapping and regionalization of the damages.

2. Diagnosis of Damages

A quantitative description of the damage mechanisms will be based on the following measurements, to be carried out on bricks, mortar and rendering, both the damaged and undamaged materials:

- chemical analysis (e.g., composition, composition variation with depth, salt concentrations),
- internationally standardized physical tests (e.g., water and vapor transport measurements, abrasion tests, size distribution of the pores, specific surface, crystallization tests),
- geological analysis (petrography, determination of the different mineral phases and their granulometry).

The run-off water from relevant buildings and test racks will be analyzed and characterized in comparison with rain water collected on inert surfaces.

Since these diverse measurements techniques are not available in every participating laboratory, it is recommended that an international cooperation should be initiated to make a maximum of analysis techniques available to every participant.

An intercomparison of test results from different laboratories on the same standard samples, which will be made available to all participating laboratories, should be carried out in an early phase of the project.

From this quantitative descriptive work it will be possible to derive a damage mechanism in many cases, hence to predict which environmental and constructional parameters are of most importance in the deterioration process and should be controlled most in simulation experiments, and what adequate measures might be taken in the conservation of certain materials.

3. Field and Accelerated Laboratory Tests

Field and laboratory exposure studies will be undertaken to brick, mortar and renderings. Racks with carefully selected specimens will be exposed to ambient conditions in field tests at the monument sites. Simultaneously, accelerated weathering will be carried out in test chambers. In these cases, the effect of frost-thawing cycles, thermal shocks, UV radiation, and pollutants (SO_2, NO_x, NH_3, chloride, oxidants) will be investigated in the presence of controlled humidity and salt concentrations. In studying the effect of pollutants, gas phase concentrations should be monitored and the exposed materials, the dew, rinse and run-off water should be analyzed. In all cases, the physical and chemical alterations of the material will be observed in detail. Damage mechanisms on the rack caused by field exposure and test atmospheres will be related to actual deposition of air pollution and to concentration conditions at relevant buildings.

Finally, all of the test experiments will be repeated after suitable treatment of bricks, mortar and rendering with specific conservation, consolidation products, in order to predict their effectiveness and durability under representative conditions for a certain building.

4. Instrumental Methods Development/Standardization of Procedures

Recent advances in analytical methods and imaging techniques should be exploited in all phases of the Pilot Study.

Standardized methods for the collection, documentation and handling of specimens will be described. Similarly, standardized methods for preparation of samples for field and chamber testing will be developed with particular reference to the intercomparability of results from different experimental programs.

The specification and documentation of microclimate will be an integral aspect of all field and chamber studies. Included are effects of orientation, shielding, etc.

Protocols for the collection and characterization of run-off water to achieve a statistically valid mass-balance for selected field and chamber studies will be developed.

Included in the protocols will be a description of the analytical methods to be employed, the sampling methodologies, and estimation of errors.

Of particular interest are nondestructive evaluation (NDE) technologies that may be in special cases applied *in situ* to brick structures. Remote sensing and analytical techniques developed for lunar and interplanetary exploration may prove applicable in such cases. Among these there are portable XRD and XRF, neutron/gamma spectroscopy, infrared thermography and ultrasonic scanning.

5. Treatment/Conservation/Restoration of Historic Brick Structures

The broad variety of responses to damage to brick structures is reflected in the many waterproofing, consolidation, salt barrier/removal systems, cleaning methods and re-placement materials applied to bricks, mortars, rendered and plastered surfaces and their mural composite structures. Though it is not feasible to undertake an experimental evaluation of there many materials and methods in the Pilot Study, a task will be the development of state-of-the-art review of materials and methods.

As appropriate, design criteria for replacement methods when new materials ar introduced in place of entirely decayed bricks, mortar or plaster will be described.

Appendix II

Experts Meetings of the NATO-CCMS Pilot Study: Conservation of Historic Brick Structures

1st Meeting	West Berlin, Federal Republic of Germany	March 30–31, 1987
2nd Meeting	West Berlin, Federal Republic of Germany	April 20–22, 1988
Extraordinary Meeting	Brussels, Belgium	October 18–19, 1988
3rd Meeting	Hamburg, Federal Republic of Germany	November 2–4, 1989
4th Meeting	Amersfoort, The Netherlands	October 25–27, 1990
5th Meeting	Berlin, Federal Republic of Germany	October 17–19, 1991
6th Meeting	Williamsburg, Virginia, United States	October 28–31, 1992
7th Meeting	Venice, Italy	November 22–24, 1993
8th Meeting	Leuven, Belgium	October 26–27, 1994

Subject Index

Author Index